THE
SPANIARDS

THE SPANIARDS

An Introduction to Their History

AMÉRICO CASTRO

Translated by
WILLARD F. KING
and
SELMA MARGARETTEN

UNIVERSITY OF CALIFORNIA PRESS
BERKELEY, LOS ANGELES & LONDON
1971

University of California Press
Berkeley and Los Angeles, California
University of California Press, Ltd.
London, England
© 1971 by The Regents of the University of California
ISBN: 0-520-01617-3
Library of Congress Catalog Card Number: 67-14000
Designed by Richard Cork
Printed in the United States of America

PREFACE

THE PURPOSE OF THIS INTRODUCTION is to clarify and complete the original eleven chapters of this book, which for special reasons had been already set in type. I have hitherto been unable to add these complementary pages as well as three new important chapters, the first one and the last two. In the book I have utilized much of the material, although not always literally, contained in the first seven chapters of my earlier volume, *The Structure of Spanish History*, translated by Edmund L. King (Princeton University Press, 1954), which has been out of print for several years. I therefore wish to express my gratitude to the publishers for allowing me to reprint and revise some of the pages and incorporate new ideas, often different from my former theories, which are now fundamental to my theses.

This new title, *The Spaniards*, indicates that I wish to accentuate and emphasize the personal, rather than the structural, nature of this history. It is not sufficient merely to narrate and evaluate what was done by the Spaniards. It is imperative especially to determine the identity of a great people. The *ser* (being) and the *hacer* (doing) of the Spaniards refer to their very mode of existence. For this reason the facts, events, and various aspects of the two facets are intimately linked to the premises that make them intelligible to the reader.

All these happenings took place in conjunction with the circumstances that gradually led to the formation of that human complex which began to call itself *español* in the thirteenth century. At the same time, however, these very circumstances were preparing the disintegration of the group comprised of peoples of three different beliefs—Christians, Moors, and Jews—who are referred to as "castes" in this work and not as "races"; for in that Spain of three religions everyone was light-skinned, with horizontal eyes, except for a few black slaves brought in from Africa. Within the human space of these three castes of believers reciprocal admiration, envy, and hatred were produced to a maximum.

The complexity and, until a short time ago, the unpopularity of my viewpoints made it necessary to reiterate and insist on them with more than the usual fervor. When one wishes to illuminate and clarify a strange and multifaceted object, it is necessary to show it in all its different and often opposing phases, making it revolve over and over again before the viewer's eyes, until it becomes intelligible to the spectator.

In this history the caste and beliefs of those persons who played a role in its development, together with their feelings of superiority or inferiority, determined the course of events much more decisively than natural or economic conditions, no matter how important these latter factors may be. The personal reactions of those directly affected by my particular approach to Spanish history are the inevitable consequences of my points of view on the problem. The "scientifically" oriented historians argue about statistics, class struggles, economic conditions, and sociological factors, but in the life of those whom I am about to describe, the foreground was always occupied by intrinsic values motivated by the desire for fame, prestige, and power over others.

Only in the light of these motivations can we explain certain situations. The Spanish language, for example, is still referred to today as "Castilian" (*castellano*) by the Spaniards themselves and other Spanish-speaking peoples. The Jews who held high official positions at court bore the title "don," similar to the English "sir," such as Don Abraham Senior, and Don Isaac Abravanel, the treasurer of the Catholic Sovereigns, and continued to bear the title "don" until they were expelled in 1492. In like manner, it was impossible to hold the solemn, magnificent funeral services for the soul of Philip II (1598) in Seville because it took Philip III several months to settle the petty quarrels and difficulties of protocol involved in the seating arrangements of ranking dignitaries. Furthermore, when Isabella, the Catholic Queen died, she clearly stated in her will (1504) that her husband, King Ferdinand of Aragon, would receive the rent from the lands discovered and conquered, but upon his death, her territories, in addition to Granada, the Canary Islands, and "all those lands discovered and yet to be discovered, conquered or yet to be conquered, shall remain in possession of *my* kingdoms of Castile and Leon."[1] As a result of this decree, not until the eighteenth century when the Bourbon dynasty ascended to the throne of Spain could the Aragonese and Catalans participate openly and significantly in the imperial enterprise of the New World.

Now in 1970 my work has been diffused by many people, thanks

---

[1] Alonso de Santa Cruz, *Crónica de los Reyes Católicos*, ed. J. de Mata Carriazo (Seville, 1951), vol. I, 95 and 355.

to the sympathy of those who have supported my theories in recent years and have not allowed themselves to be blinded by passion and dogmatic rigidity.[2] It is now possible to approach the past history of Spain without concealing anything or distorting the facts, without devaluating anything that is worthy of admiration and study. In spite of their present place in world politics, science, and technology, the Spanish people are more than the mere memory of their past grandeur. It is obvious, however, that Hispanic world continues to be outstanding today more because of its glorious past and its great individual personalities than because of the sociopolitical dimension of its nations. Picasso is outstanding in the world of art as Velázquez or Goya were in former times. In addition to those writers whose merits were officially acknowledged with Nobel prizes such as Jacinto Benavente, Gabriela Mistral, Miguel Angel Asturias, and Juan Ramón Jiménez (the latter prize awarded also in memoriam for Antonio Machado and Federico García Lorca), we should not forget others who also gained international renown such as Rubén Darío, Pérez Galdós, Unamuno, Ortega y Gasset, and Alfonso Reyes, just to cite only a few of those no longer living. The music of Albéniz and Falla is known throughout the world, just as is the scientific research of Ramón y Cajal, Bernardo Houssay (Argentina), or Severo Ochoa, Nobel laureates in the fields of biology in 1906, 1947, and 1959, respectively.

This brief reference by no means reflects all the cultural accomplishments and contributions by Spanish-speaking peoples in the twentieth century. The list of scientists, poets, prose writers, painters, and musicians would have to be much longer and drawn up at the risk of omissions. The important point to emphasize here is the marked contrast between the high level of certain sporadic, isolated notable figures and the low level of their environmental, or if you prefer, national circumstances. When we come upon a Hispanic eminence today, we are more likely to think of the phrase "in spite of" rather than "it was to be expected or logical." We tend to refer automatically, exclusively of Spain, to that continuous line of intelligence that has come down uninterrupted from the fifteenth century to the present time in Western European countries. In the final chapter of this work I attempt to clarify the reasons why the Spaniards never joined the general course of Western culture spontaneously and the motives for this particular phenomenon.

It is difficult and even painful to realize that Spain, that is, the true,

---

[2] The need to destroy the myth that all the inhabitants of the Iberian Peninsula had always been Spaniards and to take into account the beliefs and sentiments of Christians, Moors, and Jews gave rise to numerous attacks from many sides. But in reference to the absurd idea of Spain's being an "historical enigma," one may consult the work of Guillermo Araya, *Evolución del pensamiento histórico de Américo Castro* (Madrid: Taurus, 1969).

authentic *españoles*, came into being as a nation in a different way and under different circumstances from other peoples of Western Europe. For this reason, I must undertake the task of tearing down and rebuilding simultaneously, and I am not able to set forth once and for all, from the very beginning, in a well-organized whole, my ideas concerning the Spaniards' past, so intimately related to their present.

It is entirely possible that the history of the Spaniards may be uninteresting to non-Hispanic peoples, especially since Spain no longer influences the course of international politics and world affairs as she did four centuries ago. I am convinced that the Spanish contribution to universal civilization has at the same time been considerable, although not so much in the fields of science or technology. The wide diffusion of the Spanish language and the influence of Spanish art and literature, too, are quite apparent, although these aspects of culture are not my concern at the moment. I am more interested in the fact that behind the fabulous technological advances and economic progress of our time, there lies a grave difficulty: neither technology, nor economics, nor our incredibly refined armaments systems have provided an effective means to reconcile the dichotomy of how each people can situate itself in respect to its own untouchable and nonnegotiable life and at the same time live peacefully with others without mutually annihilating each other. I shall attempt to express this idea more precisely. Above and beyond the marvels of physics and twentieth-century science in general, there looms the supreme question of whether it is ultimately going to be possible to continue to exist as an American, a European, a Russian, a Muslim, an Israeli, a Chinese, or an African. Today national and ethnic problems are subordinated to ideologies and beliefs just as unyielding and combative as those that provoked the Thirty Years' War in the seventeenth century or the irreconcilable Arab-Israeli conflict in the twentieth. During Hitler's imperialistic schemes, the Germans' belief and insistence on being Aryans resulted in the extermination of millions who *had* to exist as Jews. Today Marxist-Leninist ideologies and liberal or socialized capitalism are, in the last analysis, systems of belief and being just as absolute and contrary as those that motivate the bellicose confrontations of Allah and Yahwe on opposite banks of the Suez Canal.

It becomes evident that the particular situation of human beings within their own lives is ultimately what controls, shapes, and determines the course of human events. If the Arabs and the Israelis took the same inner position with respect to their religious beliefs as the French and the English did, the phenomenon of Zionism would never exist, nor would the Muslim countries be as fragmented as they are today. By the same token, it would be difficult for the Spanish- and Portuguese-speaking nations to rule themselves democratically today.

The previous discussion may serve as a point of departure to delve into the problem of the history of the Spaniards, the entire complexity of which was born magnificently and splendidly, and sometimes painfully, as a consequence of the confrontations and harmony among the peoples of three different religious beliefs. This is only a preview of the notions about the way in which that nation which finally became wholly Spanish in the sixteenth century began to take shape, because this mixture and coexistence of differently believing peoples, though physically analogous, lent a particular shape and appearance to the life and history of the future Spaniards. At the same time, that unique social composition and its historical-economic-cultural consequences have given rise to a falsification and confusion in Spanish historiography, not only within Spain but outside as well. As a result of this "living-togetherness" in Spain of three great peoples, both under favorable circumstances and later confronting one another, not on battlefields, but in silent anger and revenge, as an outcome of the past history of present-day Spaniards, anti-Semitism and anti-Islamism hover like vultures ready to attack that very history in order to make it appealing and teachable in university courses. Voluminous works have been written to de-Islamize and de-Judaize the Spanish past, as we shall see in the course of this work; or people fall into the error of perpetrating naive frauds such as publishing *La Celestina* (1499) as an anonymous work (Barcelona, 1966) merely to avoid the explanation that this work of such major literary importance was written by Fernando de Rojas, whose Hispano-Hebrew ancestry is a well-known fact.

The obstacles one encounters upon trying to expound history are many when one wishes to offer the reader a more accurate image of what Spain and the Spaniards have been and done. On the one hand, some historians include in its history what does not exist, and on the other, they suppress important factors which undoubtedly comprised a part of the life of those who eventually called themselves *españoles* in the sixteenth century (and not before, as I shall discuss in another part of this work).

For this author the theme of history is not merely what actually happened—the events themselves—since what actually happened is inseparable from the effect that it has on its agent and on those who are affected in some way by the events taking place around them. Historiography is based both on the observation of what is offered to our own experience as well as on our questioning of what is affected directly or indirectly by the historical event. In Spanish we say that something "se le viene a uno encima" (something befalls us or comes upon us). The historical fact, someone's making or doing, penetrates or rebounds against someone else. For some it provides a healthy atmosphere and for others it is stifling and unbearable. This happening cannot be contained or defined in a single sentence with a period at the end; it is a phrase, rather, arising from or growing out of a living language, comprehensible and assimilable for some, unintelligible or rejected by others.

The original material of this book (chapters ii through xii) was translated by Willard F. King, and the newly added material (preface, chapters i, xiii, and xiv, and appendix) was translated by Selma Margaretten. I want to thank the editors of the University of California Press, Robert Y. Zachary, Vincent J. Ryan, Geoffrey Ashton, and Ernest J. Kubeck, and all who have worked on this project to bring it to a happy conclusion.

A. C.

CONTENTS

I · CONCERNING THIS HISTORY AND ITS HISTORICAL METHOD

We must begin by providing a conceptual basis for the correlation that will be established between the term "Spaniard" and the human beings so named so that we may then situate the latter in the particular time and space that are truly theirs. Since the writer of these lines, however, is himself situated in a period characterized by a general confusion with respect to the terms that must be employed in the discussion of our problem—history in general, the human dimension of history in particular—it becomes necessary to deal first in an elementary way with the subproblem that confronts us. "History" is a polysemous, hence an ambiguous, term. This fact accounts for the lack of agreement among those who speak of collective life developed in time and space, and for the strange and various interpretations which the Spaniards of today project upon their remote and even their recent past, or, what is even more serious, their ignorance of the motives for the intestine and civil wars of the nineteenth and twentieth centuries.

An indirect reflection of this enormous phenomenon has been the literature following the Civil War (1936–1939), called "tremendista," although the "tremendousness" of the phenomenon that caused this literature to appear was placed in parentheses or left shrouded in mist. Now as before, the Spaniards' reciprocal slaughter has brought forth thousands of printed pages of what I would call "dicterology" or "improperiology," not "historiology" and certainly not "humanology." Since the time of Mariano José de Larra (1809–1837) a great deal has been written about the great lack of harmony and goodwill among Spaniards. The "homo homini lupus" of Plautus and later of Hobbes might be paraphrased into something like "Hispaniolus Hispaniolo lupus." We have been content to label as "individualism" such phenomena as hatred of the state, the murder of priests in 1834, the disagreements between the various regions, or those between the haves and the have-nots, this last a problem that has been splendidly resolved in Finland, Scandinavia, and Holland, and less perfectly in England and the United States, without recourse to mass murders and concentration camps coordinated with a system of whips and gags. Extremely serious problems, although in my estimation distinct from the basic one which plagues the Spaniards, exist everywhere in the 1970s. Those serious problems which have become universalized affect each country in a particular way, just as certain epidemics wreak greater or lesser havoc according to the previous health, or lack of it, enjoyed by its victims.

My fondness for historical studies is not disinterested; it does not arise from an abstract desire for knowledge, nor does it tend to advance any particular religious or political cause. Because my attempts to throw light on certain areas of darkness are the way they are, my books have been attractive targets for the champions of the most disparate beliefs and affiliations. For some I have ascended to the high dignity of rabbi in New York (reported humorously in *El Norte de Castilla* [Valladolid], 31 December 1967), or I was a Sephardic Jew and not a Spaniard brought to Spain at the age of four by his parents, natives of the Plain of Granada. At the same time I am considered by some influential Jews (Y. Baer and I. S. Révah, for example) to be an anti-Semite. Certain sections of Catholic opinion have taken shots at my work in an attempt to destroy it, although fortunately their projectiles have been wide of the mark. My interpretation of the meaning of the Spanish cult of St. James the Greater, the Apostle (Santiago Apóstol), to cite an example which has given rise to ridiculous and even calumnious criticism, still stands undislodged.[1] To complete the picture, certain Marxist historians accuse me of violating their sacred principles because I refuse to enter the game of superior and inferior structures and to accept the dogma that economy is the center and ultimate basis of the human universe.

Since none of this is really central to my preoccupation, I continue to ask myself why in Spain, a portion of European geography, its inhabitants must settle their disputes and confront their problems by means of implacable struggles of a religious character, and not by secular discussions and formulations as is the custom in the rest of the Western world. In order that this question may be adequately answered, the historian must renounce every kind of political, religious, or sociological partisanship and allow access to what he honestly believes to be the truth, after having fired it in the crucible of logic and good sense.

Where do the Spaniards get their ideas about themselves? Why do they feel the way they do about their compatriots? Whence their col-

---

[1] See my rejoinder to Father A. K. Ziegler, "A note on the Structure of Spanish History," *Speculum*, XXXII (1957), 222–223.

lective inferiority complex, so well described by Dr. López Ibor? What motivates this desire to destroy what is already in existence, be it good or bad? What inspires the desire among the uneducated for "the pancake to flip over" magically, or that desperate phrase of Ramiro de Maeztu, a man incapable of killing anyone who, nevertheless, spoke in private of the need for "blood a yard deep"? Or, conversely, what is the inspiration for the fantastic dream of an "imperial Spain"? I can do no less than offer here an outline for the examination of these terrible questions, although my position is that of sinecure who, possessing only the rudiments of medical training, confronts the diseased body of a loved one and attempts a provisional diagnosis in the hope that trained physicians will then provide reasonable remedies. Until now there have been no such remedies, and, in fact, the patient, in moments of ill humor, even complains of the uncomfortable posture he is forced to assume in order to be properly examined.

It has been possible to achieve some results, thanks to a new formulation of the Spanish question, because this unscientific historian began from an authentic base—his own personal experience. As a young man, with the bitter taste left in his mouth by the Spanish-American War, with the vision of the repatriated soldiers wandering aimlessly, shivering in their striped cotton duck uniforms, he conceived a desire to move to a less unfortunate human climate. Nothing in the Spanish university environment made possible, or even suggested the possibility of, escaping the mediocre intellectual ambience of the turn of the century. Angel Ganivet (1865–1898) and his pilgrimage through Europe exercised a great attraction on the disenchanted, on those who could not agree that the situation I have described was normal, in spite of its vulgar approbation by those who passed inert from one day to the next. Years of rebellion, fruitless as such and for that very reason. Later, well equipped with European culture, I began attempts to find something Spanish worthy of belonging to the Europe of material progress which still seduced us half a century ago. Perhaps there existed, I imagined or wished, another Spain buried beneath the militarily or inquisitorially triumphant official society so lacking, in spite of the chauvinism of Menéndez y Pelayo, in science or workable ideas. My idea that there had been in Spain some throb of Renaissance in communion with Europe induced me to fabricate, some fifty years ago, a Cervantes who was more Renaissance thinker than artist and discoverer of new artistic horizons without precedent in any other literature. In the last twenty years I have been able to reevaluate Cervantes' artistic importance by relating his creations to the totality of Spanish life rather than to the European Renaissance.

As early as 1936 I began to become aware of our ignorance about ourselves. We did not even know who we were, let alone why we have so frequently been preoccupied with killing one another. I speak in the first person because in July 1936 I heard on the radio in San Sebastián the news of my own execution. A friend was pleasantly surprised a few days later to hear my voice. Years later I began the task— so irritating to many—of discovering the reason for our chronic Cain complex, a task made more difficult by the resistance to the idea of recognizing the need for such a discovery, and by the Spanish tendency to cut knots instead of untying them. I would have abandoned my project were it not for the fear that new acts would be added to this already overlong tragedy, and were I not convinced that my method of posing the problem was correct. Were it not correct, there would be no need to speak of it with such insistence—on the one hand to mount such inane frivolity to combat it, or on the other to recognize over and over the validity of my reasoning. In the sciences, whatever has been demonstrated and made evident is accepted as true, but in the field of knowledge of what is human, what is evident becomes obvious but frequently bothersome and even odious. In addition, we may observe in our modern age—a marvel of firm and fruitful precision—a tendency to convert what is in fact polysemous and equivocal into something dogmatic and univocal. The panoramas of history, once open for contemplation, have become schemata of pseudoprecisions, in the final analysis subordinate to political ideologies, straitjackets on free and fruitful inquiry. It is for this reason that I have attempted to offer the reader a history of Spain liberated from the puerile traditionalism of the "retrospective pan-Hispanists" (Tartessos, Viriatus, Seneca, Theodosius, Isidore of Hispalis were in Spain and were Spanish), and protected against the arrogant fallacy of the pseudoscientific historians who reduce every reality to economy, geography, and measurable material expressed in graphs. The historico-materialistic dogmas of today weigh on the historian just as the Church of Rome or of Geneva lay heavy on the inquiries of scientists and humanists like Galileo or Michael Servetus. Today's young readers frequently have no idea whom to believe or to follow. According to Pierre Vilar, for example, my history is poorly "shored up," in spite of the correctness of the way in which certain questions are posed, among them the idea of asking when the Spaniards began to exist. It is encouraging, however, that the leader of sociological history in Spain, the late Professor J. Vicens Vives, eventually joined my method of interpreting Spanish history: "In the final analysis, what weighs most in my opinion is the fact that Castro's hypothesis fits in and is more in accordance . . . with the documents on the economy, society, and culture of the fifteenth century which I have been studying thoroughly for two decades."[2]

---

[2] *Aproximación a la historia de España* (Barcelona, 1968), p. 192 (trans.: *Approaches to the History of Spain* [University of California Press, rev. ed., 1970]).

Decisive historical phenomena are neither comprehensible nor explicable by economicomaterialistic reasoning. Those who began to fight against the Moors doubtless had some kind of economic organization, markets where they could provide themselves with what they needed to subsist and to make war on a powerful enemy, but all the markets in the world would not have sufficed to unite those people, so diverse in language and customs (Asturians, Galicians, Leonese, Basques), without some central force which could bring them together and make them conscious of forming a whole with sufficient force to attack the enemy and slowly make him retreat. An elementary principle of tactics dictates that the attacked defend himself with arms analogous to those employed by his attackers. For the Muslims, the Koran was a very potent weapon which incited and helped them to procure tangible arms and to handle them with maximum audacity. Without the Koran, the Muslims would not have reached the northern part of the Iberian Peninsula. That holy text states: "Yea, if you have patience, if you fear God, when your enemies hurl themselves against you, your Lord will cause five thousand of his angels to reinforce you and attack your enemies" (III, 125). "When you sought help from your Lord he attended your plea; he sent you a reinforcement of a thousand angels, one after another" (VIII, 9). "God caused invisible armies to descend" in the aid of the faithful (IX, 26), etc. It is consequently to be expected that the various peoples of the Christian north, faced with the catastrophe which threatened them, would put into play all the sources of energy available to them. Attacked in the name of a triumphant religious faith, the Christians directed their hopes to the supernatural forces present and possible in Christianity, although not functional militarily prior to the counterattack against the Muslims. The bellicose angels of the Koran make it possible to understand the combative virtue of the Apostle Santiago. All this naturally took place in a context of economic circumstances, of supply lines, markets, and whatever. It is obvious, of course, that the hope for Moorish booty was as powerful an incitement to war as was faith in supernatural assistance. It is, however, quite evident that the reason for the political grouping of Asturians, Basques, etc., and for their feeling of collective identity, was the fact that they were *Christians*, as we shall see in the second half of this chapter and later on. What other single name could Alfonso III's chronicler have given them in 880? The further development of the cult of Santiago and its international dimension of course had economic repercussions and the pilgrimages were probably concerned ultimately more with business than with faith. Nevertheless, it would be absurd to consider the phenomenon and its consequences, prodigious in so many senses, as superstructures erected on some economic base. The economic dimension came later; it was not the primary and unifying "logos."

The theory of economic genesis, in basic connection with powerful and triumphant political systems, lacks validity outside the narrow sphere of those who indicate the general direction of historical studies today, and who unleash a fanatical arrogance against those who dare to deviate from the historicomaterialistic line. Their effects may be noted in the enormous imbalance between humanistic studies, centered in the human aspect of history and culture, and those materialistic studies, oriented by abstract sociology, by geopolitics, by economy, in short, by everything which relegates what is uniquely human in man to a secondary role. There is an apparent attempt to reduce humanity to silence or to a unisonal bleating on command of some authority. Humanity becomes a quiet sea and not a wellspring, a cascade, a clamorous torrent. My language sounds anachronistic and reactionary today. Nevertheless, the Koran has been much more useful to me than economy in understanding why those people who centuries later would be called "Spaniards" (by pilgrims from France) should choose to forge a political identity for themselves on the basis of their religious identity as Christians.

The historicomaterialistic vision of the past prefers what I call the "describable" to the "historiable," and even to the "narrable,"[3] even though in my judgment the facts and phenomena circumstantial to man are not of interest in themselves, but only insofar as they are capable of producing new and higher realities. A generic circumstance becomes part of history when it gives rise to something concrete and new, which causes us to forget what went before. Every preexistent substratum, every constant circumstance surrounding man, must occupy a decidedly secondary place in our consideration of what is truly "historiable." The materialistic historians, perhaps unconsciously, infuse the land, the mountains, and the seas and rivers with a new mythological spirit. Fernand Braudel is correct when he states that: "Ordinarily, the mountains constitute a world apart from civilization."[4] Paradoxically, however, he finds it significant that St. Theresa (1515–1582) established her first monastery of reformed Carmelite friars, one of whose members was the future St. John of the Cross, in Duruelo, a mountainous locale. Braudel then mentions another case of religious alpinism outside Christianity, among the Muslims in Corsica. Confronted with this sort of implied equivalence between physical terrain and certain human phenomena of a religious nature, the reader is invited to equate the religious sentiments of St. Theresa and St. John of the Cross on the one hand with the Muslim hermits of

---

[3] For these concepts, see J. Ferrater Mora, *Diccionario de filosofía* (Madrid, 1965), vol. I, 809–810.

[4] *La Méditerranée et le monde méditerranéen à l'époque de Philippe II* (Paris, 1966), vol. I, 38.

Africa on the other. Seduced by the actions of mountains, plains, and bodies of water, Braudel confers the function of actors in human history on natural elements and population statistics. We can glimpse a desire to reduce to spatial coordinates and numerical calculation, for those of us who are interested in what is in itself relevant, in what is unique, singular, problematical, in what has value in itself, what is simply irreducible to arithmetic, geometry, or even topology. In our humanism all cats are not gray in the dark, nor do there exist "points" determinable by the coincidence of a coordinate and an abscissa. For Braudel, the Mediterranean is a living entity which creates problems and resolves them by itself. For me it is like an empty wall on which we can hang either a Goya or a dirty rag. Over the centuries the Carthaginians, the Egyptians, the Greeks, the Romans, the Turks, the Pisans and the Spaniards, the Americans and the Russians, have used the Mediterranean in the same way as people have for millennia utilized the most varied sorts of aquatic vehicles. The Americans are in the Mediterranean because of the Russians, not because of the Mediterranean. What is significant is the life and accomplishments of the people who live around the Mediterranean, not the water. When the Pisans helped in the capture of Palermo, they sent home several Arabic ships filled with treasures which were employed to begin construction of the Duomo of Pisa—a marvel unique unto itself, inexplicable in terms of economic data. What is generic, the common denominators of history, give way, in case after case analogous to that of the Duomo of Pisa, to what is unique, impossible to explain or understand unless one begins by contemplating and admiring. Obviously what is important here is not the Mediterranean, but the Pisans.

Braudel writes: "If the Mediterranean had not been open on all sides, and especially toward the west, onto the Atlantic, *she would have probably resolved by herself* the great problem of these population surpluses, that is, to spread the people more equitably around her, which, moreover, *she managed to accomplish* in great part."[5] Anyone who does not belong to one of the Utopian or Messianic sects which base their beliefs mainly on economics and geopolitics and which today control the minds and hearts of millions of Europeans, Asians, and Americans[6] reads with stupefaction that "the proof of the overpopulation of Mediterranean Europe is the fact of the repeated expulsions of Jews, who were forced to leave Castile and Portugal in 1492. . . . In those countries overpopulated in relation to their resources, and this

---

[5] Ibid., p. 380.

[6] W. E. Mühlmann, *Messianismes, révolutionnaires du tiers monde* (Paris, 1968); O. V. Kuusinen *et al.*, *Manual de marxismo y leninismo* (Mexico, 1960); F. V. Konstantinov, *Fundamentos de la filosofía marxista* (Mexico, 1965); Eric Hoffer, *The True Believer* (Harper, 1951).

was perhaps true in the Iberian Peninsula as early as the reign of Ferdinand and Isabella, religion was the pretext rather than the cause of those persecutions. Later, the same law of numbers will come into play against the Moriscos in the Spain of Philip III."[7] None of these affirmations is true. In the first place, the Jews were not expelled from Portugal in 1492, but many years later. Second, the situation of the Jews in Spain had nothing to do with the Mediterranean but with the very innards of Spanish history. For Braudel, religion is as good a pretext as any other, since he is convinced that the decisive factor was the extrahuman "law of numbers," which in fact had nothing to do with the expulsion of *unbaptized* Jews. If Ferdinand and Isabella had wished to reduce the population of their realms, they would not have allowed even those Jews who converted to Christianity to remain there, as thousands did. The problem was not the "law of numbers," but "religious law." Fernand Braudel overlooks what happened in Spain between 1391, when massacres and expulsions of Jews began on a regional basis, and 1492. An additional proof of his disregard for facts is his statement (I, 133) that Barcelona lost its ghetto in 1492, when in fact the Barcelona Jews had refused to return there following the atrocious massacre of 1391.

What Braudel says concerning the Moriscos (baptized Moors) is no less inaccurate. They were not expelled by Philip II as a consequence of the debilitating war of the Alpujarras (1568–1571), but much later, as a result of their dealings with the Turks and other enemies of Spain. I regret having to us this sort of language, but I do so moved by suprapersonal reasons and by the incalculable damage to today's young people, growing up in an anarchistic and nihilistic period, which is implied by a theory of human history based on the "law of numbers," a theory gaining ever-increasing acceptance in the universities of Europe and America. To determine and calculate the course of human history electronically has become the dream of a large segment of humanity today. It is, therefore, indispensable to point out and insist upon this kind of fallacy in order to prevent anyone's being misled by what is in fact a kind of scholarly magic show supported by a mass of documentary erudition, impressive in its volume if not in its persuasive force. It is simply incredible that Braudel, instead of using his data to show that in 1492 the Spaniards were constrained by their environment, should deduce a population surplus from the fact of "the repeated expulsions of Jews." Common sense dictates a progression from the known to the unknown, but we are now told, in order to prove that the expulsions of Jews were occasioned by a population explosion, that the Jews were expelled in 1492, precisely when the

---

[7] *La Méditerranée*, vol. I, 380.

capture of Granada considerably augmented the geographical extension of Castile and Aragon by the addition of Granada, Malaga, and
Almeria. Braudel also fails to consider the fact that many Jews expelled from Spain came back home after being baptized and others
took refuge at the feet of the popes in Rome, where physical living
space must certainly have been at a premium.

The phases and aspects of the Spaniards' history are neither easy to
determine nor intelligible if we limit ourselves to describing or narrating mere events or happenings or to depicting peaks of prosperity
alternating with valleys of decline. What is of central importance, the
real problem behind these appearances and façades lies in the modes of
behavior of each Christian kingdom and in the way in which each
caste of believers in these kingdoms conducted itself and saw itself
with respect to the other two. In that "behavior" we also include the
effort to coordinate abilities for the common good or the attempts of
one caste to triumph at the expense of the other two. There are certain
questions which have hitherto been considered unworthy of study or
ignored by historians. For example, the fact that the Christians could
not absorb the Muslim population instead of living next to them as
Mudejars in the reconquered territories and later as Moriscos after
the conquest of Granada in 1492. Or the fact that the Jews gradually
exerted more influence in the royal courts and in Christian society in
general while the areas dominated by the Muslims began to become
narrower. The materialistic-oriented historians put forth demographic
and economic factors such as a lack of technology and unproductive
soil, but at the end of the fourteenth century the king of Castile held
land from the fertile plains of the south to the Cantabrian seaports,
and among his vassals there were many people skilled in weaving and
other types of trades and lesser professions. In spite of this, however,
the Castilians chose to export raw materials such as wool instead of
manufacturing anything. The centuries of reconquest had accustomed
the Christians of Castile to the arts of war and to employing Moors
and Jews for all types of artisanry and even for the administration of
finances. It is noteworthy, for example, that such basic pastoral terms
as *rabadán* (the head shepherd), *rehala* (a flock of sheep of different
owners under the care of one shepherd), and *zagal* (a young shepherd) are all Arabic words concerning the migration of sheep from
one part of the country to the other and indicating that this extremely
vital activity was a Moorish concern. Before 1500 the Christian of
Castile simply could not assimilate the Mudejar nor could he do without the services of the Jew.

The most popular histories currently in fashion deal with fourteenth- and fifteenth-century Spain in abstract terms of demographic ciphers as if these were the decisive factors.[8] If this were true, if the number of inhabitants determined the course of history, that "tiny corner" of land, as the Castile of the tenth century is called in the thirteenth-century *Poema de Fernán González*, should never have extended its political domain throughout the lands later known as Spain, nor spread its language throughout most of it. Nor is it possible to explain by statistics how the small numbers of Romans of the "Roma quadrata" were able to extend their power and Romanize all those people who later made up the Roman Empire. I must emphasize again, at the expense of repetition, that we are dealing here not with numerical figures but with acts of human will and volition.

The Name of the Future Spaniards

The history of the Spaniards is the most problematic and confusing of all the European peoples. In France and England it is known and taught that there were not always Frenchmen or Englishmen in the geographical territories so called today. But, as the reader will see later on in this work, both the thirteenth-century chroniclers and present-day historians assume that there were always Spaniards in the Iberian Peninsula, even centuries before the Roman conquest. For this reason, it is necessary at this point to insist that *español* is a foreign word, imported from Provence, as the Swiss philologist Paul Aebischer proved several years ago. He solved the etymological problem, but it still remains to see how and when it was possible for the inhabitants of the separate individual Christian kingdoms (Leon, Castile, Aragon) to accept as their own a name that had been imported from another land. Within this historical, and not merely linguistic, problem, we must include the strange phenomenon that although Aebischer published his study on the word *español* in 1948 in Spain[9] it still appears without any etymological explanation in the *Diccionario de la Academia española* of 1970. No less significant is the fact that in his monumental *Diccionario etimológico de la lengua castellana* Juan Corominas still did not include the word *español* in his latest edition published in 1967. Hence, I find myself faced with the double difficulty of invalidating the Spaniards' illusory past in order to be able to locate them within their proper historical being, and, at the same time, to make their authentic reality in time and space apparent to the reader.

The erroneous idea held by historians concerning the origin and

---

[8] Aragon and Catalonia had fewer inhabitants than Castile. J. L. Martín, "Los reinos hispánicos a fines de la Edad Media," in *Anuario de Estudios medievales* (Barcelona, 1966), p. 669, with accompanying bibliography.

[9] *Estudios de toponimia y lexicografía románicas* (Barcelona: Instituto Antonio de Nebrija, 1948).

identity of the Spaniards is directly related to the origin of the name that began to be applied to them in the thirteenth century and that still is. That name, *español*, as I mentioned and shall explain subsequently, was imported from Provence in the thirteenth century. Until this time the future Spaniards had been calling themselves *cristianos* (Christians), a name that appeared for the first time in the ninth century. They had not felt the need nor the possibility of giving a non-religious name to embrace that heterogeneous collectivity of peoples made up of Galicians, Leonese, Castilians, Navarrese, Aragonese, and Catalans. The authors and compilers of the *Crónica General*[10] under the direction of King Alfonso X, the Learned, utilized sources written in Latin in which the first settlers were called *Hispani* and in which the land they inhabited was called *Hispania*, a name given it by the Romans. One of these sources is the *De rebus Hispaniae*, a chronicle written by Don Rodrigo Jiménez de Rada, the Archbishop of Toledo, a Navarrese born at the end of the twelfth century and educated in Bologna and Paris where he had learned his excellent medieval Latin. (This chronicle was reproduced in *Opera* published in Madrid in 1793.) According to Jiménez de Rada, the first settlers of Hispania were descended from Tubal, the grandson of Noah.[11] The Latin text was translated thus in the *Primera Crónica General*: "Mas del quinto fijo de Japhet, que ovo nombre Thubal, donde vinieron los *españoles* . . . ," ("From the fifth son of Japheth, who was called Tubal, from whence came the *Spaniards* . . ."). The descendents of Tubal journeyed through many lands "until they came to that part of the Occident where the great mountains are called the Pyrenees" (ed. Menéndez Pidal [1955], vol. I, 6). The translator of *De rebus Hispaniae* had no other word with which to translate *Hispani*; thus he had to use the Provençal loanword *español* which had been introduced by the pilgrims to Santiago and employed by the poet Gonzalo de Berceo to refer to the inhabitants of the Christian kingdoms in the first third of the thirteenth century, as shall be explained later in this chapter. In this way a linguistic phenomenon suddenly assumes a major historical significance.

The presence of the foreign loanword, *español*, in the *Primera Crónica General* proves that in Castile neither the derivative *espanesco* (from *Hispaniscus*) nor any Castilian derivatives of *Hispaniensis* or *Hispaniolus* were used in Castile. That is to say, no name existed other than that of *cristianos* to designate that totality of peoples who began to be called *españoles* in the thirteenth century. It is not feasible to

---

[10] R. Menéndez Pidal, *Primera Crónica General de España* (Madrid, 1955), vol. I, xx.

[11] "Quintus autem filius Japhet fuit Thubal, a quo Iberi, qui Hispani (ut dicunt Isidorus et Hieronymus) processerunt," *De rebus Hispaniae* (Liber I, cap. 3), in *Opera* (Madrid, 1793).

think that the nonexistent Castilian derivation of *Hispaniolus*, that should have been *españuelo*, did not take root because the suffix *uelo* would have given the inhabitants of the Christian kingdoms a diminutive connotation. What really happened was that there was no need for a collective name at that point. From a purely abstract linguistic point of view, for example, there was nothing to oppose the fact that the inhabitants of the Christian kingdoms, from Cape Finisterre to Creus, might have called themselves *espaneses* (by analogy with *cordobeses*, as the inhabitants of Córdoba were called), *espanescos* (as the Mozarabs called themselves), or simply *espanos*, as the name *Hispanos* used to denominate the inhabitants of *Hispania* was pronounced in popular Latin. Thus, before the word *español* appeared in the language spoken in Castile, there had been no occasion for these Christians from northern Spain, nor had they felt the need, to consider themselves as a secularized, unified body.[12]

Since we are dealing with a key problem which must be the point of departure for anyone who aspires to disentangle the fabulous, fictitious clichés of Spanish history from the real ones, we must again return to the historiography written in Latin in the thirteenth century so that the reader may judge for himself. In the *Historia Arabum*, also composed by Jiménez de Rada and included in the aforementioned *Opera*, the author refers to those who fight against the Moors either as *Hispani* or *Christiani*.[13] But the archbishop-chronicler clearly emphasizes the fact that King Pelayo took refuge in Asturias for religious reasons and not political ones, which agrees with the ninth-century *Chronica Albeldense* cited in chapter iii of this book, according to which the Christians were involved in daily combat with the Muslims. Four centuries later Jiménez de Rada repeats the statement that the reason for the resistance against the Moors in Asturias was to preserve "some spark of the name 'Christian,' for the Muslims had occupied all of Spain."[14] Further on in *De rebus Hispaniae*, when he describes the defeat of Alfonso VI at Zalaca (1086), the chronicler says that the king's armies were made up of *cristianos*, and no one else (*Liber IV, cap.* 31). On other occasions the combatants are identified by the names of their respective kingdoms: "De victoris regis Aragoniae contra Gallaecos et Castellanos" (VII, 2).

---

[12] *Españón*, a variant of *español*, appeared in the thirteenth and fourteenth centuries a few times. See Aebischer, *Estudios de toponimia y lexicografía*, pp. 15, 16, 32.

[13] Abd al-Malik "pro regimine nocua coepit in *Hispanos* exercere" (ed. cit., chap. 15); in *De rebus Hispaniae*: "Taric *Christianos* fuit usque in Ecijam secutus" (Liber III, cap. 123). Such examples are plentiful and it is hardly necessary to mention all of them at this point.

[14] "Christiani nominis aliquam scintillam conservare. Sarraceni enim totam Hispaniam occupaverant," *De rebus Hispaniae* (Liber IV, cap. 1).

The *Chronicon mundi* of Don Lucas, Bishop of Túy,[15] who died in 1249, was also utilized as a Latin source for the *Crónica General*. Don Lucas uses both the words *Hispani* (p. 2) and *Christiani* (p. 75) to refer to the inhabitants of the Christian kingdoms. He concludes by citing the conquest of Cordova (1236) which put an end to what he calls the "opprobrium Hispanorum" (p. 116).

As for the Visigoths, both Jiménez de Rada and Lucas de Túy always refer to them as *Gothi*, never as *Hispani*: "Deploratio Hispaniae, et de causa exciddi Gothorum" (*De rebus Hispaniae*, vol. I, III 22). The Bishop of Túy still says that Alfonso the Catholic was elected king in 739 "ab universo populo Gothorum" (p. 73).

To further destroy the inveterate error of calling all the inhabitants of the Peninsula *españoles* with consistent retroactivity, I refer to a law of the *Codex Wisigothorum*, or *Forum Judicum* (III, I, 2), promulgated by King Receswinth (649–672) regarding permission for Romans and Visigoths to intermarry: "Prisquae legis remota sententia hac in perpetuum valitura lege sancimus, ut tan *Gotus Romanam*, quam etiam *Gotam Romanus*, si coniugem habere voluerit, premissa petitione dignissima, facultas eis nubendi subiaceat." In the thirteenth-century Castilian translation, this law in Book III, title I is numbered I, not 2, and says the following: "Tollemos nos la ley antigua, e ponemos otra mejor; y establecemos por esta ley, que a de valer por siempre, que la mugier Romana puede casar con omne Godo; e la mugier Goda puede casar con omne Romano." ("We shall strike out the former law and replace it with a better one, and establish by this new decree that is valid forever, that a Roman woman may marry a Goth; and a Gothic woman may marry a Roman man.") Significantly, in the Visigothic text the Visigoth is mentioned first in both cases. But the pertinent point here is the fact that this law does not mention *españoles*, because the legislator was very much aware that the inhabitants of the Peninsula were either Visigothic or Roman and nothing else.

These rather tedious details serve merely to show the reader that when the Castilians of the thirteenth century wrote in Latin they could choose between the nouns *Hispani* or *Christiani* to refer to that collective entity of combatants who fought in the Christian kingdoms. The Goths were called *Gothi* and the inhabitants of Roman Hispania, *Hispani*, terms which had no equivalents in spoken or written Castilian before the thirteenth century. In the Christian areas of the Peninsula the only existing common denominator within the diverse regionalisms or political "dialectism" was a religious one. Thus it was not possible, as I have said before, to coin a secular name instead of a religious

---

15 In *Hispania Illustrata* (Frankfurt: Andrea Scott, 1608), vol. IV.

one which might encompass all those variegated kingdoms and with which everyone might identify. The *Cantar del Cid* (*ca.* 1140) speaks of the "kings of Spain" in the plural, but there was no single name by which the minstrel could unite all their vassals.

In later chapters of this work I discuss in detail the pilgrimages to Santiago de Compostela in Galicia, the shrine of St. James the Greater. One important consequence of that extensive contact with Europe was the bestowal of a unifying name on the people through whose lands the pilgrims passed along the *camino francés* (the French Road). One of the sentences in the *Crónica General* gives a vivid impression of this idea of internationalism brought by those thousands of foreigners who had been crossing the northern part of the Peninsula for centuries: "The Way of St. James . . . through which Christians from almost all the lands of the world pass" (ed. Menéndez Pidal [1955], vol. I, 353). Many of the Christian pilgrims to Santiago came from the south of France where the heterogeneous populations below the Pyrenees were called *espanhols* (that is, *españols*).

Furthermore, not only foreigners visited the sanctuary of the apostle. For Christians who had been warring against the Muslims for centuries, and at the same time had been in contact with their customs, usages, and civilization, the pilgrimage to Santiago was analogous to, or probably had the same significance as, the one the Mohammedans made to Mecca, the ḥajj, a koranical precept observed by any Muslim who was able to make the journey. As the eminent Arabist E. Lévi-Provençal points out, it is no wonder that one of the campaigns of al-Manṣūr, the famous warrior, was called in Arabic *Shant Yaqub*, because its special purpose was to inflict an affront upon the whole of Christianity by desecrating one of its most revered shrines.[16] Historical parallels such as these occur constantly as we shall see, such as the ḥajj, the meaning of the names of the Christian and Arabic rulers (*malik*), etc., interpreted, of course, in their proper context within this work, particularly in the chapters dealing with Santiago and Islamic institutions.

To return to our original problem, once again language makes history comprehensible, because, in addition to being a means of communication, it is also a way of expressing and interpreting life. When they called themselves *cristianos*, the future Spaniards situated themselves with respect to some higher force beyond them, because it is not the same to live with a belief in the supernatural as it is to live in a land considered as a projection of a human group in which the speaker includes himself. When *Hispania* was a Roman province it contained *Astures* who dwelt in *Asturia*, *Gallaeci* in *Gallaecia*, or *Vascones* in *Vasconia*. Later on there were places or villages called *Romanos* or

---

[16] "España musulmana," in *Historia de España* (1967), vol. IV, 423.

Godos, or other similar names, because their inhabitants had been Romans or Visigoths.

But in none of the above cases did the correlation between the inhabitant and the land he inhabited take on an extraregional and lasting dimension, and this is one of the primary questions concerning the problematic history of Spain. Interposed between the inhabitant and the land he inhabited, there was a supernatural, or more precisely an Oriental, circumstance—a contrast-harmony between Muslims and Christians. Hence, under the influence of this particular situation, the name of those future Spaniards was bestowed upon them by outsiders. Where there was a total absence of Oriental influence, for example in France, the poet Ausonius, writing at the end of the fourth century, had already established a correlation between *Francia* and the *Franci*, which took root and multiplied, thus providing a valid cornerstone for the history of the neighboring country.

The only religious common denominator of the reconquerors or those occupying the Christian kingdoms arose as an adverse parallelism to those Moors who were already called *mozlemos* in the tenth century.[17] The fact that the word *mozlemos* is first documented in a glossary of the tenth century does not mean that the Christians had no name for their subjugators or enemies of their religious faith before then. The aforementioned chronicles were not interested in the presence of the Mudejars or the Jews. Consequently, if the political dimension of the noun *cristiano* expressed by contrast a collective identity in opposition to those who also based their own identity on a religious belief, when we reach the thirteenth century, the Provençal loanword, *español*, indirectly reflected the faith in an apostle of Christ of those who had been making pilgrimages to Galicia for many centuries. St. James or Santiago helped the Christians in their wars against the Moors and held together all those who had to find some name for the heterogeneous mass composed of Basques, Catalans, Castilians, Leonese, Aragonese, Galicians, and Navarrese. These people, in turn, saw themselves reflected as a single image in the mirror of that word so insistently repeated by the pilgrims from beyond the Pyrenees. Eventually they began to call themselves by that name that others had called them, and for the first time an agreement was reached between the words *España* and *español*.

It is obvious that the Franks, Normans, and Anglo-Saxons all had a religion, but their consciousness of their own collective identities was based on secular foundations. The identification of the personality of the State or Nation with religion (in modern times) is a Judeo-Islamic characteristic of Oriental, not Occidental, civilization.

Besides this, the fact that the term *español* was accepted in literature

---

[17] R. Menéndez Pidal, *Orígenes del español* (Madrid, 1950), p. 14.

in the first third of the thirteenth century is explicable if we recall that the memory of the great victory of Las Navas de Tolosa, won in 1212 by the "tres reyes de España" (the three kings of Spain), was still fresh in the minds of the people. From this time on the power of al-Andalus began to wane. In his *Crónica* written at the end of the thirteenth century, the Catalan Bernat Desclot, as I explain later in chapter vii, describes that victory: "Lo rey d'Aragó e *els altres reys d'Espanya* s'en tornaren cascú en sa terra" (ed. M. Coll, II, 32–37). Around the same time the *Crónica General* (p. 693) relates that before the battle Alfonso VIII addressed the Aragonese, Portuguese, and Galicians who had assembled to fight against the Almohades: "Amigos, todos nos somos *españoles* . . ." ("Friends, we are all Spaniards"). This harangue does not appear in the Latin chronicle of Jiménez de Rada and was written at the end of the thirteenth century when the strength of the Moorish armies had diminished considerably. That Spain was now a fertile land for the term *español* to take root and flourish, regardless of whether or not its *o* became diphthongized as the norms of the Castilian language dictate. Nevertheless, if a common name was used to denote the Christians beyond the Pyrenees in twelfth-century Provence, this was not true in Paris. A document dated 1292 mentions the names of the following foreigners designated by their countries: "Guillaume le *Danois*, Thomas le *Norrois*, Raoul l'*Yrais* (Irishman)"; but there is no adjective for the man who had come from Spain: "Gracien d'Espaigne."[18]

We should also bear in mind that even as late as the eleventh century the name *Spania* continued to be applied to the territory occupied by the Muslims, but not to the Christian kingdoms.[19] If the term *Hispania* was preserved in Moorish territories, the survival of its derivative *Hispaniscus* among the Mozarabs, the Romance-speaking inhabitants of the same region, is easily explained. In Mozarabic Vulgar Latin, for example, "Aredoma erea *espanesca*" meant "a *Moorish* style bronze flask."[20]

Professor Aebischer must be credited with having established the

---

[18] Paul Lebel, *Les noms de personne en France* (Paris, 1962), p. 108.

[19] In the ninth century King Ordoño I populated cities taken from the Moors (Leon and Astorga) with people "some of whom came from his kingdom of Asturias and others from *Spania*." In his commentary on this text R. Menéndez Pidal states: "It is well known that when almost all the land in the peninsula fell under foreign domination the word *Hispania* was, for the independent Christians, a synonym for Muslim territory" (*Orígenes del español*, p. 441). In the will of a Catalan drawn up on 2 May, 1010, before making a journey to Moorish territory, the merchant says: "Ut si de isto itinere quo ego facio ad *Spania* . . . ," Aebischer, *Estudios de toponimia y lexicografía*, p. 45.

[20] M. Gómez Moreno, *Iglesias mozárabes*, I, 342. Just as the lands under Moorish domination were called *Spania*, any adjective referring to the Moorish was called *espanesco*. Aebischer (p. 19) mentions "argento spanescho" (986) and "asino espanesco" (1027), that is, silver and a donkey imported from al-Andalus.

geographical region where the Provençal loanword *espanhol*, a derivative of *Hispaniolus*, the name used to designate the inhabitants of the Peninsula, originated, just as natives of Hellas would be called *Graeculi* by outsiders. Aebischer believes that the word *español* appeared for the first time "toward the end of the thirteenth century" (*Estudios de toponimia y lexicografía*, p. 32); but, as I have already said, it was in use years before and with reference to the pilgrimages to Santiago. Around 1230 the poet Gonzalo de Berceo called the Apostle whose remains were venerated at Compostela "patron of *españoles*" (*Vida de San Millán, copla* 431). Berceo, writing to glorify his fellow countryman, San Millán (St. Emilian), compares him with St. James and solicits for him the same offerings that were being made to the "patron of *españoles*." Berceo was composing his works a short distance from the route followed by the pilgrims, many of whom came down from southern France. In Provence these pilgrims had learned the name for the people patronized by Santiago, as interesting for the miracles he performed as for the economic benefits reaped by many of these same foreigners along the pilgrimage way. The conclusion to be drawn from this is that the collective name for the Spaniards was indirectly brought about by religious circumstances. Those who fought against the Moors in the eighth century were called *cristianos*; those who were under the protection of Santiago were called *españoles* by the pilgrims who came to venerate the Apostle. The secular dimension inherent in the names *Romani* and *Gothi*, which referred only to an imperial or a royal sovereignty, was soon forgotten, although traces can be found today fossilized in a few toponyms such as *Romanos*, *Romanillos*, or *Godos*, and *Gudillos*.[21]

The presence of the word *español* in the *Primera Crónica General* composed at the end of the thirteenth century has had disastrous consequences for Spanish historiography. Since, in some cases, the *Crónica* made use of the new loanword, *español*, to translate the term *Hispani* used by the chroniclers who wrote in Latin, both words became infused with the same spatial and temporal dimension. Since there had been *Hispani* in the Iberian Peninsula before the Roman conquest, it was assumed that there had also been *españoles*. Alonso de Palencia, an intelligent but misinformed writer of the fifteenth century, inserted in his *Universal Vocabulario* (1490): "Tubal was the son of Japheth from whom the Iberians who are *españoles* are descended." The different strata of populations were automatically classified uniformly as *españoles*: the pre-Roman, Roman, Hispano-Visigoth, those of the centuries of the reconquest, the imperial Spaniards with one single common belief, irreconciled to their past and present, all became fused and indistinguishable one from another un-

---

21 See Menéndez Pidal, *Orígenes del español*, pp. 505–506.

der the heading *español*. Once the Roman *Hispani* had been confused with the thirteenth-century *españoles*, it was not necessary to keep in mind that from the eighth to the sixteenth century there were three castes of Spaniards, each with its own beliefs, mission, tasks in society, and special problems. This paved the way for the absurd legend that began to take shape and become rooted in historiography that the vassals of Charles V were just as Spanish as those who had fought against the Carthaginians and the Romans before the birth of Christ.

In the *Crónica General* (p. 17) it is written that Hannibal "took those people he had brought from Africa and as many *españoles* as he wished to fight against the Romans." Nevertheless, the *Crónica* is not systematic, for it does not refer to the Cantabrians, the Asturians, or the Galicians as *españoles*. As the "Galicians were not ready to make war and were taken by surprise" they were easily conquered by the Romans (p. 29). But the *Crónica* does take the opportunity, in its account of the Punic Wars, to demonstrate an anachronistic preference for the Europeans and its antipathy for the Africans. The Romans attracted "all those excellent horsemen they found along the Ebro" because those riders "chose rightly to fight on the side of the Romans, who were Europeans, and not with the Carthaginians who had come from Africa" (p. 19). As early as the thirteenth century we find this characteristic desire for "Europeanization," at a time when that Europe which exercised such an attraction for certain collaborators of Alfonso the Learned did not even exist.

In spite of this, the *Crónica General* does distinguish the *Hispani*, those ancient inhabitants of the Peninsula whom it calls *españoles*, from the *godos* and the *cristianos* who fought against the Moors. Nevertheless, the fusion of *Hispani* and *españoles* resulted in the conversion of Quintillian, Trajan, Hadrian, Seneca, and every other illustrious Roman born in Hispania into *españoles* (pp. 129, 142, 145, etc.). The terminology changes, however, when it begins to deal with the Visigothic domination: "The *godos* elected as their king Theodisclus" (p. 256). "Now the history of the *godos* in Spain is ended and the history of the birth of Mohammed is begun" (p. 261). In 1195 "the armies of *cristianos* led by Alfonso VIII of Castile" (p. 681) were defeated at the Battle of Alarcos. The "Christian hosts" made up of Castilians, Navarrese, and Aragonese won the decisive Battle of Las Navas de Tolosa in 1212 (p. 697). Even as late as the end of the fifteenth century Mosén Diego de Valera called those who fought in the battle against the kingdom of Granada *cristianos*: "It pleased our Lord to allow the Christians to cross the pass and not suffer any harm."[22]

---

[22] Diego de Valera, *Crónica de los Reyes Católicos*, ed. J. de Mata Carriazo (Madrid, 1927), p. 135. In the *Gran Conquista de Ultramar*, a work translated from the French in the thirteenth century, the author mentions a "regiment of Spanish knights" (Bibl. de Aut. Esp., vol. XLV, 196).

These rather tiresome details concerning the names given to the inhabitants of the Peninsula in the ancient chronicles have been necessary to demonstrate that the chroniclers clearly distinguished between the pre-Roman inhabitants, the Romans (*Hispani*), the Visigoths (*godos*), and the Christians (*cristianos*) who fought to put an end to Muslim domination. Seen in this perspective, the historiography of the chroniclers between the thirteenth and fifteenth centuries is more in accordance with reality and more accurate than the writings of those modern historians who still continue to refuse to distinguish between them and persist in calling the Visigoths, the pre-Romans, and the Hispano-Romans *españoles*, putting them all in the same category.[23]

In the last analysis it is clearly evident how necessary it has been to remove some of the obstacles which prevent our uncovering the real face of the Spanish past. The initial step has been to establish precisely what is meant when we use the word *español*. This done, in the following chapters we shall address ourselves to certain phases and aspects of the Spanish past which have hitherto been poorly studied, approached from the wrong angle, or misinterpreted because of the widely held misconceptions concerning the identity and the collective personality of the Spaniards and how they came to be.

---

[23] That *español* was an imported word and not a native one is again demonstrated by the fact that the language spoken by the Spaniards was still referred to in Spain as "Castilian" (*castellano*). In Spanish America the term *lengua castellana* is still preferred to *lengua española*. Amado Alonso has pointed out that the adjective *español* does not appear in the titles of books before 1520. *Castellano, español, lengua nacional* (Buenos Aires, 1938).

II · THE PROBLEM: IN SEARCH OF THE REALITY THAT IS NOT A FABLE

MONG THE PEOPLES of the West, the Spaniard is the only one who is guided in the awareness of his past and of himself by a historiography based on fantastic notions. The Spaniard considers himself virtually an emanation from the soil of the Iberian Peninsula, or at least a being as ancient as the prehistoric Peninsular cave dwellers, those people who left brilliant and disturbing pictures of men and buffaloes on the stone walls of the caves of Altamira (Santander). Thus the Spanishness of the prehistoric inhabitants in the mountainous regions of the Province of Santander continues uninterrupted in the people who make cheese in the grottos of Cabrales, caverns not as dark but quite as ancient, geologically, as the caveman's.

Faith in the temporally uncertain biological continuity of the Spaniard has inspired the works both of respected men of wisdom and of superficial scholars. The few given to reflection on the problem quicken in this way their _faith_ in themselves, in their own _being_, rather than in whatever of value may have been _achieved_ by their ancestors. The prevailing beliefs have it that the _essence_ of the Spaniard has persisted uncorrupted, untouched, through the various peoples and events that have happened on the Peninsula since the remotest times to which the feeblest tradition refers. Father Juan de Mariana—in many ways a superior person—began his _History of Spain_ in 1601 with these words: "Tubal, son of Japheth, was the first man who came to Spain." And when he said "Spain," he was thinking of a fixed concept, as if he were speaking of the first "tree" planted in Spain. I myself was taught in school to repeat that "Tubal, son of Japheth and grandson of Noah, was the first settler of Spain." Mariana (II, 1) writes that the city of Carthage sent "two thousand Carthaginians and the same number of Spanish soldiers to Sicily," soldiers as Spanish for Mariana as those who, in his own time, manned the Spanish garrisons in Sicily. Previously Mariana writes (I, 14):

"From the intermarriage of these Celts and the Spaniards, *who called themselves Iberians,* came the name Celtiberia, by which a large part of Spain was called."

Leaping from 1600 to the present, we find a historian accepting as accurate what had been said about Muslim Granada: "Of the two hundred thousand souls in the city of Granada, fewer than five hundred were of the African nation; the rest were native Spaniards and Goths who had given allegiance to the law of the conquerors."[1] It turns out, then, that the inhabitants of the region called Granada became Muslims and spoke Arabic, and in spite of this their descendants continued to be Spaniards, like the Iberians and Spaniards of today. Sr. de las Cajigas observes that the Moors who continued to live among the Christians (the Mudejars), "conservative in sentiment," opposed "the total and rapid Christianization of the regions and cities occupied by the reconquerors." Later (between 1492 and 1609) the Moriscos (the "baptized" Moors) showed the same resistance to assimilation by the life and customs of their conquerors. "It was an uninterrupted linkage of nine centuries (from the eighth to the seventeenth), almost a millennium of popular opposition to the dominant regime. It is possible and necessary to think that the root of this resistance, tenacious and sustained, is a *surprising survival of*

---

[1] Isidoro de las Cajigas, *Los mudéjares,* I (1948), 73. The author attributes this quotation to Hernando de Baeza, Boabdil's interpreter, who composed the *Relaciones de algunos sucesos de los últimos tiempos del reino de Granada,* which appears as Volume III of the publications of the Sociedad de Bibliófilos Españoles. But Hernando de Baeza says nothing of the kind. The inaccuracy is of no special consequence so far as I am concerned, but it is of some consequence that Sr. de las Cajigas should accept such statements as true.

In reality, the quotation comes from the Granadine historian Francisco Bermúdez de Pedraza, as he is cited by F. J. Simonet, *Historia de los mozárabes de España* (Madrid, 1897–1903), p. 788: "The historian Bermúdez de Pedraza maintains that in the time of the Almohades . . . the Mozarabs [Christians living in the Moorish kingdoms] of this region had almost totally disappeared; [the latter] had renounced their faith in such numbers that when the Catholic Sovereigns reconquered this kingdom, they found no sign or trace of them. As a testimony to the apostasy of the *ancient Spanish race* [!] he cites the account made in 1311 by the ambassadors of the kingdom of Aragon to Pope Clement XI, [in which it was said] that at that time two hundred thousand people were living in the city of Granada, and among them were fewer than five hundred of Moorish birth, because they were all the children and grandchildren of Christians." In further support of his view, Simonet quotes Ibn-al-Khatib, who also said, in the second half of the fourteenth century, that the inhabitants of Granada were in large part of foreign extraction. Now, if we should apply this strange criterion to other countries, it would turn out that in fourteenth-century England there were likewise no "native Englishmen," for some were descendants of Danes, others of Normans, and others of still different "races." As we shall see, this "genealogical and biological" standard employed by Spanish historians has Semitic roots and is based on the concern for lineage, which is so intense among Jews and Muslims. In other words, this apparent nonsense takes on meaning within the caste structure of Spanish life, as will become clear in chapter iii.

the ancestral Iberian stubbornness" (p. 47). This resistance "was constantly maintained by *the same ethnic unity*" because the Mozarabs and the Mudejars "were first and above all, Spaniards, and the latter were the offspring of the former." Earlier, the Arabs and the Berbers "had been rapidly assimilated by the numerically and spiritually superior vitality of the invaded country" (p. 48), that is, of Spain, whose land, from the beginning of human time, had been inhabited by Spaniards.

This belief—that the Spanish people are as ancient as the first inhabitants of the Peninsula—is generally accepted as an unquestionable dogma. The notions of Iberia, Hispania, and España (Spain), are confused in the minds of both ancient and modern historians. Sr. Ramos Oliveira, for whom everything human depends on economic circumstances, asserts that "the moral personality of Spain in the pre-Roman epoch was already the one by which our nation has been distinguished in all epochs. The representative Spaniard is the Celtiberian."[2] According to Sr. Luis Pericot, "few differences are to be noted in the 3,000 years (a hundred generations) from the Tartessians to the modern Andalusians, not only in their temperament. Suffice it to remember that a *cheerful disposition*, skill in dancing, and the love of bullfighting were qualities that adorned them already in Antiquity. What will Tartessian texts tell us when they can speak, or, rather, when we can understand them? . . . I do not know, *but I am sure* that they will give us the picture of a perfectly Spanish society." Although Sr. Pericot writes that "Tartessus is perhaps little more than a myth, and although it would not do when we seek to get rid of myths in the history of Spain, for us to fall into another myth, no matter how pleasant it might be, . . . *in any case*, in that Tartessian kingdom, poetic because of the mystery that envelops its history, . . . lived one of the deepest roots of *the Spain of all times*."[3]

Recently (1960) a new and significant testimonial of the Spaniards' peculiar historiographic faith has appeared,[4] which adheres, like all the others, to the same school of thought: the present inhabitants were Spanish *ab initio* and were not affected by the several peoples and civilizations that have existed on the Peninsula; the Hispano-Hebrews left no deep imprint. Here are some declarations of this faith: The "demographic mobility of the region [of Toledo and Madrid], we believe, has had scarcely any effect on the firm Celtiberian base of the Meseta. Still today the dominant note in the people of Alcarria and Toledo is isolation and, in many respects, the tribal character of their organization. . . . Imbalance between heavy emigra-

---

[2] *Historia de España*, I, 232, 234.
[3] Luis Pericot García, *Las raíces de España* (Madrid, 1952), pp. 52–53. Italics mine.
[4] Criado de Val, *Teoría de Castilla la Nueva* (Madrid, 1960).

tions and almost nonexistent immigrations . . . has always been characteristic of these zones—with the exception, naturally, of the capital, be it the city of Toledo or of Madrid. All speculation concerning
racial changes or mixtures in these areas must reckon with this reality: *the population base continues to be prehistoric*" (p. 93). The
resistance of the Mozarabs was stronger than the action of the Muslims: "Mozarabism imposed its intransigent criterion. Coexistence
[between Christians and Muslims] never had anything more than the
provisional character of all military occupations. . . . Observation
of the present-day coexistence between Spaniards and Moroccans in
the old area of the Protectorate can aid us in properly conceiving the
relationship between Moors and Christians in the Middle Ages" (p.
88). "Nevertheless, this undeniable Judaism of Toledo does not play
the predominant historical role that Américo Castro assigns to it."
After the expulsion of the Jews in 1492, "the residual Jewish element
was rapidly assimilated. It is, therefore, captious to pigeonhole Christian writers alien to the Mosaic tradition along with Jews only because of their distant Jewish ancestry" (p. 92).

Similar assertions may be found in many books—large ones, small
ones, those written centuries ago, others written only yesterday. The
idea of the Iberian and Celtiberian nature of contemporary Spaniards
has at times been adopted even by some French and German scholars.

This burning faith arose among Spaniards long before the birth
in Germany of historical "science" in the nineteenth century. The
identification of Spaniards and of various Romanized areas of the
Peninsula with their pre-Roman inhabitants is as old as the beginnings
of historiography among the Spaniards. As early as the thirteenth
century, Rodrigo Jiménez de Rada believed that "Iberians and Spaniards descend from Tubal, fifth son of Japheth."[5] Later, in the
sixteenth century, a scholar as learned as Florián de Ocampo saw
Spaniards everywhere—in Ireland, in Asia. Cirot rightly thought
that the spectacle of Spanish conquest in the New World must have
given Ocampo the idea that "Spaniards" in the times of Atlas, the
Sicanians, the Siculians, and other mythical characters had been
adventurers and colonizers (*ibid.*, p. 120).

The vision of the Empire projected onto the mythical past the
imperial longing of Spaniards, both those of the Hispano-Christian
caste and those who were New Christians and saw themselves as
rivals of the former, as is explained later on. But all this is not sufficient to understand the modern Spaniard's desire to make himself
eternal in the past, to believe that he was already present in the
Tartessians, to make Emperor Trajan speak with an Andalusian accent, or to introduce into the past of the Peninsula a recurrent

---

[5] See George Cirot, *Les histoires générales d'Espagne entre Alphonse X et
Philippe II* (1905), pp. 32 ff.

rhythm according to which Emperor Theodosius—a Roman born
ca. 346 in Cauca, a town of Roman Hispania—arranged the course
of his politics in a way that anticipates the plans of Emperor Charles
V. If all this were true, those who today are called Spaniards would
possess a uniform and static reality, repeated over thousands of
years, with a magical ability to assimilate—while never losing its own
forms of life—Ligurians, Iberians, Celts, Phoenicians, Carthaginians,
Romans, Visigoths, Berbers, Arabs, and Jews. Alone among the
peoples of the West, the Spaniard would belong to a kind of man
untouched by time and circumstances, with an unchanging essence
and psychic structure, unaffected by the necessity of facing himself,
other men, and the world of which he is a part.

Human Life Is More than Geography, Biology, Psychology, and Economics

It would be foolish to waste time labeling as chimerical this way of
conceiving the Spaniard and the dimensions of his past life which are
worthy of historical consideration. This way of conceiving history
seems to me more than erroneous; it is a reflection of the way Spaniards, whether they are historians or not, are situated within their
own life, that life whose analysis and appraisal constitute the theme
of this book. If one does not stand at some distance from this life,
it is impossible to perceive its form and functioning. Spanish historiography, with its determination to include a past that does not
belong to it and to exclude the most characteristic elements of its
reality, is an inherent part of the very process of Spanish life.

In addition, current historiography has been affected by its alien-
ation from certain European ideas about the reality of man which
seem to me prerequisite to the understanding of that reality. Historiographers either do not take them into consideration or act like certain civil servants of past years with respect to royal orders: "they
respect, but do not execute them." There are even learned exponents
of pure thought, vaulting their up-to-date views, who continue to
act like Hegelians or positivists when faced with concrete problems
of history. One must remember, furthermore, that knowledge, in
itself so excellent a thing, becomes an idle accumulation of materials
without apparent purpose if it does not coalesce into a structure
within which both the parts and the whole take on meaning.

Conventional Spanish historiography builds on the supposition
that *blood*, in its transmission down the generations, *determines* the
essential constitution of Hispanic man, the Spaniard. By this route
we pass from Indibilis and Mandonius to the Spaniards who came
later without bothering to determine in what sense the term "Spanish" is employed. With the identity between the terms "Hispania"

and "Spain" established a priori, but without ascertaining beforehand the meaning of either the one or the other term, what follows may be reduced to this: we are gratified to know that we are eternal, superior to all those peoples who have trod the sacred soil of Spain, for all of them—Romans, Visigoths, Arabs—stopped being what they were and in the final analysis were incorporated into the everlasting Spanish essence—the caves of Altamira, the heroism of Numantia, Trajan and Theodosius, Seneca and Lucan, Isidore of Hispalis, the grandeur of Cordova under the caliphs, the thought of Averroës and Maimonides, the extraordinary figure of Ibn Ḥazm, the totality of Arabic and Hebraic literature; everything is poured into the undivided estate of the Spaniard's patrimony. The gaps thus become less disturbing, and we evade the anguished problem of asking ourselves in all rigor the fearful question: "But in reality what and who are we?"

The "theory" of biological continuity is combined with that of the endurance of certain characteristics of personality interpreted on the basis of a very simple and fragmentary psychology: being impetuous, proud, envious, little inclined to reflection, generous, long-suffering, and so on. But the decisive factor in this and in other instances is what man *does* with his biological and psychic abilities and weaknesses. The same is true of his natural and economic circumstances. Ancient Greece, the British Isles, and the Iberian Peninsula were not economically self-sufficient. The peoples of these three countries left them in search of better fortune and ended by constructing vast colonial empires. But how does the common denominator of economics help us to penetrate the authentic reality of the colonization of Magna Graecia, or of the Mexican New Spain, or of Canada, Australia, and New Zealand?

When I read as a proof of their Spanish nature that certain caliphs of Cordova had Galician mothers, that Ibn Ḥazm had Hispanic ancestors, and other similar facts, I wonder about the experience of life exhibited in such views. I have American friends whose grandparents were Spanish; they have lived outside the circle of those who, while in the United States, remain attached to the Spanish tradition through relatives and friends; they do not speak a word of Spanish; they are Presbyterians; it is not always easy to make them understand the values of Spanish civilization; their behavior with respect to culture and forms of life is identical with that of the purest Anglo-Saxon American. I knew intimately a man of Czech ancestry, the great president of a university in which I was a professor. He knew no Czech, and he never acted in a manner even vaguely reminiscent of his Central European forebears. Examples can be multiplied indefinitely. To be sure, if the immigrant and his descendants stay in an environment where their native language is spoken and their religion and traditional customs are maintained, then intermediate situations will be sustained for several generations, although in the long run integration with the country of residence will become complete. The same thing happened in countries subjected over long centuries to a foreign civilization. The Romans finally Romanized both the Greeks of the south and the Celts and Etruscans of the north. The Neapolitan and Sicilian dialects are derived from the Latin spoken in those regions, not from Greek. Nobody today thinks of calling the inhabitants of the north of Italy Celts or the Belgians, Gauls.

Supporters of the theory of the "eternal and immutable Spaniard" do not take into consideration the social and individual action of language, together with that of religion. Exactly like other important regions of the Empire, the greater part of Spain was in the end strongly Romanized. Had it not been for the zeal, or compulsion, on the part of historians to make Hispania a province different from others in the Roman Empire, the "Spanishness" of Seneca and Lucan would long ago have disappeared from history books. Are we to think, perhaps, that the north of Italy had less personality than Baetica, which was subdued without resistance? Cisalpine Gaul also possessed many ways of speaking and a variety of usages, forms, and dimensions peculiar to collective life. But, after centuries of Roman domination, those who were Gauls before, ended up as Romans. In other words, the horizon contemplated by the humblest peasant as he looked up from his labors was no longer Celtic but Roman. It seems to me that those who believe in eternal Spanishness do not consider the difference between the various levels and dynamic forces of collective life. Everything is measured by the same yardstick: Spanishness. When one thinks and feels this way, it is forgotten that the conditions of a certain tribe, region, or nation are independent of the biology or psychology of that person. They depend instead on the experiential awareness, the conscious experience (vivencia), of the ties that bind the individual to other members of the collectivity. Such ties have never been based on biological or corporal likeness (being strong, puny, tall, short, blond, dark) or on psychic similarities (being brave, timid, envious, long-suffering, proud, etc.), human conditions and dimensions that belong to the sphere of individuality, not to that of the consciousness of collectivity. The tribe, the region, or the nation, I repeat, has never been constituted on the basis of biological or psychic characteristics.

Man is the individual member of a tribe, of a region, of a nation because he feels himself linked to the community in manifold ways: by the manner of speaking, by a bond of common opinions and interests, because he believes in a certain way, because he reacts in like fashion when faced with circumstances that affect collective life, through a community of habits, through his consciousness of the necessity to maintain the collectivity that immediately includes him as united to some larger collectivity, through a kind of communality in preferences and in the extent to which he submits to the common scale of values, by his way of acting toward those who are not members of his group, and so forth. At the same time one must bear in mind the varying degree of flexibility and mobility in the collective and in the individual dimension; the latter is more stable and rigid than the former. It is inconceivable that the pygmy should attain towering height, and it is difficult for the envious man to stop being so; but human groups do at times change their ways of acting (e.g., the Rome of the Republic was as genuinely Roman as that of the Empire, but nevertheless the differences between one and the other were considerable). The grave error of Spanish historiography for centuries now has been to confuse individual conditions and physiognomy (psychology and biology) with the reality of the human objects we call tribe, region, nation, and state. This error in human logic and ontology—which I had never thought it would be necessary to expose so clearly—has for centuries complicated and confused the notion that Spaniards have of themselves.

No less arbitrary is the way in which Muslim al-Andalus has been made Spanish. It is said that these people who spoke Arabic and were Muslim in religion were Spaniards, that the dimension of the Islamic world formed no part of the collective dimension of their life. There is no realization of how the Arabic language molds and disposes both the internal behavior and the outward bearing of the person. When a human group arrives at the point of expressing itself linguistically in a way that is incomprehensible to another neighboring group, this announces that its collective life has in some measure become special and peculiar. For this very reason the organizers and conquerors of empires and nations have striven to impose on their subjects a uniform language. The Peruvian Incas demanded that the "common tongue" be spoken; Rome Latinized vast regions, except where the provincial language was superior in civilizing prestige to that of the conquerors (as happened in Greece) or in places like the Basque area, which was of little practical interest to the Romans. Once subdued by force of arms, the Basque region was partially excluded from Roman colonization.

When this most civilized section of the former Visigothic kingdom had been made Muslim in religion and Arabic in language, al-Andalus was converted into an extension of the spiritual and linguistic empire of Islam. After many centuries even Christians in this area expressed themselves in Arabic, for which reason they were rightly called Mozarabs, or "Arabized"; in this language the documents of Toledan Mozarabs were composed. One is therefore surprised by the insistence with which Pan-Hispanic orientalists and their followers deny the connection of al-Andalus with the Muslim East and by their attempt to link the Muslims of al-Andalus (not the *Andalusians*) to Tartessus and Celtiberia through ties of blood and biological inheritance. No account is taken—and I insist on this—of the degree to which Islam and the Arabic language mold the direction, the value judgments, and the horizon of life. Witness, for example, the view of a scholar who has analyzed the Arabic language *from within its structure*:

> . . . magical power [is] ascribed consciously and/or unconsciously to words and images of words. . . . Thoughts expressed in [Arabic] are generally vague and hard to pin down. . . . Words perhaps were never sharply defined. . . . A successful Arabic . . . has only to make [his writing] diffusely comprehensible. . . . He forces his thoughts to accommodate themselves to the ready-made linguistic structure. . . . The linguistic restrictions are at least partially responsible . . . for the general lack of organization governing life in the Arabic world of today. . . . If an Arab says exactly what he means without the expected exaggeration, other Arabs may still think that he means the opposite. . . . Arabic names of places, things, and persons are important, constituting a vital element of their integrity and influencing the attitude of people toward them. The tendency to fit the thought to the word or to the combination of words, rather than the word to the thought, is a result of the psychological replacement of thoughts by words, the words becoming the substitutes for thoughts and not their representatives. . . . [There is] displacement of the perceptual images by the linguistic ones, which for all practical purposes are treated as if they were the real thing and not just a linguistic representation of them. . . . Arabic poetry is based to a larger extent than in English or French on the effect of . . . sound combinations.[6]

These observations, for me highly useful, take on theoretical significance when related to the ontological concept on which Islamic life is based. In Arabic there is no verb "to be," and the *being* of something does not mean for the Arab what it does for an Occidental.[7] (Later on, more attention is given to this matter.)

The effect of language on the process by which collective life is constantly being made testifies to the impossibility of imagining the past as a rocklike foundation upon which there gradually settled the successive waves of human beings speaking different languages who came to the Peninsula. As has always happened, underneath

---

[6] E. Shoubi, "The Influence of the Arabic Language on the Psychology of the Arabs," *Middle East Journal*, V (1951), 284–302. Let it not be thought that the author is an unsympathetic critic of the Islamic world, for he writes from within it and in the following terms: "To a large extent, the *Qur'an* justifies the high evaluation it receives from Muslims."

[7] After the publication of the first edition of this book, I treated the problem in *Hacia Cervantes* (Madrid: Taurus, 1960), pp. 308 ff., and in "Españolidad y europeización del Quijote" (the title of the prologue to an edition of the *Quixote* published by Editorial Porrúa, S.A., Mexico, 1960), pp. xli ff.

these waves, peoples and languages of the Iberian Peninsula were constantly diminishing in their social functions and dimensions. What traces of the life in Egypt of the Pharaohs survive in the Egypt we see today? Yet that long-gone way of life possessed a unity and grandeur of civilization immeasurably superior to that of the poor, primitive, and divided peoples of Iberia. The waves of Greeks, Romans, and Muslims silenced and converted into archaeological remains that Egyptian culture which was one of the most advanced and durable of Antiquity; while over Celtiberians and Tartessians triumphed Romans, Visigoths, and Muslims, and also the forms of Spanish life, different from everything that had preceded, as I hope to make clear in this volume.

Incidental Remarks about the Basque Peoples

But there in the Peninsula we are confronted with the Basques, apparently following the trajectory of their prehistoric past, with a language that has survived, at least in part, in the wake and in the neighborhood of Romans, Visigoths, Muslims, and the Castilian-Aragonese. Thus has been created the illusion of a line continued from the shadows of prehistory to the present moment. But even in this instance the contradiction with what has been said earlier is only apparent. The Basque entered historical life, the life that would become Spanish, only after casting off his language, which was culturally fragmented and paralyzed and had never been raised beyond the oral level. In Spain, Basque was never written down until the present era and then only with effort and artificiality. At a memorable session of the Basque Academy in 1921, I heard a speech read in Biscayan Basque; it was understood neither by me, which is understandable, nor by a Basque from Guipuzcoa who sat next to me.

Without the Muslim occupation of the Peninsula the Basques would have remained isolated, withdrawn into their mountainous country, while the Romance-speaking peoples went on extending their language into the Basque areas of the Lower Pyrenees, as Menéndez Pidal has shown in a splendid study. They were strongly attached to their own soil, only slightly Christianized, and without a voice in history. But they emerge as an admirable people when they change the direction and rhythm of their life, expressing themselves in Castilian or Navarro-Aragonese on one side of the Bidassoa. Their sturdy human material does not acquire a reality worthy of historical treatment except when reincarnated in forms of life alien to its own ancestral ways—and the same is true of the neighbors of the Basques on the Cantabrian coast. The Basques, like the other peoples of what would be Spain, were molded by the personalistic system of the "castes" and developed the ability to command; like the other peoples of the Cantabrian coast, they believed themselves to be nobles (hidalgos) *by birth*, free from Islamic or Jewish stain.[8] In other words, thanks to the circumstances created by the Muslim occupation and by the new direction of life initiated by the Romano-Christian peoples in the eighth century, the Basques began to take on an active role, contrary, but comparable, to that of the Berbers who, impelled by Islam, intervened actively in the Islamic conquest and colonization of Peninsular Christian areas. The Basques molded and realized their hitherto inchoate energies in the forms of Romano-Germanic civilization; without them, neither the kingdom of Navarre nor the county of Castile would have been possible, though the ideas of "kingdom" and "county" were alien to them. The Romance-speaking peoples who had not submitted to Islam—though spurred on and influenced by it—were for the Basque people something like what the Roman invaders had been for the peoples of Baetica and Tarraconensis eight hundred years before. To the extent that the Basque, until that moment remote and strange, was Romanized and Christianized in language and in spirit—that is, to the extent that *he became different*—he emerged from his prehistory and finally was converted into one of the most valuable constitutive elements of the Spanishness that was to come.

Let us not invent fantasies. In an ideal Spain in which there fell to each region the mission for which it possesses most strength and ability, the Basques would serve as Castilians par excellence, for in truth that is what they are and have been historically. In the past, imperial gold and silver passed through their hands without soiling them, and for that reason they were entrusted in the Indies with the stupendous task of being "collectors of the king's gold and silver" (*apartadores de oro y plata*). When God so willed, the Basque functioned as paradigm of lawfulness, of Hispanic human dignity, of the mind that was generously open while governed by responsible discretion and veracity. For such reasons, kings chose Basques as secretaries. At the beginning of the eighteenth century, three Basques constructed in the city of Mexico the astonishing Colegio de las Vizcaínas, an epitome of intelligent, beautiful architecture. With tenacious and singular energy, these three Basques, possessed of a cosmopolitan rather than provincial outlook, kept their college free of both viceregal and archiepiscopal meddling though still remaining attached to religious devotion, as is evidenced by the fine chapel in which the students attended the Catholic rites.[9]

If, later on, the Basque inclusion in that Hispanic community of

---

[8] See my remarks about this matter in *Origen, ser y existir de los españoles* (Madrid: Taurus, 1959), p. 62.

[9] Gonzalo Obregón, Jr., *El Real Colegio de San Ignacio de México (Las Vizcaínas)* (Mexico: El Colegio de México, 1949).

which they were cofounders has come upon unfortunate days, the reason (and such causes are my sole concern here) must be sought in the special properties of the functioning of Hispanic life. Furthermore, if I have brought up the Basque problem, it has only been to show with precision that the presence of the Basques in Spanish life, as I conceive it, has nothing to do with the fantastic survival of Tartessians or Celts. In the eighth century the Basques continued to live in their mountains, ready, like everything really alive, to act as the basic matter for any future form, to be acted upon by it. By that time the Tartessians and the Celts were nowhere to be found.

The Psychological Bond with Pre-Roman Peoples Is Inoperative

Consequently, let us not believe that everything that happened on the soil now called Spain is Spanish, as that everything that existed on the soil of ancient Italia is Italian. The past of a people seems to be an uninterrupted continuity produced in a geographically stable space. As the historical stage is never cleared, the spectator ingenuously believes that the drama acted out there is always the same. For such reasons the paintings in the caves of Altamira are called Spanish; and Trajan, St. Isidore of Hispalis, and Viriatus are thought to be Spanish in the same way as Cervantes, Unamuno, and those members of the Royal Spanish Academy who define the meaning of the word "Spanish."

But what are the contents and the semantic limits of the word "Spanish" or "Hispanic" and the historical human reality to which these terms univocally refer? The problem is one of hermeneutics and is strictly philological, although up to now philologists have paid it little attention or have believed it to be solved or nonexistent. Given the suppositions on which conventional historiography rests, this state of affairs is natural. As a result there is no answer to the question about the meaning and precise aim of the adjectives "Spanish," "French," "English," and the like. In view of what has been said before and what I shall say later, the adjective "Spanish" cannot be applied with exactitude to those who lived in the Iberian Peninsula prior to the Muslim invasion. If we call Visigoths, Romans, Iberians, and so on, "Spanish," then we must designate in some other way the people into whose lives is integrated what has happened and been created (or destroyed) in that Peninsula from the tenth century up to the present. When it is said that the bust of the Dama de Elche or the *Etymologies* of St. Isidore are Spanish works, what is meant is that both were the product of people who lived in what today we call Spain.

The cities and persons (Gades, Hispalis, etc.) situated on the land where there exists today the *what* that we call Spanish were alone the antecedent and the condition that made that *what* possible, through a concatenation of successive possibilities and limitations. (These limitations are as real as the possibilities, despite the fact that they are seldom considered by historians.)[10] But *only by means of a crude paralogism could we identify the vital reality of the possibility with the "what" that makes it possible, which is to say, the conditioned with the condition.* Yet we do this when we believe that because the Iberians and the Romans were the condition for the existence of the future Spaniards, the former are as Spanish as the latter. In this instance historical reality is viewed as something substantial, given once and for all. To support this concept, one quotes Strabo, yet even Strabo knew that different languages were spoken in Iberia by peoples very different from one another.[11] Those along the Bastis (Guadalquivir) River "are quite transformed, and have acquired the Roman way of living; they are little short of being completely Roman; nor do they even remember their own language" (*Geography*, 3.2.15). "Even the Celtiberians," he adds, "the most savage among the Iberians, have acquired civility." Unlike these people, the mountaineers in the north, not Romanized, lived by banditry (3.3.5). We are to suppose, then, that certain inhabitants of Iberia would appear to be foreigners to their neighbors. Some were gentle and easily dominated; others for almost two centuries resisted the Roman legions, who were permanently established in the region of the north and northwest. Shall we say that the bellicose Cantabrians were Spaniards, and that the Turdetanians or the Tartessians, or Phoenicians, or Carthaginians, or Romans, successively, were not? Because it is so clearly outlined, the geographic profile of the Peninsula creates the mirage of a fixed and continued unity.

---

[10] Although the following words of Xavier Zubiri were written from a different viewpoint and with other purposes in mind, it is useful to recall them here: "Man's life is not a simple exercise or execution of acts, but a utilization of his potentialities. And we will attain the specific quality of history only when we have explained the nature of what we have provisionally called 'the utilization of potentialities,' as distinguished from the mere exercise of acts. . . . History is not woven out of facts, but out of events and happenings. . . . The acts of the animal are reactions" stimulated by the objects with which it lives. In contrast, "the most elementary of specifically human acts interposes between things and our actions a 'project.' . . . If the situation of the animal is an immersion in things, the situation of man is *his distance* from them. . . . Considered as resources, things and human nature itself are not mere *potentialities* which enable but *possibilities* which permit action" (*Naturaleza, Historia, Dios* [1944], pp. 398–402). I would add to this that the realization of such possibilities is conditioned in turn by the disposition of the "dwelling place" of life in which each people finally establishes itself, as I shall explain later.

[11] Basque was a different language from Iberian; the former was "oriented toward Eurasia, while Iberian was surely [oriented] toward Africa" (Antonio Tovar, "Sobre el planteamiento del problem vascoibérico," in *Archivum* [Oviedo, 1954], p. 231).

Justinus, author of the abridged *Historiae Philippicae* of the Gaul Trogus Pompeius, in a misleading synthesis, reduces to homogeneity not only the diverse inhabitants of Iberia but also the land and the climate with all their violent contrasts: "The healthfulness of the air is the same all over Hispania; . . . the rivers are not harmfully torrential, and they irrigate the fields and vineyards." The moderate climate, without the extremes of either Africa or Gaul, "inde felicibus et tempestivis imbribus in omnia frugum genera fecunda est, adeo ut non ipsis tantum icolis, verum etiam Italiae urbique Romanae cunctarum rerum abundantia sufficiat" (XLIV, I, 1, 2).[12] And then the well-known passage: "Corpora hominum ad inediam laboremque, animi ad mortem parati. Dura omnibus et adstricta parcimonia. Bellum quam otium malunt; si extraneus deest domi hostem quaerunt."[13] The psychobiological generalizations prevent us from getting at the functional peculiarity that we are pursuing, and, besides, it would not be difficult to find other peoples, ancient or modern, equally long-suffering and abstemious. Concerning the Scythians, the same Justinus says that "they scorn gold and silver as much as other peoples crave them. They feed on milk and honey; they know nothing of the use of wool and clothing, even when their teeth are chattering from rigorous cold; yet they wear skins" (II, 2, 3). The Moor too was not exceeded by the Spaniard in getting along with little, as Captain Aldana observed in the sixteenth century:

> It is a common rumor of the common country folk
> That the lack of water from which Spain suffers,
> And the excess of desert land and of aridity
> Provide her with a defense against whoever approaches;
> And she does not understand the skill
> Whereby the Moor appeases his hunger without food,
> As we clearly saw in earlier centuries,
> When we yielded the boundary of the fatherland.[14]

It must be understood, from what Aldana says of the Moors, that other peoples have features like those of the Hispanians, and that such features by themselves contribute nothing to the understanding of history. Justinus speaks of the inability of the Greeks to form a union almost in the same terms he applies to Iberia: "Under the rule of the Lacedaemonians and Athenians, all Greece was divided in two parts; and from making foreign wars she would turn to plunging her

---

[12] "Abundant and opportune rains make her fertile in all kinds of products, so that she can supply not only her own inhabitants but also Italy and the city of Rome."

[13] "They are made to suffer privations and travails; their spirit defies death; they are all of extreme frugality; they prefer war to peace, and if they have no enemy outside their country, they seek one inside it."

[14] Apud A. Rodríguez-Moñino, *El capitán Francisco de Aldana (1537–1578)* (Valladolid, 1943), p. 36.

weapons into her own entrails" (III, 2, 1). These and other observed qualities are useful in the understanding of history only insofar as they are explicitly articulated within a vital process and to the extent that they have led to important results, results that in the last analysis are unique and peculiar to the culture under examination. The abstemious Puritans of New England, for example, scorned the pleasures of the palate for ethicoreligious motives, that is to say, after deliberate reflection; at the same time, they cultivated capitalism, social cohesion, and the collective welfare. The insufficiency of the Hispanic diet was the unfortunate result of either not knowing how to make the land more productive or not importing food from places where it was plentiful. But this insufficiency also could give fecund support to energy of sanctity:

> I am strong like Spain,
> For lack of sustenance.
> (Quevedo)

On the one hand, there were the hunger and poverty suffered unwillingly by Lazarillo and his lordly Squire, and wistfully recalled by those little sisters of St. Theresa who were saddened by good living; on the other, heroic feats that stiffened the Spanish courage whenever a seductive goal beckoned. Abstinence in itself is an abstraction or an inadequate fragment which does not permit life in its totality to be understood. The important thing for the historian is what each people does with its abstinence, or with its indulgence—and not what might be called its "psychology."[15]

When we say "Spanish" and try to clarify what the word evokes in our consciousness, those evocations will vary with the knowledge and experience of each person, although something unique will be intuited, something difficult to define sharply when we seek to combine the several aspects that the intuition comprehends. According to the dictionary, the native of Spain is "Spanish." The definition is elusive, for to say that an object comes from a certain place, that it is produced there, is not to say what the object in question is, or what it is like. To be sure, those who are born in the Spain of today

---

[15] Much currency has been given to a statement by Firmicus Maternus, a Siculian writer of the fourth century, as if it might serve in the understanding of the historical reality of certain peoples who later would come to prominence in the area of the former Roman Empire: "Itali fiunt regali semper nobilitate praefulgidi. Galli stolidi, leves Graeci . . . , acuti Siculi, luxuriosi semper Asiani et voluptatibus occupati *et Hispani elata iactantiae praeposteri*" (*Peri Matheseos*, I, 2, 3, 4). But if we are content with the explanation that braggadocio was a Hispanic peculiarity (and not, furthermore, assigned to the ancestors of Tartarin de Tarascon), we should have to admit also that the French, the inheritors of the Gauls, are phlegmatic idiots, and that the Greeks who were preparing the imperial grandeur of Byzantium were frivolous and superficial. What is truly frivolous and superficial is the attempt to base a historiographic construction on such "psychological characteristics."

are generally Spanish. But is that all there is to it? Would it be enough to say that an alga is an aquatic plant? With algae it is a matter of little importance because the curious person will find out all he wants to know about them in a treatise on botany, but where shall we go to find out the meaning and the nature of the human object that is called "Spanish"? The difficulty is increased by the fact that we have no clear notion of the *what* and the *how* of that Spain of which the Spanish are natives. Shall we apply the idea expressed in the dictionary and say Averroës and Maimonides, born in Spain, are Spanish? May we, with any rigor, call that Cordova where they were born Spain? Those who, although born in the Spain of today, do not give the impression of being Spanish because they have been brought up in other countries—can they be Spanish? And even granting that, legally speaking, they can be, would being legally Spanish suffice to embrace the total human reality of being so in fact, authentically? This latter reality can be found in people who are not natives of Spain but whose lives have been structured within that complex we call Spanish.

Static, essentialist criteria fail to capture the fleeting reality that we pursue, the reality that can be grasped by intuition but not defined. If, for example, we take language as a norm, we shall see that in spite of its extraordinary importance, there are in Catalonia, Galicia, and the Basque country people who (despite their separatist tendencies, and perhaps, indeed, precisely because they are separatists) *are* Spanish, even though they speak Castilian badly or not at all. The historian Gonzalo Fernández de Oviedo (1478–1557) stumbled onto the problem of what a Spaniard is when he saw Galicians, Roussillonians, Biscayans, and Andalusians—all different one from another and quarreling with one another—as they reached the lands recently discovered by the Spaniards. Their Spanishness, according to Oviedo, consisted in being loyal subjects of the king of Spain. Their devotion to the king was nothing external, but an authentic *belief*, functional in the life of those people. Oviedo's explanation was of a vitalistic, not a rationalistic, type and rested on his experiential awareness of the same Spanish existence.[16]

---

[16] If we observe the phenomenon of the monarchical cult more closely, we will see that the royal power did not unite the Hispanic people by acting as a principle external to them; faith in the sovereign was the form that bestowed external reality on their longing to maintain themselves, because of certain shared desires for the future, within a collective existence. The Spaniards, given their manner of existence, were united in their estimation of the worth of their caste, of which belief in their religious faith and their loyalty to the monarch were an interpretation and a sign. In the seventeenth century no Spaniard could have written, either in public or in private, as La Bruyère did in his *Caractères*: "Royal courts would be deserted and kings would stand almost alone if men would rid themselves of vanity and mercenary interests." The courtiers "make the fashions, exaggerate luxuries and extravagance, and teach

Life in the Past Which Is Worthy of Historical Treatment Was Not a Static Reality

The historiography of a people must settle, before anything else, the identity of the people about which it is talking. Once agreement has been reached on this point, it is necessary to make clear the "historifiable" dimension of the people whose personality is already well known to the writer and to his readers. Not everything that happens, nor everything that people do, is worthy of being written down as history; the themes that belong to history possess the virtue of survival, become durable as values, and make possible the generation of other values (e.g., Greek thought; the juridical and political work of Rome; the creation of extra-European peoples speaking European languages, which was initiated by the Spaniards and the Portuguese and imitated later by the English, the French, and the Dutch; or the art of Cervantes and Goya, etc.). These and innumerable other values, as well as all that which actually made them possible, fall within the jurisdiction of historiography.[17]

The work of the historiographer consists in showing how a people went about bringing itself progressively into existence, and it cannot start from the gratuitous supposition that the people in question is an abstract substance, unchangeable from its inception and without a temporal dimension. To write the history of a people's life implies making visible its awareness of existing, the will and impulsions that are components of that existence, and the collective and dynamic structure by virtue of which the people who are subjects of history appear to be moving consistently throughout their existence in time. The people that can be the subject of a history has lived with its eyes turned toward a future, not only toward the past of daily and circumscribed routine, without visions of something beyond or values still dreamed of but not yet achieved. Those peoples who never aspired to be more than they were—and achieved exactly that—are not and cannot be the object of history. To appear now as a Spaniard, a Frenchman, an Englishman, and so on, is the result of an aim and

[the women] speedy means of consuming large sums in clothing. . . . A noble . . . , if he lives at the court, is protected but is a slave: that is the compensation" (*De la Cour*). The English killed Charles I; the French, Louis XVI. Previously the French had assassinated Henry III and Henry IV—and all this during the period of divine-right monarchy. Nothing similar happened in Spain. When the faith in the king collapsed, the vital functioning of the Spaniards led them to group themselves under local, provincial, or national bosses. It would be better to regard these *caudillos* as sought-for chieftains rather than as tyrants. This life structure is a more or less close-fitting garment for all the Hispano-Portuguese people. Nationalism is inherent in them, a nationalism based on an immersion in their own vital process, and not motivated by doing or having done this or that thing in an especially valuable way.

[17] Cf. my essay "Descripción, narración e historiografía," in *Dos Ensayos* (Mexico: Editorial Porrúa, 1956).

an effort by virtue of which a human collectivity has been formed with this particular character. So it is that deeds of the past in the Iberian Peninsula are not "Spanish" because the doers of them had always been Spaniards. The relationship must be reversed: a certain type of purpose and of activity in dealing with certain circumstances finally created a certain mode of collective awareness in those people who were carrying out that type of activity and effort. The Iberian tribes or peoples (let us call them so for clarity's sake) had no consciousness of forming a national unit coincident with the geographical limits of the Peninsula. Everything reported by Greek and Roman chroniclers and geographers testifies to the fact that those peoples were disunited and did not speak the same tongue. They lived attached to their own soil and nothing more. From what source, in what way could the awareness of being like the future Spaniards have come to them? Furthermore, they themselves have left us no records. The idea of their Spanishness and their continuity through the ages results from the anachronistic projection into the past of situations that existed many centuries afterward. The pre-Roman inhabitants of the Peninsula were called *Hispani* by the Romans because the designations applied by outsiders unify, for the sake of convenience, the differences within countries. In the twelfth century the inhabitants of Provence also used the term *espanhols* to refer to the Christians in the Peninsula, who called themselves by other names and who had not yet given themselves any common name that included all of them.

The awareness of the *human* unity among dwellers on Peninsular soil—itself so clearly set apart physically by seas and mountains—arose after the Roman conquest and was later reaffirmed, as Visigothic, during the fifth, sixth, and seventh centuries. Isidore of Hispalis wrote in full awareness of being a Visigoth, as we shall see later. But conventional historiography removes the flesh of human reality from the past and dreams up the image of an essential Spaniard, a sort of self-contained object, which may on the one hand seem metaphysical but is basically a creation of purest naïveté.

In the seventeenth century the vision of a largely rural Spain, never sufficiently counterbalanced by the urbanity of the larger cities, led to exaggerations like Gracián's statement that Spain continued to be exactly as "when God created it." The weight of the peasant element in Spanish life and the persistence of many folk traditions have contributed to the belief that Spaniards continue biologically and humanly the same type of man present in the Peninsula thousands of years ago. Ganivet said of the Spaniards: "In our old age we have come to find ourselves still virginal in spirit" (*Ideárium español*). Ortega y Gasset believed that "the Spaniard's famous lack of wants" is like that "which Hannibal had already pointed out" (*Interpre-*

tación de la historia universal, p. 360) and relates the mantillas worn by Andalusian women to the headdress of certain feminine figures in a Cretan mosaic of 1400 B.C. (*ibid.*, p. 163). Mention is also made of the continuous tradition of bullfighting, as if the spectator at today's bullfights saw them as filled with the sacred meaning they had many centuries ago. Customs and spectacles exist within a human structure; when torn out of this structure they lose reality and are deprived of their meaning. Bullfighting was once the sport of knights (cf. *The Knight of Olmedo*, by Lope de Vega); later, in the eighteenth century, it became an occupation for people of the lower classes who, for a price, put on a show. But the fact that the daring and courage of the matador, whether or not he was a "knight," should captivate Spaniards is a phenomenon that acquires meaning within the cult of the imperious power of the person, of the social dimension of the caste that was victorious over the Moors and the conqueror of worlds. To fight against bulls or Moors was all the same thing:

> "How well does he fight on his gilded saddle,
> My lord Ruy Diaz the good fighter!"[18]

Those Peninsular peoples successively conquered by Phoenicians, Carthaginians, Greeks, Romans, Visigoths, Byzantines, and Muslims did not possess the collective or social structure and physiognomy of those who slowly reconquered Peninsular territory over a period of eight centuries. The bullfight could not mean for the latter peoples what it had meant to the Cretans, simply because their social bonds, physiognomy, and interdependence were not Cretan or Tartessian. Neither can we still consider as Celts those who carry on the tradition of Halloween (the eve of All Saints' Day) in English-speaking countries, even though in the British Isles bonfires are still lit, fortunes are told, stories of ghosts and witches are related, and so on. Druidism is one thing and Anglicism is another. There are countless examples of like phenomena. The "reality" of the bullfight in prehistory is not one and the same with that "reality" in Spanish life, no more than it is with that in the life of those who enjoy this spectacle in the south of France. Any custom or institution lends itself to like observation. Ever since swords were invented, two adversaries inflamed by hatred have tried to kill each other with them; but this does not imply that the human "reality" of the duelists or the institution of the duel has continued to be the same. Consequently, in order to understand all these facts humanly and historically, one must start with the "dwelling place of life" (*morada vital*; see p. 97). Traditional

---

[18] "¡Quál lidia bien sobre exorado arzón
mio Cid Ruy Diaz el buen lidiador!"
(*Poema del Cid*, ll. 733-734)

survivals (e.g., threshing in the manner of ancient Egypt, as has been done in certain places in Spain up to the present century) do not imply that the farmer is Celtiberian or Egyptian but only that the Spanish mode of existence has made possible the preservation of many archaisms, side by side with great, and in no sense rustic, modernities of genuinely Spanish invention, such as the creation of wonderful cities in distant lands. Spanishness consists precisely in the coexistence of the most primitive rusticity with the artistic refinement of a Velázquez, a Lope de Vega, and many others. From these widely publicized traditional customs, from the intrahistory so dear to Unamuno, there would never have arisen a collective awareness capable of being elevated to the national level.

Archaic practices, preserved in one form or another in every human community, survive in Spain as atrophied elements of life, no longer connected to the structure in which they formerly had an authentic existence. The superstition about the number 13 (in many hotels there are no rooms or stories of this number) does not imply that the surrounding social milieu retains a belief in magic. Among Iberians or Celtiberians, threshing with oxen or beating the grain with a flail would never have been considered archaic by anyone, though we consider them so today, because those customs, the superstitions, and everything else were integrated into a vital system which served as the limiting horizon for the collectivity and its members. But the kind of man who later was called Spanish came to be so because he had confronted the world around him in a way that differed from the one followed by those people who had had Visigoths and Romans as the models for their lives and the horizon of their hopes. He did not become a Spaniard by continuing to cultivate the soil with a wooden plow, or by trampling his grapes with rope sandals, or by preserving traditional customs in his village; he became a Spaniard by opening a road toward the future, fortified by faith in his personal power and spurred on by the exemplary efficiency of a special mode of existing and of establishing hierarchies politically within new and fragmented political organizations. Roman and Visigothic organization had been imposed from above; that of the future Spain issued from its very heart, that is to say, from the inmost being of certain groups that were taking on form and consistency in relation to what lay beyond and within their own frontiers. The Spaniard came into existence as his conduct was more and more shaped by his awareness of the value attached to feeling self-sufficient, a "man in himself" (*hombre en sí*). The "man in himself" of whom Prince Juan Manuel speaks in the fourteenth century had spent centuries elaborating this inner configuration of the Spaniard, which becomes, as we shall see later, the "essential man" (*ome esencial*), to use a fifteenth-century phrase of the Count of Haro. Here is the word, the

formative *logos*, that gave structure, meaning, and an upward drive
to the Spaniards, to those who on this basis were created and urged
on in their Spanishness. When the President of the Royal Council
and Archbishop of Compostela dissuaded Charles V from engaging
in personal combat with Francis I of France, his principal argument
was this: "Your Majesty is not unaware that [the King of France]
is considered silly and garrulous, and judged to be inconstant and
a person *without being*."[19]

It has been necessary to insist on such details in order to disperse
and explode the compact mosaic of historiographic fantasies, in which
notions that must be carefully distinguished one from the other are
mixed up and confused. Starting from the absurdity that Spain is the
same as the soil of the Iberian Peninsula and that what is human is
no more than biology; confusing traditional practices with the attitude of men toward them; not realizing that language is inseparable
from the speaker's desire to express value judgments by means of it;
without rigorous principles as to the reality of man and of the world
in which that reality is fulfilled, traditional historiography jumbles
together a mass of human beings gathered from all epochs and capri-
ciously gives it the name Spanish. Recognition has not even been
given to—or use made of—intellectual instruments within the reach
of everyone which have been imported from outside but intelligently
reshaped in polished Castilian phrases: "If *circumstances* make the
spirit [that is to say, the I that is involved in them], they themselves
are modified by this spirit and received into it according to its own
way of being."[20] When circumstances force a human subject to re-
make them and give them form in his consciousness in such a way
that the product that results comes to acquire innovating strength
and normative value, then daily reality, in itself possessed of no upward dimension, takes on a historical dimension, is worthy of historical treatment. Before becoming perceptible and ascendant as a
fit subject for history, the Spaniard did not exist. Something that was
not the Spaniard did exist—something that was the condition and
enabling circumstance for him—but he did not exist as such; he was
something else, which is not of prime interest to me because I am not
dealing with Visigothic, Roman, or Celtiberian history, even supposing that the possibility of a Celtiberian history existed today. I
am interested in presenting a structure, not the dead bones of anecdotes, of truncated and disjointed happenings.

Before Spaniards existed in the Peninsula, there were peoples with

---

[19] *Colección de Documentos Inéditos para la Historia de España* (1842), I, 56
(the text is now more readily available in J. F. Montesinos, *Ensayos y estudios
de literatura española* [Mexico, 1959], p. 41).

[20] "Si las circunstancias hacen al espíritu [es decir, al *yo* enlazado con aquéllas],
es ['lo hacen'] modificadas por este mismo, y recibidas en él según él es"
(Unamuno, *En torno al casticismo* [1895]).

a consciousness of being something else: Goths, Hispano-Romans, Cantabrians, Celtiberians, Celts, Iberians, or whatever. The attempt to turn them all into Spaniards, besides being absurd and anachronistic in its methods, disregards the fact that, if such a claim were true, Frenchmen, Italians, Englishmen, and so on, would also be essential and immemorial beings. But a glance at any textbook is sufficient to convince one to the contrary and to stop thinking like Father Mariana in 1600. There are works in French like Ferdinand Lot's *Naissance de la France* (1948), in which one reads: "Only circumstances caused the future France and the future Germany, which had been almost twin sisters up to that point [843, the Treaty of Verdun], to see the tie that bound them broken and allowed them to become aware of their own personalities, which until then had been confused" (p. 416). These circumstances were that the Franks east and west of the line that would later divide France from Germany were separated by a strip of land. For it is men, I must add, who mold and orient the awareness of how men are to be. So elementary a book as that of M. Lot must, therefore, be read by recalcitrant historiographers: "The transformation of Roman Gaul into France is one of the most surprising spectacles in our history. How and why could *those Gauls who felt themselves Roman*—organically, one might say—who even after 410 sang of sovereign Rome, wounded but forever adored, how could they so rapidly forget her and aspire to no other goal than to be considered Franks?" (p. 135). Readers of *Naissance de la France* and of the works cited in its bibliography will realize the causes of so evident a fact. The first king of France was Charles the Bald, crowned in Rome in 875; there was nothing before then which could be called France. The very name of "La Gaule" was a literary creation which appears in the thirteenth century.

The same reasons serve for Italy, whose modern name is the same as that of a Roman province in which there did not exist the slightest hint of the future "italianità" of Dante or of the Italians of today. The reason is that "in the Empire and its governing classes there was a Roman and imperial awareness, but *not an Italian one*; [in the fifth century] maintaining sovereignty over Armorica or Valeria (north-eastern Panonia) meant just as much to those people as possessing Venice."[21] Still less can be said about the collective awareness of the peoples of the Apennine Peninsula *before* the establishment of the Republic of Rome as an "historifiable" entity.[22]

In view of a blindness that has lasted seven centuries, it must be emphasized that no historian in Italy or France today attempts to identify Italians or Frenchmen with the Roman or pre-Roman inhabitants of these lands. To base *human* and social continuity on

---

[21] L. Salvatorelli, *L'Italia Medioevale* (1936), p. 18.
[22] See *Origen, ser y existir de los españoles*, pp. 40, 64–69.

geographical, biological, or abstract psychological links (certain specified traits of character), and not on the awareness of forming part of a human community that works out and is responsible for its own destiny, is a blindness persisted in today only by certain Spanish historians.

The great poet Giosuè Carducci (1835–1907) dates truly *Italian* life from the year 1000: "In actuality there can be heard from the first years of the eleventh century the faint murmur of a life, still timid and hidden, which later will burst forth in lightning flashes of thought and of work; from this moment in truth the history of the Italian peoples begins" (*Dello svolgimento della letteratura nazionale*). No less unequivocal are the words of Giuseppe Prezzolini in his thought-provoking book *The Legacy of Italy* (1948), which begins as follows: "The Origins: Why Italians are not Romans." His reasoning is that "Contrary to the popular belief held by some self-styled scholars, many bombastic propagandists and a whole string of illustrious poets, Italians are not the direct descendents from the Romans but a new people as different from the Romans as the French, the Spaniards and the Anglo-Saxons" (p. 7). No one whose name is now respected would write today in Italy—a country that has devoted profound study to its own history—that Italians speaking a Romance tongue are linked to the Etruscans or that the Etruscans are continued by the Italians. As for the French, in addition to what has already been said, we should bear in mind the *Histoire de la civilization française* (1958) by G. Duby and R. Mandrou, which takes the end of the tenth century as its temporal point of departure. Is it possible that all these historians, whose number could be considerably amplified, are talking nonsense? Can it be that only certain Spaniards are rational historians?

Roman and Visigothic Hispania disappeared, and with it the Hispano-Roman-Visigothic dimension of its inhabitants. The name Hispania survived phonetically in that of Spain, but with varied meanings which for centuries did not come to signify what is now meant by *España*. The Spaniards are as different from the Roman *Hispani* as were the Tuscans of Dante's time from the Etruscans who once lived in Faesulae (modern Fiesole). The Romans used the term *Hispaniae* to include both *Hispania citerior* and *Hispania ulterior*; from that Latin plural is derived the habit of saying "the Spains" (*las Españas*), a name whose use by certain learned men reflects the aspiration for unity among the fragmented Christian kingdoms during the time of the reconquest. But the people who called their land Spain in the twelfth century possessed an awareness of their collective life which was totally disconnected from that of the Hispani of the Roman Empire. So different was it, in fact, that the inhabitants of that Spain were still not calling themselves "Spaniards" in the twelfth century. The term does not appear in the *Poem of the Cid* (*ca.* 1147); the jongleur speaks rather of "Galicians, Leonese, Castilians" and of "Franks" (here referring to the Catalans). As Paul Aebischer has shown, the name *español* is of Provençal origin.[23] All students of historical phonetics realized the foreign origin of the word, which would have been *españuelo* if its origin were purely Spanish; but Aebischer has made clear the Provençal derivation of *español*, which had not been observed before. Aebischer further remarks that their own unity was much less evident to the Spaniards of the Middle Ages than it was to their extra-Peninsular neighbors: "In order that the needs of an adjective 'español' should have commercial or other relations with the whole area that forms modern Spain." Those who felt that need most keenly were the inhabitants of Languedoc; and the term *español* came into general use in neighboring tongues earlier than in Castilian, because *España* meant, within Spain itself, the zone of the Peninsula occupied by the Moors.[24]

In normal circumstances I would not have to dwell at length on the origin of the Spaniards as I have done, but the antiquity and the deep-rooted general acceptance of the belief in the "eternal Spaniard" have forced me to do so. The attempt by historians, made at the same time on both the conscious and the unconscious levels, to elude a confrontation with the real past has led them to the invention of another, illusory past. But this evasion is both explicable and pardonable, for it is the direct reflection of the uneasiness felt by certain eminent thinkers of the late nineteenth and early twentieth centuries, who have even gone so far as to consider worthless and empty the three or four centuries that have preceded ours. It is a clear manifestation of what I shall later call "life as a denial of itself or the process of simultaneous affirmation and rejection" (*vivir desviviéndose*). At the moment, however, it is necessary for me to state clearly what I hope to express.

The opinion and the feeling, which to me seem unjustified, that almost all Spanish activities during the sixteenth and seventeenth centuries had been sterile led Don Francisco Giner, in a moment of irresistible love and sorrow for Spain, to write the following about certain deficiencies he had observed in other countries: "If, even outside this dark corner—and the darker, the more beloved—there still persists so much vanity and lying, out there in the sunlit empyrean of the proud, resplendent, and glorious nations, how could it

---

[23] "El étnico 'español': un provenzalismo en castellano," in *Estudios de toponimia y lexicografía* (Barcelona, 1948), pp. 13–48.

[24] Rafael Lapesa informs me that the earliest occurrence of the word *español* is as a proper name: a "domno [modern Spanish "don"] Español" had a post in the Cathedral of Toledo and signed a document of 1194 (A. González Palencia, *Los mozárabes de Toledo*, introductory volume, pp. 175–181). "For me," says Lapesa, "there is no doubt that the man in question was Provençal."

be different among a people [such as Spain] *cut off from history*, at least in the more spiritual and more profound respects, *more than three centuries ago?*"[25] Shortly afterward, José Ortega y Gasset wrote: "Three *centuries* of errors and sorrows weigh upon us. How could we frivolously ignore that centuries-old heaviness?"[26] At the opposite extreme the Fascist Phalanx, in 1937, cried out that for nearly *three centuries*, or since 1637, Spain had not been herself.[27] In 1947 Professor Pedro Bosch, a learned archaeologist, entitled one of his articles "The Contumacy of Our Historical Deviations"; in this article he affirms that in Spain, "contumacious in her errors . . . , all problems, since Ferdinand and Isabella and *even longer ago*, have either been insoluble or have been poorly solved. . . . In the crucible of Spain, the qualities of her peoples and of their character are still virginal."[28]

The grandeur of the sixteenth and seventeenth centuries was not satisfying; still less comfort could be found in the prior epoch, blemished by the Muslim occupation and by Jewish interference. For Fernán Pérez de Guzmán, writing in the middle of the fifteenth century, the occupation of Spain by the Moors was the subject for a

> Sad and tearful history
> unfit for verse or prose.[29]

As early as the fifteenth century the best and most intelligent Spaniards were beginning to contemplate the immediate past with repugnance as unworthy of being set down as history. Consequently

---

[25] *Problemas urgentes de nuestra educación nacional* (1905). The text may be read in *El pensamiento vivo de Francisco Giner*, ed. Fernando de los Ríos (Buenos Aires, 1949), p. 127. As early as 1889, Francisco Giner de los Ríos was already thinking in these terms; at that time he even added a century more to the indictment: "This morbid paralysis that our national development has been suffering for perhaps *four centuries*" (*Ensayos sobre educación*, in the edition of "La Lectura" [1917], p. 8). In the final analysis Giner felt about Spain much as had various Spaniards of the seventeenth century whom I shall quote later: "In our nation the inner grandeur of our culture from the mid-fifteenth century on helped to extend our dominion over the world; and that dominion, apparently the ultimate fruit of our progress, signaled the beginning of our ruin" (from the notes to Heinrich Ahrens, *Enciclopedia jurídica*, XXII [1879], 419).

[26] In his essay "La pedagogía social como programa político" (1910), now in the volume *Personas, obras, cosas* (1922), p. 201.

[27] "For nearly *three centuries* the true and immortal being of Spain has been in agony, torn in flesh and spirit by the poisonous *foreign* darts of an atheistic and materialistic conception of life [in 1637?]. We lost our imperial destiny and mission. . . . Now that the tradition of *this being* and power of Spain is returning, reborn, by the grace of youthful blood, the arrows of the Phalanx have become the sacred flesh of heroism" (Preamble to the Decree of 1 October 1937, inaugurating the Grand and Imperial Order of the Red Arrows, from the *Repertorio cronológico de legislación* [Pamplona, 1938], p. 994).

[28] *España nueva*, Mexico, Sept. 20, 1947.

[29] "Historia triste y llorosa / indigna de metro y prosa," *Loores de los claros varones de España*, in *Nueva Biblioteca de Autores Españoles*, XIX, 718.

they turned back to the grandeur of Roman history in the Iberian Peninsula, a grandeur vividly felt in the *Coplas* of Jorge Manrique. It was soothing to return to that grandeur as well as to the distant Celtiberian past, to Viriatus, to Numantia, to Indibilis and Mandonius. Unhappiness and anguish inspired the guidelines of Spanish historiography.

This opinion is confirmed once again by a reading of the *Descripción de España* written by the famous Portuguese humanist Damião de Góis (1502–1574) in order to defend the good name of the land he felt to be his own against the criticisms of Sebastian of Münster and Michael Servetus: "It is true that some centuries are more brilliant than others and that Spain is not now preeminent in science as she was in the past; but the nation which has produced such great figures cannot be condemned for cultural poverty, nor can the wellspring of such figures be thought dried up simply because it has not produced any for some time."[30]

With noble zeal Damião de Góis once again fills the vacuum sensed in the present with lists of names of Roman, Muslim, and Hebrew writers who lived centuries before: there appear the Romans born in Hispania, including Juvenal, who by this standard should really have been considered Italian, since he was born in Aquino. Afterward come the Muslims and the Jews of al-Andalus: Averroës, Maimonides, and even the Asiatic Avicenna. Genuine Spaniards are mentioned in this order: Alonso de Madrigal, El Tostado; Arnaldo de Vilanova, Raymond Lully, Cardinal Cisneros, Alfonso the Learned, Don Enrique de Villena, Luis Vives, Jorge Manrique, Juan de Mena, and Garcilaso. He concludes his praise of Spanish letters with these significant statements: "In the last thousand years Spain would not have been lacking in those brilliant talents which this nation has always produced had she not remained for so many years under the domination of peoples as barbarous as the Goths, the Alani, and the Saracens, who were bereft of any kind of culture; since the Spaniards are now free of that oppression, Sebastian of Münster does not doubt that they will shortly reach the very peaks of science" (*loc. cit.*). But if the Goths and Saracens were uncivilized barbarians, how does it happen that the author's list of illustrious men (p. 105) includes St. Leander, St. Ildephonsus of Toledo, Averroës, and Avicenna?

For those who have tried to judge the Spanish past with calm deliberation, it has always presented a problem difficult to solve. Some people devalue and deprive it of an effective structure; others, offended by such views, deny that there has been a Spanish decadence. When the monarchy fell in 1931, there were even some who proposed as a political ideal beginning everything "da capo," as if

---

[30] *Opúsculos Históricos*, trans. Dias de Carvalho (Oporto, 1945), p. 107.

the history of Spain had not existed. All of this strengthens my suspicion that Spanish life has been unique—in my opinion, splendidly unique.

Isolated in their historical faith, insensitive to the problems that the past had raised for peoples as close as the French and the Italians, Peninsular historiographers have gone on perpetrating down through the centuries the legendary fiction of the Spanishness of Iberians and Celtiberians. The space such a fantasy occupies in the minds and souls of those who have learned to love it from their schooldays is immeasurable. Respectable scholars and bold charlatans unite in a close defensive formation around the fantasy, and we remain ignorant of what Spaniards really are and how their existence was begun. When the first edition of this book was published, I thought it would suffice to call the reader's attention to this ancient confusion; I rashly thought that what was obvious and reasonable would make its own way. Some are now convinced, of course, but conventional, petrified historiography is still there, protected behind ramparts of pseudo-patriotism and anti-Semitism and brandishing the specters of the "Spanish" Seneca and Trajan. They mistakenly take for granted the existence of "quod erat demonstrandum"; they confuse the semantic content of the Latin adjective *Hispanus* with *español*, a foreign word of the twelfth century; they imagine that human beings living in the Peninsula have always been Spanish; they believe that the soil of the Peninsula, which today has been made Spanish by authentic Spaniards, was already Spanish before Spaniards existed. And by such begging of the question they set up the illusory figure of their "Spaniard," as if they were dealing with an object as real and visible as the cathedral of Toledo, which is Toledan because it is located in Toledo. These historians believe that the differences between the pre-Romans and the later Spaniard are due simply to the many differences between one epoch and another; sometimes one thing happens, at other times, another thing. I suppose they imagine that the "Spaniard," once having emerged on Peninsular soil, passed through various styles and circumstances of life, just as the cathedral of Toledo was first Gothic according to the style of the thirteenth century, then Gothic according to the style of the fourteenth century; while between the thirteenth and the eighteenth centuries it took on Mudejar ornamentation, Renaissance, baroque, and even rococo additions. But the difference is that we know when and how that architectural jewel was begun; the historians of the eternal Spaniard have never told us what the reality of the Spaniard is structurally and in truth composed of. They take what they term "psychological characteristics" (a vague and ingenuous notion of the nineteenth century) and project them backward onto the nebulous descriptions given in Greek and Roman texts of the inhabitants of the Peninsula—unaware

that man is not characterized by his psychology but by the value
and meaning of what he does with his psychological apparatus.

In such fashion circumstances proper to other collective subjects
(Iberians, Celtiberians, etc.) have been projected on, and added to,
the verbal image of the "Spaniard," an image that has been mistakenly
converted into an essence underlying the flow of vital time. The
magnitude of this folly and the great obstacle it puts in the way of
even halfway understanding the reality of Spaniards have forced me
to demonstrate, at the expense of being repetitious, the deep roots
of an error that is now centuries old.

III · THE SPANIARDS AS THE CONSEQUENCE OF THE INTERMINGLING OF THREE CASTES OF BELIEVERS

A PEOPLE IS CONSTITUTED when it separates from others and affirms itself with respect to them; whether or not it later acquires a historical dimension depends on the justification of its claim to surpass itself,[1] not on its attachment to age-old ways of garnering grain and warding off the evil eye, or because it is more or less moderate in diet, long-suffering of hardships, or proud. It is not merely psychic or external circumstances that give form to collective life, since the decisive factor will always be man's way of situating himself within those circumstances, whether they be material or human. Customs originating in the distant past exist in many places; but such usages are not what makes a citizen of Trieste and one of Florence share the feeling of being the product of an ancient awareness, longing, and effort which have determined the fact that both of them *want* to express themselves in the common tongue of Italy.

Spaniards were the outcome of the will and the effort of certain inhabitants of the Peninsula interested in constituting themselves as a social and political group for the sake of a future dependent on a common task. The end was achieved primarily by means of war, sometimes against Muslims, sometimes against the Christians living closest to their frontiers. They looked forward to a union that would include all the Peninsular peoples, even though in the twelfth century Portugal had already detached itself from Leon and Castile. (The subsequent union under Philip II did not bring Portugal any closer to Spain and was soon dissolved.) The unity of the other peoples of the Peninsula was fully achieved in some cases but not in others. An understanding of both that attempt at political and cul-

---

[1] As is shown later, in the thirteenth century it was felt that Castile "is better than its neighbors"; God wished to make Spain superior to "England and France," for "in all those regions there lies no Apostle."

tural unification and the reasons for disunity or faulty unification is of primary importance in the historiography of Spain.

Had the human "substance" so many people dream of really existed, the task of uniting all the Spanish peoples—still today a thankless and thorny endeavor—would not have been so hard, for the will toward both unification and disunity is inseparable from that same vital process that gave rise to the kind of people called "Spanish" by the inhabitants of Provence in the twelfth century; and no form of "Iberian particularism" intervened in the process. Let me anticipate a little of what I shall later develop: Peninsular life was reconstituted after the Muslim occupation in accordance with a system of castes based on one's being Christian, Moorish, or Jewish. After the disappearance of Moors and Jews from the social scene, respect for the pure lineage (*lo castizo*) of people—in other words, for their "Old Christian" ancestry—continued to be very intense. Awareness of the value per se of the caste now free from Jewish and Muslim contamination was strengthened and magnified thanks to imperial victories far from Peninsular soil. But within the mother country— once the coexistence of the three castes which had made possible the Christian hegemony was broken up and forgotten, once the collaboration of the Moors and Jews was suppressed—the Old Christians, deprived of common tasks, were paralyzed. The "honor" of being a Spaniard, the ideal of becoming fully one's self, of possessing "being," finally came to fill up the whole range of existence itself.

This is, in brief, the marvel and the drama that I propose to make manifest, comprehensible, and worthy of esteem in the course of this book.

The Consciousness of Caste Had a Religious Basis

The effective resistance against the Moors begun in Asturias in the eighth century had as its ultimate goal the recovery of the land formerly ruled by the Visigothic kings of Toledo. The chronicler of the Monastery of Albelda wrote in 880, during the reign of Alfonso III of Leon, that in 711 "the Saracens occupy the Spains [*Spanias*] and seize [*capiunt*] the kingdom of the Goths, which in part they still possess; against them the *Christians* fight night and day, they struggle daily [*quotidie confligunt*] until divine Providence may decree that the Saracens be implacably expelled in the future [*dehinc eos expelli crudeliter jubeat*]."[2] From this, one sees that some 170 years after the Muslims' occupation the kingdom of the Goths is remembered, but that those who fight against the Muslims are called the Christians, not Goths, in order to emphasize the contrast with

---

[2] *Chronica Albeldense*, ed. M. Gómez Moreno, in *Boletín de la Academia de la Historia* (1932), p. 569.

the Islamic adversary, as well as to indicate a common spiritual value. Even then, religious allegiance served to delimit the national and generic identity of a whole people, which was a new occurrence in the West, for no Western people had used the name of their religion to designate themselves nationally or politically. The fact that the others did not prevent its military and political physiognomy from appearing primarily as Mohammedan, as that of the people of the "house of Islam," *dar al-islam*, angered those who had found their salvation in it. As a result, calling those who fought against the Moors "Christians" was already revelatory of the presence of the Islamic Weltanschauung in the people who centuries later would be called "Spaniards." The latter name does not yet occur in the *Poem of the Cid (ca.* 1140), in which those who oppose the "Moors" are called "Christians"; when the former beat drums, "many of those Christians marveled at it" (line 2346: "a maravilla lo avíen muchos dessos cristianos"). In the *Chanson de Roland*, on the other hand, the enemies of the "Saracens" or "pagans" are called "French" (line 49: "L'ost des Franceis"), whereas the word "Chrestien" (lines 38, 102, etc.) is a general term applied to all those who profess Christianity.

I do not mean that the war against the Moors was religious in nature, aimed at the extermination of a faith that was deemed false (like the crusade of the French against the Albigensians or the Catholic wars against the Protestants in the sixteenth and seventeenth centuries). "Christian" in this instance meant that the combatants were animated and sustained by a religious belief no less efficacious militarily and politically than that of the enemy. The faith in Christ "conferred nationality" as much as did the faith in Mohammed, under which almost all the territory of the Peninsula had fallen into Saracen hands. Making the national (political) dimension coextensive with that of religious belief was the consequence of a primary and basic correlation between al-Andalus and the emerging Christian kingdoms. Other parallelisms would arise in the course of many centuries of contact.

But that the war was not exactly *for the sake of* religion is very clearly stated by Prince Juan Manuel (d. 1348), who was well informed about the past and the present of his Castile: "There is war between Christians and Moors and there will be, until the Christians have regained the lands that the Moors took from them by force; for neither because of the law nor because of the sect that they hold to, would there be war between them."[3]

Such a statement is inspired, as is explained in chapter xii, by the

---

[3] *Libro de los Estados*, in *Biblioteca de Autores Españoles*, LI, 294: "Ha guerra entre los cristianos e los moros e habrá, fasta que hayan cobrado los cristianos las tierras que los tierras que los moros les tienen forzadas; ca cuanto por la ley nin por la secta que ellos tienen, non habrían guerra entre ellos."

koranic doctrine of tolerance. And by now we are beginning to discern the outlines of a complicated system of strife and shared common life, complicated because those who lived together, in order not to lose their separate identity, circumscribed their collective being by their religious, their *caste*, affiliation. Rather than being Leonese, Castilian, or Aragonese, the varied peoples who fought against the Moors and lived intermingled with both Moors and Jews were Christians. Each one of these groups of believers had emerged and set the boundaries of its identity as the consequence of circumstances irrelevant to Peninsular life prior to 711. Their social condition resulted from circumstances that transcended politics, primarily those of spiritual lineage and, after that, of a certain type of occupation or goal. The word "caste," born in Spain, was not used in the Hindu sense, even though later the Portuguese applied it to the castes of India. (Nor is there anything strange in this, since many terms that refer to phenomena of human life have no rigorously univocal meaning: the kings of the Peninsular kingdoms did not exercise their royal powers like those of France and England, yet all of them are called kings.) The unique importance of the caste system in the Peninsula, without parallel in the West, endowed with human meaning the word "caste," which before was applied to animals, as when Bartolomé de las Casas speaks of "horses that are very *pure in blood* and noble-hearted" ("muy *castizos* y generosos caballos").

In his *Vocabulary* Antonio de Nebrija defines "caste" as "good lineage." According to Covarrubias, "*caste* means noble and pure lineage; he who comes of good family and descent, despite the fact that we say, 'he is of good caste' or 'he is of bad caste.' . . . Those who are of good lineage and caste we call 'castizos.' "[4] In the sixteenth century, speaking of the castes of India from the Portuguese point of view, Duarte Barbosa mentions families that are "noble and of good caste."[5] Antonio de Guevara says that parents, "because their honor is involved, seek a wife for their son who is prudent, rich, chaste, and *castiza*."[6] Referring to ideas about the Indians which prevailed among Dominicans and Franciscans, Gonzalo Fernández de Oviedo warned that "these things are dangerous, and not only for laymen who have been recently converted; they may even stir up many scruples in those who are *castizo Christians*."[7] The same writer makes what seems to me the invaluable observation that "in no

---

[4] *Tesoro de la lengua castellana* (1611), s.v. "casta."
[5] "Fidalgas e de boa casta" (Corominas, *Diccionario etimológico*).
[6] *Cartas*, in *Biblioteca de Autores Españoles*, XIII, 160b.
[7] *Historia natural de las Indias* (Toledo, 1526; here cited from the Madrid edition of 1851, I, 73): "estas cosas son peligrosas, no tan sólo a los legos que nuevamente vienen a la fe, pero aun a los que son cristianos castizos podrán poner en muchos escrúpulos."

Christian nation better [than in Spain] is it known who are the nobles and of good and clean *caste*, and who are suspect on points of faith; in other nations all this is hidden."[8]

The position of Christian Spaniards with respect to their caste did not proceed from motives peculiar to them, since the same thing happened among Spaniards of the Hebrew caste. The motive is to be found in the structural basis of Spanish life, in the interlacing of each one of the three peoples, all desirous of affirming themselves as a people with—and against—the other two. The forms of that contrast varied in the course of the centuries, but the point of departure and the subsequent motivations rested upon the necessity of common life among three peoples, three castes, and also upon the radical inadequacy of each one of the three.

The preoccupation, Semitic in origin, with keeping pure the bloodlines of the caste is expressed with great frequency in the literature of Spanish Jews: "The Jews said to the Holy Law: Thou art very holy, we took thee as a bride of high caste, we prize thee like a golden necklace."[9] As in the Christian examples previously cited, caste here means "lineage," in this case uncontaminated by impure blood.

In Sephardic versions of the ballad of Tarquin and Lucretia, there appear variants highly indicative of the exclusiveness of caste. Tarquin says:

Love for you, my lady, permits me no repose.
(*Vuestros amores, mi dama, no me dexan repozare.*)

---

[8] *Quincuagenas de la nobleza de España*, in the edition of 1880, p. 281. The interest displayed by Fernández de Oviedo in underscoring the "casticismo" of the Spaniards is another indication of his having been a New Christian. J. de la Peña y Cámara rightly supposes that the insistence on passing for a hidalgo and an Old Christian shows that Fernández de Oviedo was neither (see *Revista de Indias* [Madrid, 1957], XVII, 634 ff.). The objections to this hypothesis brought forward by J. Pérez de Tudela Bueso in his edition of this author's works (*Biblioteca de Autores Españoles*, CXVII, xv–xvi) do not seem to me well founded. The social and intellectual figure of Fernández de Oviedo, his evasiveness with respect to his antecedents as well as his exuberantly personal attitude, resemble the behavior of other converts in the fifteenth and sixteenth centuries.

[9] In the record of an investigation in 1592 into the purity of blood of a descendant of Diego de San Pedro (author of the *Cárcel de amor*) who aspired to the habit of the Order of Santiago, one witness said that he did not know "of what *caste* and quality of lineage" Diego de San Pedro might be. Another witness also did not know "of what lineage, or *caste* or quality of caste other people involved in the affair might be" (E. Cotarelo, in *Boletín de la Real Academia Española* XIV [1927], 311, 312). Diego de San Pedro was a convert from Judaism. The material quoted in the text is translated from a Judeo-Spanish MS from the Isle of Rhodes (eighteenth century): "Dixeron los ŷidiós ('los judíos') a la Ley Santa: Tu eres muy santa, te tomemos como una novia de casta alta, te preciamos como el oro en la garganta." This and the following ballad texts have been brought to my attention by Samuel G. Armistead and Joseph H. Silverman, to whom I here express my gratitude.

And Lucretia answers:

> And I prefer to die with honor and not live defamed,
> Rather than that my people should say I loved a Christian.
> (*Y más quiero morir con onra y no vivir desfamada,*
> *que no digan la mi gente de un cristiano fue enamorada.*)[10]

In another ballad, whose country of origin is not known, these lines appear:

> Being of the lineage you know, they married me to a Christian . . .
> I was the daughter of the high priest.
> (*Siendo hija de quien soy, me casaron con cristiano . . .*
> *Yo era hija del cohen gadol.*)[11]

In an unpublished version of the "Ballad of the Deceived Wife," we find these lines, which recall the previously cited text of Antonio de Guevara:

> I was a young man and wanted to marry;
> And I took a girl, of caste and very rich.
> (*Yo era mansevo y casarme quería;*
> *y tomí una muchacha, y es de casta y muy rica.*)

And if we return to Spain from the Sephardic east, we find the following song in Andalusia:

> You descend from a bad line, you cannot help it;
> Women and melons must be tested by their *caste*.
> (*Desciendes de mala rama, no lo puedes remediar;*
> *las mujeres y melón, por casta se han de probar.*)[12]

So sharp an opposition and so clear a correlation between peoples rested upon circumstances that had been present for centuries, even though such open talk of "caste" and "castizo" was related to the fight between New and Old Christians, which became more intense toward the end of the fifteenth century.[13] In any event, the division of society within the Christian kingdoms into three groups was bound up with what had taken place in al-Andalus, composed of Muslims, Christians, and Jews from the moment of its birth as a political entity in the eighth century. Yet before this decisive event occurred, there were inner differences in the population of the Penin-

---

[10] This version is from the Isle of Rhodes; in others from Tekirdaž (Turkey) and Salonica these variants occur:

"Que no digan la mi yente de un cristo ('cristiano') fue enamorada."

"Que no digan la mi yente de un crisiyo fue amada."

Both forms may be translated into English as "May my people not say that I loved a Christian."

[11] M. Attias, *Romancero sefaradí* (Jerusalem, 1956), ballad 88.

[12] F. Rodríguez Marín, *Cantos populares andaluces* (Seville, 1883), III, 173.

[13] See my book *De la edad conflictiva: El drama de la honra* (Madrid: Taurus, 1963).

sula for other reasons. Hispano-Romans and Hispano-Visigoths mixed with difficulty, even though intermarriage between the two peoples was finally made legal. Place names like "Romanillos" and "Gudillos," along with others noted by Menéndez Pidal,[14] reveal the separation of both types of people, who, as is now clear, did not call themselves "Spaniards," or "Celtiberians," or "Iberians," but what they felt themselves to be within their collective consciousness. But that consciousness was determined by earthbound motives, by concerns of this world, having nothing to do with religion, which would later be the crucial motivation. As for the Jews in the time of the Visigoths, their position in the society was very different from what it afterwards became, as I explain later.

The awareness of "caste" founded on religious faith gradually became a formative element of what would later be called "Spanish" life during the centuries of struggle to recover lost territory, and under the influence of the model offered by al-Andalus, where the Muslim invaders (Arabs, Syrians, Berbers) could not do without either the Christian inhabitants or the Jews. The authority of the emirs and later of the short-lived caliphate could not, and did not, try to reduce al-Andalus to religious unity. Fanatical peoples from the heart of Africa attempted it later in the twelfth century; but the social and vital structure of the Christian kingdoms was by that time already what some five hundred years of struggle and common life with neighboring al-Andalus had contributed to make it. And al-Andalus, like the Christian kingdoms, had been born under the stars of "insecurity," as we shall see later. In addition to the resistance of Toledo and Merida against the central powers of Cordova, the rebellious Umar ibn-Ḥafṣūn, and later his sons, defied the authority of the emirs for almost half a century from the impregnable fortress of Bobastro. The energy of the great 'Abd-al-Raḥmān III (912–961) was required to put an end to that dissidence, in which Christian (Mozarab) and Muslim interests were strangely mingled. The Cordovan emir 'Abd-Allāh feared in 891 that the end of al-Andalus, which had been foretold for many years, was at hand. Even 'Abd-al-Raḥmān III kept Bobastro as a refuge in case so calamitous a prophecy should be fulfilled.[15]

---

[14] Neither do such place names, still in existence today, mean that the Roman or the Gothic characteristics of the inhabitants actually continued for a long time after the eighth century. "Roman" and "Gothic" have the same value here as "Babylonian" does in reference to our duodecimal system of telling time, which was imported from the Orient by the Romans. Ramón Menéndez Pidal does not believe "in a persistent ethnic differentiation between Goths and Romans," although he cites a certain number of place-names that bring to mind the situation that existed before al-Andalus came into being (*Orígenes del español* [Madrid, 1950], pp. 505, 509). This confirms my opinion that neither the Romans nor the Goths felt themselves to be Spaniards.

[15] R. Dozy, *Histoire des Musulmans d'Espagne* (1932), II, 63–66, 273; *Ré-*

If so much insecurity was felt at the height of the Muslim domination, it is reasonable to infer that it had not been dissipated when the caliphate fell in the early years of the eleventh century. The heterogeneous demographic composition of al-Andalus contributed in large part to that lack of stability, even before the great advances made by the reconquest from about the end of the eleventh century. The Muslims included Orientals, Berbers, and converts from many places (Christians, Jews, Slavs from Europe), and they lived together, furthermore, with Christians and Jews, even though the Islamic and Oriental mode of life was clearly dominant by virtue of the prestige of its civilization. The Mozarabs acquired Arabic culture and imitated Moorish architecture rather than imposing their own on the Mohammedans; in al-Andalus, the Mozarabs were more conversant with Arabic literature than with Latin.[16] Christian magistrates and bishops sometimes bore Arabic names: one qadi was called Walid ibn Haizuran, and a metropolitan of Toledo was named Ubaid ibn Qāsim.[17] When they emigrated to the kingdoms of the north, such Arabized Christians imprinted on their new homeland the stamp of the civilization of al-Andalus, a country completely different from the present Andalusia. In view of all this, it is incomprehensible that poetry written in this area at that time should be called "Andalusian"; at the most, it can only be termed "Andalus." Such opinions as the following are astonishing:

The great majority of the Muslim population was made up of Spaniards converted to Islam, who, on adopting the religion of their conquerors, changed their inner mode of life only slightly. These converts might be of Jewish or Ibero-Roman racial extraction. . . . Their children and descendants, whom the chroniclers call *muwallad-s*, could not be distinguished after several generations from the original Muslims. Marriages between one group and the other finally produced a uniform population in which, as was to be expected, *Spanish blood predominated.*[18]

These phrases exemplify the chaotic situation in which many historians, both Spanish and foreign, find themselves. Starting with the sophism about the existence of an "eternal Spaniard," based on geographical considerations, they derive from so false a premise a series of secondary deductions that confuse *ad infinitum* everything that comes afterward. In such instances, what is understood by "inner mode of life"? Between the ninth and the twelfth centuries, the life that merits comment and in al-Andalus appears as a coherent totality, in spite of all the political and social upheavals that shook the coun-

---

cherches (1881), p. 29; M. Gómez Moreno, "Las primeras crónicas de la Reconquista," in *Boletín de la Real Academia de la Historia*, C (1932), 580.

[16] See my *Origen, ser y existir de los españoles* (Madrid, 1959), pp. 26, 48.

[17] Henri Pérès, *La poesie andalouse en arabe classique au XIe siecle* (1937), p. 255.

[18] *Ibid.*, p. 254.

try. What "Spanish" traces are there at this time in agriculture, industry, domestic and foreign commerce (especially from Seville and Almeria), the fine arts (architecture, gold and silver work, weaving), Islamic doctrine and the modes of religious sensibility, scientific and technical knowledge, philosophical thought? To understand that total way of life fully, it would doubtless be necessary to take into account Persian, Hellenistic, Byzantine, Syrian, and other contributions. But the way in which they were all combined and assimilated confers on the life and the civilization of al-Andalus a unique aspect and importance. The crucial elements in that life and civilization incline toward the Byzantine-Muslim East, despite the inclusion of certain details from the Peninsular tradition which in no way affect the splendor and originality of the whole. Should we really believe that the Mosque of Cordova, Medina Azahara (its present ruined state is of no importance to us here), the Alhambra, the astronomy of Azarquiel (Ibn al-Zarqālī), the thought of Ibn Massara, Ibn Ḥazm, and Averroës were the Islamic disguises of eternal Spaniards, Celtiberians, and Tartessians? Is it not now time to treat these matters with a certain minimum of intellectual rigor?

Many people continue to hold to the fantastic nineteenth-century conceptions of Simonet, who stated flatly that "*Spaniards* converted to Islam usually took out citizenship papers in the Arab and Berber tribes in order to make people forget their Christian origin, which exposed them to the insults and scorn of the *Old Muslims*." (Note how Simonet projects onto life in al-Andalus the sixteenth-century contrast between New and Old Christians.) "The conclusion of all this is that the Arabs did not introduce civilization onto our soil and that, on the contrary, the great splendor with which Arabic Spain [i.e., al-Andalus] shone for several centuries was due principally to the influence of the Hispano-Roman element, which [transmitted to that society] the special gifts of *the indigenous race*" (*Historia de los mozárabes*, p. 645).

For many people this empty rhetoric continues to be the truth of revealed gospel. Fortunately, those who truly know what happened in al-Andalus express themselves in a different fashion. According to M. Gómez Moreno, the Mosque of Cordova is a unique work: "Its originality [goes together with] the disturbing fact that we can find no models, either nearby or distant, that serve to explain its structure, its decoration, its peculiar aesthetics, so alien to everything consecrated to the service of monotheistic religions." Further, Gómez Moreno says this despite the mosque's horseshoe arches, derived from the Roman tradition and familiar to the Visigoths, but utilized as part of a new structure—neither Roman nor Visigothic—that lends a unique character to that monument, rising on top of the Visigothic Church of St. Vincent, which is "unrecognizable, even in its foundations" (*El arte árabe español hasta los almohades*, 1951, pp. 40, 44).

And while all this is happening within the sphere of art, the situation of philosophic thought is clearly linked to Oriental, and not mythical "Spanish," circumstances. Miguel Asín (*Abenmasarra y su escuela*, 1914, p. 17) observes that for Saíd, a historian of science and philosophy in Muslim Toledo, "the names of Seneca or of St. Isidore, the glories of ante-Islamic Spain were unknown." (Like so many others, Asín continued to cling to the Spanish character of Seneca and St. Isidore.) Precisely the same was true of the "Cordovan Ibn Ḥazm" (for Asín, the Cordova of a thousand years ago and the city of Cordova today were one and the same), who knew nothing of Romano-Visigothic culture because, as Asín says, "the native tradition had been broken without making a juncture with Islam."[19] And if we leave philosophy and turn to practical material life, agriculture departs from the Peninsular tradition in many ways (witness the importation of plants like the carob [*algarrobo*], the eggplant [*berenjena*], the orange [*naranja*], and the lemon [*limón*], all of whose Spanish names are Arabic in origin; irrigation techniques; etc.). Certain vestiges of Hellenism, which was still a living force in the Near East between the seventh and tenth centuries, were salvaged by Muslim scholars and gave rise to a scientific revival attested to by the knowledge and study of Aristotle and Dioscorides in al-Andalus. If all this should not be sufficient proof, the number and kind of Arabic words injected into the Romance dialects of the Peninsula would alone negate the outrageous claim that the Muslims, because relatively few of them were Arabic by race, did not break the continuity of life in the land that later was called Spanish. How long will books give currency to the humbug of al-Andalus as a "Spanish" country with a surface varnish of Orientalism?

The prestige of al-Andalus beyond its frontiers in the Peninsula was not incompatible with the weakness of its political structure before and after the brief splendor (scarcely a century) of the caliphate. By legalizing the coexistence of people of different religious faiths, the Islamic religion opened the way, especially in the eighth century, for the political ambitions of those who knew that they were indispensable because the number of the invaders was so small. According to Ibn Khaldūn, "Tārik installed the Jews in Toledo," and Muza did the same in Seville.[20] From then on, the Jews, strengthened by the consciousness of their high lineage, initiated a struggle for dominance and grandeur with their Muslim and Chris-

---

[19] See my *Origen, ser y existir de los españoles*, pp. 25–26.
[20] *Histoire des Berberes*, trans. M. G. de Slane (1925), I, 349–350.

tian rivals. The Mozarabs, for their part, rebelled at times, not because they were "Spaniards" but because of their Christian faith, which encouraged them to oppose their Muslim rivals. But apart from this, their customs were strongly Islamized, so that in the ninth and tenth centuries they carried into the Christian kingdoms certain practical ways of life, and at times "psychic" forms, new to those kingdoms. Through one intermediary or another, three hundred years after al-Andalus came into existence, knowledge of its forms of life was widespread in the north of the Peninsula. And in the north existence of a conglomerate of peoples of differing faiths, no one of which could survive without the other two, gave rise to the same radical "insecurity" that characterizes al-Andalus. The way was thus opened for the three divisions of "caste," for the feeling of collective importance through the mere fact of being a Christian, Moor, or Jew.

It is inexplicable that a French Arabist should think that the persistence in certain cases of Romanic names (Angelino, Yannair [modern Gener], etc.) among converts to Islam "not only is proof of the considerable contribution of Celtiberian elements to the Hispano-Muslim race but also of an undeniable influence on Arabic conceptions of genealogy."[21] M. Pérès has so absorbed the mythical view of Spanish history that he makes the Celtiberians the starting point for the consciousness of the value of lineage, which is ever present among Semites and visible to such a degree in the Old Testament. The Muslims did not fall behind the Jews in this respect. Al-Shaqundī, a citizen of al-Andalus, says about his country:

> Blessed be the Lord, who has so disposed that he who speaks with pride of the Peninsula of al-Andalus may give full tongue to his praise and be as vain as he likes without finding anyone to contradict him. . . . I praise the Lord because He fixed my birth in al-Andalus. . . . I belong to a lineage of noble and powerful people. . . . Are we not, after all, the Banū-Marwān, even though our station may change and in spite of the vicissitudes of fortune?[22]

Ibn Khaldūn (1332–1406) also alludes to the interest of the people of al-Andalus in their lineage when he describes the sad situation of Islam in that land:

> This is due to the loss of the collective spirit as a result of the collapse of Arabic power in that country and of the fall of the dynasty founded on that power. After the disappearance of the rule of the Berbers—a people in whom a strong national feeling has always existed—those Arabs have lost the spirit of collectivity and of mutual aid which leads to power; they

---

21 Pérès, op. cit., p. 255.
22 Elogio del Islam español [ca. 1200], trans. E. García Gómez, pp. 41, 44. The use of the term "Spanish" does not seem proper to me; the Muslims of al-Andalus were a different people, as Oriental as the inhabitants of the Maghreb, the Egyptians, or the Syrians.

keep nothing but their genealogies. . . . They imagine that with *birth* [the awareness of lineage] and with a government post one comes with ease to the conquest of a kingdom or to governing men. You will find among them that officeholders and mere artisans *dream of power* and try to attain it.[23]

The awareness of caste continued to be very intense even among the Christianized Moors, as may be seen in this anecdote recorded by Luis Zapata in his *Miscelánea* (*Memorial Histórico Español*, XI, 400):

On a certain occasion one lady said to another descended from the sovereigns of Granada that she was Moorish, to which the second lady answered:

"If I am Moorish, I come at least from the caste of kings."

"What does that matter to me," replied the other, "if we know that none of them was saved?"

"I much prefer," said the princess, "to have grandparents who are kings in hell than to be like you and have grandparents who are squires in Paradise." This she said to be insulting [Zapata comments], but she was much deceived in the matter.

Evident here is the consciousness of lineage, in the final analysis of "caste," in people who dreamed of exercising sovereignty over the other two castes, even when they no longer possessed the means or the strength to do so. The rebellion of the Moriscos in the time of Philip II clearly demonstrates these feelings. Expressed in a different manner, the same goal appears in the Jewish dream of elevation to the upper spheres of government both in al-Andalus and in the Christian kingdoms, a dream that inspired them for centuries, as is shown later in this volume.

The peaceful coexistence of the three castes, closely interwoven with the latent or the manifest wish to destroy that common life, brings us in direct contact with the key problem of authentically Spanish history. It is therefore necessary to anticipate some explanations of the ideal bases that made possible the establishment and maintenance of a common life among the three castes for some seven hundred years. This was something more than a mere *de facto* situation, as the person who places himself within the life manifested by such facts will understand.

Let us consider, for example, the epitaph on the tomb of Ferdinand III the Holy in the cathedral of Seville. It is written in Latin, Castilian, Arabic, and Hebrew, a surprising thing for anyone who is unfamiliar with the circumstances in thirteenth-century Castile and during the reign of Alfonso the Learned which are reflected in those four epitaphs.

To my knowledge no one has observed that the Latin and Castilian

---

[23] *Prolégomènes*, trans. M. G. de Slane (1863), I, 63.

texts do not exactly correspond to each other. Witness the passage
that concerns us here:

HIC IACET ILLUSTRISSIMUS	ULTIMA DIE MAII ANNO AB
REX FERRANDUS CASTELLE	INCARNATIONE DOMINI
ET TOLETI LEGIONIS	MILLESSIMO DUCENTESSIMO
GALLIZIE SIVILLIE CORDUBE	QUINQUAGESSIMO II.
MURCIE ET IAENI QUI	AQUI IACE EL REY MUY
TOTAM HISPANIAM	ONDRADO DON FERRANDO
CONQUISIVIT FIDELISSIMUS	SEÑOR DE CASTIELLA E DE
VERACISSIMUS	TOLEDO DE LEON DE
CONSTANTISSIMUS	GALLIZIA DE SEVILLA DE
DECENTISSIMUS	CORDOVA DE MURCIA ET
STRENUISSIMUS	DE IAHEN EL QUE
PACIENTISSIMUS	CONQUISO TODA ESPAÑA
LIBERALISSIMUS	EL MAS LEAL E EL MAS
PACIENTISSIMUS	VERDADERO E EL MAS
PIISSIMUS HUMILLIMUS IN	FRANC E EL MAS
TIMORE ET SERVICIO DEI	ESFORÇADO E EL MAS
EFFICASSIMUS QUI	APUESTO E EL MAS
CONTRIVIT ET	GRANADO E EL MAS
EXTERMINAVIT PENITUS	SOFRIDO E EL MAS
HOSTIUM SUORUM	OMILDOSO E EL QUE MAS
PROTERVIAM CUI	TEMIE A DIOS E EL QUE LE
SUBLIMAVIT ET EXALTAVIT	FAZIA SERVICIO E EL QUE
OMNES AMICOS SUOS QUI	QUEBRANTO E DESTRUYO
CIVITATEM HISPALENS EM	A TODOS SUS ENEMIGOS E
QUE CAPUD EST ET	EL QUE ALÇO E ONDRO A
METROPOLIS TOCIUS	TODOS SUS AMIGOS E
HISPANIE *DE MANIBUS*	CONQUISO LA CIBDAD DE
ERIPUIT PAGANORUM ET	SEVILLA QUE ES CABEÇA DE
CULTUI RESTITUIT	TODA ESPAÑA E PASSOS HI
CHRISTIANO UBI SOLVENS	EN EL POSTREMERO DIA DE
NATURE DEBITUM AD	MAYO EN LA ERA DE MIL ET
DOMINUM TRANSMIGRAVIT	CC ET NOVAENTA AÑOS.[24]

The Latin epitaph is clearly the reflection of one type of policy
with respect to the three castes of believers, while those composed in

---

[24] The Latin and Castilian epitaphs were transcribed by Diego Ortiz de
Zúñiga, *Anales eclesiásticos y seculares de la muy noble e muy leal ciudad de
Sevilla* (Madrid, 1795), I, 415–416. The Castilian text has been collated with the
photograph kindly sent me by the Art Laboratory of the University of Seville,
to which I here express my gratitude. The Arabic and Hebrew texts (kindly
translated for me by Professor M. Perlmann but not reproduced here because
of their close similarity to the Castilian version), as well as the Latin and Castilian, are reproduced in the *Catálogo conmemorativo del VII centenario de la
conquista de Sevilla* (Victoria: H. Fournier, 1948). The English translation of
the Castilian text runs as follows: "Here lies the very honorable King Don
Ferdinand, Lord of Castile and of Toledo, of Leon, of Galicia, of Seville, of
Cordova, of Murcia, and of Jaen, he who conquered all Spain, the most loyal
and the truest and the most generous and the most courageous and the most
comely and the most distinguished and the most patient and the most humble
and he who most feared God and he who most served him and he who broke
and destroyed all his enemies and he who exalted and honored all his friends
and conquered the city of Seville, which is the head of all Spain, and he died
there on the last day of May in the time of one thousand and two hundred and
ninety years [really 1252; the year of the text follows the medieval Castilian
method of dating the Christian era]." The italics in the Latin text are mine.

Castilian, Arabic, and Hebrew each express another policy of toler-ance and the spirit of shared common life which united all three. In the Latin text it is said that the King crushed and exterminated the *proterviam* ("shamelessness, immodesty") of his enemies, in other words, of the Muslims who occupied Cordova and Seville; it is added that he snatched Seville from the power of the pagans (of the in-fidel) and restored it to the Christian religion. Nothing of this appears in the other three epitaphs. The Church, doubtless the su-preme power, expressed its way of understanding King Ferdinand's victory over the Muslims but did so in the language understandable only to the *clerici*, not to the uncultivated masses, whether Chris-tians, Moors, or Jews. The policy of Alfonso X was not in perfect agreement with that of the ecclesiastics in his court.

The Hebrew text appears to have been modeled on the Arabic be-cause in the original the "city" of Seville is referred to as a "medina." Where the Latin and Castilian texts speak of Seville as the "head of all Spain," the Arabic says "head of all al-Andalus," which meaning the Castilian text reflects when speaking of "Spain."[25] As was cus-tomary in the formative epoch of Spanish life, the three peoples formed the social structure upon which royal power was raised; and in unison with the other two, each one rendered the homage due to the monarch.

It would, nevertheless, be insufficient to conceive Alfonso's policy of compromise as nothing more than pragmatic opportunism, for so deeply rooted a mode of common life would not have been pos-sible without some foundation in religion and ideals. Taking shelter in this fashion under royal authority and protection was also felt to be a mode of conduct pleasing to God, as I discuss at greater length in a later chapter. Suffice it to recall now that King Alfonso, who had inspired these three harmonizing inscriptions, caused it to be written in his *Cantigas* that God is

> The one who can pardon
> Christian and Jew and Moor,
> While they fix their intent
> With all firmness on God.[26]

In the same work the Learned King says that the Moors believe in the virginity of Mary because it was so written by "Mohammed in the Koran" ("Mafomat no Alcoran").[27] In a newly discovered

---

[25] The use of the word *cabeza* ("head") in the sense of "capital" is a transla-tion of the word *rās* in the Arabic epitaph; *rās* is reflected in the Spanish word *res*, meaning "head of cattle."

[26] "A carta de Pēedença" ("The Letter of Penitence"), MS of the Biblioteca Nazionale of Florence, B.R. 20, fol. 43*r*.: "Aquel que perdõar pode / christchão, indeu e mouro, / a tanto que en Deus aian / ben firmes sas entenções."

[27] *Cantiga* 329, ed. Valmar.

text of the *Chronicle of Alfonso XI*, a Moorish chieftain appoints God as the judge between himself and a Christian prince who has broken the truce agreed upon between the two, and God decides the quarrel against the Christians, whose leaders perish on the Plain of Granada.[28]

In a manuscript that the Count of Haro possessed in the fifteenth century, it was said that "some Moors and Jews claim that they can say the Lord's Prayer as well in accordance with their religion as we Christians can in accordance with our law. The Bishop of Jaen, Don Pedro, who was a captive in Granada, was inspired by their obstinacy to put this prayer of Our Father into the vernacular to show that they cannot say it."[29] Such religious infiltrations are as explicable as those that occurred in language and in customs, as I make clear later.

All these facts serve to make us realize how the belief in a higher religious harmony functioned and to perceive its reflections in both practical and spiritual life. The possibility of such a harmony is ultimately founded on the Koran (III:63) in its recognition of the spiritual communion of "the people of the Book" (*ahl al-kitab*), in other words, of Muslims, Jews, and Christians, whose beliefs are founded on a revealed book. That faith was truly "lived" by the inhabitants of al-Andalus. One of them, born in Jaen in 828 and reared in Cordova, wrote some *Ordinances for the Good Operation of Markets*[30] in which it is recommended that the following koranic precept (V:70) be kept in mind in order to prevent fraud: "If they had kept the Torah, the Gospel and what was revealed to them by the Lord, they would have eaten of what is above them and beneath their feet."

Here is the root of the social system that permitted the shared common life of the three people-castes both in the Muslim south and in the Christian north. Irregularities and vicissitudes in the practical realization of that mode of collective existence are of little importance, for everything in Spanish life and civilization between the eighth and the fifteenth centuries manifests its reality. Laws and customs do not lose their force and effectiveness because they are not universally and constantly observed. Every ideal of life shows forth its authenticity and validity when confronted with practical difficulties; nor is the ideal character of a religious or ethical doctrine negated by the fact that its functioning is connected with

---

[28] See the text published by D. Catalán, *Un prosista anónimo del siglo XIV*, p. 118.

[29] See A. Paz y Melia, "Biblioteca fundada por el Conde de Haro en 1945," *Revista de Archivos, Bibliotecas y Museos*, IV (1900), 665. The quotation was brought to my attention by Francisco Márquez.

[30] Translated by E. García Gómez and published in *Al-Andalus*, XXII (1957), 257 ff.

economic circumstances, for every plan of life is connected with the ideal and corporal structure of man. Let us not think, therefore, that the common life of the three castes by virtue of which Spanish life took on its structure was nothing more than a phenomenon of economic nature. As for the numerous instances of imperfect co-existence, let it be remembered that even in countries ruled by just laws the prisons are filled with offenders against the common law.

All these attitudes, tangent to the problem itself, prevent our seeing what really happened in the Spain of the three religions, of the three languages, and of the three castes: the three existed a sufficient number of centuries to develop and cultivate in their course a kind of upward aspiration peculiar to each one, and a kind of task directed toward self-affirmation and to persistence in the awareness of being what they personally and collectively were. From the struggle and rivalries among these three groups, from their interconnections and their hatreds, arose the authentic life of the Spaniards, which is not Tartessian or Celtiberian but simply that which is in plain view before us.

The Awareness of Collective Lineage and Its Structural Functioning

The most effective way of combating the fables about the Spanish past is to make clear and intelligible the manner in which the Spanish people came to develop as it has been and is. I am more interested, consequently, in the role played by phenomena than in the mere conceptual and isolated reality of phenomena. Furthermore, I must bear in mind—it is, unfortunately, an inescapable necessity—that many readers have grown up with the idea of the almost geological Spanishness of their ancestors and that it is extremely difficult to extract an absurdity of such proportions from people's minds.

In the midst of such conventional postures, one exception has been Ortega y Gasset's attempt, in *Invertebrate Spain*, to relate the decadent and, in his opinion, radically unhealthy tone of Spanish life to circumstances that were Visigothic rather than Iberian or Celtiberian. The Spaniards' future depended, in his view, on the fact that the Visigoths were a people deficient in vitality, weakened by long and intimate contacts with the decadent Romans. While I should not care to deny that the Franks of future France possessed greater energy than the Visigoths and that life in the Peninsula would have been different if a strong and disciplined people had prevented the Muslims from taking over what was then the best part of the land, it is no less certain that the historiographic problem is to determine the Spaniards' real identity and worth. Any history based on "if this or that had not been as it was" serves only for linguistic juggling. The history of the Spaniards must begin by determining the identity and procedures of those who initiated new forms of collective life after the Visigothic failure, a life that was tightly bound to the Semitic peoples—Moors and Jews—who for centuries maintained the civilization of the inhabitants of al-Andalus at a high level. Those Semitic peoples deeply affected the vital structure of forms of conduct of the Christians of the north. I cannot understand how Ortega y Gasset could fail to mention the role of the Hispano-Hebrews, nor how he could write these lines that still appear in the 1952 edition of *Invertebrate Spain* (p. 110) exactly as they did in the 1922 edition (p. 146): "Since we Spaniards suffer from a lack of knowledge of our own history, it is fitting to note that *the Arabs neither constitute an essential ingredient of the beginnings of our nationality nor does their dominance explain the weakness of Peninsular feudalism.*" But how could the reality of Spain be revealed to us by a history based on what the Visigoths *were not* and without consideration of nine hundred years of Semitic actuality? Despite this weakness, there are at times in *Invertebrate Spain* a number of opinions that deserve respect and consideration.

It would be a gross error to consider the pressure exerted by Semites on Christians, in this and other cases, as a "transfer of ideas" such as, for example, the adoption of the French parliamentary system by Spaniards and Italians in the nineteenth century. The inner functioning of life when faced with such phenomena as lineage, tolerance, and the like is important here as revelatory of certain value-habits. The Hispano-Christians who came up against the Moors and Jews in the eighth century and who intermingled with them had, to be sure, their own beliefs; but the tremendous usefulness of those beliefs in the furtherance of the Christians' purposes in both war and peace was revealed to them by the enemy whose life rested totally and authentically upon his religious belief. Neither the Visigoths nor the other Germanic tribes had subjugated the Roman Empire through the stimulus of any religious belief. Their wars were not waged under divine inspiration; they were not holy or *divinales* ("for a religious purpose"), the word that Alonso de Cartagena, a converted Jew, used in the fifteenth century to distinguish at one stroke the Spaniards from the other Europeans (see below, p. 151). War "for a religious purpose" was a Mohammedan invention, or at least it appeared for the first time in Europe under the aegis of Islam. Nothing like it had gone on in Iberia before the invasion of 711. Nine hundred years later Spaniards and Portuguese were conquering remote peoples to Christianize them, that is, in the full awareness that God's word and man's were the foundations of truth, and, granting no importance to the truth of things, a truth that has its foundation in impersonal logic.[31] To speak in this instance of a "transference of ideas" would imply either an evasion of the historical problem or the consideration of it from a totally irrelevant vantage point.

Living as an intermediary between Moors and Christians, the Jews presented an "Occidental" aspect lacking in the Muslim. Gifted in languages, hardworking, peripatetic, and always alert, they articulated with the Christian much more than the Moor did. The special character of their occupations, either inaccessible or contemptible to the Christian, converted them into a caste, since their different belief prevented them from gradually uniting with the Christians, who really formed likewise not another class, but a different caste. The tolerance of the Middle Ages and the intermingling of three incompatible creeds hindered the establishment of the graduated regimen that prevailed in European feudalism—peasants, artisans, nobles, clergy. Spanish society broke up into three different hierarchies, each independent of the others, and therein lies a major explanation for the absence of a feudal society.[32] If in the fourteenth century, as in the twelfth and thirteenth, Moors and Jews had held castles in fief from the king, what kind of homogeneously ordered society could have been organized on such a base?

But it is not only the fact (which might be an accident) that

---

[31] In his *História de India*, finished in 1635, António Bocarro wrote: "We may well call this conquest . . . an extension and exaltation of the Catholic faith . . . ; only, it has not been as pure as it is now, because of the great interest that commerce has had in it. . . ." The great obstacle encountered by the Portuguese was that the East Indian rulers, "out of covetousness or out of pride . . . kept neither faith nor friendship . . . , the contrary being such a firm principle among the Portuguese" that they very often missed splendid opportunities only because they would not break "the inviolable observance of their faith and word" (Lisbon ed., 1876, pp. 33, 41). It may be added that António Bocarro was a convert (see J. Lúcio d' Azevedo, *História dos Christãos Novos Portugueses* [1922], p. 231). As I indicate in chapter xi, this conception of "truth" is not Western but characteristic of the Hebrew people.

[32] The Moslem order is expressed in texts like the following: "The world is a garden, and its fence is the kingdom, and the kingdom is maintained by laws, which are established by the king, and the king is the shepherd and is maintained by the knights, and the knights are maintained by their wealth, which is gathered together by the people, and the people are the servants of justice, and the world is governed by justice" (*Buenos proverbios*, chap. xiii, ed. of H. Knust, p. 276). Similar texts appear in *Poridad de poridades* and in the *Partidas*: "The kingdom is like the garden, and the king is like the lord of the garden; and the king's officers who shall judge and assist in carrying out justice are like tillers; and the noblemen and knights are hired to protect the garden, and the laws and statutes and privileges are like fences that surround it, and the judges and courts of justice are like walls and hedges because they protect it from those who would enter there and do harm" (II, x, 3). For Arabic texts with the same idea, see Knust, p. 227. This order is horizontal, not vertical; the person who wrote the passage from the *Partidas* sensed the arrangement very clearly when he insisted upon the symbols "fence, walls, hedges." Notice how this order follows along a plane surface in the interwoven pattern of an arabesque.

there were Hebrew bailiffs in Aragon or Moorish and Jewish wardens in the castles of Castile that stood in the way of feudal organization in Spain. It is the meaning of the facts, the people who *live* them, that explain history, not the facts alone, which are in themselves merely inert appearance. Life, individual as well as collective, goes on in obedience to one hierarchy of values or another; and so the Hispano-Christian, with no other horizon than his beliefs, could not organize within the Christian community the whole of his system of values. He had to accept as inescapable realities various kinds of Moslem and Jewish superiority. Thus, the daughter of James II of Aragon, married to the highest lord of Castile, brought up her children under the tutelage of Jews. The Christian found himself in a situation of cultural colonialism, just as did the Spanish Moors and Jews, whose place was at once below and above that of the Christians. In contrast to Spain, the feudalism of Western Christianity had a tightly homogeneous hierarchic scale of respect, submission, privilege, and duty. The lord constituted a total and absolute horizon for the vassal. The Spaniard, quite differently, had to divide his loyalties among three distinct authorities (Christian, Moslem, Jewish), with no clear sense of what was owed to Caesar and what to God. In this situation, feudalism of the European type became impossible.

Laws preventing the Christians from utilizing the good services of Jews and Moors turned out to be futile. The tolerant laws of the *Partidas*, a purely theoretical code in the thirteenth century, accepted the existence of Moors and Jews, but did not suggest that the Christians should bow before their occasional superiority. The Jews were tolerated so that "they would live as in captivity forever, and would be a reminder to men that they came of the lineage of those who crucified Our Lord Jesus Christ" (*Partidas*, VII, 24, 2). Christian life was therefore the product of an inevitable custom and a disregarded legal will. Logically, this was a senseless contradiction; but since the Christian kingdoms of Spain lived this way for more than five centuries, such an easy description as "senseless contradiction" would seem inadequate, and it would be more worthwhile to think that the form of life consisted of an inescapable compromise between two beliefs, between believing that the Jew was a deicide and believing that it was legitimate to accept him. The synagogue was also a house of God, according to the *Partidas*.

By accepting the occasional superiority of his infidel fellow citizens, the Christian was not deprived of his consciousness of being lord of his land. The Christian believed himself to be superior because he had a better religion and because he did what the Moorish commoner neither knew how to, nor could, do. This explains why the Christian had more a sense of caste than of class. The social class

bases its rank primarily on its ability to govern and the amount of its
wealth; the rank of the caste depends on the mere existence of the
person: in the last analysis, all the Hispano-Christians ended up by
feeling themselves a superior caste by virtue of the fact that they
were of Christian, rather than Moorish or Jewish, lineage. The form
of their daily existence, then, was analogous to that of their literary
creation: a personal "integralism" Islamic-Judaic in root and serving
as a common denominator for the life of Moors, Jews, and Christians.
All this is made more explicit later.

Turning now specifically to how the fact of being *castizo*, of good
caste, was lived, we must bear in mind the situation of common life
and of interdependence among three peoples which prevailed in the
Christian kingdoms. The concern for being "pure in blood" (*limpio
de sangre*) which disturbed Christian Spaniards from the fifteenth
century on springs from antecedents much older than the establishment in 1481 of that form of the Inquisition peculiar to Spain. In
this instance, the Hispano-Christians imitated a system of individual
and collective evaluation very characteristic of the Hispano-
Hebrew, as hated and feared as he was admired and copied. This
phenomenon is of capital importance as a symptom of the way in
which Spanish life functioned, especially from the fifteenth century
on. The more Hispano-Hebrews were persecuted, the more the
Semitic system of purity of lineage was taken over.[33]

As is well known, it has been and still is common for primitive
peoples to assign a magic and spiritual value to blood, but the Hebrew
people regarded the communion of its "spiritual" blood in an extreme
form: "For thou art an holy people unto the Lord thy God: the
Lord thy God hath chosen thee to be a special people unto himself,
above all people that are upon the face of the earth" (Deuteronomy
7:6). "Thou shalt bring them in, and plant them in the mountain of
thine inheritance, in the place, O Lord, which thou hast made for
thee to dwell in, in the Sanctuary, O Lord, which thy hands have
established" (Exodus 15:17). From such statements arises—or they
express—the feeling of existence as a holy and closed caste. The texts
cited, and those I adduce later, are readily available; but since they
are not mentioned in discussions of the sense of Old Christianity and
nobility (*hidalguía*) among Spaniards, it was necessary to bring
them up here. If from the end of the fifteenth century Spaniards considered it infamous to mix with Hispano-Hebrews and Hispano-
Moriscos, it is because they had, themselves, fully assimilated the
Hebrew belief that had forced Jews to maintain themselves as a
caste apart. Ezra cries out in the book that bears his name: "The
people of Israel, and the priests, and the Levites, have not separated

---

[33] I have given special attention to this problem in *De la edad conflictiva*.

themselves from the people of the lands, doing according to their abominations, even the Canaanites, the Hittites [etc.]. For they have taken of their daughters for themselves, and for their sons: so that the *holy seed* have mingled themselves with the people of those impure lands: yea, the hand of the princes and rulers hath been chief in this trespass" (Ezra 9:1-2). Long before 1500 the nobles had also "trespassed" in the Christian kingdoms, so that in the sixteenth century being a great lord had no value as a sign of Old Christianity. The only valid guarantee of absolute "purity" was descent from a long line of tillers of the soil, as I point out in *De la edad conflictiva*.

Given the prejudice, confusion, and secrecy that prevail with respect to this problem, one must insist on the extraordinary character of this notion of "purity of blood." Some Germanic peoples have created for themselves an exemplary physical image of the perfect specimen of their race, but the notions about the corporal, biological manifestations of Nature present in Occidental mythologies functioned within German life in a way that was unknown to the Spaniard. The racial physical type of the "Spanish man" does not exist. From the fifteenth century on, "purity of blood" has meant consciousness of caste, of descending from the people whom sixteenth-century Spaniards came to identify also with the elect of God in the Hebrew fashion. In *El Alcalde de Zalamea* ("The Judge of Zalamea," II, 21) Calderón makes Pedro Crespo say to his son: "You are of pure lineage," even though you are a "peasant" (*villano*); therefore, the son should aspire "to be more," to surpass himself, to exalt the consciousness of his worth as a *castizo*. Pedro Crespo does not speak of *doing* but of *being*.

The feelings expressed by Calderón and in the Old Testament flourished vigorously among Hispano-Christians when they saw themselves freed from the social and economic supremacy of the Hispano-Hebrews (witness the massacres and despoilment of the latter at the end of the fourteenth century, the inquisitorial purges, the expulsion of 1492). But the hardest task still remained, for the enemy had now concealed himself under the cloak of Christianity; from the fear of such hidden Jews sprang the distrust of New Christians and the exclusion from positions of power, particularly from the priesthood, of those who were of impure lineage. Today only the clergy and a few scholars are well versed in the Old Testament, but in the sixteenth century its words were alive and possessed authority. The Book of Ezra (chap. 2) lists those who had come to Jerusalem after the Babylonian captivity and identifies their lineage and its founder. Priests had to show the register of their genealogy (in other words, as was said in sixteenth- and seventeenth-century Spain, their "ejecutoria de limpieza de sangre" ["letters patent of purity of blood"]). The children of certain priests "sought their register among those that were reckoned by genealogy, but it was not found; therefore were they, as polluted, put from the priest-hood" (Ezra 2:62). "And of the priests: the children of Habaiah, the children of Koz, the children of Barzilai, which took one of the daughters of Barzillai the Gileadite to wife, and was called after their name. These sought their register among those that were reckoned by genealogy, but it was not found: therefore were they, as polluted, put from the priesthood" (Nehemiah 7:63–64).

Here is the foundation for the statutes of purity of blood[34] in the sixteenth century, even though no reference is ever made to it, be-cause it is not a pleasing topic for either Christians or Jews. Cardinal Siliceo purged the cathedral of Toledo of impure priests in accor-dance with the model of Ezra and Nehemiah. In ecclesiastical affairs the borders between the Christian and the Jewish castes were sharply defined and corresponded to the social division expressed in literature by the terms "caste" and "castizo." "And the seed of Israel separated themselves from all strangers, and stood and confessed their sins, and the iniquities of their fathers" (Nehemiah 9:2).

The preoccupation with genealogy finds abundant expression in the Old Testament (see I Chronicles) and even extends into the New Testament. The memory persisted of the time when "all Israel were reckoned by genealogies; and, behold, they were written in the book of the kings of Israel and Judah . . ." (I Chronicles 9:1).[35]

Here is the starting point for the Hispano-Christian's identification of his manhood "in itself" (as experienced by Prince Juan Manuel in the fourteenth century and the Count of Haro in the fifteenth) with the knowledge that his bloodlines were pure and uncontaminated. Once only a reality *de facto*, in the sixteenth century caste becomes a reality *de jure*. The fear of being taken for Hispano-Jews produced a caste of Christians who saw themselves as *castizo* in the Jewish

---

[34] For the disputes that arose over these statutes, see now the important study of Albert A. Sicroff, *Les controverses des statuts de "pureté de sang" en Espagne du XVe au XVIe siècles* (Paris: Didier, 1960).

[35] The biblical commentary of Rabbi Arragel, written *ca.* 1420, indicated the persistence of this attitude toward lineage among the Hispano-Hebrews: "The uses of this chapter [of the Book of Ezra] are: first, to make us understand that he who takes a wife of an alien nation gives great sorrow and anger to God; it notes of Solomon that he took wives of alien nations, and that caused all the woe of Israel, and the falling into captivity. . . . And [Ezra] said that this sin of sleeping with women of other nations was alone sufficient that no one should remain in Israel" (*Biblia,* trans. Rabbi Arragel, published by the Duke of Alba [1920], II, 868). It is clear that long before Christian literature talks of "purity of blood," the concern over maintaining that purity was con-substantial with the very existence of the Hebrews. The thousands of converts who came over to the Christian caste injected into it the biblical ideal of purity of blood. After all, the Old Testament was also accepted as a revealed book by the Christians. But the common sacred text was not the decisive reason for the penetration of the biblical purity of blood into the sphere of Christian life in Spain.

fashion. So it is that Antonio de Guevara and others spoke of marrying their sons to *"castiza* wives," as we have already seen. The interest in thought and in the practical applications of it, as I explain elsewhere in this book and in *De la edad conflictiva*, was excluded from the sphere of activity since the majority of such endeavors had usually been Moorish or Jewish occupations. It became preferable and less dangerous to intensify the awareness of being what one was —an Old Christian. Speaking of the expulsion of the Jews, Father Mariana says that certain people reproached the Catholic King, Ferdinand of Aragon, for the loss of wealth which such a measure entailed. But the disruption of the common life of the three medieval castes was inevitable, as were the consequences of the action.

The vacuum left by the absence of Jewish, Moorish, and New Christian activities grew even wider and deeper; but it was filled by the prestige of the imperial power exercised by Spaniards in Europe and the New World. The period that we saw symbolically culminated in the quadruple epitaph on the tomb of Ferdinand the Holy is closed in the sixteenth century by another funerary inscription, the epitaph on the tomb of the Catholic Sovereigns in the Royal Chapel of Granada, whose meaning I made clear for the first time in my book *Origen, ser y existir de los españoles*. The author of this epitaph was not interested in glorifying the memory of two brilliant sovereigns who, after unifying Spain, opened grand and universal horizons for its people. The inscription mentions the destruction of the Muslim faith and of the Jewish "heresy," nothing else.

As the Christian caste emphasized the value of *lo castizo*, it came ever closer to the Semitic mode of existence, to erasing the distinction between religious and civil life, between Church and State. Responding to a mimetic impulse that was at once aggressive and defensive, Spaniards came to confuse both orders of activity almost in the fashion of the kings of Israel or the Muslim caliphs. For those who are familiar with documents from the chancelleries of the Catholic Sovereigns and Philip II, the differences in tone and style between the two reigns will provide clear evidence in support of my opinions. And let us not resort to the hackneyed excuse of the Counter-Reformation, for other sovereigns engaged in the fight against Protestantism expressed themselves in very different ways.

Before the fifteenth century neither the Castilians nor the Aragonese had poured forth their vital energies to demonstrate the purity of their Christian lineage, but the strength and vigor that artisans and peasants had been acquiring during the fifteenth century reached its peak with the accession of the Catholic Sovereigns. The superiority of the Hispano-Hebrews then became intolerable to the peasant masses, as is made clear by the chronicler Andrés Bernáldez,

Priest of the Palaces (Seville) and a passionate foe of the Jewish people:

They had the presumption of arrogance; [they thought] that in all the world there were no people who were better, or more prudent, or shrewder, or more distinguished than they because they were of the lineage and condition of Israel. As soon as they could acquire honor [high rank], royal offices, favors from kings and lords, [they did so]; some mixed with the sons and daughters of Christian knights who were exceedingly wealthy . . . *and later gained a place in the Inquisition* [which was made up of Jewish converts] as good Christians and of much honor.[36]

Jews and converts attracted the wrath of those who, through their own failings or for some other reason, were unsuccessful and had fallen by the wayside. The boastful display of lineage had become consubstantial with the very existence of the Hebrew people, especially in Spain after their common life with Moors and Christians. In the Christians this phenomenon was intensified by the example of the Hebrews, who, whether converts or not, had contributed in most effective ways to the national and international success of Ferdinand and Isabella.[37]

The Wider Effects of the Concept of a "Pure-Blooded Caste"

The new and very difficult situation of the Jews with respect to the Christians during the fifteenth century was much more decisive for the direction of Spanish life than the resurgence of classical letters, the contact with Italy, or any other of the events by which the so-called Middle Ages are customarily marked off from modern times. The savage persecution of the Jews modified the traditional relations among the nobility, the Church, the common people, and the Jews,[38] and intensified that unique form of Spanish life in which religion and nation confused their boundaries.

---

[36] *Historia de los Reyes Católicos* (1870), I, 124–134. Resentment and an inferiority complex boil beneath the not very charitable pen of the Priest of the Palaces.

[37] Miguel Pérez de Almazán, a convert from Calatayud, was the first secretary of state in Spain; with his example before them, other European kings began to have secretaries of state. Almazán was highly respected in foreign courts, and his wisdom and self-denying service considerably influenced the international policies of King Ferdinand. See the important article by P. Rodríguez Muñoz, "Un colaborador de los Reyes Católicos," in *Publicaciones de la Institución Tello de Meneses* (Palencia, 1957), pp. 117–158.

[38] The liberal professions were also affected. Regarding the riots in Toledo in 1449, the convert Hernando del Pulgar wrote: "I recall among the other things that I heard Fernán Pérez de Guzmán say, that the bishop Don Pablo [de Santa María] wrote the old Constable who was ill in Toledo: 'I am glad that you are in a city of notable physicians and fine medicines.' I do not know whether he would say so now; for we see that the famous *odreros* ["leather-

Distinguished Christian families had mixed with Jewish people during the Middle Ages, sometimes for economic motives, sometimes on account of the frequent beauty of Jewish women. Before the fifteenth century nobody was shocked by this mixing, or at least the scandal was not great enough to leave any echo in literature (save the singular case of the legendary love affair between Alfonso VIII and the Jewess of Toledo); but during this period people wrote freely on a theme that inflamed the passions, that is, on the insoluble drama that rent asunder the two inimical peoples—or, more specifically, the two castes of Spaniards. In abusive poems like the *Coplas del provincial* and others, there is allusion to the Jewish provenience of certain persons. To this certain converts make reply, as sure of their own superiority as they are of the vulgarity of those impugning them. For example, someone sent Don Lope Barrientos, Bishop of Cuenca and a partisan of the converts, an allegation against a certain Pedro Sarmiento and a bachelor of arts Marcos García Mazambrós, who incited the mob in the massacre and sacking of the Toledo ghetto in 1449.[39] In this allegation, the author's foremost objection is the use of the term "converts" to designate the New Christians, "because they are sons and grandsons of Christians, and they were born in Christendom, and they know nothing at all of Judaism nor of its rite."[40] The good converts ought not to pay for the bad ones, just as "we are not going to massacre the Andalusians merely because some of them turn Moors every day." There follows a long list of names of illustrious people who had Jewish relatives, and not excluding persons of royal blood: "*going still higher*, it is not necessary to recount the sons and grandsons and great-grandsons of the noble and very powerful knight, the admiral Don Alonso Henríquez, who on one side is descended from the king Don Alonso [XI] and the king Don Enrique [II] the Elder, and on the other side is descended from this [i.e., Jewish] lineage." We may add that John II of Aragon took Doña Juana Henríquez, the daughter of the admiral mentioned

bottle makers," one of whom had headed the uprising of the converts] have driven the famous physicians away from there; and so I believe that you are now provided with much better rabble-rousing bottle-makers than with good natural scientists" (see *Clásicos Castellanos*, vol. 99, p. 24).

[39] See the "Crónica de don Juan II," in *Biblioteca de Autores Españoles*, LXVIII, 661–662.

[40] This text was published by Fermín Caballero, *Conquenses ilustres: Doctor Montalvo* (1873), pp. 243 ff. The informant of the bishop of Cuenca calls Marcos García "the bachelor of arts Marquillos," and accuses him of having caused discord in Toledo and of being a worthless person "even as a peasant from the village of Mazambrós. . . . It would be better for him to go back to plowing as his brothers and relatives do today" (p. 252). In this and in other instances, it is obvious that rural peasants stirred up wrath against the converts. In the end, being a farmer would serve as a man's surest protection against any accusation that he was of the Jewish caste. See my *De la edad conflictiva*.

above, as his second wife, so that their son Ferdinand the Catholic turns out to be Jewish on his mother's side.[41]

In two other well-known texts of the sixteenth century, there are mentions of families with Jewish antecedents. One is the *Libro verde de Aragón*,[42] and the other *El tizón de la nobleza de España*, by Cardinal Francisco Mendoza y Bobadilla, Archbishop of Burgos,[43] in which the Cardinal demonstrates that not only his relatives, the Counts of Chinchón (accused of impure blood), had Jewish ancestors, but that almost all the aristocracy of that epoch also had them. If Spanish life had unfolded in a calm and harmonious rhythm, the mixture of Christians and Jews would not have given rise to any kind of conflict. The Jews had acquired almost as much distinction as the Christian, in spite of all the prohibitions, and the kings themselves gave to some of their Jews the title of *don*, at that time a sign of high position in the hierarchy of the nobility. For instance, in 1416 Ferdinand I of Aragon knighted the convert Gil Ruiz Naiari.[44] The mixture of blood and the interplay of circumstances already described affected the inward forms of life, and the Jew of quality felt himself noble, fighting at times in the royal army against the Moor, and building temples like the synagogue of the *Tránsito* in Toledo, on whose walls are emblazoned the arms of Castile and Leon. The greatest advantage that Rabbi Arragel assigned the Castilian Jews was that of "lineage," of having nobler blood than the non-Spanish Jews.[45] The Bishop of Burgos, Don Pablo de Santa María (who before his conversion was

---

[41] This is not a dubious inference but a known fact, as is proved by the following anecdote told by Luis de Pinedo, "Libro de Chistes" (*Sales españolas*, collected by A. Paz y Melia [Madrid, 1890], I, 279): "Sancho de Rojas [a first cousin of Ferdinand the Catholic] said to the Catholic King [while he was having a costume cut out for him]: 'I beg Your Highness that if any of that cloth is left over you will make me a present of it.' The King told him that he would do so gladly. The next day Sancho de Rojas said to the King: 'My Lord, was anything left over?' The King said: 'No, by your life, not even this much.' And he traced an o (such as the Jews customarily wore as a sign on their breasts) on his breast with his hand. The King knew what he was talking about." Another anecdote (p. 268) suggests that Jewish origin was also attributed to the Duke of Alba: "Alonso de la Caballería said to Cardinal Pedro Gonçalez de Mendoça, who had asked him what he thought of Don Enrique Enríquez, who later became an admiral, and Don Fadrique de Toledo, who later became Duke of Alba: 'I think that the farther Jews get from their origins the more vicious they are.'"

[42] Used by J. Amador de los Ríos in Volume III of his *Historia de los judíos* and later published in the *Revista de España*, CV (1885), cvi. There is a more recent edition by I. de las Cajigas.

[43] The rarity of this work has forced me to rely on a summary in the *Enciclopedia Universal Ilustrada* (Espasa), s.v. "Nobleza." See the *Revue Hispanique*, VII (1900), 246.

[44] Francisca Vendrell, "Concesión de nobleza a un converso," in *Sefarad*, VIII (1948), 397–401.

[45] *Biblia* (Duke of Alba ed.), p. 3.

Rabbi Solomon Halevi), composed a discourse on the *Origin and Nobility of His Lineage*.[46] The feeling of *hidalguía* and noble distinction was common to Christians and Jews in the fifteenth century, and accompanied the latter into their exile. Max Gruenbaum says: "Anyone who attends the divine office in the splendid Portuguese synagogue of Amsterdam will notice the difference between the German and the Spanish Jews. The solemn and tranquil dignity of the worship distinguishes it from that of the German-Dutch synagogue. . . . The same Spanish *grandeza* is found in the Hispano-Jewish books printed in Amsterdam."[47] This feeling of superiority persists still in the Jews of the Spanish Diaspora, an inexplicable phenomenon if we do not refer to their horizon prior to 1492—the belief in the seigniory of the person, which lay at the very heart of the caste system that in one way or another conferred grandeur on ancient Castile. Through that inner form of life, the Sephardim are vitally linked with their adversaries and persecutors of almost five hundred years ago, as I explain in chapter xiii.

But now I want to consider the reverse influence, the effect the converted Jews had on the Christians. Without taking the Jews into account, it is impossible to understand the birth of learned prose in the thirteenth century.[48] Likewise the literature of the fourteenth and fifteenth centuries is indebted to the Jewish people for the works, to mention only the most important of many, of Don Santob, Don Alonso de Cartagena, Juan de Lucena, Mosén Diego de Valera, Diego de San Pedro, Alonso de Palencia, Rodrigo de Cota, Hernando del Pulgar, and Fernando de Rojas. Later, Luis Vives, Juan and Alfonso de Valdéz, Francisco de Vitoria, Fray Luis de León, Mateo Alemán, Jorge de Montemayor, St. Theresa, and the anonymous author of *Lazarillo de Tormes* were to show evident traces of their Jewish descent.[49] But rather than dwell on such well-known matters, I should like to call attention to certain aspects of the Hispanic vital disposition that emerge with extraordinary vividness at the end of the fifteenth century. Among the medieval Christians of Spain, we do not find the preoccupation with what was later to be called "purity of blood." If it had existed, the strong racial mixture maliciously denounced in *El tizón de la nobleza* ("The Blight of the Nobility")[50]

---

[46] J. Amador de los Ríos mentions this work as unpublished in his *Estudios sobre los judíos de España* (1848; Buenos Aires ed., 1942, p. 333). I know of no other reference to this manuscript of the Biblioteca Nacional in Madrid.

[47] *Jüdisch-Spanische Chrestomathie* (1896), p. 4.

[48] See *The Structure of Spanish History*, p. 484.

[49] The list is far from complete. See now F. Márquez Villanueva, *Investigaciones sobre Juan Alvarez Gato* (Madrid, 1960).

[50] Among the prohibitions of the Decree of 1412, promulgated during John II's minority, is this: No Christian woman "may venture within the district where the said Jews and Moors live, neither at night nor in the daytime" (Baer, II, 268).

would not have been possible, nor would the Jews have occupied the eminent positions in which we have found them even at the moment of their expulsion.

The people who really felt the scruple of purity of blood were the Spanish Jews, as is proved by the previously cited Biblical texts, the commentary of Rabbi Arragel, and the statements of, among others, the converts Juan de Lucena and Hernando del Pulgar. Thanks to the translations of A. A. Neuman, we know the legal opinions (*responsa*) of the rabbinical courts, and these reveal unsuspected things. In these writings there is a punctilious concern for family purity and what one's neighbors will say about one, a concern studied in my book *De la edad conflictiva*. For the reasons set forth there and those already mentioned in this study, it is understandable that the Christian caste was not troubled by the problem of lineage and of purity of blood when Christians and Jews lived clearly apart from each other. If on occasions a Christian married into a Jewish family, no one was scandalized. In view of the social standards prevailing before the fifteenth century, it is unlikely that there might come to light a Christian document of *ca.* 1300 conceived in the terms of the following Jewish *responsum*, published by A. A. Neuman:

I certify over my signature to all whom this document may reach that witnesses appeared before my teacher, Rabbi Isaac, son of R. Eliakim, who was presiding at the court session, and that he received proper and legal testimony from aged and venerable men of the brothers David and Azriel, to the effect that they were of pure descent, without any family taint, and that they could intermarry with the most honored families in Israel; for there had been no admixture of impure blood in the paternal or maternal antecedents and their collateral relatives. Jacob Issachar, son of R. Shalom.[51]

This certificate of purity was evoked because someone had said that one of the forebears of the young aristocrats in question had been a slave. Not content with the finding of the local court, the plaintiff went to other eminent rabbis, and all the degrees were finally carried to the highest authority, the celebrated Shelomo ben Adret, of Barcelona, who wrote the following statement:

When your letter reached me and I opened it, I stood terrified. The author of this wicked rumor, whatever his motive, has sinned grievously and deserved severer punishment than one who slaughtered his victim in cold blood. For a murderer slays but two or three souls, but this man has defamed thirty or forty souls, and the voice of the blood of entire families cries from the earth, groaning aloud. The defamer should be excommunicated. While the sages of the Talmud stated long ago, "He who calls his neighbor slave shall be considered excommunicate," it is not sufficient to leave the culprit under the general reproach of the ancient

---

[51] A. A. Neuman, *The Jews in Spain*, II, 5. The document is one of the *responsa* of Shelomo ben Abraham ben Adret, who lived in the late thirteenth and early fourteenth centuries.

ban, but he should now be excommunicated by a living court, and I shall confirm their act and affix my signature to such a document.[52]

We have before us, then, the earliest text of a proof of purity of blood in Spain, with witnesses examined in different places, a text without parallel among the Christians of that time. In the sixteenth and seventeenth centuries, purity of blood would become a basic thought pattern of noble and ecclesiastical society as a result of the preoccupations with which the converts had, as it were, injected it. For just as the *summum jus* gives rise to a *summa injuria*, likewise the frantic opposition to the Jews was impregnated, through dramatic mimicry, with the habits of its adversary.[53]

A Jewess in Coca (Segovia) carried on amorous relations with a Christian sometime around 1319. Concerning this unnatural sin we have a decision from Rabbi Asher of Toledo, very important for the social background it reveals.[54] Yehuda ben Wakar, physician to Prince Juan Manuel, went to Coca with his lord in 1319, and there found out how a Jewish widow happened to be pregnant as a result of a love affair with a Christian, to whom, moreover, she had ceded a large part of her wealth. The Christians of Coca submitted the case to Prince Juan Manuel, who adjudged the Jewish court competent. The Jewish woman gave birth to twins. One died, and the other was taken by the Christians to be baptized. Yehuda then asked Rabbi Asher, "What should be done so that the law of our Torah [in this connection, cf. the biblical texts quoted above, p. 69] should not appear to be trampled upon in the eyes of the people? . . . All the towns in the neighborhood of Coca are talking about it, and conversations about this lost woman are going on everywhere, so that our religion has become something to be scorned. . . . I suggest that, the case being so notorious, her nose be cut off so as to disfigure the face with which she pleased her lover."[55]

Let us notice how Yehuda is more disturbed by the divulgence of the scandal than by the wrong done by the pretty Jewess whose face he wanted to make hideous. The law in the *Partidas* (see n. 54, above) put a relatively moderate penalty upon illicit relations between Christian women and non-Christian men, reserving severe punishment only for those who offended repeatedly. The law of the Jewish caste, on the other hand, emphasized the effect of transgressions of the law on

---

[52] *Ibid.*, II, 7.

[53] For other calumnies substantiated in the rabbinical courts, see *ibid.*, II, 8.

[54] The *Partidas* (VII, 24, 9; 25, 10) condemn Christian women who sleep with Moors or Jews. For the first offense they must give up half their property to their parents; for the second, they lose everything in the same way; and if there is a subsequent recurrence, they are condemned to death. If it was a case of a married woman, the husband could do as he wished in the matter—kill her or forgive her.

[55] Baer, II, 138, gives a German version of the original Hebrew.

public opinion, and identified the reputation or honor of the individual with that of the community. We do not find anything like this in the Castile of the Middle Ages, but we do among the Spaniards of the sixteenth century, who confused the honorable repute of the whole community with that of the individual, and considered it a collective disgrace for a single Spaniard to fall into heresy.[56] Just as peculiar is the fact that the Holy Office should concern itself with punishing lapses from morality such as concubinage even as it punished attacks against religion. In this the similarity to the Jewish tribunals is even closer.[57] Law, religion, morality, and social cohesion came then to be one and the same thing.[58]

Thus we begin to realize that the peculiar identification established in Spain between Catholicism and the state in the sixteenth century is inseparable from the Christian-Islamic-Judaic context, within which it was no longer possible to recognize anything that was pure and abstract Christianity, Islamism, or Judaism. The new social situation brought no change in the interplay of possibilities and impossibilities which composes the inner disposition of Hispanic history, a history made of belief and the self's awareness of how it, and not the world around it, is existing. The Inquisition and the concern over purity of blood realized to the maximum extent the possibilities and authentic inclinations of the Spaniards. Their tendencies and preferences, as they entered the sixteenth century, rested upon foundations eight hundred years deep. During that time the Peninsula had been invaded by African Almorávides and Almohades (in the eleventh and twelfth centuries), anxious to reestablish in its former vigor the Islamic faith that had become lax under the kings of the *taifas*. The Christians of the north stubbornly resisted the penetration of foreign heresies (the Albigensians, for example), at the same time that they stifled in their own minds any thought dangerous to the stability of their own belief. And it is no accident that the decisive book in bringing back those who had strayed from the faith of Moses was a work of Maimonides, a Jew of Cordova. Thus, those who have absorbed the meaning of my views about the concrete reality of *each* history will understand that the Inquisition and a zealous concern for purity of blood do not

---

[56] See Marcel Bataillon, "Honneur et Inquisition," in the *Bulletin Hispanique*, XXVII (1925), 5–17. By spreading his heresies in foreign lands, Michael Servetus was dishonoring Spain. His own family tried to lure him back to his country so they might hand him over to the Inquisition.

[57] Neuman, *op. cit.*, II, 278.

[58] The examples cited here should not be considered as isolated instances of the vindication of family honor; on the contrary, they must be included in the total picture of caste preoccupations, which we have already seen evidenced in the books of Ezra and Nehemiah, and which are still apparent in Sephardic literature (see p. 68). I do not believe that in these examples a distinction should be made between problems of honor and of lineage, as is affirmed by Sicroff (*op. cit.*, p. 88).

imply any change in the structural functioning of Hispanic history, even though new contents are introduced into it.

No kind of Machiavellian reasoning presided over the course undertaken by the Spanish kings and peoples from the fifteenth century on; there was no genuine planned effort to avoid internal disturbances and preserve unity in order to wage foreign war with undivided attention. These arguments were adduced a posteriori. To see their inadequacy, one has only to recall that the Moriscos, politically more dangerous and less involved than the Jews in the public administration, were not exiled en masse until 1609. Philip II did not carry out this move even after the bloody struggles in Alpujarra. The state-church (or theocratic state), a dual concept that actually stands for an organic unity, was a creation that came out of the spirit of those people who came to find themselves in an advantageous position for releasing impulses that they had been carrying within themselves for a long time. It was an almost revolutionary conquest achieved by resentful masses anxious to forget what they were. The molds of what had once been Jewish life were filled with anti-Jewish contents and purposes, with a fury directly proportional to their desire to get away from their origins. Centuries of tradition, Islamic as well as Judaic, had affected the spirit of the Christian caste, which now guided the destiny of a whole empire. The establishment of the Inquisition is all of a piece with the Messianism[59] that flourished in wild state in the fifteenth and sixteenth centuries, together with the mysticosensual transports of the Illuminati, whose Islamic relationships Asín has established beyond any doubt.[60]

It is therefore not a paradox but a fundamental reality that Spanish society grew more and more fanatic in its Christianity as more and more Jews disappeared or were Christianized. Sixteenth-century Spanish Catholicism, which was a totalitarian and state religion, does not resemble the Catholicism of the Middle Ages, or the Catholicism of other European countries, or even that of papal Rome, which did not scruple to grant asylum to many of the Jews expelled from Spain. Let us also keep clearly in mind the fact that Ferdinand the Catholic, in opposition to the preachments of the Dominicans, was still pro-

---

[59] See *Aspectos del vivir hispánico*, pp. 21 ff., for the Messianism of that period. There was a general belief in the superhuman mission of the Catholic Sovereigns and Cardinal Cisneros; the latter in turn protected the nun Juana de la Cruz, a prophetess who expected to bring forth a new savior (M. Bataillon, *Erasme et l'Espagne*, p. 74). A Franciscan friar believed that he was called to beget a new prophet who would save the world, and he wrote Mother Juana de la Cruz, a pure virgin, to this effect. A Franciscan, Fray Melchor, a descendant of converted Jews, started conventicles of Illuminati and found disciples among the converts (*ibid.*, pp. 65–73). In 1520 a certain Jew named Juan de Bilbao passed himself off as Prince John and the redeemer of mankind (*Aspectos del vivir hispánico*, p. 51).

[60] See *Al-Andalus*, 1945 to 1948.

tecting the Jews of Zamora in 1491, still entrusting them with the administration of the Holy Brotherhood, and still using them as ambassadors. The end of the fifteenth century was marked by an intense upheaval that made impossible what had formerly been quite usual. The infiltration of the converts into Christian society gave rise to phenomena that have found a parallel in the history of our own day, when many extremists of the "right" or of the "left" have changed their political allegiance overnight and the persecuted have suddenly turned into the hangmen.

Up to the fifteenth century, Christians had mixed with Jews without considering the crossing of blood an abomination. Thus it was possible even for the Christians of royal descent to have love affairs with Jewish women, and for the mother of Ferdinand the Catholic to have Jewish blood in her veins. The normality of this situation is indicated by the silence over such mixtures before the fifteenth century, and the outcry they provoked after that time. Naturally a number of the converts—*not all of them, of course*—behaved in a perverse fashion, and some of these turned out to be the worst enemies of the Jews and of the converts themselves, who were found everywhere, sometimes in high positions.[61] Concerning the celebrated theologian and Dominican Juan de Torquemada, Cardinal of St. Sixtus, we have the word of Hernando del Pulgar that "his grandparents were of the lineage of Jews converted to our holy Catholic faith,"[62] so that the first inquisitor, Fray Tomás de Torquemada (a relative of the Cardinal) also turns out to be a New Christian. Hernando del Pulgar, a strange and subtle spirit, was another Jewish convert, although the histories of literature do not put him down for such.[63] He wrote an ironic epistle to Don Pedro González de Mendoza, the Great Cardinal of Spain, after the families of Guipuzcoa had been forbidden to marry converts and the converts had been forbidden to go and live in Guipuzcoa:

Your Lordship no doubt knows the new statute made in Guipuzcoa, in which it was ordained that *we should not go* there to marry or to dwell. . . . Isn't it ridiculous that all, or many of them, send their sons here to serve *us*, and many of them as running footmen, and at the same time, they do not wish to be relatives by marriage of those they wish to serve.

---

[61] Strictly speaking, from the second generation on down, the converts were not Jews, but in a sense they still belonged to that caste because of their own continuing awareness that they were not Old Christian.

[62] *Claros varones*, in the series *Clásicos Castellanos*, p. 119. An historian of the Dominican Order, Fray Hernando del Castillo, denied Pulgar's veracity in 1612 (*Historia de Santo Domingo y de su orden*, p. 572); but Pulgar knew his illustrious contemporaries for what they were, while Fray Hernando was only trying to add luster to his order and remove the stain of "infamy" which had fallen upon the famous cardinal.

[63] See the introduction by Juan de Mata Carriazo to his edition of Hernando del Pulgar's *Crónica de los Reyes Católicos* (Madrid, 1943).

... These people [the Jews] are now paying for the prohibition that Moses made to his people, that they should not marry gentiles.[64]

Pulgar, secretary to the Catholic Queen, historian of the acts of the king and queen, and at the same time fond of solitude, lived the drama of the social change in Spain in all its amplitude. With an accurate eye he was able to perceive the meaning of the events taking place around him, and we must now try, insofar as possible, to see things as he saw them. With a free spirit he told the cardinal, a great aristocrat far removed from any sort of plebeian suspicion, that the exclusiveness of his contemporaries, their concern over purity of blood, was a reply to that other hermeticism of Pulgar's own ancestors. The historical reality becomes intelligible to us only when seen to be possessed of both extremes: the exclusiveness of Catholic Spain was a reply to the hermeticism of the Jewish communities.[65]

The Interweaving of the Castes

The two subject castes were joined to the politically superior caste by means of what one might call a perverted scale of values. That is, deeds and accomplishments were seen as valuable while those who performed them were held in low esteem. Artisans, businessmen, technologists, scholars, and the like produced all manner of good things, but these products were tainted from birth by the fact that their producers came from castes deemed inferior; and no matter how good the products were, the producers *were not converted into a legitimate social class.* The production of wealth did not become an index of value for the Christian caste, which both needed and scorned those who built up fortunes. If things had been otherwise, the hermetic caste of the Christians would have been broken and the infidel castes would have infiltrated it, thus endangering its existence as the ruling caste. Social functions had to be differentiated, not according to their objective value, but according to the castes that carried them out. The tailor (*alfayate*), the barber (*alfajeme*), the muleteer (*arriero*), the mason (*albañil*), the architect (*alarife*), the inspector of weights and measures (*almotacén*), and the shoemaker (*zapatero*) were Moors. The tax gatherer (*almojarife*), the physician, the pharmacist, the veterinary (*albéitar*), the tradesman, the astrologer, the interpreter (*truchimán*), and other such were Jews. The Christian played a more circumscribed role in such activities. His goal was to be a nobleman or a priest, callings that, once attained or taken up, were regarded as inherent to the person, beyond the power of re-

---

[64] *Letras,* in *Clásicos Castellanos,* pp. 149–150; italics mine.

[65] This does not mean that the inquisitorial reaction was Jewish, even though we cannot explain it without keeping in mind how the New Christians acted against the Jews.

nunciation or cancellation. Victimized by nobles, ecclesiastics, and Jews, the shapeless mass of the Christian commonalty was left outside this framework in a state of perpetual restlessness produced by the longing of its constituents to move up to the nobility through military enterprise or the priesthood and thus to become members of the ruling caste of lords. (Let us think, in this connection, of what Florence would have been if bankers and artisans had been scorned there.)

Thus a society was gradually being constructed in which, before the sixteenth century, certain types of occupations were linked, generally speaking, to religious faith. But the Moors and Jews, too, finally came to give the impression of being as "Spanish" as those who, by their imperious actions, aspired to occupy *the highest position in events,*" as Alonso de Palencia wrote. After all, the *Libros del saber de astronomía* ("Books of Astronomical Knowledge") compiled during the reign of Alfonso the Learned—based on Arabic science and written in Castilian and not Latin, because the translators were Jews—were Spanish. And on a lower plane, must not the Moorish or Jewish *alfayate* (tailor) have seemed more Spanish than the French *sastres* (tailors) and *chipeleros* (hat makers)? But in any event it is certain that for the Castilians, the axis around whom the Spain of the future would revolve, there were always certain tasks that were viewed and esteemed as of primary importance (those characteristic of the ruling classes or of those who aspired to rise to that high estate) and others of only secondary importance, which were carried on by Moors and Jews or, in certain instances, by Frenchmen and Genoese. From the thirteenth century on, the Jewish caste put forth every effort to occupy outstanding positions (so it is that Andrés Bernáldez, chronicler of the Catholic Sovereigns, spoke of the "loftiness" of the Jew), and the Christian caste would not suffer the Jews to continue in this fashion. This conflict created the drama that I set forth in detail in the chapter devoted to the Spanish Jews.

As the Cordovan Juan Ginés de Sepúlveda wrote in the sixteenth century:

In our Cordova no notice is taken of commerce, and it is considered the greatest distinction to excel at arms. And so, after the care of one's family, the greatest concern is with agriculture, an occupation that is honorable and close to nature, and which usually strengthens the body and the spirit and prepares them for travail and for war: to such an extent that the ancients preferred labor in the fields to commerce, and the Romans took many consuls and dictators from the plow. . . . Let us not worry, then, if for the moment Cordova has citizens whose strength exceeds their opulence.

(*De appetenda gloria* [Madrid ed., 1780], IV, 206)

We can now understand the broad scope of the saying "Either prince or peasant" (*O corte o cortijo*), or of this one: "Church or sea or royal house" (*Iglesia, o mar, o casa real*). People aspired to be direct administrators of the faith, or to undertake adventures that would lead to lordship, or to serve the king in some way, comfortable in the realization that they were *castizo* through their faith and nobility.

The awareness of being a nobleman by birth was especially a Castilian trait. As concerns this, Castile embraced the ancient kingdoms of Castile, Leon, and Andalusia, not excluding the Basques, always preferred by the Crown for positions of strict responsibility. The Count-Duke of Olivares, the *de facto* king of Spain more than his lord, King Philip IV, between 1621 and 1643, bears this idea out. In his instructions concerning government, written in 1625 to quicken the mind of the frivolous and passive monarch, he says: "It seems to me much to the advantage of Your Majesty that those vassals [i.e., the Portuguese] should live in the hope that Your Majesty . . . should hold your court in Lisbon for a certain continuous period of time. . . . I also deem it Your Majesty's obligation to employ persons of that kingdom in the services of this one, and particularly in embassies and viceroyalties, presidencies of the royal councils, and in some of the posts in the royal household. And I also think it a good thing to do this with the *Aragonese*, the Flemish, and the Italians . . . *who are held to be foreigners*." The Portuguese, he adds, resemble the latter-named peoples more than they do the Castilians. The Castilians comprise the best of the Spanish infantry, in which "one sees, along with their loyalty to their kings (greater than that of any other vassals), *the brio and liberty with which the sorriest commoner of Castile treats any lord or noble*, even though he be greatly unequal in power, showing in the wisdom of his impulse how much human hearts exceed human forces."[66]

Olivares was thinking about how he could use the royal prestige to bring the *disjecta membra* of the Spanish dominions in Europe into a unified relationship. The Aragonese, as well as the Catalonians and Valencians, seemed to be foreigners as late as 1625.[67] The nucleus of Spain was still Castile, as it had been since the tenth century, precisely because its men had been what Olivares said they were. The humblest peasant, *pure of blood precisely because he was a peasant*, sensed that he was a member of the seignorial caste. This notion seems to me to fit the reality better than the notion of Castilian democracy, in which democracy can have no strict meaning. The way of life in Castile was

---

[66] Page 426 of the text as published by G. Marañón, *El conde-duque de Olivares* (1936).

[67] As late as 1564 Don Martín Pérez de Ayala was reluctant to accept the archbishopric of Valencia because he disliked the idea of "living with new people *not entirely of our own nation*" (*Vida de don Martín de Ayala*, in *Nueva Biblioteca de Autores Españoles*, V, 236).

never democratic; perhaps it was, to some extent, in Aragon. The Castilians were governed seignorially by the best or more fortunate members of the lordly caste, all of whose members aspired to the same privilege. This was the basis of its grandeur and of its final wretchedness. There was never any democracy in Castile in the Greek or the Franco-English sense of the word. The inverse case, although similar in its vital scheme, was presented by the Hispanic Jews, who were likewise prisoner-defenders of their own religious belief. The reason for their existence was also their religion, just as it was for the Hispano-Muslims. Nobility, technology, and labor: these three kinds of life existed in Spain, in the highest form, and "theoretically" there was no reason why a "normal" nation should not have been the result. But unfortunately the Jews became obsessed with the idea of becoming noblemen, and the Christians were seduced by the defensive, Inquisitorial tendency and the notion of purity of blood, going so far as to invent a new historical category, the "Old Christian."

The Christian had grown accustomed to having no need for a knowledge of nature and the handling of things, because this was not required in the huge task of conquering his land and organizing his state. The rest was left in the hands of the Apostle Santiago, the French monks and immigrants,[68] the Genoese shipbuilders, the Moorish builders of houses and fortresses, and the Jews, who knew trades, who could heal ailments, who knew how to collect the money to buy the things needed by the kings, the lords, the clerics, and the "worthy men" of the cities. The urgency of getting money explains why the Jew has always appeared in front of the footlights of history. The later importance of the precious metals of America was not the result of any economic doctrine: it was simply the sixteenth-century aspect of the need to acquire by indirect means the things that could not be created, ranging from needles to costly fabrics (as Michael Servetus had pointed out as early as 1535).

In this way history is invested with meaning and explains itself. For the Hispano-Christian, peace had never been productive. The Christian in his own home felt he had nothing to do, and so stirred up trouble in the kingdom. Once Granada was conquered, the great humanist Juan Ginés de Sepúlveda sensed a danger in the lack of an adequate enterprise in which the Spaniards might occupy themselves:

According to the philosophers, nature, to enliven men's power, has endowed them with a certain inner fire which, if it is not poked and set to working, not only gives no light, but at times languishes and goes out.

---

[68] It is curious that the Hispano-Christian had no traditional word of his own for "tailor." *Sastre*, the word he uses, is a Gallicism from the south of France (see A. Steiger, *Aufmarschstrassen des morgenländischen Sprachgutes* [Berne, 1950], p. 17). The other word, *alfayate*, is Arabic. The native Spanish *ropero* has the somewhat different meaning of "dealer in clothing."

Therefore I sometimes wonder whether it would not have been better for us if the Moorish kingdom had not been preserved in Granada instead of disappearing completely. For if it is indeed certain that we have extended the kingdom, we have also thrown the enemy back beyond the sea, deprived the Spaniards of the opportunity to practice their valor, and destroyed the magnificent motive for their triumphs. Wherefore I fear a little lest, with so much idleness and security, the valor of many men grow weak.[69]

Apparently the wars of Charles V were not enough for the humanists Sepúlveda and Morales. This idea, strange at first glance, has not been an isolated occurrence, for I find it again in Fray Alonso de Cabrera, preacher to Philip II: "Our grandfathers, my lords, lamented the winning of Granada from the Moors, because on that day the horses fell lame and the cuirasses began to rust, and the shields to rot. And the most distinguished cavalry of Andalusia was finished, and it was the end of youth and all its well-known and estimable gallantries."[70]

The Spaniards had the liveliest kind of awareness that their existence was a process of self-creation and self-destruction. Ferdinand the Catholic, who knew his people well, offered them the bellicose, seignorial mission they longed for, the only thing they were really capable of. Then came the great enterprises in America and Europe, but the nation did not feel invigorated and satisfied even with them, as we are told by Sepúlveda, Las Casas, Antonio de Guevara, Father Cabrera, Quevedo, and Cervantes, all well-qualified witnesses. Gracián was to have the impression that he was living in an empty world, the same impression we get from the ascetics, the authors of the picaresque autobiographies, and Calderón's theater.

The idea of castes whose only world is that of their own self-consciousness may explain this singular history. The guiding caste thought it could live alone, welded to its belief and its sense of superiority, yet at the same time it noticed the irremediable vacuum in which it was submerged when it tried to come out of incarceration within the self.

Prior to the sixteenth century, no European country had produced such a profusion of heroes and chieftains who challenged the greatest obstacles nature could present, and always won—Vasco da Gama, Albuquerque, Cortés, Pizarro, Balboa, Magellan, Cabeza da Vaca, and a hundred others. Along with many friars fed by an equally titanic

---

[69] From the dialogue called *Gonsalus seu de appetenda gloria*, XXVI. In the preface to the *Razonamiento sobre la navegación del Guadalquivir* by Hernán Pérez de Oliva, Ambrosio de Morales writes: "At that time [about 1520] Cordova was half deserted, since the end of the conquest of Granada left her without the steady pursuit of warfare, in which her natives engaged with great honor."

[70] "De las consideraciones sobre todos los Evangelios de la Cuaresma" (1601), in *Nueva Biblioteca de Autores Españoles*, III, 60. This text provides an excellent perspective in which to situate the genesis of the *Quixote*.

energy and illuminated by their religious belief, they ceaselessly consumed their selves as in a sacrificial holocaust to that strange deity,
personal integralism, the whole living person. In opposition to the
principle inherited from Greece that reality "is what it is," the Spaniard sustained the principle that reality was what he felt, believed,
and imagined. "Having set fear aside"—a leitmotiv already in the fifteenth century—he installed himself in Italy, he rode victoriously over
the heart of Europe and over the summits of the Andes.[71]

As he felt no fear, so he felt no surprise, for everything could be
matched with fantasies already lived. Hernán Cortés' triumphal entry
into Mexico seemed to his men like an episode from *Amadis*, or like
an adventure with enchantment. Reality was a simple game between
friendly and hostile wizards.[72]

Will, courage, and imagination took the place of reflection and
created a form of life which it would be inept to characterize as primitive, backward, or prescientific, for this form of life developed according to an ascending scale of values. So-called primitive man is
not aware of the risk he runs by being primitive, but the Spaniard
has always realized the high price he has to pay for being Spanish.
To be so in the full and *castizo* measure, he renounced as early as the
sixteenth century all the learning offered him by the Spanish caste
of Hebrew origin, as I have made clear in *De la edad conflictiva*.

It has been customary to base judgments of Spanish life on the
principle that the most perfected forms of so-called Western civilization were the supreme goals toward which all the peoples of the
earth should have directed their course. Those human groups that do
not fall entirely within the area of the civilization that was begun in
Greece, given political shape by Rome, and brought to its apogee by
the dazzling discoveries of physical science, are regarded as primitive,
backward, childish, or misguided. Those who believe in the efficacy
of this form of life think that the people who are "backward" with
respect to this form are living in a limbo where they await the light

---

[71] That army was still decisive in the affairs of Europe in 1634. The Spaniards
fighting in the bloodiest battle of the Thirty Years' War, the battle of Nord-
lingen, are described thus by a contemporary German: "Then, marching calmly
and solidly massed, several Spanish regiments advanced. They were almost exclusively well-tested veterans—without a doubt, the most reliable and the
strongest infantry that I have fought against in all my life." The German-
Swedish army was routed (see Pedro de Marrades, *Notas para el estudio de la
cuestión de la Valtelina* [1943], p. 174).

[72] Piero de' Medici wrote to his son Lorenzo in 1466: "I urge you to cultivate thought and not melancholy, . . . *thoughts are useful, provided that they
are good ones*" ("Te conforto a pigliarne pensiero e non maninconia, . . . *I
pensieri sono utili, facendoli buoni*"; *apud* Edoardo Bizzarri, *Il magnifico
Lorenzo*, p. 51). The contrast with the Spanish attitude is striking; but if the
Spaniards had thought like the Florentines, they would not have created an
empire. Such is the drama of life: one thing is accomplished only by the sacrifice
of another possibility.

of a new revelation, just as the pagans, in medieval thought, had spent their lives marking time as they waited for the truth of Christ to reach them. In the eighteenth century the Christian idea was replaced by faith in progress. Those not versed in mathematics, in the French language, in the rational interpretation of the world, and in the graces of the Parisian salons were also regarded as people still waiting to be saved. Yes, the Spain of Charles V also had an absolute aspiration: to bring the whole planet into the fold of her theocratic-aristocratic faith; and thus motivated, she displayed an arrogance not exceeded by the British in the nineteenth century, or by the Americans in the twentieth.

Now such "democentric" (not egocentric) attitudes are evidence that the people who feel them and formulate them have a strong sense of their own value. But at the same time such views put a serious obstacle in the way of our efforts to make perceptible the values of a history that is strange in its course, values that reveal themselves ever more clearly as we penetrate deeper and deeper into the strange character of this history. The Spaniards' way of living "with their whole being" (see p. 39) made splendid results possible, for the total life of the self proved to be expressible in actions of singular grandeur or in artistic works of a new stamp.

Nevertheless, it cannot be denied that the Spaniards of the Christian caste suffered the consequences of their peculiar social structure more than did other western European peoples. Through their lack of interest in the production of material things or the achievements of intellectual culture, the "caste" did not become a social "class," did not break out of its silent cocoon, and there were no cultural increments (thought, technology) motivated from within Spanish life. The greater part of men's energies had to be consumed in maintaining themselves as the Christian caste in opposition to the other two castes, that is to say, in fighting and ruling over the conquered and subjugated peoples. Such a vital structure was subconsciously built within the minds of the people who did not identify themselves clearly as "Spanish" until the thirteenth century. Other western European peoples had, since Charlemagne, enjoyed a broad range of mental and volitional movements impossible for the Hispano-Christian confronted by the Moor. Other Europeans fought a great deal also, but always against enemies with whom they shared a common human base of values and assumptions, not against peoples of another caste who interpreted both heaven and earth in a wholly different manner. The very fact that Charlemagne's empire could exist, could extend so far, makes clear the difference. Charlemagne called to his court Alcuin, a cleric of the cathedral at York and a disciple of the Venerable Bede's, to found the famous school of humanities; and thus the embers of Romano-Christian cultural unity were kept burning. *If the Hispano-Christians had tried to do the same thing, they would never have progressed beyond the Mozarabic phase of Christian culture, and in the end the Islamic wave would have submerged them.*

The necessity of fighting to keep alive the geographical and spiritual identity of the self prevented the outburst of struggles of other kinds which in the rest of Europe gave rise to religious, philosophical, scientific, or economic mutations. There people were secure with respect to the firmness of their personal foundations (the Romano-Christian tradition) and could construct new horizons that did not shake that base of self-awareness. As a result in eleventh-century France, in opposition to philosophic realism, there could arise the nominalist philosophy that is the remote ancestor of modern science, and after that, all the other developments, including the distinction made by William of Ockham in the fourteenth century between theological truths and the rational truths of philosophy. And after that, the whole complex of happenings in philosophy, science, industry, and politics—in other words, in the world of the nonexpressive realities of life—which we call Occidental culture. The Spaniards could have contributed to that type of culture—which I call depersonalized—but their contributions would have been Hispano-Judaic.

Summation

Thus the basic meaning and the historical connections of the words "caste" and "castizo" have been established, though today *castizo* has a vague meaning unrelated to its origin. Unamuno wrote in 1895 (*En torno al casticismo*) that "what is *castizo*, what is genuinely *castizo*, is of old Castilian stock . . . what is Castilian is, in the final analysis, what is *castizo*." The word "caste" penetrated into the Occidental languages because the Portuguese had applied to the social system of India a term that was familiar to them, even though naturally, the castes of Spain could not have been like the Asiatic. From the meaning of "vigorous, healthful, or prolific animal," *castizo* came to designate a human excellence related to lineage (*"castizo* Christian, *castizo* woman"*) or the fine quality of something. In the seventeenth century people said "*castiza* goodness, *castizo* love." Later, "being *castizo*" came to mean "being brave and determined, daring, and generous." Under all these meanings there faintly throbs the old feeling toward the qualities and virtues most prized by the Spaniard who was an Old Christian and descended from ancestors never blemished by "heretical perversity," as the Inquisitors used to say in other times.

"Caste" and "castizo" existed as an inner reality of the consciousness of Christians or Moors or Jews, but the polemical use of such terms had no reason to take root in the spoken language while the three castes lived together or while the memory of such common life remained vivid. What we today call "country, nation, the people as a whole" appeared in the twelfth century as a conglomerate of believers of different faiths, each following his own religious law. The conjoint mention of "Moors and Christians" meant "everybody, anyone." In the *Poem of the Cid* the phrase "while the people shall be of Moors and the Christian folk" ("mientra que sea el pueblo de moros e de la yente christiana") means, according to Menéndez Pidal, "while the world lasts." "Neither Moors nor Christians" ("moros ni christianos") was used in the sense of "no one"; and "among neither Moors nor Christians" ("en moros ni en Christianos") meant "nowhere." After four hundred years of the Moorish presence, a writer of the twelfth century believed that the consuetudinary situation would last as long as his world.

The belief that the Moor was a consubstantial element in the panorama of the Christian of the north was firmly rooted in the popular imagination in the twelfth and thirteenth centuries. As Samuel G. Armistead has recently shown, the monk of Arlanza who composed the *Poem of Fernán González* toward the middle of the thirteenth century was convinced that the Visigothic king Roderic had fought against the Moors just as Count Fernán González would do later. King Roderic exclaims in the poem: "Evil fortune to the Moors who used to hold it [the land of Spain]!" ("¡mal grado a los moros que la [tierra de España] solían tener!"). Therefore the Count had to fight so that those lands might not return to the sovereignty of "their first masters" ("los dueños primeros").[73] The projection onto the remote past of the Peninsula of the circumstances that prevailed in the thirteenth century made one of the authors of the *Crónica General* of Alfonso the Learned compare the situation of the Iberians and Celtiberians in their war against Carthage and Rome with that of the Castilian Christians against Moors and Europeans. The Iberians, he says, chose the Roman side "because they held it was more reasonable to have [friendship] with the Romans, who were from Europe, than with the Carthaginians, who were from Africa."[74] What I had observed on reading the *Crónica General* is thus confirmed by this new interpretation of the *Poem of Fernán González*.

It is now easier to understand how the jongleur of the *Poem of the Cid* might use the phrase "while the people shall be of Moors and the Christian folk" as a synonym of "always." It is, however, striking

---

[73] "La perspectiva histórica del *Poema de Fernán González*," in *Papeles de Son Armadans* (Madrid: Palma de Mallorca, April, 1961).

[74] Ed. Ramón Menéndez Pidal, p. 19*b*: "porque teníen que era más razón de tener [amistad] con los romanos, que eran de parte de Europa, que non con los de Carthago, que eran de Affrica."

that the ternary expression "Christians, Moors, and Jews," so frequent later, does not appear in the *Cid*. The reason must have been,
I imagine, that the Jews lacked an epic dimension, so that mention of
them in an essentially epic work would have been out of place.

But reference to the common life of the three castes was already
usual in the time of the *Poem of the Cid*. When Alfonso VII made his
solemn entry into Toledo in 1139, the *Chronica Adephonsi Impera-
toris* relates that,

when all the populace had heard that the Emperor was coming to Toledo,
all the high officials [*omnes principes*] of the Christians, of the Saracens,
and of the Jews, and all the people of the city went out to meet him far
from it with tambourines, zithers, other instruments and a multitude of
musicians. *Each one of them praised and glorified God in his own tongue*
for having so greatly favored all the deeds of the Emperor. And they also
said: "Blessed be he who comes in the name of the Lord."[75]

From this quotation it may be seen that already in the twelfth century the three "peoples of the Book" concurred in their belief in the
same God and in the same hope for peace and mercy. If we possessed
texts from the tenth and eleventh centuries which were expressive of
collective life, the social configuration depicted by them would be
the same as that treated by texts from the twelfth to the fifteenth centuries, for thus history had evolved and in no other way. In the fourteenth-century *Libro de Buen Amor*, the Archpriest of Hita must
mention all of the three peoples when he wishes to designate the totality of the group to whom Don Carnal's letter was directed:

The letter came addressed *to all of us*:
"Powerful Sir Carnal, by the grace of God,
To all Christians, Moors, and Jews,
Greetings with all kinds of meat."

(1193)

In the mid-fourteenth century *Poem of Alfonso XI*, the King's entrance into Seville is described according to the model of the *Crónica
de Alfonso VII*, written two centuries earlier, even though here the
Christian caste is characterized by its noble and warlike games; the
Moorish, by its joyous demonstrations; and the Jewish, by its attach-

---

[75] Ed. L. Sánchez Belda, p. 122: "Cuando todo el pueblo hubo oído que el
Emperador venía a Toledo, todas las autoridades [*omnes principes*] de los
cristianos, de los sarracenos y de los judíos, y todo el pueblo de la ciudad,
salieron a encontrarle lejos de ella, con adufes, cedras, rotas y multitud de
músicos. *Cada uno de ellos alababa y glorificaba a Dios en su propia lengua*, por
haber favorecido tanto todos los hechos del Emperador. Y tambien decían:
'Bendito sea quien viene en nombre del Señor'" (italics mine). The *Crónica*
was written by a contemporary of the Emperor (p. x); but the text that I
quote does not mean that Alfonso was "tolerant," as the editor believes, but
that the life today called Spanish was structured in that fashion. The Emperor
was included within it.

ment to the Old Testament. The kings of Castile and Portugal were received by the

> Knights throwing their lances
> all with great gaiety;
> and playing on horseback
> taking up shield and spear.

> And the Moorish people
> made great rejoicing
> the Jews with their Torahs
> received these kings well.[76]

Juan Alfonso de Baena composed a poem for King John II of Castile to give him counsel and spur him on to higher endeavors, a type of activity characteristic of converted Jews in the fifteenth century. The poet addresses himself to all kinds of people:

> Then may the lords listen
> and princes and prelates,
> dukes, counts, and governors,
> the masters [of military orders] and priors,
> judges, aldermen
> of cities and of towns;
> let all hear the wonders,
> minstrels, do not marvel,
> listen, then, Castilians,
> great sages of Lully [followers of Raymond Lully]
> and subtle alchemists,
> and the rude villagers,
> *Jews and Moors and Christians,*
> friars, monks, and laymen.[77]

Although the panorama of social life has been complicated by the new attitude of the writer with respect to it, the necessity of mentioning the three castes is still felt when references must be made to the people as a totality and not to special groups of dukes, monks, scholars, or villagers. Baena mentions the Jews first, the Christians last, for reasons either of rhyme or because of his personal preference.

Only six years before the expulsion of the Jews and the conquest of Granada, the social structure of the castes in Castile continued to be the same as in the time of Alfonso VII. A chronicler from Palencia,

---

[76] Ed. Y. T. Cate, pp. 267–268: "cavalleros bofordando, / todos con gran alegrança; / e a la gineta jugando / tomando escudo e lança. / E los moras e las moras / muy grandes fiestas fazían, / los judíos con sus Toras / estos reys bien resçebían."

[77] Ed. J. Piccus, without punctuation or commentary, in *Nueva Revista de Filología Hispánica*, XII (1958), 338: "Pues escuchen los señores / et infantes et perlados, / duques, condes, adelantados, / los maestres e priores, / . . . maravillas, / non se espanten trobadores, / escuchen, pues, castellanos, / grandes sabios remonistas / et sotiles alquimistas, / et los rudos aldeanos, / *judíos, moros, cristianos,* / frayres, monges, omnes legos . . ." (italics mine).

the convert Pedro Fernández del Pulgar, describes with a certain melancholy reticence the entry into his city in 1486 of Bishop Alonso de Cartagena:

He was received with great celebrations, and the Moors and Jews who dwelt in the city rejoiced especially over him, for they were his vassals; the Moors with various dances and shows, and the Jews in processions, singing things about their law; and after them came a rabbi bearing in his hands a scroll of parchment covered with a brocade cloth. And it was said that this was the Torah. And when he came before the Bishop, the Bishop made a reverence as to the law of God, for they said that it was the Holy Scripture of the Old Testament. And he solemnly took it in his hands and then he cast it behind him over his shoulders, to show that it was now a thing of the past. And so that rabbi took it up again. Which ceremony is worthy of being recorded in this memoir because it was the last time that such a thing was done; for a few years after that, they became Christians.[78]

On their estates the great lords, whether ecclesiastical or secular, continued the ancient custom of keeping the people of the three faiths united—or at least so it happened in Old Castile, less agitated against the Jews in the fifteenth century than was Andalusia. This situation was disrupted with the exile of the Jews in 1492. At the end of the fifteenth century, when it is said in the *Celestina* (Act VII) that Pármeno's mother, for reasons connected with her witchcraft, "never failed to attend the burial of Christians or Moors or Jews," the common life of the three castes has, in fact, become a buried theme. The ternary system of the castes is no longer clearly visible in daily life and in literature but has been converted into a latent and anguished uneasiness, into the preoccupation with the purity of caste of the individual and the "cleanness" of his blood. I have dealt with the consequences—at once painful and admirable—of such a social situation in *De la edad conflictiva*.

After the fifteenth century, literary allusions to the social system of the three castes no longer proceed from the Christian side but from the Sephardic Jews. The Sephardic ballad inspired by the expulsion of the Jews from Portugal begins by describing the entry into Lisbon of Isabella, queen of Portugal, daughter of the Catholic Sovereigns:

Now the three laws come out magnificent to greet me:
The Christians with their crosses, the Moors in Moorish garb,
The Jews with guitars, so that the whole city resounded.[79]

---

[78] The text has been cited by Esteban Ortega Gato, *Blasones y mayorazgos de Palencia* (Palencia, 1940), p. 39. See also the introduction, n. 25, by Francisco Márquez Villanueva, to his edition of *La Católica impugnación*, by Friar Hernando de Talavera (Madrid, 1961).

[79] See Ramón Menéndez Pidal, *Poesía juglaresca* (1947), p. 98: "ya me salen a encontrar tres leyes a maravilla: / los cristianos con sus cruces, los moros a la morisca, / los judíos con vihuelas, que la ciudad se estrujía."

So embedded in the Spanish fashion within Hispano-Jewish life was the image of the traditional common life of the three castes that the Christians and Moors of the Moroccan version cited above are transformed into Turks and Greeks in a version from Salonica:

The Turks go to their mosques, and the Greeks go to their churches,
The Jews to the Holy Law, which guards the city for us.[80]

The Torah, as the Hebrews sang, "guards for us" the city of Salonica—a rather ineffective protection for those unfortunate people, for of the 53,000 who lived in 1940, only 1,800 remained in 1948.[81] The sinister game of circumstances was once again repeated.

But even though within the Peninsula, as I have said, the fifteenth century saw the disappearance of any literary reference to the three castes,[82] that way of feeling oneself exist as a Spaniard in a society composed of three castes was kept alive in oral tradition. In the *Vocabulario de refranes* compiled by Gonzalo Correas in the first third of the seventeenth century, we find the following proverb: "Jews during the Passover, Moors at weddings, Christians in lawsuits, spend all their money" (1924, p. 253). The fact that the Jews are mentioned first and the characterization of the preferences of each group according to an economic standard lead to the conjecture that the author of the proverb may have been a Jew. Here the Jew is shown devoting himself to religious festivities, an activity of serious and estimable purpose; the Moor, as is well known (see chapter vii, with reference to the Moriscos), took pleasure in fiestas and noisy rejoicing; the Christian appears as a litigant, concerned with making his rights prevail and affirming his personal views or interests. This characterization is based on types of value judgments, on the movement and direction of life, and not on abstract psychological characteristics; the man who invented the saying preferred the Jew and looked askance at the Christian. Furthermore, it is curious that this saying should have been preserved in the traditional store of proverbs at a time when the Jews had been absent—at least, as open practitioners of Judaism—from Spain for more than a century.

Unamuno said in 1895: "What is truly original is what is most basic, the humanity within us" (*En torno al casticismo*). The expression was too abstract, since the relevant aim would rather be to

---

[80] See S. G. Armistead and J. H. Silverman, "Hispanic Balladry among the Sephardic Jews of the West Coast," *Western Folklore*, XIX (1960), 242 n. 38: "Los turkos en las mexkitas, los gregos van a la klisa, / los ğidiós a la ley santa, la ke la sivdad mos guadra."

[81] See M. Molho, *In Memoriam: Hommage aux victimes juives des nazi en Grèce* (Salonica, 1948); Armistead and Silverman, *op. cit.*, p. 244.

[82] While it is true that Torres Naharro refers to the three castes (see below, p. 221), it must be remembered that he was writing outside Spain and that his personality had been formed in the preceding century.

return to the original sense of "caste" and "castizo"; if this is not done, Spanish history will continue to be a torrent of meaningless words, regardless of the number of facts and the amount of knowledge accumulated. Spaniards will find themselves *in* their history, in their past life, because they can in no way be both themselves *and* their history; they are not the result of constant additions but of the unbreakable fusion between people and the modes and times in which they have expressed themselves. They will find themselves in the awareness of their past, *whether they embrace it or evade it* and aim in other directions. From the end of the fifteenth century, that past did not take into account the risks and necessities of the future; the anguish of the present dominated everything, a present made up of successive points, not a continuous line. The Spaniard, isolated in his caste, aspired to making himself eternal and immutable—doubtless in one prolonged and grandiose transport—but the awareness of the past stopped functioning as "ternary" to become unitary and monolithic. So it was that history was forgotten and the vacuum filled with illusory myths about Goths, Romans, and Celtiberians. The future came to be merely imagined as desirable and not conceived as something to be built.

With better judgment than at other times, Unamuno says: "Sr. [Don Gumersindo de] Azcárate was profoundly right in believing that our culture in the sixteenth century must have been *interrupted*; otherwise we would not have forgotten it." Yet Unamuno believed that the past had not died, because "what is forgotten does not die but descends into the quiet sea of the soul, into its eternal part." In this case the phrase is graceful but inaccurate. What became of the thought of Vives, the humanism of Nebrija, Valdés, and Francisco Sánchez de las Brozas, the science of Pedro Núñez? "Culture" had to be imported in the twentieth century and in risky, always precarious, circumstances. Even the novelistic technique of Cervantes was reborn prodigiously in Galdós by way of the strong influence of Cervantes in other European literature.

The past did remain, on the other hand—in this Don Miguel was correct—like buried embers in certain peoples of Spain, especially in Castile to the north of the Duero; it endured like the sleeping echo of a voice now mute, of a clamor for greatness which was now unconscious or whispered into deaf ears. In *Nazarín*, Galdós speaks of those "Castilian types like the dried beef wrapped in tinder." Unamuno says that the Castilian "is slow in his movements, deliberate and serious in his conversation, and self-possessed as a dethroned king—all this when he is not a *socarrón* ["cunning rascal"], which word is very *castiza* and of very *castizo* character also." But Unamuno, slipping into positivism, believed that all these traits had to do with climate: "A caste of abstemious men, the *product* of a long selection by frosts of the rawest winters and a long series of periods of destitution, accustomed to the inclemency of the sky and to the poverty of life."

For my part I have preferred to subordinate natural circumstances to human ones and to return to the very roots of the feeling of "caste" and of "castizo." I have yielded to the evidence that the disposition of the life that is now Spanish was a fabric woven of three threads, none of which may be cut out. On certain occasions learned historians speak of objectivity, just as do literary critics with "scientific" leanings. They do not wish to discover their inner feelings when they face human phenomena, because such displays seem very shocking to a scholar, especially if he is German or English. On the other hand, they give free rein, sometimes very cynically, to uncontrolled hatred and rancor. As I have shown in the past and will continue to show, anti-Islamic and anti-Jewish prejudices go to comic extremes. But barricades must be set up against mythical historiography. It is necessary to probe the most sensitive recesses of the past—though they are painful to many—not for the pleasure of scholarship but to promote clearness of sight and to temper our spirits in the face of the most uncertain future that has been presented to the West since the fall of the Roman Empire. And among Europeans the Spaniard is perhaps least in contact with the sense of his own past. I am convinced that the fates will not smile in the Spanish heavens until the life that was—and still continues there latent in its consequences—is made manifest, evaluated, and transmuted into forms of activity which, without destroying the past, enable modern life to face the problems besetting the inhabitants of the Peninsula. In view of this, the first duty of the historian is to make the Spaniards turn away from their hallucinations about themselves, to stimulate them to throw off their apathy toward all planned efforts, and to take precautions against that violence which tends to fill the void in the lives of people who view existence as an end in itself. Is all this a chimera? Perhaps. But there have been others that were much less justified and whose consequences were in no small measure ruinous.

IV · THEORETICAL ASSUMPTIONS

Exposition of the Problem

I START FROM THE ASSUMPTION that the conventional psychological characterizations are insufficient: for example, that Spaniards are proud, individualistic, envious, passionate, disinclined to follow their superiors, and so on. As far as possible I should like to set forth the structure of Spanish life in such a way as to be able to relate the details to the whole in which they take on meaning and to present events as they are "inhabited" by the subject-agent of which they are the expression. A dwelling may be and actually is one even if it is universalized; a human fact, besides being old, modern, European, American, Renaissance, and so on, always is the result of the action of a human agent, either individual or collective. Consequently, it is not enough to say that a people is explicable through desirable aims that it pursues—something like "birds of a feather flock together"—if it turns out later that the historian has left in shadows the vital structure of the people who set the values. It usually happens that everything is reduced to a schematic and abstract characterization: for example, there are those who speak negatively of the Spaniards because they see them as determined not to follow certain select minorities (whose reality and possibility is never clearly defined); or people reduce being Spanish to being a "Christian knight," because that ideal type conforms to the emotional preferences of the writer, and so forth.

Neither does it suffice to attribute to economy and geography what is decisive in man's reality, while disregarding and wishing to forget that men have made themselves as they are precisely because they have triumphed over the natural circumstances of their environment.[1] But historical materialism on the one side and intellectualistic abstractions on the other, allied together, aspire to, and sometimes succeed in, reducing all men to electronic puppets well trained to bleat, laugh, and moan unanimously.

---

[1] Dan Stanislawski (*The Individuality of Portugal* [University of Texas, 1959]) explains the special characteristics of Portugal by the nature of its rivers, soil, and mountains.

Past life does not take on a historical dimension by the mere fact of having existed or of being known today; history depends on a special dimension of life, on the elevation of that life above the level of repeated and uninspired routine. The historian must make visible both the rising movement and rhythm of the collective subject of history and that subject's awareness of the process of making itself in, and with, a history. For this purpose it does not matter that there has been more or less agreement on the value of past actions and deeds, nor that it has proved impossible to make these actions universally valid. History rests upon the empirical knowledge of an experience whose most important dimension—namely, its value—is not demonstrable, though it may indeed be grasped intuitively. Judgments with regard to the Spanish action in America have been violently opposed from the sixteenth century up to the present; opinions oscillate between viewing the conquest as an act of cruel barbarism (Las Casas, Diego Rivera) and as "the noblest type of universal, generous, humane crusade that has ever existed" (José Vasconcelos). But the very fact that the topic has been discussed with such passion for four and one-half centuries demonstrates by itself the enormous human volume, the historical dimension, of the Spanish achievement.

That historical or "historifiable" dimension is what interests me now. Like a character both novelistic and dramatic, a people forges that dimension for itself as it faces the circumstances that its own actions have created. Its works continue to exist as a lasting present even though the descendants of the creators may come to exist in vital forms totally unrelated to those of their biological ancestors, and may have lost any collective awareness of resembling them. There are no longer Sumerians, or Greeks like those of Attica and Magna Graecia, or Celtiberians, or Carthaginians.

History is where are realized, in many ways, man's possibilities for achieving great deeds and works that endure and radiate their values afar, that effectively quicken and make fruitful in other men the capacity for reasoning and the longing to break out of the common round of daily insignificance; in other words, works that can affect the mind, the imagination, or the soul. The various modes of historifiable life can be extended to other areas, but not by the suppression of the political barriers that separate and distinguish peoples; rather this is achieved by the generalization of certain values. Historically differentiated peoples resemble trees touching branch tip to branch tip, but whose roots are not twined together deep down in the earth (unless one people is totally absorbed into the life of another). But certain values can be widely diffused among different peoples; one such, for example, is the Jewish belief in the Messiah (whose advent is an accomplished fact for many people); so, too, have the forms of Greek thought become universal. And many other things have spread abroad, both important and insignificant, from the use of the wheel to certain kinds of dance. In spite of all this, however, the peoples who have created or taken over certain customs and values preserve their singularity and appear as distinct units within the totality of human life, which is always pluralistic.

It is necessary, then, to presuppose the existence of a social entity and of the awareness of having belonged to it for generations, before one can set about describing and trying to understand the process of history in a human collectivity. The Castilians *knew* they were Castilians from the tenth century on, and they strove to *assert themselves*, to achieve things of value, as Castilians, not as Celtiberians. History does not consist in the mere fact of existing so that the most elementary and uniform aspects of life continue under better or worse conditions. And in any event, the chaotic confusion of unrelated facts and events unearthed by ancient and modern scholars is not in itself history, has still not achieved the status of history.

The Morada Vital

So conceived, the historian's task is risky, since he cannot achieve the sort of universally valid certitude that we are accustomed to find in the propositions of the exact sciences. Those who do not have in advance a sympathetic feeling for the historical deeds and creations of a people will not accept as valuable what was achieved by that people, no matter how great our praise. Unless it finds in the reader an adequate receptivity for a certain kind of values, the history of a people may glance off his sensibility just as Shakespeare's words did off the spirit of a number of eighteenth-century rationalists.[2] The same thing happens today all over the world, where a number of great values are either ignored or not respected.

This being the situation, I aspire in the present century to do no more and no less than satisfy the requirements I have set for myself. I am convinced, initially, that the formation of the Spanish people and their ascent to a level of life worthy of historical treatment occurred under difficult, harassing conditions. Thus it has been necessary to devise a historifiable structure that will accommodate both valuable developments and their contraries. As the center and agent of this history I have taken the whole workshop of life in which Hispanicity has been fashioning itself—not fragmentary psychological traits, always generic and meaningless in their isolation. Nor

---

[2] Leandro Fernández de Moratín, writing around 1790, said that the plays of Terence were worth a great deal more than those "of the abundant, grandiloquent, and extravagant Calderón," and that the *Burlador de Sevilla*, by Tirso de Molina, was a "foolish and indecent" work (*Obras póstumas* [Madrid, 1967], I, 361–400).

have I considered external circumstances as separable from the very course of life itself, as if the latter were a given, substantial "reality" on which causes and motives act.

Historifiable life consists in an inner trajectory or process in which external motivations acquire form and reality; that is, they are converted into deeds and events that have a meaning. These deeds and events trace out the peculiar physiognomy of a people and make evident the "inwardness" of their life, never identical to that of any other human community. This "inwardness" is not a static and finished reality analogous to the classic substance; it is a dynamic reality, analogous to a function or, as I shall point out later, to an "invariant." But "inwardness" is an ambiguous term. It may designate *the fact of living* circumscribed by a horizon made up of certain internal and external possibilities and obstacles, and in this case I shall call it the "dwelling place of life" (*morada de la vida*); or it may designate *the mode according to which* men live within this dwelling place or demonstrate awareness of existing in it, and then I shall call it "living context" or "living functioning" (*vividura*). The *vividura*, which may also be called the "functional structure," is the conscious awareness, the conscious aspect, of the unrevealed operation of the vital dwelling place.

The metaphors of the dwelling place and the functional structure will clarify, I hope, the thought that has called them forth. All peoples possessed of a historical (i.e., historifiable) physiognomy also have a vital dwelling place. Sometimes the dwelling places of different peoples appear to be similar, even to the point of having the same kind of human "furniture." Certainly we find today, almost all over the world, railroads, airplanes, churches, schools, libraries, doctors, orchestras, governors, diplomatic corps, armies, and so on. This leads us to think that the world of men is one, or at least that it will become one when the benefits of civilization (an ambiguous and fallacious term, if there ever was one) are even farther extended. It should be observed, however, that much of what we see among the vital "furnishings" in a given dwelling house does not derive authentically from the possibilities of that dwelling place. Sometimes vehicles and technical tools are mere importations; if not these, then ideas, or the conductors of symphony orchestras, or the music they perform. Examples are too obvious to require accumulation. Bringing our vision into still sharper focus, we see that even if one people produces certain things similar to the products of another (philosophy, sciences, machines, etc.), these productive activities do not occupy the same volume in the totality of the respective lives; and, especially, they do not stand in the same relationship to the respective hierarchies of value. In certain dwelling places scientific or industrial activities fill almost all the vital spectrum; in others they figure as an uncommon luxury, or are relegated to little-respected rooms, the cellar or, perhaps, the garret. The same is true of everything else that goes to make up the broad orbit of life: warlike spirit, political and social morality, sense of personality, literary and artistic distinction, encouragement of intellectual activity, a primarily spiritual or a materialized religion. Something of all these things may be found in a people, but always in an arrangement that reflects a particular system of capabilities and preferences. This means that our primary concern here is not the *what* and the *how much* of vital activities, but the peculiar way in which these activities go on. Ideas and the examples or stimuli presented by civilization function one way in one place and another way in another place.

In this book I shall use, as the occasion for them arises, the terms "dwelling place," "living context," "functional structure," and "vital disposition and way of life." I avoid the terms "character" and "psychological traits," because they point to something already fixed and given. I am interested in life as movement, course, and direction —as something variable yet joined to an "invariant" (to borrow a term from mathematics), making it possible to grasp an identity as it passes through one mutation after another. Otherwise, we could not call the Parisian of today and the one who lived in the eleventh century both "French." I am pursuing a vital constant, not a logical, univocal concept, a modality and not a substance. The dwelling places of my metaphor are not closed or cut off from those of their neighbors. The dwellers go forth and return; they possess not only "furnishings" made at home, but imports of the most varied sorts. But when such surges of activity subside and the dweller is again established in his dwelling place, he will prefer certain rooms to others as his normal habitation, for he feels more at home in them, more comfortable performing certain tasks than others. The dweller's freedom will depend upon the possibilities and limitations of his dwelling place, no matter what is imported from the outside. The awareness of the collective dimensions of the person, together with the form, and the tension or the slackness of that awareness, will profoundly affect the liberty of the dweller.

How is it possible, then, for a people's dwelling place, the awareness of being a member of a collective life, to become a new and different one? Our experience shows that some of the main Western human groups (French, Italian, Spanish) are new historical departures made visible through their new collective names (the English people began calling themselves English in the twelfth century, not before). The language that these people began to write some time after the fall of Rome was a decisive innovation and a symptom of a breach, an abrupt change, in the collective state of mind. The fact of not understanding Latin meant that people had stopped being Roman.

Centuries intervened between the time when Romance languages began to be written and the time in which orators spoke literary Latin and were understood. In the meantime an impoverished Latin was written by a minority whose daily language was no longer Latin. During this long period there were no literary works that expressed the life of the people in a language within the reach of all the people. Had such works existed, the *Chanson de Roland* and the *Aeneid* would have been linked by such a series of historical continuities as exists between the works of Marcel Proust and the *Chanson de Roland*, but this is not so. Between the Romanized Gauls and the Capetian dynasty there has been a gap in the collective consciousness. On the other hand, between the Frenchmen of the year 1000 and those of today there have been a series of gradual linguistic changes. The dwelling place of life was not torn down; its contents were renewed though, as we shall see later on, the formal disposition of its life remained constant.[3]

Dwelling places of life change as a result of great and protracted cataclysms. When such events occur, people lose the consciousness of what they have been; they speak another language; they direct themselves toward another form of collective life. Moreover, they fall under the sway of the vigorous action of other peoples whose force and prestige cannot be challenged. In such instances dwelling places have been destroyed and rebuilt in another form. A clear sign, for example, that the Romans of ancient Rome had ceased to exist is provided by the fact that the Forum and the area surrounding it were so thoroughly buried in the minds of the people that the land became a pasture for cattle in the thirteenth century, a pasture that in the eighteenth century was still called the *Campo-vaccino.*

Historical life being the way it is, the valuable activities and qualities of one people cannot always be incorporated into the life of another. The values of one dwelling place can be transplanted only to other dwelling places that are disposed to receive them. Our experience confirms this when we notice that within a particular country certain valuable activities are kept in isolation or enjoy but meager cultivation when, in respect to the country's dominant values, they are felt to be exceptional or unsuitable: technological inventions in Spain, mysticism in France, certain European modes of thought in the United States, music among the Anglo-Saxon peoples, and so forth. Contrariwise, when a phenomenon happens to be in phase with the current of a people's life, authentically cherished values are multiplied and diffused with an easy spontaneity and in terms of high achievements: natural and experimental science has flourished

---

[3] This point is further developed and illustrated in my essay "Presencia del Sultán Saladino en las literaturas románicas," *Hacia Cervantes* (Madrid: Taurus, 1960).

in England from the thirteenth century till today; theoretical thought filled nine centuries of Greek history; the all-conquering, expansionist tension of the Spaniard was maintained from the tenth to the eighteenth century in Spain or its dominions; and the same has happened in other well-known instances.

In the dwelling place of life, consequently, we find stabilized and structured habits of preference which have been created by new social circumstances. Can one imagine anything newer or more unexpected than the situation created by the Muslim conquest of almost all the Peninsula in the eighth century? The people in the north of Hispania who were not buried politically by the avalanche of new sovereignty had to assume responsibilities of command and military initiative rather than continuing their passive obedience to the kings in Toledo. Even those who had always lived in a state of chronic rebellion, like the Basques, found that their formerly pacific neighbors, peoples like the Asturians and the Galicians, were fighting now against the Muslim enemy from the south. In other words, the Basques must have felt that they were not alone in their rebellion, for the battles they were then waging against Muslim authority were not like those fought against Visigoths and Romans. When everybody rebels and the state of revolt is prolonged and not suppressed —which was the situation toward the beginning of the ninth century in all that area from Gallaecia to the southeastern part of the sub-Pyrenean region—revolt becomes a state of intermittent war and constructive disobedience. The circumstances of collective belligerence explain the birth of the future kingdoms of Navarre and Aragon and of the Catalan counties; but if we seek the reason for the fact that the Asturians, the Leonese, and the Galicians were able to form a united kingdom, it may be found in the peculiar rebellious background of the Basque Pyrenean area, a rebelliousness that was still evident in the last years of the Visigothic kingdom. The Navarrese, their Castilian neighbors, and the Pyrenean Aragonese, on the other hand, remained separate from one another and established forms of political society which differed from those of the Leonese kingdom. No one knows how people lived during the eighth century in the Pyrenean Basque region, but we are justified in seeking some explanation for the Navarrese-Castilian-Aragonese disunity as opposed to the Asturian-Galician-Leonese cohesion; and that explanation lies in the fact that the traditional rebelliousness of the Basques was now used for other purposes and in other forms—historically speaking, it had become *something different*.

However disunited these various centers of new collective personalities may have been, a common purpose spurred them all on. The future Spanish kingdoms were born disunited and would fight one another at times with great fury; but, at the same time as those battles ripped apart the social fabric, they also wove it together. The peoples in the northern part of the Peninsula had no possible exit, either to the sea like the Normans, or beyond the Pyrenees. Their horizon was the Muslim south, and that horizon forced them to fight as Christians, because their enemies did so as Muslims. Constant danger and the eagerness to survive quickened their awareness of the social dimension provided by their own group and by their contacts with those who were fighting for the same cause and against a common enemy. (The oscillation between periods of friendship and enmity with other Christian groups does not nullify the deeper and more lasting cohesive aspects of this situation.) The consciousness of the bond between groups of individuals within the smaller social units, and the extension of those ties to others who were not "different" in the same way the Moors were, gradually molded the habits of the people who existed in this state of defensive-aggressive frontier life. Thus it was that in the first centuries of the reconquest a certain specialization of social functions had already been produced among the Christian caste. Those called into combat answered an *apellido*, or "summons to battle," and for that reason the word *apellido* came finally to mean "family name" (tenth-century texts confirm the existence of *apellido* in the meaning of "summons to battle").[4] The mission implicit in that summons to battle was especially incumbent on those who were in the process of constituting themselves as the Christian caste. Other kinds of activities fell to the lot of the Mudejars and the future Hispanic Jews.

In the dwelling place of life of the future Spaniard, these kinds of activities would finally appear as present and operative or as a void symptomatic of their absence. But I must state very clearly that my notion of the dwelling place of life does not seek to outline a fixed psychology or profile for a people. The vital dwelling place becomes genuinely present for me when the life of a people attracts attention because of its valuable accomplishments in time and in space.

The dwelling place of life is worthy of mention and analysis, takes on genuine existence, when it appears as a way that leads to the achievement of remarkable, historifiable values. The vital dwelling place is interesting for its axiological dimension (i.e., for its static, moral, or simply human value) and not because of its psychological or sociological pattern. If the Spaniards, the French, and the Italians had not, in their own way, reached a summit of history, I would not have been interested in analyzing the vital dwelling place where the strategy was planned by virtue of which peoples win the battle

---

4 See V. Oelschläger, *A Medieval Spanish Word-List*, p. 17. The fact that *apellido* in the sense of "name of a person" is not found until the fifteenth century does not mean that this word, like so many others, had not been so used orally in the preceding centuries.

of their future, or, in the end, are reduced to marking time in a more or less colorful fashion, and at times to being the ghost of what they once were. But the agony of Alexandrian Hellenism, of its human agent, is as worthy of historical treatment as the radiant dawn splendor of pre-Socratic thought.

Among the various follies to which reading without understanding has given rise is that of having attributed to me the permanent "freezing" of the Spaniards' history, the predetermining or "fatalizing" of it. People who hold such opinions have never asked themselves why those who wandered along the banks of the Duero, the Seine, or the Tiber both in 1200 and 1900 are called Spaniards, Frenchmen, or Italians; they are astonished when anyone raises such a question and attempts to answer it. I believe that what is Spanish, French, or Italian is people and not the river that flows by them. And if one does not create a temporalized "form" to capture Spanish reality in time, how would it even be possible to speak of "what is Spanish"? On the other hand, no one brings up the accusation of "freezing" Spanish life against those who, welding human history to physical geography, continue to maintain that Spaniards already existed in the prehistoric epochs of the Iberian Peninsula.

A damning awareness of the possibilities and limitations of the future dwelling place of life of the Spaniards (of what they wanted and could do, or of what was less pleasing or urgent to accomplish) may first be glimpsed when the danger of a future in direct opposition to the Muslims of al-Andalus was felt. Those who would be called Spaniards in the twelfth century gained an awareness of themselves in proportion as they came to realize what their adversary was like and *what their Christian rivals were like*. There was no precedent among the peoples of the Peninsula for unified *action* in pursuit of an earthly goal such as the defeat of an enemy (I am not now speaking of psychological possibilities but of actual deeds). The Basques and Ruconians in the north of the Peninsula who had resisted the Romans and the Visigoths without being able to widen their rebellion felt bound to no common cause with the peoples of the center and the south of the Peninsula; but the Asturians, Navarro-Castilians, and Aragonese who resisted and attacked the Muslim host knew that, for better or for worse, they had to count on the other peoples of the northern zone. Thus from the eighth century a mode of conduct, not a psychology, whose dimension of value is indissoluble from its conceptual reality was beginning to be outlined. It is not only a state of "being" but also a continual "becoming," whose importance makes me consider it as a dwelling place of life and a functional structure, or consciousness of the dwelling place. In that dwelling place the innermost heart began to be filled by personal effort while other portions remained unequipped with *instruments*, with those things that are created when all of life is not felt to be constantly in peril. From the militant caste, iron-willed and disciplined in action, flowed the soaring endeavors that carried the Hispanic peoples to Greece in the fourteenth century, to Naples and to India in the fifteenth, and to America, following the call of Empire, in the sixteenth. But, as we have seen in chapter iii, the system of the three castes complicated the structure of the Spanish dwelling place of life in a highly unusual manner and forced the articulation within it of the most favored tasks and others that were complementary and indispensable. Later, after the destruction of that system, the vacuums and fissures in Spanish life point to what once existed and continued to exist *in absentia*.[5] The cardinal value that had been placed on faith and on the nobility of the caste always remained alive and operative, related as it was to those preferences that had played so large a part in constructing the Spanish dwelling place of life.

Let me emphasize that the idea of the vital dwelling place is different from the static notion of "national character," an abstract and immobile schema that takes no account of how the person lives with the possibilities and deficiencies of his chosen tendencies and of his circumstances. "National character" does not include the process of dialectic conflict which is inherent in the formation of any life, whether individual or collective. My idea of the dwelling place of life has nothing to do with the absurd notion of the *Dauerfranzose* (the eternal Frenchman) proposed by certain Germans years ago.

A people maintains its preferred forms of historifiable activity as long as its vital impetus lasts, or until it is modified internally by other peoples who come to be mingled with it, or until it is annihilated by some cataclysm. The Germanic invasions ultimately modified the functional structure of the Roman people; the Franco-Normans changed the structure of the inhabitants of the British Isles; the peoples in the north of the Iberian Peninsula, intermingled with Visigoths, Moors, and Jews, fashioned the special vital disposition of the Spaniards, which was no longer either Visigothic, or Moorish, or Jewish, but simply Spanish.

Further Explanatory Remarks

The greatest difficulty and the greatest source of confusion in conventional historical studies stem from their failure to incorporate the notion of "life." Philosophy in Europe (including Spain) has talked a good deal about "life," but in the moment of truth it has customarily acted as if such a notion did not exist. So it is that I have

---

[5] See my *De la edad conflictiva: El drama de la honra* (Madrid: Taurus, 1963) for a fuller treatment of this problem.

found it necessary to insert in this book a certain amount of material that may at first appear out of place or disjointed, but without this material I might fail to be understood even by unprejudiced readers of good will who have not already built up their own special interests within the boundaries of mythical historiography; all that I might say would fall on sterile ground.

In the following chapter (pp. 136–137) I shall try to make the reader feel the vexatious, problematical situation of those who expressed their experiential awareness of the nature of Spanish existence. Those several Spaniards living between the fifteenth and twentieth centuries show themselves, very significantly, to be caught, even imprisoned, in unhappy straits. These persons are aware that they have a past marked with difficulties and that they are colliding with a harsh present. What is their situation? What is the correlate of their awareness? The person in question does not refer to some unfortunate event that has accidentally befallen him, but rather to *the totality of his life*. The recurrence of such a phenomenon through the centuries confers on these manifestations of intimate experience the value of a historical constant: the person expresses the awareness of finding himself *in* his own life.

For this reason, in the face of the tendency to make history consist in the study of cultures only, one must accentuate the fact that cultures are inseparable from the peoples that create and sustain them and feed their own lives from them. Two centuries after the Roman Empire fell, the Romans were no longer existing as Romans. What happens to a people existing as the Roman Empire, for instance, or as a Greek city, is something singular and unrepeatable. A people wins admiration; it wins contempt; it drags along inertly; it disappears. These happenings are for each people unique. Rome and Athens, besides being different from each other because of their "cultures," possessed the singularity that their peoples existed with the awareness of being Romans and Greeks, respectively. This observation, at first simple and apparently naïve, turns into an unmanageable problem as soon as one tries to give it a justifiable meaning. Human life is not a "thing," nor a substance that can be accounted for in a definition; it is pure activity, and not a physical, psychic, or ideal object (tree, desire, triangle). Many of us believe today that the human reality is given in *life*: "The totality of the psychicophysically given cannot be said to *be*, but rather to *live*; and this constitutes the starting point of historicity. An autognosis, directed not toward an abstract I but to the fullness of my self, will *encounter* me historically determined; physics, on the other hand will come to *know* me cosmically determined."[6]

---

[6] From the correspondence of Wilhelm Dilthey with Count York von Wartenburg, as quoted by F. Heinemann, *Neue Wege der Philosophie* (1929), p.

The life that is spoken of here is not only the correlate of conscious awareness (*Erlebnis* or *vivencia*). It is, further, that which embraces humankind and in which humankind exists. In life is found the thinking I, as well as what gives rise to thought; everything exists and is given in the basic and all-embracing totality of life, which is contained in itself and which is the ultimate limit that man can reach in living and living self-consciously. The only possible way to proceed from here is to conceive (or dream) of life as being anchored in a beyond that is prior to it and ineffable; or as moving toward an indeterminable destiny.

A brief statement of what we understand by historical life must here suffice: a functional activity whose reason for existence consists precisely in its immanent continuous tending toward a future from a present that includes its past. When I use the term "form" in this connection, it is with reference to an inner arrangement, an arrangement in which form and content are inseparable both from activity and its ends, and from the structure of the function. The unrestrainable process of human existence (and we must conceive of this as the existence of a human group aware of its own collective singularity) can move either in the direction of progress or toward the stagnation and ruination of values. The different structures made perceptible by autognosis can move toward marvelous achievements or toward *abysses of horror* without there being any change in the selfhood of collective life or in the awareness of continuing to be the same.

The inadequacy of our historical ideas makes some people confuse the idea of historical structure with a naïve determinism of a biological or essentialist type, but my thought follows other paths. The life structure that I postulate is not a biologico-natural reality, in which, as Bergson would say, "its future is contained in its present." On the contrary, the human life process is, insofar as values are concerned, creation, unforeseeable and incommensurable by natural laws. The latter are an object of knowledge (*scientia*); the human element, on the other hand, is given in the *consciousness* (Bergson), in the *autognosis* (Dilthey).

The Presence of the Functional Structure

In dealing with so slippery a matter, it is a good idea to mention a few instances in which reality of what I call "functional structure" (a people's awareness of its own dwelling place of life) is shown.

---

198. Heinemann (pp. 189 ff.) has a good exposition of Dilthey's historical thought, of history as autognosis (self-knowledge), *Selbstbesinnung*: "Im Erlebnis sind die seelischen Zustände unmittelbar gegeben," in which *Erlebnis* would be the awareness of our immediate and lived experience of something.

Some historians have occasionally felt the presence of the functional structure when they have tried to make certain "facts" intelligible, that is, when they have tried to articulate the facts with the life of a people whose history they aspire to construct. Franz Cumont is the author of a splendid book of Roman history: *Les religions orientales dans le paganisme romain* (4th ed., 1929). As is well known, the Romans adopted a host of religious beliefs that came from Asia Minor, Egypt, Syria, and Persia, which interfused with the traditional religion of the Romans or displaced it. Cumont does not limit himself to recording the facts, describing the worship, and the like; he poses, besides, the problem of what the existence of those beliefs was like within the Roman life process—the question, I would say, of what is their historicohuman *reality*. The worship of the Eastern divinities spread through many countries; but the way in which the gods are articulated with the existence of the people is different in each country:

The Romans, in this respect different from the Greeks *in all the epochs of their history*, judged theories and institutions above all according to their practical results. For theorists they *always* felt the contempt that men of war and men of trade feel for them. It has been frequently observed that in the Roman world philosophy departed from metaphysical speculations in order to concentrate all its attention on ethics. Later, in the same fashion, the Roman Church [that is to say, the Christianized Romans] will leave to the subtle Hellenes the interminable controversies over the essence of the divine Logos, or over the dual nature of Christ. The questions that impassion and divide the Christians of Rome are those that refer to the conduct of life, such as the doctrine of Grace.[7] (p. 31)

The Roman gods were less poetic and more "honest" than the Greek ones; "by temperament and by tradition, the Roman spirit felt the necessity of using religion as a support for morality and the state" (p. 34). The "invariance" of the Roman vital attitude thus stands out against the variation in its contents, in this instance, religion. If the historian were not conscious of such an "invariance," he would not be able to articulate his history as Roman. The necessity to use religion for certain ends reveals the presence of an inclination to direct life through certain channels, and to this purpose religion, or any other form of culture, is subordinated. The truth of Cumont's judgment is confirmed by reading the correspondence of Quintus Aurelius Symmachus (345–405), the heart of whose existence continues to beat with a Roman rhythm when the Empire is on the verge of disappearing. Symmachus, prefect of Rome and consul (!), was building mansions for eternity (*in aevum mansura*), and he tried to combine Christianity with the traditional worship of the gods, a

---

[7] For this question see X. Zubiri, *Naturaleza, Historia, Dios* (Madrid, 1944), pp. 472 ff.

symbol of the triumph of the state: "Consuetudinis amor magnus est."[8]

The reality we are trying to grasp is in itself fleeting and hard to express, although it is not a question of any kind of "spirit" floating in the void of abstraction. The initial difficulty lies in harmonizing the idea of humankind with the fact that we can perceive only the particular forms of it, temperospatially given, that is, in collective lives worthy of being historically treated. These units or specifications of mankind are not assemblies of parts, nor are they determined by final causes. They are rather total activities in which their continuing process of life, all that is circumstantial to them, and the ends to which they are directed, all acquire meaning. These activities are unthinkable without the idea of certain constant habits that limit the action at the same time that they create it. It is not enough to reduce the modalities of life to types of *Weltanschauungen*, for the specified functional structures present themselves not only as static concepts but also as sheer dynamic play between possibilities and impossibilities.[9] To understand this, it would then be necessary to establish a correlation between a determined vital direction, and the unpredictable, historifiable value of what has been caused by that direction or tendency.

The disposition or structure of a specific historicovital activity becomes at times very obvious in what I have called the dynamic play of possibility and impossibility.[10] The Romans, to return to the preceding example, did not resign themselves to being a people of juridically and politically organized agriculturists. I do not know how a group of Italic peoples who spoke Latin acquired their efficient, expansive, cohesive, political capacity. But it is certain that the people

---

[8] Symmachus does not seem to have realized that Rome was in its death agony. Never were there more schools or more instruction. "We truly live in a century devoted to virtue," and so on. (See Gaston Boissier, *La fin du paganisme*, II, 192.)

[9] I leave to one side the fact that there are some human groups doubtless coherent and possessing a kind of physiognomy, albeit a vague one that has earned little respect. These groups are like half-finished novelistic characters whose lives are clumsily expressed or feign to be what they are not; yet they also claim to have a history. This is, however, a delicate subject that I only allude to here in passing.

[10] The following statement of Dilthey's does not seem accurate to me: "Since no nation reckons with its own death, the position of plans and ends in its life is quite different from what it is in the life of the individual. These have always only a temporal, relative relationship to the inner nation, which is capable of *unlimited possibilities*" (*El mundo histórico* [Mexico, 1944], p. 310). So long as the idea goes uncorrected that everything is possible to man (a relic, perhaps, of the immoderate pretensions of that phantom, the so-called Renaissance man), it will not be possible for historical knowledge to adapt itself to its object. Each road opened up in past ages meant the closing of serious proportions. Today men aspire to conquer astral spaces in the future, while at the same time they sense the anguish and aimlessness of their collective life in the present.

we call Roman appear living within that particular functional disposition as early as the fifth century B.C.; further, we know that their functional structure began to disappear when the Germanic tribes and Eastern peoples came to occupy the territory of the Empire and initiated ways of life affected by other functional structures.

In spite of the unvarying functional disposition, there were, to be sure, enormous differences between the Rome of the Punic Wars and the Rome of Constantine. Rome had begun to be peacefully invaded, even before the Empire, by peoples, religions, institutions, customs, and objects, proceeding from the vast extension of lands that the Roman domination was continually conquering. It has been said, and with reason, that the history of the first three centuries of the Empire was a peaceful penetration of the West by the East.[11] The Romans scorned technology and pure science, but they could not get along without importing men of learning from the East—astronomers, mathematicians, physicians, philosophers, architects, even jurists—from the third century to the fifth. Included among those who, during the Empire, passed as representatives of the spirit of the Greeks (Porphyry, Plotinus, Iamblichus, Galen, Dioscorides, Lucian) were Egyptians, Syrians, or Asiatics. The cultivated Romans knew Greek and spent their lives fascinated by the wonders of Attica. One need only read Book V of *De Finibus*, in which Cicero describes the pilgrimage he and his friends made through the "holy places" of vanished Athenian wisdom—"tanta vis admonitionis inest in locis." Greece and the Near East were present in Rome for centuries with their wisdom and their fascination, and, as was "vitally" logical, the functional structure of the Roman Empire reached the limit of its elasticity in its effort to Hellenize itself; it sought to surpass itself, and it did not succeed.[12] What ties Symmachus dynamically, vitally, with Cicero and the other Romans of the past—who are different in quality, in content, and in value—is what I call the dwelling place where Roman life took place. Without that, all that is "Roman" in the history of Rome would evaporate.

Thus we come to the conclusion that a history adequate to its historical object cannot consist simply in a relation of the successive events (in themselves nothing but meaningless anecdotes), nor in merely evaluating the achievements of a civilization out of the context of life, nor in the search for physical or socioeconomic causes,

---

[11] Franz Cumont, *Les religions orientales dans le paganisme romain* (4th ed., 1929), pp. 2–7.

[12] In a passage from Cicero it can be clearly perceived how Grecian values were articulated in the vital structure of the Roman: "Out of them [the Greek peripatetic philosophers] came orators, generals, and rulers. *Descending to a lower plane*, mathematicians, poets, musicians, and even physicians were made in that shop, as it were, of all the arts and crafts" (*De finibus*, V, 7). Such is the hierarchy of social values for a profoundly Hellenized Roman.

nor in dissolving the particularities of the life of a people in the universality of the human. History, insofar as it deals with values worthy of historical treatment, is understood if we contemplate its creating itself from within its peculiar mode of behavior, and not from without. There is no such thing as a Gothic, a Renaissance, a baroque, or a neoclassical spirit that, from an unreal space, conditions the flow of history as the moon intervenes in the tides. Nor is it demonstrable that geography or economy radically determines the future of men. These and other factors will be given *in* history, but the functional disposition of the men in each history is what will transform or will not transform, in their present and their future, the possibilities that circumstances offer them.

Historical writing misses its own theme if it is limited to presenting a mass or succession of social phenomena as having merely existed or happened, for a human action acquires historical meaning only when it is shown as being carried out against the background of public support, indifference, and resistance which leave their mark upon it. The battle, the poem, or the historifiable thought has always existed in the context of groups of partisans or opponents. The age-old image of human life as "the drama of the world" pointed toward the way by which the social phenomenon becomes historifiable—as the interweaving of deep individual factors and broad collectivity. Happenings that possess a truly historical dimension were something like dramas of lasting success which lent themselves to being "restaged" and integrated into the authentic horizon of collective life. Castile—or its Christian caste—created the epic and was re-created first in it, later in the folk ballads of the *Romancero*, and still later in the plays of Lope de Vega: the flesh became the Word, and then the Word re-created the flesh. One of the meanings of the Latin word *successus* was "ascent, the overcoming of an obstacle, a favorable outcome"; and in Spanish we still use the word *suceso* for something that attracts attention, that stands out above daily monotony. What is habitual and repeated is important as part of the social fabric and as a sociological theme, but it is not historical in the meaning here given to this term. Not all "phenomena of civilization" are of historical import. The word "historical" does not refer to any and all fruits, but to the fruits of the tree of life; it alludes to the authentic expressions of a functional context (*vividura*)—in other words, of the experiential awareness (*vivencia*) of the "dwelling place of life" —rather than only to forms of a social life viewed as a fixed object. From this angle of vision one may distinguish between the so-called history of civilization and the history of the life of a people on a "historifiable" level, which is to say, on a level worthy of historical treatment.[13]

---

[13] *Vivencia*, or "experiential awareness," refers to the active (vital, sense-

What appears to the observer as the "dwelling place of life" of a collective entity is for the latter the "functional context" immanent in the consciousness of, for example, the person who lived in the twelfth century as a Castilian, a Catalan, or a Spaniard with his vision and his soul fixed on what he was doing and had to do; neither his biological nature, nor the Goths, the Iberians, or the Franks, filled his consciousness, but what he was and continues to be. Men do not create social groups only by the way in which they satisfy their biological necessities; if they did, there would not have arisen differences as pronounced as those that in the twelfth century separated the Leonese, the Castilians, the Aragonese, and the Catalans. From this we may once again see that the myth of the "eternal Spaniard" founded on the continuity and homogeneity of "blood" runs directly against the data provided by the most basic experiences. The "dwelling place" and the "functional context" of life become visible in a people and to their historian and biographer in proportion as their form of collective existence gradually takes on a clear outline, as it throws off its muteness, and as words overflow from the fullness of the heart to express the awareness of "our selves," an awareness now confident of its own sufficiency, of its personality. The *Poem of the Cid* declares with satisfied pride:

Today the kings of Spain are his [the Cid's] relatives.[14]

Some hundred years later the *Poem of Fernán González* says:

Strongly did God wish to honor Spain
when He wished to send the Holy Apostle there. . . .
As she is better than her neighbors,
all you who dwell in Spain are better,
you are wise men, you inherited common sense.[15]

---

perceived, value-conferring) dimension of that which exists neutrally in the mind only as a concept: for example, *la esperanza* (hope) refers to the active situation of the person who is waiting for the advent of some good thing; *la espera* (awaiting) refers neutrally and objectively to the act of waiting. *Esperanza*, consequently, would be the "vivencial" form of *espera*. Similar semantic differences may be observed between Spanish *honra* ("the lived experience of having honor") and *honor* ("the objectified quality of honor"); *estar bueno* ("to be in good health or seem good") and *ser bueno* ("to be statically good"); *ricacho* ("a vulgar rich person") and *rico* ("rich, with no value judgment implied"); *compró el coche* ("he bought the car") and *tiene coche* ("he has a car"), and so on. Instances of these contraries in English are "freedom" and "liberty," "whore" and "prostitute," "fear" and "fright," and the like. Grammars have not analyzed this phenomenon systematically, but it would be useful to do so, for we would then understand better the differences between *grandioso* and *grande*, between *estar* and *ser*, and many other like pairs. In my terminology *vividura* ("functional context or living structure") is the "vivencial" or experiential form of *morada de vida* ("dwelling place of life").

14 Line 3724: "Oy los reys d'España sos parientes son."

15 Stanzas 155–156: "Fuerte mient quiso Dios a España honrar," / quando al Santo Apóstol quiso í enviar. . . . / Com ella es mejor que las sus vezindades, / sodes mejores quantos en España morades, / omnes sodes sesudos, mesura heredades."

King Peter II of Aragon fought in the Battle of Las Navas de Tolosa (1212) by the side of the Castilians of Alfonso VIII; on learning the prowess of the Aragonese and the Catalans who had attacked the rear guard of the Saracens, Alfonso said—and everyone recognized it to be the truth—"that the Saracens had been conquered by God and by him [Peter II], and that they had won the battle" (Bernat Desclot, *Crónica*, ed. Casacuberta, chap. v). And in that same century, James I of Aragon relates that the army of noblemen and of those from the *cities* besieged Valencia, "and they were fighting closer to the town than we, who had come first"; and those who came closest to the besieged city were the Barcelonese (*ibid.*). So do the Catalans express their awareness of who they were within an Aragonese-Spanish context, for at Las Navas de Tolosa they fought under the command of a man who was also called "King *of Spain.*" But they appear here expressing their consciousness as Catalans, as a federation of cities, coming nearer in that to the structure of northern Italy than to that of Castile.

Let us, therefore, seek for the historical reality of peoples in their own awareness of existing with vigor and value; let the matter of biological antecedents—that which is called race—be left to zoology, the study of what is historically human in man, for this is always based on man's consciousness of gradually making and creating himself, of lifting himself upward:

> The knights of Spain conquer by their good service.
> (*Book of Good Love*, 621)

What I call "the sovereign dimension of the person," which is as obvious in the Castilian dwelling place of life as in the Catalan, occupied a more dominant position in the past of those peoples than it did, for example, in France, where the collective consciousness expresses itself as the "dimension of radiating culture" as early as the twelfth century in Chrétien de Troyes:

> and the whole body of culture
> which has now come into France.[16]

---

[16] In French the lines are: "et de clergie la somme / qui maintenant en France est venue." For further discussion of this matter, see my *Hacia Cervantes* (Madrid, 1960), p. 72. For the antecedents of this French cultural pride, see Gustave Cohen, *Chrétien de Troyes* (1931), p. 170. The expression of that confident residence within the dwelling place of one's own life has functioned as centrally in France as imperious, dominating action has among Spaniards. The inscription over the main door of the Cathedral of Mexico (dated 1672, during the reign of Charles II and while the Marqués de Mancera was serving as viceroy) contains this phrase, so full of the awareness of grandeur: "Non taliter fecit omni nation" ("All nations have not built in this fashion"). On the other hand, a book by Mathieu de Fossey, *Le Mexique* (1857), says in the prologue: "Of what country can one speak today where the civilization of France has not spread its rays and made its influence felt?" This consciousness of the value and dimensions of one's own existence is what it is, and it is not biology or psychology or economy. It is the expression of the form of a historical life.

In this way the vision of the vital dwelling place gradually takes on form and consistency—although I realize the difficulty in using terms like "consistency"[17] with reference to something so varied in its content and so uneven on the evaluative or axiological level. But at the same time it is impossible to overlook what I conceive to be real for lack of the expressive tools with which to conceptualize what really exists. In such cases Montaigne resorted to "pointing out with his finger."

Everything Depends on How Our Idea of Life Operates

Many of us today take the idea of life for granted even though in practice we make scant use of it and have little interest in precise definitions of it. I do not propose to deal with the intricacies of such a problem but only to say that "life" refers to the reality that underlies all human activity, to what one does to "throw off care," because "avoiding care has been the common design of men . . . since God created the world." So said Ibn Ḥazm of Muslim Cordova in the eleventh century, and his thought was made a part of general European currents in 1916 when Miguel Asín Palacios translated one of Ibn Ḥazm's works under the title of *Los caracteres y la conducta* ("Characters and Conduct"). The brilliant observation and intuition of Ibn Ḥazm appeared in 1916 in a Spanish environment familiar with the thought of Nietzsche, Bergson, Dilthey, and Max Scheler (the latter's work on resentment and morality was published in German in 1912); but no one, not even Asín, Ibn Ḥazm's learned translator, made any reference to the striking parallels between the contemporary trend of European thought and that of Ibn Ḥazm in the eleventh century. The conception of life as a constant effort to prevail over the difficulty that causes concern (hunger, the enemy, one's own weakness, the necessity of expressing what has not yet acquired form in the consciousness, or of identifying and learning the nature of what is unknown, etc.) will help to trace the boundary between what is, and what is not, Spanish in time and in space. To successfully attain that distinction one must start with human accomplishments worthy of historical treatment; a problematical point of departure since, however evident it may be that values (desirable aims) serve as the stimulus and goal of life, one can only, on the other hand, arrive with difficulty at an agreement as to what is the worth of the values and the way in which they are structured. A

---

[17] Francisco de Jerez says at the end of his *Conquista del Perú*, addressing himself to Charles V: "No ruler has people / so sturdy and so brave" (*Biblioteca de Autores Españoles*, XXVI, 347), which is simply a closed and static characterization.

people may be characterized by the kind of values it pursues in the long course of years, but its history will depend on the scope and dimension of those values present in its actions and its creations. A people does not become historifiable because it weaves colorful cloths or hunts and fishes with great skill, even though such things are without doubt very valuable.

The collective existence of those who today are called Spaniards had a temporal and spatial beginning. In order to make the when and the how of this human formation visible, it has been necessary to begin with a certain idea about man and to distinguish in him between what is biological and psychic and what propels him dynamically. (Before the eighth century they called themselves Goths, and afterward *Christians*, collectively; and Asturians, Leonese, etc., regionally; see chapter i). The modes of social organization which made possible the great structure of the Spanish people were both desired and projected; all of them possess a characteristic content and profile, a political dimension, and a will toward self-expression in the forms of a valuable culture. That which is historifiable will depend, consequently, on how social groups ceaselessly conceive, with their gaze turned toward the future, the ways of life in which they exist, that is to say, on how they use their biological nature, which in itself is of no interest to history, whose theme is not merely life as physical survival.

A science of man formulated in terms that are univocal and valid for everyone still does not exist,[18] at least in written form. Conceptual rigor gradually becomes more and more lax in proportion as we draw closer to the strange and mobile reality of human life and attempt to capture the reality of the forms of collective existence. For my limited purposes and making use of what is already known, I would call man a being whose existence is anticipatory and subject to time; his present is continuously being fashioned with a simultaneous view toward his future and his past (one is concerned about doing something that still does not exist in view of what has already been done). On that basic foundation rests the life both of the man who has spent his days at a low level, desiring only not to die, and of the man who put forth every effort to make the work of his appointed days imperishable (the humble peasant as compared with Alexander the Great). But once that common denominator has been established, we must then distinguish between the vital reality of the man who existed, as we might say, by feeding on time and counting its hours, and that of the man whose existence was devoted to enriching time with contents that are lasting and visible from afar, providing delight and splendid themes for meditation and contempla-

---

[18] For an original expression of the most recent thought on the subject, see J. Ferrater Mora, *The Idea of Man* (University of Kansas, 1961).

tion, or, on the other hand, perspectives of horror and agony for those who would come later. The matter of history is not easy or democratic, although democracy, as an idea and an ideal, has its place in the human cosmos.

We must resign ourselves to reckoning with the fact that it is not possible to reduce the reality of life and human values to terms that are univocal and satisfactory to everyone; but neither have we succeeded in calculating with absolute exactness the ratio of the circumference of a circle to the diameter. But, even though we may not achieve a rigorous definition of certain objects, I believe it is important to note the evident differences among them. The individual or the collectivity that limits itself to existing in and through time, to absorbing and consuming it, is not comparable to those who, individually or collectively, create and give a meaning to a period of human time, so that it is no longer measurable only by the position of the sun but by the action of certain vital phenomena that create "eras," epochs, dynasties, revolutions—mutations that determine the ascension, the paralysis, or the annihilation of portions of humanity. It is possible to speak of the twelfth or of the fifteenth century in Western civilization because of what was achieved in these spans of time—Romanesque style, discovery of the New World—but there are no centuries in South Africa before the fifteenth. In other words, it is not the same thing for man to be a creature inherently temporal and sequential and for man, individually or collectively, to be a creator of human time that lends itself to historical treatment, or of modes of feeling himself present in time, in a time made valuable and measured by the very works of its creator. Spanish discoveries and colonization affected the consciousness of existence in other Occidental peoples (the French, the Dutch, the English), even though what these latter peoples did in their subsequent colonization is not Spanish but a part of their own history. Each people finds its unity in the dwelling place of life it has forged for itself; that dwelling place gains dimension and historical meaning, achieves full reality, when it is felt as valuable within the collective and individual conscious awareness of those who dwell in it.

If the life of man, as we have seen, is in itself the greatest problem of the humanist, the difficulties presented by the attempt to measure life's valuable dimensions are no less immense. But however the problem may be viewed, it seems empirically evident that without a faith in, and respect for, the past of a people which are in some sense "justified" and acceptable, events and facts by themselves will present an inert, opaque, and insipid spectacle. If the description or narration of events is not integrated within the total life of which they are an expression, the work of the historian will lack any historiographic dimension.

To these grave difficulties (which I do not claim to have overcome but only point out) there are also added the ungraspable, elusive nature of Spanish values and the hostility toward them in many instances both inside and outside Spain. It is even maintained that certain things are Spanish which have never been so, and scorn attached to those things that were genuinely rooted in the consciousness of people who felt themselves to be living and creating themselves in a Spanish manner, not as Celtiberians or as Roman emperors. Whole centuries of Spanish life have been denied validity, as we have already seen. Such experiences, together with many others (unconnected with Spain) through which we are passing at the present moment, force us to accept the fact that it is not always possible to demonstrate the value of what we deem to be worthy of esteem and respect. The conditions and circumstances that determine certain human results may perhaps lend themselves to calculations and measurements; but what those results may be worth is still another story. Let us remember Molière's profound witticism: "Le malade est mort selon les règles."

Cognitive apprehensions are one thing, while the bonds produced by respect are something very different. Even though they cannot be measured or manufactured, attraction and repulsion are as real as the potentiality of an explosive. We must, then, plunge into the historical task with faith and hope and without fear of the hypocritical objections of those who, as they brandish the fallacious weapons of a scientific method that, in this instance, is nonexistent, may accuse us of being relativistic or subjective. Our present world is torn apart and in peril of being annihilated precisely because the most exalted values of human civilization are not demonstrable and because the words that express value judgments have been confused as if in a new Tower of Babel. Whole peoples, races separated only by the color of their skins, social systems that have shared a common life, begin antagonistic contests, talk to one another as if they were all blind and deaf, because every object of life takes on full reality within the cognitive and evaluative boundaries of collective dwelling places of life, each one of which possesses a faculty for establishing values which is peculiar to it alone. Let us not then be astonished that the past, one and the same past, should appear to some as a magnificent spectacle—whether Apollonian or Dionysiac—and to others as a dance macabre or a rubbish heap. After Michael Servetus was burned at the stake, Calvin anxiously inquired whether his victim had held firmly to his faith; on being told that he had, Calvin replied: "He did well; I should have done the same." Everyone conceives and judges what is human from within his faith, showing by his personal judgment what he considers to be valuable rather than attempting to demonstrate the worth of anything scientifically. The

impulses in which efforts and vital purposes have their origin cannot
be axiologically linked to results, just as the son who is born is not
reducible to the interchanged first glance which bound his parents.

Human life can be the object of abstract, rigorously philosophical
analyses; but the axiological judgments about life's concrete expressions will depend on the vital position of those who formulate
them. The history of Catholic peoples will be evaluated in one way
among Catholics and in another among Protestants; the "bourgeois"
past will be refracted by the Communist prism in a very special way;
Spanish historians view the Islamic and Judaic graftings onto their
historical life with antipathy, and so forth. The attempt to construct
a rigorous system to pass judgment on human values will end by
producing a mythology that leads in the opposite direction from
that created by those who have personified nature as divine;[19] scientific treatment of what is human deforms it, just as imaginative
visions altered the reality of the stars, the forests, and the rivers.
Objects without an expressive face, glance, and voice can be captured
by means of stable, closed definitions; but the reality of any phenomenon that expresses what is human—constantly swayed by the pro-
gressive-regressive forces of future, present, and past or by longings,
desires, and thoughts—cannot be seized by means alien to its strange
rhythms. The dominion of "truth" of history for which such proud
claims are made can never be exerted with genuine effectiveness
except in more or less limited areas.

Formal Requirements of the Notion of "Dwelling Place of Life"

It is desirable to establish—or try to establish—the nature of the
conditions that must be present before we may with justification
speak of a "dwelling place of life." These conditions will prevent us
from confusing it with the empirical circumstances that have made
it possible and will rescue it from misinterpretation on the basis of
some sort of psychological subjectivism. In the first place, we assume
the presence of a human group conscious of its collective and territorial dimensions and of a past felt to be alive (just as the adult man
feels that his childhood and youth belong to him), as well as of a
future pregnant with either good or evil. The consciousness of selfhood, or the feeling that the group is both a continuation of what

---

[19] Fernand Braudel says in *La Méditerranée et le monde méditerranéen à
l'époque de Philippe II* (1966), I, 380: "Si la Méditerranée avait vécu sur elle-
même ... elle aurait dû résoudre par elle seule le gros problème de ses excédents
de population, c'est à dire, absorber ce surplus d'hommes, mieux en répartir la
masse à travers son espace. Ce qu'elle a fait d'ailleurs en partie." In such a
statement we seem to return to Homeric times, when Ocean and Neptune made
decisions that were favorable or antagonistic to mortals.

once was and an anticipation of what it is hoped will be, is expressed by an ethnic denomination, such as, for example, *Castilian*, *Catalan*, *Spanish*, or, in this special instance, *Christian*.

That the group is in the process of fashioning a dwelling place for its life is witnessed by the expansion of its geographical boundaries and by its temporal prolongation of the progressive action of its values—in other words, by the steady enrichment of those values. All this means that attention is not centered only on the maintenance of certain *customs*, or collectivized forms of behavior, which are today very like what they were in the past and will be in the future. In this dwelling place there is a variety and a hierarchy of tasks: some are customary and repetitive, others are innovative and charged with a prospective dynamism, which is to say that there comes a moment when the habitual and customary becomes *instrumental*. Language, religious belief, juridical institutions, and everything else change character; they are no longer what they have been but become the *moving force* toward goals no one had thought of before. Let us consider one example out of many: there was nothing intrinsically different about the speech of the Île de France which should make it superior to other regional dialects; but, when the noble knight Conon de Béthune, who spoke the language of his native province of Artois (not incorporated into the kingdom of France until 1659), chanced to visit the Parisian court around 1182, Queen Adèle de Champagne and her son Philip II (then only a boy) criticized the speech of that great lord who would distinguish himself later in the crusades of 1189 and 1199. In his famous "lamentation" he complains about the lack of courtesy of the king and queen:

> Who reproved me if I said any words of Artois,
> For I was not brought up in Pontoise.
> (*Qui m'ont repris se j'ai dit moz d'Artois,*
> *Car je ne fui pas noriz a Pontoise.*)

The language that before had belonged to only one region broadened its radius and would impose itself on areas that were still not dominated politically. The language was not a substance but a kind of custom that had begun to serve functionally in the realization of a political and cultural design. The vital dwelling place extended itself in space and time, and many came to reside within the limits of that spiritual enclosure. People from Artois, Burgundy, and Provençal would finally converge in it, moving in this instance in a peculiarly centripetal fashion—toward Paris. And so it was that all of them became French by adopting like modes of speech, metrical patterns, and thought. Throughout all the variations, very considerable in this instance, one design and one "planned" direction have sustained and maintained French life at a historifiable level by virtue of a chain of rules and "reproofs" such as we have already seen in the lesson given to poor Conon de Béthune.

The dwelling place of life is built in the process of transcending the routine, daily function of custom and usages. Time is not limited simply to passing through it; for it is of less importance to measure the duration of this *human* time (as the prisoner does in his cell) than to penetrate into, and participate in, what goes on in time, what flows through time, and what confers on it a historifiable dimension. The great happening—in art, science, politics, morals, and the like—modifies the meaning of all that preceded it and projects its action on all that comes afterward. To be sure, a reality that is constantly repeated—that of nature, or of those small Spanish villages observed by Jovellanos, Unamuno, and Azorín—loses its static character in the thought of the scientist or in the vision of the moralist or artist. Thus the static is made dynamic, and a historifiable *form* is bestowed on *matter* that previously had none.

What is human, like everything else, always possesses a matter and a form; otherwise, it would not be possible to talk about anything. (But our problem now is the historically worthy form of any human phenomenon.) Man is always making *use* of his *usages* as long as they have not fallen into *disuse*. But in this dialectic—given in life, not in the abstract *idea*—one special way of utilizing customs consists in employing them to express the experiential awareness of their appearance in the consciousness of the person who lives them. In the following passage Baltasar Gracián (1601–1658) expresses his feeling (his experiential awareness) about the life customarily led by the Spaniards around him: "Spain is today just as God created her, without a single improvement made by her inhabitants, except for the *small amount* done by the Romans . . . ; [human] effort has done nothing" (*Criticón*, III, 9). In the face of so inert and paralyzed a human landscape, the antechamber of the "cave of nothingness," the stern, brilliant Aragonese takes no position at all; the feeling of nothingness reinforces the writer's own nihilism. Years pass, and the immobilized spectacle of certain Castilian villages is used for other needs by Gaspar Melchor de Jovellanos: "On the most solemn days, instead of the gaiety and commotion which *should* reveal the happiness of the people, there reigns in the squares and streets a lazy passivity, a sad silence, which cannot be observed without either wonder or pity" (*Biblioteca de Autores Españoles*, XLVI, 491).

The position of the observer is no longer neutral. The nothingness seen by Gracián has become a source of distress which, together with others, contributed to make the work of Jovellanos (1744–1811) a titanic project for the moral, intellectual, and economic reconstruction of Spanish life, a project that has not lost its timeliness and continues to possess full historifiable dimensions. Among the reformers of the eighteenth century Jovellanos was perhaps the one who saw most clearly that a genuine "reform" implied simultaneous changes in habits of the mind, of practical work, and of moral sensibility; no less sweeping a program would have sufficed.

A century later the towns that had produced such differing reactions in Gracián and Jovellanos were still listening to the steady ticking of time, like the regular pulse of the blood. But now that static existence will be lived poetically, re-created by Azorín in a vision no one had seen before:

> I came at midmorning to this calm, bright little town; the sun filled the wide square with light; some cool blue shadows fell at an angle from the eaves of the houses and bathed the doors; the church, with its two squat stone towers, old towers, golden towers, rose in the background, standing out against the clean, luminous sky. . . . I have seen again in the quiet square the refreshing blue shadows, the squat towers, the closed balconies; and I have heard again the murmur of the water, the cries of the swallows that fly swiftly across the sky, *the striking of the old clock, which marks its hours rhythmically, eternal,* indifferent to the sorrows of men. (*Los pueblos*)

These widely differing versions of the same reality offer, despite their marked differences, one common characteristic that binds them to the concerns of those who reside in the same dwelling place: the Spanish village, seen in so similar a fashion by those who wonder about its meaning, endures and re-creates itself within the continuing anxiety it provokes. Its inert, monotonous customs, in themselves lacking any historifiable dimension, act like a generative logos that keeps alive the functioning of the dwelling place of life. Within it the customs are incarnated and appear afterward in this or in another form. Thanks to this process, the history of Spain exists and is something more than a description of repetitive habits like those of the Bedouin or the fellah. It is not a history of scientific inventions but of a succession of states of awareness (in Gracián, in Goya, in Jovellanos, and in many others before and after them): the nature of existence is felt to be an inescapable concern.

Within and *from* this vital dwelling place what had previously not been conceivable was gradually becoming possible in a singular and unique fashion. In contrast to the centripetal French tendency (for which France would have to pay a price), the form of Spanish life was open and centrifugal. In other words, it was not constituted around a center of rational, critical, and secularized activities from which emanated standards with respect to ways of thought and judging life. The French dwelling place of life was built up (and it is these processes by which structures are elaborated which interest me) in a series of authoritative, "dictatorial" impulses obeyed by those who yielded to the directions of people interested in creating an *élite* (the word itself is a French export), in guiding select groups in the art of being intelligent (*sages*), and in restraining passionate excesses or concupiscence (*mesure*). French asceticism was rational and secularly oriented; occasional mystic flights from the world there have also been, but French mysticism has been thin and scanty in comparison with that of the Spaniards, so filled with poetic exaltation.

Spaniards have organized themselves as a political and social community, thanks to no pedagogical dictates but to the imperious power of the Castilians. After the Catholic Sovereigns, Ferdinand and Isabella, the monarchy not only ruled by divine right but also made itself the spokesman for religious interests. The kings of the House of Austria resemble caliphs more than they do secular sovereigns; and under their spiritual power were united those who acted and governed in the lands of the Empire. As soon as authority was not felt as a power sustained by God, the Spaniard became intractable and disobedient, rebelled internally against all laws—in a word, he became an "anarchist," as I explain in more detail in chapter ix.

For the sake of clarity it must be repeated that the vital dwelling place is slowly constituted in the wake of ascending, efficacious impulses that give rise to new collective situations. The point of departure is, to be sure, established customs (linguistic, religious, juridical, economic, etc.); but these customs serve now as an instrument, not as a static base. From the first centuries of the reconquest, in a rising and progressive rhythm, there was being constituted the vital dwelling place of those who, in the thirteenth century, would be called Spaniards. The constructive impulse was not, could not be, centripetal, but something like this: an inner, confident clinging to the power of religious belief and of those who believed in it, while external activities overflowed exuberantly in response to no predetermined plan. It was felt only that one had to fight against the Moors or against one's Christian neighbors. When the last remnants of Moorish sovereignty were destroyed in the fifteenth century, the Spaniards found themselves in the ambiguous situation of simultaneously being and not being Spaniards, which is to say that they were disunited as Portuguese, Castilians, and Catalan-Aragonese. (By contrast we may compare the way in which France progressively welded onto its original center—and without a single backward step—Languedoc in the thirteenth century, Burgundy in the fifteenth, Flanders and Roussillon in the seventeenth, Savoy in the nineteenth.) Their imperious-impulsive dimension (sheer will and not calm calculation) carried the Spaniards to remote regions without taking thought for the condition of the land they left behind; they were intent only on magnifying their imperious dimension. (Unlike the Spaniards, the French, subjects of right reason and exactitude, have spent long centuries in the cultural assimilation of strange, far-off peoples, a task accomplished only in the second half of the nineteenth century by the doubtless admirable efforts of their schools.) The Spaniards had already achieved clearly visible results by the end of the sixteenth century, thanks primarily to the missionary activity of certain religious orders. Ibero-America was occupied by Spaniards whose descendants continued to exist in the Hispanic vital dwelling place and learned, *from within it*, to take from the strange culture what was possible from that point of view, from that vital perspective. It is a perspective different from that of the English and the French, but it has permitted the Hispanic-American descendants of the Spaniards utterances of compelling beauty, highly esteemed beyond their national limits—witness the process of historifiable culture which stretches from the Inca Garcilaso de la Vega and Sor Juana Inés de la Cruz to Sarmiento, Rubén Darío, and many other distinguished Latin-American writers. To understand them all and to give them their due value, one must contemplate them *from* the Spanish dwelling place of life (which has nothing to do with nationality or changes in themes and literary styles). If we try to fit these and other writers like them into other kinds of *historifiable* dwelling places (French, English, etc.), it will be seen that the results are absurd.

What I have called "instrumental" for the functions of life originating in a vital dwelling place may be something endowed with either positive or negative value (abundance or poverty, militant spirit or the lack of it, thought stemming from the Greek tradition or mythical representations of reality, etc.). But the spatial and temporal dimensions of the activities motivated by a particular dwelling place of life are inseparable from their axiological quality; they must follow a rising trajectory and be incited to further accomplishment. When the structure of the vital movement of a people is fixed or collapses and custom dictates usage, the life of a people begins to be converted into material more suitable for a chronicle than for what I call authentic history. There are today highly civilized peoples (or very backward ones, for in this respect it makes no difference) whose present existence will lend itself more readily in the future to treatment in simple narrations or descriptions than in history.

A collective life that does not make itself problematical as a collective life may provide much material for the chronicler but very little for the historian. The struggles between the Christian caste and the two others between the fifteenth and seventeenth centuries, which were basically a conflict within the Christian caste itself, make visible the functioning of the Spanish dwelling place of life both in the mother country and in the colonies. The consequences of these struggles conferred a historifiable dimension on Spanish life.

There comes a time when a people's attempts to elevate itself toward the future resemble the flight of the bustard. The animation, once so lively within that conceptual structure I call the dwelling place of life, is becalmed; its inhabitants, with respect to their histori-fiable dimension, begin to give the impression of figures in a wax museum (the simile is exaggerated and risky, but necessary). Such a state is compatible with great flashes of civilization and mighty power as well as with great wretchedness and misfortune; the whole com-plex must be carefully calibrated in all its nuances. My purpose, how-ever, is to explain insofar as possible the meaning I give to the ex-pression "dwelling place of life," the structure that announces its presence when the given circumstances function as instrumentalities in the realization of a new and high design. Primarily it is *the creation by a people of a new awareness of its collective dimension, new with respect to the awareness expressed before by those who preceded it in that geographical space*; it is, further, an awareness expressed in *works*.

The Spaniards came to be "Spanish" because those who had still not become Spanish used their religious beliefs, their militant energies, their juridical institutions, and everything else around them with the eyes of their soul fixed on *goals* neither latent nor implicit within the human medium of the Iberian Peninsula before the eighth century. But if the goals did not exist previously, the possibility of their formu-lation was, of course, present. The constitutive forces of a vital dwell-ing place, of a future existence of a people, have both anticipatory and retrospective aspects: with the *material* of a past, the *form* of a future is built. Tradition does not fall on the present by its own weight; rather there endures what a people wants and needs to pre-serve from its past for the purpose of constructing the future with materials a people feels to be its own. The future, nonetheless, will be different from the past. In such renovations of tradition we may note that the vital dwelling place is maintaining its full historifiable dimension. As an example, it may be remembered that the original expansive movement by the Christians toward Andalusia and toward the Portuguese Algarve kept on as far as Africa, the Canary Islands, and the Azores, and did not come to a halt until it had girdled the globe. Another example is provided by epic poetry: the stammering forms of the tenth century acquired a full Castilian dimension in the twelfth and thirteenth centuries; the epic then became the foundation stone and basis of folk ballads (the *Romancero*) in the fourteenth century and finally achieved a new and wholly unforeseen reincar-nation in the plays of Lope de Vega. But since the seventeenth cen-tury Spaniards have not known quite what to do with their tradition, with *what is given*, and are continually waiting for what the engineers and architects of collective life may chance to do with it. At times, as we have already seen, the last three centuries of the Spanish past have been felt to be a hindrance; yet, at the same time, it is not possible to cast them aside. But this problem does not concern me at the moment.

Nothing is per se a favorable precondition for the future, but everything may be. All that lies within man (the psyche that can never be totally encompassed) as well as what lies without him (from religious practices to natural, economic, and political conditions) has served as the means for the creation of the most varied and disparate forms of collective life. The Swiss people, for example, have constructed their vital dwelling place—limited but nonetheless genuine—by both evading and ably utilizing their French, German, and Italian components. The Swissness of this peculiar community rests, however, on the way in which the future citizens of Switzerland managed their political and economic circumstances, which were for them more important than linguistic, religious, or, in general, cultural conditions. In contrast, the ascending rhythm of future Italian life (the design of which was contemplated as early as the tenth century) was not due to unifying causes of a religious, economic, or political nature but to broadly cultural ones. Over that peninsula was projected the image of its Roman unity, an image that the Italians did not endow with effective strength through political actions but by means of aesthetic, literary, and artistic visions that were linked to the past but looked ahead to a future. No less ineffective than that image of a united Italy was the one provided by a Rome that ruled the world from the papal see; yet, despite all this, the almost inconceivably disparate peoples who lived in the Apennine Peninsula from Venice to Palermo began a battle to "reconquer" themselves with the weapons of culture: literature, art, science, and wit. With this goal in mind, the future Italians created for themselves a highly original dwelling place of life whose instrumental and axiological means resemble not at all those of Spain or France. It is like them, however, with respect to the requirements of spatial, temporal, and axiological *dynamism*. Had they been content to rest on the memory of imperial Rome or to live under the spiritual protection of the *borgo papalino*, of what had been the *urbs*, the Venetians and the Calabrians would never have created for themselves an awareness of *italianità*. The energy and the forward-looking dynamism which finally gave a certain unity to these divergent peoples were sustained and guided by the star of *civiltà*, a word that possesses in Italian life echoes and nuances not to be found in the analogous terms *civilisation* and *Kultur*. If we apprehended these words with due rigor and genuinely relived their meaning, we might come to a clear realization of how the Italians, the French, and the Germans have built their vital dwelling places.

Other peoples have acquired a historifiable dimension on the basis of a religious belief; their starting point was a divine revelation. The nearest examples of such developments for the Spaniards were those of Moses and Mohammed, who inspired vital modalities different from those of Western Antiquity and which, indeed, have survived the latter. Let us set aside for a moment the case of the Hebrew people for the reason that their nationhood was in eclipse for long centuries and, as a result, many Jews have had to mingle their way of life with forms alien to it. As for the Muslims, their historifiable dimension vanished long ago and was replaced by a vital modality which I call "narratable" because it is less suitable for historiographical treatment than for the simple narration of a chronicle. Their existence drags along in time, in a time over which they no longer exert control, even though the collective dimensions of their societies may last as long as the belief that sustains them. Their immutable literary languages rest on sacred and unshakable foundations. Even public signs in the Near East (with the exception of Turkey) continue to be written in biblical Hebrew or in koranic Arabic. The languages of Greece and Rome, on the other hand, survive in the studies of certain learned men, and nowhere else. The collectivities of which they were the expression were built up on rational forces—or, as we might say, terrains. All their works—monumental structures of beauty, inquiring thought, juridico-secular institutions—were directed from within, or with an awareness of, the problematical nature of all human things; and this is a terrain much exposed to erosion by the opinions and value judgments of people.

To live with Promethean arrogance from within man, or to live from without man, sustained by forces that transcend him: such is the dramatic choice of human destiny, of every vital dwelling place. It is of great importance for the historian to determine whether a dwelling place of life has been built up on the basis of one of these basic positions, *or on combinations of them*; and it is of special importance for the historian who tries to penetrate into the complexities of Spanish life with its mingling of Occidental and Oriental ingredients. The vital dwelling place of the Russians—about which, admittedly, I know very little—should perhaps be viewed from an Oriental-Occidental vantage point. But we must never forget that generic criteria must be sharpened and refined in every instance until they hit on the concrete reality of each individual dwelling place. No two are alike, and in their disparity and uniqueness lies the possibility of understanding their singular form of historifiable validity—in sum, the special quality of their civilization.

In our efforts to avoid the Scylla of abstract logical analysis, we should not run against the Charybdis of psychological relativism, which reduces the understanding of any civilization to something like an incommunicable mystic experience. In the vital dwelling place one or the other psychic modality is of less importance than what is caused by it, in other words, the results, which depend primarily on the way in which the future has been planned *from within* a dynamic vital dwelling place rather than on "psychology." Courage and daring became "typically Spanish" in a vital dwelling place intent, for one thing, on maintaining and exalting the prestige of a caste—on "maintaining honor," as Bernal Díaz del Castillo says—and not on stimulating technology to industrialize and commercialize the Indies, whose riches, as such, blemished the reputation of the people who possessed them, as we shall see in chapter viii.[20]

It is difficult—or at least I consider it so—to find exact modes of expression to indicate precisely what is meant by "dynamic and ascendant functioning" within a vital dwelling place.[21] What has been said earlier about "human time" and the "uses of customs" may perhaps clarify matters in some measure. I remember having read that the Chinese classify words as "full" and "empty" (something like the difference between a preposition and a noun); and there are also, within the functioning of collective life, "full" and "empty" periods of time and psychology. Notwithstanding his rudimentary philosophy, Quevedo intuited this difference when he called a work of his *Grandes anales de quince días* ("Great Annals of Fifteen Days"), which refers to a few brief days at the beginning of Philip IV's reign which Quevedo felt to represent an upheaval of considerable scope. Measuring the accuracy of that judgment about a temporal flow is

---

[20] Until now it has not been possible to understand the frequent motif of the hidalgo's poverty, which has been attributed especially to the general scorn felt by the nobles for remunerative labor; but acquired wealth was an equal or greater cause of discredit. In some *Coplas* written for King John II of Castile, the poet Juan de Dueñas says that the newly wealthy converts should not be favored at court to the detriment of "the courageous hidalgos no matter how much *poverty* they suffer" (see Francisca Vendrell, in Sefarad [1958], XVIII, 110). Such a statement is not part of "a general phenomenon in that period at the end of the Middle Ages," but an expression of the functioning of the Castilian vital dwelling place, so charged with ascendant tension in the fifteenth century. From within, and by virtue of, that tension the structure of the Spanish Empire would be planned and would function. Certain formulas that are in part valid (such as Huizinga's "Waning of the Middle Ages" or the "Counter Reform" of a number of German historians) have helped to keep alive some very naïve and generalized misconceptions.

[21] The goal toward which, consciously or unconsciously, the "dynamic functioning" of people in the making is tending may be seen only in retrospect; the tasks of the historian and the prophet are separate and different. When I speak of "dynamic and ascendant functioning," I have in mind something like a *prolonged battle*, indecisive and confused, but *through which may be glimpsed, in ever clearer outline, the shape of ultimate victory or defeat*. This internal order lends meaning to what, at first glance, seems confused and chaotic. Human time and space are the enemies against which are pitted all attempts at endowing the life of a people with historical dimensions. Juan de Lucena, a fifteenth-century convert from Judaism, put these elegant words in the mouth of Alonso de Cartagena: "Lord Marquis [of Santillana], let us [that is, Spaniards with an awareness of our cultural situation] not go after time; let us force time to turn toward us" (*De vita beata*, ed. in *Bibliófilos Españoles*, p. 112). At another point in the present study I say, for different yet analogous reasons: "Let us be the masters and not the servants of our history."

not important for us now; it is enough to perceive in it the intensity with which the Spaniard felt the creation and destruction of his own life process, and the scant attention paid to all else. That special psychic dimension of man was charged with tension, but at the cost of the slackening of interest in all things that did not pertain to that immersion in self. I would add that this phenomenon, endowed with maximum creativity, had less to do with the "baroque" than with the structure of the Spanish dwelling place and with the experiential awareness of its peculiar structure.

For the historian it is of prime importance to learn what kind of task a people assigns to its psychology, to its modes of feeling, and to its faculty for thought. Likewise it is important to know how a people fills its time. Therefore cultural typifications are not very fertile: we are little helped by concepts as broad and vague as that of "Western culture," through whose gaps and fissures there escapes the reality of the Spaniards, the Italians, the English, and many others. Instead of making so generic a characterization, I would ask myself: What was the outcome of—or what has become of—the political, caste-based imperialism of the Spaniards, or of the rationalistic and restraining French life, or of that aesthetic and intellectual "reconquest" of the Italians? And so would I proceed in all the other instances that confront us.

It matters more for the historian to capture the expression of what a people is *wanting or trying to be, or wanting to do with what it is,* than to analyze coolly and abstractly *what it is.* Therefore it is of little significance for the historic vision that the people who in the eighth century fought the Moors in Asturias and Galicia should be Christians or should call themselves Christians; it is, on the other hand, crucial that they should have been shaping their political figure *as* Christians, *knowing themselves* to be Christians, *wanting to be Christians, filling* with that very belief a given space and time—in sum, inventing for themselves a *conceptual* or *ideal* form for their human dwelling place, with doors and windows open to a future. These are the theoretical requirements, incarnate here in one concrete experience, which I deem necessary before we may speak with some basis of what I have called a dwelling place of life worthy of being treated as a historical theme—which is, we might say, the conscious awareness of the living context of a dwelling place—the human space in which the history of a people exists.

Finally, it is desirable to stress the difference, however obvious it may be, between a dwelling place of life and culture or civilization. Cultures are spoken of and viewed as finished objects of historical life, ready to be displayed in the pages of a book or the halls of a museum. The dwelling place of which I speak appears as a spatial, temporal, dialectic process that is on the way to becoming what it will later turn out to be. It is a phenomenon that submits more readily to being accompanied during its creative process than to being delimited between a beginning and an end. In the historifiable dwelling place of life, each moment affirms and opposes itself with respect to the previous one and summons toward the future. The problems involved in this process interest me more than the formulation of theoretical principles about how cultures are born and die; I prefer to stop awhile in the wonder and joy of seeing them flower and mature, while they hope and trust—or suffer anguish and despair. Such expressions may sound less than scientific, but they seem justified by the fact that, with all the "science" of the nineteenth and twentieth centuries, the history of how the authentic life of the Spaniards arose has not progressed beyond a tissue of foolish, incoherent fables.

In Search of a Meaning for the Word "Spanish"

The Spaniards are and have been those who called themselves Spaniards since the thirteenth century; and after the eighth-century Christians, Leonese, Castilians, and the like, they are those who feel and have felt part of a human community on the Iberian Peninsula, linked in a *continuity of social awareness* since the eighth century with people who have actually made that continuity possible and have given to it the mode of operation that has continually set it apart since the term "Spanish" was first used in the Peninsula. People who felt they were existing within that particular form of life considered themselves Spaniards even when they did not dwell in the Peninsula, just as in the nineteenth century English speakers in Canada thought of themselves as "British" rather than Canadian. In 1800 the inhabitants of Cuba, Santo Domingo, and Puerto Rico felt as Spanish as the inhabitants of the Canary Islands or of Seville. Despite marked regional differences, people of any real culture knew that their political unity and their ways of behaving in relation to their fellow citizens, whether from the Peninsula or from the islands, were the result of the design and action of those who, centuries before, had been continuously and steadily preparing their own present. All of them belonged to the Spanish community because certain people of authority and prestige—the kings of Castile, Aragon, and later of Spain—had united their ancestors under a human and divine faith and had launched them on lofty enterprises beyond the soil of the home country. Sixteenth-century Spaniards, whose souls united in one faith, in obedience to one monarch, and in esteem for personal bravery and ambition, knew through tradition that their collective, and at times individual, grandeur was based on the victory of their caste over those of the Muslims and Jews. The Tribunal of the Faith, or Holy Office, took care to keep that memory bright. Furthermore, the feeling of Spanishness was intensified in view of the hitherto never observed elevation of the religion of the dominant caste even above royal power. The king was sovereign over all the previously divided kingdoms; the language of triumphant Castile had become imperial and had been converted into the organ of literary expression for even Catalans and Portuguese. The awareness of Spanishness broadened out like a mighty river in response to the confluence of numerous tributaries: "Not all the vassals of the royal crown of Spain are of like customs and similar languages," wrote Gonzalo Fernández de Oviedo[22] in Santo Domingo. But a common adherence to what everyone considered lofty and full of prestige made Spaniards of them all; witness the words of the same author, speaking of colonizers in the New World: "How will the Andalusian get along with the Valencian, the man from Perpignan with the one from Cordova . . . ? Who will reconcile the Basque and the Catalan, who are of such different provinces and tongues? . . . But, since *the cause has been so great*, there has been no cease in the flow of *people of distinguished blood, and knights, and hidalgos* who decided to leave their homeland of Spain to take up residence in these parts."

Ceaseless work on the forge of the national consciousness sought to unite the disparate elements of the Peninsula which concurred in their faith and reverence for certain principles and goals that gave firm and tense outline to their conduct. Captain Bernardo de Vargas Machuca relates that two soldiers wounded by the poisoned arrows of some American Indians were dying painfully. One of them "was so badly hurt and complained so much" that his companion, Antonio de Herrera, from Plasencia, dubbed the "Bravo Español" ("Magnificent Spaniard") for his gallantry, reproached him "with very harsh words," because "with soldiers like that *one did not conquer the world*." " 'Are you well?' " he asked the other injured man. "And as the man said he was, he said to him again: 'Then may God be with you, and may He give you strength and life, for I am going to die.' And returning to his bed, at that very moment he expired; and on the following day his friend died."[23]

With such sentiments and aspirations there had gradually been formed effective Spanish links among the peoples who had appeared so diverse to Fernández de Oviedo at the beginning of the sixteenth century. The incentive provided by the gold of the Indies was doubtless a great attraction; but the dream of great personal achievement, the feeling of supremacy, was a stimulus much more in the fore-

---

[22] *Historia general y natural de las Indias*, Book II, chap. 13, p. 54.
[23] *Milicia y descripción de las Indias* (Madrid, 1599), Book II, fol. 37.

ground. It is not by accident that the *Romancero*, a story and a song of heroic deeds that uplift the imagination and the sensibilities, began to be printed in the time of Charles V. Orally from father to son there was transmitted the idea that the Spaniards continued socially the collective existence of past times under other kings. Still present in the mind were Fernán González, the Cid, and the sovereigns who had conquered those kingdoms—Leon, Aragon, Granada, Navarre—now united in sixteenth-century Spain. This was the past truly felt to be Spanish in the collective consciousness. All that which preceded the reconquest was nothing more than memories pieced together by scholars and revived through the need of creating a past in keeping with ideals of grandeur which were very much alive as early as the fifteenth century. But if Numantia was remembered for such reasons, the memory was so vague and inexact that the long-gone Celtiberian town was incorrectly located near Zamora instead of Soria.

To sum up: Being Spanish means feeling that one has existed socially in a peculiar and unique way; the awareness of the gradual unification and broadening of the original groups of Leonese, Castilians, and Aragonese with a view toward reaching set goals preceded the fact of feeling oneself *español*, an imported term, "un-Spanish" in its phonetic development. The predecessors of the Spaniards were called what Fernández de Oviedo still calls them (e.g., Aragonese, Castilians, Andalusians, etc.); but they were linked in an unbroken social continuity with the Spaniards of the sixteenth century. There was no bond between the social continuity of these Spaniards and the social awareness of the Goths, Romans, or Celtiberians, who had lived in the Peninsula and expressed the awareness of what they really were in their own languages, writing, thought, and art.

Not as an abstract psychological observation but only as the experiential awareness of a *vital dwelling place* could there be born in the sixteenth century the Spanish saying, "Church, or sea, or royal service," a saying expressive of the courses possible for the Spaniard of the time, or, in other words, of the vital panorama that, in its general lines, functioned down to the nineteenth century. Less familiar is another commentary: "[There are] six Spanish adventurers: one goes to the Indies, another goes to Italy, another goes to Flanders, another is in prison, another is engaged in lawsuits, and another is taking religious vows. And in Spain *there are no other kinds of people* save these six mentioned."[24]

Such judgments, formulated out of the conscious awareness of a

---

[24] Such is the title of a book said to have been written in the middle of the sixteenth century by an eccentric named Vasco Díaz Tanco de Fregenal (see B. J. Gallardo, *Ensayo de una biblioteca española de libros raros*, II, 784).

collective situation, possess validity as a vision of the future linked with the present. They reveal, above all, the security of perceiving the stable channels through which the lives of the people are to unroll, lives that are, at first glance, thick with unforeseeable possibilities. Such possibilities are unforeseeable as long as we think of the content of each individual, unique, unrepeatable life. Imagine the difference it makes whether it is Gonzalo de Córdoba, or Miguel de Cervantes, or the Duke of Osuna, or Don Francisco de Quevedo who goes to Italy. But it is no less certain that neither these men nor others failed to proceed according to the form of life which I call Spanish in this book. Heroic lives there were in abundance, blissfully running the greatest of risks for the God and the king of Spain. But in vain will one look for an Andreas Vesalius, or heroes in the realm of thought such as Campanella, Giordano Bruno, or Galileo, for in the sixteenth century the fear of being stamped as a Jew finally paralyzed all intellectual pursuits. This, in its turn, is another aspect of the Spanish dwelling place: "Spain is a province that is not inclined to take the point of view of reason" (Alonso de Palencia, 1459). "Let us hope that Spain, a country of light and of melancholy, may decide, one day, to rise to the level of metaphysical concepts" (Xavier Zubiri, 1933). "The capacity of Spanish-speaking people for the *other* human things . . . [is] so superior to their capacity for the sciences, in particular the exact and experimental sciences" (José Gaos, 1941). There has, then, been an awareness of Hispanic limitations as well as of possibilities. Feijoo, Father Isla, and others have said the same thing as Palencia, Zubiri, and Gaos. Such statements evidence the experiential awareness of the lasting quality of what I call residence within the historic dwelling place, a consciousness of the horizontal and vertical dimensions of the human collectivity to which one belongs.

In view of what we have already seen, it is surprising that history has continued to be written as if its theme were somehow independent of the very life expressed in history. It has gone on being either positivist (men and human societies are motivated by natural circumstances) or idealist (abstractly and extravitally, the Hegelian *idea* is realized in history). My own work attempts to follow other paths, as should be clear from the data and points of view on which it is based.

It is not hard to understand why some people consider my way of proceeding as unscientific; nor does it matter that it should be so considered, for my purpose is that the "biography" here outlined should be seen and felt as an authentic expression of the life of the Spanish people, and that their grandeur and their failure should be made intelligible. With this end in view it has been necessary to leave aside the abstract universal man and to forget for a moment the problem of whether the Spaniards were prehistoric or medieval beings situated on the margin of the Renaissance or whether they were, on the other hand, the forerunners of modern philosophic thought. The prime necessity for me has been to explain how the Spaniard has come, above everything else, to have an awareness of being Spanish, and how, from within that awareness of being Spanish he has managed, in one way or another, his own possibilities and those offered to him by people who were not Spaniards.

In my opinion, every Spaniard preoccupied with what was happening to him and others around him could have said with Quevedo, "Oh, how you slip away, my life!" (¡Oh, cómo te deslizas, vida mía!). It is impossible to forget the fact that even today there are people who do not like to be called Spanish, although, indeed, this very rejection of the term may seem to others a sign that they are affirming their Spanishness still more clearly. The awareness of existence and of the value of one's own existence takes priority over the occasional anti-Spanishness of some modern Spaniards. For this reason I do not view Spanish life from the biological, psychological, or economic vantage point. We are not dealing with a fixed object but with a continuous slipping away from a given position toward goals either longed for or imposed by circumstances. I have had to show, for example, that the peculiarities of the Spanish economy resulted more from the will that it should be as it was than from climatic conditions, poor soil, or like causes (see chapter ix). It has likewise been necessary to overcome that defensive attitude with respect to neighboring peoples which made its appearance as early as the fifteenth century in Spain; in 1609 Quevedo wrote his *España defendida* ("Spain Defended"), which has been followed by numerous attempts to rectify established opinions about the Spanish past. One such attempt, stemming from a defensive feeling of inferiority, was made by Menéndez y Pelayo in his *Ciencia española*, in which he engages in a polemic against those who have cast doubt on the worth of that science, but without coming to any convincing conclusion.[25] But for the historian, science, or the lack of it, must be considered within the framework of the Spaniard's interests and preferences and, above all, as a function of his very existence.

My history is neither patriotic nor aggressive; it tries to grasp the motive forces that have determined events and developments, some of which I consider marvelous and others of which seem lamentable and infamous. There is nothing easier than to approach the history of any people as if it were a fabric woven out of monstros-

---

[25] In *De le edad conflictiva* (1963), I have analyzed the Spaniard's position with regard to science in order to lay a firmer foundation for future discussion.

ities and stupidities. Robert Briffault has done so in *The Decline and Fall of the British Empire* (New York, 1938), and, as might have been expected, his view of England is incoherent and absurd. All history, like all human action of some scope, makes its way over ruins; indeed, it creates them. Empires, even religions, have their firm foundation in iniquities, the inevitable reverse side of their virtues. Neither glorious nor ignominious history interests me.

My history, in contrast, is founded on the assumption that the awareness of being Spanish and of acting as a Spaniard begins to make itself felt only in the tenth and eleventh centuries, for being Spanish and being an inhabitant of the Iberian Peninsula are different things. It is necessary, for my purpose, to insist on the awareness of insecurity as a line that indelibly marks the course of Hispanic existence and becomes perceptible in the very process of life. The insecure Spaniard does not yearn for a type of action or conduct *different* from that which motivates his dissatisfaction; he is not like the Roman who, during the Empire,[26] missed the political organization and the customs of the Republic. The Spaniard has not forged a life content to which he could refer as one can to a stable, objectified culture; after the fifteenth century, he sometimes missed the *persons* of Ferdinand and Isabella, which is a very different matter. What I call Spain was made and continues to be made on a loom of uncertainties. In order to survive, one corner of the Peninsula had to destroy Islamized Spain, in which even the rivers had changed their thousand-year-old names. Each of the three peoples of the Peninsula (Christians, Moors, Jews) saw itself forced to live for eight centuries together with the other two at the same time that it passionately desired their extermination. The wars of the Hispano-Christians, as Don Alonso de Cartagena said, were "holy." All life was placed, was risked, on the gaming table of the faith and in the service of the genealogical purity of the dominant caste. No important role was assigned to the peaceful human-temporal tasks. Thus there was developing a disposition of life in which the structure prevailing throughout the Visigothic centuries was forgotten, as I shall presently make clear. The principle *cedat curiositas fidei*, not functional or

---

[26] Without speaking of Cicero, Seneca, Tacitus, and other famous writers who have felt a nostalgia for the past, I shall recall a secondary figure, Columella, the author of a treatise on agriculture (*De re rustica*) composed to persuade his contemporaries to go back to the good customs of the past: "When I think of so many illustrious captains of pure Roman stock, who ever excelled in the double occupation of defending and cultivating the land (the fatherland as well as conquered land), I understand how it is that our contemporaries, abandoned to luxury and womanish pleasures, do not enjoy the vigorous and manly life of their ancestors" (Preface, par. 14). Columella then refers to the banquets, the hot baths, the lubricity, and the drunkenness of those who, in Seneca's phrase, "saw neither the rising nor the setting of the sun."

totalizing for the Visigoth, became functional and totalizing for those who appear to us today as Spaniards. These people—and this is the central point in the conscious awareness of their history—never accepted their existence simply, easily, as the Chinese naturally accepted his "Chineseness," or the Hindu, his being Hindu. For the sake of his existence in a belief (his only *raison d'être*) the Spaniard was to struggle first against the Moors, then against the Jews, the Protestants, or the agnostics. The French and English accepted in the end the compatibility of being French or English and holding a religious belief different from the traditional one, or holding none at all. For the Hispano-Lusitanian people such a situation has always meant an agonized existence: they know the price they have to pay for their belief, but they cannot help but persist in it. The gaps left by the disappearance of creeds among the English, French, and Germans have been filled with the cult of certain secular "divinities": science, sociopolitical institutions, literature (in France); the community of citizens, the protection of women, children, animals, and plants (in Anglo-Saxon countries); and so on. Nothing of this sort compensates for the disappearance of belief among the Hispano-Portuguese peoples. For them the alternatives are, and have been, either belief or nonexistence, as anyone can see who is acquainted with life in the Iberian Peninsula, Brazil, or Mexico. For underneath whatever people may wish to explain as a universal phenomenon of "these times," there lies that other thing, each people's residence within its own peculiar dwelling place of life.

This dwelling place of life makes itself visible as (*a*) a burning hope of rising to heights and destinies prefigured in a belief, be it human or divine; (*b*) an insecurity about the fulfillment of the promise implied in the belief; (*c*) the impossibility of escaping, *by one's own impulsion*, from the condition of credulity and of thereby inventing new realities, physical or ideal, forged by reasoning and experience; (*d*) the adoption, as a result of these conditions, of what, by means of experience and reasoning, has been achieved by other peoples; (*e*) the irrepressible tendency to express the complex in which the individual's vital consciousness and his internal and external circumstances are integrated. The kind of belief I am speaking of here (in addition to faith in the supernatural) is one that embraces the total vital horizon of the person: he believes in the king, in the caste, in honor, in tradition, in an imported ideology, in a Messianic revolution, in the importance of his own person, in a nationalism at times void of content, and so on.

As an example of the first manifestation of the dwelling place of life mentioned above, we may recall such passages as one from Fray Diego de Valencia (at the end of the fourteenth century): if the

Castilians should unite, he says, "I know of no single corner in the world that they could not conquer, including all Granada." Or this one, from Gómez Manrique, before 1468: "May Christ allow our king to conquer the lands Cismaritime and Outremer held by barbarous nations."[27] Many other such expressions could be cited, but I shall refrain from providing further examples at this time of what is developed at length in the course of this book.

---

[27] For these and other passages expressing the Messianic imperialism that becomes a reality in the histories of Spain and Portugal, see my *Aspectos del vivir hispánico* (Santiago de Chile: Cruz del Sur, 1949).

V · A HISTORY OF INNER CONFIDENCE AND INSECURITY

THE PEOPLE WHO around the twelfth century began to be called "Spanish" came to be so designated thanks to their faith in the vigor of their indomitable spirit and in the value of the beliefs upon which they affirmed their militant drive. At the same time the geographic and human situations created in the course of centuries as a result of that militancy never served as the basis for security and satisfaction nor gave promise of a stable, well-rounded future. For that reason we see the constant necessity of passing beyond territorial boundaries, of desiring a "plus ultra" bound by no possible limits. But in the end, as we have already seen, that past filled with so tense an existence was always felt to be dubious and, in large measure, empty. In the fifteenth century the history of the reconquest appeared to Fernán Pérez de Guzmán, a highly gifted man of no small significance, as "sad and tearful." In 1600 Mariana would remember that the Catholic King Ferdinand of Aragon was strongly censured for having expelled the Jews. In the nineteenth and twentieth centuries, the last three or four hundred years of Spanish life have been viewed with anger and disappointment. And if the past never completely satisfied the most intelligent, the future always depended for the majority on some Messianic illusion and not on what planning and quiet, premeditated effort might achieve for the welfare and profit of the kingdom or of the nation. It is this I am thinking of when I state that the history of the Spaniards has been the history of insecurity.

Life, whether it be that of one individual or of many, is always insecure, for there is nothing more problematical than the very fact of human existence. But I am not now referring to that type of insecurity. We know, or should know, that as early as the twelfth century Ibn Ḥazm, the Muslim of al-Andalus (not an Andalusian), had said that being a man consists, essentially and radically, in anxiety about one's own life and how to prolong it. Man's life is the continued striving to find an escape from, or a solution to, the difficulties, small or large, which come upon him. But that insecurity, which man must dispel at every moment, is not the object of my present concern. I am dealing with a secondary, second-rank, insecurity that has to do with the value conferred on what exists around the person, on the very possibility that the person can face up to the problems before him. Tacitly or expressly the person asks himself about the possibilities of dealing with the problems presented to him.

The Visigoths in Hispania (which was still not Spain) and the Franks in Gaul (which was still not France)—lands that until shortly before had been Roman—attempted to affirm and constitute their respective kingdoms as Goths and as Carolingian Franks. The latter succeeded in doing so, and the result was France; the former did not because they had been conquered militarily and politically by the Muslims. Those who later initiated new forms of political existence no longer did so as Visigoths but as Christians—so says the Chronicle of *ca.* 880. Islamic lights and shadows had already been projected onto a piece of the Occident in the north of the Peninsula; and the consequences would be immeasurable for the people who were beginning a plan for national life, not now as Romans or as Goths, but under a religious banner tinted with Oriental hues.

The first result of the juxtaposition and confusion of religious and secular motivations was that, in addition to the peoples inhabiting the Asturian region (to the north of the future Castile, close to the Pyrenees, in the future Catalonia), other groups resisting the Muslims came together as Christians, as united in the transcendental world of their faith, not in the world of earthly connections (under a king or an emperor). The precarious political unity of the Christian zone was a function of the divisive nature of the politico-religious structure of al-Andalus even before it was broken up into small *taifa* states after the fall of the caliphate. Thus the political disunity of the Peninsular peoples is not due to the mythical "Iberian particularism," nor do modern separatist movements have their origin in the incipient disintegration of the Spanish Empire already evident in the seventeenth century. Such separatism exists because the Empire never truly united Portugal with Spain, or Catalonia and other regions with Castile—or only unified them halfway. Evidently the problem is one of initial structure, at least in its decisive aspects. The fact that at times concomitant circumstances aggravate the difficulty does not invalidate what has been obvious for many centuries now.

Another consequence, as obvious as the previous one, was that other collectivities defined and denominated by their religion (i.e., the Moors and Jews) came to share their life with others who were fighting against their Moorish or Christian neighbors. The system of the three castes was also linked to the Islamic model of the common life of the "peoples of the book" (the Koran, the Old Testament, the New Testament). Without such a system the Christian kingdoms would not have been able to organize themselves or, in the long run, even to endure. The military caste of the knights continued to develop its energies with an intensity and a degree of specialization proportional to the freedom of movement provided it by those people in the rear guard (Moors, Jews, or French priests) who devoted themselves to technology, administered funds, and cultivated the intellectual tasks.

In the fifteenth century Gutierre Díez de Games described this process of specialization among Old Testament peoples; it is a description that applies equally as well to the society of his own day:

The patriarchs came to decide that when they should go into battle, they would set men in high places who should oversee the battles as they went on, that they might know those who fought with a good will, and gave good blows, and bore fear, and did not hesitate before death but rather were firm. And when the battles were done, they took those men and set them apart and gave them great thanks and did them much honor because they had fought so well. And they made them go with their leaders to their own lands, and commanded them *not to take up any other occupation* but that . . . , and that they should apply themselves only to that. . . . And all the peoples honored them and loved them much, and called them *hombres de bien* ["men of nobility"].[1]

These *hombres de bien* are strongly reminiscent of the *fijos d'algo* or *hijos de bien* ("children of wealthy or noble origin"), a Castilian expression translated from the Hebrew *ben tovim* or *hijo de bienes* ("son of nobility and wealth"), as I have pointed out before (see also chapter vii).

In this way a "subregionalism" was produced within each politically delimited region (i.e., each Christian kingdom); but neither the subregionalisms nor the political regions were stably constituted through a system of vertical hierarchies sustained by horizontal interrelations and interest. In Spain, from the beginning, there was a fundamental division at the political level into separate Christian kingdoms and within them into social groups that actually show a caste structure; but neither the kingdoms nor the castes (Christian warriors and hidalgos; Jewish physicians, administrators, and businessmen; Moorish artisans, merchants, and muleteers) were fused in a uniform system of social hierarchy. Furthermore, in proportion as the activities of the politically dominant caste were gaining in importance, the other two castes were losing their importance and

---

[1] *El Victorial: Crónica de don Pero Niño*, ed. J. Mata Carriazo, p. 5.

in the end were violently crushed (witness the expulsion of the Jews and Moors).

Thus, in other words, from its beginning, from the moment in which certain human groups felt themselves bound together by a common task and called themselves Castilians, Leonese, Aragonese, and so on, the lives of all of them were being established on foundations of insecurity. Interstate disunity among the several kingdoms, the risks of the Islamic frontier, and the heterogeneity of the three castes of believers within each kingdom caused internal situations of discontent. It is not possible, therefore, to attribute the consciousness of insecurity to the "decadence" of the seventeenth century because the reality of the preceding centuries was expressed in the events set forth here. After centuries had passed, it became habitual for people to feel they had to be one way and constantly comport themselves in another way. The existential anxiety became chronic and is evidenced once again in Bartolomé de las Casas' phrase that the Spaniards should "be and not be" in the Indies; they *should be* there in order to maintain the royal sovereignty, and they *should not be* there in order not to corrupt Christian religion and faith by their conduct.[2]

All that has gone before permits us to understand why even a number of illustrious writers have considered wide areas of the Spanish past worthless. There exists, for example, a "canonical" version of the history of England, or of France, based upon certain formal characteristics and upon values that are accepted by everyone as perfectly valid. The Englishman, or the Frenchman, views his past with a firm belief in its validity, a belief reflected in apparently well-established formulas such as empiricism and pragmatism, or rationalism and clarity. Until about 1935 the major peoples of Europe lived, and to a great extent still live, in the belief that they possessed a normal and progressive history founded on treasured premises that only a reckless outsider would dare to question. Every moment in the past is regarded as a preparation for a future of wealth, culture, and power.

But how different has been the history of the Iberian Peninsula. For three centuries mistresses of half a world, Spain and Portugal arrived at the present epoch with less political and economic vitality than, for example, Holland or Scandinavia, which are integral parts of highly polished Europe. The Hispano-Portuguese people have outlived the prestige of a past that is at once glorious and, for many, not a little enigmatic. The high level of their art and literature, and the personal and exemplary merit of their individuals, past and present, are widely recognized; their scientific and technical ac-

---

[2] The text was cited by Marcel Bataillon in another connection in *Charles-Quint et son temps* (1959), p. 84.

complishments have less prestige; and their economic and political competence is visibly negligible. The past, when contemplated from what might thus be called a problematical present, turns into a pure problem itself, one that compels the observer to look more sharply, for, seemingly, even the most prodigious deeds of remote Hispanic history prophesy an inevitable ultimate decline.

The past is felt to be the augury of nothing assured—nothing assured, that is, with respect to material prosperity and to the feeling of happy placidity to which the nineteenth-century European grew more and more accustomed as the century went on. But the past augurs certainly and affirmatively with respect to the Spaniard's capacity for creating forms to express the awareness of his existence, or the conflict between the stability and precariousness of human existence. The rigorous thought that served other Europeans to penetrate into the problem of being and of the rational utilization of nature had as its counterpart for the Spaniard an impulse to express the consciousness of his existence in his own world. Instead of contemplating with clear vision the timeless present of being, the Spaniard lives his life out as an anxious movement through the vast region of the ought-to-be. The characteristically European activity of doing and reasoning, in which the agent or thinker is unmindful of his presence in his work, has as its counterpart in Spain a personalized activity which is not evaluated according to its useful results, but rather according to what the person involved is or wants to be, whether hidalgo, mystic, artist, dreamer, or conqueror of new worlds to include within the panorama of his own life. The Spaniard has always lived either in the tension of the actual performance of deeds of valor or in the expression of opportunities to perform them, opportunities that, for most people, never come. The degenerate aspect of all this is to be seen in three types: the *picaro*, the vagabond, and the idler, who had all fallen into a state of inert passivity. There is a profound meaning in the Spanish saying, "either prince or peasant," that is to say, either to be exalted to the highest degree, or to sit idly by and watch the years as they move through the orbit of an indifferent destiny.

It is understandable that such a structure of life[3] should always be a

---

[3] "Life" does not mean here "biological or temporal life" but the reality of man, the human, as distinguished from the physical or animal, existence. Four main aspects are involved: (1) the inescapable acceptance or rejection of the possibilities life always faces; (2) the faculty of planning and creating even against instinctive or physical urges; (3) the incorporation of the effects of all such living activity into the very course of life's progress; (4) the appearance to our consciousness of any given life, either individual or collective, as a function whose consistency is inseparable from its structure. To illustrate, if a ship, its engine, its rudder, its captain, the shipyard, the port from which it sails, the course of the ship as determined by the ship's seaworthiness and the weather conditions could all be integrated into a single idea-intuition, the

problem for the very people who were living it, filled, as they were, with uncertainty and passionate desire. For Spain was a part of Europe, with which she was in close contact, and with which she continually interacted. In one way or another Spain has never been apart from Europe; yet her physiognomy has always been peculiar, though not with the peculiarity that characterizes England with respect to France, or France with respect to Germany or Holland. The direct consequence of such phenomena is the fact that it has not been possible to arrange the history of Spain into a structure valid for all peoples. A sharp relativism characterizes everything that refers to her: in her own people, arrogance, melancholy, suspicion, and ill temper toward foreigners; in foreigners, an air of disdain, a stubborn incomprehension, an inexactness of statement that has amounted to calumny, and at times an unrestrained enthusiasm. The Spaniards themselves, in an amazing reaction, have forged a legendary history that permits them to elude the presence of their authentic past.

If we take as a criterion of historical judgment the rich and useful pragmatism of the past century, the Spanish past consists in a series of political and economic errors, the results of which were failure and decadence, which the other European peoples avoided because they were free from bellicose-religious passion and static and seigno-rial personalism. The wonderful works whose creation has been made possible by the Hispanic life stream are admired without cavil only when they attain the extreme limits of perfection (Cervantes, Velázquez, Goya), and when they do not run against the inability to understand, the vanity, or the interests of other, more powerful, countries. But it will not be freely admitted, for example, that in several Hispanic-American countries there were cities that, by reason of their extraordinary architecture, were the most beautiful in America, for this would force the admission that the Spanish domination was not merely a matter of colonial exploitation. Similarly the surprised delight that Baron von Humboldt took in the Hispanic world a century and a half ago has not found its way into our books nor into the conversations of our contemporaries. The way has been blocked by the Anglo-Americans' attitude of superiority, and by the resentment of the majority of Spanish-Americans, who find in

---

result would be approximately the kind of notion I am trying to convey, a notion not to be grasped solely by logical reason.

The word "vital" as I use it does not mean "important." I use it in its strictly etymological sense, "of or pertaining to life," with "life" to be understood according to my explanation above. "Live," "living," and related words should be understood within the same frame of reference.

It should further be observed that I do not use the word "structure" in the sense of configuration or outline (Gestalt), but with the meaning of "functional disposition," open and endowed with movement.

the colonial past an easy excuse for their present social and technical weakness. A further obstacle is the state of awareness in which Spain has lived with respect to herself and her past. On the other hand, the missions, forts, and government buildings in Louisiana, Florida, Texas, New Mexico, and California—trifling leftovers from the banquet table of Spain's artistic greatness—are preserved by North Americans with a care and tenderness that neither Spain nor Spanish America shows with respect to her inestimable treasures.

Thus, matters that have been considered beyond dispute in the Spanish past are often not really so. For almost three hundred years the best paintings of El Greco have remained buried under indifference, paintings conceived in, and because of, Spain; and it was not until the twentieth century that El Greco's art entered the realm of universal values. So far as literary history is concerned, the value of the seventeenth-century Spanish theater was revealed by foreigners, while my own teachers thought that the *Soledades* and the *Polifemo* of Don Luis Góngora were nothing but the vagaries of a sick and capricious mind. A critical appraisal more in accord with the artistic truth, a judgment that today is beginning to be shared by Spaniards as well as foreigners, has begun to reach the public only in the past thirty years. All this proceeds from the fact that the greatest phenomena of Spanish civilization cannot be appraised rationally, but only vitally; and thus it is that nothing makes its appearance in Spanish history which is undisputed and securely established.

The fact is that Spanish life, with radical personalism as its foundation, and in contact with the European world based on the victory of man over natural obstacles, fell into a state of progressive despair and of apathy with respect to everything that did not express the awareness of the individual's life. In the seventeenth century, and even before, the Spaniard had begun to feel the inanity of his collective achievements;[4] ever since then Spanish national life has consisted in trying to ward off the blows of an evil destiny, which is to say that Spain has continually opposed the irresistible advance of those who have habitually projected reason into life and who, with their technology, have constructed the powerful Western states of modern time. But in spite of the melancholy reflections of Quevedo and many other writers, Spanish mettle continued to extend the Empire and keep it on its feet throughout the eighteenth century. When Spain lost her dominions in America in 1824, the Spaniards in Hispanic America were in a position to take over the inheritance of

---

[4] Don Francisco de Quevedo wrote on August 21, 1645: "Very bad news, and passing bad, is written in from everywhere, and the worst of it is that everyone was expecting it to be this way. There are many things that, while seeming to exist and have being, are now nothing but a name and a shape" (*Obras en prosa*, ed. Astrana Marín, p. 1616).

three centuries of civilizing colonization, in spite of the persistent attacks of England, France, and Holland. This means that the line of the critical and anguished reflections of Spanish thinkers did not coincide with the vital impulse of those other Spaniards who as late as the eighteenth century (in a nation that was on its home ground almost a desert and a pauper) pressed the extension of Spanish sovereignty in Louisiana and California, and brought about at home the cultural renascence of the reign of Charles III, with its books, sciences, buildings, and to climax the whole, the extraordinary genius of a Goya. The usual criteria lose meaning when they are applied to the history of Spain, whose existence has always been locked within the antagonistic and enigmatic embrace of living and dying, a mode of existence which I do not, by any means, consider valueless.

We find ourselves, then, facing a history that at once both affirms and destroys itself in one swan song after another. In 1499 the desperate, vanishing soul of Spanish Jewry poured itself out in the immortal *Celestina*, a work by the Jewish convert Fernando de Rojas. In 1605, in the twilight that played upon the scene where the Renaissance was struggling with forces that opposed its spirit, the *Quixote* appeared as the eternal incarnation of the rationally impossible made possible poetically. At the end of the eighteenth century, in an empire already a skeleton and shadow of itself, Goya rose above all the ruins with the unique art of his painting. Near the start of the twentieth century, Spain was described by Lord Salisbury as a "moribund nation," but precisely during this death agony a movement was gathering the strength that would enable it, in the realm of the arts, the sciences, and philosophy, to obtain for Spain by the year 1930 an international repute not enjoyed since the sixteenth century. There is no similar example of so patent a contradiction between living and not living, all the more strange if one thinks of the mass of internal and external causes that, from the seventeenth century on, "logically" ought to have reduced Hispania to a land of peasants, of fellahs, with no possibility of interesting visitors except for her ruins and her picturesque customs.

One must not be surprised, then, if so strange a kind of history can be examined only if we somewhat forget for a while ideas of material progress and decadence, political power, and technological efficiency. Since the seventeenth century, the exclusive predominance of the Old Christian caste has gone hand in hand with cultural stagnation and the decay of the collective will. Outside the Peninsula, Holland and the Franche Comté broke away from the Spanish Crown; then, inside the Peninsula, the example of the Portuguese secession in 1640 was all but followed by Catalonia. The myth of a universal empire sustained by the Catholic faith—and this faith rather as it was *felt* by the Spaniards than it was *understood* by the Church of Rome, regardless of the dogmatic agreement between one and the other—had lost its efficacy. Once the solidity of the collective will was cracked in the seventeenth century, it was never again put back together. From then on, some Spaniards would want one thing, and others, the opposite.[5] Many desired nothing at all, and lived in the inertia of custom and belief, without worrying about doing or learning anything new; in some parts of Spain in the twentieth century, people were still plowing with the Roman plow and threshing with oxen.

Although I return later on to a problem that is so central, what I have said will serve, I hope, as a warning not to apply here the usual methods for understanding history. I mean such notions as this: that civilizations are born, they progress, they wither. To understand this, let us take the example of France, in one sense near to Spain and in another, remote. The goal of the French people had been from the eleventh century to constitute a nation united under royal authority, and embracing politically everything that French civilization and language had previously conquered in a conquest that found more inspiration in earthly interests than in religious beliefs. From Henry IV on, the national aspiration was rationalized, and the learned class, strongly supported by the monarchy—following the neostoic pattern of the Renaissance—took charge of the direction of the masses. From that time on people were to live and even to talk according to rationally established principles, uniform for everyone, through whose channels authority would automatically descend from the Crown at the peak to the least of the subjects. The idea of the state (absolute monarchy) and so-called classicism in literature are aspects of the same impulse. In France, living consisted in knowing and applying the principles deduced by an autonomous reason according to a logical, rigorous, and clearly explainable process. Every human act with a collective dimension would have to fit into schemes previously worked out, even at the cost of the greatest sacrifices. All the words that the savants said should be excluded were in fact destined to be excluded from the language, and thus the French language of earlier centuries was to become unintelligible. Man was converted into a reflective being who paid scant attention to elemental, varied, and individualized living.[6] Art and public life followed rigorous norms. There came a day when

---

[5] In the eighteenth century some tried to raze the edifice of mythic and arational culture by importing the rationalist Enlightenment, but most people preferred to continue within the tradition that was falling into ruin.

[6] La Rochefoucauld's pen ran away with him once when he was writing, and his manuscript reads: "comme *les rhumes* et les maladies contagieuses." The printed text reads simply "maladies contagieuses," an abstract concept that eliminates the connotation of coughs, sneezes, and sniffling. We are in the kingdom of "bon goût."

rationalism decided that it was necessary to lop off heads, beginning with the king, and thus it was done. Later the geographical division of the country was made uniform, as were education, customs, and even manners. French history, in its essential aspects, has been lived by rule and compass, and thus France became a great nation. To articulate and explain a history that is so open and obvious in its structure is a relatively easy task. The will to power was allied with the proposal to know. Hence the heights of genius attained by rational thought (Descartes); hence the impossibility of France's producing a work of art that embraces the totality of all that is human, which is rational thought plus bold and fearless immoderation. Nothing in France is comparable to Dante, Michelangelo, Cervantes, Shakespeare, or Goya.

With an analogous method, although we would confront greater complexities, we could schematize the history of England and of the other peoples of western Europe; but when we come to Spain, such procedures serve only to a very limited extent, and we must take rougher paths. They must be taken because whatever, in the last analysis, may be the vital structure of those other peoples (it is not my purpose to deal with them), it would always be true that to their history as we view it today are conjoined the optimism and confidence of the historian, as the result of a sustained and ascending process of evaluation. The historian takes as his starting point his intuition that France (let us take her as an example) is a successful section of humanity, and thanks to this a priori optimism it can even happen that he will overvalue things that would be underestimated if nineteenth-century France had been a poor and powerless nation. When one is a great and powerful lord, even the nonsense that one says passes for wit and wisdom. Thinking coldly—that is, antivitally —one would see that the larger part of the innumerable volumes of Voltaire are full of insignificant prose and verse. But no, since Voltaire enjoyed well-deserved prestige—based on several admirable works—and also because of the intellectual rule he exercised at a time that was suited for it, it is not the custom to point out the enormous mass of commonplaces and insipidities that fill his excessive production. Yet, on the other hand, many of us have dared to attack Lope de Vega for his excessive fecundity, his haste in composing plays, his superficiality, and many other failings. Many years ago I wrote elsewhere that if Spain had possessed a powerful armed force and economic resources, the tone of foreign historians would have been otherwise. But it is so because life is so, and we can neither play with it nor escape it.

An essential factor in the history that one writes is the vital attitude of the historian within the time in which he writes. In the sixteenth century, the Seigneur de Brantôme adjudged the meals and inns in Spain to be excellent, while Cervantes and many others thought they left much to be desired. The enthusiasm of Brantôme does not surprise us, who know the vital attitude of that strange personage. And this does not mean that we are falling into any kind of relativism, and another name must be found for it. What we are trying to do, in fact, is to express in an acceptable way the integration of vital phenomena into the "dwelling place of life" which made those phenomena worthy of historical treatment.

Vivir Desviviéndose

Many people would prefer Spain's history to have been different from what it was; for centuries Spain's life has consisted in a desire to "unlive" the past, to escape from itself, as if life could retrace its steps. This process of denial of one's own life (which in Spanish I have called *desvivirse*) rises out of dissatisfaction with the course of life, out of a ceaseless wondering as to whether in truth the desired goal has been achieved—or whether it is possible to achieve it. I must repeat that the Spaniards are perhaps the only Occidental people who consider many events and entire centuries of their history to be worthless or unfortunate; they have seldom experienced the enjoyable satisfaction of living in complete harmony with their fellow citizens. In such circumstances people live with the feeling that, instead of proceeding onward, life should move backward, should begin its course anew. It is uncomfortable for the Spaniards that there should have been Moors and Jews or an Austrian dynasty; for the Catalans, that there should have been the Compromise of Caspe,[7] and so on. Time and time again the Spaniard has expressed the lack of proportion and congruity between the intensity of his impulses and the stability or worth of the results achieved. Nor should any of this be confused with the emotions described by St. Theresa with the term "desvivirse"; for her it simply meant that she lived in anguish because death would not come and allow her to see God.

Two literary characters, Don Quixote and Don Juan, are excellent examples of the Spanish attitude of "desvivirse." Don Quixote, tireless in his search for the tempestuous, active life, finally says when he is near the end of his days: "Up to now I do not know what I have conquered by dint of my labors" (II, 58). We know, though, that the greatest conquest made by Cervantes, that inventor of uncertainties, was the discovery of the awareness of human consciousness, a consciousness enriched by all the literary experiences of the

---

[7] On June 28, 1412, nine electors met at Caspe (Aragon) to select the successor to King Martin. Ferdinand, the brother of Henry III of Castile, was chosen as king of Aragon.

inner self provided by the sixteenth-century Spanish writers.

Don Juan, seemingly immersed in love affairs, scarcely touches the surface of them when he is already fleeing, unable to linger for any of them. So constant is this mode of behavior that we must ask ourselves whether his life is not defined more by repeated flight than by successful conquest, for the flight is clearly implicit in all the conquests. And Don Juan, the creator par excellence of sweet but fleeting moments of insecurity, exclaims before he dies: "Alas, I wear myself out vainly striking at the air!"

Before we can consider any single historical feature of a people, we must have a view of that people as a whole and of that people's values. Even this does not guarantee that we will be able to answer all the questions we may be asked, but it is this principle that leads me now to pursue the understanding of the facts of Spain rather than the knowledge of those facts. For many long years I have written now and again about specific aspects of linguistic, literary, religious, and even pedagogical history inside the Hispanic world. Yet, when some time ago (about 1940) I was asked to express in an essay my ideas concerning the Renaissance in Spain, I saw clearly, as never before, that such a task was impossible if it was not articulated, illuminated, in a general view of Hispanic history. Otherwise one would fall into anecdote and arbitrariness, into denigration or overestimation. For this reason, my projected article on the Renaissance has been converted into the present book—a personal detail of no interest which I mention only to emphasize the importance that I attach to insight and my lesser zeal for gathering snippets of information. It might be justly said that one of the characteristics of the present time is the imperfect balance between what we "know" and what we "understand."

Converts from Judaism Express the "Ought-To-Be" of Spanish Life

Once the meaning of events has been thoroughly examined, their ordered structure becomes apparent. After the violent reaction of 1391, the Judaic dream of grandeur and supremacy, cherished for so many centuries before, became ever less attainable. But the habit, by then so ancient, of feeling and being important was reincarnated in the converts of the fifteenth century, some of whom did everything in their power to influence Castilian policy. When this situation has been realized, a relationship derived from similarity of purpose may be established among various works that, up to now, have been looked upon as isolated phenomena that do not fit into the life of the Spanish past. In the first place, there is the *Laberinto de Fortuna* of the convert Juan de Mena, a work "planned to act on 'famous knights' and on the king, John II; the ethic defended by Mena is essentially for the nobles with special emphasis on the qualities that are most suitable for war and governing."[8] Lapesa rightly observes that the work is divided into units in each of which "a virtue or vice is defined which the king is advised in the last stanza of the section to encourage or repress" (*ibid.*). This piece of high-minded poetry was aimed—as its structure shows it—at lifting its author to the heights of the Christian caste. This seems to have been the only way for the three castes to live together at the moment when religious tolerance was at the brink of going to pieces. The convert endowed with culture sought the support of kings and grandees just as his ancestors had done, and from that eminence he set forth in his writings, for the first time in literary history, the "problem of Spain." It may thus be concluded that the condition of being a convert is not an erudite detail that can be dismissed; it is, on the contrary, a functional element that must be integrated into the very purpose of the artistic creation.

This is so generally true that, proceeding inversely, the possibility may exist of detecting Jewish ancestry in the fifteenth-century writer who is interested in political problems and in advising the king, as in the case of Mosén Diego de Valera, about whom I speak later. The chroniclers Alonso de Palencia and Hernando del Pulgar were converts; it is likely that Diego Enríquez del Castillo was one also and very probable that the furiously anti-Jewish Andrés Bernáldez, so well informed about Jewish activities, should be included among their number.

Similar in purpose to Juan de Mena's work, distinguished for its rhythm and for the lofty flight of its images, are the doggerel lines of the convert Juan Alfonso de Baena in the "Dezir" composed to move the spirit of King John II in favor of the Infantes of Aragon. The author says that he comes from Baena,

> where I learned to scribble verse
> and to eat caper berries
> many times after dinner.[9]

Baena claims to lighten the King's labors:

> Exalted King: if you read
> and observe well this my suit,
> . . . I believe you will find
> great pleasure and refreshment,
> for with it you will be eased
> of the work today you have. (st. 2)

---

[8] Rafael Lapesa, "El elemento moral en el *Laberinto* de Mena," *Hispanic Review*, XXVII (1959), 262.

[9] See the paleographic edition of J. Piccus in *Nueva Revista de Filología Hispánica*, XII (1958), 339.

He calls for the attention of Old Christians of the upper class:

> Exalted King: I beg and ask
> the nobles of condition,
> *pure-blooded hidalgos*, men
> of selected lineage,
> that they do not forget
> to observe my words. (st. 8)

Despite what slanderers may say,

> . . . I swear by Jesus Christ,
> may this work be long remembered,
> that never in all Spain,
> was such a one ever seen. (st. 9)

The author lists the writers he has read (whom some editors of this "Dezir" should identify in order to give us an idea of the scope of Hispano-Jewish cultural tradition at that moment), among them the *General Estoria*, the *Ethics* of Aristotle, Macrobius, Horace (his "philosophical" works), the Arabic astronomer Ibn-al-Zarqāli, and the "musical cadences of the Provençals" (stanzas 15–19). Equipped with so much knowledge (real or pretended), Baena feels himself authorized to tell the King:

> Your kingdom is suffering
> from so great infirmity
> that it burns more than the flame. (st. 41)

He urges the monarch to imitate the conduct of Alfonso VIII:

> and what King Don Alfonso
> has done, you should do also. (st. 51)

The memory of the Battle of Las Navas de Tolosa should inspire John II, son of Henry III, who died at the moment when

> he was going to attack
> with boldness against the Moors. (st. 119)

He urges John II to "make war on the Moors" (st. 152) and not to fall back once he has begun.

In sum, Baena addresses himself as a court counselor to the mind of the King with a view toward promoting more warlike activity and enterprises of high imperial scope. Involved in such affairs, envisioning itself to be a moral and technical instrument of Spanish expansion, the Jewish caste considered itself sheltered against the waves of "little people," "common people," all those who since the end of the fourteenth century had been preparing to devour it. With money and advice, the converts would sustain the conquest of Granada and the voyage of Columbus as well as the great international strategy of Ferdinand the Catholic, which was strongly supported by his secretary of state, the convert Miguel Pérez de Almazán.

In this light we can see better how the Castile of the fifteenth century, in the writings of some converts of more or less importance (I can mention only a few of them), shows itself to be taking on consciousness of what it is, of what it does not have, of its congenital insecurity.

The converts felt and foresaw that Castile had rounded the cape of uncertainty in its struggle with Islam, and that a splendor-filled future was approaching. Precisely at that time they made themselves spokesmen for the conscience of Spain and began to be concerned about the form of Spain's existence as well as with what Spain had to do in order to exist. In 1459 the well-known humanist Alonso de Palencia, a Jewish convert, wrote that Spain was a "province that is not inclined to take rational points of view," and this he said in a book significantly entitled *Perfección del triunfo militar* ("Perfection of Military Triumph").[10]

But much earlier, in 1434, Don Alonso de Cartagena, Bishop of Burgos, had written a famous discourse delivered by the Castilian envoy at the Council of Basel justifying the precedence of Castile with respect to England. His allegation brings us the first description of the inner functioning of Castilian society. As is well known, Don Alonso was a New Christian, or convert, and the son of another illustrious convert, Don Pablo de Santa Maria, who had occupied a very high position among the Spanish Jews and attained a rank of equal eminence in the Church. Without entering now into the complexity of that fact, let us note that Don Alonso, great jurist that he was, argued like a good diplomat filled with patriotic fervor; for centuries the Spanish Jews had stood out as excellent ambassadors of the Christian and Moslem kings. Let no one believe that the Bishop of Burgos wrote an insincere speech for the Basel audience. His works were an overflow of Hispanic awareness, and the preferences and contempt expressed in them are the very ones that were characteristically Spanish then and for long afterward: "Spaniards are not wont to prize great wealth, but rather, virtue; nor do they measure a man's honor by the store of his money but rather by the quality of his beautiful deeds; wherefore riches are not to be argued in this matter [as the English argued them]; for if we should mete out the precedences according to riches, Cosimo de' Medici, or some other very rich merchant, mayhap would come before some duke."[11] These words make it clear that the Hebrew caste, now

---

[10] In *Libros de Antaño*, V, 144.

[11] "Discurso pronunciado por don Alonso de Cartagena en el Concilio de Basilea acerca del derecho de precedencia del Rey de Castilla sobre el rey de Inglaterra" ("Discourse pronounced by Don Alonso de Cartagena at the Council

transformed into Christians, had absorbed the value judgments of the Christian caste, while preserving the Semitic tendency to speak about the real and concrete from a personal, intimate point of view.

The spirit of nobility, united with a scorn for commercial activities, already marks the abyss that will separate Spain from capitalist Europe: so far as this convert was concerned, Cosimo de' Medici was but a contemptible merchant. Don Alonso gives the impression that Castile was very sure of herself: "The kings of Spain—amongst which the principal and first and greatest one is the King of Castile and Leon—have never been subject to the Emperor; for this singularity do the kings of Spain have, that they have never been subject to the Holy Roman Empire, nor to any other, but rather have they won and raised up their kingdoms out of the jaws of their enemies" (p. 214), a very acute observation whose meaning becomes apparent later. "In the time of the Goths, many of the princes of Spain were called emperors" (p. 215). Actually, however, Leon and Castile were only nominally a continuation of the Visigothic kingdom; for their spiritual strength and their political titles, including the imperial ones, had their foundation in the city of Santiago, the resting place of St. James the Apostle, which was for those monarchs what Rome was to the Holy Roman Empire. For Don Alonso de Cartagena the strength of Castile was founded less on material realities than on the spiritual and transcendent virtue of the monarchy; otherwise it would not have occurred to him to bring up as a great Spanish merit, against England, that "the Castilians and Galicians and Biscayans are different nations, and they use completely different languages" (p. 350). In this statement is implicit the idea that was to be expressed a century later by the convert Gonzalo Fernández de Oviedo, to wit, that the only thing that harmonized the discordant variety of the Hispanic peoples was the fact that they were subjects of the king of Spain. Moreover, in the words of the Bishop of Burgos can be traced already the future imperial policy of Charles V, a policy aimed at the spreading of a belief rather than at the establishment of a system of human interests: "The lord and king of England, although he makes war, yet does not make that *divine* war, . . . for it is neither against the infidels nor for the glorification of the Catholic faith, nor for the *extension of the boundaries of Christianity, but rather is it made for other interests*" (p. 353).[12] This Semite belief is

---

of Basel, Concerning the Right of Precedence of the King of Castile over the King of England"), in the journal *La Ciudad de Dios*, XXXV (1894), 122–542.

[12] See also *ibid.*, p. 526. There are other curious observations on England: "Even though it may be a noteworthy island (for it is called *Anglia*, which some say means 'more vainglorious of' money'), there are not in it so many provinces nor such broad ones" (p. 349). I know no basis for Don Alonso's curious semantic interpretation of "Anglia," but the legend of "English gold" is, for that matter, quite ancient.

a firm base upon which rises the collective life; its efficacy in the long struggle against the infidel brought riches and power, reflected in turn in the spectacular prestige of the monarchy and its surrounding aureole of nobility: "I say nothing here concerning the beauty and grandeur of his court, for, to speak reverently and without offense of all the princes, I could say that in that part of the world known to us, except that it be for the tumult and movement of warfare, there is no prince's court so much visited and so full of so many prelates and counts and barons and other noblemen, and of such a throng of townspeople, as is the royal court of Castile" (p. 351). The court was like a temple to which one repaired to obtain earthly benefits, just as one visited the house of God to win heavenly favors; the supreme ideals that inspired the ruling caste showed their visible form in the nobility and the priesthood. Recounting such splendors, the Bishop of Burgos succeeded in persuading the Council of Basel to recognize the precedence of Castile with respect to England.

Against the Castilians, the English argued that their own land was richer and more productive, and to this the Bishop answered: "I did not wish to argue the abundance of land, because it seemed to me a *base argument* and far removed from our purpose, for it is not of peasants but of very noble kings that we are speaking; honor comes not from the abundance of the field but from the virtue of man" (p. 533). It is not easy for Don Alonso to descend to the plane of material things, but since the English wish it, he adduces

the vineyards and olive groves, of which there is a great abundance in the kingdom of Castile, and which have been exiled forever from the kingdom of England. . . . And all nations know the esteem that, amongst all the things that belong to the abundance of the earth, is enjoyed by wine and olive oil. If they should speak of those skilled in the making of cloths, I would perhaps grant them something, for *there are in our land no weavers who can make cloth so fine as London scarlet*; but even that product that we call *grana* [Kermes dye], from which the scarlet receives the sweetness of its odor and the flame of its color, has its birth in the kingdom of Castile, whence it is carried to England. . . . I might speak of metals, but in my judgment such a base and earthly argument is not proper to such an exalted subject (pp. 533–534).

In the last analysis, riches are something secondary, a possession that "abets in the exercise of virtue, but they are not to be adduced as a principal thing"; in any event, Castile is rich, perhaps in excess, since some fear lest "such an abundance of riches as there is today in Castile may do some harm to virtue." So that nothing may be lacking in this first and most faithful picture of the Hispanic soul—drawn by a Semite, it must not be forgotten—Don Alonso ends his harangue—for it is more this than an argument—with a gesture of supreme arrogance: "I shall bring no other evidence save this embassy, for from a poor kingdom such ambassadors do not usually come forth" (p. 536).

I do not believe that at the beginning of the fifteenth century any other European people had revealed so complete and precise an awareness of itself. Castile felt the ineluctable necessity to go forth into the world. With firm step and voice she faced those who tried to diminish her dignity; she recognized the primacy of the Holy Roman Empire, an ideal continuation of the Roman Empire, and of France, a direct outgrowth of the Carolingian Empire, but nothing more. Indirectly, nevertheless, the words of the Bishop of Burgos reveal, behind the arrogance of his attack, a passionate desire for justification and a defensive purpose—in other words, they reveal *insecurity*.

It is this element that appeared still more clearly in the confidential paper that Fernando de la Torre, also of Jewish lineage, addressed to Henry IV of Castile in 1455, when the latter was getting ready to inaugurate his reign.[13] This document seems to contain the first critical analysis of Spanish life and character, the first effort toward overt justification in the face of foreign censures, examples of which its author was forced to hear when he was at the court of Charles VII of France. Castile was beginning to acquire international renown, and she attracted the curiosity of other courts on the occasion, in 1453, of the execution of the constable Don Alvaro de Luna, the all-powerful favorite of Don Juan II. The French were unfavorably surprised by the fact that the constable had accumulated such a mass of riches in his castle of Escalona when not even the king of France possessed so much. Fernando de la Torre warms to the argument, highly pleased to contend "against the most great and excellent kingdom of Christians, which is that of France." What he writes is not a rhetorical harangue but rather an evaluative description of Spanish peculiarities. He mentions natural wealth: iron, steel, wool, wheat, wine, olive oil, fruit, mercury, and, to cap them all, "exceptional horses and mules." It seems at first that the author is going to give us one more version of the *Laudes Hispaniae*, so frequent in the Middle Ages, although one observes very soon how patriotism is combined with an attitude that is both critical and modern, formerly unthinkable. Besides, there is talk here not only of the products of the earth but also of the condition of the people.

The fifteenth century was an epoch of great changes, not the least of which was the incorporation of many converts into Christian society; in addition to the suprahuman, which had long been of

---

[13] See the *Cancionero y obras en prosa de Fernando de la Torre* ("Fernando de la Torre's Book of Songs and Prose Works"), published by A. Paz y Melia (Dresden, 1907).

interest, contemporary reality, that which exists within immediate time and space, was beginning to be interesting. The Marquis of Santillana composed a poem about a battle fought in his own times, the Battle of Ponza; and the *Romancero* provides a poetic gloss of events that are contemporary and nearby. The chroniclers were interested in the lives of contemporary personages (Don Alvaro de Luna, Pero Niño, the constable Miguel Lucas de Iranzo),[14] and they speak thus not only of the past but also of the current events that the people of the time had seen. It is from this new vital point of view that Fernando de la Torre launches into telling us for a second time what Spain is and how she appears to be when she is compared with other nations. His words have the tender charm of something newly born. As did Juan de Mena or Alonso de Baena—and still earlier, the Jew Santob de Carrión—a subject permits himself to advise his sovereign concerning what Castile expected of him; now, however, the argument is based on what the country really seems to be, and not on abstract ideas of virtue and good government. The thesis of Fernando de la Torre is that Castile (which to all intents and purposes was already Spain) possessed two supreme values: a provident and extremely fertile land and a magnificent courage in warfare. The fact is, nevertheless, that alongside these natural or spontaneous conditions there were rather serious limitations, for the value of Castile lay primarily in what it humanly *was*, and not nearly so much in what it produced with the labor of its people:

The vanity of the Castilians, intensified by their *pride*, and by the superabundance of their land, leads them to delight in luxuries and ostentation, and therefore they do not refrain from using the products manufactured in other lands out of Castilian raw materials. It is nothing to them to acknowledge that *such products are finished by foreigners with much finer polish.* Most of the products leave Castile in the shape of raw materials, and in the foreign lands they are turned into finished products, while in Castile people use and consume much more of such goods than in any other part of the world. As, for example, from the country of Flanders, satin, tournay cloth, tapestries, and fine cloths; from Milan, harnesses; from Florence, silk; from Naples, leather trappings for horses. They could easily do without all these things, or they could make them, *if they but wished to set about the task,* to judge by the great means that they have. For, there would be finished goods made out of wool and dyes and juicy plants and other things as are necessary, if the Castilians knew how to transform them technically as the Flemish do; for Castile has such primary materials. There would be iron and steel goods if they knew how to forge and temper them, as the Milanese do, for Castile has such primary materials. There would be goods of silk and silver with gold if they knew how to weave and fashion as the Florentines do, for it is

---

[14] The preoccupation with the biography of contemporaries appears in Fernán Pérez de Guzmán's *Generaciones y semblanzas* ("Generations and Portraits") and in Hernando del Pulgar's *Claros varones de Castilla* ("Worthy Men of Castile").

certain that the Castilians have such primary materials. There would be valuable leathers from the largest and finest bulls in the world, if they knew how to tan and dress them as the Neapolitans do, for there are such bulls and they are killed in Castile; and so with other things.

Castile *is* courageous, she *possesses* natural wealth, but she does not *make* things that demand ingenious effort. The weak style of Fernando de la Torre stiffens when he thinks of horses, the noble complement of the knight in warfare: "A perfect horse there is not in any other place except in Castile, for *heart*, body, and fleetness . . . ; for these qualities will not be found in the horses of Apulia, though they be taller and broader, and are even less to be found in the German ones, which are wild and have large heads, and still less in the Sicilian ones, which are neither swift, nor adequately suitable for battle."

But the author does not limit himself to enumerating merits and defects. With an inquiring mind and in a style inconceivable a hundred years earlier, he seeks to find a reason behind the Spaniards' lack of technical skill: "From whence does this emanate and proceed save from the fertility of the [Castilian] land and, in other kingdoms, from want. This want, the people know how, by their labors, to convert into wealth and income; and in Castile, the fatness of the land causes them, in a certain fashion, *to be proud and slothful and not so ingenious or industrious.*" That is, from necessity is born technology; and from the excess of easily obtained goods, pride and indolence. In 1455 a Hispano-Semite said for the first time and very crudely what was to be repeated for centuries both inside and outside the boundaries of Spain. The strange thing in this instance is that Fernando de la Torre, in order to compensate for the deficiencies in the deeds of his countrymen, converts the fertility of the soil into something magical and dazzling: "Not once a year but three times in some places does the earth or can the earth bear wheat, and the trees, fruit." Castile is sufficient to herself, whereas other peoples have to import what she produces. Yet even so, and in spite of the enthusiasm that he displays, de la Torre writes from a defensive position. He subtly perceives the difference between Spain and western Europe; he feels himself attacked, and he counterattacks. For the first time is posed the question, what is Spain and what is her worth, a question that is still open today. Into the conscious awareness[15] of his own history de la Torre incorporates his grief over feeling in-

---

15 "Conscious awareness" or "experiential awareness" is used here and hereinafter to translate Spanish *vivencia*, German *Erlebnis*, in the sense this word has in the works of Wilhelm Dilthey. The German word has been variously rendered into English by others as "livingness," "living experience," and "lived experience." An approximate definition of the term might be "one's awareness of one's own experience."

capable of providing certain cultural necessities; to be much, to do little.

We ought not for this reason to say that pessimism is predominant in our critic. If greatness does not come to Spain from her industrial skill and her commercial wealth, it does come from her lofty spirit and her grandeur, "for if you read the Roman histories, you will indeed find that from Castile have gone forth, and in Castile were born, men who were emperors of Rome, and not one, but seven [!]; and even in our own times we have seen in Italy and in France and in many other places very great and valiant captains."[16] This already sounds like the Messianic and imperial language that accompanied the heroic enterprises of the next century. Before Fernando de la Torre, Fray Diego de Valencia, another convert, had already said that if the Castilian people could agree among themselves,

> I know not a single corner in the world
> That they might not conquer, including all Granada.

And a little later Gómez Manrique (1468) desires Prince Alfonso to conquer Cismaritime lands and Outremer, from the barbarian nations.[17] The Spanish Empire, founded by Ferdinand and Isabella, was not a happy accident but the same form of Spanish living, enlarged at the moment when Spain was becoming conscious of herself vis-à-vis the other peoples of Europe; this consciousness, furthermore, had been expressed and enlarged by the Hispano-Semites since the time of Alfonso the Learned. A land of brave bulls, or horses with eyes and hearts of fire, a land filled with men who even in the fifteenth century caused wonderment with their deeds of prowess—was anything lacking? Impetuous valor, like boundless faith, is not satisfied with limits and national boundaries, for it seeks the infinite in time and space, precisely the opposite of what the reasoning mind pursues with its measurements, limitations, and conclusions. Castile,

---

[16] It may be noted how Fernando de la Torre confirms my belief that the conversion of the Romans in the Peninsula into mythical Spaniards arose out of the desire to compensate for certain deficiencies. The author was most likely thinking of knights such as Rodrigo de Villandrando, Count of Ribadeo, who fought magnificently in France without ceasing to be a loyal vassal of John II of Castile, or Don Pero Niño, Count of Buelna. In stanzas 198 and 199 of *Las Trescientas*, Juan de Mena mentions Juan de Merlo, a knight of the times of John II, who died fighting on the border of the Moorish kingdom of Granada, according to the commentary of Hernán Núñez, who adds that "once when there was war between the two kingdoms of France and Castile, the famous knight Juan de Merlo went out of the kingdom and, in Bala[?], a village in the County of Brabant between Germany and France, he challenged and conquered a German knight named Enrique de Remestién; and another time in Arras, he conquered an important knight named Mosior de Charni" (*Las CCC del famosísimo poeta Juan de Mena, con glosa* ["The Three Hundred of the Most Famous Poet Juan de Mena, with a Gloss"] / [Granada, 1505], fol. 99*r*). Literature does not register the activities of the Castilians in war in Europe before the fifteenth century.

[17] See my remarks in *Aspectos del vivir hispánico*, pp. 21-22.

in the middle of the fifteenth century, felt sure of her valor and her will, and she aspired to nothing less than an infinite dominion—"Cismaritime lands and Outremer." The Catalonian-Aragonese imperialism in the Mediterranean in the fourteenth and fifteenth centuries, and the Castilian and Portuguese in the fifteenth and sixteenth, provided tasks that gave satisfaction to certain wills that were untamable, and incapable of rationally modifying the natural world in which they found themselves. (The reason for this is apparent later.) The Castile of the fifteenth century craved only a leader who would bind together the dispersed wills of her people and sound the order to attack.[18] Hence de la Torre, avid for deeds of prowess, dared to advise the unfortunate Henry IV, a poor scrap of a king in a country clamoring for clear command and direction. But with great perspicacity the diligent counselor observes that the Castilian monarchy may aspire to high enterprises because it does not share its power with the great lords, as had been true of France, "for [the king] is the supreme authority in criminal and civil justice for all people; and although he may have granted a few towns and jurisdictions as favors to his dukes, counts, marquises, and other noblemen, the court of appeal and the sovereignty always remain attached or subject to his chancellery and royal crown." The king of France, on the other hand, lacked jurisdiction over the duke of Burgundy, and obtained from seven to eight hundred lances, at the most, in case of war. Thus it came about that the army of Castile was numerous and strong, for "there is not in the world another people so skillful at arms"; besides, it was the only army in which "horses and harnesses were continually maintained," even though there might be no war going on. This means that as early as the middle of the fifteenth century people noticed the Spanish peculiarity of possessing a kind of permanent army, which Ferdinand the Catholic further developed at the end of the century, thereby making Spanish expansion in Europe possible. De la Torre predicts that Castilian arms could take possession of "the nearby lands and *even those far removed*, if they would set themselves to the task with thought and hard work and unity."[19]

---

[18] Fernán Pérez de Guzmán was already lamenting that Henry III (1379–1406) did not "have the strength of body and spirit to prosecute the war" against Portugal and conquer that kingdom.

[19] Spanish Jews yearned for the imperial expansion of Castile, and wished for peace and concord inside their country—the dream of not being persecuted. Rabbi Arragel, glossing the Bible, thus ponders the fruits of harmony and mutual accord: "The people of that tower [of Babel], although they persisted against God and in their idolatries, yet were without hatred and ill-will one for another, and lived in concord, *and protected one another's goods*; wherefore our Lord wished that a memorial of them should remain; but those of the flood robbed one another, and despised one another; wherefore no memorial of them was left" (*Biblia*, trans. Rabbi Arragel [1422–1433?], published by the Duke of Alba [1920], I, 119*a*).

This does not occur "because of the sins and pride of the Spanish nobility, or because of the internal divisions among the grandees of Castile." Otherwise, the young king Henry IV would put "under royal subjection and hand that kingdom of Granada." Another convert, Juan de Lucena, urged the King on to similar militant enterprises in 1463: "The house is silent when the pigs are in the woods. . . . How glorious [would be] the king, how famous his vassals, how great the crown of Spain if the secular and regular clergy should go forth against Granada, and the knights with the king should burst through into Africa! . . . *Greater wealth would there be in accumulating kingdoms than in piling up treasure.*"[20] This passionate will to have a leader who would command and guide gave to the advent of Ferdinand and Isabella the air of a fulfilled "Semitic" prophecy, of a Messiah who at last appears. But these plans and longings proceeded from people who were urging the Christian caste on thoughtfully and with considered judgment from outside that caste. The complexity of the writers we have just analyzed, due to the fact that they belonged to two different castes at the same time, that even though members of the Jewish caste they exceeded Spaniards in their zeal for promoting Spanish greatness, could neither be seen nor evaluated so long as the composition and structure of Spanish society were ignored. The castes were integrated by the vision of great imperial enterprises precisely at the time when the shared common life of the castes was becoming impossible, and precisely at the moment when Spain was gaining an idea and an awareness of herself, thanks to certain people who would soon become the victims of their own shrewd observations and their eagerness to be preeminent.

But just as de la Torre previously described in detail the natural wealth of Spain, he now shows us with some insight the structure of the monarchical regime. The court is rich, and in its shelter live "infinite numbers of people who in time of peace are permanently employed in the royal house and court . . . ; with so much of ornaments and tapestries and tableware . . . that it is known to all people everywhere; and one must marvel at how even the common people are dressed and maintained."[21]

---

[20] *De vita beata*, ed. in *Bibliófilos Españoles*, pp. 126, 166.

[21] It is the moment of great luxury in living, unknown before John II. There is an awareness of wealth (as we have seen in de la Torre), Morisco customs are still in vogue (as I later point out), and the chivalric usages of France are imitated. The embellished expression of all this is found in the *Coplas* of Jorge Manrique:

Gifts unmeasured,	Las dádivas desmedidas,
The royal buildings	los edificios reales
Full of gold,	llenos de oro,
Dishes so burnished,	las vaxillas tan febridas,
The golden coins	los enriques y reales

Those who did not participate in such splendor, who were the majority, "*go about idly*; and not only in the court but in all towns, villages, and lands, *they are countless in number*; without robbing or stealing or doing any other evil deed, they are perpetually maintained out of the fatness of the land." It is evident that in order to dazzle the French chevaliers with whom he debated at the court of Charles VII, Fernando de la Torre sketched an idyllic picture, almost a picture out of the Golden Age, as he spoke of the host of vagabonds who simply lived off the provident earth. Although here, as before, when he spoke of the lack of technology, it is not very clear where the line is to be drawn between his praise of what Spain possesses and his bitterness over her lack of things that others possess. Concerning the people miraculously maintained in a state of idleness, he adds: "This is not done, I believe, in any other part of the world, where everyone lives, especially in France, *according to orderly rule*,[22] in the houses of the lords; and outside them, according to profession and trade."

By the middle of the fifteenth century Spain presented the same aspect that was to characterize her for centuries: a superabundance of people employed in the court, in the noble houses, and in the Church. The necessity for playing a role in society, inherent in the Hispanic condition, brought the lords to surround themselves with a multitude of servitors and minions. In the epistle of Fernando de la Torre there are precise data: a French viscount with an income of 15,000 crowns had with him only ten guardsmen at the siege of Cadillac; and in time of peace he maintained no more than ten attendants, and they and he "ate by assignment in the servants' dining room or the hall of the king." De la Torre goes on to ask, "What knight is there in Castile who with a third of the French viscount's income does not take three times as many guardsmen, and does not ordinarily maintain six times as many people, and does not regard it as degrading for him and his attendants to eat in the dining hall of His Lordship?" The Spanish knight of the Christian caste had to feel himself as if in suspension over the face of the earth—wherefore his disdain for mechanical, commercial, or even intellectual activities carried on by the other castes. Anticipating what I discuss later, I

Of the treasury,	*del tesoro,*
The caparisons, the horses	*los jaezes, los cavallos*
Of his people, and finery	*de su gente, y atavíos*
In such excess,	*tan sobrados,*
Where shall we find them now?	*¿dónde iremos a buscallos?*
What were they but the dew	*¿qué fueron sino rocíos*
Of the meadows?	*de los prados?*

[22] It is worth noting that even at that time a Spaniard should observe that in France people lived "according to orderly rule," that is, in conformity with reason.

would point out here that de la Torre is a clear example of what I later call "Hispanic integralism," for he is filled with joy and a sense of plenitude by the vital unity he observes among the prestige of the monarchy, the boldness of the knight, and the magical wealth of the Spanish earth. In Castile living was cheap, and with less money one would acquire more things than in France. "From whence does this proceed save from the noble and bountiful earth? And where are there larger incomes, and where is there *greater splendor* than there is in noble Castile?" To be sure the duke of Burgundy collects large sums in Flanders, "but these moneys come from the taxes levied on them; *the goods are not native to the place*; the Germans bring them, the Italians transport them, and the Castilians send them." Commercial traffic, evidently, uproots man from his own land, serves him from his vital context, draws him away from nature, and causes him to participate in frauds. Here we have the seeds that later were to flower in dreams of the Golden Age of Antiquity, in disdain for the court and song in praise of the rustic life, in the pastoral, and in Don Quixote's horror of firearms. Those who do not derive their whole substance from the land on which they live, in the end cease to be themselves; they disintegrate. Man was felt to be the meeting point of the strong reek of the earth with the magical beam of belief,

> for there would be no captain
> if no one tilled the soil.
> (Calderón, *The Judge of Zalamea*)

Where an earth made divine marched with a heaven made human, the Spanish soil ran its course. We have seen how Fernando de la Torre proclaimed his pride in the bounty of the Spanish earth; but before him the Arabs had already made their own theme of the fertility of the soil, cultivated in al-Andalus with loving care. The land of Seville was compared with that of Syria for its productivity, and all that "is sowed therein, bursts forth, grows, and is magnified." In some places fruit trees come up without having been planted, but only with working and improving the soil.[23] In the *Description of Spain*, by the anonymous chronicler of Almeria (twelfth century), it is related that in Saragossa, "among other extraordinary things that happen there, nothing ever spoils, neither fruits nor wheat. I have seen wheat more than a hundred years old, and grapes that have been hanging for six years. Such is the abundance of cereals, wines, and fruits that in all the inhabited earth there is no country more fertile."[24] This element of magic and marvel is lacking in the well-known *Laus Hispaniae* of St. Isidore, subsequently amplified in the *Crónica*

---

[23] *La Péninsule Ibérique au Moyen Âge*, [according to] Al-Himyarī, trans. Lévi-Provençal (Leyden, 1938), pp. 3, 5, 27, 29.
[24] See René Basset, in *Homenaje a don Francisco Codera* (1904), p. 643.

General of Alfonso the Learned: "The valleys and the plains ... bear much fruit and are abundant. . . . Spain overflows with grains, and enjoys the sweet taste of fruits" (p. 311). Here one does not yet sense the mystic trembling of the Orient. Yet according to León Hebreo, a Spanish Jew of the fifteenth century, the celestial virtues pass through the other elements, "but they are stopped only in the earth, because of her thickness and because she is in the center; and against her all the rays strike most surely. So that she is the true wife of the heaven, and the other elements are his concubines; for in her, heaven engenders all, or the greater part, of his generation; and she is adorned with so many and such divers things."[25] The sexual sublimation of the earth, in spite of Neoplatonic reminiscences, shows the stamp of Islamic-Judaic thought and feeling.

If all the references to the earth in Spanish literature were to be grouped together, the peculiarity of their approach and style would become obvious. It is even characteristic for a sixteenth-century humanist as learned as Juan Ginés de Sepúlveda to think of agriculture as an "occupation that is very virtuous and near to nature, and that usually invigorates the body and the spirit and prepares them for work and for war: to such a degree that the ancients preferred labor in the field to commerce, and the Romans drew many consuls and dictators from among the plowmen."[26] From rural life the caste of Old Christians would draw examples of men of pure blood, such as Peribáñez and Pedro Crespo.

Lope de Vega pondered the richness of the Spanish soil, with the same exaltation as the medieval Muslims:

> It is a fertile land, which never tires
> Of producing food, silver, and gold. . . .
> What think you, milady, of this land?
> Does its agreeable sight not give you joy,
> Its plants, fertile and fair,
> Such diversity of fruits and trees?
> Do you not marvel to see such grandeur?[27]

In other instances the earth appears as an "alma mater" worthy of being venerated. A victim of shipwreck in *El anzuelo de Fenisa* ("Fenisa's Fishhook") says:

> I know that land awaits me,
> Land I want to kiss. . . .
> The land is after all a mother,
> And like a mother she gives sustenance.

[25] "Diálogos de amor," in the *Nueva Biblioteca de Autores Españoles*, XX, 314.
[26] *De appetenda gloria* (Madrid, 1780), IV, 206.
[27] The examples come from the plays *Roma abrasada* ("Rome Burned") and *El molino* ("The Mill"), and are quoted by R. del Arco, *La sociedad española en las obras dramáticas de Lope de Vega*, p. 59.

Rural life was a theme of primary importance in the art of Lope de Vega, and generally in all the literature of the sixteenth and seventeenth centuries, not only because it echoed Vergil or because the Renaissance exalted nature and the Golden Age of Antiquity, but also because the peasant was felt to be the foundation of the dominant caste and the cultivator of a soil magical, eternal, and provident which gave fine-tasting fruits and wines, just as the cultivators of the invisible divinity brought down graces from heaven as the product of their labors. As early as the Middle Ages, the Castilian of the Christian caste scorned mechanical, rational labor that was without mystery, without a background of eternity, provided by either heaven or earth, to transcend it. The importance of the farmer and of everything rustic in Spanish life and letters went hand in hand with the equally pervasive presence of the priestly. Earth and heaven resolved their opposition in a unity of faith. If a passionate longing for infinitude and transcendence had not underlain the Spaniard's notion of the earth, Mateo Alemán, of Jewish descent, would not have written the following passage, as admirable as it is gloomy:

It has always been considered a hard thing to do, to find a faithful and true friend. . . . I have found only one who is the same substance as ourselves, the best, the most generous, the truest, the most reliable of all, who never forsakes us, *who stands forever unchanged*, who never tires of *giving us gifts*; and that friend is the earth. . . . She accepts and suffers everything from us, good treatment and bad. She is silent to everything. . . . And all the wealth that is ours in the earth is the gift of the earth. Finally, when we lie stinking in death, when there is neither wife nor father nor son nor kinsman nor friend who will suffer us, and all reject us, fleeing from us, then she protects us, receiving us into her own womb, where we repose under her faithful watch till she may give us up again in new and eternal life.

(*Guzmán de Alfarache*, II, 2, I)[28]

In the notion of the *patria* (fatherland) the accent fell more strongly on the land than on the ancestors. For subtle, sensitive Lope de Vega, the greatness of even a Charles V, grandson of Ferdinand and Isabella, did not make up for the defect of his being born in another country: "If it were possible for a man, he ought to seek to be born in France, to live in Italy, and to die in Spain. To be born in France because of the French nobility, who have always had a *king born in their own land* and who have never brought in foreign blood; to live in Italy for Italian liberty and fertility; and to die in Spain *because of the faith there*, which is so Catholic, so firm, and so true."[29]

---

[28] Similar words occur in the fourteenth-century *El libro del Caballero Cifar*: "For the simplest thing in the world is to cast a body into the grave especially since the earth is the home of all things in the world and receives them willingly (ed. C. P. Wagner, p. 116).

[29] *El peregrino en su patria* ("The Pilgrim in His Native Land") (1604), p.

Spain was a faith, a belief, fed by life and by death, by heaven and by earth; it was the land of the cult of the Eucharist and of the cereal that lent that sacrament its material substance. Calderón wrote *El mágico prodigioso* ("The Prodigious Magician"), a drama of complicated and highly subtle art, to be performed in the village of Yepes (Toledo) before rustics who tenderly tilled the soil; and who found in the bosom of the land a sense of eternity, not the same as the heavenly eternity, but possessed, like the latter, of an infinite perspective. Among the innumerable beliefs that make up the vital framework of Spain, the land was a very essential one; it is for this reason that the rustic and the royal-divine are always intermingled in the seventeenth-century theater just as they are in the previously quoted folk saying: "Either prince or peasant." Unamuno, with a powerful, intuitive sense for the Hispanic reality, wrote in 1927: "On few peoples of the earth has the divine, or, if you wish—it amounts to the same thing—the demoniac earth left a deeper imprint than on the peoples forged by Hispania," because Spain is "this land under heaven, this land full of heaven, this land which, being a body, and because of being a body, is a soul." This is not whimsical and beautiful lyricism but the expression of a life, and not less real and historical than that described in the chronicles; underneath this lyricism, as I have just demonstrated, throb ten centuries of yearning and insecure existence.

In the light of this, a considerable depth of meaning is to be found in the fact that Fernando de la Torre, the first Spaniard to try to reflect in earnest, if only to a degree, about his country, should take as his point of departure the Spanish earth—its reality, the emotion it evoked in him, and its magical powers. At the same time, the loyal Semitic counselor was aware of the price Castile had to pay for being what she was. De la Torre expected everything from the new young king. In spite of the blessed "fatness of the land," the solution for Spain's difficulties had to fall from heaven. Our fifteenth-century Spaniard is the first one to contemplate his country with trusting satisfaction and at the same time critically and with anguish.[30] That uneasiness with respect to one's own existence has continued in a trembling but unbroken line from the fifteenth century down to

---

304. When Lope de Vega intuits the existence of Spain as a unity, he sees it as a hollowness just as Quevedo does (a national monarchy, general welfare, and liberty are lacking); but all the negations become affirmations in his art, in a paradoxical compensation possible only in that country in which censure and praise of all that pertains to the country paradoxically coexist. Disillusion or even despair never had in Spain the consequences that modern rational thought would expect.

[30] "Anguish" is used here with the connotations it has in the writings of Kierkegaard, whose English translators have sometimes preferred the term "dread." Cf. German *Angst*. The connotation of "anxiety" as the term is used in psychology is especially to be avoided here.

the present time; it may already be glimpsed in the belief in St. James the warrior (see below, p. 380). In view of this, it seems to me that history ought first of all to take into account the following primordial phenomenon: Here is a people whose initial and constant problem is its insecurity and anguish concerning its own existence, its uncertainty, its living in a state of alarm caused by its doubt. It will be said that other peoples, even the most productive and flourishing ones, were not free from an occasional lash of dissatisfaction and self-criticism. But with them such reflections are marginal voices alongside the steady stream of the collective life, which follows its course, indifferent to the admonitions and insults that are hurled from the shore. The matter of Spain was and is something else: it is rather as if the river should never cease wondering whether its waters are really following the course they ought to be following.

A Painful Self-Awareness

Half a century ago, a book such as this would have been taken as an expression of pessimism, and the reader would have viewed with puzzlement, or with a pity verging on ridicule, the history of a culture whose primary feature consisted in its not being sure of itself. But fifty years ago it was believed that only what was clear and what was optimistic had value, and that the system of Western life bore an assurance of indefinite progress. Today, after many tragic experiences, we know that this is not true. We know moreover that there can be forms of art and life of the highest quality, whose very basis is the anguished and the radically problematical. And, besides, whatever may be the vital peculiarity of Spain, it would be senseless to approach it with any save a purely objective attitude. The person who expects to understand history must submerge himself in it, must get rid of patriotism, as well as bitterness. And especially in studying a historic life that consists in insecurity must the historian rid himself of all insecurity. He must accept the totality of the data in all their fullness, the noble with the miserable, thinking of how the two interlock.

This mode of life which consists in simultaneous affirmation and denial (*vivir desviviéndose*) and the feeling of insecurity which characterizes it have ancient roots. This insecurity did not appear for the first time in the seventeenth century when the military power of the Spaniards began to crumble in Europe; nor does it signify paralysis and inactivity, for the Spaniard went on feeding the awareness of his special deficiencies at the same time that he was magnifying the activist and sovereign powers of his person. He increased his lands and the number of his subjects, but he did not know how to fill that world around him with things. The outside world continued

to adhere to the power and the "beliefs" of the person, but the latter
lacked objectified world around him, independent of him. Additional
discussion of this condition is offered later. To feel fully and magis-
terially installed within oneself ("his laws, his own bold spirit; his
ordinances, his will," as the old ballad line runs) as a corollary carried
with it feeling oneself insufficient, denying one's own life, in a social
medium that was hollow and deserted.

All of this is not vague rhetoric. We shall see numerous instances
of the great and moving problematical nature of the Spanish past,
conceived and explained, most usually, with insufficient serenity. In
the eleventh century the Cluniac monks were imported from France
because the kings deemed them better fitted to deal with divine
duties. In the twelfth century recourse was made to the Cistercians.
The Moors in conquered territories were not exterminated, because,
as the hero says in the *Poem of the Cid*, "we shall make use of them,"
we shall see how tremendous their contribution was—and not only in
technology and learning. Ferdinand II of Leon appointed a Moorish
governor of the frontier area around Badajoz: "He put in his charge
the protection of his Moors and his city" (*Crónica General*, p. 676).
Alfonso VIII called in French and Lombard scholars to begin the
first university studies (*op. cit.*, p. 234), for the purpose of securing
a "teaching of wisdom." Around 1250 it was felt that Spain did not
possess the same rank as France and England; otherwise the *Poem
of Fernán González* would not say:

> [God] wished to raise her over England and France,
> [see] how not one Apostle lies in all those lands.

The Spaniard *had himself* and enjoyed over other Europeans the
advantage of having *his* Apostle, St. James; but it never occurred to
other Europeans to take Spain as the basis for comparisons. The
Spaniards did so because they felt insecure, as well as grand, and
with good reason for feeling both. It is high time to try to reconcile
these contradictory aspects of the Spanish past.

For the Christians insecurity meant, among other things, not being
able to do without the Jews or, later, the converts, who set forth
their vision of the innermost heart of Spain from the lofty vantage
point they had assigned to themselves, as the previous texts have
made clear. Fernando de la Torre said that everything was grown in
Spain, but manufactured products were imported. In 1535 Michael
Servetus (surely another convert) praised the empire-building drive
of the Spaniards and the Portuguese but noted that they were "always going around begging foreign books" (see the additions to his
translation of Ptolemy's *Geography*). Fertile brains, he says; grand
aspirations (*magna moliens*) and scanty knowledge (*infeliciter
discunt*).

From within the Christian caste we find like expressions of Spain's vital disposition by the admirable Fernán Pérez de Guzmán, in whose *Generaciones y semblanzas* ("Generations and Portraits") (1460) is to be found an anticipation of the thesis (expressed by some contemporary writers) concerning the Spanish hatred for any kind of select personality: "And not only was this noble knight ruined in these uprisings in Castile, but many other houses, both great and middling, were ruined: for Castile does better at making new gains than she does at keeping what she has gotten. For often *those whom she herself has built up, she herself destroys.*" The last statement is no more than a gloss of what Don Alonso Fernández Coronel said as he was going to be executed by the order of the king of Castile, Peter the Cruel: "This is Castile, which makes men and wastes them."[31]

In view of all this it is senseless to continue dully repeating that during the years of imperial expansion, before the seventeenth century, no one showed himself to be insecure and anguished, because the "decadence" had not yet begun, and so on. But the Spaniards of the past knew their own affairs and spirits much better than those who today have forgotten what really happened. Charles V, to cite evidence that cannot be scorned, was on the point of selling the Duchy of Milan in 1534 to Duke Octavio Farnese for 2 million gold escudos in order to alleviate his economic troubles. The minister Granvelle and the Council of State saw the matter clearly, and the Emperor wrote of it: "[With] the present necessity in which we are, and the condition in which our kingdoms, states, and patrimony find themselves, and [in view of] how powerful our enemies are on sea and land, [it would be] a great relief to *find ourselves out of this pit and labyrinth*, and with so large a sum of money."

Antonio de Leiva, the ambassador Gutierre López de Padilla, and others energetically opposed this disposal of the duchy; but a paper attributed to Don Diego Hurtado de Mendoza which they gave to His Majesty about the Milan problem says: "Everyone knows that you have your state in pawn, your patrimony consumed, and your

---

[31] "Generaciones y semblanzas," in *Clásicos Castellanos*, LXI, 90, 110. Other correlations no less significant could be established. Fernán Pérez de Guzmán says: "In Castile there has always been little effort made to preserve antiquities, which is a great pity. . . . Without doubt, it is a noteworthy deed and praiseworthy to preserve the memory of the noble lineages or of the services rendered to the kings and to the republics—of which little care has been taken in Castile" (pp. 50–51). Gracián is no more satisfied with the history written by Spaniards: "I assure you that there have not been more, nor more heroic, deeds than those done by Spaniards, but none have been worse recorded than by the Spanish themselves. Most of these histories are like bacon that is all fat and no lean, so that the taste palls after two bites" (*El Criticón*, III, 8). The common feature that lends unity to these foregoing quotations is that in the fifteenth century, and in the seventeenth, written history does not satisfy various ill-humored observers of the life around them.

vassals impoverished, and that only the breadth of your reputation sustains your state." Some proposed that Spain should get rid of Flanders and, in exchange, incorporate Italy, so that the Italian states "might supply all those [things] that *Spain lacks*." In 1552, in the last stages of the reign of Charles V, Luis de Orezuela wrote in a dispatch addressed to the secretary of state, Gonzalo Pérez: "Everything is crumbling and if the Prince [the future Philip II] does not open his eyes in time to remedy matters, the present times and disposition augur a *great ruin and fall*, not less than that of a great building opened from top to bottom everywhere and leaning toward its fall."[32]

Nevertheless, the Empire was being built and consolidated, thanks to human qualities stronger than the negative pressure of terrible circumstances. Anxiety and insecurity forged a type of man whose distinction and grace, combined with a serene boldness, stirred the astonishment, the admiration, and the envy of Europeans. Bernal Díaz del Castillo says: "Here on this island [of Cozumel] Cortés first gave proof of his great gift of command, and Our Lord gave him grace, *so that wherever he put his hand, things turned out well*, especially in pacifying the peoples and natives of those parts."

The Empire was born divided and hanging on the rim of a precipice; insecurity and anguish were already singing its dirge in the sixteenth century, nevertheless much of the largest and most Spanish portion of it survived intact until the nineteenth century. If economic and technological reasons alone had been decisive, the Empire should have died in the time of Charles II or long before. But the last word was always pronounced by men, those men of the caste formed to rule and to know how to command, who elevated themselves as God gave them best to understand, and who were undone by virtue of the same causes that had raised them to peaks of lofty action which lives on in history.

When the virtues of the caste were weakened, then there were no material and intangible *things* with which to replace them (money, artifacts, theories). And that lack of balance, shrewdly perceived by the Hispano-Jewish caste, explains the stumbling and falls of Spanish existence, whose insecurity has been expressed for a long time, though it has not radically affected either the rise or the fall of the Empire. The history of Spain is neither invertebrate nor mysterious: it has been the process of an inharmonious dialogue between men and things, between life like a block of marble and the mind like a chisel unable to carve it. Charles V, in a moment of depression and counseled by the foreigner Granvelle, allowed himself to be swept away by the magical jingle of a golden cascade—2 million

---

[32] The foregoing texts were cited by the late historian Federico Chabod, *Lo stato de Milano nello impero di Carlo V* (Rome, 1934).

escudos. But for the Castilian Antonio de Leiva, who had conquered Francis I at Pavia and entered into Milan, the problem was not one of golden reasons but of the heart. But let us continue hearing the voices of those who expressed the conscious awareness of their present, which is now our past.

In the heyday of the Empire (1569) the Granadine Gonzalo Jiménez de Quesada, conquistador of what was to become Colombia and founder of Bogotá, wrote: "Where is to be found today the Spaniard who can recount his deeds simply and truthfully?" Despite the Spanish victories, France did not recognize Spain's superiority. "But you, Fleming, and you others from states bordering on Flanders, can you say what Spain has done to you in order that at no Burgundian table, provided there is a Spaniard seated at it, should there be talk of anything else but of these disagreements and precedences?"[33] The Germans, he goes on, claim the major role in Spanish victories. Hungarians, Danes, and Poles "only with difficulty can listen calmly to the news of so much good fortune for the Spaniards. In Italy, the foremost province in all Europe, it will be found that they listen to nothing with greater impatience than to news of Spanish good luck in battle. Most shocking of all is the fact that the same thing happens in our West Indies, where their barbaric people try to minimize the greatness of their conquerors by offering excuses for their defeat" (*El Antijovio* [Bogotá, 1952], pp. 21–24). Jiménez de Quesada, a soldier and a humanist, felt the aching aloneness of Spanish grandeur both in Europe and in the New World that he helped to conquer and civilize. Irritated by the slanders of Paolo Giovio, he composed a voluminous reply to him which has only recently been made known. The Spaniard felt he was journeying ceaselessly, but without moving ahead, through a vast world that did not recognize the worth of Hispanic heroism. Jiménez de Quesada has had to wait almost four hundred years for even his compatriots to acknowledge the undeniable merit of his work and finally to publish it.

In 1609 Quevedo commented thus on the expulsion of the Christianized Moors: "And in the end, if the Moors who came to Spain in 711 deprived Spain of people by beheading them, the Moors that Spaniards ejected deprived it of people they themselves left. The loss was Spain's; the only difference was the knife."[34] The same nihilistic reduction of the surrounding world occurs in *El Criticón* (1657), of Baltasar Gracián, who has as one of his most significant themes the

---

[33] For a Spaniard in the time of Charles V, Flanders was simply a state in that Burgundy for which the Emperor had always longed. He would have liked to be buried in the Burgundian charterhouse of Champmol.

[34] *El Chitón de las tarabillas* ("The Babblers' Stopper"), in *Obras* (Madrid, 1936).

hatred of the common people, of what today is called the masses: "The common people are nothing but a synagogue[35] of pretentious ignoramuses who talk more about things the less they understand them" (II, 5).

Time and again Gracián denounces the multitude, smothering it with reproaches: "credulous, barbarous, foolish, loose, sensation-mongering, insolent, garrulous, dirty, loudmouthed, lying, despicable" (II, 5). The serious thing for Gracián is that "men of high birth, those of good blood, those of illustrious houses, who, however little assistance they may get, are bound to attain great worth, and who, if they are lent a hand, are bound to have a hand in all"; the grave thing is "that these yield to vices, they destroy themselves, and bury themselves alive in the cavern of nothingness" (III, 8). This whole class of people, who could become a valuable elite and did not, Gracián casts into the "cavern of nothingness." For him, as for Quevedo, the world that surrounds him is a play of inane figures, the noisy multitude of the majority opposed to the empty ciphers of the minority.

Since long before Gracián, the formless image of that nothingness had been growing ever clearer. According to the ex-Jesuit Francisco de Medrano, who died in 1607, neither peace nor war served to make Spaniards feel secure. Echoing the tone of a biblical lament, he wrote that:

> Now the softness of peace,
> Now the fury of war hurts us.
> Sad, Spain groans,
> *At the highest summit of fortune;*
> *For the weight of her great majesty*
> Is too much for her and oppresses her;
> And structures that *heaven does not support*
> Fall under their weight to the ground.[36]

Spain was not then groaning, oppressed by any error or by her departure from a preceding type of life, as had been seen to happen in imperial Rome. Spain's anguish is the very majesty of feeling herself at the pinnacle of her greatest fortune. The only support that was secure, real, was that of Heaven, and not any conceivable kind of grandiose "structure" (*máquina*). But even before Medrano

---

[35] "Synagogue" is used here in the Greek, etymological sense of "meeting, assembly." The author, aristocratic in attitude, protects himself from the lowly object he defines, removing himself some distance from it by means of a learned Hellenism, impenetrable to the mob. It is also possible that the complicated, twisted Gracián may have used against the masses, so proud of their pure Christianity, the most defamatory word of the times when interpreted in the sense understood by the masses. There is a certain amount of doubt about the Old Christian origins of Gracián himself.

[36] For the text, see the *Biblioteca de Autores Españoles*, XLI, 351a; concerning the author, see Dámaso Alonso's *Vida y obra de Medrano* (Madrid, 1948).

wrote, Spain felt that she was nothing but the hollow shell of herself and in a very precarious situation; during the war against the Moriscos of Granada, and even after that, it was feared that the Turks, in alliance with Spain's Christian enemies, would repeat the Muslim invasion. In verses addressed to Don Juan of Austria, Captain Francisco de Aldana (who died in the debacle at Alcazarquivir in 1578) said:

> Receive this tearful prophecy,
> Fulfilled in my sad, unseasonable old age:
> I tell you that I see the Iberian monarchy
> Falling at the feet of fortune;
> Rebellion and heresy are growing;
> The Gaul awakens to a moonbeam[37]
> And the people most favored by God
> Sleeps in the shadow of eternal oblivion.[38]

In the same tone he writes poetically to Philip II:

> If at the disaster in the time of Rodrigo
> When the world was still such a novice
> That the enemy knew neither firearms
> Nor any warlike device,
> Spain fell in dishonor
> Without suspecting the Turks' wickedness,
> What can she do now, so unprepared,
> Against an enemy so numerous and so well provided?[39]

According to this military expert, who died fighting heroically against the African Moors, Spain offered a superlative void as a front against her centuries-old enemy:

> What must be suspected in *such an excessive*
> *Absence of form and matter,*
> As there is between them and us?[40]

These worries might all pass as the isolated voices[41] of fainthearted pessimists, if they did not coincide with the declaration, repeated throughout the sixteenth century, that the conquest of Granada had been a misfortunate one because the great heroic stimulus for the Spaniards had thus disappeared. Las Casas and others denied the legitimacy of the Crown's imperial policy in Hispanic America. Quevedo thought that the more lands Spain conquered, the more enemies she would attract: " . . . ambition finally acquires territory that is beyond the reach of the forces necessary to maintain it. . . . America

---

[37] I.e., the French are uniting with the Turks.
[38] *Epistolario poético completo*, ed. A. Rodríguez-Moñino (1946), p. 21.
[39] A. Rodríguez-Moñino, *El capitán Francisco de Aldana (1537–1578)* (Valladolid, 1943), p. 35.
[40] *Ibid.*
[41] For other similar expressions by Aldana, see the previously cited *Epistolario poético*, ll. 91–99.

was a rich and beautiful harlot, adulterous to her husbands [the Indians!].... The Christians say that heaven punished the Indies because they worshiped idols; and we Indians say that heaven is bound to punish the Christians because they worship the Indian women" (*La hora de todos*, 1635).

What then can be the reality of a present always felt to be wanting in lasting stability? It can be nothing other than a constant process of re-creation, as if the world were beginning anew in every instant, in a continuous process of creation-destruction. And let no one think that the foregoing quotations, the expression of an "autobiographical" conscious awareness, come from nonconformists made somber by pessimism. We are persuaded of the contrary by the enthusiastic traditionalist Menéndez y Pelayo, who seriously exaggerated the amount of Spanish science and learning with the intent of filling the void of the past which afflicted his soul.

But Menéndez y Pelayo could not suspect that the science of which he talked (humanism, philosophy, mathematics, botany, etc.) was in large part the work of the New Christians and that, for that very reason, it was stifled in its infancy for the reasons explained in my book *De la edad conflictiva*.

Consequently, for long centuries now illustrious Spaniards have felt themselves to be existing in a way of life both insecure and, in the last analysis, splendid, for it must be stressed that the insecurity was an expression of the disproportion felt between aspirations and possibilities.

It is useless for my purpose to compare the chronic Spanish situation with that of other countries and to cite all the examples of persecuted and nonconformist citizens in the various European countries: St. John of the Cross, cruelly harassed by the Carmelite monks; Giordano Bruno, burned alive in Rome; Luis de León, a victim of the inquisitorial furor of the dominant caste; Galileo, tyrannized by the Roman cardinals; Michael Servetus, burned by Calvin; Descartes, a refugee in a foreign land; and so on. I must emphasize that for the purposes of my analysis it makes no difference whether the Spaniards of the fifteenth, the seventeenth, or the twentieth century have or do not have an objective basis for feeling what they feel; the important thing is to take note of the sensation of an emptiness in life which those and other famous Spaniards experienced. The *vital* truth of their judgment is what interests us.

To enumerate all the motives that at one time or another have been alleged by way of explaining Spain's misfortunes or her peculiarity would be a lengthy task. People have spoken of the climate, of her indolence, of her resistance to accepting the lights of reason, of her fanaticism, of the absence of the Renaissance. As early as the sixteenth century the Moors were blamed for the ills of Spain. Hernán Pérez de Oliva, a good humanist, says that if all the cities had resisted the Saracens as did Cordova, his ancestral home, "they would not have driven our holy religion out of our temples, they would not have given us cause to weep in the blood of our own even down to our own days."[42] The use of the word "our" four times in two lines reveals the degree to which Pérez de Oliva felt the Moors to be foreigners. Some historians of the present continue to believe that Arabic domination harmfully deflected the course of Spanish history. But the reader now knows that the Spaniard is incomprehensible unless seen in his relationship to the three castes of believers, for without them he would not have become Spanish.

Other historians have had recourse to the idea of a Spanish essence, a prior substratum, or state, of human life on which Spain has played out the game of her history. Much has been said about Iberianism, about individualism, about tendencies incompatible with the forms of good society. The ancients talked about it, and some moderns have clung to that unreal human "substantialism." They connect the Iberia known to Strabo with the Iberian Peninsula of today. Thus we fall into a mythic fatalism, into an invisible history prior to the given life in the long centuries within our reach today. The truth is that the given Spaniard, the Spaniard with whom we must deal, appears in his way of doing things, in his mode of *feeling himself* Spanish—and not in his mythical "racial" foundation.

My own purpose now is clearer and simpler, for I aspire to describe what has happened to the Spaniard, and what the circumstances in which destiny placed him offered him as bases of life. Only thus shall we be able to contemplate history as a series of worthy feats, and not as the ugly reverse side of a tapestry. What is important to us is what the Spaniard has felt himself to be and what he has done, for his achievements are indissolubly wedded to his misfortunes and failures. Rebellious to law and to any norm of the state, the Spaniard was docile to the voice of belief and to the imperative of his absolute person. If he had not been like this, the Peninsula would have been converted into a prolongation of Africa, or into an extension of France, or perhaps of England. The Spaniard made himself through his eagerness to survive and to surpass himself, *to be more*, without economic theories or ambitions. He fortified himself in the castle of his own person, and in his own person he found the impetus and faith to build a strange and immense colonial empire that lasted from 1500 to 1824. He preserved without essential changes his thirteenth-century language, and with it he hammered out artistic creations of enduring value. The Spaniards did not let themselves be unified by means of reason, knowledge, law, or a net of economic links, but

---

[42] *Razonamiento sobre la navegación del Guadalquivir,* in *Obras,* II, 2.

rather badly with the concept of "individualism," forged by nineteenth-century thought from other points of view and to solve other problems, as we shall see in chapter ix.

Those historians who have tried to explain the existence of Spain as a chronic ailment (for example, Ortega y Gasset in his *Invertebrate Spain*) now appear as outstanding instances of *vivir desviviéndose*, which is to say that their explanation of Hispanicity is a function of their Hispanism.

It has not befallen any other great civilization to live for century after century feeling all the while that the very ground under its feet was missing, and creating at the same time such first-class values. This people, on more than one occasion, has marched to its own destruction as to a jubilant saturnalia. But for the moment let us not worry ourselves about this, nor let us say whether this manner of existing is evil or good.

The paradoxical and curious aspect of this history is that the Spanish historian cannot capture its meaning unless he steps outside his own Spanish personality. If this is not done, Spanish history will inevitably appear to be either a nullity or an ailment—as Ortega y Gasset wrote—or a mythical story based on Numantia, Trajan, Viriatus, and the like. In order to avoid taking so futile an approach, we must establish precisely the theoretical bases on which it has been possible to construct this way of viewing history. Only thus will it be feasible to mark off the spatial and temporal perimeters of the authentic reality of the Spaniards, of the way of existence as a Spaniard.

VI · THE NON-SPANISH STRUCTURE OF
ROMAN AND VISIGOTHIC HISPANIA

INADEQUATE IDEAS ABOUT MAN and his life made it possible in the eighteenth century to imagine that the French were identical with Celts, and the Italians, with the Etruscans[1]—and vice versa. So naïve an illusion was finally rectified in France because the grandiose figure of Charlemagne loomed on the horizon of the French national state as we know it. From that sturdy trunk sprang the branch that was to constitute the French monarchy, and with it the consciousness of belonging to the social community called French.[2] In Italy the fall of the Roman Empire had been compensated for, in some degree, by the prestige of Rome as the spiritual capital of Western Christianity, as well as by that of the various cities where what was later called Renaissance culture was coming into being. In the Iberian Peninsula life took a different direction because men of learning—and later on the people—had had to cling to the image of a Hispania that had long since vanished but which, with the passing centuries, was sought even more tenaciously. The pre-Roman heroism of Numantia and Saguntum, Roman rule in the Hispanic provinces, cradle of illustrious emperors and of celebrated writers of imperial Rome (Seneca, Lucan, Quintilian, etc.)—all this was judged to be "Spanish." Later on, Visigothic Hispania also provided retrospective consolation; in the seventh century the Peninsula seemed on the way to complete unification, and very promising signs of culture were beginning to arise in it. This confusion between historical existence and immemorial existence springs from a logical error. People, or historical communities, are in this instance comparable to individual personalities. In both of them, it always happens that the knowledge of the ancestors is entirely different from the awareness of one's concrete existence, be it either individual or collective. A British person may know about the Picts, ancestors

---

[1] See my *Origen, ser y existir de los españoles*, pp. 64–69.
[2] "The unification of France was carried out by the Capetian dynasty" (Auguste Longnon, *Origines et formation de la nationalité française*, p. 76).

of the Scots; but this knowledge has not the same ontological nature as his feeling of his own historical existence after the Battle of Hastings. In the same way a person knows about his forefathers, but his knowledge cannot be confused with the personal awareness of his boyhood or childhood.

The Hispania, so highly praised by Isidore of Hispalis, was almost in its entirety torn violently and suddenly away from Christian Romania and converted into an extension of the Muslim East at all levels—those of religion, language, modes of living, and civilization in general. The desperate cry of the anonymous author of the *Crónica Mozárabe* of 754 continued to echo down the centuries: "Hispania, in other times a delight, is now a wretchedness; it has experienced all the horrors suffered by the Roman martyrs" (ed. Tailhan, p. 26). The consequences of so protracted a situation are mingled with the very fact of Spanish existence and with the total course of Spanish life. The awareness that the Hispano-Christians of the reconquest (the ancestors of the future Spaniards) were gradually forming about themselves grew up split at its very roots and infused with conflicting feelings: a consciousness of strength and of insufficiency; attraction and repulsion with respect to al-Andalus, which was at once frightening, dazzling, indispensable, envied, and antipathetic.[3]

The Peninsular past must be viewed from this perspective if we desire future generations to forget the historical myths still prevalent at the present time. The Castilians and Aragonese were not Visigoths or Romans or Celtiberians, for the collective dimension of a human group depends on a social form and not on a latent, enduring biological and psychic substance. The Castilians and Aragonese knew it was impossible for them to do without the Moors, even after they had conquered the cities formerly ruled by them. The economy and administration of their kingdoms demanded the collaboration of Moors and Jews. The Spanish kingdoms attracted the attention of foreign Christians by the singularity of their customs and by the appearance of their inhabitants; as the reader will see in subsequent chapters, centuries of common life with Orientals had created habits, some of which were openly visible, while others were more internal. Let us remember, for example, that royalty was sometimes buried in Moorish vestments, which were also worn by the upper classes and the people. In the sixteenth century Hernán Cortés still saw the Mexicans in a perspective shaded by his memories of the Moors: "And the clothes they wear are like very colorful *almaizales* [Moorish light veils], . . . and [they] wear over their bodies very thin

---

[3] This phenomenon, unique in Europe, is comparable to the situation, unique in America, created by the Spanish conquest of lands with an elevated cultural tradition (Mayan, Inca, Mexican). Despite wide differences, cultural and psychic analogies are clearly visible.

blankets colored like Moorish *alquiceles* [cloaks]. . . . Their rooms [are] very much in the Moorish style. . . . They have their *mezquitas* [mosques]."[4]

In opposition to the reality of the authentic form of Spanish life, there arose forms imagined and desired by people who knew, through Latin or vernacular texts, about the pre-Islamic past of the Peninsula. King Martin of Aragon (d. 1410) believed that "the Aragonese were the true Celtiberians, about whom it is written that they never abandoned their lord in battle."[5] Valerius Maximus, in his *Factorum Dictorumque Memorabilium, Libri IX*, does, indeed, relate that "the Celtiberians deemed it a crime to stay alive in battle if that man for whose well-being they had offered their lives died."[6] Caesar alludes to the same custom—apparently more Celtic than Iberian—in his *De Bello Gallico*, III, 22: the Gauls gave the name *soldurii* (a Celtic word) to those who died in this manner under the obligation of a vow of fidelity. Consequently, one cannot see the reason for converting the Aragonese into Celtiberians because some of them were faithful subjects of King Martin the Humane, even if such a custom had still been kept in Aragon, as indeed it was not. The connection of identity established by the King between the two peoples originated in sentimental motives, in the eagerness to endow his people with a pleasing collective genealogy, regardless of whether in order to do so it was necessary to surmount abysses of unreality. To imagine the Celtiberians as present in Aragon in 1400 was something like evoking today the shades of the Pharaohs roaming around their pyramids. A construction of this kind has validity as a psychic experience and may even attain a possible literary value;[7] but its validity as an objective reality existing outside desires, dreams, and books is worthless. Kings prior to Don Martin (Peter IV and James I) felt no "Celtiberian" devotion around them, for Aragon seemed to be a "rebellious and accursed" land in contrast to Catalonia, "the most honorable land in Spain, . . . blessed and filled with loyalty."[8] It should be noted further that Catalonia is a region that we do not know to have ever been inhabited by Celtiberians.

As the information transmitted by books was gradually spread by the humanists, the image of an illustrious past became familiar

---

[4] *Primera carta de relación* (Mexico: Porrúa, 1960), p. 16.

[5] J. M. Lacarra, *Aragón* (1960), I, 245.

[6] II, 6, 11; the quotation is taken from the Spanish translation of Diego López (Seville, 1631), fol. 36v.

[7] Marcel Proust played delightfully with the contradictory feelings evoked in him by the name "Guermantes" and by his actual experiential awareness of the people who bore that name in his novel: "Je les voyais tous deux [the Duke and Duchess] retirés de ce nom de Guermantes dans lequel, jadis, je les imaginais menant une inconcevable vie" (*Le côté de Guermantes* [3d ed., 1946], p. 173).

[8] Lacarra, *op. cit.*, cites these texts in another connection.

and accepted by all. Without it the authentic Spaniards, those who spontaneously saw themselves as a union of Christians, Moors, and Jews, would have been projected back toward a past filled with shadows as disturbing as they were distasteful. From the fifteenth century on the tension of empire incited and demanded the creation of glorious antecedents, heights of political prestige and humanistic culture. Trajan and Seneca turned out to be Spaniards because they had been born in "Spain," a land that molded illustrious men.

The Mythical Spanishness of the Romans Born in Hispania

The culture given expression in the Latin of Rome by those who were born in the imperial provinces (Hispania and Cisalpine or Transalpine Gaul) was not the creation of Spaniards, Italians, or Frenchmen, who represent modes of human existence without any reality at that time. Strabo, born before Seneca, says that the province of Baetica was almost completely Romanized.[9] The indigenous religion disappeared from Baetica, whose inhabitants, according to Roman usage, gave themselves three names. Only a hallucination, explicable as a kind of collective psychosis, could make of Seneca and his philosophy a Spanish phenomenon. Even if we should admit that Stoic thought had deep and original repercussions in Spanish thought (and it did not), it would no more be appropriate to deduce from that any Spanishness in Seneca, than to deduce from the Neoplatonic reflections in Luis de Granada or in Cervantes the Spanishness of Plato or Plotinus.

Seneca was a Roman, educated, like many others, by Greek masters imbued with Stoic thought, which had no specific relation to his motherland, Corduba, which since the fifteenth century has been erroneously identified with the city of Cordova after its conquest by Ferdinand III. An authority on the archaeological past of the present city says that its ruins, "destroyed and calcined, lie buried at a depth of 4 to 5 meters. What catastrophes occurred between the fourth and eighth centuries which could have produced the total razing of the Roman city and the accumulation of so enormous a mass of earth and rubble?"[10]

For those who know the literature of Rome and Greek thought,

---

[9] See Raymond Thouvenot, *Essai sur la province romaine de Bétique* (1940), p. 188, who for other reasons falls into the opposite extreme from that of the Pan-Hispanists: "Perhaps," he says, "one must attribute to Rome the birth of Andalusian particularism, which today affirms itself with such vigor in opposition to Castile and Catalonia" (p. 683). The Andalusians of today should not be confused with either the Muslim inhabitants of al-Andalus or with the Roman "Baeticolae."

[10] L. Torres Balbás, *La mezquita de Córdoba*, p. 6.

the idea of a "Spanish Senecanism" (maintained by Ganivet, Menéndez y Pelayo, and many others) would be equivalent to calling the poetry of Rubén Darío Mayan or something of the kind, revealing ignorance of the fact that Rubén's poetry was founded on Spanish and French literary models. In the same way what remains of the thought of Seneca is incomprehensible if it is not situated within the Stoic tradition of the Romans and the Greeks. Besides the fantastic conversion of Seneca into a Spaniard, the basic error rests on the use of the popular conception of Stoicism—namely, the impassive sufferance of physical and spiritual discomforts—to explain the thought of Seneca. In addition to its ethical doctrines, Stoicism was a complicated philosophical theory, which in the final analysis has nothing to do with the empirical fact of tolerating hunger and pain.

Although what has been said may suffice to show that the Spanishness of Seneca rests only on the desire to make him Spanish, it is necessary to emphasize that the critical thought of Seneca and his interest in natural science never interested the Christian caste which, from the end of the sixteenth century, was the sole representative of the Spanish form of life. If the Spaniards had been followers of Seneca, their history would have been different from what it has been and is, because their interest would have been concentrated on the rational analysis of earthly life. Seneca writes: "Death is not being: what happens after me will be like what happened before me" (*Epistulae ad Lucilium*, VI, 54, 4). For him life was a parenthetical interjection between two states of nonbeing.

The naïveté of making Seneca Spanish will finally be expelled from books when readers realize the sophism implicit in giving the same meaning to the words "Hispania" and "España," as sophistical an identity as would be involved in confusing the meanings of the "Italia" of Augustus and the "Italia" of the House of Savoy. Superimposed on that ingenuousness there appears—I repeat—the confusion between being temperate in diet, brave, and a patient bearer of all ills with the philosophy in which that mode of psychic and moral behavior took on transcendent and cosmic meaning—as if uranium deposits in a given place might imply as well the existence of a theory of nuclear fission there. The only Spanish element in the belief in Seneca's "Spanishness" is the state of mind which made the belief possible and the position such a fantasy occupies in the history of Spanish letters.[11] The fraudulent writings of Ossian, an

---

[11] My ideas about the reality of the Spaniards convince some people and disturb others. G. Borrón accepts as well founded my objection to considering the Stoicism of Seneca as Spanish; but since he is interested in Spanishness and not in Stoicism, he ventures the strange idea that Seneca was not a Stoic philosopher (*Revista de Filosofía* [Madrid; Dec., 1955]). To do so he cuts and twists the texts of the philosopher, as I have made clear in *Dos Ensayos* (Mexico: Porrúa, 1956), p. 55.

invention of James Macpherson in the eighteenth century, considerably influenced the cultivation of Romantic literature in Europe, notwithstanding the spuriousness of his supposedly Celtic poetry.

Customarily Quevedo is adduced as an example of Spanish Senecanism, although reading him is sufficient to convince one that the claim is dubious. Without doubt Quevedo treated Seneca in a Spanish fashion, just as the Spanish Erasmians (the majority of whom were converts) had done earlier with Erasmus when they tried to make him conform to the difficult situation in which they found themselves as converted Jews. They attempted to make Erasmus stop being what he was. Quevedo also would have wished that Stoic philosophy "did not lean so much toward insensitivity," for if it did not, it might "boast kinship" to Christianity; Christ, being "eternal wisdom, was pained, troubled, became angered, was afraid, and cried."[12] Quevedo struggles to derive Stoic thought from that of Job and, in doing so, falsifies Stoicism radically; in addition, he rejects suicide, which he considers nonessential in Senecan thought. But without ascetic denial and suicide, what remains of Senecan moral teachings? In the end Quevedo realizes the conflict implicit in his views and writes with praiseworthy correctness: "I am not competent to be a Stoic, but I am attracted to the Stoics" (*Nombre, origen, intento, recomendación y descendencia de la doctrina estoica* ["Name, Origin, Purpose, Recommendation and Transmission of the Stoic Doctrine"]).

The same reasons that make the belief in Seneca's Spanishness untenable require us to cast off the belief that Lucan, Martial, and other Latin-Roman writers born in Hispania possess any Spanishness. If the Celtiberians, the Iberians, the Tartessians, and all the other pre-Roman inhabitants of the Peninsula were not Spaniards, where were these later people to acquire their Spanishness?

The Visigoths Were Still Not Spaniards

The same error in perspective which has led to mistaking the Celtiberians and the Hispano-Romans for Spaniards has led also to the conversion of the Visigoths into Spaniards. If such were true, the Franks would be Frenchmen and the Ostrogoths and Longobards, Italians, as I have maintained now for a long time. The habit of

---

[12] At the end of the fourteenth century Coluccio Salutati rejected the Stoic apathy for the same reasons: "Potior est mihi veritas, quae patet ad sensum, quam opinio, ne dicam deliratio stoicorum," for whom what was felt by fragile mortal flesh was nonexistent. Its senselessness is proved by the example of Christ, who "dum de morte cogitat, in sudorem sanguinem resolutum, nec mentis tacuisse tristitiam" (*Epistolario*, ed. Novati, III, 464). See V. L. Borghi, "La dottrina morale de Coluccio Salutati," in *Annali della R. Scuola Normale de Pisa* (1934), p. 88.

speaking of Visigothic "blood" persists, as if groups endowed with a national consciousness had acquired it through biology or, ultimately, zoology. If in some Castilian village blond, blue-eyed people predominate, the fact is attributed to the continuance of the Visigoths, and it is said that their "blood" produced certain "racial" peculiarities. It is unnecessary to say that without the Goths and everyone else before them who lived in the Peninsula, there would have been no Spaniards, just as there would now be no language if some other tongue had not been spoken before; but the Indo-European was not German, nor is the German Gothic, nor is the Italian Latin. All of which means that the life structure of those who dwelt in the Peninsula in the year 700 is as different from that of the inhabitants of Castile and Barcelona in 1100 as Latin is from the Romance languages.[13]

The studies cited in note 13 confirm the fact that the Goths left clearly visible traces on Peninsular life after the eighth century: names of people; certain Gothic words in the Galician, Castilian, and Catalan languages; legal customs; some artistic traditions; archaeological objects; and the like. Rome also remained alive in the memory of the peoples of the Italian Peninsula in the Middle Ages and, naturally, in the Renaissance; but no one claims for these reasons that the Italians were Romans, or vice versa. J. M. Piel (pp. 410-411) is surprised because I have not granted the same formative importance to Gothic elements as to Arabic ones; it should, however, be noted that what is Gothic in the tenth, eleventh, twelfth, and thirteenth centuries is by then a survival which neither renews itself nor positively acts upon Christian life, while the Moors at that time are constructing houses and castles, grafting new words onto the Romance lexicon, dwelling in Christian cities, and so on. Between the Gothic and the Muslim "influence" there exists the same difference as that between the survival of the memory of older generations and a common life with one's own contemporaries. The difference reduces to nothing more—and nothing less—than that. The Hellenisms in Castilian are the subject of linguistic archaeology, while the Gallicisms of the eleventh and twelfth centuries are the result of the presence of French clerics and merchants "at that time" and "in that place" who were acting upon Castilians, Leonese, and Galicians by virtue of their prestige and their interests. The greatest tangles in Spanish history stem from a failure to keep in mind the functioning of life and its implacable logic. The Leonese, the

---

[13] This topic has been discussed recently by W. Reinhart, "La tradición visigoda en el nacimiento de Castilla," *Estudios dedicados a Menéndez Pidal,* I (1950), 535–554; Joseph M. Piel, "Américo Castros These von der 'no-hispanidad' der Westgoten," *Romanische Forschungen,* LXIX (1957), 409–413; Carlos Clavería, "Reflejos del 'goticismo' español en la fraseología del Siglo de Oro," in *Homenaje a Dámaso Alonso* (Madrid, 1960), I, 357–372.

Castilians, the Aragonese, and the Catalans were new but sturdy collectivities, no longer in need of Gothic, Iberian, or Celtiberian wet nurses. It is only fair to say, however, that Piel, with exceptional good sense, accepts without reservations my idea that the Visigoths were not Spaniards ("neither were the Visigoths Spanish, nor the Franks Frenchmen").

Carlos Clavería has collected examples of the use of phrases such as "to be of Gothic descent," "to come from the Goths," "to pretend to be a Goth" (*ser de los godos, venir de los godos, hacerse de los godos*), which were so common in the sixteenth and seventeenth centuries—a period that I prefer to call "imperial" rather than the "Golden Age." With great perspicacity he notes that these phrases "are derived from the nostalgic memory during the Middle Ages of the Spanish Visigothic kingdom" (p. 358), in which statement the word "nostalgic" is accurate and the word "Spanish," incorrect. The important thing is the nostalgia—and noticing that nothing of the kind happened among the other Romantic peoples. Dante cared nothing about either the Ostrogoths or the Longobards. "The Spaniards' pride in their Gothic origin" (p. 360) does not mean that the Goths were Spaniards, but that the Spaniards were not sufficiently satisfied with their present or their most recent past in either the so-called Middle Ages or the imperial epoch. Language expresses both optical illusions and those created by wishful thinking; but the Spaniards were not Goths—however much they might desire it—nor does the sun "rise," despite the fact that all languages have said so for thousands of years.

Accumulated Knowledge about the Visigoths Confirms What Has Already Been Said

We are interested in what the Visigoths said about themselves, not in what people hoped and imagined about them when they no longer existed as a people with a consciousness of themselves. Although Ortega y Gasset has spoken of "that fine Goth who was the Cid," such an opinion is only a reflection of a long imaginative tradition about the Spanish past. Before the eighth century the inhabitants of the Peninsula reflected the names of the places in which they lived. As Menéndez Pidal says in his *Orígenes del español* (p. 505), "Towns called *Godos* subsist up to today in Portugal, and in the provinces of Coruña, Pontevedra, Oviedo, Teruel; *Revillagodos* in the province of Burgos; *La Goda* in that of Barcelona, and *La Romana, Romanos*, in that of Saragossa; *Romãs, Romão*, in Portugal; *Gudillos* in the province of Segovia, and *Romanillos* in the provinces of Soria, Guadalajara, and Madrid; *Godinhos, Godinho, Godinhella*, and *Romainho* in Portugal; *Godones* in Pontevedra, and

Romanones in Guadalajara; *Godinhaços* in Portugal; *Godojos* in Zaragoza, and *Romancos* (*Románicos*) in Guadalajara." Traces of the settlement in the Peninsula of other German invaders have also been observed by the great philologist. *Villa Alán* (province of Valladolid) and *Puerto del Alano* (in Huesca) are an echo of the Alans. From the Suevi there have endured such names as *Suebos* (Coruña) and the port of *Sueve* (Oviedo). Even in some names of small places there still remain *Vandalisque* (which recalls the Vandals), *Godos, Godín, Romaney* (in Asturias).

As happens everywhere, place-names preserve, sometimes with an unchanging persistence, traces of circumstances and of tongues which have vanished centuries before. In Cómpeta (Malaga) the *compita* (crossroads) persists almost intact phonetically. In the place-names cited above the inhabitants of the Peninsula clearly expressed what they were as a collectivity: some felt themselves existing as Romans, as members of the sociopolitical entity created by Rome; and the others felt bound to the Germanic peoples who had settled in Roman Hispania. There was no awareness or feeling of being something else collectively. The supposed Spanishness of the Goths is nothing more than an anachronism and a phantasmagoria, based on the nostalgia and longings of later centuries.

How the Visigoths Appear to Us

The medieval Spanish chronicles called the Moorish invasion of 711 the "destruction" of Spain; and it was perfectly sensible from their point of view to give it such a name. Let us not stop to lament that remote misfortune, nor to imagine what would have been the destiny of the Iberian Peninsula without the eight centuries of warfare which ensued after the invasion. The important thing now is to make clear how from 711 on, history was to be made *by other peoples* and under different circumstances which may be linked to the succeeding period, but not to the preceding.

The inhabitants of the northern and northwestern parts of the Peninsula had never served as a support and exemplary guide to the Ibero-Romans or to the Romano-Visigoths, and we know very little of them beyond the fact that they offered strong resistance to the Romans as well as to the Visigoths[14]—which lack of information prevents our formulation of any justifiable opinions about them. When the vital dwelling place and functional structure of a people are not known, it is preferable to restrain one's imagination. The Suevi, a

---

[14] "The peoples of the Cantabro-Pyrenean mountains were a perpetual nightmare to the Gothic kings" (Ramón Menéndez Pidal, *Historia de España* [1940], III, 47).

Germanic race, were present in Galicia for 175 years, until Leovigild subjected them in 585. In the sixth century St. Martin of Braga composed his treatise *De correctione rusticorum* to depaganize the Galicians and Asturians. Helmut Schlunk wonders whether, in the realm of the fine arts, "there was in these regions a continuous tradition, independent of the so-called Visigothic art, which begins to conquer the northern regions only in the seventh century. . . . That there was in the northwest of Spain a provincial art of individual character, different from that of the center and south of the country, is indicated by the remains of decorations."[15] In the twelfth century the Basque-Navarrese still gave the traveler a strong impression of rusticity.[16] The fact that they were not linguistically Romanized shows by itself their slight participation in the life of the rest of the Peninsula.

The reconquest of Spain from the Muslims was begun in these regions—only slightly Romanized—of the northwest and to the north of what would become Aragon. The greater part of Hispania, the well-Latinized part, yielded to the Moorish pressure, as it had yielded before to the Visigoths, and before that to the Romans; further, before the Romans came, the eastern and southern coasts had been colonized by Phoenicians and Greeks. When the ten short years of Caesar's conquest of Gaul are compared with the two hundred long years that Hispania cost the Romans, up comes the mirage again of a land populated with people united and animated by a national spirit, somewhat like that of the Spain that opposed Napoleon's Frenchmen. But the Numantians and the Cantabrians went on fighting when large zones of the Peninsula were living peacefully under Roman domination. We do not know how the inhabitants of Hispalis and Corduba felt about the heroic Numantians; but the majority of the forces besieging Numantia were natives of the Peninsula fighting under Roman orders.

The people who started to make war efficaciously against the Moors were not Hispalenses or Tarraconenses, but men from the north of the Peninsula who had no <u>authentic</u> connection with the Visigothic tradition. Although they might regard themselves as the heirs of Visigothic grandeur, it is nonetheless certain that genealogical claims are not enough to substantiate the <u>structure</u> of a <u>people's life</u>. The reconquering Christians were not linked with the Visigoths of Toledo, or Caesar Augusta, or Cartago Nova.[17]

---

[15] *Ars Hispaniae* (Madrid, 1947), II, 342.

[16] *Liber Sancti Jacobi*, transcribed by W. M. Whitehill (Santiago de Compostela, 1944), p. 358.

[17] To attribute to material difficulties the absence of culture among the Christians of northern Spain does not change the reality of this fact.

The *Crónica General* of Alfonso the Learned, in the thirteenth century, saw the Visigothic kingdom as something glorious and remote, without similarity to the present:

So great was it that its dominion extended from sea to sea, as well as from the city of Tangier, which is in Africa, to the Rhone River. This kingdom was exalted in its nobility, ample in the abundance of all things, devout in religion, harmonious and united in the love of peace, made illustrious and pure by the teaching of the councils [of Toledo] . . . ; and by the great virtue of the priests that were there . . . and by the holy bishops Leander, Isidore, Helladius, Eugene, Ildefonsus, Julian, Fulgentius, Martin of Dumio, . . . Taion of Saragossa; and by the excellent school of high philosophy that was in Cordova.[18]

Yet from all that learning—more a nostalgic recollection than a well-documented living tradition—there had been no new offshoots.[19]

At a distance of more than five hundred years, the Visigothic past was clouded in a mist of legend. The mention of an "excellent school of high philosophy [in Cordova]," no longer in existence,[20] reveals the importance attached to the cultural capacities of the Visigoths. The Castilian of the thirteenth century missed that culture, which was doubtless a valuable one, but he did not suspect that in his capacity to rule and to assimilate other groups, and in the originality of his expression in epic poetry, he was already worth more than the vague and vacillating Visigoth.

The break between the Hispania of St. Isidore and the Christian kingdoms of the eleventh century is clearly perceived at precisely that point where there appears to be a link between the one and the others. The Basilica of St. Isidore in Leon, which Ferdinand I ordered to be built in 1063,[21] would seem to reveal, at first glance, that the monarch had some recollection of the great Hispalian sage. But if we consult the *Crónica Silense*,[22] we see that King Ferdinand of Leon sent the bishops Alvitus and Ordoño to Seville to get not the body of St. Isidore but that of a martyr, St. Justa. When the latter was not to be found, it occurred to them to take back the remains of St. Isidore as a substitute. According to the chronicle, the soul of the saint appeared to Alvitus and asked that his body be moved to Leon. It turns out then, if the testimony of the chronicle is not invalid, that the body of the Archbishop of Hispalis was transported to the basilica on account of his saintliness and not because of his learning.

---

[18] Ed. Menéndez Pidal, p. 305.

[19] After the Muslim occupation, ecclesiastical culture decayed considerably (see R. de Abadal, *La batalla del adopcionismo* [Barcelona, 1949], p. 22).

[20] Sidonius Apollinaris (430–488) alludes to a famous Cordovan school, about which I possess no further information: "Corduba praepotens alumnis" (see E. Pérez Pujol, *Historia de las instituciones sociales de la España goda* [1896], III, 490–491).

[21] Ramón Menéndez Pidal, *La España del Cid* (1947), I, 136.

[22] Ed. Santos Coco (1919), pp. 81–82.

Visigoths and Spaniards differ above all in their ethnic names and in the way they "dwell" in their religious belief. It is especially surprising that these presumed Spaniards were dominated in the fifth and sixth centuries by Arian heretics who denied the Catholic dogma of the Trinity; for them Christ was something like a prophet, not a divine person consubstantial with the Father. Menéndez y Pelayo had trouble with this problem for the very reason that he approached Spanish history as a continuity of orthodox Catholic believers. Granted this initial assumption, the following statement of his is logical: "Spain has never been Arian, because the Visigoths were not Spaniards."[23] But then the same historian adds, with passionate arbitrariness, that the Hispano-Romans were the "true and *only* Spanish race [!]" (p. 135). And lost and trapped in this forest of fantasy, he continues: "The race that rose up to reclaim the native soil inch by inch was Hispano-Roman; the good Visigoths [!] had completely blended with it" (pp. 185, 187, 189).

What really happened was quite different. When the Catholic prince Hermenegild rebelled against his father, the Arian King Leovigild, illustrious Catholics like the abbot Johannes Biclarensis and Archbishop Isidore of Hispalis took the part of the father against the son. Those prelates, like the Gallo-Roman bishop Gregory of Tours, did not see in Hermenegild a martyr but a rebel against the authority of the state.[24] Whether the attitude of the Catholic Spaniards might be due to the fact that there was "little of the fanatical" (Menéndez y Pelayo, *Historia de los heterodoxos españoles*, p. 171) about them, or to "Gothic nationalism" (Menéndez Pidal, *La España del Cid*, I, xxvii), it is evident that the conduct of such prelates would have been inconceivable among the Spaniards, who later came into being indissolubly bound to their religious beliefs. As Menéndez Pidal rightly says, Catholics and Arians coincided in their esteem and respect for something higher than their respective beliefs—precisely, I add, because they had a structure of life which was still not Spanish and a hierarchy of values which would later be unthinkable. A Spanish bishop has never admitted, publicly and solemnly, his agreement with a heretic, nor have a heretic and a bishop ever found common shelter under a supreme principle secular in character. The authentic Spaniards, who emerged later, no longer understood the motives of these Goths, and made a martyr out of Hermenegild and a monster out of his father: "Leovigild, king of Spains, holding his son Her-

---

[23] *Historia de los heterodoxos españoles* (1917), II, 94.
[24] "The contemporaries Johannes Biclarensis, Isidore, and Gregory of Tours, even though they were prelates full of Catholic fervor, unanimously condemned the prince as a rebel [*tyrannus* in the ancient sense] against his father and against the kingdom" (Franz Görres, "Die byzantinischen Besitzungen an den Küsten des Spanischen-westgotischen Reiches [554–624]," *Byzantinische Zeitschrift*, XVI [1907], 515–538).

menegild prisoner in the jail, as we said, slew him with an axe while he was lying therein, on the Eve of Easter, because he would not turn to the evil sect of the Arians in which the King believed; and in this way the son was made a martyr of God" (*Crónica General*, p. 262).

The behavior of the Catholic prelates in Hispania with respect to the Arian kings had a precedent in neighboring Gaul. Sidonius Apollinaris (430–488), Bishop of Clermont, protested against the ceding of his province of Auvergne, in accordance with the orders of Emperor Procopius Antemius, to the Gothic king Eurico, who was an Arian. Two years of exile in Septimania, in southern Gaul, made him change his mind; he returned to Auvergne and celebrated the heretical king in his poems. A century later Gregory of Tours (538–594) would also approve the conduct of King Leovigild toward his son Hermenegild.[25] Hermenegild was not canonized until 1586 because it was not until then that Philip II requested it of Pope Sixtus V, a thousand years after what the Visigoths considered a censurable rebellion, and the Spaniards of much later date, a glorious martyrdom.

The way in which King Reccared was converted to Catholicism in 589 is also characteristic of the life forms of the Germanic conquerors. It reminds one of the conversion of Clovis, king of the Franks, in 496 and of Emperor Constantine, which may have served the former as model.[26] Reccared's explanation of his conversion, made before the famous Third Council of Toledo, expresses the relationship between the Visigothic monarchy and the Church:

I do not believe that it is unknown to you, very reverend priests, that the object of *my having honored you* by having summoned you *in the presence of Our Serenity* is the reestablishment of the form of ecclesiastic discipline. Since the heresy that threatened the whole Catholic church has prevented the celebration of councils, God (whom it has pleased to remove the obstacle of that heresy *by means of us*) has admonished us that we should restore the rule of the ecclesiastical custom. May you be filled with joy and gladness to know that, through the providence of God, the canonical custom has returned to the paternal precinct, *to our glory*.

He then exhorts the fathers of the council to fast and pray to the end that "the canonical order so remote from the priests because of long and prolonged oblivion that our generation confesses to not even knowing it" be made manifest to them.[27]

---

[25] See Longnon, *op. cit.*, p. 62; and Luigi Salvatorelli, *L'Italia Medioevale*, pp. 69, 74.

[26] Constantine adopted the cause of the Church for political reasons, even though he was not converted until shortly before his death, as he believed that baptism would free him of all his sins.

[27] *Collectio maxima conciliorum omnium Hispaniae et Novi Orbis*, by José S. de Aguirre (Madrid, 1781), Vol. II. I have here translated more precisely the

First of all, the King speaks as if he were doing a great service to God and to his Church, *all of which* was threatened by the danger of Arianism. None of this was a fact. Reccared speaks as if he himself had not participated in the Arian heresy; instead of humble repentance, he arrogantly flaunts his self-sufficiency, for he is converted *"so that in the future our glory may shine*, honored by the testimony of the Catholic faith" (*per omne successivum tempus gloria nostra ejusdem fidei decorata clarescat*). The enormous sin of not having believed God to be as he is did not enter the King's mind; he treated the whole question as a matter of custom, ecclesiastical law, and liturgy. Instead of saying, as had been the practice among the Visigoths, "Gloria Patri per Filium in Spiritu Sancto," now the priests were required to say "Gloria Patri et Filio et Spiritui Sancto."

Whoever reads the minutes of the famous council without preconceptions will get the impression that political interests, reasons of state, take precedence over religious sentiment and worries about the afterlife. The King says: "Non credimus vestram latere sanctitatem, quanto tempore in errore Arrianorum laborasset Hispania," which does not mean exactly what Menéndez y Pelayo says in his translation ("for all the time that the error of the Arians has prevailed in Spain"), but rather "for all the time that Hispania *has suffered* [for all the travails she has suffered] for being in the error of the Arians." These travails were the civil war between King Leovigild and his son Hermenegild, and the occupation of the south of Hispania by the Byzantines, aided by the Catholics. The Hispano-Roman Isidore of Hispalis wrote: "Gothi per Hermenegildum bifarie divisi multa caede vastantur" (the Goths—he does not say the Hispano-Romans and the Goths!—divided into two bands because of Hermenegild, destroy and kill one another).[28] The conversion of Reccared and the condemnation of Hermenegild by St. Isidore lead toward the same goal, the unification and enlargement of the Visigothic kingdom. "After the conversion of Reccared," says the Catholic writer Görres, "the Byzantines offered no further attraction to the Hispano-Romans." And in the minutes of the council we read further on: "Vos tamen Dei sacerdotes meminisse oportet, quantis hucusque ecclesia Dei catholica per Hispanias adversae partis molestiis laboraverit" ("You priests should remember to what extent the Spanish Church has suffered adversity"). The conversion served to exalt the glory of the King and of the Visigoths: "Gloria Deo nostro Jesu Christo, qui *tam illustrem gentem* unitati verae fidei copulavit, et unum gregem et unum pastorem instituit. Cui a Deo aeternum meritum nisi vero catholico Reccaredo regi? Cui *praesens gloria* et aeterna,

---

passage that may be found in Menéndez y Pelayo, *Historia de los heterodoxos españoles* (1917), II, 180.

[28] Görres, *op. cit.*, p. 522.

nisi vero amatori Dei Reccaredo regi? . . . Adest enim omnis gens Gothorum inclyta et fere omnium gentium gemina *virilitate opinata"*[29] ("Glory to our lord Jesus Christ, who has united *such a number of illustrious personages,* joined in the unity of faith, established in one flock under one shepherd. To whom should God bestow the eternal reward, but to the truly Catholic king, Reccared? *Who deserves the glory* in this world and the next, but King Reccared, faithful and true glory of God? . . . All the renowned people of the Goths, *known for their courage.")* The expressive style of this passage is characteristically Visigothic. The decision taken by the King might be linked to that of Henry IV of France, which was also inspired more by political than by sentimental motives. With the Byzantines occupying a broad and rich zone in Hispania, the kingdom was being drawn away from the Roman world, which was beginning to order its vital structure under the spiritual guidance of Catholic Rome. To recover sovereignty over a kingdom undivided and in harmony with the Christian tradition of the Roman Empire, it was well worth renouncing the dogma of the nondivinity of Christ.

Let us accept with Menéndez y Pelayo the fact that the Visigoths were not Spaniards,[30] with, however, the inescapable consequence of extending the same negative judgment to the other inhabitants of that kingdom. The Hispania of the Goths was a condition for the Christian kingdoms that came later, as Germano-Byzantine Italy was for the future Italian cities, which, in the twelfth century, were no longer either Germano-Byzantine or Roman and possessed no secular capital which might unite them politically. The historical strata in such instances bring to mind certain cities of Antiquity, successively razed and "rebuilt," one on top of the other. The excavations at Ephesus have disclosed the ruins of the pre-Egyptian, Egyptian, Greek, and Roman city. Each utilized the materials of the preceding one to the end of building the new city; but none of them could have lived together with one of the older ones, nor did any one of them represent a moment in the "evolution" of those successive cities.

---

[29] J. D. Mansi, *Sacrorum Conciliorum. . . . Collectio* (Florence, 1763), IX, col. 979.

[30] In his discourse before the Council of Basel (1434), Don Alonso de Cartagena (as imperialist as all the other converts from Judaism who were interested in the politics of the kingdom) realized that it was necessary to make his idea of Spain coincide with the continuity of the Catholic faith: "After the Spaniards, in the time of St. James, received the faith, they did not depart from it," although it is true that "in the time of King Leovigild . . . *some people* were infected with the Arian heresy. . . . In the Third Council of Toledo, the Arian heresy was *completely* destroyed; but the Spaniards as a whole never strayed from the faith, for even during the time when that heresy was most prevalent, there flourished in Spain St. Isidore, St. Leander," etc. (*La Ciudad de Dios* [1894], XXXV, 537). We have already seen that the problem is slightly more complicated.

The Goths did not write, or there have not been preserved, poetic works in which they expressed the intimacy of their existence. But enough is known about them for us to affirm that their life was neither entirely Roman nor Germanic, although both elements were a condition for their existence. Isidore of Hispalis, of Roman ancestry, felt that he was a Visigoth, even though, for lack of sufficient evidence, I cannot say precisely what the collective purpose of Visigothic life may have been. I suspect, moreover, that in the confused jungle of the past there must be something to correspond to the category of a *vital structure incompletely realized* (a vital "dwelling place" that is poorly furnished), that is, peoples who move through life (in the past or today, a terrible situation) without ever recognizing themselves—within themselves and in their achievements—as completely existing and worthy subjects of history. Perhaps they dreamed, or dream, of some magic stroke of fortune which might give completeness to their existence. There are peoples who have lived like those linguistic dialects that have never served as the expression for important works. Our imperfect set of historical instruments does not permit us to capture these vital dwelling places that I would call "half finished." Perhaps these peoples have combined a yearning existence with the awareness, or with the belief, that they do exist completely. To be sure, there must be a certain structural completeness in such cases: a dwarf is completely a dwarf, although, seen in another perspective, he seems incomplete; in other words, there are peoples whose life merits treatment only in chronicles, not in history.

If we should look at the Visigothic kingdom in the perspective of the Rome of Augustus, or the Spain of Charles V, or the England of Victoria, we would get the impression that the Visigoths of the fifth, sixth, and seventh centuries were not yet preparing themselves to be very important.[31] The Visigoths themselves seem to have been aware of their difficult vital situation. Like the rest of the provinces of what was once the Empire, the Hispano-Romano-Visigoths believed that Rome had not disappeared. In the fifth century Paulus Orosius, a Hispano-Roman (whom some people anachronistically call Spanish), writes: "Rome, after so many years, continues to maintain herself and *preserves her authority intact*; the Goths and Alaric have invaded her and despoiled her of her wealth, *not of her empire*." Orosius had to feel himself as living within the vital orbit of Rome because the barbarian invaders still lacked a collective structure in

---

[31] This observation refers to what the Visigoths at a given moment felt about themselves; it is not an attempt to prophesy their future. In the seventh century no Western people presented an image that anticipated what it was going to be and do five centuries later. But from the thirteenth century on the Castilians did indeed desire for themselves an imperial future.

which one could be included, and the life of Hispania without the awareness of being Roman was inconceivable. If it was necessary for Orosius to take refuge in the vital notion of Rome in order to escape the anguish of having no place in which to be vitally "stationed," the enlightened Visigoths of that time felt the same way: they felt that they did not exist as an individuality, and in desperation they embraced the illusion of a still existent Rome, in spite of all they were doing to destroy it. A fine anecdote has been preserved by Orosius, who picked it up, when he was in Bethlehem with the future St. Jerome, from a knight of Narbonne, who had heard King Ataulf expound his political plans. This Visigothic chieftain intended to do away with even the name "Roman" (*obliterato Romano nomine*), and to replace it with "Gothic." *Gothia* was to succeed *Romania*.[32] Ataulf changed his mind when it occurred to him that the barbarianism of his Goths would keep them from obeying the laws, "without which the state is not a state" (*sine quibus respublica non est respublica*). He preferred then to utilize the power of his people to restore its former grandeur to the name Roman, for, having been unable to transform Rome (*postquam esse non potuerat immutato*), he aspired to restore her past.[33] Thanks to this flash of awareness, of Visigothic autognosis, which Orosius reported with intelligent sympathy,[34] we observe the Visigoths' entering into history sustained by the purpose of slipping into a life structure that was not their own. As we have seen, the Goths wanted to be Romans: they occupied the Peninsula in the name of Rome, they issued laws based on the Roman tradition, and they wrote in Latin and spoke something meant to be Latin even though it no longer really was. They even went so far as to continue the bad imperial custom of seeking foreign assistance in the settlement of their internal quarrels: the Byzantine invasion is an antecedent of the coming of the Arabs, whose decisive entrance in 711 was preceded by three other attempts at foreign occupation.

---

[32] This procedure was followed by other Germanic peoples, who created states with ethnic names: Lombardy, France, Anglia, Normandy, Burgundy. It is significant that nothing like this was produced in the Iberian Peninsula. Perhaps the Visigoths lacked sufficient force and personality.

[33] This important passage has already been noted by Gaston Boissier in *La Fin du paganisme* (1891), II, 409. See Paulus Orosius, *Historiarum adversum paganos libri VII*, ed. C. Zangemeister, pp. 86, 560.

[34] I do not share the view that Orosius was a Spaniard. In his *Histoire de la littérature latine* (1912), p. 914, René Pichon says that Prudentius and Orosius differ from St. Paulinus of Nola (353–431) in that the first two are Spaniards and the third is French: "It is always the contrast between the French spirit compounded of clear good sense and easy grace, and the Spanish spirit, harsher and more passionate." Seduced, like certain Spaniards, by the antiquated idea that human realities are unchangeable substances, Pichon did not realize that a history such as that of Orosius is most unlike any Spanish work: in the fifteen hundred years that intervene between Orosius and the present, no Spaniard has tried to write a universal history to demonstrate a thesis. The modern writers who resemble Orosius are Bossuet, Spengler, and Toynbee.

Yet I am not trying to present a picture of Visigothic life, or to probe into the deficiencies and incapabilities of those who lived it. I am interested, on the contrary, in bringing out some of their more valuable aspects, and to show, by these, how radical the difference is between their life structure and that of the Spaniards. It has already been seen that the conversion of Reccared and the conduct of the Catholic prelates were phenomena very closely linked to the Visigothic form of life. It is now suitable to consider the supposed theocracy of the Visigoths, regarded by many as a logical antecedent of the Spain of Philip II, even though certain Spanish historians may no longer think so.[35] The Church and the monarchy supported each other. The kings, especially starting with Reccared, preferred having the Church, united under a discipline, as their support, rather than to rely on a divided, hereditary nobility, powerful and inclined to sedition. The king customarily named the bishops. The bishops (and future saints) Braulius and Isidore on one certain occasion recommended to King Sisenand a candidate for archbishop of Tarraco (modern Tarragona), and the King named a person of his own choice.[36]

But there is something still more characteristic which brings us to the very core of Visigothic life structure, to that "dwelling place" from within which life is projected. The learned ecclesiastics of the Visigothic epoch are remembered by posterity as men of learning and not as ecclesiastics. Since them there has never been in Spain any saint who was at the same time erudite and wise, in the age-old meaning of wisdom, like St. Anselm, St. Bonaventure, or St. Thomas. The Spaniards did not canonize Father Francisco Suárez, the greatest metaphysician they had; nor even Raymond Lully, who never got above the modest category of "blessed." And canonizations in the past are a valid chart, I think, of the hierarchies of values in the Christian peoples.

The figure of Isidore of Hispalis (570?–636) clearly illustrates the split between the Hispania prior to 711 and the future Spain. He reflected the last flashes of Roman learning, now fragmentary and disconnected from the life structure it had expressed. In the words left by Isidore there are compilations and systematic reductions of the

---

[35] "The Visigothic church of the seventh century cannot be called national, in the sense of being a church directed and governed by the monarch, nor can the Visigothic state be called theocratic, if by this is meant a state in which . . . the bishops and councils hold the reins of government. . . . The Visigothic king manifestly exercised a number of rights in purely ecclesiastical matters" (Menéndez Pidal, *Historia de España*, III, 286–287).

[36] In a letter to Braulius, Isidore says: "De constituendo autem episcopo Tarraconensi non eam quam petistis sensi sententiam regis" ("As to the appointment of the bishop of Tarraco, I don't think the King has accepted your recommendation") (*Epistolario de San Braulio*, ed. J. Madoz, pp. 87–88). The King's action seems normal to Isidore, and he says nothing more about it.

Roman notions about man and nature, and the theological doctrines of some of the fathers of the Church. For the present purpose, the originality of those writings, or their possible value for modern science, is of little importance. I bring up Isidore at this juncture to put into relief the intellectual zeal that made possible his preoccupation with human-divine learning, conceived from and directed toward a horizon of international culture. After the Visigoths eight hundred years were to pass before a few Spaniards (of the Jewish caste) would be interested in secular culture, in investigating the nature of things. Isidore, Braulius, Ildefonsus, Eugene, and other Visigoths are known for their culture as well as for their sanctity.

Issuing out of Roman Antiquity, Isidore's work feeds medieval western Europe's desire for knowledge. In it and in the works of other Visigoths there is a glimmering of what the hierarchy of values might have been in the Iberian Peninsula without the Muslims—an observation offered not as an elegy but as an illustration. Isidore is neither profound nor original in his thought. He rests on Roman learning and knows nothing of that of Greece, now severed from the West and lying dormant even in Byzantium. The natural science of the Romans had very little of the scientific about it.[37]

Isidore's *Etymologies* (or *Origins*), in spite of what I have already said about him, is not an incoherent melange devoid of internal unity. A single idea, not perceptible at first glance, dominates the whole: The line of descent starts from God and goes to angels, then to men, and then to nature. The fact that the work was left unfinished does not keep us from recognizing that it contains thought ordered as a systematic whole.[38] Isidore's writings were in phase with the Occidental mind and continued to be so for centuries. Charles H. Beeson says:

> The rapid and truly gigantic diffusion of the manuscripts of Isidore is a notable event in the history of the cultural tradition. To observe the diffusion of those works and the use to which they were put is a profitable task, inasmuch as it reveals the extraordinary favor Isidore enjoyed. By pointing out the zeal with which this diligent compiler's works were read, we get an idea of the literary activities and theological preoccupations of the darkest period of the Middle Ages. The powerful influence exerted by Hispania over that world looms as the background of the picture, an influence to which Isidore contributed more than anyone.[39]

So evident a reality is accepted by scholars all over Europe, and it

---

[37] See Ernest Brehaut, *An Encyclopedist of the Dark Ages: Isidore of Seville* (New York: Columbia University Free Press, 1912), p. 40.

[38] A. Schmekel, *Isidorus von Sevilla: Sein System, seine Quellen* (Berlin, 1914), pp. 1–2.

[39] *Isidor-Studien* (Munich, 1913), p. 3. For the influence of the Visigothic writers on the European liturgy, see Bishop, in *Journal of Theological Studies*, VIII (1907), 278.

would be idle to adduce further testimony. One of them has gone so far as to try to correct the idea that Isidore knew no Greek, merely because passages can be found in his work which are translated literally from Cyril of Alexandria, at that time accessible only in Greek.[40]

Isidore was not, furthermore, a random monolith standing in desert sands. For certain Hispano-Goths it was possible to be interested in the knowledge of things. Ildefonsus of Toledo, another future saint, writes that Eugene (a bishop, d. 646) was well versed in the observation of the phases of the moon; those who heard him talk of this were left astonished and felt desirous of studying astronomical science.[41] This and other facts (the epistles of Licinianus of Cartagena, for example) reveal the presence of an atmosphere of intellectual curiosity, whose density it would not be possible to determine; the fact remains that it existed. From the city of Caesar Augusta (which, but for the Arabs, would not be called Saragossa today), Braulius wrote Isidore an epistle demanding that he remit a copy of his *Etymologies*, the great encyclopedia of knowledge of that time: "Do you think, perhaps, that the gift of your learning was granted you for yourself alone? Indeed it is as much ours as yours; it is common property, and not private."[42]

Let us forego a comparison of Isidore with other Europeans (the Venerable Bede, the Irish humanists, etc.) on an absolute scale of values. The only thing pertinent to the present problem is the will to know the natural world and the world of men, the "origin" of things, the rational—not the fabulous—history of the then inhabitants of Hispania (Isidore's *History of the Goths*), or the principles according to which the sons of the nobility ought to be educated. All this was the personal task of Isidore, who was preoccupied with certain questions and with answering them adequately. It will occur to some, perhaps, that Alfonso the Learned, a Spaniard, was also filled with scientific curiosity and composed voluminous works. And in a way this is true. But between Alfonso and Isidore there is a cleaving difference, because their functional life structures, their social dimensions, were different. The King of Castile, like an Oriental caliph, ordered the wise men of his court to undertake long pilgrimages through books Arabic and Christian, for the end of accumulating huge masses of knowledge about man as a social being and about his

---

[40] See Patrick J. Mullins, *The Spiritual Life According to Saint Isidore of Seville* (Catholic University of America, 1940), pp. 75 ff.

[41] "Idem Eugenius moribus incessuque gravis, ingenio callens. Nam numerus, statum, incrementa, decrementa, cursus, recursusque lunarum tanta peritia novit, ut considerationes disputationis ejus auditorem et in stuporem verterent, et desiderabilem doctrinam inducerent" ("Episcopi Toletani," in J. P. Migne, ed., *Patrologia*, S. L., vol. 96, col. 204).

[42] *Epistolario de San Braulio*, ed. J. Madoz (1940), pp. 80–82.

future destiny. Alfonso, with a life already hammered out on the Christian-Islamic-Judaic anvil, had an appetite for being taught what man had been like from the remote depths of time, how he was supposed to be governed morally and legally, what his future destiny might be, according to the predictions of the stars. Rational curiosity, pure and simple, was not a necessity for the wise sovereign, "al-ḥakim," of Castile. There rained down upon him the learned works that his zeal for knowledge had solicited. Yet the gigantic work he sponsored and fostered remained obscured, like an eccentric recluse, in its own land, because it was not expressed in the international language of Europe. Alfonso was not interested in including contemporary Europe in the panorama of his culture. His work was meaningful and efficacious for those in Spain who shared his life structure. The highly praised *Alphonsine Astronomical Tables*, a product of rational curiosity and thus a possible exception, are the work of Arabic and Jewish astronomers and bear the name of Alfonso only from the time-honored practice of flattery. In order to find a Castilian comparable to Isidore, we would have to come down to the humanist Antonio de Nebrija (a Christian whom I believed to be of Jewish descent), a direct and original disciple of late fifteenth-century Italian science. In the period between Isidore and Nebrija (eight hundred years) we find nothing that we can connect with the natural and rational concerns of the Visigothic vital structure.

The Visigothic ecclesiastics, as is evident from what I have said, did not scorn secular knowledge, nor did they think that this world was a vale of tears devoid of all good. A reading of the works of certain subsequently canonized Visigoths leaves the impression of serenity and peace. Let us examine, for instance, the treatise of Isidore of Hispalis on the education of the children of the nobility, based on principles fundamentally more worldly than ascetic.[43] In the human ideal of Isidore, the Greco-Roman and the Germano-Christian traditions are harmonized; virtue is conceived in a broad sense and not limited to the religious or seignorial life. Isidore's treatise presupposes the existence of a monarchico-elective regime, within which any knight excelling in gifts can ascend to the throne. A sentence from Plato summarizes the sense of these brief pages: "The kingdom is well governed when the philosophers rule and the rulers philosophize" (*Tunc bene regi rem publicam quando imperant philosophi et philosophantur imperatores*, p. 559). The sentence is to be found in many places: Boethius quotes it (*De consolatione*, I, 4, 5), and it is still recalled by La Bruyère. But Isidore makes use of it precisely at the moment when he is discussing the actual structure of the Visigothic kingdom.

---

[43] "Isidori Hispalensis 'Institutionum Disciplinae,'" ed. A. E. Anspach, in *Rheinisches Museum*, Neue Folge, LVII (1912), 556–563.

The Stoic-Christian spirit can be discerned in the insistent recommendation of chastity; wet nurses and teachers are to avoid all lewd obscenity: "The condition of the wellborn should be evident in their mode of conduct more than in the high rank they occupy." But at the same time the youth is to possess "apta et uirilis figura membrorum, duritia corporis, robur lacertorum" ("a well-proportioned, manly figure, a hard body, and strong muscles," p. 558); for this, mountain and sea sports are to be recommended. The pupil must be versed in Holy Scripture, and also in philosophy, medicine, arithmetic, geometry, and astrology; he is to be pure, wise, and of good counsel, a lover of religion, and the defender of the fatherland. The great lord will also have to restrain his greed, so as not to harm the humble: "His fields must not be immoderately extended at the expense of the poor" (*Neque rura sua, exclusis pauperibus, latius porrigentur*, p. 559).[44]

This brief treatise allows us to see something of the possible human horizon for the best Visigoths in the seventh century, not so dark as it is usually said to be. Isidore's Hispania felt itself firmly seated in this world and sure of itself. The *De Laude Hispaniae* at the beginning of Isidore's *Historia Gothorum*[45] begins thus: "Of all the

---

[44] Petrus Hispanus, since he was the author of thirteenth-century works on philosophy and medicine which were not only read and admired in the Middle Ages but were in part even translated into Hebrew, might be thought by some readers to be comparable to St. Isidore. The Germans K. Prantl in 1866 and M. Grabman in 1928 drew attention to the importance of his commentaries on Aristotle. G. Sarton, *Introduction to the History of Science* (1931), II, 889–892, mentions his writings on medicine. Subsequently, the Spaniards have treated of this encyclopedist: T. and J. Carreras y Artau, *Historia de la filosofía española* (1939), I, 101–144. M. Alonso has edited the book *De Anima* (Madrid, 1941) and has published the *Comentario al "De anima" de Aristóteles* (Madrid, 1944). It seems that Petrus Hispanus and Pope John XXI are the same person; Dante mentions Pietro *Ispano* among the major men of learning (*Paradiso*, XII, 134–135). The figure of so important a personage is surrounded by legends, and the reader can see for himself what there is of fact and fancy in the works cited above. It is enough for my purposes to point out that this philosopher, physician, and pope was born in Portugal, presumably in Lisbon, in the twelfth century; he studied in Paris, and spent the rest of his life in France and Italy. Even though he was born biologically of parents who lived in Portugal, the functional structure of his life was not Portuguese; for, if he had remained in Portugal, he would not have done what he did. There is no reason why an intelligent person born in the Iberian Peninsula today or in thirteenth century should not become a good scientist, if he incorporates into his life, either totally or partly, alien ways of life. The same thing happened to Petrus Hispanus, or Lusitanus, as he might better be called. The Spaniard has no biological incapacity for theoretical or experimental science. What distinguishes Petrus Hispanus from Isidore of Hispalis is that the latter was educated in Visigothic Hispania, there he produced his achievements, and from there his work was projected into the international world. The work of Petrus Hispanus, on the contrary, became possible and was achieved outside Spain. Spanish scholars have become aware of the existence of their "compatriot" only in recent years—and after the studies about him produced by foreigners.

[45] In *Chronica minora saec. IV, V, VI, VII*, ed. Theodor Mommsen, II, 267.

lands that extend from the west to India, thou art the fairest, Oh sacred Hispania, ever fecund mother of princes and peoples, rightful queen of all the provinces, from whom west and east draw their light. Thou art the honor and ornament of the world, and the most illustrious part of the earth; in thee the glorious fecundity of the Visigothic people takes much delight and flourishes abundantly." And the praise of Spain concludes: "With good reason in another time golden Rome, chief of the peoples, desired to possess thee; but even though Roman valor, victorious, might first take thee as a bride, the powerful race of the Goths came later and carried thee off to love thee, after many victorious wars fought over the vastness of the earth. That race delights in thee even today, secure in the happiness of its domain, with regal dignity and greatness of wealth."

It is beside the point to recall the "laudes" of other countries (in Pliny, Virgil, and other writers of Antiquity): what counts here is the fact that Isidore exalts the grandeur of the Visigothic people, the strength of their arms, before which the power of Rome had to yield. The pagan image of the rape of the bride gives to the praise of Hispania a quite earthly perspective, devoid of both anguish and uncertainty. The learned archbishop magnified the military glory of his kings, who did not fight for "divine"motives, as, according to Don Alonso de Cartagena, the Spanish kings had always done:

In the year 620, in the tenth year of the reign of the Emperor Heraclius, the most glorious Swintila, by divine grace,[46] received the sceptre. As a duke—a title conferred on him by King Sisebut—he reduced to complete submission the Byzantine armies [in the south], and he conquered the Rucones[47] [in the north of Hispania]. After ascending to the peak of royal dignity, he conquered the cities still under the dominion of the Byzantines. . . . Swintila was the first to possess the whole of Spain even to beyond the Straits of the South [Gibraltar], something his predecessors had not accomplished.

The world, according to Isidore, can be encompassed and dominated by courage in warfare, and also through knowledge and intellectual reflection. For him religious faith did not fill all the space in the dwelling place of life. The Hispano-Goth, insofar as the initial thrust of his life was concerned, was in line with the other peoples of western Europe: the Franco-Gauls, the Anglo-Britons, the Ostrogoth-Romans. Among them, the other-worldly was articulated with the this-worldly, without the exclusion of the one by the other. That

---

[46] The belief that kings receive divine grace comes from the Roman emperors, who got it, in turn, from the religions of the Orient, where the monarchs had a sacred character. See Franz Cumont, *Les religions orientales dans le paganisme romain* (1929).

[47] A people about whom little is known beyond what Isidore himself says about them.

is why the Germanicized Hispanian, Isidore, a Catholic bishop, could align himself with Leovigild, a heretical king, against the latter's son, the rebellious and Catholic Hermenegild; and other Germanicized Hispanians, as Catholic as they were learned, behaved in the same fashion. In the *Historia Gothorum*, Isidore's enthusiasm for the Gothic abductors of Hispania is not veiled in the kind of grief that a "Spaniard" would have felt over the fact that Spain had been subjected by barbarians to whom Jesus Christ was not God but a prophet, or something of the sort.

When, in the thirteenth century, the *Crónica General* of Alfonso the Learned takes up and elaborates on the theme of Isidore's "praise of Spain," the feeling is quite different, because the Spaniards were no longer Hispano-Romano-Goths. Notice how far away we are from Isidore:

Everyone must therefore learn that he should not place great value upon himself: neither the rich man for his riches, nor the powerful for his power, nor the strong for his strength, nor the learned for his learning, nor the exalted man for his high station or his goods; but he who seeks to place great value upon himself, let him do so for his service to God, for it is He who strikes and gives ointment, who wounds and heals, for all the earth is His; and all the nations and all people, kingdoms, languages, *all move about and change, but God*, the Creator of everything, *endures forever* and remains in the same state.   (p. 311)

Six hundred years after Isidore, Spain is submerged in the theological metaphysics of Islam: "For only God is, and has being." Whoever it may have been who composed this part of the *Crónica General*, he could no longer end the praise of Spain with the lucid, chiseled words of Isidore: "Imperii felicitate secura." Rather must he use these terms of trembling and anguish:

For this kingdom, so noble, so rich, so powerful, so honored, was overthrown and brought down in an outburst of discord among the inhabitants of the land, who turned their swords against one another, as if they were lacking in enemies; and in this they all lost, for all the cities of Spain were captured by the Moors, and were ruined and destroyed at the hands of her enemies. . . . Wretched Spain! Her woeful death was so complete that there was no one left to mourn it; they call her the afflicted one, more dead than alive, and her voice sounds as if from another world, and her words come forth as if from beneath the earth.   (p. 312)

This lament refers, of course, to the tragic invasion of 711; but after that event we will never find discussions of the past framed in the firm and confident words of Isidore. Thereafter, one way or another, underneath the most elevated dithyrambs will always be perceived the undertone of insecurity, dissatisfaction, and complaint. The meaning and direction of life in the times of Isidore vanished to make way for something quite different. Out of that life and on its foundations was born a new life that would bring glory and despair to the people who created it—as has happened to all the world's peoples, placed here for reasons and purposes known only to God.

From Visigothic Hispania to the Authentic Spain

The memory of the Goths remained alive among the Leonese and Castilian kings as an image of past grandeur they aspired to restore. The people did preserve a few juridical customs of Germanic origin, customs that persisted in spite of the fact that Visigothic legislation had tried to rid itself of them because they were contrary to the spirit of Roman law. It was a Germanic custom for a creditor to attach the goods of his debtor without the intervention of a judge; or for the family of a murdered person to be allowed to take vengeance on the killer.[48] The survival of these customs did not imply that the Leonese and Castilians were living according to an inner life structure analogous to that of certain Germanic peoples who had preserved similar legal usages. The Roman laws were in effect at the same time as the legal tradition of the Visigoths; and it would not occur to anyone to think for this reason that the Spaniards were Romans, for everything that is left as a residue of the past takes its meaning from the contemporaneous life disposition of a people, which determines the way in which the past and its customs are used.

The nostalgia for the idealized Visigothic monarchy nourished the belief that Christian Spain had an illustrious past, a belief not lacking in foundation. When Alfonso II (791–835) installed his court in Oviedo (Asturias), he thought he was reestablishing the "Gothic order" of Toledo,[49] and down into the seventeenth century, "to have

---

[48] See Eduardo de Hinojosa, *El elemento germano en el derecho español* (Madrid, 1915). [Alfonso García Gallo has revised Hinojosa's classic approach to this important problem. According to him, pre-Gothic Roman tradition should also be taken into account (*El carácter germánico de la épica y del derecho en la Edad Media Española*, Anuario de Historia del Derecho Español, Madrid, 1955).]

[49] "Omnem Gothorum ordinem, sicuti Toleto fuerat, tam in Ecclesia quam palatio, in Obeto cuncta statuit" (*Chronica Albeldense*, ed. Gómez Moreno, in *Boletín de la Academia de la Historia* [1932], p. 602). R. Menéndez Pidal mentions the survival of a Gothic legend in the story of Fernán González, count of Castile, to whom the King of Leon was forced to grant independence (along with that of Castile itself) because he had defaulted on the payment for a horse and the debt had increased in geometric progression over the years (*Los godos y el origen de la épica española* [1955], pp. 64–67). Other epic themes, as well as the epic genre itself, doubtless have Visigothic antecedents. Menéndez Pidal believes that I consider "that the Visigoths stand outside all that which we may call Hispanic" (p. 39); but what has gone before in this study, as well as the whole of the work, shows that such is not my opinion. In Spanish literature there are more biblical, Hellenic, and Roman themes than there are Germanic, which does not mean that the Spaniards continue the vital forms and collective dimensions of those peoples. As a literary form the epic is Indo-European, but this fact does not make the Greeks and the Germans into

Gothic ancestry" (*ser de los godos*) was a seal of glory for Spaniards. Notice, however, that (as I have pointed out before) this same animating aspiration to be like the Goths reveals that the Spaniards of the Middle Ages were not Goths; nor was the land that they were in process of reconquering and repopulating any longer Gothic. That which inspires and fascinates, and the authentic life of those who are inspired and fascinated, are different realities, just as historical condition and possibility, on the one hand, and that which is conditioned and made possible, on the other, are not the same things.

The collective dimensions and the scale of values of the Visigoths had vanished. The bishops no longer subordinated ecclesiastical power to the secular interests of the state. The cultural zeal of Alfonso the Learned would not be like that of St. Isidore. The worldly imperialism of the Visigoths had been succeeded by a "godly" war waged by people who as a group called themselves "Christians" because their enemies were called "Muslims." Whereas the Jews were violently mistreated by the Visigothic kings, they would now be protected by the kings of Spain during the eight centuries of reconquest.

In large part Christian Hispania was being submerged and broken up by the Moorish tidal wave. In the regions where the resistance against the infidels was born—on the Cantabrian coastal strip and in the Aragonese section of the Pyrenees—the perspective of life was not Visigothic. The tasks were different and very difficult on account of the loss of all the large cities and the resources of the civilization of that time. The only cities of any importance in Gallaecia were Bracara (now Braga), Asturica (Astorga), and Lucus Augusti (Lugo); the Asturian towns of the Visigothic period must have been poor and small. Both provinces were rich only in forests, mines, and cattle, whereas the richest farm lands had stayed in the hands of the Muslims. To compensate for such poverty, the northern strip of the Peninsula had a long tradition of human fortitude, of stubborn rebellion, which had shown itself in the fight against the Romans and the Visigoths, and in the assumption, or the maintenance, of discrepant attitudes in the spiritual realm. The Suevian occupation in Galicia must have contributed to increasing even more its separation from the rest of the country. Actually, the Astures and Gallaeci had lived as subject peoples without any feeling of self-determination or direction. This being so, the catastrophe on the Guadalete in 711 suddenly conferred on them the unexpected power to act, in response to external solicitation, on their own energetic initiative. Starting in the middle of the eighth century these people, forgotten by history, began to create a history for themselves parallel with the other nascent histories of

---

Indo-Europeans with respect to the form and collective dimension of their lives. "To descend from" biologically is different from feeling oneself "to exist socially and historically just like another group."

Castile, Navarre, Aragon, and Catalonia. The accords, the discords, and the discrepancies among these peoples were to fill the future of the Peninsula from that day till this. The Hispania of the Visigoths was left broken up into regions with names that had never been heard before: Castilla, Navarra, Aragón, and Cataluña. León had been the name of the encampment-city of the *Legio Septima Gemina.* Only Galicia retained her traditional name of *Gallaecia.*

The Visigothic nation sank from sight just at the moment when it was apparently on the way to establishing political, linguistic, and religious unity throughout the Peninsula.[50] When its destruction was brought about, the northern strip, from Galicia to the Mediterranean, split into segments that were to remain separate for centuries, and whose forms of speech were to be Galician, Asturian-Leonese, Castilian, Basque, Aragonese, Catalonian. Even though the Basque language may have existed since prehistoric times, what really was bound to weaken and retard the Romanization (Latinization) of those who spoke it was the fall of the Visigothic monarchy.[51] Each of those languages gave expression, in greater or lesser degree, to the life situation in which each people found itself—the needs of war, a rudimentary economy, the cultural contacts with the Moors and French. The Visigothic past, as a political and social reality, was being left in the remote distance. From now on history was going to take the form of the independent movement toward the south of six groups of people—Galicians, Leonese, Castilians, Basques, Aragonese, and Catalonians—who were starting on their course, each of them, like six horsemen, equipped with his own language and plan of life. From the crossing of their several lives, under the strong hand of Castile, would emerge the Spaniards' "dwelling place" of existence.

For the first few centuries it was Galicia that offered the most original and productive program for Hispanic Christendom: the militant cult of St. James the Apostle, conqueror of the Moors, future patron of Spain and one of the centers of her history, as I will demonstrate later.

---

[50] For a treatment of linguistic questions, see R. Menéndez Pidal, *Orígenes del español* (1929), and Amado Alonso, "Partición de las lenguas románicas de Occidente," in *Miscelánea Fabra* (Buenos Aires, 1943).

[51] And not only this: The new circumstances conferred on the Basques and their language an active and constructive role: they gave a few pronunciations to the Castilians, among others, the disappearance of Latin initial *f*, so that Castilians say *hacer,* not *facer.* The impetus of a people without a perceptible tradition of culture thus left its mark on a language of Roman ancestry. I am of the opinion that the Basques had the same kind of effect, but in small degree, on Castilian as the Franks had, on a large scale, on Gallo-Romanic, the French of today, or the Berbers had on the Muslims of al-Andalus. The presence and importance of Basque fighters left its imprint on certain phonetic characteristics of Castilian, which did not take over from the Basques the names of culturally important objects, because the Basques did not possess any such. These would be provided by the Arabs and the French.

A good many Galicians of today would have it that the mortal remains preserved in the tomb of St. James the Apostle in Compostela
are those of the famous heresiarch Priscillian and not those of the
Apostle of Christ, a claim that is not without some point. Without
getting into an argument about a suspicion that can never be confirmed by means of authentic documents, I am of the opinion that
the relation between Santiago, as St. James is called in Spanish, and
Priscillian is not corporal, but of quite a different order. Priscillian,
the leading representative of an important heresy or Christian dissidence, was executed in Trier in 385, by order of imperial authority.[52]
Priscillianist beliefs took root especially in Galicia. Thus, when the
Arian Suevi occupied that territory, they met with beliefs that bore
some resemblance to their own insofar as the Suevi themselves did
not accept the dogma of the Trinity of God, One and Indivisible.
The Council of Braga (567) anathematized those who said that "the
Son of God and Our Lord did not exist before he was born of the
Virgin," as well as those who introduced "*other* divine persons out-
side the Most Holy Trinity," errors committed by the Priscillianists.
The latter believed in "the Procession of Aeons, emanating from the
divine essence, and inferior to it in dignity." One of these Aeons was
the Son, wherefore St. Leo calls the Priscillianists "Arians."[53]

The Priscillianism of the fourth century, the Arianism of the fifth
and sixth, the adoptionism of the eighth (which maintained that Christ
was the adopted son of God),[54] and other beliefs not very far from
these, will be better understood when they can be seen in relation to
certain Oriental religions spread throughout the Roman Empire,
whose legions were often filled with Asiatics, as Franz Cumont and
others have shown. The anti-Trinitarian, or incorrectly Trinitarian,
belief of many Christians in the Iberian Peninsula—a Priscillianist belief that antedates the arrival of the Arian Germans—was not altered
overnight by the conversion of Reccared. The absence in the Iberian
Peninsula of firm ideas concerning the dual (human-divine) nature
of Christ during the Visigothic epoch and the traditional rooting of
such ideas in distant and eccentric Galicia (very much paganized
even in the time of St. Martin of Braga, later Priscillianist, and later
Arian)—all these circumstances will make understandable certain
popular aspects in the early cult of Santiago which today astonish
people who have little knowledge of these matters.

Contemplated in the perspective of the Toletum of the seventh
century, these heretical dissidences would figure with only a negative

---

[52] Information sufficient for my purpose is to be found in what is said by
Menéndez y Pelayo in his *Historia de los heterodoxos españoles* (1917), II,
chap. ii.

[53] *Ibid.*, p. 123.

[54] Ramón de Abadal, *La batalla del adocionismo* (Barcelona, 1949).

value, as a shrinking of the universal spirit insofar as they drew Hispania away from the totality of the Europe that was Rome's heir. On the positive side, the conversion of Reccared, the campaigns against the Byzantines and against the rebellious peoples of the north, traced a broad and firm national horizon. Similarly, the partisans of King Witiza who opened the ports of the Strait of Gibraltar to the Africans must have thought themselves powerful enough to cope with the claims of their foreign auxiliaries and to preserve the structure of the kingdom.

On the other hand, the perspective of the incipient Asturian-Galician-Leonese kingdom is bound to have been narrow and limited. We do not have access to the intimate life of these people between 711 and the end of the tenth century; there was no Orosius to collect such words as those Ataulf directed to the knight from Narbonne. Still, there are facts of great importance which I analyze later and which render comprehensible the passage from Visigothic Hispania to Spanish life—a life divided, anguished, wonderful in its hour, always fascinating.

Summary and a Glance Ahead

I have attempted to establish with all certainty that the past prior to the eighth century was the work of human agents whose social awareness was different from that of those who would later be called Spaniards. The human correlates of the terms "Hispania" and "España" are completely divergent. "Hispania" is, most probably, a Punic name which meant "land of rabbits."[55] Catullus called the Celtiberian region *cuniculosa* ("abounding in rabbits"). As is frequent in place names, "Hispania" was the appellation given to a land by those who did not inhabit it. The Romans gave the name "Hispania" to the whole Peninsula; in the ninth century the Christians in the north called the area occupied by Muslims "Spania."[56] During the reconquest, regional designations (Castilla, Leon, and the like) predominated, while the term "España" became generalized in the sixteenth century.

For an ingenuous observer there seems to be nothing odd about these changes of name, and the past before the reconquest seems to be no more different from the eighth through the thirteenth centuries than these latter centuries are with respect to those that follow them. But the important and decisive factor is that all the changes that have

---

[55] See A. García Bellido, *La Península Ibérica* (1953), p. 100.

[56] The *Chronica Albeldense* (*ca.* 880) says that Alfonso III, "Sarrazenis inferens bellum, exercitus mouit, et Spaniam intrauit sub era 918. . . . Almundar . . . exercitu Spanie LXXX milia, a Corduba progressus, ad Zesaraugustam est profetus . . ." (ed. M. Gómez Moreno, in *Boletín de la Academia de la Historia* (1932), pp. 605–606).

taken place since the eighth century have been changes of posture made by one and the same subject-agents, linked together within the same awareness of their selves, from that moment to the present. All these subject-agents are bound one to another without dissolution of their *internal* continuity. The deeds of the Aragonese (who begin their historical course in a corner of the Pyrenees) interlock with Catalan life, just as the decisions taken by the Castilians affect the future of the Leonese, and so on. Collective events and individual creations are all linked to situations that arose after the eighth century as a consequence of the Islamization of almost all the inhabitants of the Peninsula; they are not bound to obscure and mythical psychological characteristics of Iberians or Celtiberians. Everyone worked within the given circumstances that surrounded him. From the future Navarre to Galicia the struggle against the Moors was begun, slowly and with difficulty, with the human and economic forces available there; along the southern border of the Pyrenees, from Canfranc to the Mediterranean, defensive and aggressive actions were carried on with various kinds of outside help supplied by the Carolingian monarchs or by Aquitaine. As a result of these differing circumstances the Aragonese and the Catalans, on the one hand, and the Castilians and Leonese, on the other, pursued different courses. The relations of the Catalans and the Aragonese with peoples on the other side of the Pyrenees (which I deal with later) were not like those of the Navarro-Castilians with France. The "French Road" to Santiago entered by way of Navarre and continued to the extreme west of the Peninsula, a route that would not have existed if there had not been chronic skirmishes with the Muslims. The major aggressive impulse was that of Castile, which finally closed the way to the south for the Aragonese and Catalans, who, for this reason and not because of something that had happened prior to the eighth century, poured out their energies on other Mediterranean lands—so it is that there was an Aragonese-Catalan kingdom in Sicily, Naples, and Sardinia. As a consequence of these activities, the Aragonese and the Catalans took on something of the spirit of the maritime republics of Italy and possess civil architectural forms, combining art with mercantile interests, which are unknown in Castile. The very beautiful *lonjas* (mercantile exchange buildings) of Saragossa, Alcañiz, Barcelona, Valencia, and Palma de Mallorca are fine examples of this architecture.

But there was one common trait or, rather, one determining circumstance of the functional life structure in which, despite their profound differences, all the Christian kingdoms ultimately coincided. Their military, political, and commercial activities were conditioned by the interweaving of the life of the Christians with that of the Moors and the Jews. Without this circumstance the exterior and the interior life of the Castilians and the Aragonese is unimaginable. What conventional histories present as a juxtaposition of demographic facts is for me the very contexture and structure of an inner way of life. The Christians would not have fought effectively without the social proximity of Mudejars and Jews; and these groups would have been exterminated or expelled had they not been indispensable. When the French occasionally intervened in the war against the Muslims of al-Andalus, they killed their captives and did not understand why the Christians of Spain did not do likewise. As I further explain at the appropriate moment, the Jews had been expelled from England and France long before the fifteenth century.

Although the details of the process of Spanish life are set forth later, it was necessary at this point to destroy the fallacy that views the history of the Iberian Peninsula as a series of successive changes experienced by the same collective entity, and sees as of like nature the differences that may be observed among the Celtiberian wars, those of the reconquest, and those of the eighteenth and nineteenth centuries. This is only one of numerous gigantic obstacles interposed between the reality of the Spaniards and any attempt to reveal it to people who are blinded by the prevailing myths.

The authentic Spain has been what seems to me a splendid ensemble of humanity woven together out of three coexisting castes (as we have seen in chapter iii) and, at the same time, radically split (as we shall see). It was divided into three castes, three beliefs, into three antagonistic ambitions, in a long series of ruptures and accords. The inner configuration of the events that were taking place in the northern kingdoms was foreshadowed—in inverted form and differently shaded—in al-Andalus. The broad base of Islamic-Christian-Judaic common life in the south between the eighth and eleventh centuries is followed in the eleventh and twelfth centuries by ever more oppressive limitations for Christians and Jews under the rule of the Almorávides and Almohades.

But it is precisely in the eleventh and twelfth centuries that the Christian north (Leon-Castile, Navarre-Aragon), in contrast with al-Andalus, broadens its social horizon as it absorbs the Muslim and Jewish populations which the progress of the reconquest was displacing. To this broadening was added that provided by the French monks, knights, and merchants attracted by the various interests offered by the road to Santiago. When the limited panorama of culture and possibilities in the nuclei of resistance in the eighth and ninth centuries was opened toward the European north and the Orientalized south, the new horizons enlarged the personal consciousness of the kings and lords by whose efforts such encouraging changes had been achieved. The French immigrations had been fomented by those who were eager to "Europeanize" themselves and to resist and oppose the strongly Orientalized way of life of the Christian kingdoms. As I demonstrate later, such was the motivation behind the Cluniac "invasion" and the marriages arranged by Alfonso VI between his daughters and Counts Raymond and Henry of Burgundy—just as he himself had earlier married Constance of Burgundy. In these factors we find, too, the explanation of why, in the *Crónica General* of Alfonso the Learned, the writer falls into the strange anachronism of attributing to a desire for "Europeanism" the decision by the natives of the Ebro region to pass over to the Roman army during the Punic Wars "because they held that there was greater reason to maintain [friendship] with the Romans, *who were from Europe*, than with the Carthaginians, who were from Africa" (ed. Menéndez Pidal, p. 19). Yet all this was still compatible with the adoption of Oriental customs by both the upper and lower classes of Christian society. The Europeanism of the Church, of Romanesque and Gothic architecture, of literature in both its popular (or epic) and learned forms, in no way modified the basic Christian-Moorish-Hebraic structure of Spanish society, which continued to stand on that now traditional base in its aggressive or defensive moves against both the infidel and the neighboring Christian kingdoms.

The kings and their councillors conceived the interweaving of the three castes as a juridical and moral harmony, a conception we have seen reflected in the epitaphs of Ferdinand III (pp. 60–61) and in the traditional way of receiving monarchs when they made solemn entry into cities. That shared common life carried within it, however, the seeds of its own destruction, as has always happened in all historical situations of broad scope. Along with the interests that gave birth to the system of the three castes of believers and kept them united, there coexisted also the longing for preeminence which in the long run would utterly destroy that system, unique in the West.

The inscriptions on the tomb of Ferdinand the Holy and the concise but aggressive epitaph of Ferdinand of Aragon and Isabella of Castile in the Royal Chapel of Granada serve for me as milestones marking and dividing decisive epochs of Spanish life. Contrast with what we have seen in earlier inscriptions the words of the latter:

> Mahometice secte prostratores
> et heretice pervicacie extinctores
> Fernandus Aragonum et Helisabetha Castelle
> vir et uxor unanimes
> Catolice appellati
> marmoreo clauduntur hoc tumulo.[57]

---

[57] See my *Origen, ser y existir de los españoles* (Madrid: Taurus, 1959), p. 3. The English translation runs as follows: "Destroyers of the Mohammedan sect and the annihilators of heretical obstinacy [i.e., of the Jews], Ferdinand of Aragon and Isabella of Castile, husband and wife undivided in opinion, called the Catholic [Sovereigns], lie enclosed by this marble tomb."

The Muslim and the Jewish sects, obstinate in their dissidence, also lie buried within this tomb instead of raising their voices in praise around it in Castilian, Arabic, and Hebrew words of like meaning. An abyss separates the two situations—that of 1252 and that of the beginning of the sixteenth century—even though the subject-agent in both was the awareness and will of the caste that directed the collective life of the Spaniards.

The Spaniards were constituted as a new variety of European people by virtue of a number of blended harmonies pierced by a number of strident dissonances. The greatest creations of Spanish civilization were the expression of both the harmonies and the discords. Think, for example, of the meaning of the fact that it was descendants of Hispano-Hebrews who, in the fifteenth century, gave expression for the first time to the way in which Spaniards felt about themselves (pp. 147 ff.): Juan de Mena, Alonso de Cartagena, Alonso de Palencia, Diego de Valera, Fernando de la Torre, Juan Alfonso de Baena. In such fashion was begun the argument about what Spaniards were like and what they were worth in human terms. This is a problem that has still not been satisfactorily solved to the liking of everyone, for the task of magnifying Spain politically and creating a culture upon which to project the longing for grandeur was divided among groups of Spaniards who, from the end of the fifteenth century—exactly at the moment when the Spaniards were beginning to rise to the heights of their destiny—were incapable of coordinating their several activities. The possibility existed of developing military, economic, and intellectual power, but at the crucial moment there was lacking the channeled and cohesive force necessary so that those parallel and, at the same time, opposing energies—all of them Spanish —might tend toward the same goal. Those who gave enduring form to the words of their language around the tomb of King Ferdinand of Castile and Leon were Spaniards; the tomb and its epitaphs represent a pinnacle of Spanishness. Spanish also were the Cid, and Don Santob of Carrión, and the Moor Abderrahman (who planned the monastery of El Paular), and Gonzalo Fernández de Córdoba, and Luis Vives (who, in the sixteenth century, could no longer live in the Peninsula), and the Moors who kept the orchards and farms of Valencia and Aragon fertile and rich in the sixteenth century. All these possibilities were present in the Spanish dwelling place of life; but they came to stand in one another's way when the consciousness of lineage, of caste, had become dominant over all other considerations. For this reason we are struck by the import and scope of those words of the converted Jew Gonzalo Fernández de Oviedo (see above, p. 52) to the effect that there was no Christian nation where people knew better "who are the nobles and of good and clean caste, and *who are suspect on points of faith; in other nations all this is hid-*

den." The nobility to which all aspired depended on beliefs that could no longer live together. The circumstances of the sixteenth century were antagonistically but tightly bound to those of the eighth century.

In the formative epoch of the Spanish consciousness, the feeling of caste was a stimulus inciting people to prove their worth, something like a feeling of "noblesse oblige"; later, however, what had been the motivation became the goal, that is to say, one did not aspire to be heroic, intelligent, or industrious in order to rise as a member of the Christian, Jewish, or Moorish caste, but all effort was concentrated in the eagerness to be counted as a member of the caste that had come to stand alone—the caste of the Old Christians in the sixteenth and seventeenth centuries, the only sovereign and valued caste. Such was the upheaval that shook Spanish life, the change of direction that becomes visible, expressed and given concrete form in imperial prowess, in literature, and in the art of the sixteenth and seventeenth centuries. Doubtless the content of life had become different, but the Spaniards were aware of the connection with their immediate past, just as the branch, if it could do so, would sense and express its connection with the trunk from which it springs.

What happened after this critical change of direction cannot be discussed here. My only purpose has been to demonstrate with all clarity that the changes observable in Spanish life from the beginning of the reconquest up to the present moment are only ramifications of a basic state of awareness—of the awareness of aspiring to be Spanish, of feeling Spanish, of puzzling over who should and do have the right to be Spaniards and who should be excluded. The final judgment has not been brought in, but it has nothing to do with the Celtiberians.

It matters little that this history may seem different or unpleasant to understand for those who stubbornly persist in disregarding it. The attempt to convert Spain into a country whose structure is analogous to that of her Western neighbors has until now prevented our drawing near to the authentic reality of what has been and continues to be. The effort to suppress the past by hiding one's head in the sand like an ostrich is a foolish and ineffective activity; while the desire to begin Spanish life anew from this moment, as if nothing had happened before, is another reaction of fright which can only produce vain gesticulation. To imagine that there are "two Spains," and that one person belongs to the "good" part and another person to the "bad," particularly when the same individual is sometimes on one side and sometimes on the other, ignores the fact that such a schism is made whole by the constant underlying unity of those who have created the division. For me the only possible attitude is one of full involvement, inspired by sympathy and an ardent *caritas*, in living the problem in its entirety, from, so to say, the topmost leaves of the tree to the dark depths of its roots. One must enter into himself, return to the reality of his self, because a whole people, exactly like any single person, wastes its time and its reason if it thinks that the presence of what has actually been can be evaded. I am neither a pessimist nor an optimist. I believe quite simply that only in the full consciousness of what we have been, can we raise ourself to a higher destiny—if we really desire to improve that destiny.

VII · AL-ANDALUS AS A CONSTITUTIVE CIRCUMSTANCE OF SPANISH LIFE

The Point of View

THE IDEAS ABOUT THE REALITY of the people called "Spanish" since the thirteenth century have been rendered diffuse and opaque by the confusion that originates in the failure to bear in mind that the reality is inseparable from the way in which we attempt to apprehend it. That method of approach must be linked in some way to the mode of existence of the human phenomenon that is the object of our analysis; it must not be based only on the abstract fantasies and pious desires of the historian. But the existential mode of the vital phenomenon is, in turn, by no means obvious and is not revealed by a first glance at the mass of data lying there within reach of the observer. These data and events existed as the expression of the life of other men, of a life the historian perceives and judges from within his own life and of which, in some manner, he feels himself a part. The physicist or the naturalist finds nothing in his life analogous to what happens to the star or the plant, but the historian finds some correspondence between his own existence and that of the people who expressed their lives either in the desire to attain a goal or in dismay at not having attained it. Regardless of whether they are familiar or alien to us, all human phenomena reflect a motivation and point toward some goal; for this reason, the historian is bound to the past, not only through his knowledge of past events, but through his feeling that past life, just because it is life, functions like his own.

When we meditate on history, the themes or objects that come forward to claim our attention affect us differently from the way in which the biologist is affected by chlorophyll. Therefore the human past does not lend itself to calculations and statistical measurements allowing only one clear interpretation—not, that is, unless the past is divested of its human dimension. When it is something more than a skeletal arrangement or a figment of the imagination, the historical reconstruction of the past resembles a picture complete with foreground and distant perspectives, in which everything harmonizes by virtue of a congruent scale of values. Such a picture hopes to persuade, not to prove by means of exact and univocal arguments. The distinctions I am establishing are based on differences of position and hierarchy within the panoramic perspective I offer to the reader. The Islamic element interposed in the eighth century into Romano-Visigothic Hispania became a theme of vital moment to those who were not Muslims and were forced to adjust to those new circumstances. Thenceforward their existence would be woven from the present demands created by strange men and creeds as well as exigencies of their own traditional habits. Islam required the consideration and use of the traditional ways of existence and social tasks of the inhabitants of the north within a new perspective. Thus the obvious circumstance of being a Christian acquired a new position and dimension, for from within that religious condition it would be necessary to fight against, or in many cases to surrender to, a new and powerful faith; the alternatives were clear—either to defend oneself and to attack as a Christian, or to be converted to the faith of Mohammed. From that time forward, Christianity would take on a polemical dimension, not *within* itself, but because of its exposed frontier position and function with respect to a non-Christian world. Religious belief would become as solid and unquestionable as the sword or arrow that defended those people who found in their faith a social and political *raison d'être*; it would provide a common and unifying name for all those from Galicia to the Pyrenees Mountains of Aragon who were affirming themselves in opposition to the enemy from the south.

The novelty of this situation will be seen by a comparison of the rapid Islamization of many of the Hispano-Roman-Gothic peoples with the slow Christianization of the Hispano-Roman peoples, who adopted Christianity at the same deliberate pace observed in the other Roman provinces (Italia, Gallia). The Christianization of the Romans was a slow process, connected with the progressive infiltration of the Roman hierarchy and administration by the ministers and officials of the Church. Finally, in the fourth century, a Christian occupies the imperial throne. There was not in the Empire a military frontier between pagans and Christians. In other words, the Peninsular situation arising in the eighth century was a new phenomenon in the history of the West. From that moment on, geographical, economic, and, in general, traditional circumstances acquired a different function and meaning. Within the bosom of Romano-Gothic Hispania, formerly united under a single king, there began to germinate the various "Spains" of the future, frequently at war with one another, even though later they shared a feeling of kinship based on the possession of the same collective dimension. These feelings of relationship were at times imposed by circumstances that brought into harmony the awareness of belonging to a nearby collectivity and also to another that was more distant. For such reasons, owing nothing to the "essence" of man, the Asturians, Leonese, Castilians, Aragonese, Basques, and Andalusians came to feel themselves Spanish, possessed of a like collective dimension which was unaffected by the diversity of their habits or modes of expression, because one's inner self-consciousness of himself is independent of his awareness of "existing with others" who are felt to be related within a more ample perspective than that provided by the individual's own home territory. That collective "beyond" of social connections is finally incorporated into the area of personal self-consciousness; *feeling oneself to be Spanish*, French, or Italian consists in such an awareness (and not in any recondite, mysterious psychological makeup). Doubtless Catalan- or Galician-speaking peoples came to feel themselves possessed of a double collective dimension; but their situation differs from that of the peoples previously mentioned. On the other hand, the Portuguese zone of Galicia ultimately found itself situated in a collective frame that excluded Spanishness.

All this is discussed later. Nevertheless, I deemed it useful to stop for a moment at this vantage point to contemplate the past and survey the future. In view of the confused ideas that still prevail about the Spanish past, it is prudent to emphasize certain phenomena of collective life in order to view them from different angles, since the question of being or not being Spanish is linked to the fact that a large portion of the Peninsula was Islamized. Throughout the reconquest—and as a result of it—there came into being certain Peninsular areas where people knew everyone spoke the same language; or if the language was not the same, the pressure of common collective interests obliged people to find ways of communication. There came a moment in Peninsular history when the kingdoms next to Castile felt the need, the desirability, or the pleasure of speaking or of writing in Castilian. In the sixteenth century certain illustrious Catalans and Portuguese (Boscán, Gil Vicente, Camoens) spontaneously composed literary works in Castilian; Camoens and Gil Vicente did so before Portugal was bound politically to Spain.

We must now examine which are the aspects of Islamic life that later became visible—as an active and constitutive force—in the life we now designate and value as Spanish. As I have already pointed out in *España en su historia* (1948), religious belief played among the Spaniards a peculiar role without analogy in the other Christian peoples of the West. Today I can say with more persuasive clarity that the constitution of the system of collective life called Spanish is inseparable from the system of the three castes of *believers* discussed earlier. The magnification of Christian belief and its political and imperial dimension at the time of the Catholic Sovereigns are inconceivable without the action of Muslim al-Andalus (combined with that of the Hispano-Hebrew communities).

The poets of the caliph, al-Ḥakam II of al-Andalus, wrote in the tenth century:

> All signs announce that he will carry his flags
> as far as Bagdad, after passing through Medina.
>
> (Ibn Sukhays)

> In the Occident there has risen the sun of a caliphate
> which will shine with splendor in the two Orients
> so that it may chase away with the light of orthodoxy
> the shadows of unbelief.
>
> ('Abd al-'Azīs ibn-Ḥuṣayn Quarawi)

Without such statements and all the others that strike the same chord, how could one explain the belligerence, the political and religious exclusionism of the Christian caste?

These verses and others have been adduced by Emilio García Gómez in his fine introduction to the *España musulmana* of E. Lévi-Provençal (Madrid, 1950, p. xxvi). The famous Arabist is rightly reminded by these verses of Philip II, even though he curiously finds a basis for the manifest similarity in "the deepest substrata of the Iberian soul." Years ago I had already mentioned a ballad that expresses the feeling of religious imperialism which surrounded Charles V:

> Once the three Armenias are won,
> Arabia will not be left behind,
> Egypt, Syria, the Indies,
> All will fall to him.

Recently I have recalled another significant ballad inspired by the same spiritual attitude:

> The great Philip II,
> exalted King of Spain,
> to whom over most of the world . . .
> *God has given dominion* . . .
> For in Japan and in China
> we hope for another new religious rule . . .
> From the East to the West
> he has encompassed it all. . . .[1]

These texts, together with those of the thirteenth and fifteenth

---

[1] See *De la edad conflictiva: El drama de la honra* (Madrid: Taurus, 1963), p. 92.

centuries which I mention later, demonstrate that the religious imperialism, totalism, and proselytism of the Spanish Christians were indissoluble from the attitudes of Muslims and Jews, who had been living in the Peninsula for many centuries. What the Iberians thought and felt about such matters is unknown to us. Furthermore, the Iberians would not help to explain the special religiosity of the Oriental peoples, especially the imperial progress of the Islamic faith from Mecca to al-Andalus in the west, and as far as the Philippines in the east. It is from the starting point of that peculiar type of Oriental religiosity that one must begin in order to understand the poems cited which glorified the caliphs of al-Andalus (and not of Andalusia). It is in this light and from this point of view that I later examine the connections between Muslims and Christians in the Peninsula.

Islamized al-Andalus and the Christian Spains

The Moors came to Hispania sustained by two highly efficacious forces: the impetus of a newly born religion that was the expression of everything that the body and soul of the Bedouin could desire, and military victories that in less than a century had made them masters of a vast empire—from Persia to Hispania. They did not come like the barbarians of the fifth century, who had not left a political center behind them in Germania which might provide support; the Moors progressed elastically, with the feeling that they were moved by a central mainspring of religion; they had even begun to absorb what there was left alive of Greek culture, now Christianized, in Syria and Egypt. Moreover, Arabic literature of the seventh century, although poor in ideas, was already capable of expressing in the richest vocabulary a conscious awareness of the most intimate feelings. In testimony of this, it may be remembered that grammarians said of the poet Farazdaq (d. 732) that without him "one third of the Arabic language would have been lost."[2]

If the Strait of Gibraltar had been opposite Marseilles, France would have had a very different history, even though she was ruled by Franks and not by Visigoths. But this observation is idle. What is certain is that Visigothic Hispania succumbed, and what remained of nonsubject Christendom in the north was to initiate a course of history different from that of the other Western countries. Christian resistance made itself felt very soon, and Islam saw itself forced to start a frontier war that did not terminate until the end of the fifteenth century. Islam was incapable of creating stable political systems based on something other than a common religion and

---

[2] See Farazdaq, *Divan*, Fr. trans. by R. Boucher (Paris, 1870).

dictatorial rule; the totally religious character of Muslim life hindered the creation of secular forms of communal existence. The strength of al-Andalus lasted so long as there were leaders who could electrify with victories and dazzle with wealth the heterogeneous masses governed by their emirs and caliphs. Great masses of Christians became subject to the ruling Arabs, while retaining the liberty to practice the Christian religion, and these Christians—called Mozarabs—went on living under the protection of Moorish tolerance for four centuries, until the influx in 1090 of the *Murābits* (*Almorávides*) and in 1146 of the *Muwaḥḥidūn* (*Almohades*)—fanatical tribes from Africa —did away with that group of people, Christians by faith but Arabic with respect to certain tendencies and dispositions of their inner life.[3] For this very reason they called themselves *mozárabes*, which means "Arabized."

The struggle between Moors and Christians completely occupied Peninsular history till the middle of the thirteenth century; Cordova was reconquered in 1236; Valencia, in 1238; and Seville, in 1248. From then on, the impetus of the Christians weakened, consumed as they were by internal struggles similar to those experienced by the Moors. Much earlier than the petty Moorish kingdoms (*taifas*) of the eleventh century (there was one king in Toledo, another in Saragossa, another in Seville, and several more), there had arisen the *taifas* of the Christians (the kingdom of Aragon, Navarre, Leon, and the county of Castile). The reconquest dragged on slowly during the thirteenth, fourteenth, and fifteenth centuries, until Ferdinand and Isabella unified the Peninsula (except for Portugal), and launched a people, who were then Spaniards and already accustomed, in Oriental fashion, to boundless longings, on enterprises now known to everyone.

It lies outside the scope of my plan to recount events that are well known and which the reader will find treated in the books of R. Dozy, E. Lévi-Provençal, R. Menéndez Pidal, in the *Encyclopedia of Islam*, or in works of popularization. My interest is focused on those aspects of Peninsular life in which Islamic contacts are made evident, less to follow the footprints of Islam in Christian Spain than to attain to such a point of view as will certify the structure of Spanish life. Until some twenty-five years ago I had had more or less the same ideas about this subject as everyone else and had thought in terms of a given "content" or matter of civilization and not about the "form" or disposition of life. We had all thought at one time that Christian Spain was a given and fixed entity upon which fell the cloak of Moorish language, literature, and institutions. Only after I

---

[3] See Ramón Menéndez Pidal, *Orígenes del español*, pp. 445–449.

approached the Middle Ages in terms of "vital situations" did I begin to perceive the meaning of the Islamic in Spanish history. The Spanish Middle Ages then appeared to me as the dynamic action of groups of northern folk to subsist in the face of a world that was superior in technology and thought but not in personal fortitude, thrust,[4] commanding ability, and epic literary expressiveness. The Christians took over a host of things—material objects and institutions—created by the Moors, but they did not assimilate the activities that could produce these things precisely because it was necessary for them to take a new course of life in order to oppose and finally to conquer the Moors. It seems to me that what the Christians did not do—cut off as they were from their Visigothic tradition and because of the vital situation in which they had been placed by the Muslims—is also an effect of Islam, and to the same degree as are words imported from Arabic. In the same way, the system of values which the Christians developed (or conversely could not develop) in order to oppose their enemies is effectively again something structural that falls within the same life process. The Christian peoples who finally came to be called Spaniards were the result of the combination of an attitude of submission and wonder in the face of a culturally superior enemy, and of the effort to overcome this very position of inferiority. On this score certain lines from the *Poem of the Cid* (1140) are highly significant:

> Hear me, Albar Fáñez and all knights!
> We have taken great wealth in this castle;
> The Moors lie dead; few live ones do I see.
> Moorish men and Moorish maids we cannot sell,
> Nor by chopping off their heads will we gain anything;
> Let us keep them inside, *for we have the seigniory;*
> We shall dwell in their houses, and *we shall make use of them.*[5]
>
> (ll. 616–622)

To exercise seigniory while utilizing the services of the Moors—

---

[4] For the weakness in combat of the troops of the Umayyad Caliphate, see E. García Gómez, Introduction to the *España musulmana* of E. Lévi-Provençal (Madrid, 1950), p. xxix.

[5] The Spanish of this text is as follows:

> ¡ Oíd a mí, Albar Fáñez e todos los cavalleros!
> En este castiello grand aver avemos preso;
> los moros yazen muertos, de bivos pocos veo.
> Los moros e las moras vender non los podremos,
> que los descabeçemos nada non ganaremos;
> cojámoslos de dentro, *ca el señorío tenemos*;
> posaremos en sus casas, e *dellos nos serviremos.*

Interesting data about the agriculture and industry of the Moors in Spain may be found in César E. Dubler, *Über das Wirtschaftsleben auf der iberischen Halbinsel vom XI. zum XIII. Jahrhundert* (Geneva: E. Droz, 1943), pp. 28–66.

such was the *conscious* program (although other values held sway subconsciously, as we shall see later). It is in this respect of decisive importance that the highest value was set upon one's own religious faith, personal energy, and habits of rustic poverty. Let us look at such a delicate historical problem from the inside.

The first thing we shall do is try not to lose sight of its temporal dimension—the human content of a period, lasting until the middle of the thirteenth century, torn by war and constant anxiety. When we contemplate the past from the present moment, one hundred years, two hundred years, strike us as a long period, sufficient for the birth and rooting of new customs basic for the situation and way of life of the today in which we find ourselves included. But we are not used to proceeding in this fashion when we contemplate a long period of the past from another point in time, also past. The centuries of semi-Moorish history in Spain (711-1492) are regarded by many as a long and annoying interval, as nothing but a protracted military enterprise, slow and laborious, after which Spain returned to normality, albeit scarred and retarded here and there. The problem, however, was not to end here, because all the Moors did not leave Spain in 1492; certain of them remained—those called Moriscos, ostensibly and officially subjects of the king, and Christians, but in reality Moors who retained their religion and customs, and whose presence, as we shall see, was not negligible in matters of economics, literature, and religion. So Moorish were they that the pious King Philip III decided to expel them from his realm in 1609. But even as a consequence of this, did they all leave? It seems not, for traces of Moorish tradition are still discernible in the garden region of Murcia, in Valencia, and in Aragon.[6] Thus, the presence of Moors and Moriscos in Spain actually covers a period of more than nine centuries. Any moderately well-trained scholar knows that the hand of Islam can still be seen in the monuments of Cordova, Granada, Seville, Toledo, and other less important cities. Less well known is the existence of Mudejar architecture throughout Latin America; it is not the product of an intentional imitation of the past but the expression of the artistic sensibility of certain Spaniards who are authentically linked to centuries-old forms of art that were very much alive in all Hispano-Portuguese America during the sixteenth and seventeenth centuries. Striking illustrations of this architectural style

---

[6] See F. Fernández y González, "De los moriscos que permanecieron en España después de la expulsión decretada por Felipe III," *Revista de España*, XIX–XX (1871). Also, "Manifestación de los hijos de moriscos que quedaron en Onteniente, 1611," published by V. Castañeda, in *Boletín de la Academia de la Historia* (1923), pp. 421–427. The famous Tribunal de Aguas (*Cort de la Seo*), which settles disputes about irrigation in the Valencian lowlands, is clearly a Moorish survival. For its method of operation, see Joaquín Costa, *Colectivismo agrario en España* (1915), pp. 552 ff.

may be seen in Manuel Toussaint's book *Arte Mudéjar de América* (Mexico, 1946).[7]

In the language there exist, in either current or archaic usage, thousands of Arabic words. Works of literature have been inspired by Arabic sources from the twelfth-century *Disciplina clericalis*, which diffused thirty-three stories of Oriental provenance throughout Christian Spain and Europe, to the seventeenth-century *Criticón* of Baltasar Gracián, the germ of which is to be found in a story preserved among the Moriscos of Aragon. Yet, for all the importance this subject has and for all the vast bibliography that has grown up around it, still no sort of "vital" study of it had been undertaken until Miguel Asín Palacios began to probe about under the surface of the history of religious sensibility, and to prove—as I think he did—that the form of the mysticism of the most exquisite of mystics, St. John of the Cross, is not to be explained outside the mystic *Shādhilīya* tradition preserved by the Castilian Moriscos.

Although Paul Nwya has cast doubt upon the validity of Asín's suggestions,[8] I find justified and provocative the idea that in the mysticism and the style of St. John of the Cross there may be noted echoes and reflections of the *Shādhilīya* mystics,[9] among whom such terms as "night" and "day," "constriction" and "broadening," were commonly used as mystically symbolic. In view, however, of Nwya's objections, let us look at the facts. Certain mystic tendencies, originating in Persia, spread as far as al-Andalus and the north of Africa. According to Asín, one of these forms of spiritual life, the *Shādhilīya* (founded by the Moroccan abu-l-Ḥasan al-Shādhili), inspired certain subtle thinkers from the thirteenth century to the fifteenth, among them Ibn 'Abbād, born in Ronda in 1371. The fundamental tenet of this doctrine consists in God's being "inaccessible to his creatures; from the absolute transcendence of the infinite Being, who is totally devoid of any likeness to the finite being, it may be inferred that God is in no way what we can sense, imagine, conceive, and desire. . . . All those things that the soul may do to come to God, far from being adequate and efficacious, will be only an impediment."

---

[7] Leopoldo Torres Balbás (*Al-Andalus*, XII [1948], 250) does not consider 17 of the buildings or details among the 109 reproduced by Toussaint to be Mudejar; nevertheless, the existence in Spanish America of art that is Muslim in origin is undeniable.

[8] "Ibn 'Abbād de Ronda et Jean de la Croix," *Al-Andalus*, XXII (1957), 113–130.

[9] *Huellas del Islam* (1941), pp. 237–304. In addition to the similarity of certain expressions, doctrinal analogies are also important: "In order to effect the union with God, one must renounce all that which is not God" (p. 249). From this flows the rejection of everything tangible and all sensual desires as well as the search for the "void," for "bareness"—on these things there is accord between St. John of the Cross and the *Shādhilīya* school, of which Ibn 'Abbād of Ronda was a leading representative in the fourteenth century.

The soul of the mystic passes through a state of broadening (*bast* in Arabic) or of straining (*qabd*). God comes to the aid of the constricted soul and sends it the spiritual comfort of His favor, grace, and charisma; but afterward God places it in the tightest constraint "so that the soul may look for support only in Him."[10] Abu-l-Ḥasan al-Shādhili also makes use of the similes of the night and day, which St. John of the Cross will later convert into his "dark night of the soul."

St. John of the Cross once wrote: "The soul that seeks revelations commits at least a venial sin . . . for there is no need of anything like that. . . . Many there are who set out to seek in God their comfort and their pleasure, and to them His Majesty may grant comfort and gifts; but those who try to please him and give him something at their own expense (setting aside their own private interest) are very few in number."[11]

The bare austerity of the church constructed in the Batuecas (Salamanca) by the immediate disciples of the Saint is surprising in an epoch that sought for decorative exuberance, when the styles we call baroque were being formed in connection with the very way of life of a new form of European society. But such austerity was in accord with the structure of the mysticism and the poetry of the man who died in 1591 in a monastery in Ubeda after having suffered extremely harsh treatment from monks of his own order. The future saint had written in his prose commentary on the "Noche oscura del alma": "It is impossible in any natural way and manner . . . to be able to know and sense divine things as they are except by the illumination of this mystic theology"—in other words, except through what God himself, and not man, may deign to do. It is understandable why some people should have tried, although unsuccessfully, to have the doctrine of St. John condemned by the Inquisition[12] on the basis of its similarity to that of the Illuminati, which also had Muslim antecedents. Reading St. John's inimitable poetry one has the impression that God surrenders himself in the mystic illumination, while he remains closed up and incommunicative in the words of those who try to explain him:

> Surrender Thyself completely now in truth, [my God,]
> And will not to send me
> Henceforward messengers, [explicators of Thy infinity,]
> For they know not [with their words] how to tell me what I desire.
> (*Acaba de entregarte ya de vero*,
> *No quieras enviarme*

---

[10] *Ibid.*, pp. 249–250.

[11] Cited by Miguel Asín Palacios in *Islam cristianizado*, p. 212.

[12] *Obras de San Juan de la Cruz*, ed. P. Silverio de Santa Teresa (1929), I, 218–228.

De hoy más ya mensajero,
Que no saben decirme lo que quiero.)

In his prose commentary on the *Cántico espiritual*, St. John of the Cross reasons thus: "Because all that one may know of God in this life, however much it may be, is not the truth, for it is partial and very remote knowledge." Angels and men of reason "give me to understand marvelous things of Thy grace and mercy in the works of Thy Incarnation and the truths of the faith which they tell me of Thee,"

> And all of them wound me more
> And I am left dying
> By *I know not that which they keep* stammering.
> (*Y todos más me llagan,*
> *Y déjame muriendo*
> *Un no sé qué que quedan balbuciendo.*)

The three consecutive *que*'s express superbly the anguish produced by the stammering of those who try to say what is unsayable—to express the divine by means of human terms.

It is understandable that so extreme a position should lead to forgetfulness of the world of finite things, including the part of the Church which is visible and terrestrial; ecclesiastical organization and external practices were not attacked by St. John of the Cross, but he did fail to speak of them because they had no function in the structure of a work of profound beauty, very close to the region of utter and terrifying silence. Never in his work—not even in his letters—do there occur the words "pope," "cardinal," "bishop," "canon," "parish priest," "chaplain," "sacristan," or many others that usually appear in religious writings. Five times he speaks of "communion," but three of these passages condemn the "sensuality" and "pleasure" that it occasions or the too frequent receiving of communion. By contrast it is surprising that passages relating to direct *communication* with God are numerous, occupying ten pages in the concordance to the Saint's work prepared by Friar Luis de San José.

Some time before St. John of the Cross, Bartolomé de Torres Naharro had written sprightly verses of simple clarity about the difficult problem—which to him seemed insoluble—of communication between the human and the divine; praise of the Virgin Mary cannot, in his view, ever reach its unattainable goal:

> Here they command me to praise thee,
> Our Lady and our Glory,
> but for my words to be equal to thee,
> thou wouldst need to descend,
> which God should not permit. . . .
> No finely spun words

can here win the victory;
for praise is of no value
when the object of praise
is not given all its glory.

At first glance it would seem that the poet has limited himself to insisting once again on the contrast between human insignificance and the grandeur of the divine Mother, which may be approached only by that of her divine Son; but Torres Naharro insists on expounding the human impossibility of praising the Virgin, since

between *human knowledge*,
and *who thou art or mayst be*,
there is no proportion.

Consequently, the Virgin, as the Mother of God, could be praised only by her Creator:

by that great Maker
from whom issued such a work,
may the praise come from Him . . . ,
for all our words,
as we are sinners [i.e., men],
are a going in and no coming out,
a beginning without ending
and the painting of colors on gold.[13]

Thus it is that, for reasons we might call "metaphysical," Torres Naharro breaks a centuries-old tradition of praise to the Virgin Mary. No distinction is made here between the knowledge given by faith and that given by reason; rather it seems that the poet is content to leave open a problem that was resolved by the *Shādhilīya* and St.

---

[13] Torres Naharro here adapts to a divine subject a motif from the poetry of courtly love which had been treated by many, including Diego de San Pedro, who excuses himself for not praising a beautiful lady whose loveliness exceeded the expressive capacity of the poet:
for to do this rightly
there should be
another tongue for my desire.
And since He who visited the utmost upon you
denied to me the knowledge,
by my faith, I tell you,
let Him who made you, praise you.
(*Obras*, ed. S. Gili y Gaya [1950], p. 221)
What in Diego de San Pedro is the personal limitation of the poet is converted in Torres Naharro into the lack of proportion between human finitude and divine infinitude. With this change the motif derived from the poetry of courtly love takes on a completely new meaning both ideologically and artistically. The simple and muted melody of San Pedro's lines is now orchestrated in a rich polyphony in which a single motif, the impossibility of expressing oneself, *is expressed* in rhythmic movements without direction or way of escape: "A going in and no coming out, / A beginning without ending."

John of the Cross in the way we have already examined—that is to say, mystically and not philosophically. Obviously I am not saying that Torres Naharro was a "source" of St. John of the Cross but only that in certain Spanish circles questions like those formulated by the *Shādhilīya* were familiar—or, at least, perceptible echoes of them are heard.

We know nothing about the ancestors of Torres Naharro, nor why he remained so long outside of Spain. His biting style, his criticism of ecclesiastical life in Rome, the "intellectual" way in which he views certain problems, combined with other circumstances, seem to indicate that he was one of the many converts from Judaism who took refuge in Italy. On the occasion of the victory over the Venetians at La Motta in 1513, he composed a psalm which begins,

> Let us sing psalms of glory,
> *Let them know we are Christians,*
> Let us know this victory
> which God gives us by his hands.

Since Juan de Mena such glorification of Spanish accomplishments and of the great lords (in this case, of Ramón de Cardona) had been very much a part of the tradition of the converts. Torres Naharro begins his poem on the lance point of Longinus with a defensive phrase characteristic of New Christians:

> May God *as Trinity* preserve you,
> Oh holy blade of the lance . . .

(As we shall see later, the first thing done by a group of converts from Judaism in Barcelona after the destruction of their synagogue in 1391 was to order the construction of a chapel of the Holy Trinity.) We may also remember his "Exclamation of Our Lady against the Jews" with its typically New Christian profusion of insults. Finally, in his scandalous parody of a Church council ("Cupid's Invocation to the Council of Fops and Courtesans in Rome"), there still appears the phrase traditionally used to encompass the totality of Spaniards of the three castes (see above, p. 92):

> To all those who are lovers,
> our servants and servitors,
> *Jews, Moors, Christians.*

Torres Naharro is a complex writer, interested in presenting a clear-cut picture of the society around him, troubled about his own position within that society, careful not to reveal his personal antecedents, of refined sensitivities and intelligence. It is undeniable, furthermore, that the problem of the relation between the human and the divine aroused his interest.

After this brief digression let us return to St. John of the Cross. His work did not float free in an abstract atmosphere; it was inevitably linked to the very special mode of Spanish life. Father Nwya, and before him Baruzi, rejected Asín's ideas about St. John of the Cross because their great knowledge of mysticism was not rooted "in its own history"—in other words, in the reality of Spanish life. In the sixteenth century Jews, Moors, and Christians still lived together in some manner, and the communication among them had gained in seriousness and depth what it had lost in superficial color, as had been shown in my *De la edad conflictiva*. Father Nwya believes that Friar John of the Cross could not have known the least detail of the Muslim tradition except through some other friar of Morisco origin. In Granada, according to Nwya, there was only a certain Father Juan Albotodo, who was famous among the Moriscos; and when St. John of the Cross came to Granada in 1518, the Morisco Father Albotodo had long since left the city ("Ibn 'Abbād de Ronda et Jean de la Croix," p. 130). Hence, there was no possibility that St. John might know anything about the *Shādhilīya* doctrines (i.e., "God is inaccessible to his creatures. . . . God is in no way that we can sense, imagine, conceive, and desire" [Asín, *Huellas del Islam*, p. 249]). Or, as Torres Naharro says, to attempt to praise the Virgin adequately, who dwells in Heaven with the Trinity, "is a going in and no coming out, / a beginning without ending."

But this doctrine, reduced to simple maxims without philosophic or theological background, must have been diffused orally among certain "Jews, Moors, or Christians" just as the ballads of the *Romancero* were, just as the knowledge of the meaning of the caste to which one belonged was. Possibly the reluctance to accept the simplest facts about the Spanish reality we face is due, in the last analysis, to lack of sympathy for all things Semitic. But the truth is that there were Muslims in al-Andalus inspired by the desire to attain the divine without charismatic experiences, physical sensations and seizures, or visible images of the divine—and there were swarms of Moriscos in sixteenth-century Spain. All that, however, remains very distant from the unique oneness of the art of St. John of the Cross. In it we sense the sublime expressive form of a life that had learned how to give volume to the nondimensional, the rhythm of graceful flight to the inert, seductive charms and the fainting weakness of love to an experience of which the senses cannot take hold.

Nor do I think that the corporeal and spiritual mysticism of St. Theresa (whose Jewish, Oriental ancestry is attested to by documents, as we shall see later) can be accounted for by Christian tradition only. When we think about the historical reality of Spain, we cannot get along without those nine hundred years of Christian-Islamic-Jewish interrelationship.

As we emphasize the necessity for maintaining a lively awareness of historical time, let us not forget that some 430 years separate the arrival of the Moors and the appearance of the first Spanish literary work in the vernacular known to us, the *Poem of the Cid*—years during which the task, the inescapable obsession, of the Christians was the compulsion to have it out with the Moors. The Roman and Visigothic past must have served to keep alive the awareness that they were not Moors and the idea of a future of national unity; but with memories and longings it was not easy to conquer the Muslim lords of the larger part of the country. It was also necessary to fight some peoples who were not Muslim. Fruela I, king of Asturias (757-768), had to conquer and subdue the Vascones as well as the Gallaeci who had risen up against him (*Crónica de Alfonso III*, ed. García Villada [1918], p. 71). The struggle among the Christian kingdoms and countries was intense in the first centuries of the reconquest, which dragged along slowly until the fifteenth century because of lack of unity of purpose among the Christians.

Poor, divided, with a life whose horizon was limited to military action, down to the eleventh century the Christians had regarded the Moors as an extremely powerful enemy whom circumstances had forced them to get along with. In the tenth century, and the third century of the occupation, Cordova oppressed in every possible way the weak states of the north. In 980, seeing how Almanzor's continuous victories were bringing him far into Castile, "the King of Navarre, Sancho Garcés, [came out to meet him and] offered him his daughter; Almanzor accepted her with pleasure, he took her to wife, and she embraced Mohammedanism, and was one of the most beautiful and most religious wives Almanzor had." In 993 King Vermudo II of Leon "sent his daughter Teresa to the Muslim leader, who received her as a slave and later freed her so that he might marry her."[14] Before this, 'Abd-al-Raḥmān III (d. 961) received a Christian embassy in his palace of Medina Azahara, a wonderful prodigy of art and grandeur. The road from Cordova to the palace (some three miles) had been covered with mats; alongside the road stretched a

---

[14] Ramón Menéndez Pidal, *Historia y epopeya*, p. 19.

double file of soldiers, under whose crossed sabres the terrified ambassadors had to move. As they reached the palace, high dignitaries
dressed in silk and brocade came out to meet them. The ambassadors
greeted these people respectfully, thinking that one of them was the
Caliph; but the Caliph was found sitting in the middle of a court-
yard covered with sand, wearing rude clothing, the symbol of his
ascetic customs. In the midst of terrible threats, the Christians signed
the peace treaty imposed by the sovereign.[15]

Events of this sort are not surprising in the first three centuries of
the Moorish domination. Moreover, the Moors and the Arabianized
Jews were the exclusive repositories of science. Opulent Christians
went to Cordova to have their ailments treated, just as wealthy Europeans and Americans went to Germany in the nineteenth century.
With few exceptions, technology and trade were the heritage of
Jews and Moors. So, then, if existence was Christian, subsistence and
prosperity in the degree to which it was possible were achieved by
submitting to the benefits of the dominant civilization, superior not
only by force of arms.

For five hundred years—a long time—victory in battle went now to
one side, now to the other, until the African Almohades suffered a
decisive defeat at Las Navas de Tolosa in 1212. By 1248 the Christians
had become permanent masters of Cordova, Valencia, the Balearic Islands, and Seville. Insecurity, discouragement, and political bungling
had been considerable on both sides. I have already remarked (see
above, p. 54) on the disquietude felt by 'Abd-al-Raḥmān III, the
most powerful caliph of Cordova; after the loss of Toledo in 1085,
the dismay of the Arabs could not have been less. Thus, offsetting
Arabic faith in the certain eternity of what God had promised them
was their doubt as to the stability, durability, and tangibility of
earthly things. Let us not think, then, that the question of what happened in the first centuries of the reconquest can be answered by
saying that a weak "culture" submitted to a stronger one, and nothing more. As the Christian acquired Arabic things and ways of living
(both external and internal), he also absorbed Arabic doubt and uncertainty with respect to earthly life and would ultimately scorn
everything thought and done by people who were not of his caste.

Even Arabic science and thought, despite their volume and importance, were never entirely secularized; they were the patrimony
of a few men who were never in touch with what is called today the
"people" or public opinion. The last great caliph of Cordova, al-
Ḥakam II (961–976), so called because of his love of science, preferred piety to wisdom at the end of his life. When al-Ḥakam II died,
Almanzor handed over to the *alfaquíes* ("theologians") the best and

---

[15] E. Lévi-Provençal, *L'Espagne musulmane au Xᵉ siècle* (1953), p. 49.

largest part of the splendid library of the Caliph so that they might expurgate it and destroy by fire what was deemed harmful to the faith. Thus there was a constant oscillation between strong and renowned sovereignty and anarchic weakness, between intelligence and learning and crude fanaticism. In the Muslim civilization, visual pleasure—ornament, coloring, open spaces—was more sought after than the satisfactions provided by what we might call closed structures (compare the Mosque of Cordova with a Greek temple or a Gothic cathedral). Such primary characteristics of one and the other civilization are rooted in different conceptions of reality—what it is and what man does with it from within his individual or collective dwelling place of life. In addition to these visual delights—fabrics of fascinating color and design—the Muslim reveled in exquisite perfumes that gratified the sense of smell. All kinds of sensual and imaginative pleasure mattered a great deal more than molding vital activity into stable, closed forms (witness even the form of Arabic script, predominantly linear and open). The immediate intensity of joy or of the momentary triumph, won at times by spendthrift use of intelligence and heroic effort, was more attractive than reasoned methods of foreseeing and organizing the future (we might remember how as early as the year 1000 French kings were organizing the future development of the monarchy, the cornerstone upon which that nation was built). If an inevitable generalization is allowed, we may say that the West European was interested in existing "substantially," on a firm human foundation, while the Muslim seems to have been interested above all in what could not be enclosed within fixed outline, in what was not firmly based upon itself, for only Allah knew what the essence of things was and which things were feasible for man.

Even if, from the eleventh century, the military prestige of the Moors did begin slowly to decay and even if Christian life, thanks to its energy and dynamism, did start to ascend, not for this reason did the values of al-Andalus decline or was there any lessening of the esteem that its Christian enemy professed for it. Valor, stimulated by faith in the institution of royalty (not simply in a leader or, as the Spaniards call him, *caudillo*) and in religious belief, established more and more firmly the only superiority effective in drawing out the thousand thorns that the Spaniards had picked up in their centuries of vassalage. It was not only the enthusiasm for Christ which decided the victories in favor of the Christians; stronger than the evangelical impulse was, after all, the trust in St. James the Moorslayer—Santiago Matamoros—who lent magical aid in the destruction of the Muslims. But in the last analysis, the decisive factor would be the coincidence of religious faith and the Christian's faith in the power of his own

‑ caste. Merely by being a member of the Christian caste the individual
‑ felt himself capable of acquiring seigniory of wealth, authority, no-
‑ bility, and liberty—all thanks to vital thrust and bravery. The awareness of the commanding dimension of the person permitted him to
rise from serfdom to power, a power whose goal was more to assert
one's excellence and dignity than to create an extrapersonal culture
that would be of use to many others.

Hence, in spite of the great victories over Islam, the Castilian had,
in a certain sense, to surrender and to accept the superiority of his
enemy with regard to the ability to make use of the possibilities
around him by means of technology. In 1248 the armies of King
Ferdinand III conquered Seville after a struggle that gave definitive
proof of the military incapability of the already decadent Moors. But
these victorious armies could not repress their astonishment upon be-
holding the grandeur of the conquered city. The Christians had
never possessed anything similar in art, economic splendor, civil organization, technology, and scientific and literary productivity:
"How great is the beauty and the loftiness and the nobility [of the
Giralda].... And it has many other great and noble features besides
those of which we have spoken." To Seville came goods from all
parts: ". . . from Tangier, Ceuta, Tunis, Bougie, Alexandria, Genoa,
Portugal, England, Bordeaux, Bayonne, Gascony, Catalonia, Aragon,
and even from [northern] France."[16]

---

[16] *Crónica General*, pp. 268–269. Life in Seville a century before its conquest
by the Christians is known to us, thanks to the curious book entitled *Sevilla a
comienzos del siglo XII*, by Ibn 'Abdūn, trans. E. Lévi-Provençal and E. Garcia
Gómez (Madrid, 1948). The book is at one and the same time a collection of
municipal ordinances, a catechism of public morality and hygiene, and a description of abuses and corruption. At times it seems as if the city were confessing
its faults. The tone, which is at once intelligent, familiar, and intimate (as was
characteristic of the Muslim), reveals the high level of civic culture which
al-Andalus had achieved. A few examples follow: "The prince should pre-
scribe that the greatest stimulus be given to agriculture, which should be encouraged, as well as the farm laborers themselves, who should be treated kindly
and protected in their work" (p. 42). "Scientific books should not be sold to
Jews or Christians except when they deal with their faith, because afterward
they translate these scientific books and *attribute them to their own people and
their bishops*, when in truth they are Muslim works" (p. 173). "It would be
desirable to suppress lawyers, for their activities cause the people to spend their
money in vain. . . . But if we must have them, let them be as few as possible"
(p. 61). "Garden vegetables, such as lettuce, chicory, carrots, etc., ought not to
be washed in the pools or garden tanks, for there is no surety that these are
clean, but in the river where the water is clearest and purest" (p. 132). As is
evident, the translation of scientific books was not limited to the so-called
School of Translators of Toledo. There were Christian churches in Seville,
which the author presents as places of immorality (p. 150); Muslims and
Christians reproached each other for the same vices.

See also I. de las Cajigas, *Sevilla almohade y últimos años de su vida musulmana* (Madrid: Instituto de Estudios Africanos, 1951), an interesting study of
the political and military confusion in Seville in the years that preceded its
conquest by Ferdinand III. A firm believer in the faith of an "eternal Spain,"

In the mid-thirteenth century the opulence of the port of Almeria served as a term of reference in the measurement of economic value, just as the mines of Potosí or the treasure of Venice would do later. The author of the *Libro de Alexandre* says of the throne of Darius:

> how much it might be worth, I would not know how to value,
> the wealth of Almeria could not compare with it.
>
> (Ed. Willis, st. 2595)

Even in the fourteenth century, the Cortes (Parliament) lamented over the poverty of the Castilian land: "The earth is very sterile and very poor" (1307). "The land was very poor and needy of attention and depopulated" (1367). "Our kingdoms are poor in cattle and other foods" (1371). "Our kingdoms are very needy" (1388).[17] The principal source of wealth was cattle raising and the exportation of wool. Industry satisfied only local needs, and commerce depended in large measure on imports from foreign countries. Once the vigor of the Muslim caste had declined, the possibilities for future greatness lay primarily in the spirit of the dominant caste and in what was created by the unique interweaving of the peculiar Christian-Oriental elements with those derived from contact with European Christianity. Up to the fifteenth century, literature and art clearly testify to these characteristics of the Spanish civilization of the time. The fact that in the Mediterranean strip comprising Catalonia and Valencia things were somewhat different does not essentially alter the picture, for in spite of their greater prosperity, in large part the Christians of those regions made use of Moors and Jews for their cultural and technological activities.

It is a good idea to emphasize the fact, well known as it is, that during the Middle Ages there was not a complete separation between Christians and Moors. We have already mentioned the Mozarabs, those bilingual Christians who continued to live in the midst of the Moors, and who, starting in the first centuries of the occupation, would emigrate from time to time to Christian lands, and who moved en masse during the incursions of the Almorávides and Almohades in the twelfth century. The Mozarabs expatriated themselves from Granada with the retreating Aragonese troops of Alfonso I, who had invaded that kingdom. In 1146 there was another Mozarab

---

the author thinks, despite everything, that neither the Visigoths nor the Muslims "carried out any great urban reform that modified perceptibly the physiognomy of the thousand-year-old city of Hispalis" (p. 11). But the previously cited work of Ibn 'Abdūn makes it clear that *the style* in which the life of Islamic Seville is described diverges widely from Roman and Visigothic expressive forms.

[17] Quoted by Ramón Carande in *Anuario de Historia del Derecho*, II (1925), 267.

exodus from Seville to the lands of Castile,[18] and it is certain that such displacements must have occurred in other instances not registered by the chronicles. Besides this social class, there was that of the so-called Mudejars, the Moors who lived as vassals of the Christian kings—kings who were influenced by the tolerance of the first four centuries of Islamism, as we shall see later. To these Mudejars we are indebted for a number of beautiful monuments, including the Alcázar in Seville as we know it and the Puerta del Sol in Toledo.[19] Besides there were fugitives from one religion to the other: *muladíes*, or Christians who turned Islamic, and *tornadizos*, or Moors who turned Christian. The *Partidas*, or laws, of Alfonso the Learned say (VII, 25, 8) that at times men "ill-fated and despairing of every blessing, renounce the faith of Our Lord Jesus Christ and become Moors . . . either to live free of restraint, or to be relieved of the troubles that may have beset them as Christians." Such renegades were deprived of their property and, if they were apprehended, of their life. The same legal code speaks of the hard life of the *tornadizos* (VII, 25, 3), which discouraged those who wanted to become Christians; many would have done so "if it were not for the abuse and dishonor that they see the others receive who turn Christian and are called turncoats [*tornadizos*] and many other evil and insulting names." It is evident, then, that the two religions lived together easily, but that apostasy was not easy in either of them.

To end this list of such classes, there was a fifth, the *enaciados*, who moved back and forth between the two religions, and who capitalized on their bilingualism by serving as spies. They lived in border towns, and sometimes they formed complete communities, just as today on all the borders in the world there exist towns that specialize in smuggling. In Estremadura there is still a town called "Puebla de Naciados."

The Meaning of the Facts Set Forth Above

Despite the fact that a great deal has been written about Hispano-Muslim history, confusion still reigns as to the true nature of al-Andalus and the connection of its inhabitants with the people who clearly bore the name "Spanish" in the thirteenth century—but not before. Therefore, we must fix the outline of the human identity of those who constitute the theme of our discussion; otherwise, the more

---

[18] See Menéndez Pidal, *Orígenes del español*, pp. 445–446.

[19] See F. Fernández y González, *Estado social y político de los mudéjares de Castilla* (1866); N. Esténaga, "Condición social de los mudéjares en Toledo," *Boletín de la Real Academia de Bellas Artes de Toledo*, VI (1924), 5–27; I. de las Cajigas, *Los mozárabes* (2 vols.; Madrid: Instituto de Estudios Africanos, 1947–1948), and *Los mudéjares* (2 vols.; Madrid: Instituto de Estudios Africanos, 1948–1949).

data and information are added, the less will be our understanding of the social condition and dimensions, that is, the authentic human reality, of the people who are the object of study.

Little light will be shed on the medieval history of the Peninsula as long as distinguished Orientalists and others continue to write that the "Spanish *race*" remained Spanish while it lived under the domination of peoples of Arabic *blood*. F. J. Simonet wrote about the population of Granada at the very moment of its conquest (1492) that, according to certain Aragonese ambassadors who had visited the city in 1311, "at that time two hundred thousand people lived [there], of whom fewer than five hundred were Moors by birth, for all of them were the children or grandchildren of Christians."[20] Simonet did not dare to write that not being "Moorish by birth" meant that a man was "Spanish," but only that he was of Christian "birth," a foggy concept based on ideas about the social reality of people that I now consider invalid. On this basis and in the belief that "blood" and "psychology" mold the structure and character of human collectivities, a distinguished Arabist wrote recently: "This huge mass [of descendants of Christians], growing constantly by natural propagation and with a great capacity for infiltrating, through marriage, all lineages including the royal family—this multitude of *good Muslims*, who were, however, *Spaniards by race* and therefore ruled by another psychology and different atavistic instincts, . . . is the group *responsible for the true physiognomy of Muslim* Spain."[21]

Spanish Arabists apply to all al-Andalus the same criterion of "españolización" ("conversion to Spanishness"), regardless of the number of generations separating the Muslims from their Christian origins. Whenever Moors from al-Andalus go to fight in Morocco, they are called "Spaniards"; Ibn Ḥazm was a "Spaniard," and so on. If such standards prevailed, the Muslim would lose any clear historical reality, for in Morocco they would be Berbers, near the Nile they would become Egyptians, and so forth. The same thing would happen to imperial Romans if such a concept were justified, which it is not. Those who adopt the language, the religion, and the system of politico-administrative hierarchies of another human collectivity become a part of the latter, no matter what the human condition of their grandparents may have been. In large majority the Romano-Goths adhered to the cause of the invaders and adopted their language and their religion; and religion, in the case of the Mohammedan peoples, is a decisive factor because of the all-encompassing nature of Islamism. According to Lévi-Provençal, the converts to Moham-

---

[20] *Historia de los mozárabes de España* (1897), p. 787.
[21] García Gómez, Introduction to the *España musulmana* of Lévi-Provençal, p. xix.

medanism "more and more lost the sense of their own origin as time went on." Some of them "paid large sums in gold to have genealogies fabricated for themselves which would permit them to boast of Arabic lineage." The ancestry of others was given away "by their names, by their obviously Roman surnames, as happened with the Banu Angelino and the Banu Sabatico of Seville." One Arab chronicler of the tenth century, Don al-Qutiyya (i.e., "the son of the Gothic woman"), prided himself on descending from King Witiza; but in short order there came about such an ethnic jumble among the peoples of al-Andalus "that it became ever more difficult to distinguish in them the native elements from foreign ones" (Lévi-Provençal, *España musulmana* p. 47). Furthermore, even if many Muslims had descended directly from the Gothic kings, by what right are they called "Spaniards" when the Gothic kings themselves were not Spanish? Ibn al-Qutiyya called himself "son of the Gothic woman," and not "son of the Spanish woman," because there were no Spanish women then.

Al-Andalus becomes intelligible when viewed not from within its heart but as the outer border of something it was not. Because of the special position of al-Andalus with respect to the other Islamic countries (Egypt, too, was a border area with respect to Iraq and Morocco), we are struck by

the highly respectful and in some ways filial attachment maintained by al-Andalus throughout its existence toward the rest of the Arabic world and to the authenticity of its civilization. This attachment was revealed especially in the field of religion. Once Islamized, al-Andalus[22] showed itself to be resolutely conservative. . . . Up to the end of its history, the Malikite school dominated al-Andalus, and [the theologians] exerted themselves ardently and without faltering to the destruction of all attempts to diffuse new currents, to the extirpation of heresy, and to the maintenance of an extremely strict orthodoxy. . . . In al-Andalus this conservative tendency is evident not only in the field of religion. Any close examination suffices to reveal the archaic character of its social life —at least until the twelfth century—a social life preserved until recently in Morocco, the direct heir of the civilization of al-Andalus. . . . A great many archaic Muslim institutions subsisted in al-Andalus, while in the rest of the Arabic world they were gradually dying out.[23]

Such was the human world in which the Muslims of al-Andalus existed. The analysis of their blood would be a task for biologists, but certainly not for historians. The people of al-Andalus were not Spaniards, nor did those who fought and fraternized with them before the thirteenth century, in Muslim or Christian lands, feel them-

---

[22] Influenced by the pernicious habit of calling al-Andalus "Spain," Lévi-Provençal actually writes here "l'Espagne."

[23] E. Lévi-Provençal, "Le rôle spirituel de l'Espagne [?] musulmane," in *Islam d'Occident* (Paris, 1948), pp. 310–311.

selves to be Spaniards. The *Crónica General* (in the part composed during the reign of King Sancho IV) imagines the speech of Alfonso VIII, king of Castile, before the Battle of Las Navas de Tolosa (1212); first he exhorts "his own people," the noblemen (*fijosdalgo*) of his kingdom and the "men of arms" who fight under his orders; then he directs himself to those who had come from other kingdoms to aid in the battle against the Almohades, the supreme test for the Christians after five hundred years of struggle and common life with al-Andalus:

> After King Alfonso had made sure of the readiness of his troops in this fashion, he drew aside the next day with those from Aragon and the Portuguese and the Galicians and the Asturians, all those who had come there, and King Alfonso spoke to them thus: "Friends, *all of us are Spaniards*, and the Moors entered into our land by force and conquered it from us, and *the Christians at that time* [500 years before!] were weak, for they did not expel the Moors and throw them out of the land."
>
> (Ed. Menéndez Pidal, p. 693)

The "Christians" of five centuries earlier—and note that they are thus termed, rather than Goths—now appear as "Spaniards." The reason lies in the fact that for five centuries (711–1212) the Christians had needed aid, since at the beginning they felt themselves weak: "Certain groups joined with others and helped each other, and were a match for the Moors, always conquering lands from them, until affairs have come to the state in which you see they are today. And you have all heard sufficiently of the harm they did to me [Alfonso VIII] in the Battle of Alarcos."

For this reason, in order to unify his allies politically and morally, King Alfonso uses a term that is secular and less generic than the traditional one of "Christians," used to designate the whole mass of those who were opposed to the Moors. The memory of the disaster at Alarcos now incited the Aragonese and Navarrese to join themselves to the Castilians; the lands conquered during a period of more than a century were in danger of being lost if what had happened on the ill-fated and burning day of July 19, 1195, should be repeated. The Berber caliph, Abu Yūsuf Ya'qūb al-Manṣūr, destroyed the Castilian host and King Alfonso himself very nearly fell prisoner. The castle of Alarcos, to the west of Ciudad Real, was razed. According to Rodrigo Jiménez de Rada, whose account is here followed by the *Crónica General* (p. 681), King Alfonso IX of Leon and King Sancho VII of Navarre "pretended to come to the aid of this King Alfonso [of Castile] at the Battle of Alarcos." As if this treachery were not enough, "once the noise of the battle was over, a few days afterward those two kings, of Leon and of Navarre, began to make war and to run through the kingdom of Castile like a *horde of enemies*. Further: King Alfonso of Leon fixed his love on the Arabs, and he took many of them with him and entered the kingdom of Castile . . . sacking and destroying all that he found" (p. 682).

Against this background the words ("we are all Spaniards") directed by Alfonso VIII in 1212 to Aragonese, Portuguese, Galicians, and Asturians stand out sharply and take on meaning. The Asturians had come without their king, Alfonso IX, who felt less "Spanish" than purely Leonese, and therefore hostile to his Castilian rival. The reconquest lasted eight centuries precisely because the Christians did not truly feel themselves to be Spaniards; to think otherwise would imply the admission that the "Spaniards" had lived in civil war and enmity for eight hundred years, which would be absurd in the extreme. The truth is that the patterns traced out by the collective dimensions of each group lacked a fixed, fully defined outline and did not yet fit that mode of shared common life in which groups were tied to one another by mutual bonds, a mode of life that is evident and inescapable by the sixteenth century and is today called "Spanish." That modality of life took on its shape slowly, because what is designated by the term "Spanish" affirmed its reality above all on the basis of a community of belief, including that overarching belief in which, as I have already said (p. 130), it was hoped that the three castes of possible Spaniards might be brought into accord; furthermore, that collective modality was being forged in the common task of fighting and conquest rather than by means of the interlocking peaceful tasks of secular intellectual activities. (One of the principal supports of "Italianness," on the other hand, has been the intense attraction exerted by superior models of literary and artistic beauty.)

In contrast with the lack of "Spanish" feeling displayed by the king of Leon in 1195 and 1212 (other like cases could be adduced), there may be cited the Aragonese-Catalan reaction of the chronicler, Bernat Desclot, after the victory of Las Navas de Tolosa. According to him, the three kings of Spain returned to their own lands after having routed the Saracens and conquered a large number of cities, towns, and castles: "And when the King of Aragon had returned into Aragon, he found there French and English and German knights and many other people who had come to fight; but they had come too late, and they came before the King and asked him what had become of the Saracens. And he answered them that they need not go farther, because the Saracens had been defeated and killed *by the kings of Spain*" (chapter VI). The awareness of being Spanish was alternately split or made firm by the very force of circumstances (the way of dwelling and of creating oneself in one's own life). These realities have never been rigid and given from the outset; they are problems of the life process, not of geography or biology. My exposition of the problem here leaves the outcome open; the process is observed only to understand the past and to give some insight into the future.

Lévi-Provençal has called our attention to the human complexity of al-Andalus—without naïvely relating everything to the Celtiberians, even though he does use the term "Spanish" imprecisely:

A Muslim Spaniard [in my terms, an inhabitant of al-Andalus] and a Christian Spaniard [i.e., a Leonese, Castilian, or Aragonese, on the way to becoming what is today called Spanish] were not so foreign to each other or so different as might be thought. From early times, as is already known, the kingdoms of the north had Muslims among their subjects; on the other hand, Muslim Spain [i.e., al-Andalus] always had among its peoples a large proportion of native elements who faithfully maintained their Christianity.

And he adds that usually only the political development of the Peninsula during the high Middle Ages is studied, while its human problem remains in the shadows, perhaps in total darkness.[24]

The answers to such intelligent observations will help in the understanding of the past of the Peninsula if they are based on the initial supposition that the Moors and the Christians were oriented toward opposite poles (Muslim Asia and Christian Europe) at the same time that they found themselves in confused, insecure situations, in a state of irresolution, of deficiency. Al-Andalus could not maintain the caliphate or fuse the disparate elements that had permitted her to attain the pinnacle of her prestige. From the eleventh century on, the culture of al-Andalus and her political structure were at once sustained and destroyed by invasions from Africa.

While this was going on in the south, the Christian north was opening wide to French penetration, related, as we shall see later, to the pilgrimages to Santiago de Compostela. Cluniac and Cistercian monks invaded the lands and cities of Navarre, Castile, Leon, and Galicia for the official purpose of correcting the ways of that European sub-Christendom, whose kings and great lords judged it much in need of direction. The Gallic imprint was deep, but the Christians of the north could not develop a culture consonant with that of European Christendom in philosophy, learning, and technology precisely because of the system of the three castes, a system whose analysis and evaluation is the subject of this study. To maintain their independence, the kingdoms of the north had to make use of their Moors and Jews, who were as Spanish or non-Spanish as the other inhabitants of the Christian kingdoms in their reciprocal contacts. It is imperative to keep in mind this total picture of Peninsular life in order to make meaningful the data of social and political history (see chapter ix). We must not lose sight of the essential uniqueness of the phenomenon if we do not wish to fall into misguided opinions

---

[24] *Islam d'Occident*, p. 161.

and to waste time and effort. I imagine the situation of the Christian kingdoms after the fall of the caliphate in the eleventh century had opened up the hope for a better and more exalted future to be something like that of an architect forced to choose between roofing over his building to protect it from the elements and establishing it on solid foundations so that it might not tumble down. The roof in my simile is European Christian culture; the foundations correspond to the system of the three castes. If the Christian kingdoms had been able to rid themselves of Moors and Jews in the eleventh century— but I do not construct history on the basis of what might have been desirable, but on very simple realities in full accord with the ideas that make them perceptible—everything would have been different.

Spanish history must take into account the imprecision, during centuries, of the boundaries that separated the relatively limited social awareness of the Galician, Castilian, Catalan, and the like from the wider awareness represented later by the term Spaniard. The names themselves—let me emphasize this fact—tell us enough: "Don Pascual Espaniol" (recorded in 1161) and "Don Espannol" (in 1212)[25] must have been so called (either they or their ancestors) by some foreigners for whom "España" designated, in vague terms, the lands south of the Pyrenees. "Espanesco" (in 996) meant "Moorish."[26] At that time the Christians of the Muslim zone called themselves Mozarabs, and those in the Christian zones were Galicians, Navarrese, and so on. Non-Christians in the Christian kingdoms were Moors and Jews, who experienced the same state of fluctuating within a caste, a religious community, a kingdom, and, finally, Spain. Would not the Jew Abrahám Senior, whose baptismal sponsors were the Catholic Sovereigns, feel himself to be fully Spanish?

Such fluctuation and elasticity were correlates of the insecurity created by the separation into castes and the inevitable harmonies created among them. Once religious differences had "officially" disappeared, the task of unification, of making everything "Spanish," depended on common occupations. The imperial enterprise of the sixteenth century contributed toward erasing regional particularisms. Nevertheless, it is to be noted that only the Castilians and the Leonese had the *legal* right to go to the Indies. The fact that *in practice* Navarrese, Aragonese, and Catalans went to the New World and held distinguished posts there does not lessen the exclusionist intent of the laws, which as late as the sixteenth century still looked upon those who were not Castilians or Leonese as foreigners.[27] The

---

[25] See V. Oelschläger, *A Medieval Spanish Word-List*, p. 84.

[26] See M. Gómez Moreno, *Iglesias mozárabes*, p. 342.

[27] In this connection, see the sensible comments of Salvador de Madariaga, *Cuadro histórico de las Indias* (1950), p. 106. I do not, however, consider entirely accurate his assertion that "if more Catalans did not go to the New World dur-

laws of the Indies in the sixteenth century were not promulgated for a population felt to be uniformly Spanish. The problematical issue of the *limits of an individual's Spanishness—when it had begun and where it stopped*—began to appear in the high Middle Ages and had still not totally disappeared in the sixteenth and seventeenth centuries. This problem must be kept in mind if we are to understand the very special nature of manifestation of Spanish civilization, whether it be the disunited kingdoms of the Middle Ages, the partly united, partly discordant castes, the fragmented republics of Spanish America, or the echoes of all these things throughout the twentieth century in Spain.

The reality to which the various national names refer is based on the belief held by those included in the group that the people bearing such names are closer together, with respect to collective relationships, than any other class of human beings. The semantic boundaries of such designations rest more on axiological than on logical foundations. In Argentina the Galicians and Asturians, though separated from each other in different regional clubs, are grouped together socially as Spaniards as their collective dimension is extended to the maximum limit. A Spaniard, a Mexican, or a Chilean appears as such when seen at close range; from a more distant viewpoint they are all felt to be Spanish Americans and nearer to the Spaniard than any other people outside Spain. For this reason the Spaniard finds the term "Latin American" artificial.

This common feeling with respect to the collective dimension is independent of congeniality, or of any kind of "affinity by choice," or of the sameness of political sovereignty. It is more a value than a substantive reality—I insist on this point—and for this reason it is elastic. For the same reason the national names appear in one form when they are "lived" from within, and in another when they are observed from without and are the subject of reflection. The Irishman established in England will be British officially but Irish in his heart of hearts; similar situations may be observed in the United States. The dimension of value and the substantive dimension of the national designation are fused into one when a nation completely absorbs regional differences (in Portugal, Denmark, and other like cases). When such absorption is not achieved, a certain wavering is inevitable, even in closely knit countries like France, where many Alsatians and Bretons are more sensitive initially to their regional dimension than to that of the official nation. Similar hierarchies of value may be found in Spain, Italy, and other countries.

---

ing the first two centuries, it was simply because they did not choose to go" (p. 107). On this point see the introduction to Madariaga's work concerning the lack of cohesion between Castile and Aragon after the discovery of the New World.

On the eve of the famous Battle of Las Navas de Tolosa, King Alfonso VIII called the Asturians and the Catalans "officially" Spaniards; both the particular and the general designations were real and effective, but in different ways. Let us keep this in mind as we enter the labyrinth of regional nomenclature among the inhabitants of the Peninsula in the epoch of the three castes and the several kingdoms.

The Moriscos

After the political domination of the Moors came to an end, a considerable number of Mudejars (now called Moriscos) stayed in Spain. About them I shall say only what is necessary for my purposes. They revolted more than once, and the armies of Philip II had to fight strenuously to reduce the Alpujarra rebellion, in southern Granada.[28] As everyone knows, the Morisco population, except for those who were priests, monks, or nuns, was expelled by Philip III in 1609. That unhappy breed survived the spirit that had made living together possible for Christians, Moors, and Jews; once the model of Islamic tolerance, with all its prestige, had disappeared, there was no ideal vertex at which Christians and Moors could converge. As will be remembered (see above, p. 89), there had been attempts to draw the three castes of believers together under the same merciful God as well as under the same political leadership. In 1098 and in 1104, for example, Alfonso VI subscribed certain royal patents—some redacted in Latin, others in Arabic—as "King of all the Christian and pagan kingdoms of Spain" and "Emperor of the two religions" (Ramón Menéndez Pidal, El imperio hispánico y los cinco reinos, p. 110).

But, like many other problems in Spanish life, this one was insoluble, and it is idle to argue the point whether the Moriscos ought or ought not to have been thrown out of their native land. They doubtless were a political danger, and they did have intelligence with foreign enemies of Spain, who herself was beginning to feel frightened and weak,[29] so weak that it was necessary to bring home the regiments in Italy because the forces available in the kingdom

---

[28] In the Guerra de Granada of Diego Hurtado de Mendoza, the fight that went on from 1568 to 1571 is described with a full awareness that it was a civil war of "Spaniards against Spaniards" (Biblioteca de Autores Españoles, XXI, 73). The Moriscos were dispersed to remote places: "It was a most pitiable departure for those who had known them well off and comfortable in their homes; many died along the roads, from labor, from weariness, from grief, from hunger; killed by the very ones who were supposed to guard them; robbed, sold as captives" (ibid., p. 92). Luis del Mármol recounts the revolt in Granada in detail in Rebelión y castigo de los moriscos de Granada, in Biblioteca de Autores Españoles, Vol. XXI.

[29] See above, p. 170, and Juan Reglá, "La cuestión morisca ... en tiempo de Felipe II," Estudios de Historia Moderna, III (1953).

were not sufficient to guarantee security against the risks of the expulsion. The war in Granada in 1568 "revealed that our Spaniards are not worth so much on their own soil as they are when transplanted to the soil of other people."[30]

The Moriscos were hard and skillful workers, and it is a commonplace to lament the disaster that their removal brought on agriculture and industry. This was expressed once and for all by Diego Hurtado de Mendoza in words of polished steel, when he spoke of the Alpujarra as being "naturally sterile and hard, save where there are valleys; yet under the diligence of the Moriscos—who allowed no piece of ground to be wasted—usable and cultivated" (*Guerra de Granada*, in *Biblioteca de Autores Españoles*, xxi, 75). The Moor excelled at manual labor, scorned by the Christians, and for this he became, in Christian eyes, as useful as he was contemptible.

But the subject of the Moriscos will continue to float in a historical fog as long as we limit ourselves to nothing more than describing and presenting external aspects of that unfortunate people. Friar Marcos de Guadalajara, a resentful writer who both knew them well and hated them cordially, believed that the cause of the expulsion "can be no other than that, since the [Moriscos] have taken over all the tasks of artisans, and business dealings, and likewise the service as peons and day laborers; and since they do all this with greater advantage to the buyers, for they are so parsimonious and greedy that they neither eat nor drink nor dress themselves, it has come to pass that the Old Christians (who formerly earned their livelihood by working) find no one who will take them as day laborers; and if they are taken on, it is for so low a wage that they cannot live; and so it is that they leave their lands and go off ruined."[31] The same writer adds that "with their exile the price of wheat came down, merchandise moves freely over land and sea, the sea is navigated without so much worry; agriculture is of more profit and pleasure with the benevolence of the heavens; long trips are made without fear of enemies; travelers enjoy the beauty of the Most Holy Cross; the towns where they [the Moriscos] lived are honored by the Company of the Most Holy Sacrament of the Eucharist; fine coins of copper [*vellón*], gold, and silver circulate; the holy days are celebrated generally throughout Spain, and with approbation; our enemies do not know the secrets of the country; we are free on our coasts and river banks from African insults and robbery; our Spain is raising up . . . an abundance of new soldiers; unrest and differences of opinion are settled with facility; the land now rests secure from

---

[30] Marcos de Guadalajara y Xavier, *Memorable expulsión ... de los moriscos* (Pamplona, 1613), fol. 79v.

[31] *Ibid.* This passage is cited by J. Caro Baroja in *Los moriscos del reino de Granada* (Madrid, 1957), p. 219.

treason and uprisings; we live here in one Apostolic Roman Catholic faith; and, finally, we all have security in our homes" (cited by Florencio Janer, *Condición social de los moriscos* [1857], p. 169).

Had all this been true, a new Golden Age would have reigned in Spain after the explusion of the nefarious caste in 1609. This was not so, of course, even though the impassioned outcries on both sides at that time must be included in the total reality of our subject. The lamentation and the insults mean that, around 1600, the normal common life between Old Christians and Moriscos had become impossible. In 1497 the Catholic Sovereigns had still authorized the Moors expelled by the king of Portugal to "enter, *live*, and come into our kingdoms and dominions for all the time you may wish and find it convenient; and if you wish to depart from them, you may do so."[32] The Moriscos continued to be in the situation of the Mudejars (those who lived in Murcia were still so called) but within a social framework now broken because of the disappearance of the possibility of that common and harmonious life with the Christians which had existed in the twelfth, thirteenth, fourteenth, and fifteenth centuries. Friar Marcos de Guadalajara either was unaware of all this or preferred to forget it.[33] He no longer understood that the Moriscos were still attached to the religious ideal that had made possible, both in theory and in fact, the common life of the three castes of believers: "They were certain that every individual could be saved under the law of Christ, [under that of] the Jew, and [under that of] the Moor if he kept the precepts of his religion faithfully" (Janer, *op. cit.*, p. 169)—an invaluable confirmation of the survival of a spiritual situation created centuries before. Their hope of recovering political power by force of arms had vanished, but there were still certain Moriscos in Granada who believed they could regain by theological tricks something of the position that had been lost politically. These hopes explain, indeed, the meaning of the apostolic texts counterfeited by them which appeared during the excavation of the ground underneath a tower on what was afterward called, precisely for that reason, the Sacro Monte (Holy Mountain) of Granada. Between 1595 and 1597 there appeared, written in Latin

---

[32] Quoted by Henry Charles Lea, *The Moriscos of Spain: Their Conversion and Expulsion* (London, 1901), p. 404.

[33] As one example among many, here is how Peter II of Aragon addressed the Mudejars of Valencia, whose help he needed, in 1286: "We are at war with the French, as you will have heard, and we need your services and that of other loyal vassals of ours [*et dels altres feels nostres*]. We send you our faithful emissary, Don Samuel, and we ask that from the communities selected by him you send us archers and lancers of good spirit and discipline; we shall give them good pay and, further, we intend to reward them well so that they may be content" (*Documentos inéditos del Archivo de la Corona de Aragón* [published by P. de Bofarull], VI, 196).

and Arabic, texts of the Gospels in which Christianity and Islam were strangely syncretized: for example, "There is no other God but God and Jesus, the spirit of God." References to the Trinity were very superficial, so that the Muslims would have less difficulty in swallowing it.[34] The Incarnate Word was "the Spirit of God,"[35] but not one of the persons of the Trinity, by which token this special religion of the Moriscos came close to Arianism.

Though the Jews were not mentioned, the aim of that naïve theological fraud was to propose a God acceptable to the three monotheistic religious beliefs. Prudent and well-educated people pointed out the crudeness of the deception, which had been accepted as a divine message by the archbishop of Granada, Pedro de Castro y Quiñones.[36]

Belief in the authenticity of the "books" that certain astute Moriscos had buried on what is today called the Sacro Monte took hold among the clergy of Granada and in other places. The learned biblical scholar Benito Arias Montano (of Jewish descent) chose not to declare himself either for or against the discovery, which some people had judged to be an obvious fraud. The matter was submitted to Rome, and the books of the Arabic gospels were taken there in 1641 after much delay and resistance. But the Church did

---

[34] For all this problem, see J. Godoy Alcántara, *Historia crítica de los falsos cronicones* (Madrid, 1868), pp. 44–128. This work stands out in its time for the sober clarity of the author's thought and for the absence of the cloying rhetoric that was then so usual.

[35] What the Koran actually says (IV:169) is that the Messiah, Jesus, is the Word that God had sent to Mary, "and a Spirit proceeding from Himself"— that is to say, a Being endowed with Spirit.

[36] This saintly and naïve gentleman came to accept as his own the "doctrine" of those "evangelical" texts, written in Arabic on leaden tablets. We know this thanks to an anecdote related by Gregorio de Morillo, a chaplain of the Archbishop: "In his presence, in 1603, they carried to the Sacro Monte during a period of nine days a woman possessed of evil spirits, and the devils were refractory and would not come out, even though they had recited a thousand Gospel texts over her; and the Archbishop went there, and with the *Libro de la Nómina de Santiago* ["Book of the Names of St. James"] he made the sign of the cross from her forehead to her breast, saying in the Arabic tongue: 'Non est Deus, nisi Deus Jesus, Spiritus Dei,' and the enemies, wailing terribly, abandoned that body" (*apud* F. Rodríguez Marín, *Pedro Espinosa* [Madrid, 1907], p. 81, who gets his material from a document written by Dr. Barahona Miranda, canon of the Sacro Monte of Granada). The instrument productive of this miracle was one of those leaden books fabricated by the Moriscos and whose title is *Prayer and Defense of Saint James, Son of Xamech [sic] Zebedee.* The book ends as follows: "This is the sign that was written with shining light on the back of Jesus, son of Mary, true spirit of God, and which defends against all adversity, sickness, fits, madness, and *devils*, those who carry it with them, and it is as follows: 'There is no God but God, Jesus, the spirit of God, truth made manifest, true certitude'" (in Godoy Alcántara, *op. cit.,* p. 53). That syncretized faith of Christianity and Islam had become operative in the soul of an illustrious archbishop.

not pronounce on the case until 1682, when Innocent XI declared that it was a matter of a fiction invented "to ruin the Catholic faith," and "that many things smelled of Mohammedanism . . . , it being obvious that they were taken from the Koran and other highly impure Muslim books" (J. Godoy Alcántara, *Historia crítica de los falsos cronicones*, p. 127). The Pope observed with great perceptivity that the Spanish society was "very concerned with the supernatural and the marvelous, and very little or not at all with doctrines." In Rome it was said that "the piety of the Spaniards is injudicious."

Menéndez y Pelayo passes a very superficial judgment on these events as he ends his investigation of a phenomenon of such importance with this phrase: "So it was that this absurd attempt at *religious reform* failed: a notable episode in the history of the aberrations and weaknesses of human intelligence."[37] As a result nothing takes on reality in his history; it remains floating in the imprecise, abstract fog of "human aberrations and weaknesses," which is to say, in a meaningless vacuum. In the last analysis the problem presents at least three aspects: first, a final residue of the will toward common life (conscious or subconscious) on the part of certain Muslims and some Spanish Christians; Miguel de Luna and the Moriscos who collaborated with him in the fantastic deception felt, in addition to their practical interest, that such a fraud was *possible*, given the traditional interlocking of the spirituality of one religion with that of the other. The fact that this subject has been studied only sporadically and partially does not mean that such interlockings did not exist; here is a task to be carried out by future Orientalists and Hispanists. That cross-fertilization between the two religions was possible is evidenced by the blind faith with which an archbishop and many other clergymen accepted the famous leaden tablets—or by how certain Muslims recited the Lord's Prayer (see above, p. 62).

A second aspect is the trusting receptivity toward whatever was supposed to have come from the supernatural beyond, all of which seemed based on a surer and more efficacious reality than what was known about the world below heaven. And finally, we must remember one last aspect, of a social nature: the situation in which the Collegiate Church of the Sacro Monte of Granada found itself after the Holy See had declared the famous leaden tablets written in Arabic to be a ridiculous farce. On the other hand, the condemnation did not extend to the tablets written in barbarous Latin, in which it was said that on that spot several disciples of the Apostle James, among others St. Cecilius, had suffered martyrdom—an account, however, filled with so many "incongruities and anachronisms that its falsity

---

[37] *Historia de los heterodoxos españoles*, V (1928), 348.

leaped out from the first lines" (Menéndez y Pelayo, *Historia de los heterodoxos españoles*, v [1928], 344). But in spite of everything— indeed, precisely because all this happened—the canons of the church of Sacro Monte had published in 1741 a biography of Archbishop Pedro de Castro, entitled "A Mystical Bouquet, Historical, Chrono- logical, and Panegyrical, Woven from the Three Fragrant Flowers of the Most Noble Ancient Origin, the Most Exemplary Life, and the Most Deserved Fame" of the Archbishop who had founded their church. With so important a publication, truly the product of de- lirium, they rescued the sacred character both of the mountain and of the relics preserved in the church. As is said in a note to the reader, called "Explanation of the Work," "One must distinguish between the tablets [in Arabic] and the tablets [in Latin] which were found there." The latter "are stamped with papal approval, are allowed, and are kept along with the sacred relics to which they refer on the high altar of the Collegiate Church of Sacro Monte. Other tablets in strange Arabic and Oriental characters which con- tain various dogmatic and doctrinal points are prohibited; . . . there- fore we treat with special care those that are permitted, *without entering at all* into the question of those that are prohibited and reserved for the judgment of the Church in the Archives of the Vatican."

It was neither possible nor prudent to "enter into" the matter of the authenticity of the tablets, for then it would have been neces- sary to recognize that all those documents were a farce invented by some Moriscos at a moment of anguish for their caste. But under the shadow of such a fraud there had arisen something very real: a splendid church, great sums in ecclesiastical properties, and the faith of a whole city in its patron saints. Even the Holy See did not dare to declare apocryphal the inscriptions in lead by virtue of which St. Cecilius, patron of Granada, was believed to have suffered martyrdom on a spot called "Holy" precisely because of a Morisco deception. Vital truth is seen through moving and irregularly shaped prisms and cannot be reduced to the abstract judgments of reason. The reality of history does not fit into the framework outlined by two opposed terms: "it is true, it is false"; "it is right, it is sinful"; "it is beautiful, it is repulsive"; "it is essential, it is accidental." The "truth" of the Arabic exorcisms pronounced by Pedro de Castro, of the religious syncretism of the Moriscos, of the "holiness" of the mountain where the dramatic farce of those inventions was acted out—that truth is inseparable from the reality of Spanish life, which we may live with, love, and suffer but never confine or dissect in judgments that, in the last analysis, crush and destroy what I hope to keep alive.

Some Morisco Achievements in
Sixteenth-Century Spain

Because they were the strongest, the Christians had put an end to the always unstable equilibrium of the three castes; but the Moors continued to live in Spain—now in a much diminished fashion—as they had been living for many centuries. Their craftsmanship and their taste for agricultural activities (love of trees, of all the products of the land) had a religious basis. The individual did not become unworthy because his ancestors were manual laborers. Doing things well was a moral duty much emphasized by the laws and ordinances with regard to good conduct in the practice of the arts and crafts.[38] Ibn 'Abdūn says: "It shall not be permitted that anyone pass himself off as a master in a thing he does not do well, especially in the art of medicine. . . . Let the same be said of the carpenter" (*Sevilla a comienzos del siglo XII*, p. 145). In certain "Laws of the Moors" written in Castilian at the beginning of the fourteenth century, it is ordered that "the masters of the trades are guarantors of doing well what is given to them to do," and detailed instructions are set forth about the harvesting of wheat, the gathering of dates, and the drawing of water from wells.[39] In the twelfth century Ibn al-'Awwām wrote a treatise on agriculture, which was translated into Spanish in 1802; and the first book on this subject published in Castilian, the *Obra de agricultura* of Gabriel Alonso de Herrera (Alcalá, 1513), was based on Arabic works about agriculture.[40]

But economics and all the rest must be situated *within its* history; otherwise we shall be speaking of meaningless abstractions and not of human phenomena. The expulsion of the Moriscos was provoked by something more than intolerance, economic rivalry, and governmental bungling; we must consider, instead, the structure of Spanish life and its way of functioning—unique, *sui generis* with respect to the values created and destroyed by it.[41] Human phenomena must

---

[38] See E. Lévi-Provençal, *Un manuel hispanique de ḥisba (Sur la surveillance des corporations et la répression de fraudes en Espagne musulmane)* (Paris, 1931). Another treatise of this kind is that of Ibn 'Abdūn, *Sevilla a comienzos del siglo XII.*

[39] *Tratados de legislación musulmana* (n.p.: Real Academia de la Historia, 1835), p. 112.

[40] For an overall view of the economy of al-Andalus, see J. Vicens Vives, *Manual de historia económica de España* (Barcelona, 1959), pp. 98–115.

[41] F. Braudel thinks that the expulsion of the Jews in 1492 was due to "the overpopulation of southern Europe," without bearing in mind the long and now familiar gestation of that extremely complex event (*La Méditerranée ... à l'époque de Philippe II* [1949], p. 357). Christian intolerance in Spain was not the "offspring of population crowding" (*fille du nombre*, in *ibid.*, p. 598); intolerance is not a fixed and historically valid entity. Tolerance was the expression of a situation of mutual needs, of the ability of each social group to

be observed from within their reality so that history does not become for us a ghostly matter, a question of abstract numbers and mirages that deprive life of its meaning as value, aspiration, drama, and novel. The Jews and the Moriscos lived articulated into the ensemble of the total life of the Spaniards; they strove for, and dreamed about, the acquisition of prestige and dominion. The image they had formed of themselves (without analogy, I insist, in Orient or Occident) was shattered because next to them there lived another kind of people aspiring to surpass their own limits, *to be more*, and the Jews and the Moors (later the Moriscos) were a serious obstacle in the way of that goal. Philip III, great-great-grandson of the Catholic Sovereigns, no longer saw anything but danger in the presence of the Moriscos within his kingdoms. Almost 300,000[42] of them were forced to leave the land that had been theirs, which they had always dreamed of recovering, as we shall hear Abén Humeya say later (p. 249). Long before, in a Castilian text written in Arabic characters, it was said that "the time draws nigh . . . Allah will become enraged . . . against them, the worshipers of the cross, and will seize their property, their houses, and their women."[43] Friar Marcos de Guadalajara knew that when the Moriscos celebrated their Easter "they prayed to Mohammed for the sake of the fortunate years of the Muslim Sultan to subject the Christians. . . . After a long lament and weeping that they made over this, the *alfaqui* ["theologian"] came out saying to them: *Be consoled, friends, for this land has been yours at another time, and shall return without any doubt*" (Janer, *op. cit.*, p. 171). In a *Discurso antiguo en materia de moriscos*, published by Janer (*op. cit.*, p. 266) without indication of its origin, the greatest danger pointed out is "having in the heart [of Spain] so many enemies of our holy faith and special enemies of ours, who know that their ancestors were the lords of the land in which they now see themselves enslaved and oppressed in a thousand ways." The author of this temperate discourse criticizes the lack of interest in converting the Moriscos: "How many prelates and priests there are who, instead of thinking about pursuing souls, which is their profession, think about planting lettuce . . . , and they apply their thought, and what is worse, the blood of Jesus Christ, to their relatives, and to their houses, and to their pleasures. It is impossible for

---

develop one kind of activity or another, of how each group was aware of its life. The Jews were as much a small minority group before 1391 (when the serious persecution began) as the Moriscos were before 1609.

[42] The exact number was, apparently, 272,140, according to Henri Lapeyre, *Géographie de l'Espagne morisque* (1959), p. 205. In his *Discursos históricos de la ciudad de Murcia* (1621), Francisco Cascales had already given the "very account of the Secretariat of State" (Lapeyre, *op. cit.*, p. 206). But the Morisco problem, rather than being a matter of figures, is a living human phenomenon and vitally connected to others.

[43] *Tratados de legislación musulmana*, p. 403.

us to convert the Moriscos without pacifying them first and taking from them the fear, hatred, and enmity that they hold for the name Christian, for the first precept of rhetoric is that he who wishes to persuade must secure the good will of his audience. . . . There are also persons who have spent enormous numbers of ducats on other pious works who, if they had spent them on the conversion of the Moriscos in their diocese in the fashion set forth above, I believe would have done much greater service to God and to His Majesty."

The calm good sense of this anonymous critic's exposition (which I have much shortened) recalls the style of certain Erasmians of the sixteenth century. But the moment was no longer propitious for reasoning quietly. The Moriscos were conspiring with Moors outside the country, the Turks, and the French in order to harass an enemy they believed to be weak and saw to be very worried. Philip III knew about the Moorish conspiracy to invade Spain just as it had been known at the time of the Visigothic king Roderic; "Now," the Moriscos said, "there are many fewer people as a result of plagues and the war in Flanders; for if then [at the time of Roderic] there were no arms or people skilled in their use, now there are many fewer, and of less spirit and valor." All this was reported to Mulay Zīdān in Morocco by "fifty Moriscos who passed from these kingdoms to Barbary." And Mulay Zīdān answered them that "he could not fail to endeavor to make himself lord of the kingdoms possessed by his ancestors" (Janer, *op. cit.*, p. 275). On September 11, 1609, Philip III communicated to his council that the Moors of Barbary "have conversation and intelligence with heretics and other princes who hate the grandeur of our monarchy. . . . And if these people and our other enemies fall upon us at the same time, we shall see ourselves in the danger that may be anticipated" (*ibid.*, p. 298). In August of that year the King had written to the archbishop of Valencia that the Moriscos were assuring possible invaders that they would find in Spain "150,000 people as Moorish as the Barbers, who will gather to them with their persons and property; declaring to them to move them to action how lacking are our kingdoms in soldiers, and how ill equipped in arms and munitions; and all [of the possible invaders] have offered to do it" (*ibid.*, p. 332).

It is not my purpose to set forth facts that are already known but to make evident how two of the three castes of Spain were still fighting to affirm or recover their supremacy at the beginning of the seventeenth century. The remnants of the Jewish caste were attacked by the Inquisition through the New Christians of Jewish ancestry, while the real Spanish Jews helped to worsen the international situation of Christian Spain from Turkey, Holland, and, later, from England. In view of all this, it is not very fruitful historically to insist on whether or not the Moriscos monopolized agricultural activity and crafts in the regions where they lived. The personalism of the Christian caste had been sharpened by virtue of imperial grandeur within an environment limited in economic well-being and socially impoverished. The way toward subsistence without oppressive burdens was blocked for those who were not landed gentry or of the clergy. The Church came to possess almost half the arable land of Spain (see chapter ix). By the side of these economically powerful classes (with their seigniorial mansions, their splendid churches) the rest of the victorious caste of Old Christians felt itself afflicted. The idle hidalgo, as full of conceit as he was lacking in means, is a well-known literary theme in the literature of the sixteenth and seventeenth centuries. What there was of banking and large-scale trading activities rested in foreign hands, which channeled into foreign countries the gold and silver from Mexico and Peru. The Spaniard who had made a fortune in the New World became an object of scorn. In other words, once again it is evident that the economy of a country is above all the result of what people want and are able to do with it. As Quevedo said, in former times, "Spain, which possessed genuine wealth . . . , preferred to conquer Moors rather than to amass ducats" (*Epístola al conde-duque de San Lúcar*).

More and more, as the sixteenth century wore on, gainful labor degraded the individual, because accumulating money and doing business with it were the activity of Moriscos and of New Christians of Jewish ancestry. The Moriscos were "so industrious that, despite having come to Castile [when they were expelled from Granada] only ten years ago without a span of land, and despite the unfruitfulness of those years, they are all influential, and many of them rich, to [such a] degree that, twenty years from now, it may be expected that the natives will serve them" (Janer, *op. cit.*, p. 272, citing a certain Dr. Liébana).[44] Here is the crux of the question: how people conduct themselves in and from the intimacy of their dwelling place of life—in this instance, in view of their awareness of caste. The Supreme Commander of Leon wrote to the King on August 28, 1609: "Although in view of the *little skill with which the Old Christians apply themselves to working the* land, it will cost effort to settle what is left vacant; *still it is of much greater concern to remove the apostasy and heresy of this people* by whom Our Lord is so ill served and to be made safe from the danger in which we are with this people" (Janer, *op. cit.*, p. 282). The King noted in the margin:

---

[44] Henrique Cock, a member of Philip II's noble guard, wrote that Torrellas (Saragossa) was "all populated by Moriscos, like many other [towns] of that region, because it has much irrigated land. In Torellas there is much production of bureaus and desks and little boxes made of different-colored woods set into walnut panels" (*Jornada de Tarazona hecha por Felipe II en 1592*, ed. A. Morel-Fatio and A. Rodríguez Villa [Madrid, 1879], p. 77).

"I have seen all this [and] it is very well advised." Such was the authentic hierarchy of values which determined the functioning of life within the Old Christian caste—that is to say, among those who came finally and totally to be "Spanish." It mattered little that "a titled lady, who is a very respected woman, crying a great deal," should go whining to the Archbishop of Valencia because the departure of the Moriscos "was the complete ruin of her house" and made impossible "the settlement of her towns" (Janer, *op. cit.*, p. 305).

It is, then, in no way mythical that manual labor and craftsmanship meant much more and were of more value to the Morisco than to the Old Christian. It is not a question of numbers and statistics (phantasmal and skeletonized history) but of the *fact* of the direction of inclinations and values. If the Morisco had worked for the Christian as the Indian of Mexico and Peru did, Spanish life would have been different. But the tradition and the awareness of Islamic prestige permitted the Morisco, notwithstanding his decadence, to build a life of his own, to a certain degree independent in economic relationships and in the more or less obvious practice of his religion. They did not eat pork, nor did they drink wine. Against this the "imperious dimension" of the Christian caste availed little. The Moriscos were not isolated like the American Indian, for they could depend on African and Turkish Islam and French hatred of the Spanish monarchy.

The Morisco relied on a tradition of economic activity which the Christian lacked. The Cortes of 1582 called Philip II's attention to the increasing number of Moriscos in the kingdom of Granada and to the fact that they were "in possession of all trade and contracts, especially the supplying of provisions, which is the crucible where money is melted down; for they gather it in at harvest time and hide it. . . . And in order to make better use of it they have become shopkeepers, bakers, butchers, tavernkeepers, and water carriers—by which means they likewise gather in and hide all the money. For none of them buys or has real estate, and with this they are so rich and powerful."[45] To work, to earn money, and to hoard it up appears here as a grave sin, because at that time the Christian could not do it as efficaciously as the Morisco. Before Spain became a vast empire, the Morisco did all that to serve the Christian, who did not force him to change his religion, language, and customs—that was the radical difference. After the capture of Granada, the Christian tried to keep on being served by the Moor (as the Cid had said in the *Poem*) while emptying his life of all its familiar content, of all heartening stimuli. In the sixteenth century the Marquis of Comares had a castle of his in the Alpujarra repaired, just as the Cid had done

---

[45] Janer, *op. cit.*, p. 270; Caro Baroja, *op. cit.*, p. 222.

in the lands he conquered in the eleventh century: He ordered "the Moriscos to repair the walls, and they did it by providing peons and beasts of burden to labor in bringing materials, so that in a short time they made it [the fortress] secure in its darkness. . . . Among those mountain people there were many men of good intelligence who, hiding their true concerns, appeared to accede in the carrying out of the ordinances [of the king against them], although they were greatly bothered by the language problem [i.e., the prohibition against speaking Arabic]."[46] The absurd attempt was made to make the Morisco stop being a Moor and at the same time function within Spanish life just as when he was a Mudejar.

It is futile to attribute the radical and violent solution of the Morisco problem to the political ineptitude of the Duke of Lerma. Once the Old Christian had adopted the Semitic tradition of the unity between the state and *one* religious faith, it was impossible to do anything. Worldly exigencies had to be subordinated to those of the faith; and in that of the Spanish Catholic there was no room for the sanctification of productive labor. In addition, the imperious and imperial dimension of the triumphant caste rendered impossible the acceptance of the high value set on work by the two castes that had been conquered and were finally eliminated; nor was it feasible to imitate intellectually and artificially the Protestant idea that manual labor was a task grateful in the eyes of God, an idea proposed, as we shall see later, by the Jesuit Pedro de Guzmán. Religion had been made consubstantial with the state, and in their faith those who had extended the power of the king over much of the New World—and a good deal of the Old—affirmed themselves. When the basic differences in dogma are set aside, the friars and bishops who directed and, in the last analysis, determined the policies of Philip III (as they had done before for Philip II) resembled the theologians (*alfaquís*) of al-Ḥakam II or the rabbis of Amsterdam who condemned Benedict Spinoza to a kind of civil death. The Spanish Empire had taken on the appearance of a huge synagogue.

Proposals for humane solutions—doubtless there were some—to the bitter problem presented by the Moriscos were chimerical. In actuality, the journey of the ejected people to the places of their exile is marked by a succession of atrocities committed in defiance of what had been mercifully ordered by Philip III.[47] But not all that was written about them was inspired by incomprehension and a total lack of clarity. The most humane description of their skills and aptitudes is found in the *Historia de Plasencia* by Friar Alonso Fernández:

[46] Luis del Marmol, *Rebelión y castigo de los moriscos*, in *Biblioteca de Autores Españoles*, XXI, 264.

[47] Janer, *op. cit.*, presents documents about the murders, rapes, and robberies suffered by the unfortunate Moriscos (pp. 307, 308, 311).

"They were diligent in the cultivation of gardens, and lived apart from the society of Old Christians, preferring that their own life not be the subject to observation. Others were occupied in trade. They sold foods at the best stands in the cities and villages, most of them living by the work of their own hands. Others were employed at manual trades such as tinkers, smiths, shoemakers, soap makers, and muleteers. They all paid their taxes and assessments willingly, and were moderate in their food and dress. . . . They had no use for begging among their own people; and all had a trade and were busy at some employment" (Janer, *op. cit.*, p. 162).[48] They propagated abundantly, "because none of them took up the sterile calling of monk, cleric, or nun. . . . All married—poor and rich, sound and lame. . . . And the worst that can be said of all this is that some Old Christians, even while they claimed some trace of hidalgo blood, married Morisco women in order to gain insignificant portions of wealth and thus spotted their already tarnished lineage."[49] The last phrase is not very clear, though interesting. How could an Old Christian with claims to nobility be considerably tainted in lineage? Here there shines through, unconsciously, the misgiving so common at the time that even those who boasted of being Old Christians and noble were not free from suspicion unless they were peasants. And marrying a Morisco woman, which was not an unusual occurrence, revealed that one had a little to lose with regard to purity of blood (see my *De la edad conflictiva* [1963], pp. 177, 206).

So far as their customs and character were concerned, "they were

---

[48] Books about the Moriscos were numerous and passionate at the time of the expulsion, and even the scholars who discussed it in the nineteenth century took sides in the matter. I have already cited Florencio Janer, *Condición social de los moriscos* (1857), a mediocre book but containing important quotations; it is favorable to the Moriscos. The two volumes of P. Boronat y Barrachina's *Los moriscos españoles y su expulsión* (1901), polemical and well documented, justify the expulsion. Boronat believes that the grandeur of the Arabs (not very evident to him) was due to Spain: "What did the eighth-century invaders bring from Africa? What prosperity did they produce in Africa when they returned from here [Spain]?" (II, 350). This is a historical sophism. The Arabs came to al-Andalus at a high point in their history when Islam was flourishing in other places; they fell into decay later, just as they did in Syria, Egypt, and so on. The Morisco form of life had been integrated for many centuries within the life lived together by Muslims and Christians, and in 1600 the Moriscos were doing about the same thing as before. In Africa, lacking the soil of Spain and Christian markets, they were no longer themselves.

Recently there have been published several important studies, which do not, however, necessitate the modification of my point of view about the Moriscos, that is to say, about their ultimate meaning within Spanish life. See especially T. Halperín Donghi, *Un conflicto nacional: moricos y cristianos* (Buenos Aires, 1955); Caro Baroja, *op. cit.*

[49] Thus wrote Pedro Aznar de Cardona in *Expulsión justificada de los moriscos españoles* (1612), quoted in Janer, *op. cit.*, p. 160. This must be the basis for what Cervantes says of the Moriscos in *Persiles y Sigismunda*: "They are not plucked off in their prime by any religion . . . . they all marry; all, or almost all, beget children." (See my *El pensamiento de Cervantes*, p. 294.)

quite fond of burlesques, tales, and boasts, and they were inordinately fond of dances and songs (so that they usually had bagpipes, timbrels, and tambourines). . . . They preferred work that required skill rather than brawn; they were weavers, tailors, rope makers, sandal makers, potters, shoemakers, veterinaries, mattress makers, gardeners, muleteers, olive oil peddlers" (Janer, *op. cit.*, p. 159).[50]

In sum, the relation between Moriscos and Christians still recalled that of the Middle Ages, with the difference that the literary and scientific culture of the Moriscos now boasted no Averroës or Ibn Ḥazm, and that their writings (preserved in Spanish as spoken in Aragon and written in Arabic characters—that is, *aljamía*, as this written language is called) are lacking in any special value. By this time the New and Old Christians were dominant over them with respect to both political and cultural grandeur. In any event, the number of books written between 1610 and 1613 on the subject of their expulsion (some twenty, counting both those in print and those in manuscript) demonstrates the great importance such an event had in public opinion. It had proved impossible to assimilate the Moorish caste through either persuasion or violence. These people felt themselves to be as Spanish as the Old Christians, and their consciousness of nationality had its roots in a glorious past.[51] Their virtues as diligent workers and the wealth that those virtues signified were sacrificed by the Spanish monarchy, which considered wealth and welfare to be nothing as compared with the national honor, with its foundation in religious unity and the indisputable seigniory of the royal power, as we have already seen. Pacts and agreements with infidels were the practices of bygone times. In the last analysis, the Moriscos had become an irremediable anachronism—even though, on the other hand, the pattern of national life was much as it had been in the Middle Ages: in a more limited and humble way than in 1100,

---

[50] The words of Janer's original text are very significant: "Eran muy amigos de burlerías, cuentos, berlandinas, y sobre todo amicísimos (y así tenían comúnmente gaitas, sonajas, *adufes*) de bailas, danzas, solaces, cantarcillos, albadas. ... Eran dados a oficios de poco trabajo: tejedores, sastres, sogueros, esparteñeros, olleros, zapateros, *albéitares*, colchoneros, hortelanos, *recueros* y revendedores de *aceite*." *Adufe* ("tambourine"), *albéitar* ("veterinary"), *recua* ("mule train"), and *aceite* ("olive oil") are Arabic. *Sastre* ("tailor") and *ollero* ("potter") were formerly, and to some extent still are, called by their Arabic names of *alfayate* and *alcaller* or *alfarero*. Again, *burlería* ("droll tale") is the original of *bulería*, which the dictionaries do not give, although it is a well-known form of *cante flamenco*. The Moriscos were, as we see, very fond of singing and dancing, and the words *zambra* ("a festival with dancing and merrymaking") and *zarabanda* ("the dance") are also Oriental. For centuries the Moors had received their kings with dancing, music, and rejoicing (see above, p. 92).

[51] "Don't you know that we are in Spain, and that we have owned this land for nine hundred years?" Thus spoke Don Fernando de Válor (Abén Humeya) before he unleashed the rebellion of 1568. (See Antonio de Fuenmayor, *Vida y hechos de Pío V* [1595], quoted in Janer, *op. cit.*, p. 144.)

the Moor continued to work and create wealth at the beginning of the seventeenth century, and the Christian continued to lord it over him in full consciousness of his personal superiority.

In the time of Charles V, Spain felt strong, and a residue of flexibility still permitted her to carry the burdensome legacy of tradition. In the time of Philip II, a shared common life between New and Old Christians became ever more difficult, intolerance toward the Moriscos grew stronger; and the Moriscos themselves rose up in arms when the first whiff of the decay of the Spanish Empire reached their nostrils. Abén Humeya, in the harangue that I have quoted previously (n. 51), expressed himself thus: "The broad Empire of Spain is nothing to me, because, believe me, when states reach the pinnacle of their grandeur, they must decline. Powerful forces are destroyed by the refinement, voluptuousness, and pleasure that accompany their prosperity. . . . We are no band of thieves but a kingdom; nor is Spain less abandoned to vices than was Rome." In truth, Phillip II needed all the strength he could muster to put down the Moriscos in the mountains of Granada, and to reduce their poorly armed bands he finally had to call on no less a military expert than Don Juan of Austria, after other distinguished generals had failed in three years of fighting.

That civil war and the final expulsion of the people that could not be subdued were what had to be, given the terms of the problem up for solution. Yet the Morisco continued to feel that he was Spanish: "Wherever we are, we weep for Spain, for, after all, there were we born, and it is our natural fatherland. Now do I know and feel what is usually said, that the love of the fatherland is sweet." Thus speaks the exiled Morisco in the *Quixote* (II, 54)—which complements what was felt by Christian souls of delicate temper. Hernando de Talavera, the first archbishop of Granada, was of the opinion that if the Moriscos and other Spaniards were to be good Christians the Moriscos "would have to have some of our faith, and we would have to do some of *their good works*."[52] This was not political sentimentalism of the moment, for in 1638 the historian Bermúdez de la Pedraza observed that if "faith was lacking and baptism abundant" among the Moriscos, it was equally certain that "they practiced *good moral works*; they showed much truth in their dealings and contracts and great charity toward their poor; they were little given to idleness; all worked hard" (quoted by P. Longás, *Vida religiosa de los moriscos*, p. lii).

Here is one more conflict in a time that has its very roots in conflict, an epoch that will find its expression, finally, in the so-called baroque styles. It will not do to oversimplify the question and reduce

---

[52] According to F. Bermúdez de la Pedraza, in *Antigüedades y excelencias de Granada*, fol. 91, quoted by P. Longás, *Vida religiosa de los moriscos* (Madrid, 1915), p. 75.

it to the fact that Spanish intolerance overwhelmed Moorish obstinacy, rebellious against the religious unity imposed by the Christian caste, when the decisive thing was really the clash between
reason and life, a clash of which some were aware who dreamed of
ideally harmonizing the "faith without works" of the Old Christians
and the "works without faith" of their adversaries. So long as faith
and works remained separate from each other, the social catastrophe
was inevitable. In 1614, the Jesuit Pedro de Guzmán observed that
certain Protestant "heretics" owed the "happiness" of their states to
the practice of industry—to works—as a constructive social virtue.[53]
Always, some way or other, some Spaniards knew and *felt* what
would be good to do in Spain, unrealizable though it might be; *and
this polemical dualism between consciousness and conduct is precisely the premise from which derives the permanent and universal
quality of Spanish civilization*—"vivir desviviéndose"—*one* of whose
expressions is the literature of the so-called Golden Age. Such a
dualism, let us note in passing, is not primitivism, for primitive peoples do not turn their own existence into a problem.

During the sixteenth century certain Aragonese lords accepted
with some irritation the inquisitorial pressure against the Moriscos,[54]
who were the main tillers of the soil: "Since the lords have no other
more appreciable incomes on which they can live and maintain their
houses and estates, they deeply regret that the Inquisition punishes
their vassals in their property or persons; whence many unjust complaints against the Holy Office and against those who are in it." Thus
writes an inquisitor in Saragossa to the Supreme Council in Madrid
in 1553. Later, in 1569, no less a personage than the admiral of Aragon, Don Sancho de Cardona, was tried by the Holy Office for his
excessive tolerance toward the Moriscos, for whom he had gone so
far as to have a mosque rebuilt. To him was imputed the intention
of going to the Pope and even to the Sultan of Turkey in protest
over the forced baptism imposed on the Valencian Moriscos.[55] But
just as it was not possible to bring together faith without works and

---

[53] "In many kingdoms, not only of the faithful but even of infidels and of
heretics (such as those of La Rochelle), the rulers thereof take especial care
that there be in their cities no idle people; and in this consists a large part of the
happiness of those people" (*Bienes del honesto trabajo y daños de la ociosidad*
[Madrid, 1614], pp. 119–120).
[54] In 1508 Ferdinand the Catholic had already forbidden the forced conversion of the Moors of Catalonia. The protest against the violent acts of the Inquisition had originated with the viceroy (the Duke of Cardona) and other
lords whose lands were worked by Moorish vassals. The ideas of tolerance
which I analyze in chapter xii are here voiced, I believe, for one of the last
times: "No one is to be compelled to be converted to our Holy Catholic Faith
and to be baptized, for only when conversion comes freely and from a pure
heart is it service to God" (Archivo de Simancas, *Inquisición*, Libro 926, fol.
76, quoted by Lea, *op. cit.*, p. 407).
[55] See Longás, *op. cit.*, p. 57.

works without faith, neither was harmony possible on the plane of economic interests, since the "things" of this world, tangible and interchangeable, were never decisive within the Hispanic "dwelling place," where, ultimately, the individual decided matters by looking within himself and not toward the outer world.

The leaders of public life could not at the time see anything in the Morisco except a rebellious will; no common field of activities and interests existed in which the Morisco's love for Spain could be linked with the esteem that a few spirits of delicate temper felt for the Moriscos. The conflict was converted into a clash of wills bound to the longing for the preeminence of their caste and cut off from the exigencies of the external, neutral world that belongs to all, but all of which belongs to no one. The result of this clash of naked wills could be nothing but the annihilation of one of the groups; compromise was impossible. The lords of Aragon were overwhelmed, and their fields fell into a wretched state for long years. I am inclined to see a residue of Aragonese animosity toward the central authority of Castile in the fact that during the seventeenth century the Aragonese printing presses were a refuge for bitter, satirical books, in which the existing order did not come off too well. The first editions of Quevedo's most mordant and caustic works appear in the kingdom of Aragon, not in Castile. The unifying policy of Philip II, which contravened the provincial prerogatives of Aragon, together with the expulsion of the Moriscos, contributed to shaking the precarious union among the various kingdoms of Spain. Catalonia, which had very few Moriscos, held itself aloof from controversy over the expulsion.

Now, it seems to me, the distance can be calculated that separates the expulsion of the Moriscos in 1609 from that of the Jews in 1493. The Moriscos had been reduced to carrying out practical tasks—very useful but lacking in prestige—and this explains the aforementioned attacks and praises; the Jews made others feel inferior by virtue of their own intellectual and administrative superiority. The common people never esteemed the Jews highly, and no one, really, ever had the courage to defend them openly after their expulsion. Only the kings and the upper classes accepted their indispensable services without snide reservations.[56] Their social function was different from that of the Moriscos, who were highly useful and even amusing pariahs, encased for centuries in the national life. In spite of their suspect faith, the Moriscos challenged the severities of the Inquisition for more than a century; they enjoyed strong protection, they seduced more than one Old Christian with their enticing sensuality, as well as their cleverness in making money. Their presence is even

---

[56] See my *De la edad conflictiva* (Madrid, 1963).

~ visible in Illuminism and in certain aspects of the mysticism of St.
- John of the Cross; in ways that are imperfectly known to us they
~ funneled the themes and expressive forms of the Arabic tradition
into the literature of the sixteenth and seventeenth centuries. A centuries-old tradition protected them, because important zones in the
Hispanic soul had been conquered by Islam, as we shall presently
be seeing. The cycle that begins in the eighth century with the
Mozarab Christians subject to the Moors closes in the seventeenth
with the Moriscos subjugated and finally expelled by the theocrats
of a weary Spain, bowed down under the weight of her empire.

With those nine hundred years unfolded before our eyes, it is obviously impossible to disregard the presence and intermingling of
the three castes of believers if we hope to make clear why the very
special Spanish mode of life and civilization is as it is. And we shall
try to keep this problem in mind as something that gives a structure
to history rather than as the factual content of a national life. Let me
repeat that Christian Spain was not something that preexisted in a
fixed reality of her own, upon which there fell the temporary "influence" of Islam, as one "mode" or result of the life of "those times."
Christian Spain "became"—emerged into being—as she incorporated
and grafted into her living process what she was compelled to by her
interaction with the Muslim and Jewish worlds.

I do not intend for a moment to analyze in detail the Moorish,
Judaic, and Christian civilization in medieval Spain. I aspire to do
no more than explain to myself the formation of the way of life
called Spanish by those who for nine centuries intermingled their
castes in a social structure of unique form.

Islam and the Spanish language

Words of Arabic origin in Spanish are interesting now less as linguistic "elements" or components than as the reflection of an important human presence that is clearly visible in the course adopted
by the collective life of those who were later called Spaniards. Like
the other Romance languages, Castilian in the beginning was a form
of Latin spoken by rustic people unaffected by the prestige of those
persons who possessed a modicum of culture—and these latter were
few in the Visigothic era and still more infrequent between the eighth
and the tenth centuries. In addition to Latin words, there remained
in that dialect some words of Greek, Germanic, or pre-Latin origin,
now completely severed from the human circumstances that had
determined their adoption. The spoken language maintained certain
words from the written language, thanks to the influence of the
clergy and of the few others who knew how to write; therefore,
epístola ("letter") did not become *ebicha*, and *evangelio* ("gospel")

is not now *vanijo*. In any event, those who spoke the Romance dialects no longer associated them with the Roman atmosphere and modes of life; nor did those who said *robar* ("rob"), *luva* ("mitten"), *guardia* ("guard"), or *Gontruda* (a woman's name) relate those words of Germanic origin to the Goths. Words of Arabic origin, on the other hand, could be related to the Moors and Mozarabs and their customs, just as today Spaniards know that a *football* and the sport so called are English. A municipal statute granted to the Moors of the Val d'Uxó by James I of Aragon in 1250 and written on his orders by "Salamó, son of Alquizten," began with the phrase, "En nom de Deu tot piados e miserocordios" ("In the name of all compassionate and merciful God"),[57] because such was the opening formula of Muslim documents. The Latin and Castilian versions of Ferdinand III's epitaph, referred to above (p. 60), employ the same accumulation of laudatory adjectives which is characteristic of Arabic missives addressed to illustrious personages. A king of Morocco wrote to James II of Aragon in 1308 in the following fashion: "Al rey alt, lo exelsat, lo honrat, lo preciat, lo noble, lo precios, lo be costumat, don Jayme, rey d'Aragón"[58] ("To the high, exalted, honored, respected, noble, esteemed, courteous King James, king of Aragon").

The vocabulary of the building trades was in large part Arabic because the Moors were the ones who customarily constructed houses and castles. So it was in many other instances. A phenomenon comparable, though on a lesser scale, to the adoption of Arabic words is that of the Gallicisms accepted into Spanish between the eleventh and the thirteenth centuries, which came into the language through oral communication more than through literary works. People who began to call the *decano*, *deán* ("dean"); the *cantor*, *chantre* ("precentor"); the *huerto*, *jardín* ("garden"); and the *camena*,[59] *chimenea* ("hearth"), did so because they had heard the French people who traveled through the country say these things. All this means that both the Arabisms and the Gallicisms make visible the action of some of the social forces that helped to build and mold the complex figure of the future Spanish life, which is incomprehensible if we bear in mind only

---

[57] *Colección de Documentos Inéditos para la Historia de España*, XVIII, 42.

[58] See A. Giménez Soler, "La corona de Aragón y Granada," *Boletín de la Academia de Buenas Letras de Barcelona*, III (1905), 344. Another document begins as follows: "Al rey alt e noble e honrat e poderos e verdader e nomenat lo rey de veritat, don Jayme, rey de Aragón" ("To the high and noble and honored and powerful and true king and the one called the king in truth, James, King of Aragon") (*ibid.*, IV [1907], 54).

[59] "Todo omne que fragua fezier o *caminada* [variant of *camena*] en el castannal, pecho VI moravedis" ("Any man who builds a forge or a hearth in the chestnut grove shall pay VI maravedis,") (*Fuero de Salamanca*, ed. Onis-Castro, p. 111).

the Romano-Visigothic tradition. Arabisms and Gallicisms expressed the modes of an ineluctable common life. From the eleventh century the people of Romance (or Basque) speech who had not been submerged by the Islamic inundation appear as three, four, or five Christian kingdoms with a population made up of Christians, Mudejars, and Jews (this final group was, in addition, quite Arabized linguistically and culturally). The two last-named castes were oriented, as might be expected, toward al-Andalus in the south, for from there proceeded what made them valuable and indispensable to the Christians. The latter, in their turn, gravitated toward both al-Andalus and Christian Europe. For Castilians and Leonese the European horizon was, above all, that of France; Aragon and Catalonia turned, in addition, toward the Italian cities, principally the maritime republics. From Europe people sought what did not exist in the deficient Roman tradition of the Christian kingdoms, whose original literature in the Latin language was scanty in comparison to that of Italy, France, and England.

Let us observe from this point of view some aspects of the social action of Islam on language, customs, and at times, even on literature.

Numerous Arabic words are found in Spanish and Portuguese (and, to a lesser extent, in Catalan) as a reflection of inescapable necessity, just as Latin likewise had to accept thousands of Greek words.[60] Many Arabisms have persisted both in dialects and in the literary language.[61] The grammatical structure of Spanish and Portuguese was not affected by Arabic, although sometimes Arabic syntactical peculiarities appear in literary works translated from that language.[62] But however strong the linguistic pressure may have

---

[60] The terms *préstamo, loanword, emprunt,* and *Lehnwort,* used in linguistics, are inexact because the words I wish to categorize by means of such terms are acquisitions that are never returned. They ought to be called "linguistic adoptions or imports."

[61] After Latin itself, the Arabic vocabulary is of most importance in Spanish: there are more than 4,000 words of Arabic origin, including derived formations (see Rafael Lapesa, *Historia de la lengua española* [Madrid, 1960], p. 97). There is no complete list of Ibero-Romanic words of Oriental origin. See Dozy and Engelmann, *Glossaire des mots espagnols et portugais, dérivés de l'arabe* (1869); L. Eguílaz, *Glosario etimológico de palabras españolas de origen oriental* (1886); P. Ravaise, "Les mots arabes et hispano-morisques du 'Don Quichotte,'" *Revue de Linguistique* (1907–1914); J. Corominas, "Mots catalans d'origen arabic," *Bulletín de Dialectologia Catalana,* XXIV (1936), 1–81; A. Steiger, *Fonética del hispano-árabe* (1932), important work with extensive bibliography; José Pedro Machado, "Alguns vocabulos de origem árabe e comentarios a alguns arabismos" (from the *Diccionário* of A. Nascentes), *Boletim de Filologia,* VI (1940), 1–33, 225–238; E. K. Neuvonen, *Los arabismos del español en el siglo XIII* (Helsinki, 1941); Lapesa, *op. cit.,* pp. 95–110.

[62] See Alvaro Galmés de Fuentes, *Influencias sintácticas y estilísticas del árabe en la prosa medieval castellana* (Madrid, 1956). The author pays special attention to the versions of *Calila e Dimna* and refers to the *Crónica General.* Sr.

been, the structure of the Peninsular languages of Latin origin continued to be Romanic. If the whole Peninsula had been overrun by the Muslims as England was by Normans, then the structure of the language would have been profoundly altered; but the Christians adopted Arabic words because they shared their lives with Muslims and Jews and not because of the pressure of any conqueror. The English had to say "veal" and "beef" because the lords who had authority in the cities spoke thus, and it was to the lords that such commodities were to be sold. The Norman element in English was to a large extent the result of an imposition; the Arabic element in Iberian Romance was due to the necessity of filling deficiencies. These lexical adoptions refer to extremely diverse zones of life: agriculture, the construction of buildings, arts and crafts, commerce, public administration, sciences, and warfare. Furthermore, one must bear in mind that borrowed Arabic words could be the result of Jewish activities as well as those of Mozarabs and Muslims, for the language of Jewish culture in the Peninsula was Arabic, at least until the thirteenth century. The Romance dialect spoken by the Jews was filled with Arabic words.

It is significant right off that *tarea* (Portuguese *tarefa*), meaning "task," is Arabic. The *alarifes* (architects) planned the houses and the *albañiles* (masons) built them;[63] wherefore the Arabisms *adobe* (unburnt brick), *alcázar* (castle), *alcoba* (bedroom), *zaquizamí* (garret), *alacena* (cupboard), *azulejo* (tile), *azotea* (roof terrace), *baldosa* (fine paving tile), *zaguán* (vestibule), *aldaba* (door knocker), *alféizar* (windowsill), and many others. The excellent Moorish technique for the control and supply of water is evident in *acequia* (irrigation ditch), *alberca* (artificial pool), *aljibe* (cistern; adopted in

---

Galmés rightly observes that the syntactical Arabism reflects "the more or less conscious intention of letting oneself be influenced," an attitude motivated "by the prestige of a superior culture" (p. 219).

[63] In the records of the town hall of Seville, a century and a half after the city was conquered, we read that in 1393 "two *moros albañíes* ["Moorish masons"] undertook to start and finish this piece of *albañería* ["masonry"—it is a question here of a water distribution system], and they made the aforesaid *alcantarilla* ["water conduit"]. . . . And besides, these two master craftsmen undertook to start and finish all the superarches that were to be made over again." In their work they used *aceite* ("olive oil") and *azulaca* ("plaster")—two Arabic words. (Text published by R. Carande in *Archivo de Historia del Derecho Español* [1925], II, 399.) In fifteenth-century Burgos, Moorish master craftsmen were still in demand. Here are some data that I find in L. Serrano, *Los conversos D. Pablo de Santamaría y D. Alonso de Cartagena* (Madrid, 1942): Three Moorish artisans report, in 1492, on the poor quality of the "machinery and arms deposited in the Castle of Burgos" (p. 73). In the same year some Moors are recorded as supplying the royal army with flour; they also furnished carpenters (p. 95). Houses for the cathedral chapter are contracted for with Moorish architects and workers in 1379, 1398, 1435, 1436, etc. (p. 257). The program formulated in the *Poem of the Cid* ("We shall dwell in their houses, and we shall make use of them") was still being carried out.

French in the form *ogive*), and in a multitude of other words. Because the tailors were often Jews, they were called *alfayates* (Portuguese *alfaiate*).[64] Barbers were called *alfajemes*; goods were transported by *arrieros* (muleteers) and *recueros* (tenders of the *recua* or
caravan); they were sold in *zocos* and *azoguejos* (market squares), in
almacenes (warehouses), *alhóndigas* (granary markets), and *almonedas* (public sales; originally, in Arabic, "book of accounts"); weights
and measures were in *arrobas* (quarters, that is, fourth parts of a
quintal, an Arabic hundredweight), *arreldes* (weight units equivalent
to 4 pounds), *quintales* (weight units equivalent to 46 kilograms),
adarmes (weight units equivalent to 179 centigrams), *fanegas* (vol-
umetric units equivalent to 55.5 liters; originally, in Arabic, sacks),
almudes (units of dry measure, varying in equivalence), *celemines*
(the name of various dry and area measures, derived from the Arabic
word for eight), *cahices* (the name of various units of dry measure),
azumbres (units of liquid measure equivalent to 2.006 liters; originally, in Arabic, the eighth part of a certain jug); these weights and
measures were inspected by the *zabazoque* (originally, in Arabic,
"chief of the market") and the *almotacén*; the *almojarife* (originally,
in Arabic, "inspector") collected the taxes, which were paid in
maravedís (originally, in Arabic "of or pertaining to the *Almorávides*") or *meticales*. Cities and fortresses were governed by *alcaldes*
(mayors; originally, in Arabic, "judges"), *alcaides* (defense officers
of castles or fortresses; originally, in Arabic, "chiefs"), *zalmedinas*
(magistrates with criminal and civil jurisdiction; originally, in Arabic,
"chiefs of cities"), and *alguaciles* (lieutenants of police). Accounts
were kept by means of *cifras* and *guarismos* (numbers—Arabic, of
course), or by means of *álgebra* (which meant "reduction" in Arabic); the *alquimistas* (practitioners of *alquimia*, or alchemy) distilled
alcohol in their *alambiques* (alembics) and *alquitaras* (stills), or they
prepared *álcalis* (soda ash), *elixires*, and *jarabes* (sweetened and
fruit-flavored or medicinal potions; originally, in Arabic, "bever-
ages"), which they put into *redomas* (flasks). The cities were divided
into *barrios* (originally, in Arabic, "exteriors"), and *arrabales* (sub-
urbs); and the people ate *azúcar* (sugar), *arroz* (rice), *naranjas*
(oranges), *limones* (lemons), *berenjenas* (eggplants), *zanahorias* (carrots), *albaricoques* (apricots), *sandías* (watermelons), *altramuces*
(lupines), *toronjas* (grapefruit), *alcachofas* (artichokes), *alcauciles*
(wild artichokes), *albérchigos* (clingstone peaches), *alfóncigos* (pis-
tachio nuts), *albóndigas* (meatballs), *escabeche* (souse), *alfajores*

---

[64] Because the Portuguese clings even more than the Spaniard to tradition,
Arabic words persist in his language which have been replaced by Romance
words in Spanish. In Portuguese one still says *alfaiate*, as well as *alface*
("lettuce"), *ceroulas* ("underdrawers," called in Old Spanish by the Arabic
word *zaragüelles*), etc.

(pastes of almonds, walnuts, honey, and pulverized toast), and many other things with Arabic names. The plants mentioned above grow on irrigated land, and since the rainfall in Spain is light (except in the northern part), irrigation requires a great deal of work and skill to channel and distribute the water, a skill in which the Moors excelled, for they needed water to keep their bodies religiously clean and to fertilize the soil. For this reason the Arabic names for the irrigation system have persisted rather than those of the Roman tradition. I have previously cited *alberca, aljibe, acequia*; but the vocabulary relating to irrigation is very rich: *noria* (irrigating wheel or draw well), *arcaduz* (water conduit or bucket), *azuda* (Persian wheel, to raise water out of a stream), *almatriche* (canal), *alcantarilla* (bridge, sewer), *atarjea* (a small drain), *atanor* (water pipe), *alcorque* (hollow to hold water around the base of a tree), and so on.

The names of articles of clothing would take up considerable space: for example, *albanega* (a net to bind the hair), *alcandora* (a kind of shirt), *almaizar* (a gauze headdress), *almalafa* (long cloak), *alfareme* (hood to cover the head), *marlota* (an outer skirt or tunic), *albornoz* and *almejía* (short cloak), *jubón* (doublet), *alpargata* (rope-soled sandal; a word of pre-Latin origin taken over by the Arabs), *zaragüelles* (wide, short, plaited breeches), and so on. Some of these articles of clothing were a part of the Duchess of Albuquerque's wardrobe in 1479, according to the inventory cited below.

Let it be observed that I have not mentioned the military vocabulary (*adalid, algarada, rebato, etc.*)[65] nor the vocabulary of industry and the crafts (*almazara, aceña, alfiler, argolla, ajorca, tabaque, adarga, azafaya, azafate, etc.*). On the basis of our knowledge, it turns out to be an inadequate description to say that the Christians adopted the names of things, or that they underwent "influences," for what these words reveal is that area in Christian life occupied by Islamic civilization. It is a question of the projection of a certain type of Muslim life in which the cultivation and the cult of the earth mother, the taste for physical and aesthetic pleasures, and the practice of warfare were important. Arabic technology contributed to the luxury of the upper classes, as can be seen if we probe a bit into the intimacy of that life. Among the property left by Doña Mencía Enríquez, Duchess of Albuquerque, who died in 1479, there were the following articles made by the Moors: "Two chemises from *Almería*. One dark red *almalafa* [robe] of silk and gold thread. One *alfareme* [gauze head

---

[65] The Portuguese word *arraial* comes from Arabic *arŷāl* ("a large number of animals," or "an army"). *Arŷāl* is the plural of *riŷl* ("the hind foot of an animal"), so that *arŷāl* with the meaning of "herd of bulls or cows" seems earlier than *arŷāl* with the meaning of "army." In Portuguese the basic meaning has been extended in such phrases as "campos cheios de pacificos *arrayaes* de gente" ("fields full of peaceful *flocks* of people"; see the *Diccionário* of Moraes).

covering] thirteen and one-half 'varas' long, with white, gold, and crimson piping. One white Moorish *almaizar* [gauze veil] with trimmings of crimson and dark green edging. One small chest with a flacon of *almisque* [musk]. One perfume box with some *algalia* [civet]. One *marlota* [close-fitting gown] of crimson satin, adorned with pearls and *aljófar* [seed pearls]. Some skirts of blue *aseituní* [a rich Oriental fabric] with edging of crimson satin. Two *guadamecires* [pieces of embossed leather], one blue and white, and the other blue and red. One *almarraxica* [perfume vial] of enameled gold. Some small *alcorques* [overshoes with cork soles] of Don García. One *almofrej* [covering for a travel bed]. Twelve *alhombras* [carpets]."[66]

The Christian of the first centuries of the reconquest (a very long period) allowed himself to be dragged along by the practical aspects of Muslim life; he did not, on the other hand, adopt the science and philosophy of the Arabs, flourishing as they were between the tenth and twelfth centuries, for reasons that we shall see. His great task was to repopulate the no-man's-land between the two frontiers and to press his advance as much as possible. The Christian lived inside his Christianity, and never employed Arabic religious words except to refer to the religion of the Moors (*alquibla*, the point on the horizon toward which they turned to pray; *azala*, prayer; *almuédano*, muezzin). With respect to science, Alfonso the Learned adopted many names of stars (e.g., *Betelgeuse, Aldebarán*).[67] There are, moreover, adjectives such as *jarifo* (showy), *zahareño* (wild and incorrigible), *rahez* (cheap), *mezquino* (wretched), and others. The names of certain sicknesses are also Arabic: *alferecía* (epilepsy), *almorranas* (hemorrhoids), *jaqueca* (headache), *zaratán* (cancer of the breast), and others. Likewise Arabic are the names of some vices and virtues: *gandul* (idle), *aleve* (perfidious), *hazaña* (heroic deed); see J. Corominas' *Diccionario etimológico*. Various exclamations were expressed in Arabic too: *albricias* (to indicate joy at the receipt of good news); *olé* (enthusiasm), *ojalá* (wistful longing), and so on. It is not my purpose, however, to list all the words of Arabic origin which were spread throughout the Peninsula.[68]

---

[66] In A. Rodríguez Villa, *Bosquejo biográfico de don Beltrán de la Cueva* (1881), pp. 239–245. Or we may study the requests made in 1418 by Alfonso V of Aragon of Mohammed VIII, king of Granada, in preparation for a joust in the Moorish style (published by A. Giménez Soler, in *Boletín de la Academia de Buenas Letras de Barcelona*, IV [1907], 369). When a thorough study of the private life of Spaniards in the past is made, the Arabic contribution to it will loom large.

[67] See O. J. Tallgren, "Los nombres árabes de las estrellas y la transcripción alfonsina," in *Homenaje a Menéndez Pidal*, II, 633–718.

[68] For Arabisms in the Aragonese dialect spoken in the Pyrenees region, see J. Corominas, in *Nueva Revista de Filología Hispánica*, XII (1958), 69.

When the totality of Oriental elements is gathered together and analyzed, it will be possible to discover phenomena that are not yet taken into account. One aspect of the problem which has scarcely begun to be observed is that of pseudomorphosis—or parallel expressions—a linguistic peculiarity that originates in the Christians' having adopted certain vital attitudes of the Arabs. Here we are confronted with the phenomenon of like spiritual feelings and value judgments, which is different from the importation of words along with the objects they represent. It is, therefore, desirable to cite some examples of semantic crossing between the Arab and the Spaniard. Some are difficult to put one's finger on because the words seem fully explicable within the Latin and Romance traditions; at other times the Latin meaning clearly coexists with the Arabic, just as in the door of Baeza Cathedral the Gothic and Moorish styles are brought into harmony.

An instance of this kind of phenomenon may be found in the use of *poridad* with the meaning "secret" (rather than that of Latin *puritas* [purity]). There are abundant examples of this usage in Spanish and Portuguese texts of the Middle Ages: "to speak in *poridad*" (*Poem of the Cid*, 104); "He knows the condition of his friends and their *poridad*" (Calila e Dimna, ed. Alemany, p. 65); "all the poridat [secret] was later to be discovered" (*Book of Good Love*, 921). The examples are numerous, and these from the twelfth, thirteenth, and fourteenth centuries suffice. Still in 1505, however, in Pedro de Alcalá's *Arte para ligeramente saber la lengua arábiga* (Granada) there appears the definition "*poridad* or secret." The same form occurs in the *Amadís* (1508), and not until almost a century later does the spelling with *u* (*puridad*), reflecting the influence of Latin, become generalized: for example, "Time which discovers the *puridades*" (Mariana, *Historia de España*, Book 14, chap. 16). The expression *en puridad*, as used in such phrases as *hablando en puridad* ("speaking clearly, without evasion"), preserves an echo of the old meaning: "loyalty, frankly, without trickery."[69]

Therefore, to say that *poridad* is the same as Latin "puritatem" is

---

[69] Portuguese also has *poridade* ("*Poridade* vos terrei," "I will keep your *secret*" [*Cantigas de amigo*, ed. J. J. Nunes, II, 231]) alongside of *puridade* ("Se preguntar quisierdes, / en vossa *puridade* / saberedes, amigo, / que vos digo verdade" [*ibid.*, II, 294]). Nunes indicates that *en vossa puridade* means "in your consciousness," which demonstrates that *puridade* was felt to be a phenomenon of inner, spiritual life. It may be that the form with *u* is due to a learned restoration, or to the attempt to emphasize the relationship *puro* ("pure") when the meaning of "secret" was not intended. In his *Sacrificio de la misa*, however, Berceo uses *puridad* in the sense of "secret" because the Latin form of the word has remained in his mind: "Buena es de saber esta tal *puridad*" ("It is a good thing to know this *secret*"; ed. Solalinde, p. 213). In modern times Portuguese uses the form *puridad*. As late as 1666 the meaning of "secret" is preserved in the title of a work by Friar Francisco do Santíssimo Sacramento: *Epítome das excellencias da dignidade do ministro da puridade* ("Epitome of the Excellencies of the Dignity of the Minister of Secret Affairs").

only a half-truth, given the difference in meaning between "purity" and "secret." The old post of "secretary of the king's *poridad*" cannot be understood by reference to "purity." Nor does any extra-Peninsular Romance language help us out of the difficulty. On the other hand, the Arabic verb *khalaṣa* ("was pure") has derivatives that signify "sincerity": for example, *kholūṣ* ("friendship"), *mojliṣ* ("sincere friend"), *khālaṣa* ("to deal sincerely with someone"), *jālaṣ* ("purity"); see R. Dozy, *Supplément aux Dictionnaires arabes*.

Pure friendship has a considerable value for the Muslim. Arabic had other words meaning "secret," but apparently in this instance what prevailed in conversation (because we are dealing with an oral process) was the identification of the secret, the *poridad*, with the purity of friendship,[70] an identification that is at once very Islamic and very Spanish. In the Latin and Romance environment the secret was an objective reality, the result of putting something aside (*secernere*); it was what was set apart (*secretum*). But for the Arab the secret was related to dealing sincerely, intimately, and loyally with someone; it was a problem of life, a personal question dependent on friendship. In this attitude toward friendship the soul of Iberia is set off—for good or for ill—from the world of the Occident.

The fact that *poridad* is an echo of Arabic takes us to the very heart of this historical problem. In *Calila e Dimna* (p. 388) we read that harm comes to "el que dize su *poridat* al *mesturero* que sabe que non gela terná" ("the man who tells his *secrets* to an *informer*, for he knows that the latter will not keep them").[71] In *poridad*, along with the idea of secrecy, there was an implicit awareness of one's friend's worthiness of that proof of friendship. The supreme value for the Arab was esteem for the human person. Unlike the ascetic Christian, described in the *De contemptu mundi*, the Arab of whom we are speaking here was "the noblest and best creature to be found in this world" (*Calila e Dimna*, p. 51). Life was not lived in rational

---

[70] *Poridad* occurs, as noted above, in *Calila e Dimna*, which was translated from the Arabic in the thirteenth century: "Sabe el estado de sus amigos e su *poridat*" (p. 65), which in the Arabic is "Arafa bāṭina amri sāḥibibi bima yaẓharu minhu" (literally, "He knew the interior [*baṭin*] of his friend's affairs through what this affair showed") (ed. L. Cheikho [Beirut, 1923], p. 68). *Poridad* here, then, translates "the internal, the intimate," something not exactly like "what is secret" in Romance, and which approximates, on the other hand, Arabic *khālaṣa* ("intimate friendship, purity"). We are constantly dealing, in the case of these pseudomorphisms, with an "external aspect" that corresponds to another "internal aspect" and vice versa.

[71] The association of the two words, *poridad* and *mesturero*, was common. The *Partidas* of Alfonso the Learned say with reference to scriveners: "Ca maguer el rey e el chanceler e el notario mande fazer las cartas en *poridad*, con todo esso, si ellos *mestureros* fuessen, non se podría guardar de su daño" ("For even though the king and the chancellor and the notary may order that letters be composed in *secrecy*, despite that, if they [the scriveners] should be informers, it will be impossible to prevent them from doing harm"; II, 9, 8).

dealings with things but anchored in the longings of one's own heart, in one's own intimate privacy (*poridad*) and in that of one's friend or faithful lover. *Poridad* has both an "inwardness" from the heart and a social "outwardness": for example, the phrase "Secretary of the King's *Poridad*." Thus matters had to be, because the heart is, technically and not only metaphorically, the seat of religion and morality. Suffice it to recall the treatise on mystic and moral theology, *Deberes del corazón*, by the tenth-century Spanish Jew Ibn Paquda, which is related to the famous Islamic mysticism of the heart.[72]

Some meanings of the verb *correr* (to run) provide another example of Hispano-Arabic coincidence. The *Poem of the Cid* says: "Davan sus *corredores*" (1159), that is "They sent out soldiers to make forays." Menéndez Pidal notes that this curious meaning of *corredor* ("runner") lasts until the sixteenth century, but he does not explain it. It is, however, understandable if we take *corredor* to be a translation of *almogávar* ("raider"), from Arabic *mogāwir* ("mounted raider" and "runner"), a derivative of *gāwara* ("to run" and also "to raid"), with a double meaning that is injected into the Spanish word *correr*.

In Tirso de Molina's *Cigarrales de Toledo*[73] it is said that a sleeping beauty "mostraba en los *aceros* con que dormía, que era aquel el primer tercio de su sueño" ("showed in the *steel* [i.e., strength] with which she slept, that that was the first third of her sleep"). Once again we are puzzled by the fact that *aceros* means both "energy, strength," as occurs so frequently in seventeenth-century language, and also "the well-sharpened blades of a steel weapon" (cf. "the extremely thin blades [*aceros*]" of some knives mentioned by Lope de Vega in the *Pastores de Belén*, Book 2). The explanation is provided by the fact that Arabic *dokra* means "blade of the sword," "sharpness of the blade," and, in addition, "vehemence and force of spirit." The same root found in *dokra* provides the basis also for words like *dakar* ("strong, valiant, ardent") and *madkīr* ("testicles"). A similar development takes place in the Arabic word meaning "iron," *hadīd*, from whose root come also *hadd* ("blade of the sword") and *hidda* ("sharpness, vehemence, force"). *Aceros* is, then, an Arabism.

Another example of Arabism is found in certain meanings of the word *vergüenza* ("shame") which fit with difficulty into the Romance tradition: for example, "En la delantera o en la zaga ... debe poner ... los mas esforzados, et homes más de *vergüenza* et más sabidores"[74] ("In the vanguard or the rearguard ... one must put ... the

---

[72] *Duties of the Heart*, trans. M. Hyamson (New York, 1925).
[73] Ed. V. Said Armesto, p. 35.
[74] Juan Manuel, *Libro de los Estados*, in *Biblioteca de Autores Españoles*, LI, 320a.

most daring men, and those who show most *shame* and are the best-informed"); "Et aquestas pocas de compañas que avían fincado con el Rey eran caballeros et escuderos, et otros que el rey avía criado en la su casa et en su merced; pero eran todos omes de buenos corazones, et en quien *avía vergüenza*"[75] ("And those few companions who had stayed with the King were knights and squires, and others whom the King had reared in his house and in his grace; but they were all men of good heart, and in whom *there was shame*"). The meaning of *vergüenza* here is really "honor, loyalty," an active and working virtue, not a feeling of restraint (modesty, embarrassment, or an inhibiting respect). Such a shade of meaning is not contained in the concept of *vergüenza* in other Romance languages; it is meaningless to say "un homme de honte" or "un uomo di vergogna." I think it possible, then, that *vergüenza* with the meaning of "point of honor, loyalty" contains an injection of Arabic meaning. Pedro de Alcalá, whose vocabulary reflects the Arabic spoken in al-Andalus,[76] notes: "*verguença: aar; verguença* with infamy: *aar.*" E. Westermarck has described for us the institution called *'ār*:[77] for the Moors it represented the very special obligation one person finds himself in with respect to another. "I am in the *'ār* of God or in your *'ār*" means that a man must aid me; if he does not, he is in danger of suffering some misfortune. The word also designates the act by which one person places himself under the obligation of aiding another; *hādā la 'ār 'alayka* means "this is my *'ār* with respect to you." All of this fits perfectly with the text of the *Crónica de Alfonso XI*, for "en quien avía vergüenza" is a translation of "in whom there was *'ār.*" This Arabic institution implies also the transference of a conditional curse: if you do not do what I desire, you may die, or something very bad may happen to you. In the text quoted we have seen that the chronicle explains the reasons why the few knights with the king should have *vergüenza*, or, in other words, *'ār.*[78]

---

[75] *Crónica de Alfonso XI*, in *Biblioteca de Autores Españoles*, LXVI, 327a.

[76] *Arte para ligeramente saber la lengua arábiga* (Granada, 1505).

[77] "L-'Ar, or the Transference of Conditional Curses in Morocco," in *Anthropological Essays Presented to E. B. Taylor* (Oxford, 1907), p. 365.

[78] Westermarck's study helps, in addition, to explain something that has always seemed peculiar to me in the legend of the *Seven Princes of Lara*. Doña Lambra ordered one of her servants to fill a cucumber with blood and throw it at one of the princes; so it was done, "and he dirtied [the prince] all over with blood." Outraged by so dishonorable an attack, the princes killed the servant, even though he had taken refuge under his mistress' cloak; she in turn was covered with the servant's blood. These violent actions determine the subsequent revenge. Menéndez Pidal says (*Infantes de Lara*, p. 6): "I know no other example of this singular type of insult." But Westermarck observes (p. 365) that no means of transmitting a curse is more efficacious than blood because it contains *ŷunūn*, or evil spirits. In Morocco it is believed that shed blood contains *ŷunūn*, or evil spirits. Doubtless for this reason the malignant Doña Lambra

Still more likely, perhaps, than the explanation based on '*ār* is one suggested by James T. Monroe. In Arabic, *ḥayaya* means "to live, to preserve life, to be ashamed." The derivative *moḥayyat* has the sense of "protection, the fact of being ashamed." The ninth-century Arabic historian Ibn-Qutaybah speaks of the noble who "defends his vassal and his companion with his *moḥayyati*," in other words, with "his protection" and with "his shame." By one route or another we come to the conclusion that the active meaning of *vergüenza* is not Romance.

There is one Spanish expression that is *koranic in origin*, and surely anyone who carefully compares the holy book of Islam with Spanish sayings and proverbs will find others. To say of a person that, however much he knows, his intellectual and human value is only slight, one says that "he is an ass burdened with knowledge" (*es un burro cargado de ciencia*). Here once more is a reflection of the longing for "integration," the ideal condition in which there is a perfect coincidence between the person's existence and his action, the inward and the outward. In the seventeenth century Alonso Núñez de Castro writes: "They confirmed it in Madrid by calling him an ass loaded with letters."[79] The dictionary defines *burro o asno cargado de letras* as a "scholar with a limited grasp" (*erudito de cortos alcances*). There is no apparent justification for such an extravagant metaphor, nor is it clear how an immaterial reality (letters or knowledge) can be loaded upon the rude and tangible materiality of a donkey; but if we move into an archaic zone of the language, we begin to see more clearly. In Portuguese there is a quip that goes "a donkey loaded with books is a scholar" (*um burro carregado de livros e um doutor*), and the matter now begins to take on meaning. The meaning becomes perfectly clear from a passage in the Koran (62:5):[80] "The likeness of those who were charged with the observance of the law, and then observed it not, is as the likeness of an ass laden with books." Mohammed censures the Jews here for not carrying out the precepts of the Bible even though they know them; this incongruity, which destroys the integrality of knowledge and conduct, is expressed in an image that was meaningful in a land where the donkey was a means of transportation. Later, the books in this metaphor (started

---

had Prince Gonzalo González dirtied with blood; he was the youngest of the brothers and the one most loved by his mother Doña Sancha, who was bitterly hated by Doña Lambra. Other Arabic pseudomorphisms are *plata* with the meaning of "silver" (see Paul Aebischer, " '*Argentum*' et '*plata*' en ibéro-roman," in *Mélanges de linguistique offerts à Albert Dauzat* [Paris, 1951]) and *adelantado* ("advanced") in the meaning of "adelantado de la frontera" ("governor of the frontier"); see H. L. A. van Wijk, "En calco árabe en esp. 'adelantado,' port. 'adiantado,' " in *Neophilologus* (1951), pp. 91–94.

[79] See *Diccionario histórico de la Academia Española, s.v.* "asno."

[80] Professor G. L. Della Vida has kindly supplied me with this reference.

on its worldly career by someone who must have known the text in the Koran) were replaced by letters or knowledge, and thus it was converted into something barely intelligible.[81]

The effects of the long Muslim domination are further reflected in geographical and place names: *Trafalgar* (the "white cape"), *Guadalquivir* (the "great river"), *Guadarrama* ("river of sand"), *Albufera* (the "lagoon"), and so on. A list of such names may be found in Miguel Asín Palacios' *Contribución a la toponimia árabe de España* (1940), which is a very useful work though far from complete. Not included, for example, is *Andalucía*, which in the fourteenth century still kept the Arabic article in such phrases as the following: "el rey de al Andalucía" ("the king of Andalusia").[82] Ibn Baṭṭūtah, the famous traveler from Tangiers in the fourteenth century, uses both *al-Andalus* and *al-Andalusiyya* to designate the Muslim zone of the Peninsula. When the names of towns and those of small places are carefully catalogued, the breadth and depth of Muslim domination in the land of the future Spaniards will appear in its full scope. A comparison with Germanic toponymy—which abounds in Galicia and other regions—would permit us to understand the different nature of the traces left by the Suevi and the Visigoths on the soil of Hispania.[83] No river, mountain, cape, or lagoon today bears a Germanic name.

These linguistic phenomena have not been presented here as interesting curiosities or as philological data. My purpose is to make evident the breadth of the contacts between Islamic and Christian society, so that later on we may not be surprised when we see the action of the Muslim presence in the deepest areas of life, such as literary expression or the social functioning of religion. If the Christian invoked Allah when he said *ojalá* and *olé*, he also followed the Arabic model when he used such swear words as *carajo* ("membrum virile") and *leche* ("milk"),[84] when he used *padres* ("fathers") as the plural to refer to both the male and the female parent when they were considered together, and when he said *huevos* ("eggs") for "testicles,"[85] or *grandes* ("great") in the term "grandes de España" ("the grandees

---

[81] There are other references of the same kind in Arabic literature: "Those who collect books without profiting from what they contain have by a certain poet been called mules loaded for a trip, who know as much about the usefulness of the cargo as a camel does" (Masudi, *Les Prairies d'Or*, trans. C. Barbier de Meynard, III, 138). In Spain students' books were transported by donkeys; Ignacio de Loyola left Salamanca for Barcelona "walking behind a donkey loaded with books" (P. de Rivadeneira, *Vida de Ignacio de Loyola*, I, xvi).

[82] *Crónica del rey don Pedro*, in *Biblioteca de Autores Españoles*, LVI, 439a.

[83] See Georg Sachs, *Die germanischen Ortsnamen in Spanien und Portugal* (Jena, 1932).

[84] See M. L. Wagner in *Volkstum und Kultur der Romanen* (1933), VI, 23.

[85] "'Bayzatan' (the two eggs), a *double entendre* which has given rise to many tales," says R. F. Burton in a note to his translation of *The Book of the Thousand Nights and a Night* (1885), II, 55.

of Spain").⁸⁶ The "grandees of Spain," who appear as a formal institution in the sixteenth century, are mentioned in literature as early as the thirteenth century: "The king himself could find none among the *great men* [*grandes omnes*] of Castile who dared to stand against the danger of that place [Calatrava]" (*Crónica General*, p. 666b).

Hijodalgo

If we had not been brought up in the mythical belief that the Spaniards were eternal beings, or could at least trace their direct lineage back as far as the cave dwellers of Altamira, the nine centuries of peaceful and belligerent common life with the Muslims would not have been felt as episodic and external to the vital structure of the Peninsular peoples. Then, too, we would not have been shocked by the fact that *hijo d'algo* ("son of worth"; modern Spanish *hidalgo*) is not explicable within the Latin and Romance framework.⁸⁷

The sons of the great Visigothic lords for whom Isidore of Hispalis wrote a treatise on education (*Institutionum disciplinae*, see above, p. 194) were not the sons of property nor of moral abstractions. As I have already said, St. Isidore refers to the circumstances of their birth, but he does not make them sons of those circumstances: "The condition of the well born should be evident in their mode of conduct more than in the high rank they occupy" ("Bonorum natalium indolem non tam dignitate magis quam moribus animi debere clarescere," p. 557 in the edition of Anspach). The "filial" manner of designating the condition or quality of a person is Semitic, that is to say, both Hebraic and Arabic. The rich man, in Arabic, is the "son of wealth," and according to this model, Castilian formerly said *hi de malicias* for "malicious" and Catalan used *fill de caritat* for "charitable" (see Corominas, *Diccionario etimológico, s.v.* "Hijo"). These instances of generation of something transcendental which acts as a creative principle are, of course, different from *hi de puta* (French *fils de putain*), in which the social infamy of the mother is empirically proved to have passed to the son. In this instance we are dealing with a fact of biological generation and not with an immaterial process. But the Arab even interprets the relationship among material objects in a way that seems metaphorical to us, though for him it is not. T. E. Lawrence recounts in his *Seven Pillars of Wisdom* that, when the first bicycles came to Arabia, the people called them "children of

---

⁸⁶ James T. Monroe tells me that Burton translates *akābir ad-daulati* ("the great men of the state") as "grandees" in the phrase "and the king called together his grandees." The *Arabic-English Dictionary* of J. G. Hava does, indeed, translate *al-akābir* as "the chief men, the leaders, the nobility."

⁸⁷ The Semitic nature of the linguistic form *hijo-de-algo*, suggested by me in earlier editions of this work, has been accepted by J. Corominas in his *Diccionario etimológico* and Rafael Lapesa in his *Historia de la lengua española*, p. 109.

cars."[88] In Hebrew the arrow is the "son of the bow"; in Arabic the thief is occasionally called "son of the night," just as what is ephemeral may be called the "son of the day." These phrases are more than linguistic data, for they are linked to a concept of the reality of things and of man which differs from the Occidental view. For the Oriental the existence of beings is based either on a process of creation which guarantees their reality, or on the immanent virtue of the object itself which providentially makes it be as it is and have the value that it has. In the final analysis there is a divine action that guarantees the essence and the worth of reality from within or from without that reality; things have an outwardness and an inwardness that, as we shall see later on, are always reversible. From this view results the constant invocation of the revealed word of God; and from this concept proceeds the necessity for these "filiations" or "paternities," for seizing on the infinite threads which, spun from earth to heaven and from the present to the beginning of things, lead to the primal design that makes of all reality something conditional and transitory. Or, in other terms, things are or exist because it has been so willed, never in and of themselves.

The Western mind, on the other hand, adopted an attitude we might call suspicious: nothing is justified a priori, and reality and evaluations depend more on what man may have invented with his mind and incorporated into his life than on what was given and already existed in that life. The civilization of Western man has been the result of the conflict between the spirit already incarnate within him and the critical examination of the rewards each man deems himself to deserve. If we approach from this angle the problem of how the noble rank of a person was expressed, we will see at once the difference between the Occidental and Oriental modes. On the one hand there appear those names expressive of objectivized actions: the *baron*, among the Germans, was the free man who was good at fighting; the *count* (from L. *comes*, "he who goes with one") was the one who accompanied the king in his palace and in battle; the *duke* (from L. *dux*, through OFr *duc*) was the one who led as commander and chieftain; the *marquis* (from the Provençal) was something like the governor of the frontier, or march; the Spanish title *ricohombre* ("rich man"), whose rank was higher than that of the *infanzón* or the hidalgo, seems to have entered Castile by way of Navarre and to have come originally from France (see Menéndez Pidal, *Vocabulario del Cantar de Mio Cid*, p. 82).

In all these instances the noble rank, the elevation above the common people, was due to the quality of a person's deeds or to the wealth that permitted him to act nobly. In other instances, however,

---

[88] "Bicycles they called . . . the children of cars, which themselves were sons and daughters of trains" (New York: Doubleday; p. 172).

noble rank was the result of accidental or, as we might say, "existential" virtues derived from the circumstances of birth. The *infanzón* was, originally, the son of noble parents; in a document of 1093 (cited by Menéndez Pidal, *Vocabulario del "Poema del Cid,"* p. 719) they are designated as soldiers (*milites*) "non infimis parentibus ortos, sed nobiles genere necnon et potestate, qui vulgari lingua *infanzones* dicuntur" ("born not of base stock, but of noble lineage, with social authority, called in the vernacular *infanzones*"). This word is related to *infante* ("son of a noble father"), as in "Infantes de Carrión" (the noblemen to whom the Cid's daughters were married), and to *infante* in the meaning of "son of the king." All these titles have to do with the fact that, in Arabic, *al-walad* ("the son"), designates by itself the heir to the throne (see Dozy, *Supplément aux Dictionnaires arabes*). This derivation is in no way invalidated by the fact that in Old French the *jeune homme noble* was called an *enfant*; in the eleventh and twelfth centuries the Pyrenees did not constitute a barrier against the diffusion of Hispano-Orientalisms (we have already seen that Arabic *aljibe* became the French *ogive*).

To return to *hijo d'algo* (or *fijo d'algo*), the fullest definition of the term is given in the *Partidas* of Alfonso the Learned: "And because these [the *fijosdalgo*] were selected from *buenos logares* ["good places"] and *algo* [literally, "something"], which means the same thing in our language as 'bien' ["material and moral worth"], they were called *fijosdalgo*, which is the same as *fijos de bien*.... The *fijosdalgo* should be selected from the direct descent of the father and the grandfather" (II, 21, 2). This definition, or rather description, is considerably confusing to the Western mind. Since whenever a problem arises, the solutions proposed may be more or less fortunate, I at first glance chose the wrong road in attempting to find an Oriental origin for the word *algo* ("material or moral worth") instead of limiting myself to proving the Oriental nature of the connection between the meanings of *algo* and *hijo*. In reality, there is no reason why Latin *aliquod* ("something") should not have developed from its original indefinite meaning into other very concrete meanings.[89] The Spanish

---

[89] Where the Bible says, "Ut faciam cum eo misericordiam Dei" (II Regum 9:3), the thirteenth-century Spanish translation reads, "A quien fiziesse yo algo," which is to say, "That I may show kindness unto him." *Algo* has the same meaning in the following passages: "El rey ... fazedor d'*algo* a sus pueblos" ("The king . . . who does good things for his people," *Calila e Dimna*, ed. Academia Española, p. 49); "Yurámosle todos que uos fiziessemos *algo*," *Crónica General*, 506b, 6). Cf. also the Portuguese like development: "E esto vos damos por muito d'*algo* e d'amor que sempre recebemos de vos. ... Com obrigação de fazerdes *algo* a melhoramento em essa nossa heredade" ("And we give this to you for the many goods and favors and love we have always received from you. ... With the obligation of showing contributions to and improvements of our inheritance," *Elucidario de Santa Rosa*).

indefinite demonstrative pronouns *aquel, aquello,* and *aquello otro* ("that one," "that thing," "that other"), as well as *al,* acquired extremely concrete senses (*tener mucho aquél,* "to have a lot of it"; *quillotro, quillotrar,* "lover," "make love to"; *lo al,* "the carnal act," etc.).

Both Arabic and Hebrew conditioned the formation of *fijo d'algo,*[90] which is perfectly understandable for anyone familiar with the peculiar structure of Spanish life. The *fijos d'algo,* according to the *Partidas,* came from "buenos logares" and were *fijos de bien,* that is, of *algo,* in the double sense of material and spiritual worth. In the fifteenth century these "sons of worth" (*hijos de bien*) were called "men of worth" (*hombres de bien*) by Gutierre Díez de Games.[91] These men are the "good people" (*los buenos*) in the Spanish proverb "allégate a *los buenos* y serás uno de ellos" ("cling to the good people and you will become one of them"), a plan for life which is satirized in *Lazarillo de Tormes.* These "buenos" must correspond to the Hebrew expression *ben tovim* ("son of the good" and "son of wealth").[92]

In a text from *Midrash Rabbah* which I adduce on page 13 of the article cited in note 90, Israel is symbolized as a woman of noble family, a *bat tovim* and a *bat genosim*; which is to say, "daughter of good people, of material and spiritual worth, and of noble lineage." Noble lineage is expressed in the same way in two texts (of 985 and 1020) in which the idea of *fijo d'algo* ("son of worth") appears for the first time in the phrase *filii bene natorum* ("sons of the well born"). This form of expression seems "odd" to Menéndez Pidal (*Vocabulario del "Poema del Cid,"* p. 691). The *benē tovim,* "sons of wealth or of good people," formed an institution among the Jews, a noble class to which the Talmud and the biblical commentaries of the *Midrash Rabbah* allude. But, in addition to this, it is possible that the nobility originally projected by the Jews onto the individual by circumstances outside himself (good ancestors, good places, good things) may have found expression in the Spanish *fijo d'algo* on account of Arabic as well as Jewish models. On the one hand, *los buenos* ("the good people") in the sense of "nobles" appears in various Spanish phrases copied from *benē tovim,* as is evident in this text from the convert Dr. Francisco de Villalobos: "If a [poor muleteer] sets out to trace down his ancestry, it will be found that he descends in the direct line from pure blood, and the proverb runs that many *sons of nobles* [*hijos de buenos*] are reduced to such a state, and that even

---

[90] See my article *"Hijodalgo:* Un injerto semítico en la vida española," in *Papeles de Son Armadans* (Madrid: Palma de Mallorca, 1960), pp. 9-21.

[91] See my *Origen, ser y existir de los españoles* [Madrid: Taurus, 1959], p. iii.

[92] *Tovim* is the plural of *tov,* "good, beautiful, excellent, outstanding; wealth, property, happiness, health" (E. F. Leopold, *Lexicon hebraicum* [Leipzig, 1910]).

though they may be seen wearing a tattered coat, not for that reason should they be despised."[93] As we have seen before, *buenos* had the same meaning in proverbs like "Allégate a los *buenos* y serás uno de ellos." In *Guzmán de Alfarache* (II, III, v), Mateo Alemán says that his protagonist's father-in-law, "even though an innkeeper, was a good man," for not all innkeepers rob their guests; "and if there is some [stealing], they are not to blame for it, nor should such be thought of my people, since they were all *nobles from the mountain regions* [*de los buenos de la Montaña*], *hidalgos* like the Cid, but through misfortune and poverty they had come into that business." The "Montaña" included, besides Santander, the territory north of Burgos and the Basque provinces; because people believed that there had never been any Moors or Jews there, it was considered that the Christian caste proceeding from that region was free of any taint: "Even though we are cobblers, if we come from Montaña, we are all hidalgos" (L. Vélez de Guevara, *El diablo cojuelo*, Tranco V). The equivalence established between "*los buenos* de la Montaña" and hidalgo undoubtedly reflects the Hebraic *tovei*, whose genitive form *tovim* occurs in the phrase *benē tovim* ("sons of material and spiritual worth").

In Hebrew "the good people [*los buenos*], the leaders of the city," are called *tovei ha-ir*; this expression was crossed in Spanish with imitations of Arabic expressions which are identical in meaning to *benē tovim*. In Arabic, ni'mat means "wealth, cattle, grace, favor."[94] One of the titles given to sovereign in Arabic is actually *wa-liyy-alnni'am* ("the benefactor"), which reminds us of the passage in *Calila e Dimna* (quoted above, p. 268, note 89) in which the king is called "the one who does *good things* for his people" ("fazedor d'*algo* a sus pueblos"). This *algo* (*ni'mat*) that the king dispenses to his people is also *ni'mat allah* ("the grace of God"). In sum, the *fijo d'algo* is the son of all that worth, grace, and favor represented by the Hebrew *tovim* and the Arabic *ni'mat*; the person of the *hijo d'algo* is permeated by nobility, haloed by it, and, thanks to that nobility, he enjoys exemptions and privileges in the same fashion as *benē tovim* ("the children of the good").[95]

---

[93] *Los problemas de Villalobos*, in *Biblioteca de Autores Españoles*, XXXVI, 425.

[94] I owe my knowledge of this to the young Arabist James T. Monroe, whose help in this matter has been most useful.

[95] Centuries ago nobility was conceived as a *spirit* infused into the person, and which could depart in the same way it had come. In the *Fuero Viejo de Castiella* ("Old Statutes of Castile"), we read: "They say of Castile: That the noble lady [*fijadalga*] who marries a peasant shall pay taxes on her property [*algos*]; but this property shall once again be exempt after the death of her husband; and the lady must take a packsaddle on her back and must stand on the grave of her husband, and she must say three times, striking the grave with the edge of the packsaddle: 'Peasant, take back thy mean estate; return to me my

The Arabic phrase *awlād ni'mati* ("sons of worth") corresponds exactly to Spanish *fijos d'algo*. In the story of "Ghanim bin Ayyub" in the *Thousand and One Nights* (at the end of Night 43), where the Arabic says *awlād ni'mati*, Burton translates "they are *people of condition* and show signs of former opulence." In other words, *awlād ni'mati* is something like "rich people" and, by extension, "those of good family." The *awlād ni'mati* did not, however, form a separate social class like the Hebrew *benē tovim*.

Consequently, in *fijo d'algo*—the word and the institution designated by the word—we are afforded a characteristic example of the intimate connections among the castes which constituted the authentic reality created by the shared common life among Christians, Moors, and Jews in the tenth century. The individual rose above the common social level by virtue of the parents who had engendered him; it was as if he had been annointed by a grace that as it elevated him, magnified him and made him grand—*a grandee of Spain*—just as in the case of *akābira ad-daulati* ("the great men of the kingdom") or the "great men of Castile" (see above, p. 266).

---

nobility'" (Book I, title V, xvii). For a like case of loss and recovery of nobility by the hidalgo, see Book I, title V, xvi. The magical nature of nobility evidenced here and the Oriental origins of the concept of nobility are mutually complementary.

VIII · ISLAMIC TRADITION AND SPANISH LIFE

NSUFFICIENT OBSERVATION and interpretation have been devoted to certain Spanish ways of living and speaking which have no meaning when removed from their Islamic frame of reference. For my purpose it makes no difference that such practices are also found in other countries likewise touched by Oriental civilization (Byzantium, India, Russia, etc.), since I am not interested in folklore but merely in making evident the effects of nine-hundred years of Christian-Islamic interaction on the modes of life of the Hispanic peoples. For this purpose it likewise makes no difference whether the Muslims of al-Andalus owe some of their customs to Byzantium, to Persia, or to any other country. The customs of the Spanish Christians in the first years of the reconquest were a vivid reflection of the Moorish prestige, which at times "depressed and humiliated" them (Menéndez Pidal), but which, in spite of this, forced an unconscious imitation, even after the political and military splendor of Islam had vanished.

Moorish habit may account for the fact that in little towns in Castile where today probably very few people bathe in hot water there were *public baths* in the thirteenth century. Municipal ordinances provide us with our information: The ordinances of Zorita (Guadalajara) require that "viri eant ad communem balneum in die martis, et in die jovis, et in die sabbati. Mulieres eant in die lune, et in die mercuri. Iudei eant in die veneris, et in die dominica. Et nemo det sive sit mulier, sive vir, pro introitu balnei nisi obolum tantum."[1]

---

[1] *Fuero de Zorita de los Canes* ("Ordinances of . . . "), ed. R. de Ureña, pp. 67–68. For a more complete record of references to public baths in the municipal ordinances, see A. Ruiz-Moreno, *Cuadernos de Historia de España* (Buenos Aires, 1945), III, 152–157. According to an Arabic geographer of the eleventh century (Bakrī), the Galicians (northern Christians were all so called) "ne se nettoient et ne se lavent qu'une ou deux fois dans l'année avec de l'eau froide. ... Ils prétendent que grâce à la crasse, due à leur transpiration, qui les recouvre, leurs corps se maintiennent en bonne forme physique" (Al-Himyarī, *La Péninsule Ibérique au Moyen-Âge*, trans. E. Lévi-Provençal (Leyden, 1938), p. 83).

"The keeper of the bath shall provide the bathers with those things that they may need, be they water or other necessaries. . . . Any person who takes anything from the bathing pools will be punished by having an ear cut off" (Al-Himyarī, *La Péninsula Ibérique au Moyen-Âge*, p. 69). The same text is to be found in the ordinances of Cuenca. The ordinances of Brihuega (Guadalajara) make the observation that "neither the manservant nor the maidservant that are brought to the bath will pay anything."[2] Even an insignificant town like Usagre (Badajoz) had its bath: "The women will go to the bath on Sundays, Tuesdays, and Thursdays; and the men on the other days." Whoever went to the baths was allowed to bring as many as three servants, including "one to bathe the master."[3] In these ordinances the keeper of the bath was usually required to provide the bathers with hot water, soap, and towels. The baths gradually fell into disuse among the Christians, who in 1526 started trying to suppress those of the Moriscos. This measure was not put into effect until 1576, when the Moriscos were punished for the rebellion of 1568 by being prohibited from practicing their customs. One of the Moriscos, a gentleman named Francisco Núñez Muley, replied thus to the royal mandate: "The baths were built for the cleanliness of the body; and to say that couples get together there is not to be believed; for where so many people go, there can be no secret. . . . There have always been baths *throughout all the provinces*; and if at one time they were taken away in Castile, it was because the baths *weakened the strength and the spirit of the men for war*. The men who were born in this kingdom of Granada have no need to fight, nor do the women need to have strength, but rather to be clean; if they do not wash in the baths (and since it is forbidden them to bathe in brooks, springs, and rivers, and in their houses), where then are they to go and bathe?" In 1567 a solemn ceremony took place, and "all the artificial baths" that there were in Granada were destroyed.[4] The people forgot the custom of washing themselves frequently, in Spain as in the rest of Europe, until well into the nineteenth century.[5]

---

2 *Fuero de Brihuega*, ed. J. Catalina, p. 162.

3 *Fuero de Usagre*, ed. A. Bonilla, p. 48.

4 Luis del Mármol, *Rebelión y castigo de los moriscos de Granada*, in *Biblioteca de Autores Españoles*, XXI, 161, 162, 164.

5 Although at times there were probably public baths in Hispania as a part of the Romano-Visigothic tradition before the arrival of the Moors, their existence among the Christians in the reconquered lands reflected the Muslim usage. When Prince Sancho lost his life in the Battle of Zalaca in 1086, his father, Alfonso VI, inquired of his wise men why the ability to fight had grown weaker in his knights; "they answered him that it was because many went frequently to the baths, and gave themselves too much to vices. The King then had all the baths in his kingdom destroyed" (*Crónica General*, p. 555). Very likely all the baths were not destroyed, and this anecdote is probably apocryphal. But even so, the idea remains that the baths, to which the Moors were much addicted, were regarded in this particular instance as a cause of weakness and vice; if it

Also, I think that the *ritual washing of the dead* was very likely an imitation of the Muslims. In the *Poema de Fernán Gonzalez* (*ca.* 1250), the Castilian count had the corpse of his enemy, the Count of Tolosa, solemnly washed before it was dressed in a rich silk cloth.[6] The *Crónica General* relates that Count Fernán González "himself disarmed with his own hands the Count of Tolosa, there where he lay dead; and he caused him to be bathed" (p. 399a).[7] In a version of the Joseph story recorded in Hebrew characters, we read that before Joseph had his father Jacob embalmed, he had him bathed ("Yoçef su mandamiento fizo may priado, / Fizo vannar al muerto, luego fue pimentado"). The same thing can be found in the *General estoria* of Alfonso the Learned: "And they bathed him very, very well, and then they embalmed him" (p. 256). Petrus Comestor thought that this was a pagan custom, a "mos ethnicorum"; and Sr. González Llubera thinks that the custom is rabbinical.[8]

To be sure, many of the customs that I am analyzing were also found among the Spanish Jews, who were highly infused with Muslim life. The custom of having *women cover their faces* was still practiced not long ago in Mojácar (Almeria), Tarifa (Cadiz), some Peruvian cities, and, I imagine, in other Hispanic areas. In Argentina a women's coat is called a *tapado* (past participle of *tapar*, "to cover up"), a word that comes from the *manto tapado* (a kind of cloak), mentioned by Tirso de Molina in *El burlador de Sevilla* (II, 101), with which women covered their heads and faces.[9] Dozens of seven-

---

had been thought that the baths were a traditionally Christian custom, they would not have been considered in this way. The reality of something in the past or the present depends on the vital context within which it exists. (Cf. the curious instance of the Spanish word *albaricoque* ["apricot"], which is an Arabism, even though its ultimate origin is the Latin *praecox* [*malum praecox*]).

[6] "Lavól e vestiól de un iamete preçiado" (373).

[7] There are many references to ritual washing among the Muslims in El-Bokhâri, *Les traditions islamiques*, trans. O. Houdas and W. Marçais (1900), I, 405 ff.: "The one sent from God came into our house while we were washing the body of his daughter. He said to us: 'Wash her three times or five times. . . . Begin with the members on the right side and with the parts of the body that are washed in ablutions.'"

[8] See I. González Llubera, *Coplas de Yoçef*, pp. 19, 42. Antonio de Guevara, bishop of Mondoñedo, was quite familiar with the customs of the Moriscos and the Jews. He mentions some of them in the *Constituciones sinodales*, which he gave to his Galician diocese in 1541 (in R. Costes, *Antonio de Guevara: Sa vie* [Bordeaux, 1925], pp. 57 ff.): "When a man expires and dies, certain persons who do not rightly understand their faith, wash his whole body, thinking that they are washing away his sins; more than this, they shave off the hairs of his beard, which they then keep to make charms; and since this is a Jewish, and even a Morisco rite, we do excommunicate all those persons who henceforth do this. . . . Many men and women also have the custom in time of lightning and thunder of holding up their skillets and tripods to heaven, thinking it certain that thus the thunder and lightning are mitigated. And since this is a Morisco superstition, we do order and command that from henceforth no one dare to perform such an action."

[9] See L. Pfandl, *Introducción al Siglo de Oro*, p. 273.

teenth-century plays contain situations based on the woman's custom of covering her face when she went about town: for example, Tirso de Molina, *El amor médico* (in which occurs the exclamation "Oh tapada a lo morisco!" ["Oh lady covered up in Moorish fashion!"]) and *La celosa de sí misma*; Calderón, *El escondido y la tapada*, and so on. Thus Christian women went on doing what had been prohibited to Morisco women in the sixteenth century: "For to want women to go about with their faces uncovered, what is this but to give men occasion to fall into sin by looking upon the beauty that they usually cannot resist?"[10] It should be remembered, of course, that prohibitive regulations frequently do not reflect the reality of the events.

The custom of having *women sit on the floor*, as they are said to have done down to the eighteenth century, was a Moorish reminiscence. The proper place for women to sit was the *estrado*, a low platform only slightly raised from the floor and covered with a rug and cushions. In an early fourteenth-century text we read: "The lady realized that he was the king, and she rose up, and went forward to kiss his hands. The king refused, and went to sit with her on her dais."[11] The family of Domingo Sarmiento still lived this way at the beginning of the nineteenth century in San Juan (Argentina), according to his account in *Recuerdos de provincia*. Cervantes knew from his own experience that the dais on which the ladies sat was an Oriental institution: "An *estrado* with more velvet cushions than any Moor ever had" (*Quixote*, II, 5). Sancho Panza aspires to have his wife sit in church on *alcatifas* ("carpets"), *almohadas* ("cushions"), and *arambeles* ("cloth hangings") (*ibid.*), all three articles having Arabic names. This is why the sofa and armchairs in a drawing room are still called an *estrado* in Spanish; and for the same reason, to the grandee's ceremony known as "covering oneself" (*cubrirse*) before the king there corresponded a ceremony for the ladies of the court known as "taking the cushion" (*tomar la almohada*) from the queen.[12]

A great many of the forms of *courtesy* acquire meaning only when we examine them under the Islamic light. If you are a Spaniard and you show a friend something of value which he praises, you must, to be correct, say: "It is at your disposal" (*Está a su disposición*). It has happened once in a while that a foreigner, not knowing that these words are only ritual, has asked whether the valuable object was

---

[10] Luis del Mármol, *op. cit.*, p. 165.

[11] *El libro del Caballero Cifar*, ed. C. P. Wagner, p. 100.

[12] The reader not intimately acquainted with Spanish custom and tradition will perhaps need a further explanation here. When noblemen were invested by the king with the *grandeza*, or grandeur, of Spain, they were granted the privilege of keeping their hats on in the presence of the king. The queen, for her part, invested noble ladies with the same dignity by allowing them to sit on cushions in the royal presence.

really being offered to him, and this has created more than one embarrassing situation. In the *Poem of the Cid* one is told that King Alfonso VI praised the Cid's horse as well as the one who rode it: "This horse of which I have heard such good report . . . ; in all our lands there is no man so valorous" (3510). To this the Cid replied with a Muslim courtesy that had by then become thoroughly Hispanic: "I give him to you as a gift; have him taken away, my Lord" (3115). As was *de rigueur* in the eleventh century—just as it is today—the king did not accept the gift: "For I have no liking; if I took the horse away from you, it would not have so good a master" (3517).

The Muslims still use today these formulas of purely ritual offering of what they possess, formulas that they have had to repress at times when the interlocutor is a foreigner; this at least is what has happened in French Morocco.[13]

The custom of saying "This is your house" (*Esta es su casa*) to one who is visiting it for the first time is Muslim. When the visitor departs, you say to him: "Please know that you have taken possession of your house" (*Ya sabe que ha tomado posesión de su casa*). In Portuguese you say: "Disponha da casa como se fosse sua, é uma casa a sua disposição." In Catalan: "Ha press possessió de casa seva." All this belongs to the Arabic heritage—"al-bayt baytak" (*this house is thy house*)—so that foreigners are astonished when they hear in Lisbon, Madrid, or Barcelona that the house they are visiting for the first time belongs to them.

When you are about to eat or drink in front of someone who for some reason or other is not going to participate in either the eating or drinking, you must say to him, "Would you care for some?" (*¿Usted gusta?*). In Andalusian towns people who are eating will say to a passerby: "Come and eat!" (*¡Venga usted a comer!*), though no one accepts, of course. In Portuguese you say, "You are served" (*Você é servido*), or "Will you keep me company?" (*Quer fazer-me companhia?*). In Galicia you say, "Stay with us" (*Quédese con nosco*); in Catalonia, "Are you pleased [to join me]?" (*Sou servit?*). The proper replies are: "May it profit you" (*Que aproveche*), or

---

[13] As a consequence of the long Spanish domination of Italy, some of these Hispano-Islamic customs were eventually adopted there too, especially in the ancient kingdom of Naples, which was Spanish for more than two centuries. When King Victor Emmanuel visited the newly annexed kingdom of Naples in 1860, it is told that the Neapolitan mothers showed their children to the new sovereign, who could not say enough in praise of the beauty of his little subjects; this caused the mothers, in a transport of enthusiasm, to say, "They are yours, my lord!" The Arabic origin of some of the usages that I mention has already been noted: for "besar manos y pies," see G. Rittwagen, *De filología hispano-arábiga* (1909), p. 57. "Está a su disposición" and "venga a hacer penitencia con nosotros" have been commented on by M. L. Wagner, in *Volkstum und Kultur der Romanen* (1930), III, 115–116.

"May it aid your health" (*De salud sirva*), depending on the region, the social class, and so on. In Portuguese you answer: "May it be good for you" (*Bom proveito*). In the large cities, or among those who have picked up foreign customs, such uses do not persist with the same intensity as among the village folk. In Italy, for reasons previously mentioned, one also finds a reflection of the Spanish epoch in the expression "Will you favor me?" (*Vuol favorire?*), which a man will say, for example, on the train when he sits down to eat in front of other travelers. And thus it happens in the whole Muslim world.

One frequently hears "if God wills" (*si Dios quiere*, or *si quiere Dios*): for example, "Hasta mañana, si Dios quiere," "A ver si quiere Dios que llueva," and the like. At first glance it would seem that such a phrase is the outgrowth of Catholic piety or religiosity, so deeply rooted in Spain; but when we recall the presence of Spanish *ojalá*, from Arabic *wa shā'a-l-lah* ("and may God will that . . ."), we are getting at the true origin of the phrase. It is a matter of another pseudomorphosis (like *almogávar*, *corredor*, "raider"), which appears now with a Christian meaning.[14] One proof of this is the difficulty of translating literally into any other European language the expression "Hasta manaña, si Dios quiere" ("Until tomorrow, if God wills"), which is quite naturally used by numbers of Spaniards. The purely Christian invocation to God may be found, of course, in medieval Latin expressions such as "Deo volente," or English "God willing." We must keep in mind, however, what has been said before concerning the habit of bathing. It seems to me that the Spaniards use, or have used, the name of God more than the other Romanic peoples: the reader who compares the noun "God" (Dios) in the dictionary of the Spanish Academy with the corresponding noun in Littré's French dictionary will understand what I mean. And I believe that in many instances behind the Christian "Dios" vibrates the echo of Allah, present even in the interjection, *¡olé!* (*wa-l-āh*, "for God's sake") with which audiences shout their encouragement to dancers and bullfighters.

Connected with all this is the existence of greetings and formulas

---

[14] This linguistic pseudomorphosis is confirmed by the Morisco account of the peoples of Gog and Magog as given by F. Guillén Robles, *Leyendas de José, hijo de Jacob, y de Alejandro Magno, sacadas de dos manuscritos moriscos de la Biblioteca Nacional de Madrid* (Saragossa, 1888), p. liii. Those cursed people, shut up by Alexander behind walls of iron, "unceasingly lick the wall with their tongues that are coarser than files; at times only a thin layer remains to be punctured; and they leave it till the next day, saying: 'Tomorrow we shall penetrate this dike.' But since they do not add, 'If God wills,' when they start to work on it again at dawn, they find the wall of the same thickness as when they began; only on the day appointed by Allah, when, recognizing their error, they add 'If God wills,' will they break down the iron barrier."

of respect which include the name of God. In the thirteenth century the Mozarabs said, "May God defend, may God preserve." about which Ramón Menéndez Pidal comments: "To be sure, this custom may be more general than the influence of the Mozarabs, for even today we preserve some trace of it in the phrase 'may God protect him' [*que Dios guarde*] in official mentions of the king."[15] It seems as if the great philologist did not find the Muslim influence sufficient to explain both the modern *and* the Mozarabic custom. The question is clarified when it is realized that *Dios guarde* was a general formula of Muslim origin, and that there are relics of this sort of thing in the royal chancery, and in the greeting of Andalusian peasants, "May God protect you, gentlemen" (*Dios guarde a ustedes, caballeros*), which I have heard in the Province of Granada, where the language is very archaic. From the same source comes "God preserve" (*Dios mantenga*), which was already regarded as rustic usage in the sixteenth century, and therefore was so annoying to the punctilious squire in *Lazarillo de Tormes*.[16] Andalusian peasants still say today, "To the peace of God," which sounds, to be sure, like the ecclesiastical "Pax Domini sit vobiscum," but which in reality is a tracing on the Arabic *al-salām 'alayk* ("peace be with thee").

Only in Spain has *besar la mano, besar los pies* ("to kiss the hand," "to kiss the feet"—the latter in the case of ladies) been preserved as an epistolary formula. At the beginning of the twentieth century ladies still took leave of gentlemen by saying, "I kiss your hand"; and the gentlemen answered with "I, your feet, señora." Mariano José de Larra (1807–1837) still knew the tradition of the child's kissing the father's hand: "The father, who was not called *papá* then, went about with his hand more kissed than an ancient relic" (*El casarse pronto y mal*). And it will also be found that among the Muslims a son will end a letter to his father with the formula "after having kissed your respectable hand."[17]

In a letter to Philip II written in 1566, Don Luis de Requesens signs thus: "Your Majesty's creature, vassal, and servant, who kisses Your Majesty's very royal feet and hands" (*De V. M. hechura, vasallo y criado que sus muy reales pies y manos besa*).[18] In the Spanish

---

[15] *Orígenes del español*, p. 460.

[16] See my "Perspectiva de la novela picaresca," in *Revista de la Biblioteca* (Madrid: Archivo y Museo, 1935), II, 138 ff.

[17] "Ba 'da taqbīli aydīkum al-girām." E. W. Lane states: "It is a common custom for a man to kiss the hand of a superior. . . . To testify abject submission, in craving pardon for an offence, or begging any favor of a superior, not infrequently the feet are kissed instead of the hand. The son kisses the hand of the father." (*Manner and Customs of the Modern Egyptians* [London, 1836], I, 252.)

[18] Letter on display in the Museum of the Hispanic Society of New York.

theater of the seventeenth century, a usual formula is "Give me your feet" (*Dadme los pies*), when an inferior wishes to show reverent gratitude to the king: "Dadme, gran señor, los pies." In the *Quixote* (II, 16), Sancho Panza "again and again *kissed* the feet" of Don Diego de Miranda, a statement that has seemed so normal to the commentators that they have let it pass without explanation. Yet earlier, in the *Poem of the Cid* (1140), the hero tries on one occasion to kiss the feet of King Alfonso VI, and the King will not permit it: "Kiss my hands, not my feet."[19] When Blanquerna (in Raymond Lully's book of the same name) takes leave of his father to go and live as an anchorite, "on his knees, he kisses the hands and feet of his father."[20] The fact that the Muslims had acquired this custom through contact with Byzantium or some other civilization is irrelevant here. What is important is to observe that the Spaniard Christians took it from the Spanish Muslims. The formula of vassalage—"I kiss your hand"— is not connected with European feudalism but with Oriental life.[21] How normal it was among the Arabs for one to kiss the hand of another as a sign of submission and homage is seen in the following passage from Ibn Darrāj (d. 1030): "Thou makest me fear the length of the journey; but the journey is worthy of being made only in order to kiss the hand of the 'Āmirī" (in Al-Šaqundī, *Elogio del Andalus*, trans. E. García Gómez, p. 61).[22]

I do not know whether *kissing the bread* that is picked up from the ground or floor is a Christian influence on Islam, or the reverse. In Andalusia when a piece of bread falls to the ground, one picks it up and kisses it, saying that "it is God's bread" (*es pan de Dios*). The Moors do and say the same thing, *'āysh Allāh* ("God's bread"). What is evidently Moorish, though, is the practice of excusing oneself from giving alms to a beggar by saying, "Forgive me for God's sake, God protect you, succor you, help you," and so on, which is

---

[19] "Besad las manos, ca los pies no" (2028). In his *Cantar de Mio Cid*, Ramón Menéndez Pidal cites (pp. 507–508) numerous examples of such usage, but he does not refer to its Moorish origin.

[20] "De agenollons, besà les mans el's peus a son pare" (*Evast e Blanquerna* [Barcelona, 1935], p. 84).

[21] At the beginning of the fifteenth century, Rabbi Arragel says: "Rabbi Abraham [Ben Ezra] says that it was the custom in those days to put out his hand and for the lord to put his on top of it, the one signifying subjection, and the other, seigniory; and he even says that it is still customary to do this in the lands of India" (*Biblia*, trans. Rabbi Arragel, published by the Duke of Alba [1920], I, 133).

[22] Kissing the hand as a sign of respect was also practiced by the Spanish Jews. The *Coplas de Yoçef*, written in Spanish with Hebrew characters, say:
He went out to receive his honored father,
He asked for his hand, then he kissed it.
(*A reçebir saliera a su padre honrado,*
La mano le pidiera, luego la ovo besado.)
(Ed. I. González Llubera, p. 7)

the same as the Arabic "God give you alms, help you, sustain you, make you content."[23]

It is hard not to relate the clamorous, spectacular forms of alms begging—still observable in Spain, especially in the south—to the Christian-Muslim life of the Middle Ages: "God preserve your sight!" the blind man will say; frequently the beggars will refer to the holiness of the particular day, especially on Maundy Thursday and Good Friday and on the patronal festival of the town, and the like. In the *Buscón* (1608) Quevedo speaks of prayers invented to stimulate charity; the beggars allude to the "ill wind" (*aire corruto*) and the "fatal hour" (*hora menguada*) in which they suffered the mischance that deprived them of their health. The Archpriest of Hita (fourteenth century) composed songs "such as those the blind beggars recite" (*de los que dicen los ciegos*, stanza 1514). These beggars formed an important social institution, just as they did in the nineteenth-century Egypt described by Lane, who quotes many beggars' cries similar in form to those heard in Spain: "O Exciter of compassion! O Lord! For the sake of God! O ye charitable! I am seeking from my Lord a cake of bread!"

The *blessings* and *curses*[24] (see p. 263), so numerous and expressive, must also be rooted largely in Oriental life. In Spanish (and also Italian) the lower classes praise a woman's beauty by blessing "the mother who bore thee" (*la madre que te parió*). And here, for comparison, is what Caliph Al-Mansūr (in Bagdad) said to someone: "May the mother who bore you be for God," that is, may she be blessed.[25]

He who proposes to lengthen the list of similar facts will find the task easy, for there is much to be added; but my purpose is only to open up perspectives that will make manifest the form and the peculiar value of Spanish life and civilization. The words and phrases cited above reveal aspects of country and city life, make visible the daily concerns of those who bought and sold, transported merchandise, built dwellings—or, on the other hand, of the aristocrats who possessed elegant objects and clothing for use in the home or in their games and sports. Practical utility and aesthetic pleasure made the tasks of the Moor desirable and necessary; thanks to Muslim activities, the Christian caste could develop its talent for expansion

---

[23] *Allāh yu 'tika* (in less formal Arabic, *Allāh ya 'tik*). See J. Østrup, *Orientalske Høflighedsformer* (Copenhagen, 1927), p. 76. Cf. further Lane, *op. cit.*, II, 23.

[24] The tendency to curse God is more frequent and violent in Spain than in other Occidental countries. The *Jewish Encyclopedia*, s.v. "Cursing," says: "The Orientals have an ineradicable proneness to curse God . . . on the slightest provocation in daily life."

[25] See Gerardo Meloni, *Saggi di Filologia Semitica* (Rome, 1913), p. 145; he refers to Ṭabarī, III, 413, 1.

and sovereignty, could come one day to the political and juridical organization of vast areas of the planet. Without trying to set up historical parallels, which are always inaccurate, we might say that the Christians made use of the Moors and the Jews, incorporating them into the functioning of their life in ways that resemble the Roman grafting of Greek art and learning, or the religious concepts from the Orient, onto their own Latin modality as tillers of the soil who were at the same time warlike and legally minded. Without Greece and the Orient, Rome is as incomprehensible as Spain without the shared common life of its three castes.[26] The imperial institution, to give one striking example, itself came from the Orient.

Insofar as she was a people of universal dimensions, Rome functioned as a Latin-Hellenic-Oriental human ensemble. I therefore find incomprehensible, or childish, the question put (sometimes in all good faith) by those who would like to know *what is purely Spanish* once the bothersome, sticky Moorish and Jewish patches have been peeled off.

In Spain there were both linguistic and spiritual symbioses. Kings and royal personages were buried in Christian fashion but with Moorish vestments, as may be seen in the pantheon of the Convent of the Huelgas Reales in Burgos (which has best been studied by M. Gómez Moreno). John II of Castile ordered the construction of the original monastery of El Paular (in the Sierra de Guadarrama) about 1440; but "we find in the registry of the monastery that the principal architect was a Moor from Segovia called Abderrahman, who must have lived for a long time, for references are made to him over a great span of years."[27]

And just as the Moor Abderrahman is intimately linked to the construction of a Carthusian church, the Moorish girl Moraima becomes the subject of a ballad—that poetic form whose existence expresses the epic soul of Castile, though in the fifteenth century that epic spirit was much tempered by lyricism:

> I was the Muslim Moraima,
> A Moorish girl with a pretty face;
> A Christian came to my door,
> To deceive me, oh wretched girl.
> (*Yo me era mora Moraima,*
> *morilla de un bel catar;*
> *cristiano vino a mi puerta,*
> *cuitada, por me engañar.*)

---

[26] Roman history is far better known than that of Spain, so that the passing comments I have just made are sufficient. It should be remembered that in Rome the apricot was called *armeniacum*; string bean, *faba Judaea* or *Syriaca*; the peach, *persicum*, etc.

[27] Antonio Ponz, *Viaje de España* (1784; I quote from the Aguilar ed. [Madrid, 1947], p. 881).

The souls—and the bodies—of Christian men and Moorish women had been joining together for centuries; and now in the fifteenth century, when the Moor no longer appeared as a serious threat, poetry expresses orally, in the ballad rhythm and melody accessible to everyone, the delights and the dangers of love for both body and soul. Alonso Alvarez de Villasandino (d. *ca.* 1427) fixed forever in beautiful verse one of those blissful dreams for which men have always gambled their hopes of eternity:

> Quien de linda se enamora,
> atender deve perdón
> en caso que sea mora. ...
> Linda rosa muy suave
> vi plantada en un vergel,
> puesta so secreta llave
> de la linia de Ismael. ...
> Mahomad el atrevido
> ordenó que fuese tal,
> de aseo noble, complido,
> albos pechos de cristal:
> de alabasto muy broñido
> debíe ser con grant razón
> lo que cubre su alcandora. ...
> Por aver tal gasajado
> yo pornía en condición
> la mi alma pecadora.[28]

In other words, the poet says that he would risk his sinful soul for the perfect body of a certain Moorish woman, "a most delicate rose planted in a secluded garden." Mohammed, daringly, bestowed all graces on her, graces barely concealed under her alcandora. The Christian who loves such a beauty deserves to be pardoned.

In the fifteenth century, which saw the beginnings of the great stream of Castilian lyric poetry, there appear many anonymous songs with Morisco themes, some of which may well have been composed by Moriscos; many of them had so forgotten their own language that in 1462 the chief *alfaquí* ("theologian") of Segovia had to issue a Castilian version of the *Suma de los principales mandamientos* ("Summation of the Principal Commandments"), of koranic law.[29] In the brief song reproduced below, apparent naïveté of form is combined with much premeditated art. The ternary rhythm—of going, not finding, returning—leads us gradually from the high, clear note of deep melancholy: from "tan garridas" ("so graceful") to "las colores perdidas" ("their bright color lost"). The three delightful Moorish girls, each with a name like a tinkling bell—Aisa, Fátima,

---

[28] See *Poesía española (Edad Media)*, ed. Dámaso Alonso (Buenos Aires: Editorial Losada, 1942), pp. 175–176.
[29] See *Memorial Histórico Español* (1853), V.

Marién—mingle together in the final chord of their common misfortune. All their world had been summed up in a few olives, and the olives are no longer there but have disappeared with the bright colors of their blooming cheeks.

> Tres morillas me enamoran
> en Jaén:
> Axa y Fátima y Marién.
> Tres morillas tan garridas
> iban a coger olivas,
> y hallábanlas cogidas
> en Jaén:
> Axa y Fátima y Marién.
> y hallábanlas cogidas,
> y tornaban desmaídas,
> y las colores perdidas,
> en Jaén:
> Axa y Fátima y Marién.

These and many other things like them make up the history that can neither be narrated or documented; they compensate for all the defects in what was, for all that which could not be. But the "feeling" itself no one can take from us, because it is ours and goes with us always, and is greater than all those other things, so grand and powerful, which so many times leave us in desolate solitude.

During the reign of Henry IV (1454–1474) there were Moriscos and Jews at the court, and some persons connected their presence there with the unbelief of certain courtiers. A group of prelates and wealthy men directed an insolent protest to the King: "It is very notorious that in your court there are persons, in your palace and near your person, who are infidels, enemies of our Holy Catholic Faith; and others who, although Christian in name, are very suspect in their faith, especially in that *they believe and say and affirm that there is no other world, but only being born and dying like animals.*"[30]

A Czech traveler, the Baron of Rosmithal, visited Castile toward the middle of the fifteenth century, and recorded in his diary certain curious notes on the life he observed. Morisco customs had infiltrated private life; or rather, these customs had been Spanish for centuries, but in the fifteenth century people wrote about the matter, because

---

[30] See A. Paz y Melia, *El cronista Alonso de Palencia*, p. 61. I do not know what the basis was for the accusation, which alludes to both Moriscos and converted Jews; it is, however, possible that in the Jewish camp there were signs of the rationalism that later appeared among the Jews of the emigration. The beginning of Spinoza's philosophical reflections was to be found in (or was prompted by) certain Amsterdam marranos, among them Uriel da Costa and especially Juan de Prado (I. S. Révah, *Spinoza et Juan de Prado* [Paris: Mouton and Co., 1959], p. 53). The *Celestina*—which I cannot discuss at this juncture—provides an example of this phenomenon.

that was the time when writers were beginning to be interested in what was going on around them, to be conscious of themselves as human beings in a vital situation, in a given time and space. Let us then have a look at the Baron's diary: "There now resides in Burgos a powerful count, who took my lord and his company to his palace," as one of the Baron's secretaries writes; "there also came beautiful damsels and ladies richly adorned in the Morisco fashion, who, in *their whole appearance and in their eating and drinking followed that fashion.* Some of them danced very lovely dances in the Morisco style, and all were dark, with black eyes. They ate and drank very little, they greeted my lord gaily, and they were very friendly with the Germans."[31]

If this happened in Burgos, where there had been no Moors since the tenth century, one can imagine how in vogue Morisco fashion must have been in zones more recently reconquered. It is obvious, for that matter, that in the first half of the fifteenth century there was an increase of wealth in Castile; and the luxury in dress and customs promoted Morisco practices, which, for more than five hundred years, had been representing an ideal of wealth and distinction. Henry IV's favorite, Miguel Lucas de Iranzo, rode horseback "a la *jineta*" (what would in America, oddly enough, be called English style, that is, with the leg from hip to knee horizontal and from knee to foot vertical) "with a Morisco *aljuba* [jubbah, a long garment with short, close-fitting sleeves] of multicolored silk."[32]

But I do not claim to be tracing out a picture of private life in the fifteenth century. I have wished only to make the picture complete enough to show that the Muslim customs were not a fad, something superimposed on Christian life, accepted as an elegant concession that the conquerors made to the conquered. This type of concession explains the favor enjoyed by the Spanish colonial style in architecture and other forms of civilization in the North American West. But it is not what happened in Spain, where Muslim life continued to be an active and felt presence during the sixteenth and seventeenth centuries; witness the already mentioned, important example of the leaden tablets from the Sacro Monte in Granada.

---

[31] Edition published in *Libros de antaño*, VIII, 162.

[32] *Memorial histórico español*, VIII, 262. *Jineta* is a style of riding taken from the Moors, with short stirrups and drawn-up legs; the word is Arabic, just as is *jinete* ("horseman"); see A. Steiger, *Fonética del hispano-árabe*, p. 146. The African tribe of the Zanata provided the Moorish kings with their best *jinetes*, a word that imposed itself on Castilian, Portuguese, and Catalan, thanks to the fact that *caballero*, originally "horseman," came to mean "a member of the noble class." French resolved the problem with *cavalier* doubling *chevalier*, but Spanish was confronted with the vital fact that those who rode most and best were the Moorish horsemen or *jinetes*, and the Spaniards continued to use the word as their own. *Aljuba* is also Arabic and the origin of Spanish *jubón* ("doublet").

Nor is it my purpose to deal at length with Morisco subjects in literature but only to point out the meaning of their presence. In addition, this problem formed the basis of a recent study which is both clear and comprehensive.[33] I shall speak with equal brevity about reminiscences of Islamic art in that created by the Christian caste. For my purpose it may suffice to refer to the book by O. F. L. Hagen, *Patterns and Principles of Spanish Art* (University of Wisconsin Studies, 1936), which says (p. 34):

As far as Spanish ornamentation can be reduced to abstract linear motives and color patterns, its fundamental scheme is best recognized in walls adorned with colored tiles, so-called *azulejos*. The habit of sealing the walls of houses or courtyards with glazed tiles originated in ancient Mesopotamia. . . . The age-old Oriental habit was bequeathed from the Sumerians to the Assyrians, thence to the Persians and the Moslems who carried it to Spain. Here we are at the roots of Spanish decorative imagination. Without the Oriental tradition there would not be any glazed tiles in Spain and without them, I dare say, neither the particular character of Spanish ornamentation nor the particular color-taste would have come to what it is.

I am not competent to measure the extent to which Professor Hagen's idea may be pushed; he himself sees Oriental influence even in "the surface-pattern of a Spanish painting—no matter whether this be a Primitive, an El Greco, or a Velázquez."

The Impact of Islamic Religion

In no Catholic country does religion displace a greater social volume than in Spain and in the Hispano-Portuguese nations; and the truth is that religious belief has never been replaced by anything that is equivalent to it in extension and force. This is not to say that the majority of Hispanic people think that they must live according to Christian norms, or that didactic and literary expressions are affected now by religion as they were in 1700. The domes of transcendence under which everyone felt that he had his place and was protected have disappeared, and with this transcendence has also been lost the pure prestige of the values incarnate in it. But in spite of all this, with all this, the religion of the Spaniard, the Portuguese, and the Ibero-American is something that is ever present, as a permanent and infrangible reality, although it may become noticeable and although we may realize the tremendous dimensions of its existence only when someone tries to suppress it. Indeed, the Hispanic people in their great majority are convinced that the Hispanic Church no longer incarnates values comparable to those reflected in the artistic

---

[33] María Soledad Carrasco Urgoiti, *El moro de Granada en la literatura* (Madrid, 1956).

creations of two centuries ago. But the proof that religion is there, whatever its form, is that every effort to combat or silence it unleashes catastrophe. Mexicans, Spaniards, and other Hispanic peoples have written this chapter of their history with torrents of blood. The Hispano-Lusitanian people still live in a nonrational world, without earthly autonomy, without a foundation in objectives *originally created* by Hispanic man. And this must be recognized, without acrimony and without melancholy, today more than ever.

Some of the most important creations of Spanish civilization during the sixteenth and seventeenth centuries, and even during the eighteenth, are nothing but aspects of the singular religiosity of this people. The most visible part of this creation consists in extremely beautiful churches and religious works of art in Spain and in what was once her Empire, enough by themselves to demonstrate the worth of any culture. In addition, many of the universal figures of Spanish letters were friars, nuns, and clerics: Fernando de Herrera, St. John of Avila (whose works inspired the seventeenth-century Jansenist, Antoine Arnauld), Juan de la Cruz (St. John of the Cross), Teresa de Jesús, Luis de Granada, Luis de León, Francisco de Vitoria, Francisco Suárez, Juan de Mariana, Lope de Vega, Calderón de la Barca, Tirso de Molina, Gracián, Sor Juana Inés de la Cruz, Feijoo, and others. Hispanic history is essentially the history of a belief and of a religious sensibility, and, at the same time, of the grandeur, the misery, and the paralysis provoked by them.

The members of the Christian caste lived their religion with all its consequences, knowing at every moment what they were risking in such a gamble with destiny, and playing this game with a greater seriousness than some of the Roman popes showed at times. Some popes were willing to go to war to defend their temporal interests, but they did not ruin or depopulate their states by fighting against heretics and infidels, as Spain did. For many of the popes, religion was a worldly and political business, an intelligent bureaucracy, a subtle dogmatism without warmth of heart, and a marvelous "secularism"—and these things are not said here in a tone of criticism and contempt, which are entirely absent from my motives.[34] Rome fought

---

[34] When I take intelligence and the cult of beauty as bases of Italian religious life, I use these terms without any derogatory accent whatsoever. I use them to make a simple affirmation. Precisely because such was her nature, Italy was able to humanize the coarse Europe of the sixteenth century, which, without Italy, would have preserved its medieval tone. Neither the intellectualist skepticism of Jean de Meun nor the lyricism of Provence (dear to exquisite and solitary souls) had the requisite strength to displace the axis of the "vital situation" of the so-called Middle Ages. Italy manufactured the serum that made the European mind change its course completely: she did this by humanizing, "secularizing," the divine without breaking away from it. Pontifical Rome found the common denominator between Greek man and modern man, bridged the gap between the until then "illegal" instincts and faith, and left the "heretics"

at Lepanto (1571) under the leadership of a Spanish prince, Don Juan of Austria. But in 1611 the Duke of Osuna, Spanish viceroy in Sicily, heaped reproaches upon the pope, whose galleys would come to load silk at Messina but would refuse to fight the Turk at the same time that the Spanish fleet was rushing into battle (see my *Santa Teresa*, pp. 245-246). That man of genius, Machiavelli, had already written that "those people who are closest to the Roman Church, which is the head of our religion, have the least religion" (*Discourses on the First Ten Books of Titus Livius*, I, 12). Roman religion was not inalterably caste-bound.

The Reformation deflected religious interest toward the conduct and social efficacy of man; but with this, the way was eventually closed to the affective soliloquy of the soul with God. The religion of the Reformation ended up by being converted into a theology applied to practical life with a view to restraining any attitude of the individual which tended to break his interconnections with society. France is without doubt a Catholic country, although she has caused her Catholicism to infiltrate itself with whatever substance it has found useful in the rationalism of its enemies; thus it was possible for enlightened Catholicism to emerge in the "Institut Catholique" of Paris, alongside the traditional Catholicism of the rural masses. From the end of the sixteenth century, French Catholicism placed itself at the service of the national state that its kings personified,[35]

---

with the illusion that they were the ones who were changing the course of history. But without the secular "life" of Catholic Italy in the fifteenth century, the heresies (actually as old as Christianity itself) would have been reduced to sterile efforts—rather like the anarchism of the nineteenth century—with many adherents, with many martyrs, but without effective transcendence. Rome offered Luther both reasons to deny her and, in equal measure, possibilities to affirm the purely human value of man.

[35] The splendid funeral oration of St. Francis of Sales in honor of the Duc de Mercoeur (1602) is the discourse of a politician and courtier who is more concerned with human interests than with the divine at any cost, who no longer believes that earthly values are to be scorned and forgotten as the meanest dust: "Je connois bien que mon office n'est pas maintenant (et ju vous supplie, *Messieurs*, de ne la pas desirer de moi), de vous representer les raysons que nous avons eu de regretter et plaindre. . . . Soit donq que je jette les yeux sur son bien pour nous consoler ou sur notre mal pour nous affliger, je ne puys eschapper de l'abisme de ses vertues infinies, dont la grandeur et l'esclat est insupportable a la foiblesse de mes yeux. ... En ceste occasion, que j'estime aussi digne d'une grande eloquence qu'aucune autre qui se soit presente e siècle; en ceste assemblee, qui est presque toute la fleur de ce grand royaume; [he is preaching in Notre Dame, to the Court of France] et en ce lieu, auquel *mille beaux esprits* eussent ambitieusement recherché de faire paroistre tout leur art et leur science de bien dire, etc." (*Oeuvres de Saint François de Sales* [Annecy], VII, 401-402.) The whole sermon is a canticle to the glory of the deceased nobleman as the hero of France's imperial cause. How different from another funeral oration, one delivered on the death of Philip II (1598), to which I refer elsewhere and in which the preacher presents the king as one put to death for the crime of being mortal and a sinner, and points to the catafalque as if it were a symbolical scaffold.

and on the margin of that Catholicism there was emerging more and more a rationalized world, eccentric to religion. By the sixteenth century, cultivated France regarded the religious theater as an intolerable anachronism, and it was finally suppressed by the Parliament in 1584. In Spain the same variety of spectacle lasted until 1765, when the foreign intellectualist pressure of the period forced a reaction against the traditional tendencies.

Spanish religion, we may then conclude, is based on a Catholicism very different from that of Rome and France—not to mention the Catholicism of the United States. It is a form of belief characteristic of Spain, intelligible only within the peculiar *castiza* structure of her history. Spanish religion—like her language, her institutions, her very limited capacity for objective science, her prodigality of expressiveness, and her integral personalism—must be referred to the nine hundred years of Christian-Islamic-Jewish interaction. The Hispanic theocracy, the impossibility of organizing Spain or Hispanic America as a purely civil state, founded on objective interests and not on the magical power of individuals, are an expression of the functioning, disposition, and limitations of Spain's vital dwelling place.

As a social institution, the Spanish Church is something that nobody and nothing have succeeded in suppressing or replacing. This failure is, after all, probably quite normal: other religions likewise continue to exist in other countries, and there is no reason to regret it. But the peculiar thing about Spain is not this, but rather that the Church continues to be a power there set up against the State, in a form that is not known to either France or Italy, the other great Catholic countries.[36] As a nation included in the circle of Occidental culture, Spain has possessed a state; this state, however, has existed

---

[36] The extranational character that the Spanish Church presented at the beginning of this century is observable in a criticism of the Library of the Cathedral of Toledo made in purely scholarly work by an author who subsequently figured in what might be termed the far-right wing of Spanish politics: "At the present time (and it is to the shame of the Chapter of the Cathedral of Toledo and of Spanish ecclesiastical culture that I say so), it is all but impossible to get into the aforementioned Chapter Library, which, acting like a dog in the manger, neither does any work itself nor allows anyone else to do any there. . . . Thanks to the beneficial orders of the revolutionary government of 1868, Sr. Octavio de Toledo went to that place and in a few days, amidst grave dangers, compiled that part of the *Catalogue* that has recently been published by the *Revista de Archivos*. It is certain that among valuable codices that belong to that Library (whose contents ought to be moved, *legally* or *illegally*, in the interests of culture, to the Biblioteca Nacional in Madrid) there are many that include works of Toledan translators" (A. Bonilla y San Martin, *Historia de la filosofía española* [1908], p. 322). I have omitted part of Sr. Bonilla's violent attack, which, as is evident, proposed that the state, although it might not have the right to do so, should take possession of a valuable property of the Church— because the Church did not know how important the property was and was incapable of administering it. This is one of the innumerable examples of what I call "reciprocal illegality" in the relations between Church and State, of which the tragic denouement was the Civil War of 1936.

even in recent times as a co-power alongside the Church, which still preserves the memory of the time when Spain was governed inquisitorially. The efforts to dispense with ecclesiastical power have had only a passing and superficial effect. Deprived of her properties in 1836, the Church succeeded, through the religious orders, in acquiring again a considerable economic power and in exercising a very broad influence through her educational centers. It is useless to resort to explanations of an external kind to account for a fact of such scope. What happens in reality is that the masses continue to find inspiration in a static and immutable belief, and not in objective realities governed by the play of human actions and interests. Spanish capitalists very often preferred to keep their money in bank accounts or to invest it in government bonds instead of risking it in industrial enterprises. The great industries, the richest mines, and many railroads belonged to foreign concerns. In 1935 there were 17,000 foreign technicians in Spain. There has prevailed in Spain a quietist apathy, faith rather than the cognitive attack on reality. Earlier (p. 277) I cited the expression of Islamic origin "if God wills" (*si Dios quiere*), to which should be added at this point, "it is the will of God," "it was the will of God" (*está de Dios, estaba de Dios*), rooted in the bowels of the people, and used at every turn.[37]

Over against the quietist apathy—old and deeply rooted—of many powerful people there rose up the Messianic hope of the mass of the people, founded on a belief opposite in sign but analogous in root. Among the popular beliefs, anarchism, as great an enemy of Occidental legality as certain very Hispanic fanatics are in other ways, has attracted many followers. Several old forms of anarchism, under the disguise of foreign ideologies, have recently rent the soul of Spain in the atrocious conflict that went on from 1936 to 1939. The Spaniard does not think that he is a member of the national collectivity, or that the progress and destiny of this collectivity depend on the actions of the people in concert and as individuals; he waits for things to happen, or for some leader with thaumaturgic gifts to rise up. The people who fought against fascism thought, and in good faith in many instances, that they were offering their lives for a universal cause, and that the sacrifice of the poor Spanish masses would bring about a change in the course of history. This is not new: at the

---

[37] A folksong goes:

> You'd live without troubles?
> Let the ball roll;
> Whatever God wills
> Will fall into your hands.
> (*¿Quieres vivir sin afanes?*
> *Deja la bola rodar;*
> *que lo que fuere de Dios,*
> *a las manos se vendrá.*)
> (F. Rodríguez Marín, *Cantos populares*, IV, 143)

end of the fifteenth century the Spanish masses believed that Ferdinand and Isabella had been sent by God to establish happiness on the earth and to put an end to the tyranny of all the powerful. A few Renaissance thinkers *wrote* Utopias, but the Spaniards *have* shed their blood for such dreams on more than one occasion, thus erasing the boundary between the possible and the impossible, the real and the imagined. (This central theme of Spanish history is treated at length in chapter ix.)

It will be said that something similar has happened in every human society; but the chief differences between the Spaniards and the other Western peoples is that the history of the latter is made up not only of persons who fire with their ideals and disenchant with their failures (Cromwell, Napoleon, etc.), but also of extrapersonal activities (economics, original political concepts, scientific and industrial changes, etc.). Phenomena of this kind are scarce in Hispanic history, and when they have been present—always as an importation from the outside, not as an innovation emergent from within—their influence has been slight: in Spain the "personal element" contrasts strikingly with any idea or plan founded solely on "reasonableness" and the healthy desire to produce things useful and efficacious for everyone.

History thus turns into an alternating process of illusions and disenchantments, the products of faith or disillusion with reference to the leaders of the nation, and inspired by Messianic hope or fears of the "Antichrist," by the exaltation of an idol or of the vituperation of the guilty. From the depths of the Middle Ages till the nineteenth century, literature continued to occupy itself with Roderic, the last king of the Goths, and with the traitor Julian, who opened the gates of Spain to Islam to avenge the outrage of his daughter by the lustful king. Both were held guilty of the ruination of Spain, and the legend of the wicked king was expanded with exquisite stories of revenge. Some centuries later another "personal" explanation of history's course was forged. In 1497 the crown prince Don Juan—only male child of Ferdinand and Isabella—died, and to this misfortune has been attributed the tortuous course of subsequent history, a course for which, it is said, the House of Austria is responsible. In another sense, an example of transcendent personalism can be found in the enthusiasm of the Spanish people for King Ferdinand VII, who (though he had congratulated Napoleon on his victories over the Spaniards) was called nothing less than "the longed for"—out of pure pleasure in Messiah-seeking, since he was the most villainous and perverse monarch conceivable. Yet in spite of this, that monstrous figure served as an incentive for the Spanish masses to throw out the armies of Napoleon (1808–1814). And again, the

cultural splendor of Spain during the eighteenth century is attributed
to Charles III, whose only merit was that he did not disturb the constructive work of a group of aristocrats won over to the cause of
intellectualism.

In what other Catholic country is there anything like the processions in Seville during Holy Week? The images vie with one another
in luxury and splendor, and the rival confraternities in charge of the
different ones carry on psychological and sentimental warfare with
each other. Among those who carry the images in such spectacular
and dramatic processions there are men of the people who, as people,
may very well be anarchists (indeed, sometimes they are) who dream
of razing the social structure and with it the Church; but they are
capable of killing each other in defense of the honor and supremacy
of "their" image, the sculptured figure (such as the "Jesús del Gran
Poder," the "Virgen de la Macarena," etc.) of which they are the
bearers. It is customary to explain such behavior frivolously by referring to the "superstition" of the people, an explanation that clarifies nothing, for there is as much superstition in England (witness
the belief in ghosts), in southern Italy, and in Poland as there is in
Spain, yet nothing comparable takes place in those countries. A person is superstitious when he is motivated by the harm or good that
may come to him through unknowable and indomitable forces, while
the man who helps to carry a religious image in Seville becomes one
with his "superstition," converting it into the substance of his own
existence and suffering trials and tribulations for it. I do not think,
needless to say, that many of the "Catholics" who participate in the
processions in Seville believe in, and approve of, everything that the
Church commands to be believed—among other reasons, because
they do not even know what these things are. What is important
is that the person includes himself in a halo of transcendence, in
something that is "his" and at the same time beyond him—a little
like a parachutist forever suspended in the air. He lives trusting in
something that is located outside him and that operates outside what
he himself does. He lives off what the earth, like a generous "alma
mater," gives him. When her fruits are not easily produced, he has
recourse to foreign capital and technology. Therefore, in the Hispanic countries, the great industries, the mines, and the oil wells
usually require the aid of foreign technicians. Or the individual may
live off the magical munificence of the State without bothering very
much about the efficacy of the functions that are performed by it.
He floats on the belief in the providential care of the State, just
as he does on the previously mentioned religious belief. In either
case he is shut up within himself, in his faith and hope—which has
little to do with what popular, superficial thinkers have called indi-

vidualism.[38] Shut up in himself, with his eyes fixed on each of these transcendent objects (Church and State), Hispanic man lives by expressing his inner life, presenting and acting out his existence in gestures, in words, in attitudes, as if he were the stage of his own life; sometimes these representations result in prodigious works of art or in beautiful and unselfish moral acts. The part of the Spaniard's life which is not an expression of his inner life or an acting out of his existence—I repeat—is or has been imported from other peoples, which is not to say that Spaniards cannot create original science on the basis of what is imported, but the usual, the fundamental, is the other.

A way of life with this kind of structure is bound to defend its special form of religious transcendence with tooth and nail, and is bound to oppose every effort to create political forms based on "neutral" reasons that tend to make the life of all Spaniards possible and mutually shared. This is why the Hispanic states are shot through with inefficiency and immorality, and it has been impossible for them to be ruled by civil and religious standards that are objectified and the same for everyone. The Hispanic religion is a personalized belief, not a guide for conduct; but the Hispanic man is capable of killing and being killed in the defense of "his" religion, of that world of his in which reign his will, his dream, and his caprice. He would feel lost in a world governed by norms that he thought not subject to his will. To keep such a world from eventuating, he can commit the most horrendous crimes and atrocities, incompatible with the most elemental Christianity. Seen in this light, the Civil War (1936–1939) was a struggle between the old religiosity of the "caste," petrified by the centuries, and an effort toward a new religiosity, toward the creation of another transcendent orbit, vague and misty, in which the Spanish "I want to" (*me da la gana*) was to be combined with a utopian project for universal happiness. The other ideologies—fascism, communism—are systems imported with the purpose of filling the vital vacuum created by the dominance—in the final analysis, Semitic—of belief. In 1931, when the Spaniards saw themselves deprived of the protective cover of the monarchy, no group or party had sufficient strength and skill to channel public life in such a way as to make possible a shared common life within the country or harmonious relations with democratic nations. The masses were divided, and in general they attempted to direct matters in a confused fashion rather than to be guided. Further, the Republic was attacked by those who resisted the acceptance of any economic or religious change. For their part, the popular masses, whether or not they were organized into parties, were in reality anarchists and

---

[38] I discuss the special form of Spanish individualism—in my opinion a pseudoindividualism—in chapter ix.

interested only in sudden and Messianic changes. Those who thought or felt in other ways were few in number and lacked the means to make themselves obeyed. In the end the situation began to resemble a bullring where the spectators, and not the *toreros*, were attempting to fight the bull. And what I call anarchism was as much of the right as of the left. With all this a power vacuum was produced which could not, of course, be filled by any system of democratic life brought in from the outside. Democracy has never been exportable, for it rests upon habits of ordered and conjoint behavior, on mutual concessions and enterprising tasks carried out in the interests of all, and, finally, on reciprocal tolerance. Complete democracy exists nowhere: it is an idea that must be pursued constantly with a view toward approaching it as closely as possible. Violent regimes, on the other hand, fill all the points within the social space: they are omnipresent. And, above all, they possess formulas and mechanisms that are easily exportable, and which either fall like a yoke upon a nation or are easily seized upon by peoples in a state of political vacuity, lacking governmental forms that are visible nationally and internationally.[39]

I have alluded to certain facts of political history because of their distant but unequivocal connection with the ways in which the existence of the Spaniards was constituted. Let us remember that the people who fought the Muslims gave themselves, as their ethnic designation, the title of "Christians" (p. 11). The compenetration with the Moors in the centuries following the conquest is reflected in the multiple phenomena with which the reader is already familiar and in others he will soon see. All this does not mean, obviously, that the Spaniards were, or lived, in every respect like the Moors; but that in order to stand out clearly against them, the Spaniards accented, brought into the foreground, that which most characterized them *as not Moorish*—to wit, their religion. All that conglomerate of Arabs, Berbers, renegades, slaves, and so forth was unified in one common faith; in like fashion, the tie that closely bound together Leonese, Castilians, and Aragonese was their Christianity. Politically divided, often fighting among themselves, religion made them one, "nationalized" them spiritually. There still exist as a popular spectacle (in Mallorca and other places) fights among "Moors and *Christians*," not among "Moors and *Spaniards*."

The paradigm of the collective framework was neither Visigothic, nor French, nor English, all systems in which the political dimension predominated over the religious. In Spain the basis of the nation was the circumstance of having been born within one of the three

---

[39] This topic is further discussed in chapter ix.

castes of believers; therefore, one still says in Spanish things like "to be blind *by nation*" (ser ciego *de nación*), which is to say, "from birth." Don Fernando de Válor was chosen king of the rebellious Moriscos of the Alpujarra because he was the "king of his nation," according to Hurtado de Mendoza in his *Guerra de Granada*; that war, he also says, was one of "Spaniards against Spaniards" (*Biblioteca de Autores Españoles*, XXI, 73, 74). The "nation" was determined by belief, while in France *nation* referred to the land in which one had been born: the *quatre nations* in the old University of Paris designated the students from France, Picardy, Normandy, and Germany. In the inquisitorial proceedings against the Portuguese canon and convert António Homem, who had reverted to Jewish practices, it is said that he often went around "in the company of persons of his *nation*," in other words, with Jews,[40] and the meaning is the same as saying that he frequented the company of people "of his *caste*." When Lorenzo Escudero, a Sevillan, tried to become a Jew in Amsterdam in 1658, the rabbis said that they did not know he was "of the *caste* of the Jews."[41] There were, then, "nations" within the Spanish kingdoms before these kingdoms formed one "nation" in the geographical or political sense. And I must insist—because it is a central matter for those who try to understand the Spaniards—that the political *function* of religion among the Spaniards is a tracing, a copy, of the function that Mohammedanism and Mosaism performed for the Moors and the Jews; it is a Semitic tracing in the same way that *hijosdalgo* (the *hijos de buenos*) and the name of the "*grandes*" of Spain are. The half political, half sacred nature of the royal institution in the time of Philip II manifests clearly that the spirit of the caliphate had slipped into it, much as the supernatural halo of the Persian emperors and the Pharaohs was reflected in the divine character of the Roman emperors ("numen imperatorum"). Historians speak abstractly about divine-right monarchy, but there was nothing abstract about the feeling of the people as expressed in the *Romancero*:

> The great Philip II,
> exalted King of Spain,
> to whom over most of the world
> *God has given dominion* ...
> and so our invincible King
> wishes to be ever occupied
> in spreading over all the world
> the Holy Evangel ... [42]

---

[40] See António Baião, *Episódios dramáticos da Inquisição portuguesa* (1919), I, 108.

[41] See I. S. Révah, *Spinoza et Juan de Prado* (1959), p. 62.

[42] *Biblioteca de Autores Españoles*, XVI, 189.

Here also is the explanation of the strange text of the epitaph for the Catholic Sovereigns (see above, p. 205), in which no reference at all is made to the great political labor of those monarchs; it is only said that they crushed the Moors and the Jews, the two castes who by that time were the object of hatred and scorn. The Christian caste had surpassed the other two after the astounding Spanish accomplishments in the Old and New Worlds; but in the epitaph those accomplishments are passed over in silence, even though they are latent as the invisible foundation upon which rises, filled with prestige and defiance, the monumentality of the victorious caste.

Other aspects of the impact of Islamic life upon that of the Christians—which up to now have been virtually ignored—are revealed in the course of this work. The Christians conquered—and unconsciously allowed themselves to be conquered. The Muslims are, after all, as Messianic as the Jews, though in different ways. Despite the fact that according to Muslim orthodoxy Mohammed was the last prophet, and inspired by God, the Muslim did not for that reason stop, nor has he yet stopped, nourishing his spiritual quietism with the hopeful longing for a Messiah-Mahdi.[43] But together with the attitude of "flight from the world" maintained by those who put all their hopes in God and not in the perishable things surrounding us, Islam also values highly whatever exists, beginning with man himself, because it is God's creation. *Calila e Dimna* thus says in the Spanish version (see Solalinde [1917], p. 17) that the human person is "the noblest creature and the best that may exist in this world." This route leads to a reverence for man because of what God has put into him, which is very different from the value conferred on the human being by the rationalists because man was capable of penetrating with his intelligence into the essence of the universe, an essence kept secret by God—for six thousand years, as Kepler said. And while I do not say that the two intensely Spanish traits of expecting everything from divine grace merely because the individual feels himself to be a "son of God," and the supreme value put upon one's self are exclusively Oriental in their motivation, I do believe that the long centuries of contact with the Orient provided a medium most propitious to their becoming dominant characteristics. Messianism and esteem for the self may well be universal; but when we find those modalities of conduct much accented and not sufficiently opposed by others that might neutralize them, then it is permissible to attribute to those vital situations a very special character.

My opinions are based on the evidence that the Spaniards did not

---

[43] See E. Bloch, *Le messianism edans l'hétérodoxie musulmane* (Paris, 1903).

live their religious beliefs as the Italians, the French, the English, the Germans, and the Scandinavians did; little historical knowledge is required to perceive the differences. Outside Spain there was an "other world" (*más allá*) and also a "this world" (*más acá*). The stimulus for the Italian life structure has been essentially this-worldly —commerce, luxury, technology, art, inquiring thought, scant enthusiasm for war, sensuality, absence of national spirit and, consequently, of epic poetry, and so on; religion was not a stimulus of major importance in building the structure of the history of Italy, which was often a theater of war for foreigners covetous of the wealth of her soil and her industry as well as of the fine fruits of her intelligence and art. France's structure grew out of the centripetal force of the capital city of her kings, whose dynasty (injected with divine powers, as we shall presently see) served as the country's spinal column. England, Germany, and the other nations of western Europe, in one way or another, built their existence on earthly foundations; but Spain rests on "divine" foundations, as we have heard Don Alonso de Cartagena put it so well (p. 151) when he distinguished the motives behind Castilian wars from those "other interests" that impelled the English to fight. The history of Spain is in essence holy or *divine*, and only by accepting this evidence without reservation will we attain to an understanding of that history. From the ninth century to the seventeenth, the axis of Hispano-Christian life—of what there was in it of the affirmative, the original, and the grandiose—was an ultramundane belief that emerged as a heroic reply to other, hostile beliefs under whose impact the Hispania of the Visigoths finally disappeared.

Belief and Confidence in the Inherent Virtue and Sufficiency of the Person

Secure in our knowledge of the situation of the Christian caste— its political and social dimension, its basing of the person's value on the fact of being Christian—it is to be hoped that we can propose a plausible explanation for the most characteristic forms of Spanish behavior since the sixteenth century. The Spaniard, everyone says, is an "individualist," rebellious against authority, inclined to do what "he pleases" (*le da la gana*),[44] quick to join himself enthusiastically to whatever anarchist doctrines—never invented by him—are current. But the mere psychological analysis or moral judgments (even the high evaluation) of such an obvious phenomenon leaves shadowy the

---

[44] *Gana* expresses the "experiential" (*vivencial*) aspect of the word *voluntad* ("will"), being related to it as *honra* is to *honor*, as *estar*, in many cases, is to *ser*, etc. It seems to me that *vivencial* (for the meaning, see note 13, chap. iv) should be incorporated into the vocabulary of linguistics.

reason for their existence—to wit, the satisfaction and pride in living that way. It is doubtless useful to broaden our observations and express our opinion about how certain aspects of a civilization appear to us; but in the end the decisive element in the historian's task must be the attempt to make evident the historicosocial assumptions and human connections of a given society which may help to render comprehensible those things that are still not understood. To this end an understanding of the phenomenon of belief, of its organization function—that is, of its ability to make people who had before existed in accordance with other sociopolitical dimensions function socially and politically as Christians (intermingled with Moors and Jews)—must doubtless make a large contribution. But first it is desirable to broaden the angle of our vision.

When we compare the "modern" way of life with the existence of the Hispanic peoples, the latter has the appearance of an escarpment against which the seas of European history since the sixteenth century have been dashing with little effect. The curious thing about this situation is that the Hispanic peoples have neither adapted themselves to alien usages nor resigned themselves to a tranquil acceptance of their own peculiarity. They have juxtaposed their perennial techniques and certain foreign ideas and way of life, and at the same time have defended themselves against any attempt at radical foreignization. Spain has been attacked in every possible way since the sixteenth century, and she has always maintained her right to live on the margin of scientific and industrialized Europe with the same tenacity that Don Quixote displayed in protecting his Quixotism against all the priests, barbers, bachelors, and canons of rationality.

The position adopted was to become immutable because the basis upon which the Christian caste had affirmed itself was immutable.[45] For the reasons set forth in note 45, the inhabitants of the Spanish Empire did not unite with one another by means of economic and intellectual interests; they were, rather, like bundles of ascending lines that converged in a belief—in the *caudillo*, in the king, in artistic grandeur and beauty, in God. Neither in Spain nor in Hispanic America did the various regions weave themselves together in a network of mutually complementary tasks. It is therefore quite normal, "historically" speaking, that there should be all kinds of separatism in both Spain and Hispanic America. The regions were united either

---

[45] I shall not repeat in detail here what was fully set forth in my book *De la edad conflictiva: El drama de la honra* (Madrid: Taurus, 1963): any intellectual exercise or technological labor was considered a task characteristic of the Jewish caste and, consequently, dishonorable. Awareness of this attitude makes clear, at last, one of the most confused and debated aspects in the history of all the Hispanic peoples.

by their faith in the crown or by some kind of external force imposed upon them, but never by some common task to be accomplished.

It will be said, however, that the Hispania of today is not like the Hispania of the sixteenth or even the eighteenth century, because now there are trains, telegraph lines, automobiles, deputies, senators, airplanes, vitamins, and so on; but all these things are imported, just like hundreds of things in the seventeenth century which then seemed like innovations: "Spain exports wool, wine, olive oil, gold, and silver, as well as other products *of intrinsic value,* and she takes in coarse Angevin linen, thread, eyeglasses, pins, inkstands, glass beads, jew's harps, flutes, whistles, and dolls, as well as thousands of other foolish things that would be scorned by the most barbarous tribes of Ethiopia."[46] The situation in the preceding centuries had been essentially the same, with the difference that the producers of things had then been inside the country—the Moors and Jews, who were already *being used* by the Cid in the eleventh century. The Christians both then and later lived behind the barricade of their sense of the "intrinsic value" of their land and their persons, and thus the inner posture of the Christian caste turns out to have the same form in the tenth century and in the nineteenth: in the earlier period, adoptions from the Muslims; in the later, European importations. When in 1909 Unamuno uttered his much disputed exclamation "Let the others do the inventing!" he was speaking from the depths of *castiza* history, a history interested in promoting, from a fixed position and a longing for eternity, a series of changes in scenery which did not affect the capacity for altering the course of that history. The simultaneous existence side by side of the authentically permanent and the mutable has quite naturally given rise to the illusion that there have been two Spains. However, we have only to remember that this phenomenon has been going on for a thousand years and we will realize how unfounded such a notion is.

Every important innovation in Spain that has not been based on the intention to broaden the imperious dimension of the self and to express what that self is and feels has always had its origin outside the Christian caste, even though the will toward adoption of such changes has always come from within. The following "things" have been desired and sought (as we shall see later) by the Spaniards: the Cluniac monks in the eleventh century, the Cistercians in the twelfth century, the Jews down to the end of the fifteenth century, the Moors till 1609, Erasmianism in the sixteenth century, literary Italianism in the same period, Italian techniques (in navigation, commerce, and industry) even earlier, French ideas and institutions from the end of the seventeenth century on, the sciences and technology

---

[46] Pedro Fernández de Navarrete, *Conservación de monarquías* (1626), in *Biblioteca de Autores Españoles,* XXV, 533.

of all Europe in the eighteenth and nineteenth centuries, German philosophy in the nineteenth century (Krausism) and the twentieth (historical vitalism, phenomenology, etc.). I consider it an inadmissible abstraction to say that Spain has been a crossroads for the "cultures" of the world, where the natives of the land have met and fused with Phoenicians, Romans, Goths, Moors, and so on. This approach makes for confusion in the concept of culture and, ultimately, for chaotic thinking, because it deprives us of a *subject*, an agent, and an intelligible center to which we may refer this alluvion of events and "influences."

The medieval Christians decided to practice tolerance and establish a code for it, to have military orders, to found schools like the Estudios de Palencia; and at the same time they had little use for many things that they could have had and did not (such as a literature in Latin like that to be found in the rest of Europe, philosophy, etc.). The fact that such decisions were imposed by unavoidable circumstances is no reason for denying the existence of a constant will, any more than we would deny the presence of a skillful captain on a ship being tossed by a storm, or in the doldrums. The decisive moves did not always originate in the same part of the social organism, and a detailed history of Spain would have to make it clear just which individuals and groups started what. The lower classes, not the upper, were behind the expulsion of the Jews, who were protected by the upper classes for centuries against all manner of attack and abuse. In the fifteenth and sixteenth centuries, the New Christians of Jewish origin took one of two opposite directions: either they ascended to the peaks of culture, or they gravitated toward the Inquisition. They are to be found both on the side of enlightenment and with the partisans of obscurantism. This sort of thing is often called a cultural crossing, but it would be better to understand the creation of Hispanic values as the result of the conflict between the opposing castes: within the boundaries of the dominant caste, individuals either shrank into themselves or strove to move outward and breathe another atmosphere.

This constant polarization of the vital activity of Spanish Christians, this tension whose opposing forces draw their energy from the same source, continues to be evident in the eighteenth and nineteenth centuries and among the cultivated citizens as well as among the common people. Thus, in the eighteenth century we have Moratín, the *Caballeritos* of Azcoitia, and, on the other hand, Ramón de la Cruz's "Majos";[47] and in the nineteenth, both the so-called *afrance-*

---

[47] The name popularly given to a small group of aristocrats ("little gentlemen") in the Basque country who sought to promote the Enlightenment in Spain. The Majos signalized the end of the eighteenth century; they were certain people of the "gentry" who dressed as members of the lower class.

sados, that is, the Gallicized, who were the modern spokesmen for the spirit of Sancho the Great of Navarre and Alfonso VI (who had Gallicized the Church in the medieval Christian kingdoms), and the guerrilla fighters in the War of Independence, as hostile to France as was the champion Bernardo del Carpio. It took two bloody civil wars to establish something like a constitutional regime in the nineteenth century. After that, Spain went on importing and imposing on herself alien things and institutions deemed necessary by certain persons who were not satisfied with the life of a nation that did not seem to change with the changing ages but always to live in her own changeless age. Thus there came socialism, communism, and fascism, or the replacement of the traditional faith by the type of free thought which had originated in France at the end of the eighteenth century. What is there about the Spain of today that could be called authentically Hispanic? Probably these things among others: monarchism and syndicalism (to be discussed later) which would organize the country as a conglomerate of human units with no state over them— a structure in which the dream of a stateless self-rule by spontaneous virtue might become real, though physical violence would be used, when necessary, to secure the dominance of that dream (see chapter ix).

So-Called Spanish Individualism

"Experience has shown that obedience to decrees and corrective laws is of short duration in Spain; for every private citizen [*hombre particular*] makes it a point of honor to go against them, deeming it an act of positive nobility to refuse to submit to laws."[48] These are the words of Pedro Fernández de Navarrete, writing at the beginning of the seventeenth century. Writing at the end of the nineteenth, Galdós has one of his characters say: "What the government says belongs to it doesn't really belong to the government but to the nation, that is, to John Private-Citizen ['Juan *Particular*']. And to defraud the government is to give back to John Private-Citizen the stuff that belongs to him."[49]

In these two quotations the word "private" (*particular*) implies the lack of a social dimension or ties. In modern times the Spaniard's way of conducting his life has been called "individualism," but this term is so vague as to be almost meaningless. Everyone is an individual, a human being who in one way or another individualizes his life without ever breaking his ties with the life of other men. What separates and characterizes peoples is not their singular or collective individuality, which is always present. Rather, it is the way each

---

[48] Fernández de Navarrete, *op. cit.*, p. 529.
[49] *Fortunata y Jacinta*, in *Obras completas* (1942), p. 36.

individuality is given a content of values. Cases of extreme individualism abound outside Spain. Take, for example, the repellent but at the same time admirable Oscar Wilde: "I am far more of an individualist than I ever was. Nothing seems to me of the smallest value except what one gets out of oneself. My nature is seeking a fresh mode of self-realization" (*De profundis*). Oscar Wilde aspired to forge his own life and express it in symbols, just as an artist conceives the realization of his work in a particular style of his own. The validity of what the artist creates will depend on whether the value of his creation is meaningful for others. His individualism is thus the cause and condition for obtaining a result that is not individual at all, the social objectivity of his work.

Those who have branded Spain with the mark of individualism have not usually had in mind artistic or creative individualism, and the term is used just as readily to describe the British attitude in favor of free competition, free trade, and the differentiation of the worker's tasks. When it is applied to Spaniards, it is usually with reference to their rebelliousness against any rule, a rebelliousness devoid of any view to establishing a different set of regulations. With a kind of personal separatism they rebel against rules as such. This is evidently what is meant by describing Spaniards as individualists. And if it is, let us say so, and dispel the linguistic error that blurs our vision of reality. Concerning the Spanish, I would rather speak of a certain withdrawal and small interest in the world outside, qualities to be discerned in the Hispanians' limited involvement in the exploration of other peoples' cultures, even when the peoples are those formerly ruled by Spain and Portugal. If I had to locate, as it were, that which is most characteristic of Hispanic life, I would put it as a median between a kind of withdrawn inertia and the willful outburst through which the person reveals what there is—be it something insignificant or something of value—in the depths of his soul, as if he were his own theater. Visible examples of this enormous contrast are the peasant and the conquistador; the insurrections and convulsions of the blind mass of the people, destroying everything; apathy toward the transformation of natural resources into wealth, and the use of public wealth as if it were private; archaic and static ways of living, and the hasty adoption of modern devices produced outside Spain. The electric light, the typewriter, and the fountain pen were popularized in Spain more quickly than in France. On the plane of the highest human values we find a manifestation of this sharp contrast in the poetic inwardness of St. John of the Cross or of the quietist Miguel de Molinos, and the series of daring assaults on external reality to be found in Quevedo, Góngora, or Goya.

Unamuno illustrates the problem of so-called Spanish individualism more than with his thought, in this bare analysis of himself:

"Of all tyrannies, the one most hateful to me is the tyranny of ideas. . . . [On the other hand,] I never protest when someone declares himself superior to me. If he succeeds, I thank him, for he has proved himself my superior, and he has actually come to help me in my inferiority" (*La ideocracia: Más sobre la crisis del patriotismo* in his *Ensayos*). Spaniards feel themselves, then, to be like so many radii whose very existence depends on a center in the form of another person. When these radii are numerous, the circle of political dictatorship emerges—sometimes as a kind of patriarchy—a political form highly expressive of the Hispano-Portuguese life structure, and within which little margin is left for the individuality of citizens, just as in the case of religious belief. No new religious doctrine has ever prospered in Spain, nor has it ever occurred to anybody to invent one. (Mysticism, needless to say, is not an objective system of beliefs.) Only the Jewish caste seemed to be groping toward a new faith, but its attempts culminated in the religious and philosophical thought of Benito Spinoza, which could have no effect in Spain.

It would seem, then, that the following conclusion could be drawn from these observations: The Spaniard gives up his individuality and disciplines himself as he enters the community created by faith in God or in the personal power of another man; or he assumes strong individuality when he accomplishes something of value—acts and creations that endow him with an individual personality as rich as that of any other European (the examples would run from Fernán González and the Cid in the tenth and eleventh centuries to Ramón y Cajal and Manuel de Falla in the twentieth). In contrast to these courses of action, the so-called Spanish individualism—the blunt rejection of ideas and rules—would consist in a vital emptiness, in an attitude devoid of all *individualizable* content, that is, in the Spaniard's *no me da la gana* ("I just don't want to"), which admits of no answer. Unamuno, who did not approach this problem the way I do, nevertheless made certain observations that I find useful: "It is hard to understand how a person, without speaking, without writing, without painting anything, without chiseling a piece of sculpture, without playing any music, without transacting any kind of business, *without doing anything at all*, can expect that by the single act of being present he will be regarded as a man of extraordinary merit and outstanding talent. Nevertheless, here in Spain—I do not know whether such is the case elsewhere—more than a few examples of this extremely old phenomenon are known" (*El individualismo español*).

The phenomenon observed by Unamuno and others is indeed hard to understand if we look for a logical motivation behind a person's assumption of merits that he does not have. It will not do simply to admit that Spaniards are this way because an abstract psychological pattern has been made concrete in them. The truth is that in many Spaniards there survive the spectacular posture and attitude of the victorious caste of yesteryear—now without a basis in the reality of accomplishment.[50] The Spaniard has preserved certain inner and outer ways that were proper to the time when he felt himself the member of an imperial caste, aware of his innate merit and of the effective power of his mere presence. How can this be understood any longer in a technocratic world with which the Spaniard has always lived at odds? And yet we should try to make clear the blurred perspective—blurred even for Unamuno—of an age in which legitimate efficacy was granted to a sword upheld by personal power, by faith, and backed up by the skill of men who knew how to command. It must not be forgotten that the Spaniard began to be aware of the imperial power of his nation long before the discovery of America. The conquest of Naples by Alfonso of Aragon, followed at the end of the fifteenth century by the capture of Granada, the victories of the Great Captain, the discoveries across the sea, and the accession of Charles V—all these confirmed the Spaniard in his belief that Spain was predestined to be the guiding center of world politics. The will to seigniory became a reality in the Empire, just as the wing of the bird and the air around join constantly in the action of flying. Likewise, being Spanish and acting with imperious authority became, in the end, reciprocal functions of the same person. It is not, then, that Spain, an abstract national entity, had an empire; rather, it is that Spain, when she was acting imperially, achieved the maximum expression of her possibilities, of her *vividura*, at the same time that the Empire itself was taking on Hispanic form. As the conquistadors brought the lands of America under Spanish dominion, they effectively converted the mass of the Indians into people of partially Hispanic blood, Hispanic language and manner, and Hispanic religion. There is no way to understand Spain and write her history without reliving the state of mind of a people who knew that the royal standard was flying from Antwerp to Sicily, and from St. Augustine and Santa Fe to Buenos Aires and Concepción (Chile). This titanic effort, without precedent in its time, is still evident in the commanding beauty of many fortresses, churches, and palaces, and in millions of people vitally molded to the Spanish pattern, re-

---

[50] In *La Prisonnière* of Marcel Proust, Albertine responds to every statement with "Is that so? Is it really so?" even when someone says to her, "It is raining." "The lovely girl gave the strange impression of being a person who is not able to observe things for herself." The truth is that Albertine had acquired that irrepressible habit in the days of her precocious beauty when, sure of fascinating everyone who talked to her, she answered phrases like, "You know that I have never found anyone as pretty as you," with a doubting "Is that true?" which concealed a satisfaction that was not at all doubtful.

gardless of whether they feel sympathy or antipathy toward their Spanish past.[51]

A meaningful history of this tremendous Hispanic expansion would make evident how, as the outward movement progressed, the way of life forged during the reconquest became ever more fixed. Without realizing that he is doing so, the Spaniard, secure in the conviction that he belongs to the best caste—be he a great lord or a ragamuffin, dull or intelligent—goes on nourishing in his soul the void of the vanished Empire, the dream that the self, the person, by virtue of his mere existence, is at once everything. Thus it is possible to understand how a few naïve Spaniards have lately been able to believe that they have an empire just because they have shouted a pair of magic words: "Imperial Spain." The person is everything, can do everything, and needs only himself. "Let *the others* do the inventing," said Unamuno; and one of Baroja's characters exclaims: "Ten men with talent and initiative, and the revolution is made!" Don Quixote was also persuaded that he could stop the Turks' advance by hurling a handful of knights errant against them. Yet it must be remembered that in 1686, when their monarchy was bleeding to death from the wounds inflicted by Louis XIV, the Spaniards contributed insofar as they were able to the liberation of Budapest from the Turks.[52]

Let us not go on calling this rebellious and proud aloofness "individualism." It would be better to view this strange and sometimes splendid kind of existence as a "personal absolutism." "I am the master of my hunger" was the answer of one very poor Spaniard to men who wanted to buy his vote for a deputy he did not like. This is not Stoicism or Senecanism, for this same Spaniard, master of his hunger, can abandon himself to instinctive rage when the imperialism of his person so demands. The abstract reason of the Stoics or of legal codes is not very appealing to the Spaniard, whose *ideas about justice* would support what I have been saying. Laws

---

[51] The Arch of Triumph built for Alfonso of Aragon in the Castel Nuovo in Naples was the work of Italian artists. Triumphal arches had not been raised in Italy since the time of the emperors, and this one would not have existed except for the will of the king to have a "Roman triumph" after his entry into Naples on June 2, 1447—ALFONSUS REX HISPANUS SICULUS ITALICUS PIUS CLEMENS INVICTUS. In order to be authentic, the triumphal arch must include both the material structure and the triumph that passes beneath it—art and life. It was built between 1452 and 1468 by Pietro Martino and Francesco Laurana (see Ricardo Filangieri, in *Dedalo* [Milan, 1932], XII, 439).

[52] *Diario puntual de quanto ha passado en el famoso sitio de Buda; y relación cumplida de su presa por assalto el día 2 de setiembre del año presente 1686* ("A Detailed Journal of What Happened during the Famous Siege of Buda; and a Full Account of Its Capture by Attack on September 2 of This Year, 1686") (Madrid: Melchor Alvarez, 1686). Spaniards served in the army of the duke of Lorraine, and the exhausted treasury of Charles II gave a huge sum toward that honorable undertaking for reasons of imperial prestige.

and judges do not take into account man's complex and unstable situation, said Pero López de Ayala in the fourteenth century: "They have forgotten the soul, they take little pity on it." A judge, if he were to be acceptable to the Spaniard, would have to be like the superhuman daimons in Plato's *Laws* (IV, 713). The Spaniard wants a system of justice based on value judgments, not on firm and rationally deduced principles. It is not, consequently, an accident that casuistry was fostered by the Spanish Jesuits, or that the Frenchman Pascal should find this casuistry perversely immoral. It is the written law that the Spaniard fears and despises: "I find twenty chapters against you and only one that is with you," says a lawyer to the unfortunate litigant in the *Rimado de palacio* by Pero López de Ayala. According to Juan de Mena (1411–1456), justice consists in "a hundred thousands deceptions, schemes, and tricks"; legal works, "fuller of opinions than a basket is of grapes," foster a cheating spirit in judges and lawyers. And so it was that the "land of the Moors" was longingly thought of as the place where justice was truly just; for with the Moors the same judge disposed of both civil and criminal cases, basing his opinions not on laws but on "discretion and good doctrine." Even Cervantes expresses more than once a longing for Moorish justice, in spite of his long captivity in Algiers: "Among those barbarians, *if they are barbarians in this regard*, the qadi is a competent judge in all cases, and he sums them up on his fingernail and gives sentence with a single breath, and there is no appeal of his sentence to any other tribunal" (*El amante liberal*). This praise of Muslim justice signified a fleeting receptivity to the possibilities of another caste as well as a protest against having to submit to laws that had little effective power in the eyes of either judges or litigants. Cervantes, Quevedo, and Gracián all express their emphatic contempt for courts of law. Gracián says that the judge exiles the thieves "because he wants to be the only one" (*Criticón*, II, 7). And in 1903 Miguel de Unamuno writes: "In Spain, whenever there is talk of governmental programs it is time to start trembling, and the moment we hear that such and such idea is going to be applied, we had better run for shelter. I prefer the application of what is called the 'loyal wisdom and understanding' of any old judge, *whatever the quality of his culture*, because this wisdom and understanding, when it is really loyal, is usually the expression of a whole real man, and not of an abstract entity" (*Sobre el fulanismo*). Unamuno says the same thing that Juan de Mena had said four centuries earlier.[53]

---

[53] I am familiar with what has been written by Rabelais, Montaigne, and others about the justice of judges and the excellencies of free and spontaneous justice. Nothing in their ideas authentically enters into a system of "personal absolutism" like that of the Spaniards, who, when they speak of justice, do so from the fullness of their lives, and not merely from rational thought.

Joaquín Costa, the great agitator of the Spanish conscience at the end of the nineteenth century, followed the same centuries-old line of scorn for official justice. According to him, those juridical institutions founded on an oral tradition are perfect: "The *comunidades de agua* [societies to regulate the fair distribution of water among farmers] are never professional, nor are they *superior* in dignity and social position to the people whose affairs they administer; as a rule, the office is filled by farmers, . . . elected by the vote of all those who use water for irrigation. . . . The platform on which they sit is not guarded by doorkeepers, bailiffs, armed guards; they do not disguise themselves under judicial robes; . . . They are not surrounded by that grotesque Congolese apparatus with which official justice so frequently hides its crimes, its negligence, and its ignorance. *The proceedings are oral, extremely brief, public, and free. . . .* Its jurisdiction is not obligatory, but voluntary." If an irrigator does not wish to appear, "then the judicial proceedings are passed on to the judge of the primary court of claims. As anyone would suppose, the cases in which this occurs are extremely rare: [in choosing] between rapid, free, human, and honorable justice . . . and officially sanctified justice, addicted to legal formulas, obscure, offensive in its manners, larcenous in its proceedings, . . . and adept at all kinds of prevarication, only demented people fallen from another star would hesitate" (*Colectivismo agrario en España* [1915], pp. 542–543).

Costa, Unamuno, and the other enemies of organized authority believed in the "innate virtue of the person," based on the mere fact of his existence. Justice dispensed by the unlettered was more just in their eyes than that of learned lawyers, in which opinion they are at one with St. Theresa, who scorned those who "assign all seigniory to *false signs of authority*." The future saint preferred, naturally, divine justice: "O King of Glory, [how marvelous it is] that thy kingdom, because it has no end, is not built upon such a fragile ground." The flesh-and-blood king must be surrounded by hosts of people and great pomp, for otherwise one would not know that he was king, "and so it is right that he should have these *false signs of authority*" (*Libro de la vida*, chap. 37). St. Theresa and all those Spaniards who have felt like her found in the society around them no sparks of the divine perfection, but only deficiency and evil. Consequently, the only possibility was either to place oneself totally in God's hands, as the mystics did, or to strive to find something authentically just in social institutions that had grown up among countryfolk and thus were uncorrupted by the evil tricks of urban man. Costa and Unamuno obviously constructed their Utopias out of Rousseauian and post-Romantic materials; but in doing so they found themselves in accord with ancient Spanish modes of thought, whose roots must be sought in the tension created by the conflict between the inner law of belief (one was a Christian, a Moor, or a Jew) and the often bothersome external aspects of that law. Existence within a medium simultaneously governed by three divine laws hindered any attempt to govern oneself according to the legal modes of human reason. Ultimately, traditional customs born out of the spontaneous agreements made on the spur of the moment were more respectable than written laws.

We have already seen the great attraction to Muslim justice felt by the people who viewed the system from the outside—an attraction due to its simple, autonomous, and oral character. Among neither the Moors nor the Jews was there any distinction between religious and civil law. The Christian caste, on the other hand, was governed by both an ecclesiastical law (tithes, offering of the first fruits, etc.) and a secular juridical tradition that had been inherited either from Rome or from the Germanic peoples. Despite this, however, let us see what actually happened in the countryside and in the towns. When the Christian awoke to the consciousness of living within a social unit, he saw himself surrounded by Mudejars and Jews, with whom he had to reckon in one way or another. This situation cannot be ignored if we wish to understand how the channels of the Spaniard's inner and outer life were formed and where they led. The Christian defined and affirmed himself within the social space of his belief; he shared his life, sometimes willingly, sometimes unwillingly, with people of other beliefs. He felt himself better than, and superior to, the other castes because the king and the nobles were Christians and ruled over the other castes. Furthermore, the Church was, without doubt, very powerful. But if we descend to the tiny details of everyday life, it was considerably more difficult to discover who really held the reins of power. To penetrate into that daily life—which provides the foundation for our life today—the language itself serves as a most truthful chronicler. When a public function or post does not bear a Castilian, Portuguese, or Catalan name, but rather an Arabic one, we may assume that such posts and functions were originally in the hands of Moors or Jews. At times the Christian must have felt that the *law* was applied, or even promulgated, by peoples who were not of his own *law* or faith. And this state of mind, operative for centuries, must be incorporated into our view of the Spaniard's history if we are not to go astray.

The paying of taxes was a very burdensome obligation for all commoners. Note, then, the number of Arabic words connected with this and other hated activities. The *Partidas* of Alfonso the Learned (2, 9, 25) inform us that "*almoxarife* is an Arabic word, which means the official charged with collecting for the king the taxes on land." The subject payed the *almojarife*, and the king received the *alcabalas*, or the taxes imposed on selling and bartering. The *alamín* and the *almotacén* inspected weights and measures. Two important words connected with the administration of justice are *alcalde* (judge) and *alguacil* (the constable who executed the orders of the court and put criminals in jail). The *alcaide* gave orders in the castle; the *almirante* did the same aboard ship; the *almocadén* guarded the frontier (the Spanish "adelantado" of the frontier is a tracing of this Arabic term).

In addition to these terms, we may add that an *alfaqueque* was the man sent to redeem captives, while raids on enemy territory were made by *almogávares*, commanded by an *adalid*. Further, if Islamo-Judaic tasks and functions filled very important and immediate zones in Christian life, such contacts were not cut off at the moment of death: *ataúd* (coffin) is an Arabic word (Portuguese, *ataúde*; Catalan, *taüt*). The survivors needed an *albacea* (executor) to divide the inheritance—and not because there were no Romance words to designate this function; but for reasons we do not know the Romance designations, *cabezalero*, *testamentario*, *mansesor*, were supplanted by *albacea*.

For many centuries the Christian must have felt happier and more secure while exercising authority than when respecting it; he served his own interests better by being one of *los buenos* and a *fijodalgo* —in other words, when he knew himself to be exalted internally— than when he joined his interests to those of the people who were giving orders around him. To move about with ease the Christian did not look for some sedentary activity in which he would find himself very much dominated by the other castes but rather escaped into the free and open field of military adventure, in which he had dominion over his rivals of the other *laws* in both material profits and prestige. Disciplined in combat, he was not accustomed to be so within the limits of his city when he was simply a "civilian"; for after all, even in the spiritual sphere, we might ask what must have been the inner attitude of those who saw Christian churches and monasteries filled in the eleventh and twelfth centuries with so many foreigners, in large majority Frenchmen, whose terminology finally won out over that of the natives, as had happened before in the case of the Arabs. The spiritual invasion of the Cluniac and Cistercian orders, which I shall discuss later, motivated the introduction of *monje* (monk), *monja* (nun), and *fraile* (friar)—words that pushed aside the original Castilian *mónago*, which survived in *monaguesa* (a cleric's concubine) and *monaguillo* or *monacillo* (acolyte). By the twelfth and thirteenth centuries various positions of ecclesiastical authority, such as those of the *deán* and the *arcipreste*, were already designated by such French terms.

I insist on the fact that sources of wealth and prestige, primary goals for the overwhelming majority of people, lay hidden in the distance, beyond the civil perimeters. Just as in Italy commercial dealings carried people far and ultimately overflowed into the magnification of the city (Amalfi, Genoa, Venice, etc.), in Castile men threw themselves into great deeds of bravery in order to magnify their names, their personal prestige, and their nobility. The Archpriest of Hita summed it up once for all in a line which it is always pleasant to recall:

> Con buen servicio vencen caballeros de España.
> (By their good service the knights of Spain conquer.)

Instead of feeling themselves a complement of their city as the Italians did (e.g., the Médicis in Florence), the Spaniards preferred to annex cities unto themselves, to create them like the halos of their own persons, within which their own authority might reign, since at home no other authority seemed sufficiently worthy. It is of primary importance to bear all this in mind in order to understand the meaning of the reconquest and of the constitution of the empire, which differed so greatly from the Roman expansion. The Romans were constantly extending the augustan prestige of their emperor, while the Spaniard sought to immortalize his own name, or that of his native city, or that of his personal circumstances. Examples such as that of the *Philippine* Islands (named for Philip II) are infrequent; in any event they are not comparable to the weight given to the prestige of Augustus in Rome, as the following topographical names witness: *Augusta* (Aosta), *Caesar Augusta* (Zaragoza), *Bracara Augusta* (Braga), *Augustodunum* (Autun), *Lucus Augusti* (Lugo).

As the Castilians advanced southward in the eleventh and twelfth centuries, they frequently gave their own names to the places they were repopulating: *Gomecello*, which originally was Gómez Tello (in Salamanca); *Gómez Sarracín* (in Segovia). In the Province of Cuenca there are *Martín Miguel, Sanchonuño, Urraca Miguel, Diego Alvaro*, and numerous other examples that have been pointed out to me by Rafael Lapesa. "They are extraordinarily frequent in the southern basin of the Duero, populated about 1088," I am told authoritatively by Menéndez Pidal. Nothing like this took place in the other Romanic countries; and if on occasion, in the United States or elsewhere, we run across what appear to be similar examples of towns bearing the names of individuals, the phenomenon has a different meaning. The way of life of the person who gives his name and the importance of such an act within the context of his dwelling place of life are very dissimilar. The reconquering Castilians were thinking more about their own names than about the nature of the terrain or any other objective circumstance. The meaning that I attach to these facts is confirmed by what happened during the Spaniards' imperial expansion. The English and the Dutch, when they called many places in America New-this-or-that, were reflecting the Puritan belief that they had come to a *new* world, free of the old spiritual oppression. *Newark* meant "New Ark of the Covenant." In this case, the religious belief and the word *new* that expresses it, have a generic character and are not personalized or concretized. In contrast to this, Garcilaso el Inca tells us that Bartolomé Colón called the city he founded Santo Domingo "because he got there on a Sunday [*domingo*], the Feast of the Saint Dominic, and his father's name was Domingo; thus three causes coincided to make him call it thus." Or, again, "The city of Cartagena [in Colombia] was so called because of its good harbor, which, since it was much like than of Cartagena [in Spain], caused those who first saw it to say: 'This harbor is as good as that of Cartagena'" (*Comentarios reales*, Rosenblat ed., I, 24–25). The city of *Osorno*, in Chile, owes its name to the fact that the mother of its founder, Don García de Mendoza, was Countess of Osorno. The Granadine Jiménez de Quesada remembered his own *Santa Fe*, near Granada, when he founded *Santa Fe de Bogotá*; the Spaniards from the Cordova in Andalusia gave the name *Córdoba* to various cities situated, like their own home city, at the foot of a mountain. Garcilaso explains that the effort to give the name *Nuevo Toledo* to *Cuzco* failed "on account of the inappropriateness of the name, because *El Cuzco* has no river to gird it like Toledo, nor does it resemble Toledo in its situation" (*ibid.*, II, 101). In this and many other instances, the place-names are a reflection of a particular person's emotional experience as he faced the place to which he was giving a name. So it happened that names came into being that were expressive of the personal religious devotion of the sponsor: Sierra de la *Sangre de Cristo* (*Christ's-blood* Mountains), River of the *Mother of God*, and the like; or they were expressive of what the discoverers fancied about the places and peoples they discovered: *Amazonas*, *Argentina*, and so on. In all these instances the names express, directly or indirectly, personal circumstances.

It is no less curious that also in Arabic Spain there was an abundance of place-names formed from the names of persons. The Arabist Miguel Asín wonders what the explanation is of "this plethora of personal names in the Arabic toponymy of Spain. Attachment to the land, the deeply rooted right of property, attributes common to all races and peoples, would not give us a full explanation of a phenomenon that, like this one, is so peculiar to our own soil."[54]

---

[54] M. Asín Palacios, *Contribución a la toponimia árabe de España*, p. 35. A

Asín tries to explain the phenomenon as the result of the distribution of part of the Spanish territory among the Muslims that conquered it in the eighth century; but since the same thing is found in Muslim Asia, we should rather consider the phenomenon as evidence of an "autobiographical" expressionism, a frequent tendency among both Muslims and Spaniards.

From what has been said, then, it would follow that the Spaniard feels himself united with other people only when, in his view, they amount to a magnification of his own person, and not because they may represent ideas with a universal validity.[55] It has not been the Spaniard's habit (though I do not say he is incapable of such behavior) to accept plans of collective life based on continuous effort and good sense. Rather, he has given himself to those who have proposed Utopian projects because, without wondering about the possibility of their achievement, he has *believed* in them: magical changes in society, a new world empire, and the like. On the other hand, nonsubmission to laws has been regarded as a "positive act of nobility" (remember the words of Fernández de Navarrete).

The individual never gets outside himself but aspires to draw the surrounding world into his own self. The only social life he really believes in and participates in is based on coincidences of feeling, without any background of depersonalized ideas or enterprises. This explains the social groupings whose unifying center is a *caudillo*, the local political boss, or a common Messianic hope. On the other hand, Spaniards do not join together to carry out the anonymous and, for them, cold task of making the life of their cities richer and more comfortable. Ganivet wrote in 1896 that he had seen some of the "ancient free cities" of Europe and was delighted by "their family-like attitude toward everything inside their walls, as if these were the walls of a single house," and by the citizen's faith and confidence in his city. But Granada, the beautiful city that Ganivet loved so much, "what can she do but beg the national government if she is lacking in means? If she turned to her own inhabitants, which of them would feel any confidence in her? There is little

---

comparison with Roman and Visigothic toponymy would make evident the peculiarity of the Islamic and Castilian practices.

[55] People have often noted this fact, although they have not fitted it into the whole structure of Spanish life. In 1896 Ganivet observed how secular societies failed and religious communities prospered: "We are rebellious toward association, and in fact, all the organizations we found perish in a short time; and, nevertheless, we are the country of religious communities. . . . We understand and practice community of property when there is an ideal goal; but we do not know how to bring funds together to make them grow and prosper. We revolt against all authority and organization and then voluntarily despoil ourselves of our civil personality and accept the hardest slavery" (*Granada la bella*). Ganivet attributed this strange way of life to mysticism (which was, according to him, "sensuality restrained by virtue and poverty").

confidence in the nation; but in the city, none at all" (*Granada la bella*).

Now the historian, besides noting and evaluating facts as isolated or successive units, must arrange them in a vital structure. And when this is done, the important conclusion is reached that the history of a people cannot be constructed on universal and abstract patterns. The history of Spain becomes meaningful when it is conceived not as a unified continent of objectively organized culture but as an immense archipelago of great individual and collective figures who have created few extrapersonal or social and secular values, such as science, economics, and the like—heroes, kings, saints, religious leaders, great lords, poets in prose and in verse, artists, guerrilla fighters, insurrectionists, and every other kind of thing along this line. Persons and entities emerge from a collective background that is static but at the same time longing for a hope and a promise in this world or the other. Each person, each generation, has the sense of arriving at the world "anew" when the decision is reached to break out of the timeless immobility. In the middle of the seventeenth century Baltasar Gracián said that "Spain is today just as God created her, without a single improvement made by her inhabitants." And Quevedo formulated a judgment that did not reflect the intellectual situation of contemporary Europe but perfectly described that of Spain: "Few there are today who study something for its own sake and for its rational content and owe some truth to their own experience; for, captive to the authority of the Greeks and Romans in matters touching the natural world, *we take pride only in believing* what they said; and so it is that the moderns deserve the name of *believers* as the ancients did that of learned" (*La cuna y la sepultura* [1634], chap. iv).[56] Like his compatriots, Quevedo is included in the censure he formulated; in his art he was a great innovator, but he introduced nothing new in thought or science.

Throughout the nineteenth and twentieth centuries it has been customary to say that in Spain "everything is still to be done." The generations have not bequeathed to one another a tradition of enterprise and purposes, save the tradition of belief that immobilizes and the art of expressing the awareness of the continuity of one's existence. Even so, we have seen that many people have considered the past three hundred years to be a period of little value in Spanish life. Fusion between the castes of Old and New Christians having become impossible in the sixteenth century, since then the empty spaces between one generation and another have usually been filled with other peoples' cultures, with what Unamuno would call other peoples' inventions. There is, to be sure, a literary tradition, that is,

---

[56] Apparently Quevedo was unaware of what had been done in the sixteenth century by certain Spaniards whom I discuss later.

an expression of the absolute consciousness of the person, of how he feels within himself and in his world of feelings, cares, and hopes. Starting with Lope de Vega, we can contemplate the whole past of the Christian caste, continued later in the writings of the Romantics and even in contemporary poetry. With Ganivet, Unamuno, or Antonio Machado we can go back through the centuries and hear time and again the troubled, noble voices of which they are a magnificent echo. But it is useless to look for Spanish antecedents of Menéndez Pidal's philology or Ramón y Cajal's histology. And if Spanish history *is* this way, why should we not write it in accordance with its truth?

My history based on great writers and artists, on heroes, antiheroes, saints, apostles, martyrs, or exalted nincompoops has its own traditional antecedents in Fernán Pérez de Guzmán's *Generaciones y semblanzas*, in certain autobiographies, and in certain pages of Quevedo. Many Spaniards have done with their lives, and with the lives of others that have come within their embrace, what the artist does by means of verbal or pictorial expression. But how is it possible to bring these stars of greater and lesser magnitude together in one historical system? In spite of the difficulty of such a task, it is worthwhile to undertake it, leaving aside for the moment such artificial notions as the Middle Ages, the Renaissance, baroque, and the like. It is especially necessary to separate clearly the continuing values of this history from the discontinuous scientific, political, and economic culture that has come out of this self-consuming life, out of the conflict between personal longing for "the absolute" and the conviction that this absolute leads, in the end, to paralysis.

Let Us Be Masters and Not Servants of Our Own History

All the good and the bad things that have happened to the Spaniards are ultimately linked to the fact that people who were not yet Spaniards had to confront the disastrous circumstances created by the Muslim occupation of the land of Hispania, a Romano-Visigothic country. That overwhelming event forced the adoption of new collective attitudes which, in the course of time, became fixed and habitual. Then those human horizons began to be drawn—at once clear and shallow of perspective—against which the system of castes we now know well gradually took on shape. This centuries-long process occasioned the Christian caste's affirmation of its existence by virtue of circumstances against which, at the same time, it had to react; as they mingled with the Moors and Jews, the Christians both shared a way of life and consumed their own lives. But in that very feeding of life upon itself (*desvivirse*), in that eagerness to escape from the given, the inevitable daily situation, there arises the element of "willfulness," not the fatalism, of Spanish life. In the final analysis, the Catholic Sovereigns and the large majority of their people *willed* to have done with the Jews and the Moors. Later, in 1609, Philip III and many other Spaniards willed to suppress the last Muslim remnants in Spain. And along with those happenings, a great number of Spaniards decided, *preferred*, not to engage in intellectual and technical activities so as not to be charged with Jewishness. These states of mind and the situations created by them were not the result of an inescapable destiny or a biopsychology conditioned either by the far-off Iberians and the even more remote Neolithic inhabitants of the Peninsula or by the climate and geography of the land.

The outlines of the historical panorama are now being sketched out with ever greater clarity; within that panorama everything will finally be explained and understood by virtue of plausible reasons that eliminate the necessity of appealing to adventitious circumstances or to psychological determinism (abstemiousness in food and drink, envy, outbursts of intense emotion, etc.). But even though what has happened in the past may profoundly affect the course of the vital process, the action of our preferences, the receptivity to novel ideas, suggestions, and examples can change the course of individual life and even induce us to "furnish" the rooms of our vital dwelling place in a somewhat different fashion or to carry out collective actions informed by one or another dimensions of value.

I do not believe that history is the "master of our lives," as was customarily said in the nineteenth century. But there is no doubt that the extent to which the future of a people may be planned, or clearly obvious defects may be remedied, is much reduced if those who are capable of understanding such reforms possess no clear idea about the peculiarities—and the reasons for them—characteristic of the people whose ways of life they hope to modify. As long as the Spaniard's past is covered by the shadows of myth, whatever may be said about the *way of being* of the Spaniard and his possibilities will simply lack meaning; for if the future can be envisioned only as the most problematic of realities, the present and the past from which we proceed in the formulation of any future project must not be totally veiled in mist. Among all the European peoples, the Spaniards have been the most criticized, censured, lamented, and counseled. And I insist that it is astonishing that in the twentieth century people of undoubted eminence have considered the past three or four hundred years in Spain as a negative factor. In certain political harangues some thirty years ago it was said that the only counsel of prudence would be to treat the past of Spain—all those years preceding 1930—like a blotted copybook, tear out the soiled pages, and begin again. That, of course, is as monstrous as it is childish. If we feel this way, if the past seen from our present is going to be like that contemplated by Fernán Pérez de Guzmán in the fifteenth century—a "sad and tearful history"—each generation will continue to pass on to the next an inheritance of myopia and incoherent proposals, which is what has constantly happened heretofore.

The most enlightened and the best intentioned have preferred to cover their eyes, to make no reasonable response to the question of how and why, since the end of the sixteenth century, the Spaniards have been culturally—in thought, in science, in technology—among the most backward nations in Europe. We now have the answer, thanks to an operation of careful historical probing which had to be undertaken, however painful it may seem to many; and the results of this probing of the past must be accepted if the Hispanic world truly wishes to escape in the future from the consequences of the situation voluntarily created and not imposed by fate, in the sixteenth century. The Spaniards of the Christian caste took a vow of ignorance: they identified personal dignity with complete mental quietude. When this did not occur, it was almost always a Spaniard of Jewish ancestry who set himself intellectual problems: "The blessed will know in the future celestial life these aspects and laws of nature, and from such knowledge they will receive intense pleasure. . . . They will know much greater and more recondite things: that is, the causes of everything there is on the earth and the internal principles appropriate to each thing, . . . which *causes and laws*, because they are so hidden, will produce so much the greater joy when they are known." Such were the sentiments, written in Latin, of Luis de León,[57] a New Christian who had to purge himself of his excessive intellectual curiosity in the prisons of the Inquisition. Father Juan de Mariana would write later, also in Latin,[58] that with such an example before them, "it was inevitable that the zeal of many distinguished men should be dampened, and that their strength should falter and die."

The whole question as to whether or not there was a Spanish science, and whether or not men of learning were persecuted by the Inquisition, was badly formulated almost a century ago by the opponents of Menéndez y Pelayo. Science there was, as well as intellectual zeal and attempts to carry research forward; Menéndez y Pelayo was right. But the most distinguished representatives of that learning almost always have turned out to be Spaniards of Jewish origin: Luis Vives, Francisco de Vitoria, Gómez Pereira, the mathematician Pedro Núñez, and so on. Whenever by chance we come across a

---

[57] Rafael Lapesa quotes this passage for the purpose of literary analysis in his "Las odas de Fray Luis de León," in *Homenaje a Dámaso Alonso*, II, 312.

[58] See *De la edad conflictiva*, pp. 168–169.

text expressive of intellectual eagerness, the author is most frequently a convert; witness, for example, Pedro de Medina, one of the converts protected by the Duke of Medina Sidonia[59] and author of the *Libro de grandezas y cosas memorables de España* (Seville, 1549), in which he shows great pride in his cosmographic learning:

> It is a wonderful thing that with a round instrument a span in width, which is called an astrolabe, the arc of the heavens may be measured, though it is so large that man's understanding cannot grasp it or even imagine it; and that with this instrument the height of the sun may be taken by passing its rays through a very narrow opening, even though the sun is many times larger than all the earth and the sea, and that by this it may be known how far away or close to us the sun is at each day at any spot a man may be. (1944 ed., p. 95)

The Spanish Old Christian did not make himself "nobly" idle intellectually through any desire for comfort, but out of a need that was as spiritual (let us not bother if this seems facetious) as that of the Calvinist who labored at technical jobs with his hands in order to make himself pleasing to God. Anyone who does not understand this had better renounce the attempt to understand Spanish history after the sixteenth century.

Now, of course, there are no longer either New or Old Christians, or empires whose superhuman conquest may grant to one caste an advantage of value and honor over its rival; no longer are there hidalgos or *hijos de buenos* whose lineage the resentful peasant might find it worth his while to examine closely so that he could oppose the noble lord or the man of learning. All of that has passed and left in the history of Spanish civilization traces that are as positive as they are negative; and it has all passed because people willed that it should. With that background now vanished, the Spanish people of the nineteenth century—so much in need of culture, with that quietist lassitude described in unforgettable words by Galdós, Unamuno, Azorín, and before them, Jovellanos—seem to me like a fencer deprived of his sword who continues waving his arms and shouting *his words* with the same vehemence as when he was crossing swords with his adversary, though he too has now disappeared. If there are no longer castes, if we are nothing but Spaniards, why should we not direct our will constructively toward the periphery of the person and not toward the immovable center? The cult of one's own personality for the sake of personality made possible an empire that no longer exists and brought with it miseries better not spoken of because they are so willfully destroyed. Within the vital dwelling place of the Spaniards there continue to reside the will of yesteryear and the eagerness for a future—and with all that, the

---

[59] Information supplied by Claudio Guillén.

feeling that today, as never before, being a man is not an easy or negligible task. But for the moment, let us continue to observe the affirmations and negations, the yes and the no, of the past—which is my undertaking. The rest devolves upon those who are experts in the efficient and practical management of human multitudes.

Hidalguismo

The reader by now knows a good deal about the originally Semitic character—ultimately, the "magical" nature—of the relationship implied in the old terms *fijo d'algo* and *fijos de buenos* (see above, pp. 266–271). The Christian caste built up a way of life like that of the conquering warrior and entered history with the dangerous assurance that it was possible for this caste, in one burst of energy, to scale the greatest heights. As early as the year 1000, the Castilian was beginning to think that he could really "take" the Moor, and that fabulous Cordova was within reach of his sword. The conquests of Toledo and Valencia (although the latter conquest was temporary) provided an eleventh-century confirmation of his feeling of superiority, based on an awareness of his "intrinsic value." This attitude predisposed the Hispano-Christian to adopt whatever might reinforce it, even though it might come from the camp of the enemy. Thus he was ready to adopt Arabic ways of expressing personal value (*fijodalgo*), or what there was good in Arabic actions (*fazañas*). *Fazaña* ("feat, prowess," originally "model of goodness, generous act") comes from the Arabic *ḥāsanah* ("good act, generosity").[60] *Fijodalgo* and *fazaña*, together with the special sense of *grandes* ("grandees") which has already been noted, are clear evidence of the impression of superiority which the Muslim made on his rival a thousand years ago. Then, the Christian's feeling of superiority grew stronger and stronger. This must be the point of departure for understanding the inordinate urge to nobility and the sense of being God's chosen caste that took possession of the Christian and convinced him that only prowess in war and the exercise of authority were valuable activities. I shall begin by citing texts that will put us in contact with the reality of daily life.

In a proclamation made in Valencia in 1410 against blasphemers who "soiled their lips and tongues by speaking ill of God and the Virgin Mary," plebeians were condemned to be publicly flogged and pilloried; "but if it be a *person of honor who does not work with his hands*, let him pay as a penalty 50 gold maravedís."[61] An abstract

---

[60] J. Corominas, *Diccionario etimológico*. Note that the Arabic *ḥāsanah* did not mean "prowess"; but the Christian associated it, for reasons of like sound, with his own word *hacer* ("to do").

[61] F. Danvila, in the *Boletín de la Academia de la Historia* VIII (1886), 338.

conception of history would treat such an idea as a "theme" or "commonplace," and would relate it to Plato's contempt for physical labor and his low regard for crafts, which reappears in the Middle Ages: "Opus humanum, quod natura non est, sed imitatur naturam, maechanichum, i.e. adulterinum vocatur"[62] ("A human work, not natural but an imitation of nature, mechanic—that is, counterfeit"). But what good would it do here to compose a study of the contempt for manual labor through the ages? We are actually faced with a caste of people who composed their existence out of the vital "impossibility" of working at tasks deemed not honorable. "You have always kept me busy with the base things of your mechanical job," says the soul to the body in the Diálogos de la fantástica filosofía de los tres en uno.[63] The author might have taken his idea from a repertory of medieval commonplace, but in its historical context the idea has a peculiarly Spanish meaning, for it implies that great value was attached to that which was not mechanical work, that is, the intrinsic value of the person.[64]

That value was not only a matter of high spirits, courage, or brio, predicated as attributes of the person. It was the very substance of the person, that which made him "whole" and conferred on him "integrity," that which made him "all of a piece"—peculiarly Spanish concepts.[65] The Spaniard has been the only example in Western history of a man whose purpose in life is founded on the idea that the only calling worthy of a man is to be a man, and nothing more. When Pedro Crespo entrusts his son to the general, Don Lope de Figueroa, he reasons thus: "What would he do here with me but idle his time away in a life of profligacy? Let him go and serve the king."[66] Pedro Crespo, a successful peasant, feels that the value of

---

[62] Hugo of St. Victor, in Patrologia, vol. 176, col. 747 (quoted by E. R. Curtius, in the Zeitschrift für Romanische Philologie, LVIII, 23). With great good sense Joseph Conrad once observed: "The value of a sentence is in the personality which utters it, for nothing new can be said by man or woman" (Nostromo, p. 200).

[63] By Francisco Miranda Villafañe (Salamanca, 1583), fol. 21r.

[64] Don Artal de Alagón, count of Sástago, wrote: "I am not trying to condemn all combat between individuals or to discourage men from preserving their honor and standing up for the honor of God and of themselves in the way that one should . . . ; rather I would want to encourage them and give them enthusiasm for these purposes, such enthusiasm, I understand, being more necessary than cooling their blood, which is already so cold that it is pitiful to see how intrinsic value has grown weak in those men in whom it should be most whole" (Concordia de las leyes divinas y humanas [Madrid, 1593], fol. 126r).

[65] This is something different from the "moral integrity" that preserves intact the moral principles on which conduct is based. The idea of integrity or "wholeness" refers to something that implies active fortitude and courage and leaves everything else in shadow.

[66] Calderón, El alcalde de Zalamea, II, ll. 765–768.

his prosperity lies not in the fact that his life has been materially productive but in the fact that his wealth will assure his son a career in the ennobling service of the king.

No other European country so stigmatized manual labor, which was not accorded legal dignity until the reign of Charles III in the eighteenth century, in the course of the invasion of rationalist ideas from foreign lands, an invasion that affected only the epidermis of Spanish life. But it is also certain that belief in intrinsic value was continually shaken by the uneasiness of those who found themselves locked up in their consciousness of caste as well as by the similar disquiet of those who realized the grave dangers of Spanish exclusionism. Pedro Fernández de Navarrete writes: "This court has been filled with many other persons of low degree: lackeys, coachmen, saddle boys, water carriers, wafer peddlers, porters, collar stretchers. . . . The harm that comes from the fact that these people are leaving the work in the fields undone need not be emphasized." The porter is singled out for special censure: "With the introduction of this not very ancient occupation, it has begun to be the custom that, if a servant buys a real's worth of fruit, he must give half to the porter who carries it, *a vanity and extravagance tolerated only in the court of Spain.*"[67] This criticism is closely connected with another: "No sooner has a merchant or a worker or a peasant enough to buy a government pension worth 500 ducats a year than he buys with this income a pension for his eldest son, whereupon not only this son but all his brothers become ashamed to occupy themselves at the humble tasks with which that money was originally earned," for "those who are not nobles aspire to make themselves nobles, and those who are, aspire to rise to higher places still" (Fernández de Navarrete, *Conservación de monarquías* [1626], in *Biblioteca de Autores Españoles,* xxv, 473, 475).

In 1541 there were already in Castile and Leon 781,582 taxpaying commoners and 108,458 hidalgos; that is, 13 percent of the families in the kingdom paid no taxes and, most commonly, performed no work of any kind.[68] Some people observed, however, that it was not possible "to preserve in good condition a republic that consists entirely of nobles, for, to assure mutual assistance between citizens, it is necessary to have a head to rule, priests to pray, counselors to counsel, judges to judge, noblemen to provide prestige, soldiers to defend, farmers to till, tradesmen to do business, and artisans to

---

[67] Fernández de Navarrete, *op. cit.,* p. 504*b.*

[68] "Relación de los vecinos no pecheros que hay en las 18 provincias del reino para el repartimiento del servicio de 1514, y de los hidalgos que se presupone podrá haber en cada una de las dichas provincias," in *Colección de documentos inéditos para la historia de España* (1848), XIII, 521–528.

take care of mechanical matters."[69] The last two classes of activity had been precisely the ones that had belonged to the Moors and Jews.

When the Spaniards got to the Indies, they implanted and perpetuated their way of life there, as might be expected. In 1590 the inhabitants of Buenos Aires wrote to Philip II in desperation, complaining of the poverty of the Argentine land (which for the English Puritans would have been a paradise, because it is not the land that makes the man but the reverse, even though the importance of natural conditions and the historical moment are not to be denied). In Argentina there was no gold or silver, nor were there native cities, as there were in Mexico and Peru, and the Spaniard, scorning commercial and technical tasks, did not know what to do: "We are so poor and needy that we could not be more in want, in proof of which, *we do our plowing and digging with our hands. . . .* Such is the need from which the settlers suffer that *their own women and children bring their drinking water from the river. . . .* Spanish women, noble and of high quality, because of their great poverty *carry their drinking water on their own shoulders.*" The superior of the Franciscan monastery who was the author of this letter sorrowfully confirms that "the people do their own work and [take care] of their cattle *with their own hands,* for I have seen it happen thus, and it is a pitiable state of affairs; the people wait on themselves as if it were the tiniest village in Spain."[70]

I know no document more significant for the understanding of the history of Hispanic America and the contrasts it presents with the rest of America. The Christian Spaniard moved into the region of the Plate River in the sixteenth century just as in the tenth and eleventh he had spread down over the south of the Iberian Peninsula, with the object of gaining honor and maintaining seigniory for himself.[71] Since there were neither Moors nor Jews to do the work in Buenos Aires, and since the Indians quickly fled out into the pampa, what was eventually to become the Argentina we know today remained in rather a wretched condition until a century ago. Houses in Buenos Aires, a region without rocks and stones, were straw-covered adobe huts, for this was the only kind of masonry the conquistador knew how to make without wealth and vassals to carry out his orders. As late as 1852, the future great city was a pest-ridden village: "The skeletons of oxen and horses lay about in the mud

---

[69] Fernández de Navarrete, *op. cit.,* p. 472.

[70] Emilio A. Coni, *Agricultura, comercio e industria coloniales* (Buenos Aires, 1941), p. 15.

[71] I am cognizant of the importance of immigration into the Indies by many New Christians (of the Jewish or Moorish castes); but the matter has not been sufficiently studied, and I do not propose to discuss it at this time.

in the middle of the street; even in front of the doors of some of the houses you could see the putrefied remains of animals."[72]

But at the same time people in America and Europe were already familiar with *Facundo*, a brilliant historicocritical picture of Argentine life by Sarmiento, for to produce such a work of personal integration and expression there was no need of *base* manual labor. But work with the hands was precisely what Sarmiento was later to propose as the remedy for his country's ills, a program similar to that proposed in Spain by Fernández de Navarrete in 1626: Bring people in from the outside, make others work, give foreigners special privileges, let them "make the rivers navigable and dig ditches for irrigation. . . . The children of these foreigners would, in the second generation, be Spaniards who would fill out the population of Spain, which is the object toward which this discourse is directed" (*op. cit.*, p. 478). He went so far as to advocate the importation of Negroes "to improve some of the many rich mines that Spain possesses." These Negroes would "by the second or third generation be white; if they were not, it would make no difference, since they were apt at manual labor and the cultivation of the soil" (*ibid.*, p. 482). Fernández de Navarrete foresaw what was to happen in Brazil.

At first glance this program looks like an attempt to correct the course of Hispanic history. More closely examined, it turns out to be the contrary; in typically Spanish fashion, Fernández de Navarrete trusts that *others* and not *he himself* will do things, while he blames *others*, not *his own kind*, for what is happening. His negative criticism and lamentations over the poverty and depopulation of the land could have been the utterances of any representative of the Enlightenment, with the sole difference that the author did not in the least suspect that the lack of things, the sense of emptiness, were part and parcel of the very direction of Spanish life. The proposed solutions implied mechanical juxtapositions; that is, they called for the addition of people to do what the Moors and Jews had long been doing without any thought that the dominant caste would cease to be what it was. That it was the working castes that were missed is clearly seen in this statement of utopian and nostalgic longing: "I am persuaded that if, before they [the Moors and Jews] had reached the *state of desperation* that inspired such evil thoughts in them, a way had been found to admit them to certain honors, to avoid keeping them under the brand and stigma of infamy, it would have been possible for them to enter *through the door of honor* into the temple of virtue and into the bosom and obedience of the Catholic Church" (*ibid.*, p. 466). Fernández de Navarrete's ignorance

---

[72] Rafael Alberto Arrieta, *Centuria porteña* (Buenos Aires, 1944), p. 37.

of his own history and the rationalistic naïveté of the statement are obvious. He was also dreaming of a Utopian single caste, without realizing that if the Moors and Jews had attained an awareness of their "intrinsic value" (see note 64), they would have ceased to do the work whose lack was then ruining Spain.

In fine, this treatise is indispensable source material,[73] not only on account of its proposals, but also because it reflects the anguish of a person who sees clearly what he is like and would prefer to be different. Fernández de Navarrete is like the madman in the asylum (*Don Quixote*, II, 1) who, just after he was adjudged sane and was about to leave, said to one of his companions: "If that man is Jupiter and won't rain, I, who am Neptune, . . . shall rain whenever I feel like it." According to Fernández de Navarrete, advisor to the king, the pursuit of letters "usually engenders a certain melancholy that weakens the spirit by opposing the cheerful impulsiveness with which dangerous adventures are undertaken *when reflection does not cause them to lag*. And that is why the goddess of wisdom was called 'Minerva, *quasi minuens nervos*,' for the peoples that indulge excessively in the pleasure of learning easily forget the practice of arms. Spain has examples enough of this, *for as long a time as the throwing off of the Saracens' heavy yoke lasted, she was rude and lacking in letters*, and to remedy this the universities and schools were founded by the kings" (*op. cit.*, p. 542)—as a foreign importation, it might be added.

Similar observations might be made about the writings of Diego de Saavedra Fajardo, Spain's representative at the preparatory conference for the Peace of Westphalia (1648) and a man widely read, widely traveled, and well-versed in foreign languages. He too laments the harm and poverty suffered by his country, and at first we might expect to find in him an advocate of Europeanization ready to shatter the forms of traditional Spanish life; but nothing of the kind. When the time comes to face the decisive issues, Don Diego feels like a Spaniard of the tenth century. His world is the world of belief: "Don Juan de Austria commanded his banners to be embroidered with the cross and this motto: 'With these arms I have conquered the Turks; with them I expect to conquer the heretics!' . . . I avail myself

---

[73] The work even proposes the creation of shipbuilding schools "through which Spain would be freed from dependence on the help of foreigners, who, because they are foreign and without obligations or pledges of faith or love, are apt to undertake any kind of treason" (Fernández de Navarrete, *op. cit.*, p. 542). The work of Fernández de Navarrete should be given serious attention by all those who have to do with the government of the Hispano-Portuguese peoples, who are all alike in this respect. In the twentieth century (just as in the seventeenth or in the twelfth), no Hispano-Portuguese country is capable of building its own ships without foreign help.

of these arms and of the standard of Constantine to . . . signify to the princes the confidence with which they should raise the banner of religion against their enemies. . . . Heavenly spirits will attend this standard; *two riding on white horses* were seen fighting in the vanguard when King Ramiro II conquered the Moors near Simancas. . . . At the battle of Merida in the time of King Alonso IX there appeared that divine lightning bolt, Santiago, the son of thunder, the patron of Spain [see chap. x], leading the squadrons with his blood-stained sword."[74]

---

[74] *Idea de un príncipe político-cristiano, representada en cien empresas,* No. XXVI.

IX · IN SEARCH OF A BETTER
SOCIAL ORDER

Anarchism

THE UTOPIAN VISION of a society organized politically without the coercive action of the state (as proposed by Bakunin, Kropotkin, Reclus, etc.) found ardent supporters among the peasants and laborers of Spain, especially in the southern and eastern regions. This ingenuous and Messianic faith[1] bears a certain relation (in its juridical and social ideology) to the doctrines of eminent sociologists and jurists of the late nineteenth century which were in no sense revolutionary or linked to the violent action of "practical" anarchism. Such violence (e.g., the assassination of Cánovas del Castillo in 1897, and bombings in Barcelona and Madrid) was carried out or inspired by foreign anarchists, like those who made attempts against the life of several sovereigns and chiefs of state in the rest of Europe. In reality, it is necessary to make a sharp distinction between anarchism organized as a political movement (anarcho-syndicalism) and certain modes of thought which have been present in the Spanish tradition for a long time. Doubtless, however, the fact that such traditional attitudes came to the fore in Spain at the end of the nineteenth century was due to the flourishing growth of anarchist ideas elsewhere, especially in France, Germany, and Russia.[2]

Long before the political and social doctrines called anarchist had been formulated, the Spaniards, without supecting it, had expressed their anarchical proclivities in many ways. And this "native anarchism" is the aspect of the problem which concerns me now; for in the final analysis those attitudes discussed in chapter viii—self-

---

[1] "Andalusian peasants today *believe* in 'Mother Anarchy,' as some of them call her, as ingenuously as their grandparents *believed* in the Immaculate Conception. They are absolutely convinced that one fine day, after a brief peasant revolt, the state will disappear with all its faults, the land will all be tilled communally, and all men will be happy forever" (J. A. Balbontin, *La España de mi experiencia* [1952], p. 250).

[2] For an interesting exposition of this problem, see Peter Heintz, *Anarchismus und Gegenwart* (Zurich, 1951).

sufficiency (pp. 296 ff.), so-called individualism (pp. 300 ff.), the idea
of a justice independent of written law (pp. 304–308), and an *hidal-
guismo* conceived as the valuable autonomy of the person (pp. 308
ff.), which even impelled people to demonstrate such autonomy
ostentatiously[3]—are an expression of, and lead toward, anarchism.
In view of all this, and without losing sight of the connections between "anarchism" and the caste structure of society, it is necessary
for us now to situate within its own vital dwelling place the longing
to regulate collective life without the hindrances imposed by the
requirements and privileges of the state, to create, in other words, a
social order free as a star, able to do what it liked, as Juan Martí says
(see n. 3).

Fascism, communism, socialism, and constitutional rule were all
injected into Spanish society as the result of inspirations proceeding
from without; anarchism, on the other hand, was the emanation and
expression of the structure, the situation, and the functioning of the
Spaniard's social life. Politics was polarized either around the magic
halo of divine-right monarchy or the imperious center of the individual himself. The "grace" emanating from the king was comparable
only to that dispensed by God: "It was necessary to win his grace
like that of God himself; and if it was lost, there was nothing to do
but resign oneself."[4] And so things actually were, even though the
awareness of living a life sustained by transcendent grace must be
complemented by that faith in the "grace" emanating from one's
own person, especially when the individual's ego was felt to be
empty of other content. In the absence of other points of support
between the two extremes, the alternative was: either God and the
king; or one's own consciousness. To be sure, obedience to the word
of God and that of the king was never denied; under these two
powers the white Spaniard and the Indian joined in one belief which
made possible the constitution and stability of the Spanish Empire.
And the dismembering of that empire into numerous small regions
was the indirect consequence of the same complex of attitudes: when
royal authority disappeared after the French invasion in 1808, the
lack of cohesion among the crown dominions on the American continent became evident. The viceroyalties lacked any common tasks,
and the republics that arose shortly afterward were never intent on
creating such common endeavors. The groups that appeared had

---

[3] Juan Martí tells us in the second part of the *Guzmán de Alfarache*: "What
things I might relate which I have experienced and seen on this journey to
Valencia. . . . We need not consider the grandees of Castile, *for they are as
stars and are great princes and can do as they will*; I speak only of certain
people who swell with pride at *their high-sounding lineage* and the giddy pride
of being taken [for grandees], spending more than they could and they should"
(in *Biblioteca de Autores Españoles*, III, 404*b*).

[4] Gregorio Marañón, *Antonio Pérez*, I, 36.

been formed around *caudillos* able to extract obedience from those who bent before the prestige of an imperious voice and glance. The great size of Hispanic America and its mountainous terrain are reasons given to explain the fragmentation of the area by people who forget that the Incas had managed to keep closely unified a territory that is now divided into three nations.

The *caudillo* whose only law is that of his own strength or personal cunning, the man who organizes guerrilla bands and military uprisings in Spain or mounted insurrections and military revolts in Latin America, rules and commands obedience by virtue of the "grace" projected onto his followers; he fascinates and bewitches people accustomed for centuries to being swept along by the power of a grace that descends from above—and not by a horizontal system of mutual interests that are clearly visible and constantly being tested.

Changes motivated by such a system of mutual interests have never occurred in Spain because its social and national structure was founded on the primacy of belief. For this reason Spain has experienced no real revolutions but only chaotic revolts and uprisings without well-coordinated goals. When the period of chaos has terminated, the situation continues just as it was or even worse. All this is only too well known, but the reason for such behavior has never been clearly demonstrated. A revolution is like a surgical operation *performed for the first time* and never before described in medical literature, the result, with regard to its method and its purpose, of a highly original design; it is a bloody affair, but the blood is shed by people who know how to staunch the flow, as well as how to restore the patient, a whole people, to health. Those who are unable to wield so sharp a knife had much better remain quiet.

When the Christian Spaniards decided around 1500 that the Jewish and Moorish castes were not as Spanish as their own,[5] they did so not to free themselves from the bonds that linked them to the other castes (namely, a confusion of their national identity with their religious identity) but to make these bonds, that peculiar type of confusion, a still more integral part of the very core of their lives. In other Catholic countries (including Italy), politics, public administration, intellectual culture, commerce, and industry were activities separate from religion and not antagonistic to it; but the Spanish Christian caste fell into the regrettable error of scorning and rejecting the customary occupations of the Moors and Jews instead of taking them over (what they did was more on the order of the destruction of the houses and property of the conquered and the expelled rather

---

[5] It will be remembered that Diego Hurtado de Mendoza—who witnessed it all, knew the facts, and was intelligent—called the war against the Moriscos a war of "Spaniards against Spaniards" (*Guerra de Granada*, in *Biblioteca de Autores Españoles*, XXI, 73).

than their profitable acquisition). On the other hand, the custom of allowing civil life to be ruled, in the last analysis, by ecclesiastics became greatly intensified—just as the Moors had been ruled by their theologians and the Jews, by their rabbis. So it was that the Inquisition was reinstituted and gained absolute dominion over Spanish society from the end of the fifteenth century on. Precisely because people have not seen this matter clearly or deduced the chain of circumstances arising from it, Spanish historiography remains a worrisome tangle and puzzle.

But from the favorably located vantage point we now enjoy, we can perceive clearly the full scope of the crisis suffered by the Spanish people at the beginning of the sixteenth century. The problem was whether one must, following the demands of the caste structure, accept the "casticismo" of a *reinforced* belief or, on the contrary, follow ways of life of a secular nature. The two attempts to achieve this last purpose—the civil war of the *comunidades* (1512), about which I shall have something to say later, and the Erasmian movement—ended in complete failure. As J. F. Montesinos rightly says, the common characteristic that links the Erasmian Alfonso de Valdés and the agents of Charles V in Italy "is the hope that the Emperor, the secular authority and not the ecclesiastical, may be the one to trace out the definitive shape and structure of the Catholic world."[6]

But what spurred the Erasmians on (many of them, like Alfonso de Valdés, converts from Judaism) was not the transformation of the structure of Europe, but of that of Spain, so that they might escape from inquisitorial oppression and secure greater civil liberty, which had been severely limited after the failure of the *comunidades*. Alfonso de Valdés carried Erasmian spirituality to the extreme and dreamed of a church lacking all visible external signs: "There being many good Christians, wherever two or three of them might be gathered together in His [Christ's] name, would be a church" (*Diálogo de las cosas ocurridas en Roma*, p. 170). "If [the Emperor] reforms the Church at this time, for we all know by now what great need there is of it, . . . it will be said until the end of the world that Jesus Christ formed the Church and Emperor Charles V restored it. . . . The Emperor is a very good Christian and a prudent man, and he has very wise people in his council. I expect that he will dispose everything for the glory of God and the good of Christianity" (*op. cit.*, p. 222).

In 1526 Lope de Soria, Charles V's ambassador, wrote from Genoa: "It seems that all the harm Your Majesty may do to His Holiness will be licitly done, in view of his ungratefulness and the small respect that he shows for the service of God and the good of Christians."

---

[6] J. F. Montesinos, Introduction to the *Diálogo de las cosas ocurridas en Roma* of Alfonso de Valdés (Madrid, 1928), p. 53.

According to this ambassador (using the same language with which Charlemagne had addressed the pope in the eighth century), the pope should only "look after spiritual matters and leave temporal affairs to Caesar."[7]

Under the protection of the imperial power of the Emperor and the spiritual authority of Erasmus, some converts dreamed of directing the kingdom from the court, as their ancestors had done centuries before in the court of Alfonso X. But now the principles of tolerance reflected in the epitaph of Ferdinand the Holy (see p. 60) were no longer dominant: the possibility of changing and upsetting the very bases of the criteria of authority. People sought and vainly hoped to create a new regime of just legality to replace the prevailing system of justice, divine and *castizo* in nature, with another system founded on human and objectified reasons.

Joaquín Costa, Francisco Giner de los Ríos, Pedro Dorado Montero, and other eminent writers of the late nineteenth century were surprised as they kept turning up antecedents of modern libertarian doctrines in sixteenth-century writers. Since nothing was known about the Spanish past except what had been written polemical intent (either to praise or to excoriate), it is understandable that these ideas, opposed to the authority of the state and aimed at the exaltation of the spontaneity and "legality" of the inner decisions of the individual, should have been considered as nothing more than rootless abstractions which had turned up from time to time in the past. No one bore in mind the strife-torn reality of which those ideas were the expression, from which they had burst forth. The Holy Office was praised or condemned, but eyes and minds were closed to the meaning and implications of that monstrosity—which represented an unbearable and chronic situation. On the one hand, the Old Christians refused to tolerate any longer the authority of the New Christians, many of whom had been elevated to the highest positions in the court of the Catholic Sovereigns. The New Christians, on the other hand, did not respect the authority of people who subjected members of their caste to intolerable infamy and torture and kept them in a state of agony and despair from which there was no possible escape.[8]

---

[7] Quoted by Montesinos, *op. cit.*, p. 51.

[8] On February 12, 1486, in Toledo, 750 people, men and women, were forced to march in a procession from the church of San Pedro Mártir, "the men without wraps, their heads bare, their feet without shoes or stockings; and on account of the great cold they were ordered to wear some thin soles underneath their otherwise bare feet, and [they carried] unlighted candles in their hands; and the women [went] coatless without any sort of wrap, barefooted, their heads bare like the men, and [carrying] their candles. *Among those people there went many distinguished men of that group* [i.e., New Christians] *and men of honor. And because of the great cold and the dishonor and disgrace they suffered on account of the great numbers of people who were observing*

The spectacle described in note 8 was repeated in many places, and the reactions provoked by such things are known through the works of those who were capable of putting them into words. In a short treatise the poet Juan Alvarez Gato lamented the attempt on the life of Ferdinand the Catholic in Barcelona in 1492 and took advantage of the opportunity to say that through that crime, regretted by everyone, God was warning Ferdinand and Isabella to be "on the alert, and [to have] their royal consciences prepared, examining them frequently and taking accout of *certain failings* in order that they might increasingly purify and enlighten them." And he adds: "It also seems that thou hast done it, Lord, so that from their humility they may remember that, in this wretched life, *all of us, both great and small, have need of each other*."[9] The social order was radically split; the group that we would today call "middle class" had profited not at all from having become Christian: it was crushed between the rancor of those below it and the sadism of those above it. The chronicler Gonzalo de Ayora, a convert who had been educated in Italy and had taken part, like so many others of his caste, in the war of the *comunidades*, addressed a pamphlet to Ferdinand the Catholic in 1507 in which he protested against the conduct of the inquisitor, Rodríguez Lucero; from it comes the following testimony: by means of threats, torture, and flattery, false evidence was secured against "people who were wealthy and appointed to high offices and dignities, . . . they tortured women when they were naked in order to shame them more; and they dishonored many of them."[10]

Such is the social and moral climate of the late fifteenth and early sixteenth centuries which gave birth to the ideology now called anarchist. As early as 1492 Juan Alvarez Gato could write as a result of the attempt on the life of Ferdinand the Catholic: "No condition of life or person is secure, whether great or small; *for all there is on the face of the earth is danger and strife*, and happiness is not within human powers."[11] Against this background the rhetorical phrase Fernando de Rojas employs in the introduction to the *Celestina*, "All things are created as if in contest and battle," seems to take on vivid meaning. Other observations of Alvarez Gato would seem, on the other hand, to anticipate the previously mentioned words of St. Theresa about *false signs of authority* (p. 306): for example, God is a

---

them, . . . they went along screaming and crying: some tore their hair; it is believed more for the dishonor and disgrace they were suffering than on account of the offense they had given to God." Afterward in the cathedral the priests of the Inquisition said mass for them and preached to them, and they read out publicly to each one the respects in which he had lapsed into Judaism. (Fidel Fita, "La Inquisición toledana," *Boletín de la Real Academia de la Historia*, IX, 295; also, Francisco Márquez, *Juan Alvarez Gato* [1960], p. 295.)

9 See Márquez, *op. cit.*, p. 297.

10 *Ibid.*, p. 407.

11 *Obras completas de Juan Alvarez Gato*, ed. Jenaro Artiles, p. 185.

lord "Who will never turn a deaf ear to your pleas, Who will not turn his face away from you, or withdraw from you, or Whom you will need to pacify, *nor is He of clay like these* [*lords*]."[12]

These last words of Alvarez Gato are extremely significant; they indicate that, in defense, the soul of the convert was falling back upon itself. The New Christians were convinced of the righteousness of their cause and of the injustice of the treatment given them by a society that was as much theirs as the Old Christians'. In so bitter a situation one of the possible modes of escape was an ascetic flight from the world and the illumination of the soul by the spark of justice immanent within one's own consciousness. Among those who had something of a genius there arose a convulsive search for God, who possessed none of the failings of the lords "of clay," or of the "false authorities," with whom Teresa de Jesús debated before the bar of her own conscience. The court of one's own conscience was also deemed a competent tribunal by another despairing soul, Friar Luis de León (called a spiritual "libertarian" by Joaquín Costa), who edited St. Theresa's works in 1588.

The withdrawal into one's own soul was intensified in direct proportion to the pressures brought to bear upon it, pressures that were in no sense generic and indeterminate but entirely concrete and clearly expressed, as may be seen in the work of Luis de León, whom I discuss presently, and in numerous events and documents before and after him. Withdrawal into the self is part and parcel of the attacks against society and against the princes who exerted an oppressive authority over it. The New Christian and Erasmian, Alfonso de Valdés, exclaims: "Do you understand that princes have the same dominion over their subjects that you have over your mule? . . . Beasts are created for the service of man, and man *only for the service of God. . . . The good prince, without regard for his private interest, will be obliged to seek only the good of the people, since the kingship was established for their benefit*."[13]

Today we can no longer doubt that the spiritual attitudes of the Spanish Erasmians are a continuation of those of the converts of the fifteenth century, of those who had sought the quiet solitude of the heart, known only to God: "God understands the language of the heart, *which is the same in all men* and in all angels. *In our wills we all speak one language and no other*, by which we understand ourselves. This is the language God understands and not that of the lips."[14] In the phrase "the same in all men" we hear the cry for unity in justice,

---

[12] From a letter written before 1480, in Márquez, *op. cit.*, p. 285.

[13] Alfonso de Valdés, *Diálogo de las cosas ocurridas en Roma*, ed. J. F. Montesinos (Madrid, 1928), p. 109.

[14] Juan de Lucena, *Carta exhortatoria a las letras*, ed. in *Bibliófilos Españoles*, XXIX, 213.

achieved from within, since all external manifestations—whether of the law, the princes, or the rancorous masses—offered no guarantee of justice.

In sum, the literature of the spirit (from mysticism to the pastoral novel and poetry) and such aggressively critical works as the drama of the first half of sixteenth century and the picaresque novel are branches from the same trunk, from one and the same human situation. Once the brightness of the law had been obscured (whether that of the Church or that of the State), the only light came from within one's self, the light of those who were *illuminated* directly by God.

The possibility that the sect of the Illuminati may well have had Muslim origins (as Miguel Asín thought, in my opinion rightly) is as meaningful for me as the fact that Illuminism became especially intense in the sixteenth century. The Illuminati were also fleeing toward the secure haven of their own souls; and the suggestion that Moriscos and converts from Judaism should have been especially interested in that mode of religious spirituality (which Marcel Bataillon has shown to be related to Erasmianism) is corroborated in a curious reverse fashion by the surprising fact that a New Christian of Morisco origin should have felt inclined toward Judaism after reading the works of Friar Luis de Granada, in which the Inquisition had observed certain signs of Illuminism. A certain Lorenzo Escudero, an actor from Seville, "and who was nothing but a Morisco, the son or descendent of a Muslim," went to Amsterdam in 1658 with the purpose of becoming a convert to Judaism, "giving as his reason that reading the books of Friar Luis de Granada had made him a Jew, and that what he desired was to secure salvation."[15] The Spanish world of the three castes is at times as unpredictable as it is inscrutable.

Those ideas that sounded to some modern writers like anarchism must be set into their own vital context; they are incomprehensible without bearing in mind the social position of the Old Christians and of the converts, the indiscriminate punishments of the Inquisition and the reaction against them, the stimulation of perversity among the confused masses,[16] the exaltation of religious spirituality and of evan-

---

[15] Archivo Histórico Nacional de Madrid, "Inquisición," Book 1123, cited by I. S. Revah, *Spinoza et Juan de Prado* (The Hague: Mouton et Cie, 1959), p. 62.

[16] Children played a game called *jueces y penitenciados* in which some acted as judges of the Inquisition, others as people condemned to punishment by it. Even the young Prince John and the pages who played with him engaged in such sport and on one occasion came close to strangling a *penitenciado*, who was indeed, as we know now, a New Christian. Fortunately Queen Isabella intervened after having been aroused from her siesta: "Raising her skirts a bit and without her slippers, she went into the back court where the game was going on, which had reached the dangerous point when they were about to strangle the relapsed Christians and, in view of the way the affair was going, they might

gelical Illuminism. Juan Alvarez Gato, a contemporary of Henry IV and of the Catholic Sovereigns, was aware of the existence of "certain devout people who were already called *Illuminati*" (Francisco Márquez, *Juan Alvarez Gato*, p. 280): "What shame for those who are *illumined* by the doctrine of the Gospels, for we know that by following it we shall not only pass through this brief flight in peace but that, adhering to it, we shall enjoy everlasting life." From such statements as these and the circumstances discussed earlier, it may be deduced that the Erasmian movement and the so-called Spanish pre-Reformation were based more on peculiar Spanish conditions than on apparently similar circumstances elsewhere in Europe.

It has been necessary to place ourselves in the center of the most painful conflicts of the late fifteenth and early sixteenth centuries in order to understand the "libertarian" sense of certain opinions expressed in the works of highly serious authors. Specially notable among these is Luis de León, about whom Joaquín Costa said:

> The ideal of Friar Luis is a society without a state or, rather, a state we might call, in the modern fashion, "libertarian," in which divine grace, illuminating the soul from within, should take the place of laws, and where the duties of the governor should be like those of the shepherd.[17]

Luis de León, commenting on the name "Pastor" (Shepherd) given to Christ in the Holy Scriptures, says:

> His government does not consist in giving laws nor in setting up commandments, but in grazing and nourishing those whom He governs. . . . At all times and on every occasion He orders His government in conformity with the particular case of the person over whom He rules. . . . For these reasons His is an extremely perfect government; because, as Plato says, the best government is not that of written laws. . . . Perfect government is that of the living law . . . , so that the law may be the good and sound judgment of him who governs, which judgment adapts itself always to the special situation of the person ruled (*Republic*, Book IV).[18]

If Luis de León had gone no further than this, his opinions might be explained as an echo of Platonic doctrines, and the "libertarian" element in his thought would fall into place in the so-called history of ideas;[19] but he does not deal with this problem only on a theoretical

---

truly have done so. . . . [The Queen] went up to the Prince and struck him and took away the prisoners, and carried them off with her wrapped in capes. All this was found out, and apologies were made to Fernán d'Álvarez [father of the presumed criminal] for that game" (cited by Márquez, *op. cit.*, p. 94).

[17] *Crisis política de España* (a speech read at the *Juegos Florales* ["Poetical Festival"] of Salamanca on September 15, 1901); it appears in *Historia, política, social: patria*, ed. José García Mercadal (Madrid: Aguilar, 1961), p. 250. References to Luis de León may also be found in Pedro Dorado Montero, *Valor social de leyes y autoridades* (Barcelona: Manuales Soler, 1903), p. 16.

[18] Luis de León, *Nombres de Cristo*, ed. F. de Onís, Book I, pp. 131, 147.

[19] Francisco Giner de los Ríos quoted Plato in connection with anarchism in his article "Para la historia de las teorías libertarias," *Boletín de la Institución Libre de Enseñanza*, XXIII (1899), 88.

basis or as a part of the Christology of the time. The theme of law and justice has here a vital, autobiographical dimension and takes on meaning when it is related to other passages in his *Nombres de Cristo*. "Christ," he says, "ordered His kingdom for our benefit . . . ; but these [kings] who rule us now reign for themselves." And since they have never had "personal experience of how affliction and poverty hurt," they impose "on their subjects . . . the heaviest of yokes, . . . rigorous laws," which they apply with "cruelty and severity." Anguish presses in ever more closely upon him, and gradually there begins to appear the real motivation for his comments on justice and laws: What should be the nature of "the condition of those who are subjects in this kingdom? And, in truth, they may almost all be reduced to this one, which is that everyone should be magnanimous and noble, and *of the same lineage*."

Here is the problem, the painful wound that makes many excellent Spaniards cry out in 1583 just as they had done a hundred years before. This is the anguished center from which the so-called libertarian theories irradiate. Since the fifteenth century the New Christians had been brandishing one defensive weapon, the argument that God did not distinguish between one Christian and another: "In Christ Jesus," Friar Luis recalls, "neither circumcision availeth any thing, nor uncircumcision, but the new creature" (*Galatians*, 6:15). Great is the nobility of Christ's kingdom, "in which no vassal is base of lineage, or insulted on account of his condition, or less well born than any other. And it seems to me that this is the way of being a king *rightly and honorably—not having vassals who are base and subject to affronts*." This radical opinion is cautiously moderated by one of the interlocutors in the dialogue, who alleges that "sometimes it is desirable to treat one part [of the kingdom] ill in order that the other parts may not be lost. And so our princes do not deserve reprehension with respect to this"—in other words, when they allow the Inquisition to persecute those of us who are Christians of Jewish origin. But Sabino replies vehemently: "I do not reproach them now, but I lament [what happens to] their quality, for by reason of the exigency that you, Juliano, have mentioned, *they necessarily become lords of base and mean vassals*." Friar Luis' voice becomes ever more emphatic. It may perhaps be necessary, Sabino goes on, for kings to authorize such great cruelty: "But if there are certain princes . . . who seem to feel that they are greater lords when they find better ways not only to affront their own [vassals] but also *to make that affront extend to many generations, to make their infamy endless*—of these princes, Julian, what can you say to me?" Juliano replies:

What? Why, that they are anything but kings. For one reason, because the goal toward which their office is directed is to make their vassals happy, *and it would be a miracle if humbling and debasing them should have any connection with that goal.* And . . . they harm and decrease themselves. Because, if they are the heads, what honor lies in being the *head of a deformed and vile body?* And if they are shepherds, of what value to them are *mangy sheep?* . . . Thus it is not possible to bind together in peace a kingdom *whose parts are so opposed and differentiated, some* [having] *great honor and others, marked infamy.* . . . That kingdom in which *many classes and kinds of men and many families* are as if offended and hurt[20] and in which the differences imposed for these reasons by fortune and *the laws* do not permit certain groups to mingle and be at harmony with others, is a kingdom subject to infirmity and *armed strife* over any question that may arise. . . . Because of man's weakness and his inflamed tendency toward evil, *laws* for the most part *carry with them one very great disadvantage:* for while the intent of those who establish them is . . . to pull men back from evil and induce them to good, at times the opposite result is achieved, and the very fact that a thing is forbidden arouses the appetite for it. . .

For that reason, he continues, St. Paul says (Romans 5:20) that "the making and giving of laws many times gives rise to the breaking of the laws."

With his followers Christ made use of a new and strange law, "not only teaching them to be good, . . . but in effect *making them good,* which no other king or legislator has ever been able to do." Consequently, there are two kinds of laws: some "speak to the intellect and illuminate it as to what, in conformity with reason, should or should not be done . . ."; others cause the will to be fond of, and inclined toward, "what merits being desired as good. . . . *The first law consists of orders and rules; the second, in a celestial quality and wholesomeness.*"[21] (These words clarify and confirm what is said above, p. 333.)

Friar Luis prefers the law of grace, the law inspired by God, because the other laws either are corrupt in themselves or corrupt society when they are applied. Long before, another New Christian

---

[20] For different reasons another cleric, the Jesuit Pedro de Rivadeneira, speaks of the small affection felt for Philip II in 1580, shortly before the conquest of Portugal. Everyone, he says, "is bitter, displeased, and irritated with His Majesty." There were manifold reasons: in the towns people complained about the tax they had to pay on everything they sold (the *alcabalas*); the ecclesiastics protested against having to give to the king two-ninths of the tithes collected; the friars, "against the reform which has been attempted in their orders"; the grandees, because "no attention is paid to them"; the knights, because "they receive few benefits" (*Biblioteca de Autores Españoles,* LX, 589). The reasons adduced by Father Rivadeneira are not the same as those mentioned by Luis de León, but the lack of a sympathetic bond between the people and its sovereign confirms, from another point of view, the existence of ill will in those who had to obey the commands of the royal authority, "so that, though the king is so powerful and so much obeyed and respected, he is not as much liked or loved as was the custom, nor so much the master of the will and hearts of his subjects."

[21] Luis de León, *op. cit.,* Book II, pp. 83–103. The entire chapter should be borne in mind.

and Erasmian, Alfonso de Valdés, had written: "We call ourselves Christians and we live worse than Turks and brute animals. If this Christian doctrine seems to us some kind of fairy tale, why do we not forsake it completely? ... But since we know [it] to be true ..., why do we live *as if there were among us neither faith nor law?*"[22] But Alfonso de Valdés was more concerned about the conduct of the popes than about what was happening around him in Spain. Friar Luis, after a long century of the Inquisition, was contemplating the painful lacerations of Spanish society; his own trial by the Inquisition and that of his companions, which had been authorized by iniquitous laws, led him to trace out the structure of the life he knew in the words we have quoted, phrases whose violence is equaled nowhere else in that epoch: "vassals who are base and subject to affronts"; "base and mean vassals"; generations of "endless infamy"; vassals who are "humbled and debased"; a social body that is "deformed and vile"; "mangy sheep." Certain types of occupations, certain professions ("classes and kinds of men") are "offended and hurt"—which means that intellectual and technical tasks, as well as many families, are despised and scorned. Perverse laws make it impossible for "certain groups to mingle and be in harmony with others." Never has life in the time of Philip II been judged more directly and bitterly: Christian laws were not obeyed; and those of the state, which sowed discord among the castes by confusing moral and civil values with genealogical ones, were creating a society that was "mean, vile, infamous, leprous"—and, as we may add, despairing. The allusion to *"armed strife* over any question that may arise" clearly refers to the situation of the Moriscos.

When the words of Luis de León are related to the ideas set forth in my *De la edad conflictiva*, it is easy to perceive the meaning of certain texts that up to now have been considered as precursors of nineteenth-century anarchist concepts. But the truth is that the Spaniard was not an anarchist and could not even suspect what such forms of sociopolitical life might mean. What really happened was that many Spaniards endowed with sufficient culture and sensitivity to express in words all those things that stung their souls, withdrew into an inner solitude, each one *illuminating himself* by the light available to him; and in that light he found reasons to reject the visible and immediate *law* and yearned for others, better legal forms: the law of Christ, above all, but also the legal forms of Muslim justice, or of the Muslim Illuminati, the spiritual Utopia of Erasmus, or the social Utopia of Thomas More (the ideas of the latter were, indeed, put into practice by Bishop Zumárraga and Vasco de Quiroga in New Spain). "Flight from the world" was not just a peculiar notion of

---

22 Alfonso de Valdés, *op. cit.,* p. 94.

those "bygone times" but a reaction against all that which made it impossible for the Spanish castes to continue to participate in a shared common life. It is, therefore, entirely clear why the expression of such anguish should have arisen among the most intelligent members of the oppressed castes. In this connection we should also bear in mind the fantastic attempt at a Christian-Islamic syncretism conceived by the Granadine Moriscos, in which Archbishop Pedro de Castro had so blissfully trusted (see p. 241).

In sum, we must distinguish between those reactions against the law which are of Platonic origin[23] and those that had been provoked by the total state of affairs which actually existed around those who rebelled against a legality felt to be perverse, a legality that urged men to be disobedient and to dream of other ways of being ruled. Furthermore, this latter type of reaction is badly understood if we say only generically that the oppressed (the humble and destitute) always and everywhere have tried to rebel against tyranny; for in sixteenth-century Spain the oppressed were learned and intelligent men who, though themselves victims of these iniquitous laws (the statutes of purity of blood; and, before them, the ordinances against the Jews; the failure to observe the terms of the surrender of Granada;[24] the inquisitorial law itself), still were able to rationalize their agonizing situation. Luis Vives, for example, certainly looked back to Plato and Isocrates when he wrote that "without laws people live well, with right-minded and circumspect customs" when "children have been accustomed to finding pleasure in good things and repugnance in evil ones."[25] But the Vives who thought that "where love for the good and hatred of evil have become second nature in man, laws are not needed in order to live with rectitude and order," is the same man who dedicated his De pacificatione to Alonso Manrique, archbishop of Seville and inquisitor general, with the following words: "We can but wonder at the latitude given to the judge, who is not lacking in human passions, or to the accuser, who many times is urged on to slander by a hidden hatred, an unconfessable hope for gain, or some other perverse motivation."[26] Some members of Vives's family had been burned at the stake, others dispossessed of their property, by the Holy Office; in such passages as the last quoted, deep personal motivations prompt his comments on the corruption of judicial proceedings.

---

[23] See Dorado Montero, op. cit., p. 14.

[24] A Granadine nobleman, Yusé Banegas, expresses thus his sadness at the failure to abide by the terms of the surrender: "If the king who gained the victory does not keep faith, what can we expect from his successors?" (see Márquez, op. cit., p. 303).

[25] Cited by Joaquín Costa, La ignorancia del derecho (Barcelona: Manuales Soler, 1901), p. 37.

[26] Obras completas, trans. L. Riber, II, 274–276.

Another precursor of libertarian doctrines is the Mercedarian friar Alonso de Castrillo, author of a *Tratado de república* ("Treatise on the Republic") (Burgos, 1512). Friar Alonso took some part in the war of the *comunidades* (the uprising in 1520 of the cities of Castile against the government of their new king, Charles V), which was closely connected with the cause of the converts, for one of the petitions of the *comuneros* was that inquisitorial legislation should be modified. Alonso de Castrillo asserts that in the beginning the *comuneros* were asking for a "very just justice," though he criticizes the subversive violence with which they made their demands. Understandably, the author wavers between affirming that without a king "there is no peaceful republic" and maintaining (perhaps more spontaneously) that obedience "has been introduced *more by the force of positive law than by natural justice*" (chap. 6); and he insists that "with the exception of the obedience of children to their parents and the respect shown by young people for those who are older, *all other kinds of obedience are by nature unjust, because we all were born free and equal*" (chap. 22).[27] Friar Alonso, forced by his vows to obey in spiritual matters, rebels against all other forms of obedience; and he does so, to be sure, after the revolt of the *comunidades* and after his unsuccessful mediation during the rebellion, in a book that is rightly termed "cryptopolitical" by Tierno Galván.

According to Friar Alonso, the conflict was provoked by "strange and foreign men, enemies of our Republic, and of our people (Preface). Here he alludes directly and clearly to the predatory courtiers of Charles V, many of whom were not Spaniards; the outrages perpetrated by them incited people "to do harm, to burn houses, not so much out of devotion to justice as out of greed for booty; and as men *weary of obedience* they desire by means of rebellion to ascend to equality with more important men, for nothing can be so powerful in man's perdition as the equality of men. And once the tumult has been started, the very men who intend to be the first to flee say 'let [the tyrants] die.' "

The *comunidades* took up arms to put in order what they felt to be an evil government, but the immediate result was a chaos without form or direction. The phrase underlined above, "weary of obedience," is pregnant with meaning. Given the system of the castes, the lack of a just justice was a chronic and inevitable sickness; and it is necessary to accept this reality without confusing what "really happened" with what "should have happened." Such a confusion leads

---

[27] Eduardo de Hinojosa referred to Alonso de Castrillo's book in his *Influencia que tuvieron en el derecho público ... los filósofos y teólogos españoles* (Madrid, 1890), p. 79. See also E. Tierno Galván, "De las comunidades," an essay included in his *Del espectáculo a la trivialización* (Madrid, 1961), pp. 287–317.

either to a history without meaningful content or to a prejudiced history bent solely on defending the position of either the rebel or the tyrant. Spanish life was rejecting its own bases and suffered from a radical insecurity precisely because the Spaniards had not created for themselves, whether by peaceful agreement or by genuine revolution, a social system based on effective obedience. Therefore, the social situation came to be that we have seen described by Luis de León. Members of the Christian caste tried to force those of the other two groups into their own caste mold by means of the magic action of the water of baptism; they sought to transform Jews and Moors overnight into convinced and faithful practitioners of the religion of the most powerful caste. The problem was lucidly explained by Francisco de Cáceres, a Jew who returned to Spain in 1500 and fell into the hands of the Inquisition:

> If the king, our lord, should order Christians either to become Jews or to depart from his kingdoms, some of them would become Jews, and others would leave; and the [Christians] who left, when they saw themselves lost, would become Jews in order to return to their native land, and they would be Christians, and they would deceive the world; it would think that they were Jews, but within, in their hearts and their wills, they would be Christians.[28]

The Moriscos, for their part, must have thought and said the same thing. It was impossible, therefore, to create a justice that was socially just, but only pragmatic arguments and legal criteria based on force whose worst defect consisted in their claim to be just and holy. So there arose the nonconformist, at times self-contradictory, attitudes of men like Luis de León and John of Avila, both of whom were New Christians. John of Avila, for example, deemed it a sin to store up hatred against those who had been punished by the Holy Office and "to fail to consider such people as one's fellowmen."[29]

Abuses, unlawful acts, and outrages were as common in other countries as in Spain—there is no doubt of that; but the special factor in the case of Spain was the loss of the notion of what was just and what unjust and the complete confusion with respect to the bases of "obedience." The result of this chronic situation was the lack of esteem for the law and for those who administered it, whether they were Christians, Jews, or converts. The only form of justice which inspired an illusory nostalgia was that of the Moors (see p. 305). In the sixteenth century those who pressed the justest of claims tried to gain favor by means of corruption and bribery. Charles V wrote to Pope Leo X in 1519 that the converts had offered Ferdinand the Catholic, "my lord and grandfather—may he dwell in glory," 300,000 ducats in order that those who were punished by the Inquisition might not have to

---

[28] Fritz Baer, *Die Juden im christlichen Spanien*, I, 545.
[29] Márquez, *op. cit.*, p. 294.

wear *sanbenitos* and that the placards with the names of penitents and their penance might be removed from the churches. But it was fruitless for those "of their lineage" (the converts from Judaism) to say that *"harm and injustice* had been done to them" and that they were attempting to free themselves from *"the misgivings and fear in which they live."* The Emperor was violently opposed to the Pope's granting a bull to modify inquisitorial proceedings, "as secrecy is the strength of the Holy Office."[30] Both the converts from Judaism and the Moriscos requested that "witnesses and jails [of the Inquisition] might be publicly known," so that judges could not see "young unmarried women and the wives of good, upright men" in secret.[31]

But if royal power was deaf to the demands of those who were persecuted and martyred by the Inquisition, the anarchical behavior of the converts, firmly entrenched in a large number of municipal councils, was no less disturbing, as the converts Alonso de Palencia and Mosén Diego de Valera state without reservation in their chronicles. In Cordova the New Christians, "made extraordinarily wealthy by some curious means, and then become haughty and aspiring with insolent arrogance to get public offices into their hands, [and] after New Christians in spite of their low extraction had, through money and against all regulations, achieved the order of chivalry," stirred up "revolts and rebellious factions"; all this was done by "men who before had never dared [to make] the slightest movement toward liberty." With the aid of Alonso de Aguilar, "whom they provided with funds when he was obliged to pay the extraordinary expenses and high wages of the troops, they had enlisted . . . three hundred well-armed cavalrymen; and venturing greater daring, they exerted no caution about practicing Judaic ceremonies as they pleased." As for the Bishop of Cordova, "with the increase of his honors, his way of life and his customs began to degenerate in his old age," and he was finally expelled from his diocese.[32] The chronicle of Diego de Valera, likewise cited by Francisco Márquez in *Juan Alvarez Gato*, reinforces the impression that the New Christian oppressed the Old in a variety of ways. I consider invalid the usual explanation that these and other disorders in the fifteenth century were the result of the weak government of King Henry IV or merely the reflection of what Huizinga has called the "autumn of the Middle Ages." The social chaos of the times was tightly linked to the conflicting inter-

---

[30] The text of Charles V's instructions to his ambassador in Rome, Lope Hurtado de Mendoza, with regard to this matter has been published by Fidel Fita in the *Boletín de la Academia de la Historia,* XXXIII (1898), 330–345.

[31] From a petition presented by the Granadine Moriscos to Charles V in 1526, in Henry Charles Lea, *History of the Inquisition in Spain,* I, 585.

[32] For this whole problem, see Francisco Márquez, "Conversos y cargos concejiles en el siglo XV," *Revista de Archivos, Bibliotecas y Museos,* LXIII, no. 2 (1957), 503–540.

ests of the opposed castes—a conflict that, indeed, was translated into the enmity of the lower classes toward the bourgeoisie of the cities, who were qualified for leadership by their culture, their economic power, their administrative and technical efficiency, and who were, irremediably, Hispano-Judaic.

The situation of the municipal councils changed little during the reign of the Catholic Sovereigns or even in the sixteenth century. As Márquez says, "The cleverness of the converts was almost always able to leap over any kind of restrictive barrier" ("Conversos y cargos concejiles en el siglo XV," *Revista de Archivos, Biblioteca y Museos*, LXIII, no. 2 [1957], 539). This whole problem is related to the complex phenomenon of the comunidades—complex because in that turbulence there mingled in one and the same outburst the interests and the passions of both the victims and the creators of this chronic state of illegality.

It is logical to suppose that the converts incited and aided the revolt insofar as they could, for among the petitions of the *comuneros* there appear these:

That the Inquisition should have a new organization, for the greater glory and honor of God.
They asked further that many persons of these kingdoms who have been defamed might be heard and have their wrongs righted.[33]

Pero Mejía comments that "with regard to the Inquisition I have not been able to find out what they were requesting" (*Relación de las Comunidades de Castilla*, in *Biblioteca de Autores Españoles*, XXI, 370); but today, thanks to the instructions given by Charles V to his ambassador in Rome (cited above, p. 339), we do know that the *comuneros* were asking for the Holy Office to proceed openly and not in secret and for the removal of the *sanbenitos* (the defamatory placards in churches listing names of those found guilty by the Inquisition and the practices that had occasioned their sentencing). There is no doubt that certain rich converts gave Juan de Padilla, head of the Toledan *comunidad*, a great sum of money so that he might work for the inquisitional reforms; it is said that Padilla refused to help them, but he did accept their gold.[34] According to Pero Mejía, "most of the councilmen [of the cities] approved of the uprising against the policies followed by the Emperor" (*op. cit.*, p. 368); since

---

[33] Pero Mejía, *Relación de las Communidades de Castilla*, in *Biblioteca de Autores Españoles*, XXI, 369. For the problem of the *comunidades* and the New Christians, see also my work *La Celestina como contienda literaria*, p. 41 ff.

[34] See Fidel Fita in *Boletín de la Academia de la Historia*, XXXIII (1898), 307–326. From the documents published there we know that the New Christians called the Old Christians *negros* ("black men"); Juan de Padilla was a *negro* (p. 319). As soon as the uprising of the *comunidades* had begun, two Jews, one a former member of the Spanish Royal Council, returned from Fez; they were both burned in Seville in 1521 (p. 339).

many of the municipal councillors were New Christians, the cause of municipal liberty became confused with the interest of the converts in maintaining within the cities their own often abusive and anarchical power.

If the movement of the *comunidades* was clear and justified with regard to its motivations, it was chaotic with regard to the formulation of its goals and the search for means by which these goals might be carried out. Economic power lay in the hands of the *comunidades*; but the energies of aggression and command were possessed by others. In the end it became clear that in Castile only royal authority and the nobles in its service possessed the genuine gift of leadership. One detail related by the convert Alonso de Santa Cruz reveals only too well the inexpertness of the *comunero* leaders, who sallied forth from Torre de Lobatón (in Valladolid) only to be put to rout in Villalar on April 23, 1521: "They were to blame for all this [their economic difficulties], because in Torre de Lobatón they found 20,000 *fanegas* of wheat and more than 30,000 *cántaras* of wine, all of which they dissipated in two months, for the soldiers would give a cask of wine for a pair of hens; and they would exchange a load of wheat for two geese."[35]

The *comunidades* were a poor patchwork of contrary aims: the promotion of just tax and administrative reforms; the elimination of the oppressive meddling of Chièvres (grand chamberlain of Charles V) and his men; the chimerical attempt to make certain Castilian cities into political entities like the municipalities of Italy;[36] the Hispano-Jewish illusion of escaping from the undoubtedly evil clutches of the Inquisition; the longing to satisfy the mutually unrelated ambitions of various individuals or groups. Furthermore, the *comunidades* made possible the revelation of certain individual ways of thinking and feeling, which circumstances had not previously permitted: for example, among the professors of the University of Alcalá, most of whom were *comuneros*, there flowered that Utopianism and Messianism so characteristic of Erasmian circles and of New Christians. The famous humanist Hernán Núñez (called the "Comen-

---

[35] Alonso de Santa Cruz, *Crónica del Emperador Carlos V* (Madrid, 1920), I, 458. As is well known, the author was Charles V's chief cosmographer, but earlier he had accompanied Sebastian Cabot as treasurer on the latter's expedition to the Spice Islands in 1525. See A. Morel-Fatio, *Historiographie de Charles-Quint*, p. 100. Santa Cruz has all the earmarks of being a convert.

[36] Antonio de Guevara says in a letter supposedly addressed to the *comunero* Antonio de Acuña, Bishop of Zamora: "I have also found amusing the cunning you displayed in deceiving and stirring up Toledo, Burgos, Valladolid, Leon, Salamanca, Avila, and Segovia by saying that henceforward they would be exempt and free, as Venice, Genoa, Florence, Siena, and Lucca are, so that they should no longer be called cities but dominions and that they should not have councilmen but consuls" (*Epístolas familiares*, in *Biblioteca de Autores Españoles*, XIII, 142a).

dador griego" or "Greek commander"), an enthusiastic *comunero*, said that "he would turn Muslim if within a year he did not see the noblemen humbled and if anyone should remain who had more than 100,000 maravedís of income."[37]

"Weary of obedience," as Friar Alonso de Castrillo had said, groups of disunited Castilians thought they could overthrow the hierarchies in power at the time. But Castile had been constituted as a state and as the center of the future Spanish monarchy, thanks to the commanding power of the people who had succeeded in overcoming caste divergencies and their conflicting spiritual hierarchies. What tyrannical oppression may have been required to achieve this goal is not pertinent to the discussion at this point;[38] but it was utterly fantastic that in 1520 some thousands of Castilians should have thought it possible to order their lives in accord with their horizontal interests: economics, cooperation among artisans, autonomous municipal administration. These levels of coincidence formed no sort of united whole, primarily because of the opposing interests of the castes: Juan de Padilla, a "negro" for the New Christians, hungered for the jingling gold coins of the latter, but he refused to take any steps toward the reformation of inquisitorial proceedings. In addition, another obstacle was that the "cellular" units of the councils could not form a whole fabric among themselves. This Spanish dream of forming a state (or a nonstate) on the basis of fractional units operating under different laws may be effective locally, but not beyond the limits of each council. Furthermore, from what we know about the inner workings of the councils,[39] the shared life within them left much to be desired.[40] In the final analysis, the unifying authority was that of royal power and of those who represented it in Castile (i.e., Admiral Fadrique Enríquez and Lord High Constable Iñigo de Velasco) who *at that time* genuinely embodied the power of command and organization of the nascent empire. The *comuneros* lacked cohesive powers; and in the final analysis Friar Antonio de Guevara—verbose, cynical, and, at times, clear-eyed—was right: "I do not know," he said, "how you hope to reform the kingdom,

---

[37] M. Danvila, *Historia de las comunidades de Castilla*, III, 676; *apud* Tierno Galván, *op. cit.*, p. 311.

[38] The occasional attempts (see p. 89) to direct the three castes toward the same vertex of religious belief had failed. Ultimately that illusion was related to the Sufi longing (more an aspiration than an idea) to make all loving searches for the divine meet in one and the same God (see chap. vii).

[39] See especially the previously cited article by Francisco Márquez with respect to the council offices.

[40] Cervantes, whose ideas about justice and authority greatly resembled those of the writers I have been quoting, makes Sancho say jokingly, on the occasion of the famous adventure with the lost donkey and the braying councilmen: "It is of no importance to the truth of the history whether those who brayed were mayors or councilmen, but only that they brayed, for a mayor is as much in danger of braying as a councilman" (*Quixote*, II, 27).

for with all your help there is no subject who recognizes his prelate,
. . . nor is there a vassal who keeps his faith . . . : so that, under the
color of liberty, *everyone lives according to his own will*" (*Epístolas
familiares*, in *Biblioteca de Autores Españoles*, XIII, 150).

The *comunidades* expressed through violence the dissatisfaction
felt by the Castilians with the way they were being governed by the
first of the Hapsburg kings. Once that uprising had been put down
(as well as that of the Valencian *Germanías*, which was even more
chaotic and popular in character), the protest and suspicion with
respect to the lack of justice and the rationality of the laws continued
to be manifested both in works of a literary nature (for example, the
picaresque novel) and in juridical and sociological treatises. A contemporary of Friar Luis de León, Dr. Tomás Cerdán de Tallada,
states that it is well known that "good laws were born out of the
evil customs of men, for, if there were no such evil ways, and if we
all lived well, *and if republics were maintained with order and under
a good administration, laws would be superfluous.*"[41] He adds further
that "the excess of laws" multiplies the number of lawsuits.

In 1901 Joaquín Costa—who, without being an anarchist, came
close to the doctrine in some of his opinions—wrote that in Spain
"men could live in society in an orderly fashion almost without
having any dealings with the laws: free, therefore, from the necessity
of knowing them; nor would that state of affairs—let it be clearly
understood—lead to conflicts among the multiple individual spheres
[of interest] or to a weakening of the tendency to form various sorts
of unions—as has been done in the past and will always be done—
[such as] the municipality, the nation, the state."[42] A regime based
on good customs would make the work of the legislator unnecessary;
Costa called attention to many of these good customs, for example,
that of the Valencian court which regulated irrigation (see above,
p. 306); but he reinforced his own doctrine mainly by that of certain
Spanish jurists who had maintained that "the legislator promulgates
the laws tacitly, *ad referendum.*" Among others, he cites texts from
Diego de Covarrubias, Martín de Azpilcueta, Juan de Caramuel (who
maintained that "the acceptance of the law by the subjects must be
free"), and Gregorio de Valencia ("the prince cannot decree laws
except under the condition that the people accept them").[43]

In the nineteenth century modern thinkers sought the support of

---

[41] *Verdadero gobierno desta monarquía* (Valencia, 1581), fol. 60; *apud*
Dorado Montero, *op. cit.*, p. 15. Cerdán de Tallada was a member of the Royal
Council.

[42] *La ignorancia del derecho*, p. 43.

[43] *Ibid.*, pp. 101–110.

those of the sixteenth: Luis Vives, Luis de León, and many others. Without having any clear idea of the inward feelings of those sixteenth-century Spaniards who were aware of their own lives, Francisco Giner de los Ríos intuited, and set forth in sharp and precise words, the basis for the ideological similarities between the moderns and their predecessors: "Day by day coercive power seems to be losing the special position it has held from Thomasius to Kant . . . ; people are beginning to turn their eyes toward other, more solid guarantees: especially *toward the inner self*, the disposition of the spirit, the motivation of conduct, and, therefore, toward that [type of] contemporary education whose general outlines we have just traced out."[44]

I know, of course, that the moral form and content of the *inner self* were not the same in the nineteenth century as in 1500, though in both eras that inwardness served as the pole star and the haven of many shipwrecked travelers deprived of all other hopes of salvation. The *inner self*, illuminated by divine grace, strengthened those who were oppressed from without and was the first step on the mystic ladder of liberation.[45]

In my *Aspectos del vivir hispánico* (1949, pp. 25 ff.), I have outlined the Messianic hopes that agitated the souls of various fifteenth-century writers: "The birth of Prince John [son of the Catholic Sovereigns], 'the prince the people longed for,' was compared with that of St. John. The *bachiller* Palma, in a style characteristic of the convert, . . . expresses himself according to Pauline spiritual forms." Spiritual freedom—the redemption of religion—was confused with secular liberty. The chronicler Enríquez del Castillo writes to Queen Isabella that Jesus Christ came to free us from "the tyrannical servitude of the world, so that no one should be compelled to serve without [being given] a daily livelihood." In one of his eclogues, Lucas Fernández says that "the world is now freed from tribute, and restored." Friar Francisco de Osuna maintains in his *Abecedario espiritual* (so severely expurgated by the Inquisition) that the grace of the Holy Ghost "is communicated more to the lowly and scorned than to the vain and haughty." All this inward and spiritualized

---

[44] Francisco Giner de los Ríos, *Acerca de la función de la ley* (Madrid, 1932), p. 47. This essay was first published in French in the *Revue Internationale de Sociologie* (Aug.–Sept., 1908).

[45] Further confirmation of such inner ways of feeling is provided by certain early sixteenth-century oaths and forms of blasphemy uttered by people who believed themselves unjustly deprived of the support of grace and hope. They rebelled against God for having taken away his grace and hope, leaving them "disgraced" and "desperate." In 1525, for example, "there was ordered the public proclamation in the square of the Zocodover, of the City of Toledo, that no one should dare to say 'I disbelieve in God' . . . or 'there is no power in God,' and 'I do not believe in the faith of God' . . . and 'I deny the faith and the chrism I have rejected'" (Alonso de Santa Cruz, *op. cit.*, I, 146; II, 360).

Christianity, as I have said before (*Aspectos del vivir hispanico*, p. 35), is very like that of the Erasmians.

The dream of a Messianic redemption that would be visible and tangible as well as spiritual is sometimes expressed in frenzied terms by these writers, some of whom were ecclesiastics, others laymen. In view of the identity between "redemption" and "liberation of the peoples" in certain Jewish mystics, it is altogether natural that the Messianic ideal should have flourished vigorously among the converts: "Redemption had both a political and a historical content. The hope that peoples might be freed from their yokes and emerge into a new liberty stimulated the Messianic idea with great and powerful efficacy."[46]

The situation in Spain became very complex—and is difficult to understand at first glance—because the currents of spirituality (both European and Oriental) converged in the same polemical area in which the opposed castes were conflicting. Very little of those inward attitudes was externalized; new types of religious belief did not emerge, nor was the political or social structure visibly modified. At the most we might mention the unsuccessful and confused action of the *comunidades*; or the plans of Friar Juan de Zumárraga and Bishop Vasco de Quiroga to make the Indians of Michoacán live according to the rules outlined by Thomas More in his *Utopia*[47] so that they might thus return to the uncorrupted purity of the Golden Age. As a result of the conflicting tensions of Spanish existence, in the end everything was translated into the enrichment of the dramatic, poetic, and novelistic possibilities of the *inner self*. Once aware of all this, we can understand the broad scope and the profundity of sixteenth- and seventeenth-century literature, which includes works ranging from *La Celestina*, the *Quixote*, and the drama of Lope de Vega to the mysticism of St. John of the Cross.

What Is "Spanish Anarchism"?

Here we must stop a moment to check our bearings and make sure that we do not stray off our course. All the matters discussed in this chapter are in some way related to the ideological and social movements called "anarchism" in the nineteenth century; but that relationship is like the one between a waterfall on the one hand and the channel and the turbine that turn the potential force of the water

---

[46] Gershom Scholem, *Die jüdische Mystik in ihrem Hauptströmungen* (Frankfurt a/M, 1957), p. 334. See also p. 268: "If the spiritual process of existence were carried back to its primary bases, one would come to the idea of Redemption, in the sense that the world would return to its original unity and purity."

[47] See Silvio A. Zavala, *La "Utopía" de Tomás Moro en la Nueva España* (Mexico, 1937), and my *Hacia Cervantes* (1960), p. 101.

into industrial power on the other. Since this step, from the will to revolt to the theory of revolution, was never taken by the Spaniards, it is not surprising that in this instance they never transformed into objectified anarchist *ideas* their yearning for a terrestrial redemption, their repugnance toward the laws, and their Messianic dreams of a just collective life not imposed from without. If we apply to this situation the age-old distinction between "matter" and "form," we may observe that the Spaniards possessed the first without ever arriving at the invention of the second. Let us remember those *comuneros* who were reduced to bartering with the products they possessed in such abundance instead of making use of them in a less primitive economic fashion.

Spanish "anarchism" is a phenomenon much like the presumed Romanticism of Spain's literature and customs in the sense that the latter, *in order to become Romantic*, had to be seen from the viewpoint of the philosophy of Rousseau, Schelling, and the like. In other words, to call the Spanish past of any period anarchist, baroque, or Romantic is imprecise and naïve, though we all tend to make such loose statements. The modalities of Spanish existence penetrated deeply into the awareness of the *inner self* (witness the spiritualism of the converts, the imported Erasmianism, the pleasure in solitude, the quietism of Miguel de Molinos, etc.); or the anguished tensions of the inner self were discharged outward against the spectacle of a broken social order, without proper harmony between the individual and the collective, between inward situations and the transcendent forces by which they were sustained. From this situation flow the repeated protests against the laws, against those who apply them badly, and even, in moments of exasperation, against God; from it also, however, proceed the possibilities and the richness of literary expression, which are inexplicable if we take into account only more or less abstract concepts, such as the Middle Ages, the use of certain ancient or modern *topoi*, the Renaissance, or transitional periods— all those things, in short, with which we tend to play at times a kind of "historical solitaire."

An Economy Free of Laws and Pure in Blood

The anarchist doctrines of the nineteenth century fell upon a human soil well prepared to receive them. The Spanish state had never been closely united; it was made up of kingdoms and viceroyalties that met at one vertex, the royal institution, and within the separate parts there had been chronic complaints about the injustice or deficiency of the laws and the authorities who applied them. (The laws of the Indies were of more theoretical than practical value.) In the seventeenth and eighteenth centuries the circumstances of Spanish life had certainly not contributed to the modification of the opinions expressed by Luis de León, Quevedo, and so many others.[48] The agrarian reform planned by the Count of Aranda in the second half of the eighteenth century, "in view of the notable decline suffered by agriculture in these kingdoms," could not be put into effect.[49]

It is now time to examine, along with these criticisms of evil laws and their evil application, the reasons for Spain's having been converted into a country whose economy was primarily agricultural, in which the traditional crafts and industry had fallen into almost total desuetude. We must hear, in this regard, not only the critics of evil or impotent governments, but also those who had been predicting the economic ruin of Spain since the sixteenth century. It will then be seen that it does not suffice to speak in generic terms and to apply to Spain criteria prevailing in the rest of Europe at any given moment.

It is said, for example, that the poverty of the state and the lower classes was due to "a bourgeoisie ruined by its own enterprises and an inactive but dominant aristocracy, [who] had sadly deformed the mentality of the working classes."[50] I would prefer to focus the economic history of Spain on the social condition and function of individuals rather than on generic concepts of bourgeoisie, aristocracy, and laboring classes which are of little use in the situation of the Spaniards of the seventeenth century, the period to which Vicens Vives refers. The Spanish economy was as firmly anchored in caste and in people's faith as were literature, art, politics, and all the rest. The production and use of wealth depended in the first instance on the awareness of one's personal dignity, on one's honor and reputation. When the Spaniard who had become wealthy in the Indies re-

---

[48] "To find out whether Satan [and not Christ] governs a republic, there is no surer sign than to see if needy people go around seeking relief without finding a way in to the princes" (Quevedo, *Política de Dios y gobierno de Cristo*, in *Biblioteca de Autores Españoles*, XXIII, 34).

[49] See Joaquín Costa, *Historia política, social, patria*, pp. 197 ff. The legislators during the reign of Charles III (1759–1788) were as able as they were well-meaning, but, as Costa says, "the purely intellectual guidance of the legislator was not sufficient" because "the same slave traders who had the rural masses chained to their service were the very people entrusted with breaking the chains by their own hands. The Council of Castile was moving in a vicious circle" (p. 206).

[50] J. Vicens Vives, *Manual de historia económica de España* (Barcelona, 1959), p. 378. Sr. Vicens Vives, the famous Catalan historian and sociologist, whose untimely death was a great loss for Spanish scholarship, wrote in one of his last works these generous words in support of my theories, which he had formerly opposed as intuitions without documentary support: "In the final analysis, what weighs most in my opinion is the fact that Castro's hypothesis fits in and is more in accordance . . . with the documents on the economy, society, and culture of the fifteenth century which I have been studying thoroughly for two decades" (*Aproximación a la historia de España* [Barcelona, rev. ed., 1968], p. 192; trans.: *Approaches to the History of Spain* [University of California Press, rev. ed, 1970]).

turned to Spain, he was held in scorn; even today the word *indiano* carries this connotation in northern Spain.[51] In other words, the first thing we must do as we examine the problem of Spanish wealth and poverty is to determine what significance and value they possessed within the vital dwelling place of the Spaniard. Many preferred to die of hunger rather than to lose status—that is, not to "maintain honor"—in the opinion of their neighbors. Cervantes refers ironically to the situation of people who preferred to fall prisoner to the Barbary pirates rather than set hand to oar so that their galley might proceed more rapidly:

> for to seize an oar in a perilous moment
> to them appears to be dishonorable.[52]

European models aid us little in knowing and understanding the economy of the Spaniards. In the seventeenth century everyone desired to make it known that he belonged (or to feign that he belonged) to the chosen caste, to that of the Old Christians, to those who were not Jewish. As late as the nineteenth century, Simón Bolívar boasted of his "pure blood." It is a commonplace to speak of Spanish pride, as if this psychic trait had come down from the Celtiberians; in reality, this pride was the haughty gesture made by members of the triumphant caste as they struggled to avoid confusion with those who were not pure in blood. Purity of lineage was affirmed positively by judicial inquiries and reports on the purity of one's blood; negatively, it was asserted by abstaining from any display of interest in the tasks that were deemed characteristic of Moors and Jews, or by demonstrating that one's ancestors had been unlettered peasants. The highest position in the social scale was occupied by ecclesiastics; within this group, the regular clergy possessed in fact more strength and economic power than the secular, so that the desires of those interested in spiritual calm and economic security pushed them toward the monastic life. Those who did not follow this route and possessed no royal post set out for the Indies, thus fulfilling the terms of the proverb mentioned earlier: "Either Church, or sea, or royal house."

Once Spain was reduced to an economy based on the cultivation of land, ownership of the land more and more came to be concentrated in the hands of the great lords and, especially, in those of the ecclesi-

---

[51] I have already pointed out in *Hacia Cervantes* (1960), p. 339, that "wealth acquired by anyone not of noble lineage (the noble had inherited it, or acquired it in the service of the king) was not respected, whether it was that of the *indiano* ["the man who had made a fortune in America"] or that of the banker; the *Cortes* of 1566 proposed to the king that bankers should be expelled [from the country] as the Jews had been earlier, for banker and Jew were all one." In the literature of the time, those who had grown rich in the Indies were assigned ridiculous roles.

[52] See *De la edad conflictiva*, p. 124.

astics. About 1618 the University of Toledo informed the king as follows:

Though the population has decreased by more than half, there are twice as many members of religious orders, clerics, and students of grammar, because *they now find no other way to live or support themselves.* The basic reason is that until a few years ago the nerve and sinew of the republic consisted in artisans, since so much was manufactured for Spain, all of Europe and all the Indies; and an artisan would marry his daughter to a poor young man, but one who had a craft, by means of which he earned his livelihood so regularly that it seemed a fixed income . . . ; and now, seeing that no one can earn a penny, *they do not wish to besmirch their daughters or their sons,* [and] they seek to have them study (because they see that all ecclesiastics are rich) to become nuns, members of religious orders, clerics.[53]

This anonymous report could be accused of inaccuracy or bias if other evidence did not confirm that such was the general impression of those who observed the alarming economic condition of the kingdom. Fernández de Navarrete calls attention to the fact that "while Spain is so in need of people to cultivate the land and to practice the arts and crafts, it possesses in 200 square leagues more than nine thousand monasteries, without taking into account the convents for nuns, which are likewise very numerous" (*Conservación de monarquías* [1626], in *Biblioteca de Autores Españoles,* XXV, 540). Gil González Dávila states in his *Historia de Felipe III* that "in the Orders of St. Francis and St. Dominic alone there were 32,000 friars in Spain" (A. G. de Amezúa, *Introducción al epistolario de Lope de Vega,* p. 208).

But the complaints about the superabundance of religious orders and their exemptions from taxes had already begun a century earlier. The Cortes of 1523 in Valladolid warned that "at the rate at which the churches and monasteries are buying, and at which gifts and legacies are made to them, in a few years the major wealth of the kingdom could be theirs"; they proposed that the Pope be asked to forbid churches and monasteries to acquire real estate, to which Emperor Charles V replied: "Sobeit . . ., and we have already written to His Holiness that he may confirm it" (*ibid.,* p. 215). Nothing was done, however, because the Holy See never consented to it, and the sovereigns in truth ruled Spain through a semiecclesiastical state; it was unthinkable that they should rebel against the very principles upon which their authority rested. The Church constituted a kind of state within the secular state. The cry of the deputies in the Cortes fell on deaf ears; to the Cortes of 1566, Philip II's response was that it was not desirable "at this time to introduce a change or make another declaration." Cristóbal Pérez de Herrera, a doctor whom we

---

[53] See A. G. de Amezúa, *Introducción al epistolario de Lope de Vega* (Madrid, 1940), p. 208.

might today call a "sociologist," asked in the Cortes of 1617 "that it should be seen what measures might be taken in order that the great number of common people, children of farmers and of craftsmen, who were entering religious orders and becoming priests, might be reduced; leaving behind the duties and trades of their fathers, they study, or enter religious orders, or are ordained as priests" (*ibid.*, p. 218). In that same Cortes, Jerónimo de Cañizares, the deputy from Guadalajara, stated that "vassals are lost when they become friars and priests, and *estates that originally were obliged to pay taxes to His Majesty are being incorporated into the Church* under the cover of these friars and priests, and if the situation is not remedied, within a very few years His Majesty will have no one to serve him." An alderman from Toledo, Gerónimo de Zevallos, wrote in his *Arte real para el buen govierno de los reyes y príncipes* (Toledo, 1623) that the excessive accumulation of property in the hands of the Church was an evil so great "that if some medicine against this damage is not considered, this monarchy will be wholly ruined, for that damage is like a woodworm, which, however small it may be, in the end destroys a beam" (fols. 122–135). Archbishop Gaspar de Criales wrote to Philip IV in 1646 that those who entered the religious orders were "the bravest, healthiest, best-formed men, those with the best faces and those of the best wit and ability, without there being among them a single cripple, and scarcely any small, ugly, dull, or ignorant ones"; among the laity there remained "the dregs and dross of men." A Franciscan friar, Luis de Miranda, says in a *Memorial* address to the king that there is "a huge quantity of property *which is being converted from secular to ecclesiastical*"; from the abundance of friars proceeds "the great lack of people in our Spain for trade . . . , and [the fact] that there is no one to till the soil, to cultivate the vineyards and farms, *because those who could work have sought asylum* (as they say) *in the Church*; some, unlettered, as lay brothers; others, mayhap with very few letters, as ecclesiastics . . . , simply *in order to have by this means an honorable life. . . .* So it is that *the whole weight of imposts and sales taxes comes to rest on the weak shoulders of the poor*, the unfortunate and miserable peasants, who, no longer being able to support it, throw down the burden, desert and abandon their fields and farms, as experience shows us, for the villages are almost all depopulated and deserted." According to this Franciscan, around 1625, three-fourths of the land was uncultivated, as a result of which "the monarchy of our Spain is hour by hour and minute by minute being consumed and wasted away, and morally speaking, it is impossible that it should last if with all speed and diligence we do not have recourse . . . to the remedy of our very great ills" (*apud* Amezúa, *op. cit.*, pp. 210–213).

Deputies from the cities in the Cortes, the monks from their monasteries, and certain writers (directly or ironically) made the same judgment about the ills that monastic exuberance entailed for the economy and the good government of the kingdom. Mateo Alemán— in his moralizing, insistent, and extravagant style—makes a comparison between the traitor Judas and "all those who may try to be ordained as priests or become friars with an eye only on having enough to eat, to wear, or to spend. . . . God is the one who must call, and he who anointed David; he is the one who chooses priests. . . . Parents should not think that, in order to provide their children with food, they must put them in the Church."[54] Lope de Vega makes a similar comment, though in a totally different style, in a private letter to the Duke of Sessa (ca. 1617): "Friars are the most prudent men in the world: they do not go to war, *they do not pay milliones* [consumption taxes on wine, vinegar, oil, meat, soap, and tallow candles], they enjoy the best things and people give them money . . . ; they engender children and other people raise them. . . . This applies to the bad ones; there are many saintly ones."[55]

In *El licenciado Vidriera*, Cervantes juxtaposes popular anticlerical criticism and the very ironic commentary of the Licentiate; someone says—employing an untranslatable pun—when he sees a very fat friar pass by: "The father cannot move *de ético*" ["because he is moral" and also "because he is consumptive"], to which Vidriera replies: "Let no one forget what the Holy Ghost says: *Nolite tangere Christos meos.* . . . The religious orders are heaven's rich gardens of pleasure, whose fruits are set on God's table." In the preceding quotations I should like to point out only the common characteristic that binds together all the critical opinions about the religious orders in the sixteenth and seventeenth centuries: they enjoyed a comfortable economic situation in the midst of an impoverished society; they benefited from the same financial privileges as the nobles and hidalgos with respect to exemption from state taxes; their high rank rendered them untouchable, for they formed a sphere of authority free from state intervention and, to a certain degree, also free from that of the secular Church.

The economic reality of seventeenth-century Spain now begins to take on clear form and vivid hues and foreshadows what was to happen later. The sources of wealth were being exhausted, and landholdings were monopolized without producing profits either for the people—other than the famous *sopa boba* ("thin soup") dispensed by the monasteries to the poor—or for the state, whose worldly needs were not attended to. Those who were not friars passively contemplated the swift passage through Spain of the gold and silver from

---

[54] Mateo Alemán, *Guzmán de Alfarache*, in *Biblioteca de Autores Españoles*, III, 336–337.
[55] *Cartas completas*, ed. A. Rosenblat, II, 11.

the Indies, wealth that did not rest in Spain but was expended in
other countries for the payment of debts and the importation of
indispensable objects. Wealth was of value as the institutional attribute of the nobility and the Church, not as the expression of the
productive activity of individuals, for whom being rich and nothing
else could earn only insults.

In *La pobreza estimada*, a play by Lope de Vega written before
1604, two young men seek the hand of Dorotea. One, Leonido, is a
poor hidalgo, while the other, Ricardo, is very rich and of Jewish
ancestry:

> LEONIDO: Is Ricardo basely born?
> FELISARDO: He is a confessed convert
> by testimony of the *sanbenito*.[56]

Leonido, fearful that Dorotea prefers the New Christian, says that
he would trade his letters patent of nobility "for his [Ricardo's]
rich infamy"; but his friend Felisardo replies that Ricardo would
give his inheritance and "a thousand loads of Doroteas" in exchange
for pure blood. Dorotea, to be sure, ends up marrying the poor
hidalgo. What is worthy of note—we are not now interested in the
literary analysis of the play—is that Lope de Vega, so well informed
as to the situation and feelings of Spanish society, should have made
the rich man a member of the Hispano-Judaic caste. When Ricardo
learns that Dorotea is extremely poor, he tries to make himself pleasing to her by giving her a purse filled with gold coins, which he
sends to her by way of Leonido's servant and accompanied by the
following message: "Your suitor has left you because you are poor.
. . . Make use of this, and ask for what you may need in his absence,
so that he may enjoy you while I pay for it." Dorotea reacts with
burning indignation:

> O scoundrel, I will have you killed.
> Out of my sight, and to the *Jew*
> return the money for which you sold,
> by ugly crime, your master Leonido.
> (in *Biblioteca de Autores Españoles*, LII, 158a, b).

With emotional force Lope de Vega makes evident the fact that the
money of the Spaniard belonging to the Jewish caste availed nothing
either to dignify him socially or to capture the heart of a pretty
Valencian girl.

The source of this work is a story from the *Conde Lucanor* inspired by a legend about the sultan, Saladin,[57] and in which the

---

[56] *Biblioteca de Autores Españoles*, LII, 146a. The last line quoted ("por boca
de San Benito") contains an untranslatable pun. "San Benito" is St. Benedict
and also the placard bearing the names of people sentenced by the Inquisition
which was hung in churches.

[57] See *Hacia Cervantes* (1960), pp. 79–82.

author, Don Juan Manuel, personifies in the successful lover the Castilian ideal of the "man in himself," the integral man, but without setting him off against an opponent. That "man in himself," the backbone of Spanish history and life, appears now as an Old Christian hidalgo and polemically opposed to a New Christian; the conflict is between honorable poverty and base wealth, base because it does not appear as the attribute of the noble or ecclesiastical class, because it is not institutionalized.

The Spanish economy did not depend in any decisive way on either natural circumstances or any historical turn of events (gold from the Indies, Mediterranean trade, etc.). It moved in accordance with the way in which the Spaniard set value upon wealth: hence it was possible for the religious orders to gain possession of so enormous a quantity of productive land. Ramón Carande speaks aptly of "an economy in the divine manner,"[58] which reminds me of the "divine" character Alonso de Cartagena assigned to Spanish wars, waged for the "exaltation of the Catholic faith."[59] Furthermore, Carande is right in stating that it is not "surprising that the wanderlust of the nomadic shepherd, the mystic, and the soldier, in view of the importance [of these figures], helps explain the lack of longing for "the controls of a systematic and productive economic order" (*La economía y la expansión de España bajo el gobierno de los Reyes Católicos*, p. 48). I believe, however, in spite of everything, that the center of the problem must be sought in the *inner* condition of the Christian person, and in the necessity felt by him to affirm himself polemically against the Hispano-Hebrew, whose economic attitudes and values were *felt* to be opposed to his own. We have just read Lope de Vega's intuitive analysis of the situation; Alonso de Cartagena had already expressed the same value concept in the fifteenth century: "The Castilians were not accustomed to hold wealth in high esteem, but virtue" (see above, p. 150). Don Alonso, born a Jew,

---

[58] Ramón Carande, *La economía y la expansión de España bajo el gobierno de los Reyes Católicos* (Madrid, 1952), p. 47.

[59] Alonso de Cartagena, *España en su historia* (Buenos Aires, 1948), p. 27. A good example of this economy "in the divine manner" is provided by a ship owner who had twelve or thirteen vessels engaged in trade with Spanish America. These ships he never insured commercially at the *Gradas* ("gallery") around the Cathedral of Seville where "merchants had set up an exchange for their transactions" (Mateo Alemán, *op. cit.*, 191). Rather, this ship owner, "lord of Cantillana and other towns," preferred to insure his maritime property on the *gradas* ("steps") of the altars, for "many people prayed to God . . . for a favorable voyage. He gave something of every cargo to hospitals and monasteries, and even a portion to the poor and widows; . . . the ducat and the real he had given to an old woman [so that she might pray for the good fortune of his ships], because the voyage was successful, gained for her the sum of 12 or 20 ducats when his ships returned; and the vessels were brought back safely by her prayers. Never did he lose one" of them (see *Miscelánea de Zapata*, in *Memorial histórico español* (1859), XI, 240).

bishop of Burgos and, at the time of this comment, ambassador of the King of Castile, becomes the spokesman for the feelings of the Christian caste for obvious reasons whose sincerity I would not deny. The consciousness of religion and of caste were so closely united that the New Christian on occasion became a priest or even an inquisitor—or he returned to Judaism when his inner self pushed him toward his native caste rather than toward his adopted belief.

Because the opinions about the value of wealth were as we have seen, all that avalanche of criticism and complaint which fell upon the monastic orders in the sixteenth and seventeenth centuries never went beyond a mere *flatus vocis* and gesturings of no efficacy. The plethora of monks was the expression of the power of a caste that had succeeded in raising itself to the pinnacles of a world empire. The monks were nobles of the divine order, who made a positive contribution to the organization of the empire in distant lands, and to the saving of the lives of the American Indians.[60] To wish that there had been fewer monks in Spain is merely to reveal ignorance of the structure and life course of the Spaniards. A comparison with the situation in the United States might be helpful. Here we have an abundance, perhaps a superfluity, of government bureaucrats, some of whom are accused of corruption, while the farmers have a hard time finding hands to help with the crops. The Spanish Empire was a religious institution, and the horizon of the Spanish mind was also religious, so that facing his horizon, the individual felt that he was living shut up within himself in hermetic isolation; yet at the same time he had a full awareness that the religious life was stifling the secular life, a secular life that no one in Spain could conceive of as valuable for itself alone, as a rational and reasonable organization of human stimuli. The critics of the friars would themselves not have known what to do in a land without friars. Like authentic Spaniards, the friars who criticized their own brethren would have themselves liked to be the only monks. If by some magic art the patrimony of the Church had been disentailed in the seventeenth century, the state would not have known how to take advantage of it. An ever increasing flow of men and women entered monasteries and convents, because people—or the majority of them, at least—move down the path their own history prepares for them. The deputies in the Cortes and all the rest who cried out and hurled criticisms against the superabundance of monks and nuns were lamenting the pleasant pain of their own special way of life, the constant modality of which was the denial of its most basic characteristics. Those who do not

---

[60] Marcel Bataillon has written enlightening pages about this; in the end "the spirit of peaceful conquest" triumphed in America ("La Vera Paz: Roman et histoire," *Bulletin Hispanique*, LIII (1951), 235–300).

understand the nature of this process had best renounce the attempt to understand the Spanish past.

The same impulses, preferences, and virtues that made it possible for the Spaniard (or the Portuguese) to extend and maintain his empire in Italy, Flanders, America, Africa, Asia, and Oceania prevented him from inventing and putting into practice in Spain economic forms similar to those of the Western Christian countries. The first thing that those who raised their voices against the superabundance of monks would have had to do was to set aside the guiding principle of their own conduct: "Oh, how great is all that beyond this world! Oh, how little the things of this world!"[61] The other Christians in Europe preferred to employ the word "great" to describe both worlds.

It seems to me that these opinions are confirmed by the fact that the public treasury gained only minimal benefits from the disentailment of ecclesiastical property and the suppression of the religious orders in 1836—accompanied by the senseless executions of monks in July of 1835. Lamentation, despoilment, and destruction do not fill the vacuums created by the absence of thought and of intelligent, prudent, and effective work. The French and the Russian revolutions destroyed old regimes, but eyes were turned toward the design of the new construction (whether good or bad is not a matter for comment now) which was to occupy the place of the old. In Spain, however, the criticism or the attack against the economic structures that were judged harmful was focused on the possible value of the latter as booty. The nomadic habits acquired during the centuries of the reconquest impelled the Spaniard to avail himself of the mineral and agricultural wealth of Hispanic America by making use of the work of the natives, just as earlier in the Christian kingdoms he had made use of the labor of the Moors or the Moriscos; but he did not learn, therefore, to profit by the inventive use of the possibilities of his own land, which was generally abandoned to the competence and greed of foreigners. Future generations of young people who may read these pages should enter into a quiet dialogue with their own inner selves as they confront the economic complexities that for a long time still must continue to assail the body and the soul of the Spaniards.

Modern Forms of Anarchism

The antiauthoritarian and antilegalistic attitudes of the sixteenth and seventeenth centuries linked easily to the anarchist doctrines of the

---

[61] "¡Oh, qué mucho lo de allá! ¡Oh, qué poco de acá!" At the beginning of this century these words were still engraved on the facade of the seminary of Vergara, where I read them for the first time.

rest of Europe in the nineteenth century primarily because of the uncomfortable lack of balance between the needs of the majority of Spaniards and the inept actions on the part of the state to satisfy them.[62] People looked within themselves for what the social milieu did not provide, in a way somewhat similar to that of Luis de León and other Erasmian converts in the sixteenth century. It was no inexplicable accident that Francisco Pi y Margall, president of the ephemeral Republic of 1873, should have written a prologue twenty years earlier for the works of St. John of the Cross and made there the following comment: "Today when we rebel against all authority and believe that the source of all certitude and legal right exists only within our own *ego*. . . ."[63] The ego referred to here was, to be sure, that of rationalist and Romantic philosophy and a concept unknown to the mystics of the sixteenth century; but Pi y Margall, who had read Hegel and the *Paroles d'un croyant* of Lamennais, thought that Christ should be considered as "a reformer in the religious and in the social order." St. John of the Cross interested him because he had expressed "his own individuality," because he was not obliged to "have recourse to *anything but himself*." He adds further that "since we are in a period of social revolutions, of revolutions that sooner or later will do away with the hydra of immorality and injustice," poetry will make its voice heard (in *Biblioteca de Autores Españoles*, XVII, p. xvi).

In the nineteenth century, as in the seventeenth, people cried out against evils and sought the remedy against them in the inwardness of the *self* or in the advent of some Messianic solution. Along with these negative or passive manifestations (the discontent and malaise so obvious later in the work of Galdós and in that of the Generation of '98), we may note the active search for a fulcrum upon which to rest the social reformation of Spain in the example of certain institutions that had habitually operated without inter-

---

[62] In the *Cortes* of 1855 Antonio Ríos Rosas said that a law establishing freedom of religion would not attract foreigners to Spain, for "Spanish Americans do not immigrate to this country, whether they are rich or poor," because there were "so many, such great, such sad, and such absurd reasons why nothing can be developed. . . . Freedom of worship! The worship of liberty, the worship of law, the worship of justice is what can restore our past greatness to us" (*apud* Menéndez y Pelayo, *Historia de los heterodoxos españoles* [1932], VII, 292). Such was the social medium in which the anarchist movement was incubated. Ríos Rosas apparently did not understand that religious intolerance implied the loss of liberty, law, and justice.

[63] *Biblioteca de Autores Españoles*, XVII, xviii. The prologue is unsigned, but Menéndez y Pelayo says it and the prologue to the works of Father Juan de Mariana published in the same *Biblioteca de Autores Españoles* were written by Pi y Margall (see Menéndez y Pelayo, *op cit.*, p. 262). See also Marcel Bataillon, "Les idées humanitaires de 1848 et les valeurs littéraires de l'Espagne," *Actes du Congrès International d'Histoire Littéraire Moderne* (Paris, 1948), p. 229.

ference by the state and without coercion from the law. Joaquín Costa knew that according to usual custom in the Basque provinces tenant farmers pass on the lands they cultivate to their children, and no landlord dares to interfere with the custom even though legally he might do so.[64] This and numerous other facts demonstrate, he says, that *"without going outside ourselves,* we find all that world of immanent individual law, . . . over which we are the sovereigns and masters; we are the only people responsible, but also the only judges" (*Teoría del hecho jurídico,* p. 20); because "law is an order of liberty: coercion is not law" (*ibid.,* p. 19), whether in the individual or in the social sphere. In his *Colectivismo agrario en España* (1915), Costa describes certain institutions in which the economic ends and the effort of the individual to achieve them are juridically and morally integrated; in these consuetudinary institutions, the lands benefit those who cultivate them and not the idle owner who ordinarily receives the income. One example among many is that of the *senaras concejiles,* certain portions of land which "the farmers till cooperatively, normally on holidays, some contributing their own labor, others their plows and other equipment" (*ibid.,* p. 310). These instances of free and cooperative cultivation would serve as an excellent example to modern Spanish anarcho-syndicalists. Costa mentions the work of Martín González de Cellorigo (*Memorial de la política necesaria, y útil restauración de España* [1600]), a book dedicated to Philip II which would be considered subversive today, which says that it is already enough for the "poor people" to pay the tithe due to God without having to pay in addition *"another, much heavier one to the owners of the property;* on top of which they are beset by innumerable debentures . . . , besides imposts and obligatory royal and personal taxes" (*Colectivismo agrario en España,* p. 85).

In different places in Spain there were, or used to be, instances of collective exploitation of the land, of corporations for the use of water for irrigation of the land, of communal labor for the benefit of the confraternity or brotherhood to which the worker belonged. In other words, alongside the prevailing system of property established by the civil code, equal for everyone, there continued to exist special private forms of landownership and use which were sanctioned by unwritten custom. In such cases the state and its abstract laws became unnecessary—an ideal situation for certain Spaniards who for long centuries had been "weary of obedience," as Friar Alonso de Castrillo had written in 1521.

---

[64] Joaquín Costa, *Teoría del hecho jurídico* (1880), p. 22. Costa's work precedes that of Jean-Marie Guyau, *Essai d'une morale sans obligation ni sanction,* which appeared in 1883 in the form of separate articles in the *Revue Philosophique.*

All the comments made by Joaquín Costa and others in favor of a cooperative system of landownership and use, independent of the state and its written laws, are related, of course, to Spanish anarcho-syndicalism; likewise we must bear in mind the direct contacts between certain Spanish propagandists and agitators and various nineteenth-century European doctrines that leaned toward anarchism. One of the most famous of these propagandists—and one of the men most respected today by Spanish anarchists—was Fermín Salvochea, who had been educated in England, where he became familiar with the writings of Robert Owen, whose agnosticism and cooperative socialism Salvochea made known in Spain in the second half of the nineteenth century.[65] But despite all this, the fervent acceptance of the anarchist creed by many farmers and workers is not only the result of intellectual conviction or adherence to political systems dominant somewhere else on the globe. If communism had not triumphed in Russia, what strength would European communism have today? But the anarcho-syndicalist has no need to refer to any dominant example, for his political attitude rests on no dogma or model as does communism, whose "Gospel" was written by Marx and Engels, and whose "Church" pronounces on dogma from Moscow. The anarcho-syndicalist is a believer who adores the figure projected out of his own soul, as Don Quixote loves Dulcinea; and he rebels when anyone asks him to produce a portrait, even a very tiny one, of that figure. Communism proposes closed schemes and admits no spontaneous attitudes and suggestions, which would be very dangerous for its dogma. The doctrine of the Spanish anarchist, however—if he has one—would be projected in open figures, in the hopeful faith in a beyond, a faith that quickens longing and incites to sacrifice.[66] In contrast, the inner self has no role to play in Communist dogmatics.

The decisive factor in Spanish anarchism consists, more than in ideologies expressed in books, in its links with a continuum of vital situations and reactions which, intermeshed in space and in time, have given rise to inner modes of *being situated* in life. What is serious and grave about Spanish anarchism is its authentic Spanishness. Behind it there pulsate centuries of despairing and hopeful solitude, of confidence in illuminations from within, of suspicion toward all external justice and order. The greatest danger in the conventional application to Spaniards of the label "individualist" is that it prevents our seeing how, in certain given circumstances of time and space,

---

[65] "Fermín Salvochea en su 114 aniversario," in *España Libre* (New York, March 17, 1956). See also Gabriel Jackson, "The Origins of Spanish Anarchism," *Southwestern Social Science Quarterly* (Sept. 1955).

[66] As late as 1960, it should be noted, Spanish *émigrés* in Europe and America were publishing four anarchist newspapers.

there have arisen habits of disbelief in the legality of the state, habits of inward disobedience, of rejection of all rules imposed from above which do not lead to personal benefit.

History is usually written as if the Spaniards had not been actors and sensitive spectators in all that happened in the land that for eight centuries they were tearing little by little from the hands of tenacious enemies. The reports to the king and the books written about the agonizing situation created by the excessive number of monks referred to something that was really going on and affecting the state of mind of the people; there were situations that made it obvious that wealth was running in one direction only and leaving vast areas in the Spanish land and soul in arid poverty. The economic dominion of the monks grew so monumentally that Isabella the Catholic herself was moved to comment on it: "She said, that if they should wish to put a fence around Castile, they ought to give it to the Hieronymites."[67] If this remark seems ironic, the following comment of the Queen mentioned by Captain Bernardo de Vargas Machuca is totally serious: "The Catholic Queen Doña Isabella said that in order for Spain to be extremely productive, it would be desirable to give it to the Benedictine monks, since they were great farmers."[68] For reasons with which the reader is now familiar, it is idle to compare the Spanish situation with that of other Catholic countries, where the state and cultural and economic activities possessed a different meaning. Secular interests absorbed the energies of Cardinals Richelieu and Mazarin much more than ecclesiastical ones; nor did the king of France, the emperor of Germany, or the doge of Venice move in a monastic atmosphere.

In every city or town in Spain surrounded by fertile lands, there were several monasteries; the monks (save in exceptional instances of criminality) were not subjected to the justice of the kingdom, nor did they pay taxes. They worked corporately under a freely chosen rule (that of St. Augustine, St. Benedict, St. Bernard, St. Francis, etc.) and were untroubled by poverty or anxiety about the future. Oral or written criticisms of moral excesses among the monks referred to particular instances, not to the totality of the monastic institution, except during the brief period of intense Erasmianism. Be that as it may, now we can ponder how the "underdogs" felt as they contemplated, century after century, the comfortable existence of those above them: oppression and poverty contrasted with liberty and ease.

---

[67] *Apud* Melchor de Santa Cruz, *Floresta general*, I, p. 16, no. 68. The Queen was referring to the proverbial acquisitiveness of this order and the notable care they took of their own property.

[68] *Milicia y descripción de las Indias* (Madrid, 1599), fol. 212; *apud* Gallardo, *Ensayo de una biblioteca española de libros raros*, IV, 915.

No one spoke of the affirmative aspect of the monastic institution, the fact that the monks created a great part of the artistic grandeur of Spain and the Indies.

The ecclesiastical and moral situation of Spanish society in 1551 and 1561 is vividly illuminated by the *Memoriales* of St. John of Avila, which were sent on to the Council of Trent.[69] In them from the beginning there appears the problem of the inefficaciousness of laws when prevailing customs are opposed to their fulfillment: "The way used by many to reform decadent customs is usually the making of good laws and ordering, under penalty of severe punishments, that they be kept. . . . But as long as there is no foundation of virtue in the subjects which leads them to abide by these good laws . . . , they will perforce seek out tricky ways . . . for breaking them" (in *Miscelánea Comillas*, III, 3). The examples of such "decadent customs" are abundant: If the one who holds the cure of a parish is a monk, the bishop can exercise no authority over him, "and from this exemption result many scandals" (*ibid.*, p. 32). There is obvious in these *Memoriales*, as in so many other works that testify to how people lived, the lack of accord between religious faith and the conduct of its ministers and believers; the consequences of such a situation were immeasurable, for the horizon of social concerns was almost wholly religious. Like many others, John of Avila believed that one of the causes for the rise of Protestantism was the conduct of the "ecclesiastical estate," which had caused the spreading of "unhappy reports"; and "the sound that now is spread abroad has been such that it has been sufficient to provoke the wrath of God upon the said estate and even upon the people." The ministers of God, according to this New Christian, had been "made slaves of evil" (*ibid.*, p. 138).

The Church lacked power over those clergy who maintained concubines when they were "distinguished by blood, ecclesiastical position, or wealth, and when the prelate was unable to subject them" (*ibid.*, p. 132). For these reasons John of Avila wondered whether it might not be more effective to do away with the celibacy of the clergy, thinking that it might be better "for them to be married in order to avoid the great evil that today exists" (*ibid.*, p. 30). Furthermore, the ignorance of the clergy was so abysmal that one bishop was moved to say to John of Avila that "these unworthy men are destroying my diocese" (*ibid.*, p. 143).

The Tridentine reforms must have corrected matters somewhat, although Lope de Vega's conduct as a priest and what he reveals with respect to the public opinion about monks make it likely that the lack of harmony or dissociation between belief and conduct prob-

---

[69] The only published version of them is the one prepared by Camilo M. Abad, S. J., in *Miscelánea Comillas* (1945), III, 3–171.

ably was not much changed. It is, further, naïve and shortsighted to continue calling opinions like those of John of Avila either "Erasmian" or anticlerical, for they are an integral manifestation of the social history of the time. We must place ourselves inside the minds of those who were living in Madrid in 1561, 1661, or 1761 and face what was clearly obvious to everyone: crimes against the faith were punished by torture and burning at the stake, while the action of the civil authority created neither a disciplined government nor any kind of harmonious justice or morality in the civil sphere. There is no doubt that in other Catholic countries the Church also exerted a strong influence over the state and social life;[70] but when we group Spain along with France, Belgium, Southern Germany, and the like in this respect, we forget the decisive fact that no human phenomenon takes on reality within itself and in isolation. No such phenomenon is, then, reducible to statistics; historical positivism and materialism fall into a major error when they try to do so. In other "civilized countries" (the phrase used by the author of the pamphlet mentioned in note 70), there were, in addition to religion, cultural modalities and intellectual and social customs that differed widely from those of the Hispano-Portuguese peoples. The reality of the human phenomenon consists in a simultaneous *living with* and *living without*, which is to say that it must be viewed not only in relation to the other factors present in contemporaneous society, but also to those that are absent from a given society. If the historian does not bear all this in mind, his history becomes nothing more than empty words.

As a social phenomenon, the contrast between the common people and the exalted monks is comparable to that which had existed earlier, in the fourteenth century, between the oppressed and angry "little people" and the powerful, opulent Hispano-Hebrews. One popular proverb, indeed, equated the two groups: "Neither friar nor Jew is ever a good friend."[71] The "little people" could not, of course, hope to enter the economically privileged caste of the Hispano-Hebrews; but it was indeed possible for the peasant or the aimless hidalgo to penetrate into the area of placid monastic joys, more and more coveted as the possibility of financial comfort for the layman became more limited. As we have seen, many people grew alarmed and made their outcries heard, because Spain was in danger of being converted into an Occidental Tibet. Such a situation went dragging on, for

---

[70] See *Del excesivo desarrollo de las órdenes religiosas en España* (Madrid: Imprenta de la Revista de Archivos, 1910), a work by an ecclesiastic who preferred to remain anonymous. His conclusion is: "Spain is not in an exceptional situation with respect to other civilized countries in the number of its religious orders" (p. 85).

[71] Gonzalo Correas, *Vocabulario de refranes* (1906), p. 207. The first edition of this work appeared in the first half of the seventeenth century.

better or for worse, while the gold and silver from the Indies continued to serve as a financial *deus ex machina*. But when imports from Peru and Mexico ceased in 1810, and when the oppressive regime of Ferdinand VII came to an end in 1833, the religious orders suddenly appeared as the perfect target for the dammed-up greed and rancor of a people made callous of soul, who had not even been shaken by the loss of the overseas empire in 1824.[72] In 1835 large numbers of monks were shamefully massacred, while the survivors were forced to flee the country. *Mutatis mutandis*, the tragedy of the Jews and the Moriscos was repeated.[73] According to some authorities, the massacre of the monks was organized by the Masons; it is also said that the Archdeacon of Ecija inspired the extermination of the Sevillian Jews in 1391. What is certain, however, is that such extravagant excesses were never the work of one man or of one group but the result of deep and widespread states of mind.

In the popular imagination there floated the picture—as Gil de Zárate says—of "their former superiority," and, furthermore, I believe, another more pleasing image, that of a life founded internally on a beloved faith and not imposed by a law adverse to one's personal interests. The populace thought of the friar as exempt even from hierarchical fetters, for the monasteries were ruled by their order, and in the final instance, by the pope, who lived very far away. From the point of view of nineteenth-century anarchist ideology, the monasteries looked like guild associations. More than once the disseminator of anarchist ideas was compared to a lay monk, agnostic but virtuous: he did not drink wine, he did not smoke, he shared what he had, including the clothes he wore, with others. Anarchist ideas took hold especially in the south and in the east, regions endowed with a lively fantasy; the Andalusian and the Levantine are more impressionable, sentimental, and less circumspect than the Castilian. The promise of liberation, spread by people of irreproachable conduct, found an echo in those who thirsted after a new justice, a communal regime, fragmented and cooperative, like that of the very Spanish and very familiar system of the hated and envied monks.

---

[72] See Melchor Fernández Almagro, *La emancipación de América y su reflejo en la conciencia española* (Madrid: Instituto de Estudios Políticos, 1944). The criticisms of this study seem to me largely baseless.

[73] In *Los españoles pintados por sí mismos* (Madrid, 1851), pp. 149–153, Antonio Gil de Zárate (a second-rate dramatist) described the "secularized monk," a characteristic figure of the time; certain phrases in the description reflect the feelings of liberal writers at that juncture: "If on occasion I also happened to present on the stage the passions and crimes of men whom the cloister had enclosed, delivering them over to public execration, I yielded perhaps with great facility to the flood that was then sweeping us all along; my mind was still concerned with ideas about *their former superiority*; and most of all I had not seen those unhappy creatures covered with rags, dying from hunger, or begging alms in the streets."

Like a new maternalistic Church, "Mother Anarchism" smiled mercifully on those who had never heard a sincere and altruistic voice
but only the confused and incomprehensible noise of abstract laws,
backed up by the armed force of a stern state interested only in
maintaining the *status quo*. St. Theresa, Luis de León, Quevedo, and
many others had written against that disagreeable and flinty state.
It is not surprising that, in a Spain reduced by 1850 to a hollow
simulacrum of itself, many Andalusian peasants should have accepted as true the fantastic message of a well-ordered society free
from awkward meddling by the state. After all, such credulity was
no stranger than the eager acceptance in 1938 of the pleasing news
that Germany and Italy were ready to "make Spain a gift" of an
empire, a promise held as an article of faith, not by ignorant peasants,
but by university graduates.

Only in Spain today does the anarchist faith possess deep roots, a
phenomenon understandable only if seen in connection with its historical context. Anarcho-syndicalism, unlike communism, contains a
minimum of foreign ideology and a maximum of Spanish spontaneity.
Fundamentally it is more a phenomenon of faith than of reasoned thought; there is no "treatise" explaining Spanish anarchism,
nor have the organs of anarcho-syndicalist propaganda formulated
clearly and rigorously how it is possible for a whole people living
under anarchism to coexist side by side with other Europeans who
are not. Once again we may observe here that when one path of
belief is closed to the Spaniard, he immediately invents another for
himself. Of great symbolic value in this regard is the conversion to
Judaism of that Christian of Morisco ancestry (see p. 331) after the
reading of Friar Luis de Granada.

The Spaniard holds tightly to faith in the Spanishness of Numantia
and Viriatus (when no one else in Europe believes anything of the
kind), just as today, out of harmony with the rest of the world, many
believe in "Mother Anarchism"—or as they believed, a few years
ago, in a Fascist empire fallen like rain from heaven, or in the benefits that would ensue from turning into citizens of a province imperially ruled from Moscow. In what I have said there is no political
aim; I propose only to put an end to the fiction—for it is not the
history—of the Spanish past. I do insist on the impossibility, or the
extravagance, of undertaking any political task, or even of attempting to interpret the existence and civilization of the Spaniards, without a precise notion of how the Spaniards first appeared on the stage
of history and of the inner shape and process of their life. Imperial
triumphs confirmed the Hispano-Christians in their belief that the
other two castes were superfluous, and they were eliminated, but
the conquerors could never rid themselves of the idea that they were
a caste whose purity of blood was open to question. Thus they were

forced to establish themselves on the basis of the inner self, on the way of *being* of the person and not on the *doing*, for by *doing things* one ran the risk of not appearing to be an Old Christian.

The result was the progressive debasement of all activities whose ends were economic, and the impossibility of making use of the immense commercial and industrial opportunities of Hispanic America. The converted Jew Hernando del Pulgar said "that in order to become wealthy in a short time, two 'littles' and two 'greats' were needed: little shame and little conscience; great greed and *great diligence.*"[74] "For forty years now," wrote Juan de Mal Lara in 1568, "there have been new kinds of people, who do not direct themselves toward heaven, because they are not saintly enough that their purpose should be the conversion of the infidel into a Christian, but go down the road toward hell, *which is [the road] to acquire gold and silver*. . . . To bring gold and silver . . . is a wealth that falls to pieces in the hands, and, in fine, it is devils' treasure that turns into lumps of coal. . . . The tyrants who have risen up in the Indies, . . . even though they were *children of worth [benē tovim;* see above, p. 269], went to seek their perdition, *called wealth by the common people.*"[75] The hidalgo, the son of worth, loses status, becomes common and plebeian, when he enriches himself in Hispanic America. The father of the picaresque protagonist in *Guzmán de Alfarache* (1599) lived in Genoa: "His business was . . . making exchange of money everywhere in the world. Even for that they persecuted him, insulting him as an usurer."[76] The picaro's mother, a prostitute, thus had married a man who dealt in money, so that Guzmán's parentage was dishonorable on both sides. In 1617 Cristóbal Suárez de Figueroa inveighed fiercely against *indianos*, the men who had made fortunes in Hispanic America: "How devoted they are to mercenary affairs, to thrift! . . . I have never seen an estate acquired in those parts which came to a good end in ours."[77] And still in the nineteenth century people were writing in a tone reminiscent of the opinions of Hernando del Pulgar about those who make their fortunes in busi-

---

[74] Melchor de Santa Cruz, *op. cit.*, p. 85, no. 418.
[75] *Filosofía vulgar*, ed. A. Vilanova, III, 85–86.
[76] In *Biblioteca de Autores Españoles*, III, 189.
[77] *El Pasajero*, ed. F. Rodríguez Marín, p. 147. In a play by Lope de Vega, *El premio del bien hablar* (written in 1624 or 1625), Leonarda states that her father is noble because he is a Biscayan; he could therefore enrich himself in Hispanic America without being debased:

> My father's ancestral home
> is the noblest in Biscay:
> if he goes to the Indies,
> what honor can it take from him?
> If the sea has enriched him,
> it can't prevent his being a gentleman.

(Act I, scene 2)

ness: "To be a banker in Spain one needs a great deal of the first [boldness], very little of the second [money], and a total lack of the third [heart]."[78] In *Los españoles pintados por sí mismos* (1851), the type of the *indiano* was described by Antonio Ferrer del Río in half-ironic, half-despective fashion, much as we refer today to the presumptuous *noveaux riches*; in his words there still seems to persist something of the attitude of Mal Lara and Suárez de Figueroa: "For the Indies, as for the kingdom of heaven, many are called but few are chosen." The newly rich man returns to Spain with an opulent exterior that does not wholly conceal his native vulgarity: "The tavernkeeper wears frock coat and tie, and even though he is not gracious or polished, his form has been impregnated with that kind of varnish distilled by wealth" (pp. 17, 19).

In sum, even in the mid-nineteenth century Spanish society did not accept as normal and respectable the class of people who had become rich in business, banking, or working far from the fatherland. Attention continued to be concentrated on the intrinsic qualities of the person and not upon what the person had acquired; activities of sufficient interest to elicit attention were lacking, and the well-to-do man moved within the vacuum of his wealth, used for his own comfort, without promoting social goals of greater transcendence. The projects for collective life so vividly outlined in the time of the Catholic Sovereigns produced consequences tightly linked one to another. Precisely at the time when the economic horizons of Spain and Portugal were widening marvelously in the sixteenth century, the roads that might have led to wealth, to modern capitalism, were being closed in their technological and moral aspects. The stimuli of invention and intellectual activity—those that did exist and might well have multiplied—were reduced to insignificance through the lack of an object upon which to act.[79]

Spain, the creation of the Spaniards I have been talking about, disdained wealth when it could have produced it in rapid progression; it preferred to sacrifice riches on the altar of its belief in the absolute value of the person, in a way of existing (not of doing) which was hermetic and incompatible with any other. When it is said that will was the primary dimension of life for the Spaniard, it should be added that the willful act takes on meaning and reality as the force that sustains faith in the absolute, caste-determined primacy of the person, an absolute that consists in being as one is because that was the way one was. The caste-determined condition was not a tem-

---

[78] *Madrid al daguerreotipo* (Madrid, 1849), p. 39. The same work says: "We never hear the word *rich* pronounced without there coming into our mind the idea of an *American* [i.e., a Hispanic American]." And also: "On the Stock Exchange a fortune is lost with much greater ease than it is won" (p. 38).

[79] See *De la edad conflictiva*, p. 169.

porary or accidental phase of Spanish life, but an introverted mode of perceiving that one existed *in that way*, as a person of one faith, of one law,[80] independently of goods possessed or of the action and creation that might be carried out. The awareness of the individual's being is dissolved in the awareness of the society of which he forms a part. Spaniards no longer live in this fashion, and the awareness of personal dignity is affirmed individually, regardless of how much infamy the social group to which one belongs may attempt to cast upon that personal dignity; but the consequences of the original, *constitutive* mode of existence of the Christian Spaniard have continued to live on in the collective subconscience, in the habitual ways in which value is judged, in modes of living and working. In Asturias and Galicia people still call disdainfully those who return after having made a fortune in Latin America "indianos."

The will of the caste—energetic and tenacious—erected a protective and impregnable wall around that ultimate and sacred inclosure of the person. So it is that Lope de Vega, whose works are the most vivid and trustworthy document with regard to Spanish values, says that the convert Ricardo (in the previously cited play) would have paid "a thousand loads of Doroteas"—in other words, of pretty and adorable girls—in addition to his entire fortune if that would have served to erase the infamy of his origins.

Personal worth, that is, the idea that one had reached fulfillment simply because one knew himself to be a member of the chosen caste (an idea constantly and tensely at war with the opinions of the society around the individual, in Spain and out of it) delighted in turning back upon itself over and over again, expressed itself in ornate and punctilious formulas of courtesy,[81] turned inward and

---

[80] In Lope de Vega's novelette *El desdichado por la honra*, Felisardo leaves the service of the viceroy of Spain in Sicily on learning that his parents had been included in the edict of expulsion of the Moriscos, "a thing [being of Moorish origin] which had never been known to me; rather I considered myself a knight and hidalgo, and *in this faith* and confidence I treated myself exactly like those who were [noble]. . . . It seemed to me I should leave Your Excellency's house . . . , for it is not right that a man to whom people may throw up this infamous stigma whenever the occasion offers should live in it" (*Biblioteca de Autores Españoles*, XXXVIII, 18).

[81] See, for example, the *Diálogos familiares* of Juan de Luna, Paris, 1619. After a long conversation, one lady takes leave of another in the following fashion:

DOÑA MARÍA: I kiss the hands of your grace for the grace you have done me . . .
DOÑA ANA: Your grace knows what you deserve.
DOÑA MARÍA: My worth derives from being your most humble servant.
DOÑA ANA: I am your most humble servant.
DOÑA MARÍA: I kiss the hands of your grace a thousand times.
DOÑA ANA: And I [kiss] those of your grace a hundred thousand.

contorted itself in an endless ornamentation without reference to anything but itself.

Even religious belief seemed at times to be subordinated to the primacy of the person, to his imperious will, to the purpose of maintaining oneself in an exalted position, superior to everything else. But this mode of being is *not*, it must be emphasized, "individualism," which implies an interest in the existence around the "individualist" of a society able to offer him some content that he may make his own; such an attitude is characteristic of England, where there has been so wide a variety of individual activities. What seduced the Spaniard was making his supremacy as a person prevail, and he demonstrated the ability to do so in numerous extraordinary cases: at times he even attempted, in an imaginative way, to appear as God's antagonist; this is precisely what Don Juan tries to be in *El burlador de Sevilla*. On the other hand, the Spaniard of the Christian caste never took the initiative or argued spontaneously against belief in God (whenever such attacks appear, they rest on ideas imported from abroad).

The premium set upon the will that affirmed the absolute value of the person had fatal results for the logical, rational effectiveness of that absolute person, but admirable ones for his expressive capacities. Spaniards in the future should not forget either side of this human problem in order, first of all, not to scorn a past so rich in works and actions of truly universal dimensions; and, secondly, to be aware of the risks inherent in the extravagant cult of what I would call personal absolutism, not individualism. Around this absolute person there was produced an alarming vacuum with respect to things and to the possibilities for a frugal way of life. To this modality of life— and not to other factors—are due the fact that Spain was converted into the ruralized country of the nineteenth century described by so many people (see n. 62 [Ríos Rosas]); that time and again so much blood has been shed stupidly, uselessly; that a nation once so powerful has had to let itself be managed by the caprice, the selfish interests, or the sadism of foreign forces. History is not a "guide to life," but those who hope to occupy themselves with Spain's future should first forget Numantia and Viriatus and bear in mind what the Spanish caste system has created and destroyed in the land of Spain.

(*Apud* J. M. Sbarbi, *Refranes, adagios y proverbios castellanos* [Madrid, 1891], p. 132.)

The overelaborate, labyrinthian forms of so-called baroque architecture presuppose an attitude of wonder and ecstasy shared by artist and public. That art, today so external and inexpressive for many, must have invited the Spaniard to contemplation and communion with himself; elsewhere it probably served the ends of ecclesiastical or noble propaganda, or of sensual enjoyment, or of mere gesticulation. But we cannot enter here into a discussion of the intricacies of "baroque" sentiment and art.

During the three centuries of the fabulous Spanish Empire, successes and failures bore an evident relationship to the incontrovertible fact that God was the sole spokesman whom the Spaniard truly heeded, and the only one to whom he responded with exalted fervor. Dialogue with his fellowmen, or *with his circumstances*—eager to be known and interpreted—usually took the form of either an indifferent monologue or a pure fantasy. As religious exclusionism (which is the dominant note, the concrete Spanish form, in the abstract period of time called "the seventeenth century") was intensified, the replies to God's demands for tribute were formulated in pyramids of printed paper full of naïve and ineffective, empty words;[82] for the term "the work of God," as well as the concept of "century," is not univocal in meaning. What the Spaniard deemed to be "the work of God" was not what Galileo and Kepler felt it to be: namely, to try to discover the thought of God as expressed in the magnitudes and movements of the stars.

Not everything, however, was inane vacuity. Benito Feijoo and some of his disciples were as Spanish as Salvador Mañer, their obtuse antagonist, though it is evident also that the habitual course of thought and value judgments suffered no appreciable change as a result of the labors of Feijoo. Furthermore, it would be a serious error and omission not to bear in mind what the inner self of the Spaniard had gained in dimension during those centuries of solitary dialogue with God. The eighteenth century abounds in heroic figures who by their own unaided efforts achieved prodigious things in remote parts of the Empire: certain Mexican viceroys, the missionaries in California, the titanic struggles of people like Blas de Lezo, who successfully defended Cartagena de Indias, and so on.

Doubtless one expression of the attempt to raise oneself up to God was the architecture of the seventeenth and eighteenth centuries, often viewed as an abstract kind of art or as evidence of "bad taste," and not as a stimulus to contemplation or as an effort to escape annihilation by the corrosive action of the fleeting moment, a moment, like that of childbirth, replete with fatal barbs. In his dialogue with God, the Spaniard intensified his artistic forms and affirmed his confidence in his own worth and certitude, in his lack of need for other company. But when circumstances shoved him about, he came to find

---

[82] Here is one example among hundreds: Salvador José Mañer, *Dissertación crítico-histórica sobre el juicio universal, señales que la han de preceder y estado en que ha de quedar el mundo, con el destino de los niños del limbo* (Madrid: Imprenta del Reyno, Calle de la Gorguera), 1741. This adversary of Padre Feijoo uses the "rationalized" language of his age to say things like this: "Noah's Ark was begun one hundred years before the Flood . . . ; and if we favor the opinion of those who say that the blows struck in its construction were heard all over the world, everybody must have been warned" (p. 4).

himself defenseless. Only so can we explain how it was that the insistent protests and complaints I have cited should have remained floating in the air like a mystic soliloquy, like a prayer offered up to good sense: they were never translated into effective action and thought.[83]

Pedro de Guzmán, who has been quoted earlier (p. 251, n. 53), was a Jesuit with an open mind and a critical attitude; he attributed the ills of Spain to idleness,[84] but without recognizing the reasons for it. He contrasts the enormous extension of the monarchy, "twenty times larger than that of Rome," with the sparse population of the Peninsula, which, he says, would not total four million inhabitants (*Bienes del honesto trabajo y daños de la ociosidad*, p. 126), a population decline due to the magnitude of the Empire. "And I do not take into account," he adds, "the people lost on account of the expulsions carried out, both in our own times and in those of our grandparents, of the people who by their infidelity deserved that we throw them out [of Spain], *although they were the ones who most tilled and cultivated* [the land]. Now if the few people who remain do not apply themselves to work and to the husbandry and cultivation of the land, which in large part is either mountainous or bleak plateau, it will become worthless soil. . . . And I shall say of the Spaniard what the Holy Ghost says of the lazy man: 'I passed over the land of the lazy man, and I found that it was covered with weeds and thorns'" (*ibid.*, p. 130). Pedro de Guzmán contrasts the industry of Jews and Moriscos with the idleness of Catholics, as before he had cited the example of the Protestants of La Rochelle, whose governors "take the most special care and pains that there should be no idle people in their republic, for in that [lack of idleness] consists a large part of their happiness" (p. 119).

This broad-minded Jesuit was even familiar with the form of work in China, yet he abstains from mentioning the ecclesiastical overpopulation of Spain, and it is surprising that he should not have realized that Christians of pure blood repudiated industrious activity

---

[83] It was useless for Joaquín Costa to speak to his people at the dawn of this century like a new prophet out of Israel: "On the day of the rout in Santiago de Cuba, the sons of privilege remain triumphant and unhurt . . . , those who shout *La Marcha de Cádiz* [a march played during the Spanish-American War], those who have failed their baccalaureate exams, the spoiled young gentlemen from the towns, the dandies on the sidewalks of Las Calatravas [a church on Alcalá Street in Madrid], . . . the dregs of society who fill the bullrings, drunk on wine and savagery; and yet there is no one in the government who will take up the whips of Christ in the temple to slash the faces of the mob." ("Crisis política de España," a speech read at the *Juegos Florales* of Salamanca on September 15, 1901; in *Obras completas*, VI [Madrid: Biblioteca "Costa," 1914], 59).

[84] *Bienes del honesto trabajo y daños de la ociosidad* (Madrid, 1614).

in order not to be confused with the infidels expelled from the kingdom. He and others were seeking to make walk people whose feet had previously been shackled.

Without the French Revolution and the unfortunate Napoleonic invasion of Spain, it is most likely that Spanish society would have kept its ecclesiastical, nobiliary, and rural aspect for a considerable length of time. And in any event the changes introduced in the first half of the nineteenth century, after the death of Ferdinand VII,[85] were, despite the expulsion of the religious orders, more superficial than profound. After 1833 neither constitutional government nor European theoretical thought sent down vigorous roots in Spain; on the other hand, there was a curious revival of attempts to probe the _inner self_ in the hope of finding there a solution to the problems that continued to trouble the souls of the most enlightened Spaniards—problems that today are taking on increasing actuality, despite the dominance of our technologically created automatism, the horrible risk of which is nothing less than the self-destruction of mankind. In other words, total inward isolation in the Spanish manner may be no more dangerous than total surrender to the anonymity and unawareness resulting from sociological abstractions and the machine-based technology that produces physical comfort—and this is the surrender characteristic of peoples we call "civilized" and leaders of the world.

But to return to Spain, I repeat that the changes introduced in the first half of the nineteenth century were more apparent and superficial than effective. No positive, constructive reforms of the religious position of the state or its citizens followed upon the expulsion of the religious orders. Things had been destroyed solely for the pleasure

---

[85] In 1827 the University of Cervera displayed its gratitude and allegiance to Ferdinand VII in a famous document, which has not always been quoted accurately. The professors of that university, founded by Philip V, did _not_ say: "Far from us the regrettable madness of thinking." What happened was that the attempt by the Portuguese government to promulgate a "constitutional letter" provoked a spirited reaction in the court in Madrid at the beginning of 1827. Partisans of the absolutist regime sent King Ferdinand statements of allegiance; among them appears that from the University of Cervera, published by the _Gaceta de Madrid_ on May 3, 1827. The most striking passage of this document is the following: "We are all of one heart and one soul: _far from us the dangerous novelty of invention_, which has burrowed away for a long time, bursting out finally with the result no one can deny of depraving customs, [which has led] to the total upheaval of empires and of religion in every part of the world." The wise teachers of Cervera were referring to _innovations_, to political upheaval, about which they did not wish to "reflect," or, in other words, which they did not desire, or wish to plan. In this instance they were in harmony with the reactionary policies of the rest of Europe, especially with those of Charles X of France. Cervera's professors could not have referred to general freedom of thought, which was not practiced by them; they did know, however, and fear the excesses and disorders that had occurred in Spain during the brief constitutional period from 1820 to 1823.

of destruction, and the religious orders would again become very influential. The constitutional system (in defense of which many lost their lives during the war against the Carlists) failed to achieve genuine dominance in any Spanish- or Portuguese-speaking nation. Nor was Spain fully opened up, after Ferdinand VII, to foreign science or the technology developed as a consequence of the industrial revolution. The only innovation really accepted, on occasion with genuine enthusiasm, was the Romantic point of view, utilized for the literary expression of contemporary or past life.

On their return to the fatherland after more or less protracted residence abroad, the political exiles either did not try to import, or did not succeed in harmonizing to the Spanish milieu in any significant measure, the science of the countries in which they had lived; they did, however, help to modify and renovate public administration and the orientation of politics. The émigrés succeeded in familiarizing the average Spaniard with the image of a Europe different from that of the ancient regime.[86]

By the middle of the nineteenth century movements outward, to foreign countries, began to occur more frequently under the stimulus of intellectual curiosity; the ideas imported were, nevertheless, those that best conformed to the traditional preferences and temperament of the Spanish people. I have already called attention (p. 356) to the reaction of Pi y Margall to certain European ideas that lent themselves to a new interpretation of the mystic poetry of St. John of the Cross and to the discovery of possible solutions for the political and social difficulties of the moment. In other instances, the anarchist doctrines—corporative and antagonistic to the state—of Owen, Proudhon, and others possessed a familiar ring for a people who had been cursing the state for centuries and holding fast to the author of salvation offered by the feelings of the inner self, listening to their own souls rather than obeying the helmsman of their reason. Once again they fell back on the refuge provided by the sacred precinct of the person, where man dreams of the beyond and frees himself ideally from the material and moral poverty in which he is suffocating. Fundamentally, anarcho-syndicalism is nothing more than a lay version of the Spanish monastic tradition, impregnated as it was with asceticism and mysticism and abounding in sharp criticism of the conduct of certain clerics,[87] of their excessive numbers and their tax exemptions, so harmful for the economy of the kingdom.

[86] See Vicente Llorens, *Liberales y románticos* (Mexico, 1954).

[87] One example is a book entitled *Espejo de la conciencia*, written by "a Minorite, resident in, and subject of, the Custodia de los Angeles," in other words, in the Franciscan monastery of Guadalcanal (Seville). It was published anonymously and, according to V. Barrantes, by a clandestine press in Estremadura about 1502 or 1503; the book itself carries neither place nor date of publication (*La imprenta en Extremadura*, p. 41; see also "Libros de Antaño,"

We should recall at this point that the expulsion of the Jesuits in 1767 (whatever the motivation of Charles III's action) was strongly supported by the other religious orders: "The Jesuits had stirred up hatred among these monks and possessed bitter enemies."[88]

Once almost all the religious orders were abolished in 1835 and their financial holdings had vanished, the memory of their wealth and way of life remained vivid. For the man who considered the unique position of the Spanish monasteries, without taking into account their extraterrestrial goals, they must in fact have superficially seemed like the very model of syndicalist organization, fragmented into corporate units similar to those later described by Joaquín Costa. Each monastery organized its labor autonomously and made use of the produce of the land, which was itself communal property, for the benefit of the community. Faith, virtue, and mutual agreement, arrived at spontaneously and without coercive pressures, made private property unnecessary, while the sources of wealth and the means of production were utilized to the advantage of all. It is no accident that Rabelais (despite his insolent antimonastic remarks) should have conceived as an abbey the Utopian residence whose only rule was that dictated by one's own will (*Thélème*, it should be recalled, derives from the Greek word for will, *thélēma*).

Foreign libertarian doctrines offered a structured theory for ancient and thoroughly familiar Spanish habits and tendencies. Joseph Proudhon found in Sancho Panza the perfect expression of justice unconnected with the state, unsystematic and concrete in the sense that each case required new rules, a new debate:

He never seeks, like the ancient philosophers, the Supreme Good, nor, like modern socialists, Happiness; he has no faith whatsoever in the absolute and rejects, like a mortal enemy, contrary to his nature, all a priori and definitive systems. His deep intuition tells him that the absolute, just like the *status quo*, cannot enter into human institutions. For him the abso-

---

XII, 400). Later there were editions in Logroño, 1507; Seville, 1512; Toledo, 1513; Seville, 1516; Toledo, 1525; Seville, 1531; Seville, 1543 (according to Nicolás Antonio, *Bibliotheca Nova*, this edition attributes the authorship to Juan Bautista de Vinones); Seville, 1548; Medina del Campo, 1552 (both these late editions are once again anonymous). This work, which no one reads today but which was widely read and freely circulated in the first half of the sixteenth century, addresses the bishops in the following fashion: "Oh, my lords, may your lordships observe and note well for what you spend the possessions and income of your bishoprics, and may you [not] indulge in extravagant revels or go about with great retinues or possess wonderful tableware; otherwise, in truth you are stealing the property of the poor: and their blood cries out against you each day before God" (1507 ed., fol. 92). "They [the bishops] have allowed them [the poor] and still allow them to perish from hunger. . . . They must yet be reproached for their cruelty and tyranny over their subjects as long as everyone confesses and says that the most cruel seigniory in the world is that of the ecclesiastics, . . . and if they could, they would tear out of the poor indigent his vitals" (fol. 94).

[88] François Rousseau, *Règne de Charles III d'Espagne* (Paris, 1907), I, 135.

MANUEL PELLICER.

FIGURE 1.
Epitaph of the
Catholic Sovereigns
Ferdinand and
Isabella at
the Royal Chapel
of Granada.

FIGURE 2.
The Crucifixion, by Giovanni del Biondo (14th century).
The face of the apostle James (holding a pilgrim staff)
is a replica of Christ's.
(From the journal *Dedalo* [Milan, 1931], p. 1289.)

lute is life itself, diversity in unity. As he accepts no formula as final, it thus turns out that the mission of the explorers who precede him consists solely in widening the horizon and clearing the road for him.[89]

About the same time that the "good news" of anarchism was beginning to be known and spread in certain rural areas,[90] Julián Sanz del Río was starting his explanations of Krausist philosophy at the University of Madrid. There was no intentional coincidence between the two phenomena, but it is clear that the motivation of both is inseparable from the "inner" situation of those who yearned to find a possible solution for the difficulties presented by the "new" political and social regime. The panorama that for centuries had seemed consubstantial with the Spanish mode of existence had undergone wide change. The monks had vanished from the previously numerous and powerful monasteries. After a long and bloody civil war (1833–1839), the constitutional regime had clearly won out over the absolutist. Without an Inquisition, without monks, and without an absolute monarchy, it seemed as if Spain had been reborn from its own ashes. The actual events of the time—the policies of Martínez de la Rosa, the government of Isabella II, and the satirical articles of Larra which mirror these events—do not concern us here, for I am not narrating the history of Spain but only trying to render visible and comprehensible the position and directions of Spanish life.

The enlightened and reflective men did not find the panorama of 1850 as disheartening as that of the years encompassing the tyranny of Ferdinand VII, when on rainy or disagreeably cold days public offices hung on their doors this sign: "Closed on account of inclement weather." But even so, it was difficult to see how anything efficacious might be done with a people exhibiting, in both the cities and the country, such economic and cultural decadence. Ways of action toward the outside world were, in truth, obstructed; there was a lack of teachers, public officials, and citizens determined to put an end to an inertia and apathy whose origins were centuries old. The phrase so frequently repeated later was beginning to be heard: "Everything is yet to be done." The truth was—and this is the structural theme that had been debated for so many years—that those things that happened and had to happen in the *outer*, social zone were of little moment to the man interested solely in the drama, novel, or farce acted out *within* his own self. Such was the vital dialectic of the Spaniard, the dialectic that for centuries had set in motion those intricate debates between the value of the things that might be done

---

[89] *Idée générale de la révolution au XIXe siècle; apud* Peter Heintz, *Anarchismus und Gegenwart*, p. 60. Heintz states shortly before that "the anarchist revolutionary in modern times would be like a living portrait of Don Quixote."

[90] See Juan Díaz del Moral, *Historia de las agitaciones campesinas andaluzas* (Madrid, 1929), and the bibliography cited by Jackson, *op. cit.*

374 · IN SEARCH OF A BETTER SOCIAL ORDER

and the hierarchical arrangement of those who had to do them: "Good lineage is like a light that illumines the good things done by those of illustrious family, and therefore the lineage of the lower classes is called dark."[91]

The value of the "thing" to be done did not matter, but only the value of the autonomous and inner process of its doing, the *point from which* it was done. With rare exceptions the Spaniard was not interested in a task the importance of which consisted in an idea, a theory, a common utility rather than in the role he himself would play in the task; material advantage mattered less to him than the fact of his personal intervention. Centuries of hidalgo status, of caste-determined rank, were for him like the tables of his own law of evaluation, of his hierarchies of value judgments.[92]

The categorical imperative of Kant left the possible Spanish Kantians cold, while the Hegelian theory of the absolute state, so Germanic and so attractive to the Germans, had no greater success. Both these philosophers spoke above all to the reasoning mind, and thus neither Kantianism nor Hegelianism left deep traces on nineteenth-century Spanish thought. Quite the opposite, however, occurred with the Romantic philosophy of Krause (d. 1832), which conceived the state as a relativity, as a medium that made possible the open and limitless goals of the person, the family, the corporation, the nation. In other terms, for Krause the value-creating and structurizing movement passed from the base upward, like an ethical impulse, like a hope. And while the pantheistic metaphysics of Krause (connected with Spinoza's "deus sive natura") stimulated little talk or action in Spain, the ethical, juridical, and educational derivations of his theories (spread especially by direct disciples of Krause) stirred keen enthusiasm in many and gave rise in the second half of the nineteenth century to a cultural revival unprecedented in the history of Spanish thought.[93] Francisco Giner de los Ríos, the most distinguished and worthiest among those influenced by Krause's thought, considered it an error to affirm that the state was "merely a social institution, as if the individual were not, just like society, a person also and the active subject of the law"; the immediate object of the state's activity is "that each person, by all the means within

---

[91] Luis Zapata, *Miscelánea*, in *Memorial Histórico Español*, XI, 271.

[92] Once a man introduced himself to Joaquín Costa in the following fashion: "I am a Galician, I live in Barcelona, I have served the state for twenty years."
"You had better say," Costa replied, "that the state has served you for twenty years" (cited by J. García Mercadal in his Prologue to the *Historia política, social, patria* of Joaquín Costa, p. 24).

[93] Pierre Jobit, *Les éducateurs de l'Espagne contemporaine: Les Krausistes* (Paris, 1936); Juan López Morillas, *El krausismo español* (Mexico, 1956). See also the article "Krausismo" in the *Diccionario de filosofía* of J. Ferrater Mora.

his reach, may serve the rational aim of his life." On another occasion, while examining the problem of the relations between the individual and the state, he says that a trait common to "all modern liberalism [is] the suspicion with which it views the corporative element and all those social circles that aspire *to live and to govern themselves by themselves, independent of the central state.*"[94]

Giner and Costa were not anarchists, for both men justified the permanent function of the law and of the state; but, as Dorado Montero has observed, "Giner taught insistently . . . " that "coercion in its various forms, even in its material aspect," is nothing "but one of a number of necessary means or conditions, in given circumstances, for achieving the rational aims of man."[95] Although in his philosophy of law Krause admitted coercion, the basis of his thought is that "law is an *ethical order*, [based on] positive cooperation, *voluntary* donation of the conditions for life, charitable sacrifice of means on the part of those who have them to benefit those who need them; an order whose right guarantee is, in reality and in the final analysis, *not found outside the conscience of individuals*" (*Valor social de leyes y autoridades*, p. 194).

Here, I think, is the basic reason for the success of Krausist thought in Spain: the call, the stimulus to set in motion the spontaneity of the personal conscience, to make of each person a kind of creative artist and director of his own life. The analysis or evaluation of Krause's philosophy is not my task; but I am interested in making evident the point at which it makes contact with the tradition of life that I have been expounding in the preceding pages. The revolutionary anarchists (like those described by Blasco Ibáñez in *La bodega*) had nothing in common, with respect to their practices, with nineteenth-century thinkers such as Pi y Margall, Giner, or Costa; but both Krausism and anarchism signified a retreat to the only refuge that had remained intact and secure after the destruction of all the revered values of Spanish life. Confidence could be placed only in the person's inner self, not in the things outside that self. Long ago, when the tired and hungry traveler was about to cross the threshold of an inn, he used to cry out: "Mistress, what is there to eat?" And the reply would come back: "Whatever your grace brings with you!"

Like Luis Vives and Luis de León before him (see above, p. 332), Giner de los Ríos falls back on Platonic thought to make evident the inanity "of wishing to make up for the lack of education and of inner judgment, which is the fruit [of education], by piling regula-

---

94 *El pensamiento vivo de Giner de los Ríos*, ed. Fernando de los Ríos (Buenos Aires, 1949), pp. 202, 203, 242; the italics are mine.

95 Dorado Montero, *op. cit.*, p. 194.

tions on top of regulations, adding corrections on top of corrections, *which achieves nothing but a worsening of the illness.*[96] For Giner both coercion and rivalry served for nothing in education. So it is that, without ever declaring himself a partisan of anarchism, he stated that it "is a doctrine, exact or inexact, correct or mistaken, as respectable as any other, and which has no more to do with the brutal and stupid crimes committed in its name by a few unhappy people than other political or religious doctrines" have to do with the excesses to which they have given rise ("Para la historia de las teorías libertarias," *Boletín de la Institución Libre de Enseñanza*, XXIII [1899], 88). And Giner was right: in the name of Christ countless people have been tortured and burned; European democracies, as well as dictatorships, have established themselves on the basis of crimes and all kinds of wickedness.

If, as we look back on them now, it may be seen that the anarchism and the Krausism of the past century were oriented toward the same existential possibilities and needs, they were likewise in agreement with respect to some of the sociological theories to which they gave rise: "From Ahrens, disciple of Krause and professor at Brussels, Proudhon seems to have received the encouragement that induced him to conceive a professional organization of society."[97]

Once we have succeeded in endowing our image of a people's temporal and spatial dwelling place of life with a concrete reality, the present and the immediate past of that people are seen to be tightly intermeshed with the more distant past. The irremediable rupture of the shared common life among the castes toward the end of the fifteenth century caused each generation to pass on, by means of its most qualified spokesmen, a legacy of characteristically Spanish anxieties to the next generation. The gap between the concept of justice and the experience of it became ever more unbridgeable; the contrast between inner grandeur and the inability to act is expressed in a thousand ways in seventeeth-century literature. The individual felt his neighbor—the man nearest him—to be ever more distant from him.[98] Three long centuries of existence under a regime of mutual

---

[96] "Para la historia de las teorías libertarias," *Boletín de la Institución Libre de Enseñanza*, XXIII (1899), 88. See Dorado Montero, *op. cit.*, p. 11.

[97] *El pensamiento vivo de Giner de los Ríos*, p. 53.

[98] Two characters in Tirso de Molina's *La celosa de sí misma* converse as follows:

> DON SEBASTIÁN: As time passes so quickly
> in Madrid, there is no occasion
> for neighbors even to meet
> each other, or be able to talk. . . .
> DON JERÓNIMO: . . . .
> In one house sometimes
> there may live

suspicion and distrust (not to mention the usual battle, waged in Spain and every other country, between the poor and the rich, the tyrants and the slaves) explain the inner and public situation of those who in the mid-nineteenth century were "officially" declared free—without an inquisition, without monks, without an absolute monarchy.

With regard to Spain it is no longer permissible to write the history of the past as nothing more than a connected narrative, a myth, or a series of anecdotes. If we react with rage or impassivity toward the past, we are only assuming masks that prevent our seeing that what is indeed there reflects *uniquely Spanish* circumstances; it is a past that cannot be described by general terms, such as medieval, Renaissance, Counter-Reform, or what you will. For me at least, that past holds countless moments of inexpressible delight and reverent admiration, but also—it could not be otherwise—of painful feeling. If I have spent so long a time on the historicovital analysis of anarchism, a form of social organization which attracts so many Spaniards (for good or bad reasons), it is because in that *punctum candens* lies the possibility or the impossibility that the future of a whole people should be chaotic, a permanent servitude, or, on the other hand, an opening out toward days of justified hope. The fact of the matter is (and it is not just the lesson of history but a question of opening one's eyes to reality, of contemplating with the mind) that it is now impossible in the twentieth century to cultivate, without enormous

---

eighteen neighbors, as I have seen,
and they pass a whole year
without talking to each other,
or knowing of one another.

DON SEBASTIÁN: . . . .
. . . I chanced to see
in one house, on one day,
weddings, burials and births,
weeping, laughter, mourning and party dress,
in three adjoining parlors,
and another three adjacent rooms,
without one group's knowing of the other,
nor within one room,
would this confusion have given them
occasion to know one another.

DON JERÓNIMO: One wall here
is farther from the next,
than Valladolid from Ghent.

(*Biblioteca de Autores Españoles*, V, 128–129)

All this is not a picturesque anecdote revealing local customs but one expression of the theme of inner cleavage and splitting; the most exalted expression of this theme is that of the "divided heart" (cf. the lines of verse which state, "the knife of jealousy / splits the very heart"). In any event, the modalities of civic life offered "matter" for that "form" of art we are accustomed to call baroque. The schism in Spanish society had already been expressed by Luis de León in *Los nombres de Cristo* (n. 21, p. 334), and Tirso makes use of it in this delightful symphony of discord and disagreement.

risk, forms of life based exclusively on the *inner self*. I do not deny that the existence of the Spaniard's *inner self* may be more necessary today than ever before, as a counterbalance to the inordinate externalization of man in these declining years of the twentieth century, when we are able to use physical energy as never before, but are also abstracted from ourselves as never before. But when the problem is presented in this fashion, it becomes too broad for us and slips out of our hands. Every people, every individual, can face up to only a certain number of difficulties, those of the most immediate concern in the given instance; and the most urgent problem for the Spaniard is to realize that his present condition is caused by the situations in which his inner self has constantly placed him. For the Spaniard, *inward states* have been more decisive than *surrounding conditions*, which is to say that the light of illumination has been focused inward rather than outward. The preceding pages have borne witness to the ways in which the future became steadily more hermetic (the seventeenth century more so than the sixteenth, the nineteenth more than the eighteenth). It requires no prophetic gift to see that the future now before us will become still more oppressive and hermetic as long as we do not open up broad highways leading to work in the world outside the self, while we do not create concepts, ways, and modalities that permit life under the law, a life shared with our neighbors, within an order that renders sterile the unholy alliance between authority and injustice. Exclusionism and the sealing up of man within himself have failed—though the inner self as such has not failed and will not do so if it decides to open outward toward the circumstances.

We have had to gain a sharp view of the guiding forces that determined the structure of the past to the end that the remainder of this work should be intelligible. Instead of taking inspiration from the famous title "The Spaniards *Painted* by Themselves" (*Los españoles pintados por sí mismos*), I have preferred to transform that title into a longer one that more nearly states my purpose: "The Spaniards expressing their lived experience, their inner reactions, on finding themselves situated in the awareness of their grandeur and their weakness." Instead of narrating or describing, I have also preferred to let the Spaniards write the novel of themselves. It is a type of history which differs from the narrative chronicle or the miscellany of anecdotes much as the Cervantine novel does from the book of chivalric adventures or the medieval tale. The author relates—and controls—Amadís; Don Quixote and Sancho relate themselves, tell the story of their own lives. Each point in the history depends on a system of vital forces and value judgments; and each point interacts with all others. All the possibilities offered by the wealth deriving from Hispanic America were affected by the judgment of value made with respect to the man who acquired wealth and by that man's own reactions. In order to understand the Spaniards (or the French or the Italians), it is necessary to upset the rhythm of historical time —as Proust has done—to interweave memory with the vision of the future, to inject into the "before" the lived experience of the "after" (and vice versa). In this fashion history takes on the flesh of real life, of empirical (temporal and spatial) experiences as well as of conceptualized projections, and of the firm bonds between *inward states* and *outer conditions*. From the point of view of such a history there is more sense than nonsense in the well-known ridiculous remark made by a character in a bad historical novel: "Let us set out for the Thirty Years' War." The historian must keep in mind the remarkable and tremendous consequences of the fact that those who fought against the Muslims twelve centuries ago called themselves "Christians"—with an ethnic and national connotation. If those men could have called themselves "Spaniards," their future would not have been made up of such grandeur or such disasters.

"Belief, caste, economy"—conceptual terms we must employ now in order to understand one another—were expressed in a conscious awareness and in external actions which, as their radius was extended, gradually created the protective, and entangling, net of life —both the tolerant sharing of a common life with other castes and inquisitorial narrowness; the spontaneity of certain juridical customs and the legal rigidity that destroys them; the exultant grandeur of empire and the indifference toward its loss. And always, when fortune's tide was lowest, the Spaniard has sought within himself, turned over within the interstices of his inner self, the means of escaping from himself; or he has sallied forth in search of foreign vestments to cover and protect his nakedness. Of such events and feelings does this history consist, and it has no possible fixed point of termination; for, as the hardened picaro Ginés de Pasamonte says to Don Quixote about his autobiography, "How can it be finished, if my life has still not ended?" Indeed, his life was so far from ended that we later see him standing before his puppet stage and dreaming of marvels more real and *historical* than his former picaresque frauds. Spain can still choose among various wonderful destinies. Why should it not?

X · THE BEGINNINGS OF THE CHRISTIAN AND EUROPEAN REACTION: ST. JAMES OF GALICIA

The Belief in the Apostle St. James (Santiago)

> "By whom are the Spains loosed from the yoke of bar-
> barian furor, and freed."
>
> (Luis de León)

> "So firmly linked were the interests of Heaven and
> those of Spain that Heaven manifested itself as Spain's
> ally in her greatest afflictions. What grandeur equals
> that witnessed by the Spaniards when the two celestial
> champions, St. James and St. Emilian, mingled with
> their squadrons?"
>
> (Feijoo, "Glorias de España,"
> in *Teatro Crítico*, IV, disc. 13, par. 16)

T HE NUMBER, THE SIZE, and the magnificence of certain Roman cities are due to their having been constructed on what had been the camp site of a famous legion. In like fashion, Santiago de Compostela ("campus stellas") rose over the space occupied by an encampment of the spirit; it was the result of the homage offered to the sepulcher where lay the body of one of Christ's greatest Apostles. There are, to be sure, other Spanish cities in which the relics of some saint are venerated; but Santiago's peculiarity consists in the fact that the cult of the Apostle for eight hundred years inspired architectural marvels—many of which, fortunately, still stand. Pilgrimages made them possible, and they, in their turn, were an expression of the lasting prestige of the belief in the presence there of the remains of an Apostle no less important than Sts. Peter and Paul, who were venerated in Rome. In the eleventh century, according to the *Codex Calixtinus* (ed. Whitehall, p. 149), one could hear spoken in Santiago the languages of very different and strange peoples: Germanic, English, Greek, "and [the tongues] of other peoples coming from all the regions of the world"; and "just as the sun makes the moon shine, so does the immense power of the Apostle illumine Spain and Galicia" (p. 148).

The history of the Spaniards would not, in truth, have taken the course it did without the belief that there reposes in Galicia the body of one of Christ's disciples and companions, beheaded in Palestine and carried to Spain by miraculous means; thus he returned to the land formerly Christianized by him, according to a tradition about which there would be no point in arguing, a tradition that had existed since before the arrival of the Arabs. Faith in the physical presence of the Apostle gave spiritual support to those who fought against the Moors; the extraordinary veneration in which he was held led to the erection of marvelous buildings both in Santiago and along the routes of the pilgrims, and it had cultural consequences both inside and outside Spain. The Order of Cluny and others of no less importance were established in the north of the Peninsula, attracted by the success of the pilgrimages; millions of people moved along the *via francigena*, or the French Highway, and those people kept up the connection between the Christian Spanish kingdoms and the rest of Europe. Art, literature, institutions, customs, and forms of linguistic expression interacted with religious belief in that prodigious historical event, which took place in the northwestern corner of Spain, the *finis terrae* of Christian Europe, where the outlines of the countryside are blurred by mists in which the land itself appears to be suspended.

In spite of all—and there is much—that has been written about Santiago of Galicia, we continue to wonder how such an event was possible.[1] It is understandable that Rome, the head of an empire, should be continued by Christian Rome, and that Jerusalem should take on exceptional prominence. Galicia, on the other hand, had been completely lacking in importance; she was not perceptibly significant under either the Romans or the Suevi or the Visigoths. We would expect, then, that such a miracle as took place there would have only local authority, and that it would have even been rejected as illegitimate when it came to be known outside Spain. This did not happen, so we must reconsider this event of such huge proportions and try to remove it from the category of arbitrary and puzzling chance happenings.

---

[1] See L. Vázquez de Parga, José M. Lecarra, and J. Uría Ríu, *Las peregrinaciones a Santiago de Compostela* (Madrid, 1949), 3 vols.

At the beginning of the ninth century, near the ancient city of Iria Flavia, a sepulcher was venerated which was said to contain the body of James the Apostle. Orthodox opinion always admitted that the Apostle was James the Greater, the son of Zebedee. Gonzalo de Berceo and the *Poema de Fernán González* both speak of him as such in the thirteenth century, in agreement with ecclesiastical tradition; but popular belief, in defiance of the learned, adored a St. James who included the Greater (Matt. 4:21) and the one called the brother of Christ in the Gospel (Matt. 13:55), a description taken literally, as we shall see, by those who venerated the sepulcher. For centuries this fraternal relationship, forgotten by orthodoxy, formed the core of that belief, which acquired considerable dimensions, especially because it concerned a brother of the Saviour. Such a belief bore a resemblance to certain pre-Christian cults of twin divinities like Castor and Pollux—the Dioscuri or sons of Jupiter—one of whom ascended to heaven while the other remained on earth (at least for some time) as a protector of man. Like St. James, both Castor and Pollux descended from heaven on their white horses to fight for the army they favored.

If Spain had not been submerged by Islam, the cult of Santiago of Galicia would not have prospered; but the anxiety of the eighth and ninth centuries fortified the faith in a Santiago the brother of Christ, who, like a new manifestation of Castor, would achieve magnificent victories, riding his shining white charger. Similar miracles had occurred elsewhere occasionally, but without taking on transcendent importance; on the other hand, the peculiar circumstances in the northwest of the Peninsula transformed this miraculous appearance into an indispensable aid, consonant with forms of belief oblivious to the boundaries between heaven and earth, between miracle and the reality of experience. Indeed, with the belief in Santiago there appears a most original type of existence, something that I shall call integral "theobiosis," without an exact parallel in Christian Europe though probably akin to ways of life in Muslim and Jewish states where the notions of state and religion are confused. The cult of Santiago was not a simple manifestation of piety eventually useful in the struggle against the Moor. The truth is, on the contrary, that the belief emerged out of the humble plane of folklore and assumed immeasurable dimensions as an answer to what was happening on the Muslim side: a type of war sustained and won by religious faith was to be opposed (not rationally, of course) by another fighting faith, grandly spectacular, strong enough in turn to sustain the Christian and carry him to victory. In the same way that the Moors had been unconsciously imitated by those who called themselves "Christians" (a term used to designate both ethnic and national distinctions) rather than Goths or "Hispanians," a correlation was also established with respect to the military use of religious beliefs.

At the beginning of the ninth century, some hundred years after the Saracen invasion, the Christians in the northwest of Spain must have felt themselves very weak materially and spiritually. They were already seriously isolated from the rest of Christendom in the Visigothic period. Now this isolation must have been almost complete, and the restoration of the ancient monarchy of Toledo on Spanish soil probably seemed impossible. But, behold, at the beginning of the tenth century the Christians began to raise their heads, and under Alfonso III (866–910) they considerably extended the boundaries of the Asturian-Leonese kingdom. Alfonso's sons and subjects speak of him in 917 as "magnus imperator."[2] No longer did the Christians feel themselves humbled in the face of the Moors: their monarchs, once simply *principes* or *reges*, they now called *imperatores*. What justification could be found for such an elevation in rank? I would venture to say that the title of *imperator* is inseparable from the title of *pontifex* ("pontiff") given to the bishop of Santiago with great verbal pomp. The first indication of this that I know of is in a document from the year 954, most likely not the first one: "I, Ordoño, prince and humble servant of the servants of the Lord, desire for you, illustrious and venerable father and Lord Sisnandus, bishop of the see of our patron Santiago and *pontiff of the whole world*, eternal health in God Our Lord."[3] The person who wrote

[2] R. Menéndez Pidal, *La España del Cid*, pp. 74, 77, 710.

[3] *España sagrada*, XIX, 366; A. López Ferreiro, *Historia de la Iglesia de Santiago*, II, 319; Menéndez Pidal, *op. cit.* The Latin text says: "totius orbis Antistiti." The decisive effect of Santiago on the political and ecclesiastical life of the kingdom of Leon has been acknowledged by R. Menéndez Pidal, who, having been previously informed of my views, says in a new edition of *La España del Cid*: "The discovery of the sepulcher of Santiago and the empire [of the kings of Leon] are two correlated facts" (p. 69). In another recent book by Menéndez Pidal we read: "With the discovery of Santiago's sepulcher the small Asturian kingdom did not feel, as it did before, in a condition of oppressive inferiority; they already possessed something very great to outdo the old Visigothic court in dignity" (*El imperio hispánico y los cinco reinos* [Madrid, 1950], p. 22. My idea of the outstanding part played by the belief in Santiago could not find better or higher recognition.

In its entirety the Latin text reads as follows: "Ego exiguus et servorum Domini servus Hordonius Princeps vobis inclyto ac venerabili Patri Domino Sisnando, Episcopo hujus Patroni nostri et totius orbis Antistiti." The sense is quite clear: ". . . for you, illustrious and venerable father and Lord Sisnandus, bishop [of the see] of our patron [Santiago] and supreme prelate of the whole world"—that is to say, "pontiff." Despite the simplicity of this text, Father A. K. Ziegler has misinterpreted it in *Speculum*, XXXI (1956), 148–149; the meaning is distorted in order to contradict the evidence that the bishops of Santiago believed themselves to be—and called themselves—pontiffs in the tenth, eleventh, and twelfth centuries. Father Ziegler overcomes his difficulties by mistranslating the text under discussion and another cited below in note 7, in which the word *culmen* obviously means "the highest point" and not simply

after such a fashion was King Ordoño III of Leon, who must have had powerful motives, and not only political ones, for giving the papal title to the bishop of Santiago, and consequently not recognizing the hierarchy of the Roman pontiff.[4] The King could permit himself such magnification because the bishops of Santiago believed themselves to be pontiffs. And they believed it because Santiago was a higher-ranking Apostle than Peter: he was a protomartyr, a favorite of God, the brother of Christ, and the "son of the thunder," according to the Gospel; popular belief (which was subsequently to be reflected in the liturgy) had indeed converted him into the twin brother of the Lord.[5]

Compostela's rivalry with Rome in its pontifical and apostolic pretensions was not an idle gesture in the tenth century, for these claims were at times accepted as valid beyond the limits of the kingdom of Leon. In 956, for example, Cesáreo, an ambitious Catalan and abbot of St. Cecilia in Montserrat, came to Compostela for a Church council and took advantage of the occasion to have himself "consecrated by the Galician and Leonese bishops, the metropolitan of

---

"high," as Ziegler would have it. Further, Ziegler ignores the remaining material adduced here about the pontifical claims of the bishops of Santiago. It would be pointless to mention so gross an error if it had not appeared in a periodical published by the American Medieval Society; but it must be said that everything Father Ziegler says in his review is as inaccurate as his Latin translations. See my note in *Speculum*, XXX (1957), 222–223.

[4] If we bear in mind what the Roman pontiffs were like in the tenth century, and how they must have looked from the point of view of Leon and Santiago, we will be in a better position to understand the claim of the Compostelan prelates. "In that epoch popes appeared and disappeared according to the whims of the feudal factions. There were some who died at the hands of assassins, or ended their days in prison. In that Roman milieu, demoralization went hand in hand with brutality. More than once, feminine intrigues decided who should wear the tiara, for Marozia and Theodora, utilizing their lovers or their successive husbands, had their sons named pope" (H. Pirenne, *Histoire de l'Europe* [1936], p. 115). Marozia, who enjoyed the title of *senatrix* and who was the real power in Rome, had one son who governed the capital of Christianity from 932 to 954. While this son, Alberich, exercised his tyranny, another son, closely supervised by Alberich, was occupying St. Peter's chair (931–936). In his lifetime Alberich named the following popes: Leo VII (936–939), Stephen VIII (939–942), Marinus II (942–946), and Agapetus II (946–955). For a few short years Agapetus II restored to some extent the fallen prestige of the pontiffs, but his predecessors obeyed the tyrant in silence and had no relations with the outside (F. Gregorovius, *History of the City of Rome in the Middle Ages* [London, 1895], III, 321; Luigi Salvatorelli, *L'Italia Medioevale* [Milan], pp. 530–542). There were not many mortal obstacles, therefore, to keep Santiago from strengthening its apostolic pretensions. The Rome of St. Peter (an Apostle of less importance than Santiago, as we shall see, for the Leonese and the Galicians) appeared to be weak, isolated, and depraved, lacking in the moral force necessary to arrest the advances being made by the see of the "son of thunder." Santiago and Rome were now islands of Christianity which, during the tenth century, knew little about one another. In the eleventh century the Cluniac order instituted a change in this state of affairs.

[5] This belief gained currency throughout Europe because of the bold attempt to create in Spain a duplicate of the correlation between pontificate and empire.

Lugo, and the apostolic bishop of Santiago—in the presence and with the endorsement of King Sancho the Fat"—as nothing less than "metropolitan of the Province of Tarragona, with jurisdiction over the dioceses of Barcelona, Tarrasa, Gerona, Ampurias, Osona, Urgel, Lérida, Tortosa, Saragossa, Huesca, Pamplona, Oca, Calahorra, and Tarazona." Cesáreo was attempting to reinstitute and bring under his spiritual authority that immense section of the former Visigothic Church. But, as Ramón de Abadal, the source of my information, says,[6] none of these previously named prelates (especially Archbishop Aimeric of Narbonne) accepted the consecration of Cesáreo as valid, because the apostolic see called both the See of Hispania and the See of the Occident was not founded by Santiago, who "had arrived there when he was already dead." Consequently, the ordination of Cesáreo was not legitimate. He continued, however, to call himself "archbishop" in documents emanating from St. Cecilia, though, of course, the title had no force outside his own abbey.

This incident reveals the vibrant feeling of prestige in Galicia and how that prestige exerted itself on the spirit of the kings of Leon. While the Catalan counties lived under the sovereignty of the Frankish kings, Galicia and Leon permitted themselves attitudes of imperial universalism; for if Bishop Sisnandus was not the first to believe himself entitled to the universal pontificate, there are certainly documents that prove that he was not the last. In 1049 Bishop Cresconius was excommunicated by the Council of Rheims "because against Divine law he arrogated to himself the highest apostolic title."[7] During the episcopate or pontificate of Diego Gelmírez (1100–1140), a period of maximum splendor for Santiago, that magnificent personage established pontifical pomp and honors in his court. He was censured for this by many, who reminded him that some of his predecessors "had claimed nothing less for their church than its equality with the Church of Rome" (A. López Ferreiro, *Historia de la Iglesia de Santiago*, III, 274). Gelmírez named cardinals, and his cardinals wore the purple; he received the pilgrims "Apostolico more," as if he were indeed the pope.

The foregoing data, which encompass a period of three centuries, will suffice to prove the constant, zealous longing on the part of the prelates of Compostela to establish themselves as heads of a universal hierarchy. I am aware that not only Santiago disputed Rome's supremacy during the Middle Ages, and that at one time Milan and

---

6 *Els primers comtes catalans* (Barcelona, 1958), p. 280.

7 López Ferreiro, *op. cit.*, II, 483. A more accurate version of this text is given by Caesar Baronius, *Annales Ecclesiastici*, ad annum 1049, no. 17 (XVII [Parisii, 1887], 30A): "Excommunicatus est etiam Sancti Iacobi archiepiscopus Galliciensis [Cresconius], quia contra fas sibi vindicaverat culmen Apostolici nominis."

Ravenna thought their own titles superior. Moreover, the legend of the Grail presupposes that the axis of Christianity did not pass through Rome alone. But none of these ideas took concrete shape in a claim so thoroughly sustained as that of Santiago nor so closely bound up with a popular state of feeling and with forms of liturgy and worship. Those who believed that Santiago was the center of Catholicism felt that truth and justice were on their side. Such a sentiment must already have been strong around Alfonso III (866–910), who is precisely the one who had the first proper church built in honor of the Apostle: "And he caused the church of St. James to be built, all of carved stone, with pillars of marble; *for the one before this had been made of earth*."[8]

The presence of the body of Santiago in Iria Flavia is not mentioned before the ninth century, although the coming of the Apostle to Spain for the purpose of Christianizing the Peninsula had been spoken of; even then the two Santiagos were being confused,[9] as they continued to be subsequently.

In martyrologies prior to the year 1000, the passion of St. James is dated March 25, although in these terms: "Passio sancti Iacobi Iusti, fratris Domini, sicut in Actibus Apostolorum continetur" ("the passion of St. James the Just, brother of the Lord, as it is contained in the Acts of the Apostles")[10] But the passion spoken of in Acts (12:2) is that of St. James the Greater, whereas the brother of the Lord (Matt. 13:55) is St. James the Just, that is, the Less. The juxtaposition of the two Apostles was nothing unique: the same thing occurred with almost all the rest.[11] In the present instance, however, it happens that this third Santiago, the result of the fusion of the two, suffered his passion on March 25, on the same day as the commemoration of the Passion of Christ (López Ferreiro, *op. cit.*, I, 311–312), a circumstance that accentuated the brotherhood of the two. The so-called *Codex Calixtinus*, falsely attributed to Pope Calixtus II and composed in the twelfth century, still had both passions coinciding on March 25. Later, either because it was no longer urgent to emphasize the divine brotherhood of Santiago, or because the double celebration was in fact perceived to be inadmissible, the Feast of St. James was transferred to July 25.

---

[8] *Crónica General*, p. 369b. This king was a great builder of churches. As the chronicle says (p. 379a), "He also built a church, well wrought, over the bodies of St. Facundus and St. Primitivus, on the bank of the river Cea." This was the shrine of that pair of twin saints on the route of Santiago.

[9] The *De ortu et obitu Patrum*, an apparently spurious work of St. Isidore, already demonstrates this confusion, which is also to be found in the Byzantine text on which it is based. Monsignor L. Duchesne (*Annales du Midi* [1900], XII, 156–157) describes such an error as enormous.

[10] According to López Ferreiro, *op. cit.*, I, 63, which refers to martyrologies of the eighth century and later.

[11] Rendel Harris, *The Twelve Apostles* (Cambridge, 1927), *passim*.

If Santiago of Galicia was a fusion of the two Jameses of the Gospels, the military and equestrian activity of "Santiago Matamoros," St. James the Moorslayer, as he might be called in English, presupposed in the Christian Apostle certain characteristics entirely foreign to everything that is said about either James in the Gospels, the Acts of the Apostles, the ecclesiastical history of Eusebius of Caesarea, and other hagiographical sources. The Santiago in whom the ninth-century Spaniards believed is the one who later is mentioned in the *Crónica General* of Alfonso the Learned in the narration of the miraculous apparition of the Apostle at the Battle of Clavijo (822), in terms corresponding to what was expected by the people, accustomed by tradition to imagine Santiago, and before that the Dioscuri, as descending from above mounted on a white horse to favor his protégés. The Apostle appeared to King Ramiro I and said: "Our Lord Jesus Christ divided between all the other Apostles, my brothers, and me, all the other provinces of the earth, and to me alone he gave Spain for me to watch over her and protect her from the hands of the enemies of the Faith. . . ."[12] And so that you may doubt nothing of this that I tell you, tomorrow will you see me go into battle, *on a white horse, with a white standard and a great shining sword in my hand*" (p. 360). Then the Christians, "trusting in God's help and the help of the Apostle Santiago," conquered the Moors.

In 449 B.C. the twins Castor and Pollux had also appeared on their white horses and in the same way decided the victory in favor of the dictator Postumius Albinus at Lake Regillus.[13] Strabo (VI, 261) speaks of an altar erected on the bank of the river Sagra to commemorate the victory won with the help of the Dioscuri in a battle in which 10,000 Locrians conquered 130,000 Crotonians.

The most obvious example of an apparition like that of the Dioscuri

---

[12] The chronicle translates the Latin text of the so-called Vows of Santiago, which may be found in E. Flórez, *España sagrada*, XIX, 331. From the Latin text it is evident that the sending of Santiago to Hispania was felt as a militant action related to the mission of the reconquest; but Jesus did not send forth his Apostles to take up arms and fight, but rather to teach the people with gentle words: "Go, and teach all nations."

[13] "The gods have appeared to us, to Postumius on Lake Regillus, and to Vacienus on the Salarian way. . . . Do you think that they were riding white horses when they appeared to Vacienus?" (Cicero, *De natura deorum*, III, 5; II, 6). *De natura deorum*, II, 6, states that in the battle of Lake Regillus, Castor and Pollux "ex equis pugnara visi sunt"—were seen fighting on horseback. For these and many other references, see the excellent article on the "Dioskuroi" in Pauly-Wissowa, *Real-Encyclopädie*, IX, col. 1091: "Since early time the appearances of the primitive pair of gods have been connected with horses, especially white ones." Euripides calls them λευκοπώλω . . . ἔκγονω Διός (*Heracles furens*, vv. 29–30). The gods were even conceived of as two white horses, although later the horses were converted into their attribute. In Sparta they were the models and protectors of every kind of equestrian or military exercise. There was an altar dedicated to them at the entrance of the hippodrome in Olympia (Pausanias, V, 15, 5), etc.

in Spain is found in the *Vida de San Millán* of Gonzalo de Berceo in the first half of the thirteenth century. Count Fernán González won the Battle of Simancas (939), according to the poet, thanks to the help of Santiago and St. Emilian. The Christians feared the numerical superiority of the Moors, and,

> While the good people were in this doubt,
> they turned their gaze and thoughts to heaven:
> they saw two persons fair and shining,
> much whiter were they than the recent snows.
> They rode *two horses whiter than crystal.* . . .
> their faces were angelic, their forms celestial,
> they came down through the air at great speed,
> they looked at the Moors with fierce glance,
> the swords in their hands were frightful to see.
>
> (437–439)

The defeat of the Moors was complete: "With God and the saints the battle was won" (452).[14]

Once established in the imagination and the memories of people (whether there are many believers or only a few does not matter), myths leap over tremendous geographical distances and slip down through the generations. Countless changes occur in both their form and their content, so that myths lend themselves readily to the expression at a given place and time of whatever conforms to the vital situation of those who make use of them. Like customs and language, myths (their distinct elements, the separable threads forming the tissue of what is believed and imagined) are one of the bases that have made possible the existence in time of the human qualities of man, who without them would have continued to be an animal. That basis (myth) is at once continuous, changeable, and shifting (all human things are paradoxical), even though its presence can be discerned down the long course of the millennia and has enabled historians to perceive the structure of man's past.

Let us look at one example among hundreds of possible ones: in 1902 Ramón Menéndez Pidal demonstrated that the theme of Tirso de Molina's *Condenado por desconfiado* ("Damned for Lack of Faith") appears for the first time in the *Mahabharata*, composed some 1600 years earlier.[15] In Tirso's play the Hindu Brahman has,

---

[14] The Dioscuric character of this apparition has already been mentioned by A. H. Krappe, "Spanish Twin Cults," in *Studi e materiali di storia delle religioni* (1932), VIII, 13. In Gonzalo de Berceo's *Milagros de Nuestra Señora*, stanza 198, Santiago saves one of his pilgrims whose soul some demons were going to carry off; but in the Latin source followed by Berceo (a work probably written by Hugh, abbot of Cluny), Santiago effects the miracle in the company of St. Peter (I am indebted for this information to Professor Raymond S. Willis). The tendency to pair saints appears on other occasions and reflects a pagan tradition.

[15] "*El condenado por desconfiado*, de Tirso de Molina," in *Estudios literarios* (Madrid, 1920), pp. 9–100.

naturally, become a Catholic and no longer recites the Vedas but prays according to the commandments of his church; the Hindu hunter who engages in sinful activities (doing harm to living beings) is in the Spanish version Enrico, a bandit who steals and commits other crimes, and so on. By way of Oriental and Christian-European literatures, the theme came down to Tirso de Molina.

It is surprising that the scholars not acquainted with such basic principles of cultural continuity should be scandalized and upset to find out that a long time ago several cultural historians related the warlike figure of Santiago and his white horse to the ancient tradition of the Dioscuri.[16] This relationship is not arbitrary or "grotesque"— as Father Justo Pérez de Urbel says—but a simple, normal phenomenon within the broad picture of connections between Christianity and earlier religions. The existence of such connections has been known for centuries and has been accepted in recent times by eminent Catholic historians. Long before them Alfonso de Valdés had written in the sixteenth century:

We have divided among our saints the duties held by the pagan gods. St. James and St. George have succeeded to the place of the god Mars; St. Elmo, to that of Neptune; St. Martin, to Bacchus; St. Barbara, to Aeolus; the Magdalene, to Venus. The function of Aesculapius we have divided among many: St. Cosmas and St. Damian are encharged with common diseases; St. Roch and St. Sebastian with pestilence. . . .[17]

Father Hippolyte Delahaye, the well-known Bollandist, says in *Les légendes hagiographiques* that the miraculous arrival of Santiago on the Galician coast is a pagan survival: "There is nothing more common in popular hagiography than the theme of the miraculous arrival of an image, or of a holy body, in an abandoned ship. . . . Pausanias (VII, 5, 5–8) describes in like form the arrival in Eritrea of the image of Hercules. . . . Let us remember the coming of Santiago to Spain, of St. Lubentius to Dietkirchen," and so on.[18] Father Delahaye further clarifies the meaning of his remarks with the discreet addition that "it was natural for the new religion to appropriate finally the totality of a ritual that needed only right interpretation to be converted into the language of the Christian soul in its elevation to the true God. All the external signs that did not imply the express acceptance of polytheism were bound to find favor in the eyes of the new religion" (1906 ed., p. 169). "I would not wish to deny that at times popular devotion has allowed itself to be impregnated in certain places with the still living memory of ancient

---

[16] See my book *Santiago de España* (Buenos Aires: Emecé Editores, 1958), pp. 89–91.

[17] *Diálogo de las cosas ocurridas en Roma*, ed. J. F. Montesinos (Madrid, 1928), p. 206.

[18] Edition of 1906, pp. 34–36. For more details, see H. Usener, *Die Sintflutsagen* (Bonn, 1899), pp. 136–137.

superstitions . . . ; that, for example, St. Cyrus and St. John have ended up by being converted into something like healing saints, unselfish doctors, like *Cosmas and Damian*, and that the latter pair . . . have taken on, in the popular imagination, a new and definitive form as spirits who aid mankind, *like the Dioscuri*. But if we keep our feet on the ground of fact, there is no reason to say that the Church has systematically practiced these transpositions of names which allowed the thing itself to live on" (*op. cit.*, p. 195). In other words, those transpositions happened within the subconscious of people who passed from paganism to Christianity in a brief period of time; the Church did not order that this god or the other one should be venerated as Christian saints.

With regard to the passage, or transposition, of Castor and Pollux into the figures of apostles or saints who hurl themselves down from the heavens on horses shining with whiteness in order to exterminate the enemies of their faithful worshippers, signs of that transposition (though without the Dioscuric horses) may already be found in the Gospel according to St. Mark: "And James the son of Zebedee, and John the brother of James; and he surnamed them Boanerges, which is, the sons of thunder" (3:17).[19] Now "sons of thunder" corresponds in meaning to the Greek *Dios-kuroi* or "sons of Jupiter the Thunderer"; or to *Bana-ba-Tilo*, "sons of heaven," in Mozambique.

James and John are brothers and sons of thunder; in the Gospel according to St. Luke (9:54), they ask Jesus if he wishes them to bring down fire from heaven to consume the Samaritans: "Lord, wilt thou that we command fire to come down from heaven, and consume them . . . ?" Jesus does not accept so frightful an offer, because his mission is one of love and peace. But it is undeniable that both evangelists introduce into their account the figures of two brothers, characterized as "sons of thunder" by Jesus himself, even though in the course of time he refused, in "Christian" fashion, to make use of the awesome power that, it is suggested, the brothers possessed.

Outside the Gospel texts the correlation between a pair of Apostles and the dual group of Castor and Pollux had been established by the people who erected the church of San Paolo Maggiore on the site of the pagan temple of the Sons of Jupiter the Thunderer which had been built by T. Julius Tarsus, a slave liberated by Augustus. "The portico and eight Corinthian columns [of the ancient temple] still existed in the seventeenth century, as well as the inscription designed to perpetuate the name and titles of the man who had dedicated the

---

[19] Rendel Harris, *Boanerges* (1913), pp. 2–4, showed that *Boanerges* is a Semitic word whose first part contains a plural of *bn*, "son" (Hebrew *ben*, plural *bnaym*); the second part, *rges*, corresponds to the Hebrew ra'am, "thunder"; *raŷasa* in Arabic means "to thunder."

temple. In 1688 an earthquake left standing only two columns, which are set with their architraves into the facade of the modern church. The statues of Castor and Pollux, bereft of their heads, arms, and legs, lie on their sides in a small niche dominated by the statues of St. Peter and St. Paul."[20] Two Latin distichs, engraved in stone above the mutilated statues of Castor and Pollux, say that just by appearing and opening their mouths the two Christian Apostles made themselves heard by the two pagan gods in spite of their deafness. The latter disappeared:

> Audit vel surdus Pollux cum Castore Petrum;
> Nec mora: praecipiti marmore uterque ruit.
> Tyndaridas vox missa ferit; palma integra Petri est:
> Dividit at tecum, Paule, tropaea libens.

Thus it was, adds M. Albert, that "these Christian Dioscuri had taken the place of the pagan Dioscuri"; although this authority states that St. Michael and St. George have represented the sons of Jupiter in popular imagination, he did not think of adding to this the figure and warlike activity of Santiago. In the Catholic encyclopedia *Reallexikon für Antike und Christentum* under the heading "Dioskuren,"[21] it is clearly recognized that the pair St. Peter–St. Paul corresponds to that of the Dioscuri; with regard to the pagan twins, "the Church took, according to its custom, two positions: one polemical, the other favorable to the ineradicable Twins who were thus appearing under the aspect of martyrs or saints. . . . We limit ourselves to mentioning the instances in which Christian veneration of the Greco-Roman gods is attested to or may be deduced with certainty. The Neapolitan church of San Paolo Maggiore, consecrated to the Apostles Peter and Paul, was raised over the temple of the Dioscuri. Both of the apostolic princes carried out their common mission in Rome; their names bore the same initial; in other words, everything favored their being seen as a pair, and as a pair fitted to substitute for the Dioscuri in their capacity as protectors of sailors. Both Apostles had made sea voyages . . . , and St. Paul came to Italy in a ship whose sign was Castor and Pollux ["navigavimus in mavi Alexandrina . . . cui erat insigne Castorum," as the Vulgate reads], according to the Acts of the Apostles, 28:11. In Rome itself Pope Damasus I (366–384) calls the two Apostles 'nova sidera' ['new stars'], recalling the Dioscuri (see E. Caspar, *Geschichte des Papstum* [1930], I, 252). Another pair of saints who occupy the place of the Dioscuri is that of the medical saints Cosmas and Damian."

All of this is a truth well known to scholars, but it has been neces-

---

20 Maurice Albert, *Le culte de Castro et Pollux en Italie* (Paris, 1883), pp. 47–48.
21 (Stuttgart, 1957). The author of the article is W. Kraus. P. Laín Entralgo kindly provided me with this quotation.

sary to insist on it because of the rude outcry and the thick clouds of dust raised by the ill-informed. The temple of the Dioscuri in the Roman Forum lasted as long as the empire of which Hispania (and not "Spain") was a part. "Wherever Roman arms spread and triumph, the Dioscuri go with them; the latter are imposed on the conquered peoples, first in northern and southern Italy, and then in all the provinces conquered afterwards" (M. Albert, *Le culte de Castor et Pollux en Italie*, p. 41). As was customary, the two divine brothers were venerated in Hispania, and votive inscriptions abound there. For example, an official offers an ex-voto in memory of the public dinners given to celebrate taking possession of his office; a mother, Sulpicia, gives thanks because her son has recovered his health:

> CASTORI ET POLLVCI DIIS MAGNIS . . .
> OB FILIVM SALVTI RESTITVTVM.
> (THIS VOTIVE TABLET TO CASTOR AND POLLUX, THE
> GREAT GODS, FOR HAVING RESTORED HEALTH TO MY SON . . .)
>
> (M. Albert, *op. cit.*, p. 50)

Toutain[22] found two other inscriptions in Baetica (which was still not Andalusia)—a pointer to, along with the general form motivated by the healing powers of the Dioscuri, a power later exercised among Christians by the saints Cosmas and Damian. And as protectors of sailors they were venerated in Galicia, as José Filgueira Valverde[23] showed in a learned study to which I can only allude here. The "Fraternity of the Holy Body" in Pontevedra is related—in its remote origins and through a series of, as might be expected, complex detours—to the cult of the twins Castor and Pollux. Pontevedra is, of course, part of the region in which Santiago rode on his white, Dioscuric horse for the purpose of exterminating Saracens. It was in Pontevedra also, in the town of Portosanto, that Alfredo García Alén[24] found in 1956 a Roman ring of very rough workmanship on which may be seen two figures wearing conical caps "which recall the representations of the Dioscuri." On the basis of such scanty evidence it seems difficult to make a definite identification (Sr. García Alén does not do so), but the fact that the figures form a pair and are identical is an important sign.

It was not necessary, after all, for visible signs of the existence of the cult of the Dioscuri to appear in Galicia in order to relate

---

[22] *Les cultes païens dans l'Empire Romain*, I, 411. I have found another inscription, from Tortosa, in the *Corpus Inscriptionum Latinarum*, II, suppl. 6070: "Castori et Polluci M. Valerius Votum Solvit Libens."

[23] "San Telmo y la advocación del 'Corpo Santo,'" *Revista general de Marina* (Madrid) (March, 1943).

[24] "Dos anillos romanos del Museo de Pontevedra," *Cuadernos de estudios gallegos* (1959), p. 355.

to them the equestrian figure of Santiago and his militant protection of those who invoked his name.[25] Georgiana G. King[26] made the connection in 1920, and before her J. R. Mélida had noted the relationship between the horseman so often shown on Iberian coins and the cult of Castor (Georgiana G. King, *The Way of Saint James*, III, 298, 299).

It was not only in Spain of the reconquest that there remained latent (in some form or another) the Christianized image of the Dioscuric friend to man who aids him in his hour of need (in sicknesses, on stormy seas, in war). The traces of Castor and Pollux are also perceptible in St. Cuthbert and St. Wilfrid, who died, respectively, in 687 and 719 and were famous for their evangelical work in England. Their memory remained very much alive among the Anglo-Saxons and led to their being invoked in grave circumstances. In the second half of the eleventh century, King Malcolm of Scotland ordered the extermination of the inhabitants of Hexham because that town of Englishmen had killed his messengers. On the eve of the day fixed for the execution, all the people took refuge in the church of St. Wilfrid. Overcome by fatigue, one of the priests fell asleep during the night, and in his sleep "there appeared to him two horsemen, one of whom said: My name is Wilfrid, and I come in the company of St. Cuthbert, whom I took with me as I passed through Durham. At dawn I shall stretch a net all along the river Tyne, and your enemies will not be able to cross it." And so it came to pass.[27]

The Comte de Montalembert, a Catholic writer, and M. Albert after him, related the two horsemen who appeared to the inhabitants of Hexham in the eleventh century to the ones who appeared to the Romans in the Battle of Lake Regillus in 449 B.C. And I would add

---

[25] Only ignorance of the connections between the pagan and Christian worlds has led certain people to seek in Revelation (19:11-14) the model for the image of Santiago and, in so doing, to sever it from its pagan antecedents. But the Book of Revelation refers to something entirely different: "And I saw heaven opened, and behold a white horse; and he that sat upon his was called Faithful and True, and in righteousness he doth judge and make war. His eyes were as a flame of fire, and on his head were many crowns: and he had a name written, that no man knew, but he himself. And he was clothed with a vesture dipped in blood: and his name is called The Word of God. And the armies which were in heaven followed him upon white horses, clothed in fine linen, white and clean." According to the commentators, this vision refers to a battle "between God and His creatures" (see the edition of Revelation in the *Biblioteca de Autores Cristianos* [Madrid, 1958]). Santiago, on the other hand, is not God, nor is he "dipped in blood." He fights alone or in the company of one other saint in favor of one army and against another; he intervenes in human affairs. It is amazing that so absurd an interpretation as the identification of Santiago with the apocalyptic vision has been maintained by at least four different people.

[26] *The Way of Saint James* (New York: Hispanic Society of America, 1920).

[27] Aelred Rievallensis, *De SS, Ecclesia Hagolstad*, cited by the Comte de Montalembert, *Les moines d'Occident* (1875), IV, 375.

that the Dioscuric model is evident also in the two horsemen who appeared to Emperor Theodosius,[28] and, in the persons of Santiago and St. Emilian, to the Christians of Spain, according to the previously quoted text from Berceo.

Despite the Dioscuric tradition of appearances of paired figures, it is understandable why Santiago of Spain should usually have had to appear unaccompanied, for his body was the object of a devotion addressed to him alone. Nor was his appearance an accidental or fleeting one but that of a body come to its Compostelan sanctuary and which made itself visible in its celestial aspect when there was need. Furthermore, appearances belonging to the Dioscuric tradition could even include three figures, as was observed at the Battle of Antioch (1098), when St. George, St. Mercurius, and St. Demetrius, mounted on white horses, fought by the side of the soldiers of Christ:

Tunc autem [the enemy] praeliati sunt cum illis [with the Crusaders] et sagittando multos occiderunt ex nostris. . . . Exibant quoque de montanis innumerabiles exercitus, habentes equos albos, quorum vexilla omnia erant alba. Videntes itaque nostri hunc exercitum, ignorabant penitus quid hoc esse et qui essent, donec cognoverunt esse adjutorium Christi, cujus ductores fuerunt sancti Georgius, Mercurius et Demetrius. Haec verba credenda sunt, quia plures ex nostris viderunt.[29]

(At that moment, however, [the enemy] fought [the Crusaders] and with their arrows killed a good many of our men. . . . Innumerable masses of fighters came out of the mountains on white horses, and their banners were also white. When our men looked at this army, they had no idea what they could be or who they were. They nonetheless, realized them to be sent by Christ and whose leaders were Sts. George, Mercury, and Demetrius. And this word should be believed because many of our men saw it.)

This account, as well as that dealing with Sts. Wilfrid and Cuthbert, is well known and has been generally accepted as a reflection

---

[28] The Apostles John and Philip had aided Emperor Theodosius (375–395) just as the Dioscuri had come to the aid of the pagans at Lake Regillus. According to Theodoret of Cyrus (*Historia Ecclesiastica*, V, 24), an historian of the fifth century, Emperor Theodosius found himself in difficult straits while he was battling against the rebel Eugenius, a Christian who had usurped the imperial title with the support of the pagan Flavianus. The Christian Theodosius went to spend the night in a chapel—doubtless in order to consult an oracle, says Theodoret—and in his dreams there appeared two men dressed in white and mounted on white horses who revealed themselves to be the Apostles John and Philip. They ordered him to attack at dawn and assured him that he would triumph, for they would be his aids and champions. The Apostles unleashed a dust storm against his enemy which was so violent that the arrows and spears they hurled against Theodosius' army wounded the assailants themselves (see my *Santiago de España*, p. 98).

[29] *Gesta Francorum et aliorum Hierosolymitanorum seu Tudebodus Abbreviatus*, in *Recueil des Historiens des Croisades, Historiens Occidentaux* (Paris, 1866), III, 157.

of Dioscuric traditions. For example, Father Franchi de'Cavalieri says:

Capisco altri ravvisi i Dioscuri nei ss. Giorgio, Mercurio e Demetrio, comparsi a cavallo nella grande battaglia de Antiochia, l'anno 1098, o nei ss. Wilfrid e Cuthbert, che una volta gli abitanti de Hexham in Inghilterra, minacciati dagli scozzesi, avrebbero veduto trascorrere su bianchi cavalli a tutta corsa. Capisco anche, fino ad un certo segno, come l'Harris [J. Rendel Harris] possa aver creduto riconoscere gli equestres fratres nei tre fratelli Cappadoci. . . . In alcuni luoghi di Grecia si venerarono, è vero, tre Dioscuri in vece di due.[30]

(I understand that others recognize the presence of the Dioscuri in Sts. George, Mercury, and Demetrius, who appeared on horseback in the great battle of Antioch in 1098, or in Sts. Wilfrid and Cuthbert, whom the people of Hexham in England, while threatened by the Scots, were supposed to have seen dashing on white horses at full gallop. I also understand, to a certain point, that Harris [J. Rendel Harris] may have recognized the "brother horsemen" in the three brothers Cappadoci. . . . As a matter of fact, in some places in Greece, they worshiped three, instead of two, Dioscuri.)

When we locate the faith in Santiago in space and time, in a cultural tradition and a vital structure, its reality becomes convincing and important. The necessity, the imagination, and the will of the besieged people in the northeast of the Peninsula injected new life—Christian life—into a traditional motif, latent in Hispania just as it was in all that part of Europe which belonged to the Greco-Roman tradition. The Dioscuric pattern, provided with Christian meaning, was revived in Christian Rome, in Syria, in England, or in Hispania.

What happened in Spain with respect to Santiago is a particular instance of the generalized tendency to interpret in Christian fashion what was once a pagan belief; but the truly important matter for me is what the Galician-Leonese, and later the Spaniards, did with that belief. The historical antecedents of a phenomenon like this interest the historian of religion a great deal, but are of less moment to anyone specifically engaged in the observation of how the life of the Spaniards was being formed and acquiring historifiable value. These two fields, or directions of interest, must be clearly distinguished. It should be noted to begin with that the known instances of apparitions of what might be called the Dioscuric type are isolated phenomena and, in the last analysis, are of only anecdotal significance; in Spain, on the other hand, we are faced with a functional and basic "Jacobean" force testified to by the existence of the splendid city of Santiago de Compostela—a city created in some sense by the belief in St. James and an outstanding example of a value I would call historifiable.

---

[30] See *Nuovo Bolletino di Archeologia Cristiana*, IX (1903), 118.

What happened with respect to Santiago in Galicia did not occur because certain myths or beliefs had been wandering in folkloric fashion through the memory and imagination of a series of generations; faith in the image and in the virtues of the Apostle was a theme of prime importance for the continued existence of a people, and thus it became a central theme in the occupations and preoccupations of that people, in their collective consciousness. In turn, the communal awareness actively reworked the traditional theme and was not content with what tradition or legend was building up at random in the memory of certain individuals. Instead of being diluted and scattered, the belief in Santiago became ever more concentrated and acquired new dimensions. For this reason it was not enough that the Apostle should fight upon a white horse (the people concerned had not the slightest suspicion that such a figure was a pagan heritage); to this version was added, in order to increase the Apostle's power, another aspect of age-old traditions which had originated in Syria and Palestine and been shaped by the cult of the Dioscuri. The concept of twin divinities was projected onto the heterodox belief that certain Apostles were twin brothers of Jesus. The Church had always interpreted such a brotherhood as being spiritual only, but the people (whose point of view is reflected in the apocryphal writings) ingenuously accepted it in the physical sense. The name of the Apostle Thomas means twin brother in Syriac. In the previously quoted *De ortu obitu Patrum* (see p. 386) we read: "Thomas, Christ's Apostle, called Didymus, which means [in Greek] twin brother of Christ and like unto the Saviour."[31] The famous Galician heresiarch Priscillian, a great reader of apocryphal writings, identified the Apostle Judas of the canonical epistles with the Thomas of the fourth Gospel, and thus converted him into the twin brother of the Lord: "Judas the Apostle, the twin brother of the Lord [*didymus Domini*], who had a stronger belief in Christ after he touched the wounds he had suffered."[32]

Both these passages taken together prove that the belief that Christ had twin brothers had spread over Spain, and that, although the belief was heretical, apparently some, and perhaps many, accepted it in the atmosphere of religious syncretism of the end of the Roman Empire. Some texts make the twin brother one Apostle, others another. St. Matthew had already said (13:55): "Is not this the carpenter's son? Is not his mother called Mary, and his brethren James, Joses, Simon, and Judas?" We are not concerned with the scriptural

---

[31] "Thomas apostolus Christi, Didymus nominatus, et juxta Latinam linguam Christi geminus, ac similis Salvatoris" (in Harris, *The Twelve Apostles*, p. 55).

[32] Shepss ed., p. 44. Harris, *Boanerges*, p. 408, observes that Priscillian found no difficulty in harmonizing the fact of Christ's divinity with the fact that he had a twin brother.

problem of what "brother" means here, but with what the popular opinion of the meaning was—that popular opinion that had fused the two Jameses. What was understood by "brother" may be seen in an apocryphal epistle of the pseudo-Ignatius, addressed to John. After he expresses his desire to see the Virgin in Jerusalem, he adds that he would also like to know St. James, "the venerable St. James, called the Just, who, I have heard, is as like Christ Jesus in his life and his way of conversing with people *as if he were a twin brother born from the same womb*; they say that if I see him, I shall see Jesus himself, without finding any difference in any feature of his body."[33]

This Apostle, the presumed twin brother of the Lord, suffered his martyrdom in a form parallel to the passion of Christ, according to the account in the *Historia Ecclesiastica* of Eusebius of Caesarea (II, 23). Bishop J. B. Lightfoot (*The Apostolic Fathers*, I, 596) says that throughout the history of the Church, from its earliest times, there was the tendency to find in the lives of the saints and martyrs a literal conformity with the sufferings of the Lord. The enemies of St. James the Just are the scribes and Pharisees; he dies during the Passover; for his executioners he prays: "Father, forgive them for they know not what they do"; the destruction of Jerusalem is punishment for having killed him. The same story has been told of other martyrs, and we shall presently see the reflection of the same tradition in the case of Santiago of Galicia.

In other apocryphal writings there is a continued insistence on the brotherhood of Jesus and James: "Is this not the carpenter's son, and is not Mary his mother, and are not his brothers mentioned in Matthew 13:55 are reduced to two.[34] For those who venerated the sepulcher in Galicia in the first centuries of the cult of Santiago, the Apostle was both "the son of thunder" and the brother of Jesus. Thus there were relics of Santiago, the brother of the Lord—"Sancti Jacobi, Germani Domini"[35]—which we may assign to Santiago of Galicia and not to St. James the Less, not only because of all that we have seen up to now, but also because of the testimony of Arabic historians who write—only because it is what they have heard—that the St. James venerated in Galicia was "the son of the carpenter."

The belief that Jesus and Santiago of Compostela were twins is

---

[33] "Similiter et illum venerabilem Jacobum qui cognominatur Justus; quem referunt Christo Jesu simillimum vita et modo conversationis, ac si ejusdem uteri frater esset gemellus; quem, dicunt, si videro, video ipsu, Jesum secundum omnia corporis ejus lineamenta" (in J. B. Lightfoot, *The Apostolic Fathers*, Part II, Vol. II, p. 655).

[34] "The Acts of Andrew and Mathias," in A. Walker, *Apocryphal Gospels* (1873), p. 354.

[35] Part of a text written in Visigothic script, and therefore earlier than the twelfth century, found in the cathedral of Leon (see J. E. Díaz-Jiménez, in *Boletín de la Academia de Historia*, XX [1892], 126).

reflected in painting. Karl Künstle (*Ikonographie der Heiligen* [Freiburg im Breisgau, 1926], II, 318) says: "The portrait of St. James by Giovanni Sancti in the sacristy of the Cathedral of Urbino is distinguishable from the figure of Christ only by the long pilgrim's staff. Martin Schaffner represented him with the features of Christ in the Germanic Museum in Nuremberg." Illustrations of this important similarity are a fourteenth-century crucifixion (in the journal *Dedalo*, XI [Milan, 1930], 1289) in which the St. James at the foot of the cross has the same face as Christ, and a painting of St. James which, as in the example to which Künstle refers, is distinguishable from the Christ in the same painting only by the pilgrim's staff (*Florentine Painting*, III, 2 Pt. I, folder 33 [3], by R. Öffner).

If for the Christian people Santiago was the brother of the Lord, what were the Muslims of that time thinking of their rival, the Galician Apostle? The encyclopedist Mas'ūdi, a native of Bagdad, who wrote in 943 a work called *The Golden Meadows*, speaks a great deal about the disciples of Jesus, though news of the miracles of Santiago had not yet come to him; he knew that Peter and Paul were buried in Rome, and that Thomas had gone to India to preach the law of the Messiah; he says that another disciple had gone as far as the farthest reaches of Persia, and "the place of his tomb is venerated by the Christians. . . . Mark died in Alexandria, where his tomb is found."[36] It would seem, therefore, that special beliefs with regard to the tombs of the Christian Apostles were not rare, even though none of them had taken on a militant and national character, as in the case of Santiago.

Mas'ūdi speaks about the Apostles of Jesus because the Arabs felt a lively curiosity about everything religious; the first historian of the religious beliefs of his time was a Muslim from al-Andalus: the Cordovan Ibn Ḥazm (994–1063). In his famous work whose Arabic title reads in English "The Decisive Word on Sects, Heterodoxies and Denominations" (translated into Spanish by Miguel Asín Palacios as *Historia crítica de las ideas religiosas*), Ibn Ḥazm speaks of certain Spanish Christians who attributed brothers to Jesus. He cannot understand this, "unless they say that Mary engendered them by Joseph the Carpenter, for this is what is affirmed by a certain sect of ancient Christians, one of whom was Julian, metropolitan of Toledo."[37] Ibn Ḥazm mentions St. James the Less as the son of Joseph the Carpenter (III, 109), but I have not found in his work any concrete reference to the shrine at Compostela. Other writers, on the other hand, give very important references to it. Ibn 'Idhāri wrote a history of Africa

---

[36] *Les Prairies d'Or*, trans. Barbier de Meynard, II, 300–301.

[37] III, 58. Asín notes that no such opinion is to be found in the writings of St. Julian of Toledo, but that it was held by Apollinaris, who had a pupil named Julian, and that this is the root of Ibn Ḥazm's confusion.

and Spain in the thirteenth century, in which, according to the Arabic custom, he gathered up fragments of earlier writers. According to him, "Santiago is the *most important Christian shrine*, not only in Spain, but in all Europe. The church in that city is for them *what the Kaaba is for us*; they invoke Santiago in their oaths, and Christians come on pilgrimage to his shrine from the most remote countries. ... *Some Christians say that Santiago was the son of Joseph the Carpenter.* ... The devout come to his temple even from Nubia, the land of the Copts."[38]

Even more important is the testimony of Ibn Ḥayyān, the Cordovan historian (987–1076), recorded by Al-Maqqarī, at the beginning of the seventeenth century, in his famous *Analects*:

Santiago is a city in the most remote part of Galicia, and one of the shrines most frequently visited, not only by Christians from Spain, but also from Europe; for them Santiago is as venerable as the Kaaba in Mecca is for the Muslims, for in the center of their Kaaba is also to be found the object of their supreme adoration [*al-mathal*]. They swear in his name, and they go there on pilgrimages from the most distant parts of Christendom. They claim that the tomb located in that church is that of St. James, one of the twelve Apostles and the most beloved of Jesus. *The Christians call him the brother of Jesus*, because he never forsook Him.[39] They say that he was bishop of Jerusalem, and that he went about preaching the Gospel and making converts until he reached that remote corner of Spain. Then he returned to Syria, where he died at the age of 120 solar years. They also claim that after his death his disciples brought him and buried him in that church because it was the most distant place in which he had left the imprint of his preaching. Never did any Moorish king think of penetrating that far or of subjecting the city to Islam, because of the inacessibility of its location and the perils of the road. This undertaking was reserved for Almanzor.[40]

Ibn Ḥayyān was the son of one of Almanzor's secretaries, so that he must have heard a great deal about Santiago, both from Moors and from captive Christians, after the famous expedition that no one had dared to undertake before Almanzor. Ibn Ḥayyān gathered the impression that Jesus and Santiago were considered as brothers because *they formed an inseparable pair*. This was the belief and feeling in Galicia around the year 1000, and it must have been the belief for centuries before. Ibn 'Idhāri knew that Santiago was the son of Joseph the Carpenter, and Ibn Ḥazm was surprised that Christian

---

[38] *Histoire de l'Afrique et de l'Espagne*, trans. E. Fagnan (1904), II, 491, 494.

[39] The Arabic text uses the word *lazūm*, which means, according to Lane's *Lexicon*, "one who keeps, cleaves, clings or holds fast much, or habitually to a thing."

[40] I have followed the translation of P. de Gayangos, *The History of the Mohammedan Dynasties*, II, 193, but correcting it somewhat (with the help of Professors Hitti and Ziadeh), on the basis of the Arabic text as found in Al-Maqqarī, *Analects sur l'histoire et la littérature des Arabes d'Espagne* (Leyden, 1855), I, 270.

people should accept the belief that Christ had brothers. From different directions, the three Arabic writers confirm our suppositions as to what the Galician-Leonese really felt in the ninth, tenth, and eleventh centuries.

In the sermons falsely attributed to Pope Calixtus II, forged by twelfth-century ecclesiastics in Compostela to add still more importance to the cult of the Apostle, we find allusions to his brotherhood with Jesus, although translated into allegorical language: "It is more important to be the brother of the Lord in the spirit than in the flesh. Consequently, *whoever calls St. James* [the Greater], *the son of Zebedee*, or St. James [the Less], the son of Alpheus, *the brother of the Lord speaks the truth*."[41] The two beliefs remained alive then, the one in the brotherhood of Santiago and Christ, and the one that confused the identity of the two Santiagos—and this fits in perfectly with Arabic testimony. Moreover, the sermons of the pseudo-Calixtus are important for the form in which they express what survived of the belief in a Dioscuric Santiago. Carolina Michaëlis de Vasconcellos, who did not suspect any connection between Santiago and the Dioscuri, perceptively mentions "the great inclination of the coastal peoples in the northwest of Spain to sidereal superstitions."[42] But Santiago's being a "son of thunder" and his presence at the Transfiguration on Mount Tabor had already established the connection, not with superstitions, but with actual beliefs, of which there is an echo in the style of the forged sermons: "He shone in his conversation like the bright star of the morning amidst the other stars, like a great sanctuary lamp."[43] With the same spiritual and allegorical meaning it is said that Santiago "thundered, by command of the Lord, in all Judea and Samaria, and even to the farthest limit of the earth, which is to say, in Galicia; he hurls thunderbolts of terrifying sound, he waters the earth with his rain, and he emits great flashes of light." Both Boanerges "watered the earth with their rain as they communicated the rain of divine grace to the faithful with their preaching" (col. 1383). Still today the Portuguese peasant speaks of the thunder as if it were produced by Santiago.

---

[41] "Majus est esse fratrem Domini spiritualiter quam carnaliter. Quisquis ergo aut Jacobum Zebedaei aut Jacobum Alphaei *fratrem Domini* dicit, verum dicit" (*Sermones quatuor de Sancto Jacobo Apostolo in Gallaecia habiti*, in J. P. Migne, ed., *Patrologia*, S.L., vol. 163, col. 1387). Another proof of the confusion between the two Jameses is given us by the *Historia Compostellana*. Mauritius, bishop of Coimbra, discovered the head of St. James the Less in Jerusalem and brought it to Spain (*España sagrada*, XIX, 252); but the *Historia Compostellana* (*España sagrada*, XX, 222) believes that that head belongs to the body entombed in Compostela. This proves that there was no difficulty in attributing to the patron saint of Spain the head of Jesus' brother, that is, St. James the son of Alphaeus (St. James the Less).

[42] C. Michaëlis de Vasconcellos, *Cancioneiro da Ajuda*, II, 842.

[43] *Patrologia*, Vol. 163, col. 1398.

Each of these beliefs had traveled a different road: they belonged to different epochs. There was no rational connection of any kind between them. The ambivalent Santiago of Galicia might be for some the brother of Jesus; for others a half-brother, the son, that is, of Joseph by a previous marriage—an idea rejected by St. Jerome (346–420) and replaced by another more in accord with the latter's love of virginity, namely, that the so-called brothers of Jesus were only his cousins, for Joseph had no other wife save the Virgin, and he always remained a virgin himself. But in the fourth and fifth centuries a *History of Joseph the Carpenter* was current in Arabic according to which Joseph lived for forty-nine years with his first wife, who bore him Judas, Just, James, and Simon.[44] In this enumeration St. James the Just splits into two persons, whereas in the epistle of the pseudo-Ignatius he is converted into a twin brother of the Lord, a relationship that certain Christians believed in.[45]

The divine office as sung in the cathedral of Compostela in the eleventh century, and presumably for many years before that, exalted the merits of the Apostle to a degree that was later judged excessive, for the office was changed in the twelfth century. With Mark 3:17 and Matthew 20:21 ff. as their inspiration, the offices said:

Jesus called Santiago Zebedee, and gave him Boanerges for a name. *He called the blessed Santiago* aside on the high mountain, and He was transfigured before him. Santiago and John said to Jesus: "Grant us to sit in thy glory, one upon thy right hand and the other upon thy left." "Can ye drink of the cup whereof I must drink?" But they answered: "We can."[46]

In the sermons of the pseudo-Calixtus, an effort was also made to enlarge the role of Santiago in the scene of the Transfiguration, but there is at least a mention of the fact that Peter and John were witnesses of the occasion ("testibus astantibus Petro et Joanne cum eo," J. P. Migne, ed., *Patrologia*, S.L., vol. 163, col. 1393). The pseudo-Calixtus, although forgetful of the sweet words of the Saviour (Matt. 20:23), "but to sit on my right hand, and on my left, is not mine to give," likewise corrects the exorbitant claim to be seated on the right

---

[44] Cf. E. Amann, *Le protévangile de Jacques* (1910), pp 216–217; P. Santyves, *Deux Mythes évangéliques* (1938), p. 89. It is probable that this Arabic history is of a later date; see *The Muslim World* (April, 1955), p. 187.

[45] I shall omit here a number of other texts that substantiate this point and pass on to what I consider more important, the function of that belief within the vital dwelling place of the Spaniards.

[46] "Ihesus uocauit Iacobum Zebedei et imposuit eis [sic] nomina Boanerges. Eduxit Ihesus beatum Iacobum in montem excelsum seorsum, et transfiguratum est ante eum" (López Ferreiro, *op. cit.*, I, 427). The *eis* ("to them") betrays the fact that in an earlier version John was also mentioned, since John was present with Peter and James on Mount Tabor (Matt. 17). But the author of these antiphons was disturbed by the presence of Peter and John along with James, and he converted the Transfiguration and the privilege of contemplating it into a grace granted exclusively to St. James.

hand and left hand of Christ. The sermon says, in fact, "that it seems impossible for anyone to sit between the Father and the Son, seeing that the Son Himself is at the right hand of the Father, and the Father at the left hand of the Son" (*ibid.*, col. 1394).

But everything seemed justified to the worshipers of the Apostle when the Bishop of Compostela raised himself to be the pontiff of Christendom and the pilgrims were coming to Compostela in increasing numbers.

Dazzled by the marvelous halo that had surrounded their Apostle for centuries, his adorers did not limit themselves to singing the foregoing antiphons on the day of his feast—originally March 25, later July 25. There was also a "Passio Sancti Jacobi," in which the parallel with the Passion of Christ was accentuated in the manner previously alluded to. The brotherhood was thus complete.

"The passion of Santiago . . . which he suffered under Herod the king" is composed in a style recalling that of many apocryphal gospels: "In those days the Apostle of Our Lord Jesus Christ, Santiago, brother of John, Apostle and evangelist, would visit all the land of Judea and of Samaria and would enter into the synagogues." The Apostle works great miracles. Before he is beheaded, he asks his executioner for water just as Christ did (John 19:28). Praying before his torture, Santiago reminds Christ of how important his own person is: "Thou didst deign to show us the mysteries of the marvelous works. . . . Whilst thou wast on Mount Tabor, and wast transfigured in the divinity of thy Father, to no other Apostle didst thou grant to contemplate such prodigies, *save to me*, to Peter, and to John, my brother." When Santiago died, "a great earthquake was produced, the heavens did open, the sea was roiled, and intolerable thunder was heard; when the earth did open, the larger part of the evildoers was swallowed up, and a brilliant light shone upon that place." His body was taken by his disciples: "They put his body and his head in a bag made of the skin of a deer, with exquisite perfumes; accompanied on their voyage by an angel of the Lord, they carried it from Jerusalem to Galicia, and they buried it in the place where it has been venerated from that day until this."[47]

So it was not merely a question of the usual devout enthusiasm of those who venerated a certain saint or virgin and trusted in that saint's extraordinary power. What characterizes the cult of Santiago down to the twelfth century is the intent to emphasize his close and intimate connection with Jesus Christ.

Eminent Catholics have cast doubt upon the existence of the body of an Apostle of Christ in the shrine in Galicia. The reaction against the cult of Santiago gained strength in the seventeenth century, when

---

[47] Latin text in López Ferreiro, *op cit.*, I, 392–405.

there were no longer any Moorish enemies against whom to make holy war, and when Spanish religiosity was certainly not what it had been in the tenth and eleventh centuries. In 1601 the great Jesuit historian Juan de Mariana doubted the authenticity of the tomb of Santiago: "Certain grave and learned persons in recent years have found it difficult to believe in the coming of James the Apostle to Spain; other persons, if not the same ones, have found it difficult to believe in the discovery of his sacred body, for *reasons* and writings that move them to hold their opinions."[48] Years later another Jesuit, Father Pedro Pimentel, adjudged it more advisable for Spain to put her trust in the protection of St. Theresa: "He who invokes St. Theresa will often obtain better favors than he who invokes Santiago."[49] A few years ago the Jesuit Father Z. García Villada insisted on the slight probatory value of the documents that relate the discovery of the body of Santiago, because the most ancient ones are from the eleventh century, and the suspicion is inevitable that they were forged to provide a posteriori justification for a popular and very ancient belief; these texts "indicate the motive that occasioned the formation of the tradition that in that tomb were enclosed the remains of the Apostle. This motive is the testimony of the angels and the lights that were seen on certain nights over the place where the tomb is. We cannot certify the degree of veracity in the marvelous account."[50] A Catholic, Monsignor L. Duchesne, thus sums up his disappointing search for rational proofs for the great miracle of Santiago: "In the first third of the ninth century veneration is given to a tomb dating from Roman times, which at that time was believed to be the tomb of Santiago. Why was this believed? We do not know at all."[51]

The error of these learned ecclesiastics consisted in trying to demonstrate what was rationally undemonstrable. Beliefs are established in the vacuum left by another belief, and they take root and gain strength by virtue of well-defined necessities and circumstances that exist independently of all demonstration. Vital phenomena (despair, hopefulness, the acceptance or rejection by the credulous or the skeptical person of the beliefs prevailing around him) cannot be treated as physical objects. Let us consider how absurd it would be to try to demonstrate "scientifically" that the body of an Apostle was brought from Haifa to Galicia in A.D. 44, in the custody of angels, and that some eight hundred years later it gave signs of its presence. History, that is to say, the life of a people which is perceptible in its connected sequence of values, is not a sequence of "events," isolatable by means of logical abstractions. The important thing in the present

---

[48] *Historia de España*, VII, 5.
[49] *Biblioteca de Autores Españoles*, XLVIII, 445*b*.
[50] *Historia eclesiástica de España*, I, 93.
[51] *Annales du Midi* XII, 179.

instance is the intensity of the belief in Santiago and its immeasurable consequences; for it is conceivable that a marvelous occurrence might be "authentic" in the way in which the aforementioned ecclesiastics demand, and at the same time insignificant and sterile as an event connected with human actions and the creation of human values.

The boundaries between the real and the imaginary vanish when what is imagined is incorporated into the very process of collective existence; Shakespeare, anticipating modern philosophies, has already said that "we are such stuff as dreams are made on." When the substance of one of these dreams is accepted as truth by millions of people, then the dream is real, and reality is a dream. The Christian martyrs lived in the reality of Christ as they smiled beatifically while their flesh was torn apart by wild beasts. Peoples incapable of dying for a faith have never attained a complete, historifiable reality. Even the most "positive" and materialistic forms of collective life have ultimately been resolved in the devotion to intangible deities, albeit these have the exterior of a tractor, a five-year plan, or electronic automation.

Santiago's shrine arose to face the Mohammedan Kaaba as a display of spiritual force, in a grandiose "mythomachia" or struggle between myths. The city of Santiago aspired to rival Rome and Jerusalem, and not only as the goal of a major pilgrimage. While Rome possessed the bodies of St. Peter and St. Paul, and the Islam that had submerged Visigothic Hispania fought under the banner of her prophet-apostle, the ninth-century Hispano-Christians unfurled in their small Galician homeland the ensign of a most ancient belief, magnified in an outburst of defensive anguish. The presence of a powerful race of infidels over almost the whole face of Spain would necessarily enliven the zeal to be protected by divine powers in the Galicia of the year 800.

There is no way of reconstructing today the map of religious beliefs and cults diffused among the Christians at the time the country was invaded by the Saracens. In the book by St. Martin of Braga, *De correctione rusticorum*, some of the beliefs of the Galician peasants of the sixth century are described, and these attest to the prevalence of ancient pagan divinities: "Many of the devils expelled from heaven hold sway in the sea, in the rivers, in the springs, and in the woods, and they cause themselves to be adored like gods by the ignorant. The people make sacrifices to them: on the sea they invoke Neptune; on the rivers, the Lamiae; at the springs, the Nymphs; in the woods, Diana."[52] So it was that, despite almost six centuries of Christianity, the

---

[52] See M. Menéndez y Pelayo, *Historia de los heterodoxos*, II, 261. This valuable text should be read in the edition of C. P. Caspari, *Martin von Bracara's Schrift De correctione rusticorum* (Christiania, 1883). The work was written between 572 and 574 to convert the peasants of the northwest region (diocese of Astorga and Braga). Besides the passage transcribed by Menéndez y Pelayo

FIGURE 3.
The apostle James as a likeness of Christ.
(From the book *Florentine Painting*, III, 2, part I, illus. 33 [3].
Courtesy of the author, Prof. R. Öffner.)

FIGURE 4.
Master Antonio de Nebrija teaching classical humanities
to the Grand Master of the military order of Alcantara
and to his family.

Roman religion, or at least a goodly part of it, continued to live. (Among the Indians of Guatemala also, who were converted to Christianity in the sixteenth century by the Spaniards, Mayan religious rites are still today strangely intermingled with Catholic beliefs.)

It is undeniable, however, that these and other circumstances only served as the instrument of, the condition for, future situation and actions, since the vital process of a people and its historifiable existence (the creator of values) are separate realities from that of the elements that have made them possible. In themselves, these elements might have given rise to unforeseeable dispositions of collective life. What the people in the northwest of the Peninsula finally became—their language, their special sensibilities, their way of forming social links with their neighbors—was not a *necessary* product of their misty climate, of the Celts, of Priscillian,[53] or of the Suevi. As always, our problem consists in organizing the known facts into a meaningful chain of relationships rather than in basing our interpretations on vague and unrelated prehistorical motives. The existence of a human event, Santiago or something else, does not consist in elements that the historian separates with his method of dissection, for what happens then is dissection indeed, which is to say, work on a cadaver. We must begin by not calling the belief in Santiago belief in a legend. The term "legend" is simply the epitaph inscribed over what was once a belief, and the belief is intelligible only if we intuit it while it still is a part of human reality and feeling. The history of Santiago of Compostela would consist, simply, in reliving what people *did* with the belief that the body of the Apostle had been found in Galicia.

No study of comparative religion permits one to see the veneration given to the tomb of the Apostle for what it was, as an example of the opposition and struggle of beliefs. Beliefs are not born and do not prosper because of the caprice of fantasy, or the malice of priests, or mere economic motivations, but as something that grows out of the longings, necessities, and limitations of man. The medium in which they live is the masses, infantile or adult, rustic or polished, national or universal. It is not infrequent that what are called legends today were born as a reaction to other, rival beliefs. Monsignor Duchesne, educated in French positivism and rationalism, did not see how it was

---

from the old edition of *España sagrada*, XV, the following should be noted: "It is great madness for a man baptized in the faith of Christ not to celebrate the Lord's day [Sunday], on which Christ was raised from the dead, and for him to celebrate on the other hand the days of Jupiter, Mercury, Venus, and Saturn, who have no proper days, and who were adulterers, magicians, and evil creatures, and died an evil death in their own land" (p. 12). Leaping from the sixth century to the nineteenth, Señora Michaëlis de Vasconcellos mentions the Portuguese custom of putting a piece of money in the coffin, so that the deceased will be able to pay for his passage on "Santiago's ship" (*Cancioneiro da Ajuda*, II, 806).

[53] E. Ch. Babut, *Priscillien et le priscillianisme* (1909).

possible for a Roman tomb to be changed into the tomb of St. James the Apostle; but if we now approach the question by thinking of life processes, the answer seems simple. The Muslims, moved by a militant faith that had its inspiration in Mohammed, the Apostle of God, had extended their dominions from Coimbra to India. The Christians of the northwest had little strength with which to oppose such an irresistible landslide, and thousands of voices must have clamored for celestial help that would sustain their hearts and increase their strength. In the time when wars were made more with valor and singleness of purpose than with complicated armaments, the temper of the morale of the combatant was a decisive factor. It was indispensable to have confidence in a visible, nearby power that could be opposed to the deadly shout of "Mohammed" uttered by the enemy. It was urgent to fortify the courage of a people cornered and in constant agony, and whom the collapse of the Visigothic kingdom had left in the first line of defense. For centuries it had been a current belief in Spain that St. James the Greater had come to preach the Christian faith there. St. Julian, archbishop of Toledo, was familiar with this tradition and did not accept it; according to him, St. James preached in Palestine and not in Spain,[54] which reveals that in 686, before the Saracen invasion, the Visigothic Church did not feel any special interest in fomenting certain popular beliefs. But in the ninth century, not only was the preaching of a living Santiago urgent; equally urgent was the presence of his sacred body. There was no ecclesiastical guile in this, but rather the historical development of very old beliefs, both pagan and Christian, that had existed for centuries in a form we can know only through their results. If people believed that St. James had come to Spain during his mortal life, they could the more readily conceive that he should return there after his death, although on this second journey the figure of the Apostle was crossed with those of Castor and Mars.

This instance in which a belief owes its origin to polemical motives is not unique. Everyone knows that the fabled personage Bernardo del Carpio emerged in opposition to Roland and Charlemagne, who were glorified in poems humiliating to Spain. About 1110 the Monk of Silos protested, in his chronicle, against the French epic stories that tried to convert Charlemagne into the liberator of Spain: the Emperor did not conquer the Moors, nor did he rescue the road to Santiago from their control; the Spaniards owed nothing to Roland and his lord. Toward the end of the twelfth century a Spanish minstrel launched Bernardo del Carpio against the arrogant French, in a Battle of Roncevaux conceived from the Spanish point of view—

---

[54] Cf. Duchesne, *op. cit.*, XII, 153.

Roland perishes and Charlemagne flees.[55] A ballad derived from the ancient, lost poem was later to put it thus:

> A bad time you had of it, you Frenchman,
> In the Battle of Roncevaux.

But since it was not a vital matter in the thirteenth century to believe wholeheartedly in the deeds of Bernardo del Carpio, King Alfonso the Learned casts doubt upon the accuracy of the accounts: "Some say that the Battle of Roncevaux was in the time of this king, Don Alfonso [III, the Great], and that it was not with Charles the Great but with Charles whom they called the Bald. . . . And if anyone knows how to explain this better, and can state it more truthfully, he must be heeded, for we say only what we find among the Latin writers, in the ancient books."[56] The learned king washes his hands of the matter, because annihilating Frenchmen was not a task of the first order for Spain. The people always regarded the French with special antipathy, while the governing classes were rather, in one way or another, under their enlightening guidance. Even though Alfonso the Learned's vassals might take the songs of Bernardo literally, the monarch did not find it urgent to make them feel that they were right in doing so.[57]

Another example of the belief inspired by polemical needs is provided by King Arthur of England. Chronicles prior to the twelfth century spoke of that fabulous monarch, but they did not make him out to be a personage of major importance. Yet suddenly between 1136 and 1138 Geoffrey of Monmouth issues his *Historia regum Britanniae*, destined to immortalize the (rationally) nonexistent king and to influence the poetic sensibility of Europe profoundly. The motive behind this event was the fact that the Norman dynasty felt itself humilated before the kings of France, who were rich in prestige because they count Charlemagne as their antecessor. The subject Britons had little to put up against the French until Geoffrey of Monmouth provided them with a sovereign more ancient and more illustrious than the great Emperor.[58] The Britannic people thus appeared to be

---

[55] Cf. R. Menéndez Pidal, in *Revista de Filología Española* (1917), IV, 151 ff.

[56] *Crónica General*, p. 376a.

[57] This was true to such an extent that a Navarrese minstrel of the thirteenth century could allow Charlemagne, in the Spanish *Roncesvalles*, to say: "I repaired the roads of the Apostle Santiago." The same poet recognized the French Roland theme as legitimate for a Spanish poem (cf. Menéndez Pidal, in *Revista de Filología Española* (1917), IV, 151 ff.). The author of this *cantar de gesta* very likely had some sort of connection with French monasteries, which were more interested in the success of the pilgrimages than in the rehabilitation of the good name of Castile.

[58] Cf. G. H. Gerould, "King Arthur and Politics," *Speculum*, II (1927), 37. It has been known for a good while that King Arthur was the English counterpart of Charlemagne: cf. W. A. Nitze, in *ibid.*, p. 318.

rehabilitated and glorified, and showed for the first time its clear will not to let itself be humiliated by the Continent.

Long before this in Spain a St. James who was a peaceful Apostle had been converted, thanks to circumstances more dramatic than those that determined the diffusion of the belief in King Arthur, into a martial and invincible Santiago. The militant Santiago had probably not yet penetrated into ecclesiastical literature in the eighth century; a hymn of the time of King Mauregatus (783–788) makes no reference to the tomb, but it does refer to his preaching in Spain, the country that had been assigned to him: "eiusque [i.e., St. John's] frater potitus Ispania."[59]

In this hymn the Apostle is already called "Spain's golden and shining head," and he is implored to spare Spain from the plague and from all manner of evils.[60] A half century later he will be implored to exterminate the Saracens, and he will be converted into a counter-Mohammed, and his sanctuary, into the counter-Kaaba. Against this background the meaning of such an enormous belief, and its reflections inside and outside Spain, can be understood. The torrent of that faith burst forth from remote, popular springs; its channeling was an ecclesiastical and political task, at once national and international. Down to the twelfth century we can perceive the equivocal interplay between the unrestrained and heretical cult of a multiple St. James and the orthodox idea that was gradually confining him within his role of St. James the Great, who retained even so the additional title of the Moorslayer (Matamoros). An analogous ambiguity appears in the claim made by the bishops of Compostela to the universal pontificate between the tenth and twelfth centuries, a claim that never reached the critical point of a schism from Rome; nor did the bishops of Santiago even rebel violently against the primacy of Toledo, her not very beloved rival. The extravagant aspirations of the Santiago prelates were above all a spectacular gesture, altogether fitting and proper to the cause of the holy war and for attracting innumerable pilgrims, but they never amounted to an effort toward the establishment of a schismatic hierarchy. The belief in the invincible warrior was something that the Moor understood and an effective shield for the Christian. Thus it was that fantasy ran away with those who saw

---

[59] *The Mozarabic Psalter*, ed. J. P. Gilson (1905), pp. 208–209.

[60]   O uere digne sanctior apostole,
          caput refulgens aureum Ispanie,
          tutorque nobis et patronus uernulus,
          uitando pestem esto salus celitus,
          omnino pelle morbum, ulcus, facinus.   (p. 210)

The reason for dating this hymn between 783 and 788 is the following acrostic: "O rex regum, regum pium Mavrecatum [an Asturian king who reigned from 783 to 788] exaudi cui probe hoc tuo amore prebe."

in the Apostle a divine force, a rider on a snow-white, immortal horse, a protector of agriculture,[61] and a consummate thaumaturge.

How the Presence of the Apostle Was Imagined and Felt

The ninth century saw the composition of numerous martyrologies, that is, calendars with information about the martyrs commemorated (and even of saints who were not martyrs).[62] Deacon Florus of Lyon (d. 863) composed one that was added to by Ado of Toul between 830 and 860;[63] in this work we read that the bones of the most blessed Apostle Santiago were carried to the farthest limits of Hispania and buried by the "Britannic Sea" ("contra mare Britannicum"); the devotion and veneration in which they are held are exceedingly well known ("celeberrima illarum gentium veneratione excoluntur"). We do not have information about how the Galicians and Asturians of the ninth century conceived the figure and mission of the future Santiago of Spain, but we may draw some conclusions about this period from later expressions in literature and art. The chronicle of Sampiro,[64] which is the first to mention the existence of the sepulcher, is not contemporaneous to its discovery; nearer to that time is a document of the year 885 in which King Alfonso III grants some lands and a village to the monks living near the sepulcher (see L. Vázquez de Parga, José M. Lacarra, and J. Uría Ríu, *Las peregrinaciones a Santiago de Compostela*, I, 30) and says that, after God, Santiago is his most merciful patron ("nobis post deum piissimo patroni"). From the beginning (that is, from the first half of the ninth century, a little more than a century after the Muslim invasion), the cult of Santiago must have had enormous political and religious significance. Mounted on a horse and armed with a heavy sword, the Apostle appears on a tympanum in one of the transepts of the cathedral of Santiago; it is a work of the mid-twelfth century and was made a part of the very structure of the church. On the standard that the equestrian figure sustains with his left hand there is written: "Sanctus Jacobus Apostolus Christi." In the archivolt of the tympanum, ten angelic figures observe the portentous scene.

The artistry of those who carved this tympanum is far inferior to the splendor of the Portico of Glory, one of the supreme achievements of Romanesque structure. In the Portico is expressed the learned

---

[61] See Michaëlis de Vasconcellos, *op. cit.*, II, 834, for the question of the protection given by Santiago to plants and cattle.

[62] See the bibliography in Grober, "Grundriss der roman," *Philologie*, II (1902), p. 144.

[63] Váquez de Parga, *et al.*, *op. cit.*, I, 34.

[64] Dated as of the end of the tenth century or the beginning of the eleventh (B. Sánchez-Alonso, *Historia de la historiografía española* [1941], I, p. 114).

position of the Compostelan Church, according to which Santiago occupies the subordinate place assigned to him in the Christian hierarchy, next to the prophets and Apostles of Jesus Christ. There is no allusion to the militant character of the Boanerges, the sons of thunder. Thus there coexisted in the Compostelan basilica two opposed representations of Santiago: the learned and "canonical" one, we might say, and that of the people, with their traditional attachment to the image of the celestial horseman. It was not possible to eliminate either the one or the other.

The semicircle of the tympanum, as well as the smaller ones around the angelic heads, must have served as the symbol of the visible curve of celestial space, the home of the blessed and the well of good fortune for those who, sustained by hope, directed their faith and their prayers to Santiago, messenger of God, powerful, invincible. The miraculous apparition of the Apostle on this tympanum is seen in two ways, from heaven and from this base earth: the angels contemplate it without leaving their glorious world—like an eternal prodigy which contemplates itself—while the mortals, humbled, stand in supplication before it, rather than merely observing. In the eleventh and twelfth centuries of Christianity, the beyond, what is now called the supernatural, was felt to be more real than what is called "natural." Much more was known about that other invisible "nature" than about its tangible aspect; when the moment of truth arrived, the theological heavens turned out to be nearer than the earth upon which people walked. It was not possible at that time to contemplate a miraculous event as the Toledan knights who were contemporaries of El Greco and firmly grounded in their earthly existence, would do centuries later in the *Burial of the Count of Orgaz*. The miracle of this burial gravitates toward this near world of here and now, which coexists with the world of the beyond. But those who prostrated themselves before the equestrian Santiago still did not possess a place all their own *from* which to contemplate the divine. The only possibility was to surrender before it, to pray and to wait. All else was sinful disorder, a symbol of which may be seen in the monsters crushed under the pillars of the central arch of the Portico of Glory.

The theme of the equestrian Santiago was not just the happy idea of a Compostelan sculptor of the twelfth century, for its bases and antecedents are found in popular devotion, in what was hoped from the militant Santiago—or from the extreme and heretical belief in his brotherhood with Christ. No sculptor had to invent a theme that had been present continuously from Roman antiquity to the Christian epoch of the Empire and had later spread throughout Christian Europe (see pp. 387–388). Literature and art of later centuries bear clear witness to the startling success achieved by the tomb of Santiago as early as the ninth century. The *Poem of the Cid* (*ca.* 1140) makes matters perfectly clear:

> The Moors shout: Mohammed! and the Christians: Santiago![65]
>
> (l. 731)

I have already quoted (p. 388) the lines from Berceo's *Vida de San Millán* which describe how Santiago and St. Emilian came down from on high "on *two horses whiter than crystal*" and routed the Moorish host. In the *Poema de Fernán González* (from the thirteenth century, though based on a much older *cantar de gesta*), the Apostle aids the Count of Castile to conquer Almanzor:

> There will the Apostle Santiago be called,
> Christ will send his servant to protect us:
> With such aid Almanzor will be stopped.

And, indeed, at the moment of hardest fighting in the Battle of Hacinas, the Count

> raised upward his eyes to see who was calling,
> saw the holy Apostle who was there above him,
> and the knights with him formed a great company . . .[66]
>
> (st. 561)

In the account given by Rodrigo Jiménez de Rada in *De rebus Hispaniae* of the Battle of the Navas de Tolosa (1212), Santiago is not mentioned, nor does he appear in the translation of this text included in Alfonso the Learned's *Crónica General*. Jiménez de Rada, who was archbishop of Toledo, probably was little interested in mentioning Santiago to the ecclesiastical primacy of Spain. But in another version of Jiménez de Rada's chronicle, entitled *Estoria Gótica*, the translator links Santiago to that memorable battle: "The kings' standard bore the image of the holy Mary of Toledo, with which they had always conquered. And saying: 'May God and Santiago help us!' [while] others [shouted] 'Castile, Castile'; others: 'Aragon, Aragon!' and others: 'Navarre!' they attacked boldly" (ed. E. Lidforss [Lund, 1876], p. 123). Perhaps it was the Leonese knights who invoked Santiago in this text, since they could not say, "Leon, Leon!" because

---

[65] It seems best to me to punctuate the original Spanish line as follows: "Los moros llaman: ¡Mafómat!, e los cristianos: ¡Santi Yagüe!"

[66] Stanzas 413 and 561 of the Menéndez Pidal edition of the *Poema*, which read in Spanish as follows:

í ['allí] será el apóstol Santiago llamado,
enviarnos ha Cristo valer a su criado:
será con tal ayuda Almoçor embargado

alçó suso los ojos por ver quien lo llamava,
vio el santo apóstol que de suso le estava,
de caveros con él, grand compaña levava ...

their king had not come to the battle—even supposing that "Leon!" had ever served as a battle cry. In any event, the cry of "Santiago!" appears in the foreground of the scene.

As literature gradually widened its expressive scope, the meaning of the Apostle became ever more explicit; what was in the consciousness and on the tongues of all was then set down in writing. By the middle of the fourteenth century, Castilian literature had taken on lyrical dimensions, apt for the expression of the innermost feelings, of much greater amplitude than ever before; it was, therefore, to be expected that the traditional meaning of Santiago, which I have been calling attention to for years, should manifest itself in very clear and express form. In the *Poema de Alfonso Onceno*, the Moorish King Yuçaf speaks after the defeat of Salado (1340):

> Into the Alhambra of Granada
> he entered with very great sorrow,
> he broke his sword,
> and he began to make moan . . .
>
> "I, your king, am conquered,
> I know not what to do,
> for I have lost my power,
> I cannot defend you.
>
> *Santiago of Spain*
> killed my Moors,
> scattered my company,
> broke my standard.
>
> *I saw him well that day*
> with many armed men,
> the sea appeared dry
> and covered with knights."
>
> This king spoke truly;
> know this without fail,
> for God, king of mercy,
> would gain the victory.
>
> To show His kind favor
> and aid the good king [Alfonso]
> he would send there
> the Apostle of Spain.
>
> Glorious Santiago
> made the Moors die,
> *Mohammed, the lazy one*,[67]
> tardy, would not come.
>
> (st. 1879–1888, ed. F. Janer)

---

[67] In the Province of Granada a lazy person is still called a *majoma* ("Mo-

In this same poem King abu-al-Ḥasan invokes Mohammed before beginning the battle against the Christians (st. 1572–1575). Without the circumstances evidenced by this invocation, without the necessity of a militant faith to oppose against Islam, the Christians in the northwest of the Peninsula would not have shaped and valued as they did the traditional theme of the Dioscuric horsemen; otherwise these mythical figures would have followed the path of development of those dialects that wither away and finally die out for lack of expressive needs that go beyond the daily commonplaces or naïve imaginings whose time is always in the present and whose horizon includes no future of lofty flight. Folklore may be collected and classified, may serve to attract tourists; but it is of no use for the creation of history.

By virtue of his active presence over long centuries and the extremely diverse radiations of that presence, Santiago is one of the pillars of Spanish history. However important they may have been at some moment or in some place, the other saints around whom cults developed are today like impoverished dialects in comparison to what might be called the "literary" impetus of the belief in the Apostle, who, there in his basilica in Compostela, brandishes an enormous sword, without which the pilgrimages, the grandiose cathedral itself, and all the rest would not have existed.[68]

The battles with the Moors ended centuries ago, but there still remains the solemn beauty of Santiago of Compostela and of the ancient abbeys of Celanova, Osera, Samos—and of so many other churches which neglect has allowed to fall into decay. But the city of Santiago, a glorious place, one of the centers and vertices of Spanish life, has been kept whole and in unshaken dignity. The profusion of royal coats of arms there—of the Catholic Sovereigns, of the House

---

hammed"), though people are unaware that they are using the name of the Muslim in this instance; neither did the Leonese and Castilian Christians suspect that their equestrian Santiago owed his origin to a Dioscuric horseman. The evolution through time of language, customs, and beliefs has always been like this.

[68] Themes of this kind must be seen in their structured and coherent form; the artistic and literary form in which Santiago appears after the eleventh century cannot be explained except by a long, slow oral gestation, for, before being fixed in written form, the most revered beliefs had been present for a long time orally. Hastings' *Encyclopaedia of Religion and Ethics* (XI, 458) says about the dogma of the Holy Trinity: "In the New Testament we do not find the doctrine of the Trinity in anything like its developed form . . . [but], if the doctrine of the Trinity appeared somewhat late in theology, it must have lived very early in devotion." Santiago and his sword are not, of course, part of dogma; but for that very reason it is illuminating to observe what has happened to beliefs that did become dogma, so that those who are little acquainted with these matters may not bewilder readers with their ignorance. For some aspects of the belief in the Holy Trinity before the Council of Nicea, see Adolf von Harnack, *Handbuch der Dogmengeschichte* (1931), I, 575–577, where he deals with "the doctrine of the logos in Tertullian and Hippolytus."

of Austria, and of the Bourbon dynasty—demonstrates this truth. In various epochs Spain sought her own self in Santiago, in whose diverse styles bold chords are harmonized: the Romanesque capitals of Archbishop Gelmirez's palace, the Portico of Glory (an expression of faith and hope unstifled by the decorative richness), the serene magnificence of the neoclassic palace of Rajoy. In the light of Santiago the spectator feels that the stone, humanized by art, comes to life and constantly recreates its beauty.

Military and Political Consequences

Because the religious and the militant elements were integrated in the belief of Santiago, that double dimension was present also in the clergy and the lay worshipers. Santiago was a reflection of the Muslim holy war, and a support for the holy war that the Christians were to wage against it. At this point the Apostle of the Gospels was converted into the ex-officio master of the military orders, long before such orders had any kind of legalized existence. The old saying went: "Bishop of Santiago, now the sword, now the crosier,"[69] because those prelates fought against the Norman invaders, the Moors, or the rebellious members of their own flock as readily as they held the crosier, the symbol of their spiritual authority. In 942 Bishop Rudesindus (later St. Rosendo) conquered the Norman invaders by invoking the name of the Lord.[70] In 968 Bishop Sisnandus died fighting against the same Nordic peoples, *sagitta percussus*[71] ("wounded by an arrow"). Such behavior was frequent, and it came to be normal for bishops and abbots to fight like undaunted chieftains, to intervene in politics as counselors of the kings, or to direct military campaigns. For this reason the ecclesiastical element predominated over the civil, just as the inspiration and assistance of heaven were more valuable than were such abetments when they were of a purely earthly sort. And thus there was slowly taking shape the outline of what the vital disposition of the future Spaniards would be.

The capture of Coimbra from the Moors by Ferdinand I in 1064 is an excellent example of this peculiar vital process, of what I call "theobiosis," which is something different from theocracy. As a preparation for the difficult conquest of the city, strongly walled and situated on an eminence, the King spent three days before the tomb of the Apostle, in the hope that the latter would obtain the much desired victory from God. The offerings were made and the army

---

[69] In Spanish: "Obispo de Santiago, ora la espada, ora el blago." In Portuguese: "Bispo de Santiago, Ballista e bago." (Cf. Michaëlis de Vasconcellos, *op. cit.*, II, 816.)

[70] *España sagrada*, XVIII, App. XXXII.

[71] *Ibid.*, XX, 13.

marched to war, sure of divine protection.[72] The siege began in January of 1064 and on July 7 of the same year hunger forced Coimbra to surrender. The *Chronicle of Alcalá (Cronicón Complutense)* says that the King was accompanied by the Queen, Doña Sancha, and by the following prelates: Cresconius, of the Apostolic See of Santiago (the one who was excommunicated in 1049 for using the title he was still using in 1064); Vestruarius, of Lugo; Sisnandus, of Viseo; Suarius, of Mondoñedo; the abbots Peter of Guimarães and Arrianus of Celanova. After these a large number of noblemen are mentioned, but as a group and without the citing of any names. Not even one secular name attracted the chronicler's attention.

During the long months of the siege the royal-episcopal army had passed through serious difficulties because its food supplies were exhausted; but this shortage was relieved by the monks of Lorvão, a Mozarabic monastery enclaved in Muslim territory, thanks to the well-known tolerance of the Saracens. These monks had hidden reserves of cereals in their great silos, and at the opportune moment they were able to supply the Christian army. Thus, combat operations were in charge of bishops and abbots while the services of supply were in the hands of a monastery. Where could we find an event that would be more illuminating for the understanding of such a special way of life? We may relegate to the background the fact that Santiago was a survival of, or reincarnation of, age-old beliefs. The essential thing is rather that the very conditions of Spanish life had made possible a mode of existence by virtue of a belief in which the dividing line between the human and the divine was erased. From the historical and the human point of view, the Dioscuric origins of Santiago have here the same value that the chronicle of Saxo Grammaticus has with respect to her son Napoleon Bonaparte. Life—the life of art or any other kind of human life—has its foundation in circumstances that are no more indispensable than they are dispensable.

The Chronicle of the Monk of Silos[73] completes our description of the conquest of Coimbra with a stroke of inestimable value: while the seven months of the siege passed, the people of Santiago were also besieging the Apostle with petitions for prompt and efficacious aid. A Greek pilgrim who was praying day and night by the sacred relic heard people imploring Santiago to fight like a good soldier. He could not conceive how one of Christ's Apostles, a fisherman by trade and a man who had never been on a horse, could be transformed into an equestrian soldier. This story seems truthful; the pious Greek was probably not the only one to be surprised by a cult that had so little scriptural foundation. The chronicler adds that the Apostle hastened

---

[72] The texts are to be found in López Ferreiro, *op. cit.*, II, 486–489.
[73] *Crónica Silense*, ed. F. Santos Coco (1919), pp. 74–76.

to set aside the doubts of the pilgrim. By the time the account of the Monk of Silos appears in the translated and ornamented version of Alfonso the Learned's *Crónica General*, the pilgrim has been converted into a bishop and is called Estianus:

While he was there, watching and praying, one day he heard the village folk and the pilgrims who came there say that St. James appeared to the Christians as a horseman in the midst of their battles. And the bishop, when he heard this, was troubled, and said to them: "Friends, call him not a horseman but a fisherman." Forasmuch as he persisted in his obstinacy, it pleased God that he should fall asleep; and St. James appeared to him in a dream, with keys in his hand, joyful of countenance, and said to him: "Estianus, you regard it as unseemly for the pilgrims to call me a horseman, and you say that I am not one, wherefore I have come to you now to show myself to you, so that you may never doubt again that I am one of Christ's Knights and a helper of the Christians against the Moors." And the Apostle having thus said, a *very white* horse was brought to him, and he mounted it in knightly fashion, with all manner of arms, *shining* and beautiful, and in that dream told him how he wished to go to the aid of the king, Don Fernando, who for seven years had been encamped above Coimbra: and "so that you may be more certain of this that I tell you, with these keys that I have in my hand, I will open tomorrow, at the hour of tierce, the city of Coimbra. . . ." And it was found that it truly happened thus later, just as he had said.

(p. 487*b*)

When he had won Coimbra, the king, Don Fernando, "went to Santiago, and there offered his gifts and kept his vigil" (p. 488*a*). The account of this magnificent feat included thus the event itself and its Spanish perspective, its full historical and unique reality. The "fact" that a king succeeded in capturing a city is in itself an abstraction, that is, something insufficient as a human reality.

If a medieval bishop was physically apt, he went into battle like any other *hijodalgo*. If Santiago was a warrior-Apostle, why should the priests in charge of his cult not be soldiers? And if the bishops and abbots were men of war, it seems obvious that the lower clergy would be too. The latter did not customarily wear their long cassocks and cloaks or habits; rather they wore beards and went about armed. This we know because these practices were censured and prohibited by the Councils of Compostela in 1060 and 1063: "Bishops and clergy will wear long outer garments [*usque ad talos induantur*] . . . they will be tonsured, and they will cut off their beards . . . they will not bear arms."[74]

In the tenth and eleventh centuries the clergy of Santiago already have the air of knights of the military orders, whose character and origin I discuss elsewhere. To be sure, the discipline in Santiago was less rigid than in the cloisters of the primitive orders of the twelfth century, because of the excessive confidence in the power of the

---

[74] López Ferreiro, *op. cit.*, II, Appendixes, pp. 229, 231, 239.

Apostle and the copious income from the prigrimages. The essential thing, however, was the interconnection between the military and the divine, which led to a scorn of contemplation. The belief in the "son of thunder" was developed during years of anguish and oppression, which grew less and less as the reconquest progressed in the eleventh and twelfth centuries. What had once given courage to the faithful later turned into laxity and an excess of confidence. The most exalted of Apostles brought security, well-being, and an international prestige almost magically won, somewhat as Peter's Pence converted Rome into a center of debauchery and spiritual indifference until a good while after the Council of Trent. The Archbishop of Santiago, Diego Gelmírez (1100–1140), had to forbid his clerics to appear in the choir dressed like secular folk, ill-kempt, wearing beards, or colored clothing, and spurs, and giving the appearance that the Church of the Apostle was manned not by clergy but by knights.[75] It would be a pure and naïve abstraction to speak only of the "relaxation of customs." The reality was that an essentially military saint brought forth fighting prelates and clergy armed and mounted. Diego Gelmírez would first of all have had to change the character of his magical Apostle, thanks to whom he could be surrounded with pontifical pomp and rank. But the vital disposition of the future Spaniards was gradually being shaped. Four hundred years in a state of war had fixed the course of the preferences of a people.

The Spain of the eleventh and twelfth centuries was the land of St. James, "Jakobsland," as it was called by the pilgrims from the north of Europe. One can imagine what the faith of the people was like and how much they trusted in their patron saint when the king of Leon, Alfonso VI, granted certain charter privileges in 1072 to the city of Valcárcel, near Santiago, because of his love for "the Apostle on whose power the land and the *government of all Spain* are founded."[76] In 1087 his sister, Princess Elvira, as she lay dying, made an offering to Santiago: "To thee, Apostle Santiago, *my most invincible lord and glorious victor.*"[77] In 1170 King Ferdinand II promised to endow the church of Merida, a dependency of the See of Compostela, as soon as it was reconquered, and thus to continue the good works done by his royal ancestors for the Apostle, "confiding in whose protection, we will conquer the Moors."[78] In his last will and testament Alfonso the Learned (d. 1284) prayed to Santiago, "who is our Lord and father, whose Alfonso we are."[79]

---

[75] *Historia Compostellana*, II, 3, in *España sagrada*, XX, 256.

[76] "Sancto Jacobo Apostolo in cuius ditione terra vel regimen consistit totius Hispaniae" (Michaëlis de Vasconcellos, *op. cit.*, II, 797).

[77] López Ferreiro, *op. cit.*, III, Appendix, p. 25.

[78] *Ibid.*, IV, Appendix, p. 108.

[79] Echoed by Quevedo in his *Su espada por Santiago*, in *Biblioteca de Autores Españoles*, XLVIII, 443*b*.

It would be useless to adduce further testimony to the vital connection between Leon and Castile and the Apostle, the one adored in Santiago ever since the ninth century, not only as a pious relic, but as a real force that guided the political direction of the Christian kingdoms. For those monarchs "non erat potestas nisi a Jacobo," and on him were founded the power, the prestige, and the hope of the kingdom.

We have lost the key to the understanding of such a strange form of religiosity and its anomalous mixture of motives. The body of one of Christ's companions was adored with such enthusiasm that the disciple left the gentle doctrine of his Master in the shadows. We can understand how medieval Spanish Christianity was more productive of holy wars, propaganda, and thaumaturgy than of reposeful contemplation and of mystic emotion. In the ambit of such religiosity scarcely any room was left for a St. Bernard, a St. Francis, a St. Thomas, or a Roger Bacon. The Spanish saints with an international dimension were St. Domingo (Dominic) de Guzmán in the thirteenth century and St. Vincent Ferrer in the fifteenth, both of them the scourge of heretics and infidels, who foreshadow St. Ignatius in the sixteenth century—and let this be said without subtracting from their own greatness, for without them the history of Europe would not have been quite the way it was. But contemplation and technical activities continued to be a task for the other two castes.

The Spanish Santiago is inseparable from the sustained longing of those who sought and found in him a support and meaning for their existence; it is inseparable from the lives of those who lived their belief, a defensive faith, worked and reworked by the very need of the people to hold fast to it. The Moors in al-Andalus felt this so acutely that when Almanzor, at the height of his power, judged it necessary to strike the coup de grâce against the Christianity of the north, he destroyed and dispersed the religious communities of Leon and Castile and finally destroyed the temple of the Apostle (997). Here is proof from the enemy camp that the Muslims considered Santiago to be Mohammed's rival. He respected only the clearly defined area in which the holy relic was kept, for the Muslim knew that the power of sacred objects was not limited by the confines of Islam. He had the bells of the shrine brought to Cordova as a trophy, on the shoulders of captives, and there he had them melted down and turned into lamps for the great mosque of Cordova. The damage wrought by this Islamic thunderbolt increased the faith in the holy relic, so holy that not even Almanzor himself had succeeded in destroying it.

The diffuse and vaguely defined belief in Santiago, extremely ancient albeit not highly regarded by the Visigothic Church, as we have seen, acquired volume and structure as a faith opposed and, in a certain way, similar, to the faith of the Muslims. Unlike the shrines of the Virgin in Guadalupe, Saragossa, Montserrat, and many other places, it cannot be disposed of as a pious fable. Santiago was a positive creed launched against Mohammedanism; there was nothing illusory about the battles won under his banner. His name was converted into the national war cry, in opposition to the cry of the Saracens.

T HE SHRINE OF GALICIA stood out in various
perspectives. To the Saracens it seemed to be a Christian Mecca, whose
efficacy they sensed and sought to destroy. For the Spanish Christians we now know what it was. For foreigners who knew the
strength and splendor of al-Andalus, the tomb of the Apostle became a place of pilgrimage as venerable as Rome. In the struggle
against the infidel, one of the Lord's Apostles was making war in
behalf of the good cause, and this miracle was taking place in the
land of Galicia, a place hospitable to miracles and that also provided
an opportunity for the improvement of material fortunes. When the
monks of Cluny, in furthering the secular interests of the dukes of
Burgundy, undertook the task of restoring scourged Christianity,
they must have quickly seen the value of the pilgrims' route as a
means of international expansion for the order. Through the diplo-
macy of the spirit, France got more effective results than she did by
fighting the Moors. The crusade into Spain never won the hearts of
the French people.

The Spanish Christian kingdoms found in France the magnet they
needed if they were to pull away as much as possible from the attraction of Islam. The kings knew that their power rested only on faith
and pure personal courage, while for everything else, their cultural
horizon was largely limited to that provided by Muslim lands. But
now, thanks to Cluny's imperialism, the Christian kings from Navarre
to Galicia would strive to draw closer to France, whose civilization
was to lend its distinctive color to Hispano-Christian life in the
eleventh, twelfth, and thirteenth centuries.[1] These Spanish kings used

---

[1] But it did not decisively Westernize the disposition of the Spaniards' vital
dwelling place. France superimposed certain words, objects, literary and artistic
forms onto the Christian Spanish caste, but the caste system prevented the
Christians from following paths parallel to those taken by the other Romanic

Santiago as a source of international prestige, which they were badly in need of. Since the tenth century, Europe had known of the immensely valuable material and intellectual achievements of Muslim Cordova, and it was to this city that European eyes turned when they were looking for things of this world. Islam made enormous contributions to European life in mathematics, philosophy, medicine, poetry, and various crafts, and presented, besides, the lovely spectacle of cities like Seville, Cordova, and Almeria, which were in commercial contact with Italy and the north of Europe. But the Christian kingdoms of Hispania could offer to other Europeans almost nothing at all save the extraordinary favor that God had shown them in the gift of the body of Santiago.

We can no longer understand clearly what a relic of such great spiritual volume meant in those centuries, when the tokens of divine favor were worth more than any conquest by human effort. God was an authentic power in society. He may be on the lips and in the hearts of many today, but war and peace are now determined by other motives, and faith in God does not lead to meetings of chiefs of state. But in 1010, Alduin, abbot of Saint-Jean-d'Angély (Charente-Inférieure), announced the discovery of the head of John the Baptist, and called several sovereigns together for the purpose of showing it to the faithful. There were Robert II the Pious, of France; Sancho the Great of Navarre; William V, Duke of Aquitaine; as well as princes, counts, and prelates, among whom the most conspicuous were Odon of Champagne and Landulf of Turin.[2] So dazzling was the assemblage that it ought to have given strong support to the authenticity of the relic and won respect for it with the ignorant as well as with the learned, but this was not so. The head of John the Baptist begot only a limited cult, and this caused the inestimable merit of the Sepulcher of Compostela to stand out all the more sharply. It was useless to try to compete with it and, without more ado, to try to launch a new belief of international scope. The *Acta Sanctorum* call the account of the discovery a fable; but even without this condemnation, how was a relic to gain universal belief for itself if it was already considered an imposture by its French contemporaries? Adhemar de Chabannes (988–1034), a monk of St. Cibar of Angoulême, observes that "it does not appear at all clear who brought the head to this place, nor when, nor whence it was brought, nor whether it belongs to the forerunner of Jesus Christ."[3]

---

peoples. Later on I discuss the differing ways in which Castile, Aragon, and Catalonia maintained relations with France.

[2] Ernst Sackur, *Die Cluniacenser*, II, 68.

[3] "A quo tamen vel quo tempore vel unde huc delatum, vel si praecursoris Domini sit, haudquaquam fideliter patet" ("Historiarum libri tres," in J. P. Migne, ed., *Patrologia*, S.L., vol. 141, col. 67).

Let us observe first of all the facility with which French monks wrote about religious subjects at the beginning of the eleventh century. Still close to the year 1000—when the millennial fears were at their strongest—a French monk was already reasoning in terms of clear and incisive ideas in a way that would confirm—if it were not a waste of time to do so—that it is no mere accident that Descartes's philosophy is French. If a Father Adhemar or a Monsignor Duchesne had lived next door to the tomb of Santiago in the ninth century, the belief in the "son of thunder" would not have passed beyond the boundaries of Iria Flavia. But the history of each people has been wrought within a different disposition of life.

Very likely the basic motive behind the appearance of the Baptist's head in Saint-Jean-d'Angély was the fact that that abbey was located on the road that brought the pilgrims to Santiago by way of Blaye and Bordeaux. It is well known that since the eleventh century miracles blossomed along the *via francigena*, one of whose starting points was St. James Street, *rue Saint-Jacques*, in Paris (the street owes its name, of course, to the connection with the famous pilgrimage). The celestial route of Santiago traced in the Milky Way had its terrestrial counterpart in a *via miraculosa*, on which one set out in Paris and ended at the tomb of the invincible Apostle. This is the explanation I find for the sudden appearance of the head of John the Baptist and for the fact that William V of Aquitaine, with such close ancestral ties to Cluny, should immediately call upon Abbot Odilon to introduce the Cluniac observance in Saint-Jean-d'Angély, which was raised overnight to the rank of an apostolic church; that is, its efficiency and rank were increased because of its strategic location.

At this point the presence of Sancho the Great of Navarre at that meeting of sovereigns in France becomes especially interesting, because, as is well known, shortly after that the Navarrese monarch gave to the monks of Cluny the monasteries of San Juan de la Peña and of San Salvador de Leyre (1022). The pilgrims came upon these monasteries soon after crossing the Pyrenees, as they went along the route that joined the main road in Puente la Reina. The Benedictine order of Cluny had been founded in 910 through the initiative of William the Pious, Duke of Aquitaine, even though from the outset the purpose of the order probably was to make the sovereignty of the Church prevail over that of secular powers. From the beginning of the ninth century until the middle of the eleventh, as we know, the papacy was of secondary importance with respect to the Holy Roman Empire. While the popes were engaged in exhausting struggles with the Roman nobility, Cluny began to extend from Burgundy energetic activities of a political nature whose effects were felt far from the famous abbey in the tenth and eleventh centuries. According to Albert Brackmann the germs of the ecclesiastical and imperial policies of Pope Gregory VII (1073–1085) may be seen at an earlier date in Cluny.[4]

The new Christian states in the northern part of the Iberian Peninsula were bound to attract the attention of Cluny very soon, especially the Hispanic March (primitive Catalonia), which had been politically joined to the Carolingian Empire.[5] But the later foundations in Navarre, and afterwards in Castile, resulted from the attraction exerted by the great miracle of Compostela, whose occurrence was known in northeastern France almost a century before the foundation of Cluny (see p. 422). Even though the presence in Hispania of a powerful Muslim state kept pontifical Rome in a constant state of alarm,[6] it had not given rise to any crusade to liberate so many oppressed Christians. Yet, for one reason or another, the fact that the sepulcher of an Apostle of Christ had appeared in a zone already liberated from the infidel must have aroused the interest of the abbots of Cluny, who were eager to develop a spiritual and economic policy that was not practicable for Rome under the circumstances of the times. Abbot Odilon (994-1048) had sent to the altar of St. Peter (the one belonging to Cluny, not the altar in Rome) the gold and silver collected from the Moors which the kings of Leon and Castile paid to his order as a spiritual tribute.[7]

The religious and political intervention of the Order of Cluny was motivated both by the Catholic ideal of the monks and by the desire of the Christian Sovereigns (in Navarre, Leon, and Castile) to counteract the inevitable cultural pressure of the Muslims.[8] To be sure, the decisive incentive for Cluniac intervention, from Navarre to Galicia, was the Sepulcher of Santiago, whose ideal image entered combat on behalf of those people who fought as Christians in a region almost totally deprived of contact with the center of Christianity for more than two hundred years. A relic of such magnitude meant as much in the tenth century—when the boundaries between the spiritual and the material were blurred—as the petroleum of Iraq does in the twentieth; that is to say, it served as the incentive for intelligent

---

[4] Albert Brackmann, *Zur politische Bedeutung der kluniazensischen Bewegung* (Darmstadt, 1958), pp. 13–14.

[5] In 962 there were already Cluniac monasteries south of the Pyrenees, according to J. Pérez de Urbel, *Los monjes españoles en la Edad Media* (1933), II, 416 ff.

[6] "Opposition to the Muslim peril was the keenest concern of papal policy until well into the eleventh century: southern Italy and Spain constituted for a long time the major worry of the Roman Curia" (P. Kehr, "Das Papstum und der katalanische Prinzipat," in *Abhandlungen der preussischen Akademie der Wissenschaften* [Berlin, 1926], p. 4).

[7] Sackur, *op. cit.*, II, 112; Brackmann, *op. cit.*, p. 18.

[8] With respect only to the form of the social phenomenon, we may compare this reaction with the interest shown by Ibero-American countries in affirming their cultural contacts with Europe for the purpose of escaping the seduction of the ineluctable models provided by North American life.

and courageous enterprise. The enterprise undertaken by Cluny consisted in directing into suitable channels, for the good of their souls, the devotion of those who wished to make the pilgrimage to Compostela.

A further—though fortuitous—motive for the coming of Cluny to Navarre, point of entry into Hispania for the pilgrimage, was the friendly relationship between King Sancho the Great and Duke William V of Aquitaine, whom we have already seen in Sancho's company in 1010 during the meeting held to discuss the discovery of the relic of John the Baptist. By bringing in Cluny, Sancho initiated an international policy designed to shatter the isolation from Europe suffered by Christians from Navarre to Galicia. In truth, of course, the new relation to Europe was linked to those earlier contacts already established by virtue of the road to Santiago. Although Sancho the Great may at that time have been the most important of the Hispanic kings, it was the pilgrimage that raised him to a position of international eminence, because he ruled the zone through which, as early as the beginning of the eleventh century, the increasing numbers of people going to Compostela entered Spain. The Duke of Aquitaine (*ca.* 959–1030) was among these: "Since the days of his youth he had been in the habit of visiting the resting place of the Apostles in Rome every year, and if he happened not to go to Rome then he substituted for that holy pilgrimage the one to Santiago of Galicia instead."[9] William lived and traveled more with the dignity of a king than of a duke, and his pilgrimage was therefore an event that attracted attention. Because of these journeys, friendships grew up between him and both Sancho of Navarre and Alfonso V of Leon (999–1028): "He had captured the sympathy of those kings to the point of annually receiving their ambassadors, who brought him precious gifts, to which he responded with even more valuable gifts."[10]

In these gifts to the Duke of Aquitaine, I see the foreshadowing of the contributions that Sancho the Great, his son Ferdinand I, and his grandson Alfonso VI later paid to Cluny. In any event, in these frequent visits of the Duke of Aquitaine, so closely allied with Cluny, are to be found the motives immediately behind the introduction of the French order into Navarre, Leon, and Castile.

For the Hispanic monarchs the pilgrimage was a source of holiness, prestige, power, and wealth, which the national monasticism was not in condition to take sufficient advantage of. It was necessary to bring in "engineers" from the outside to organize an adequate system of *do ut des* between Spain and the rest of Christianity and thus

---

[9] Adhemar de Chabannes, in *Patrologia*, vol. 141, col. 56.
[10] The biography of William of Aquitaine can be found in the *Histoire littéraire de la France*, VII, 284, or in *Patrologia*, vol. 141, col. 823.

to elevate the importance of the Peninsular kingdoms both with respect to Islam and to Europe. The razing of the city of Santiago by
Almanzor, who at the same time left the holy relic untouched, propagated the fame of the Apostle and provided a unique excuse for
bringing in clergy well instructed in matters pertaining to God.
When Sancho the Great gave the Monastery of Oña to Cluny in 1033,
he said that "at that time the monastic order, the most excellent of
the orders of the Church, was unknown in all our fatherland,"[11] an
opinion shared generally by kings and great lords in that century.
The fact that many of the monasteries were "double," that is, for
both monks and nuns, had given rise to disorders that, if they were
not exclusively Spanish, justified the monastic policy of the sovereigns, whose basic idea was to attract distinguished people and the
wealth and culture of Europe. In an anticipation of enlightened
despotism, Spain for the first time and through the energetic action
of her kings revealed her intention of "Europeanizing" herself, of
assuaging the pains of isolation and self-deprecation. The Monk of
San Pedro de Arlanza, who composed the *Poem of Fernán González*
around 1240, stated (as has been noted above, p. 111) what had been
felt for centuries and what may be deduced from everything that I
have written on this subject: God favored Spain with the body of
the Apostle, for

> Greatly did God wish to honor Spain,
> when He chose to send the Holy Apostle there,
> *He wished to raise her over England and France,*
> See how not one Apostle lies in all those lands.[12]

It is indeed worth noting to what an extent Santiago was felt to
give support to the Christian caste, as well as how Spain was already
experiencing in the thirteenth century its anguished sense of life, was
already aware of its insecurity.

The prestige had come from God himself, and now the monks of
Cluny were bidden to organize it from the point of view of human
interests. As the eleventh century went on, the French infusion became more perceptible. The first bishop of reconquered Toledo
(1085) was French, as were many monks and canons. An echo of
this religious colonization is heard in the considerable number of
French words that entered the language earlier than the thirteenth
century. The introduction of French words into Spanish and Portuguese is not comparable to what happened in England, where French

---

[11] A. de Yepes, *Crónica general de la orden de San Benito* (1615), fol. 467.
[12]   Fuerte mient quiso Dios a España honrar,
quand al santo apóstol quiso í enviar,
d'Inglaterra y Francia, quísola mejorar,
sabet, non yaz apóstol en tod aquel logar.

(st. 154)

and Anglo-Saxon were mixed to produce a third language; Castilian went on being essentially what it had been in linguistic structure, although augmented by French words (things) which in the eleventh and twelfth centuries corresponded to what had been taken from Arabic in the three hundred years preceding.

With the Cluniac invasion and what followed, the Mozarab-Islamic aspect of the Christian zone of the Peninsula began to be modified. The Roman rite, used in Cluny, replaced the Mozarabic rite; the script and the style of architecture were changed; literature, highly original as it was (the *Poema del Cid*, written around 1140, was among the greatest literary works of its epoch), turned to French sources and forms (the religious theater; the poetic stanza of four fourteen-syllable verses in monorhyme, called *cuaderna vía*;[13] international themes of both religious and profane nature). But whether the Spaniard slept on an Arabic *almadraque* ("mattress"), or on a French *colchón*, the personal tension of the heroic caste continued to be the same. The Christian—whether Leonese, Castilian, or Navarrese—kept his distance from things Arabic or French.

The Cluniac monasteries marked the way of the pilgrims from San Juan de la Peña to Galicia. Although they practiced charity with the needy, the essential thing was that there should be "no lack of rich travelers and pilgrims who would pay generously for the hospitality that was extended to them."[14] Monasteries like Sahagún came to own immense properties, gifts from people who hoped to attain eternal salvation through the prayers of the monks. This demonstrates that if the people in general looked askance at the monks, the wealthy did not feel the same way. Countess Teresa de Carrión, the great-granddaughter of the Leonese king, Vermudo II, and the widow of the powerful Gómez Díaz,[15] made a gift to Cluny in 1076 of the magnificent monastery of San Zoil de Carrión, on the road "qui discurrit ad Sanctum Jacobum": "Dwelling in Spain, we heard of the fame of the town of Cluny and of the lord abbot Hugh, a holy man of that community, whose monks live in the service of God, under the discipline of His rule and turning their steps toward heaven without flagging." In 1077 the Countess confirmed her donation in a document signed by the Bishop of Santiago, Diego Peláez,[16] to prove, if it were necessary, that the whole matter of Cluny and the pilgrimage to Santiago were one and the same thing.

---

[13] The *cuaderna vía* was used in religious and learned poems (lives of saints, Poem of Alexander, etc.). French origin of this form of poetry has been proved by Ramon Menéndez Pidal, *Poesía juglaresca* (1947), pp. 353–354.

[14] Pérez de Urbel, *op. cit.*, II, 446–448. For this period, see Marcelin Defourneaux, *Les Français en Espagne aux XIe et XIIe siècles* (Paris, 1949).

[15] A relative of the famous Infantes de Carrión in the *Poema del Cid*; cf. Ramón Menéndez Pidal, *Cantar de Mío Cid*, pp. 540 ff.

[16] *Recueil des chartes de l'abbaye de Cluny* (1888), 604, 622.

The aristocracy followed the example of the kings. Ferdinand I (d. 1065) paid Cluny an annual tribute of 1,000 gold dirhems. In phrases of sweet submission, his son Alfonso VI doubled the sum, in testimony of even firmer spiritual vassalage: "To Hugh, abbot of Cluny, torch quickened by the divine fire, river of honey and sweetness." The motives behind such vassalage are already familiar to us. But it must be borne in mind that there was no sense of self-deprecation in this attitude, since the sincere feeling of Catholicity erased any notion of frontiers in the kingdom of God. In any event, the submission to Cluny implied a cession of what we would today call areas of sovereignty, because the monks formed a completely autonomous institution. But it was necessary to raise the Christian kingdoms with their intermixtures of Moors and Jews and inadequate inner stability to a level of stability beyond that provided by their kings; that is, they had nothing like the feudal structure of the French states. One obvious reason for the absence of feudalism was the fact that the royal power at times reached the people by way of officials and institutions that were not Christian (e.g., *almojarife*, the royal tax collector; *almotacén*, the inspector of weights and measures; *alfequeque*, the agent who redeemed captives; *zalmedina*, the governor of a city or castle). Further, the amount of stable secular wealth possessed by the Christians was limited, whereas there was a torrent of divine marvels. Santiago was the supreme thaumaturge, and after him, in each region there existed other promoters of miracles: St. Facundus and St. Primitivus, in Sahagún; St. Aemilianus, in La Rioja; and a hundred others. There were also miracle workers of flesh and blood; in 1083, Alfonso VI gave "the chapel of St. John and an inn at the east gate of Burgos,"[17] a place where the pilgrims passed, to a French hermit who worked miracles in front of the monarch while riding on his little donkey. The Christian population lived its belief with an ardor equal to that of the Mudejar or the Jew.

It is not, then, the religiosity of the Middle Ages, more or less uniform throughout western Europe, that determined the peculiarity of Spain. The concept of the Middle Ages is an abstraction that is of little use when we confront the immediate reality of a human group at a given moment in time. What characterized the Christian caste at that time was not an abstract medievalism but the predominance of belief over human deeds (even over theological thought), just as, later, literature and art would predominate over science during the seventeenth century. In any historical unity (that of a people), each particular manifestation of life depends on what coexists around it. In this sense, the religion of eleventh-century Spain is not identical with that of the same period in France; nor was seventeenth-century

---

[17] Ramón Menéndez Pidal, *La España del Cid* (1947), p. 273.

Spanish literature produced and lived like contemporary literature in the rest of Europe. We have seen the effort to establish in France a cult around the head of St. John, an effort that at first glance seems to be a generic medieval trait. But following hard upon this came the monk Adhemar with his demolishing criticism. At the beginning of the twelfth century the monastery of St. Médard (Soissons) exhibited one of the Child Jesus's milk teeth, and in the face of this exhibition up rose the Abbot of Nogent-sous-Coucy and charged the other monks with imposture: "Attendite, falsarii . . . "[18]—rivalries among the monks, say those who cling to the externality of "facts." But did not such rivalries go on in Spain too, and fierce ones at that? Accuracy requires us to think that the French monks of the eleventh and twelfth centuries already moved in the same life disposition (see chap. iv) that was later to manifest itself in Jean de Meun, Descartes, and the Encyclopedia. In other words, what is peculiarly "French" (with regard to the form taken by the dynamic thrust of French life) existed in the eleventh century as well as in the eighteenth, with more difference in content than the space of seven hundred years implies. Because France was like this, the *Chanson de Roland* is not the *Poema del Cid*; nor is there in France a national hero of flesh and blood like Rodrigo Díaz, or writers like St. Theresa and Cervantes; but there is indeed a Descartes, a Racine, and also a Bossuet and a Voltaire.

I have had to insist on the preceding points in order to open the way to new modes of writing history and to assail the belief that "facts" are something absolute, shaped in no way by the circumstances that make them possible—as if a river could be isolated from the shape of its bed and from the downgrade that causes it to flow. Santiago, the pilgrimages, and all the rest, are unintelligible if we speak of them, as is the custom, as *things* that exist and happened apart from everyone else. Santiago of Spain was a unique phenomenon, functionally related to that special way of *feeling one's own life*, of being situated in life, which today we term "Spanish."

It is, therefore, necessary to sharpen our focus a little more to see quite clearly that the modalities of religious belief in Spain and in France diverged considerably, in spite of the uniformity imposed by the not very exact concept of the Middle Ages. In 996 Robert II, called the Pious, was anointed King of France, and this monarch is the first to appear gifted with the virtue of curing scrofula, by the laying on of hands and the making of the sign of the cross. This miraculous faculty continued to be an adjunct of the French monarchy, and it was exercised in the eleventh century just as it was in the nineteenth. Robert II, who was the son of the usurper Hugh

---

[18] Migne *op. cit.*, vol. 156, col. 652, Cf. M. Bloch, *Les rois thaumaturges*, p. 29.

Capet, did not feel very secure on his throne. Fearing lest the legitimacy of the new dynasty should be disputed, his more faithful partisans thought it advisable to attribute to the new monarch the power to cure scrofula. If the monarch had been a usurper, God would not have granted him the miraculous gift of healing the sick.[19] Later I have something to say about how that surprising innovation originated, but what interests me here is its connection with the French life structure and the meaning of the strange fact that the Capetian kings should arrogate to themselves the power to cure scrofula.

Toward the year 1000, when the people were transformed with terror and awaiting the end of time, and trusted in everything except themselves, certain Frenchmen deemed it useful and possible to incorporate divine powers in a human being and cause him to work miracles reserved only for the chosen of God. This decision to endow the kings of France with thaumaturgic power implied a sanctification *en bloc* and a priori of a whole dynasty, of a national cause anchored in human time and space. Purely earthly realities were injected with divinity. If the miraculous faculty of curing scrofula seems at first glance to be more thaumaturgic than the intervention of Santiago, a little thought will lead to exactly the opposite conclusions. With the practice of such a rite, *a supernatural power was secularized and regularized* in a way impossible even for popes or religious orders. The kings of Leon or Castile would have done something similar if they had arrogated to themselves the power of winning battles merely because they were kings, rather than *hoping* to win them thanks to the intercession of Santiago.

In a recent book the genesis of the thaumaturgic power of the French kings has been studied.[20] Apparently its origin may be found in Germanic superstitions which survived in unknown ways in the royal circle of the Capetians. From the belief in the curative power of one's own lineage (*Stippenheil*), people came to believe in the healing power of a specific lineage, that of the Germanic kings and, later, that of the Capetians. There are accounts of how the magical strength of lineage worked among the Franks: a Frankish woman cured her son by touching him with the fringe of the mantle of the Merovingian king, Gunnthram. It is noteworthy, however, that in the atmosphere of a Christian court there should have survived a popular superstition supporting the idea that God had elevated the kings of France over other kings by virtue of their consecration with holy oil brought from heaven and not purchased in any pharmacy (Percy Ernst Schramm, *Der König von Frankreich*, I, 153). This

---

[19] Bloch, *op. cit.*, pp. 79–81.
[20] Percy Ernst Schramm, *Der König von Frankreich* (1960).

anointment conferred on the French king a distinction superior to that of priests, for they were anointed with the chrism and could now work miracles; the king, on the other hand, was consecrated with celestial oil (*Himmelöl*) on the head, the breast, between and on the shoulders, and in the joints of the arms (*ibid.*, p. 158).

To be sure, this practice was tied up with faith in the "grace of God," but it was a naturalistic and pagan faith (Germanic in this case) in which the distinction between gods and mortals does not appear very clearly, a distinction very sharply drawn by the three castes of believers who made up the Hispano-Christian kingdoms of the eleventh century. For that reason—as we shall shortly see—the miraculous power of the French kings seemed sheer nonsense to Alfonso the Learned. I therefore persist in my belief that the decision of Robert the Pious to take up the task of curing scrofula was due to a rational calculation and not merely to the survival of a superstitious tradition. The decisive factor here is not the existence of a given custom (see p. 403), but the way in which that custom was utilized. Saints work miracles without consciously setting themselves the task and do not arrogate to themselves a divine power that disturbs the order of nature. Neither do they assume the ability to transmit those superhuman powers to other people, whatever their social rank. What is characteristic in the case of the French king was the energetic audacity of the people who set down this major premise: "All the kings of France, *ipso jure*, possess the virtue of curing certain diseases," which produced the following logical deduction: "I am anointed as king of France, and *therefore* I will cure diseases." Beyond the act of anointing the king, the Church had no part in the matter. Reason, secularized judgment, prevailed over the acceptance of what was demanded by faith, which is above all reasoning: the action of divine grace is necessary in the first instance but has been conditioned or limited by those who are the beneficiaries of it. The kings of France decided, *motu proprio*, how much curative power they necessarily possessed. The fact that those royal powers were linked to a magical tradition does not explain how it came to pass that such a tradition was used by French kings for nonmagical purposes. The problem has not been envisioned in this form by those who have dwelt with the "thaumaturgic" power of the kings of France.

The Norman dynasty in England saw later how useful it would be to possess the same divine virtues, and Henry I Beauclerc initiated the miraculous cure of scrofula in the twelfth century with the same success as his continental colleague. His only precaution was to invent the fiction that the last Anglo-Saxon king, Edward the Confessor, had already cured scrofula. With this, and with the opportune resurrection of belief in the mythical king Arthur, the Norman dynasty sent its roots down deep into English soil, without the need to seek support from heavenly divinities. France and England started their modern life anchored in human interests, in the extraordinary power and prestige of their monarchs.

The French kings dispensed their therapeutic grace liberally. There were even Spaniards who went to be touched by the king. We have testimony of this as late as 1602.[21] But the general reaction of the Spaniards makes clear instantly the distance that separates Spanish religiosity from the French form. It was a skeptical and ironic reaction, one example of which may be found in the 321st *Cantiga* of Alfonso the Learned. A certain child in Cordova was suffering from

> A very grave illness
> That she had in her neck;
> It was called *lamparones* ["scrofula"].

The physicians did not succeed in curing her so she was taken to the king, because

> All the Christian kings
> Have that as one of their powers.

Here is the monarch's reply:

> To what you say to me
> I answer thus and say
> That what you counsel me
> Is not worth one rotten fig.
> Your tongue is too loose
> And you talk as lightly as a swallow.
> For you say I have that power,
> And you speak nonsense.

The "good man" was speaking as lightly and stupidly as a swallow. Instead of the nonsense of claiming that the king would cure her, the king himself ordered the child be taken to "Her Majesty the Virgin,"

> Who is clothed
> In a mantle of scarlet.

They washed the holy image and the Child Jesus with water; they poured the water into a chalice "in which God's blood is made from the wine of the grape," and they let the little sick girl drink of it for as many days as the word *María* has letters; on the fourth day, the scrofula disappeared.

It is an excellent anecdote. To believe that a human being, just because he is a king, can work miracles, is nonsense; but it is wisdom

---

[21] Bloch, *op. cit.*, p. 312.

to cast a real spell with Christian ingredients, handled in the manner of the best Judeo-Islamic magic. Let us now observe that the whole process takes place as a play of forces and actions detached from the person. The very language of the *Cantiga* expresses this: the Virgin appears "clothed" (*envolta*) in a scarlet mantel, and she releases her powers through the water that touches her, the water receiving in turn the powers of the chalice, which is the crucible of divine transmutation. Nor do the letters of the name of Maria have, as such, any power of their own to work a miracle, but only by the fact that they are five in number. Things, then, are not things per se but, rather, detached aspects—ghosts—that float about as forms without matter, shadows without substance. Each of these forms glides over the other, for, as in Islam, the only thing substantial and unmoving is God. The reality of nature is nothing but the flux of aspects, and each thing is cast in an "exterior" so that it can have contact with the "exterior" of other things, and so on, to the infinity of the decorative arabesque, which has no content except its own flux. Such was the structure of the natural world for the Learned King. The important point here is that the spell I have described appears in a work written by the King himself. It is not a tale such as old women tell by the fireplace, because there was no line that absolutely divided the learned from the popular, either then or later. Thus it is understandable why the effort of the French kings to cure scrofula was treated as nonsense. Those kings evaded the magical construction of the world; they absorbed and rationalized the supernatural and converted it into an attribute of royalty (like the crown and the scepter), not into a play of appearances floating over man. In Spain, it was impossible to humanize or regulate the divine, because that would have destroyed the whole Spanish system, beginning with Santiago, a belief to which no one had openly attributed a taint of falsity before 1600. The kings of Spain did not arrogate to themselves divine powers; they acted by virtue of the grace conferred on them by God.

It was easy to bring pilgrims to Santiago, and it was possible to conquer the Moors with naked energy and heroic exaltation. It was a more arduous task to bring the powers that came down like rain from heaven into articulation with everyday existence, and it was in order to accomplish this task that the Cluniac monks were brought in, those monks who "sine taedio ad caelestia tendunt." On the other hand it would have been unjust to expect the Castilian-Leonese monks to organize spiritually kingdoms with depopulated frontiers and lands milked dry by an endemic war and sorely lacking in productive capacity. Christian wealth usually came from booty captured from the Saracens, or from the pilgrimage, a tourist traffic that, like the wars against the Moors, was also *divinal* or "holy." Alfonso VI believed that in the same impulse the Cluniac monks would resolve both the problems of heaven and those of earth,[22] and he was deceived. An individual monk can be a saint or an original thinker; but a religious order is an institution tied to worldly concerns, and the Cluniac monks were first and foremost at the service of the political interests of the duchy of Burgundy. History cannot be constructed out of sighs of lamentation and hymns of joy, and the truth is that the most important consequences of the coming of Cluny to Spain were, regrettably, political. The Abbot of Cluny promoted the marriage of Alfonso VI to Constance, the daughter of the Duke of Burgundy; later the daughters of the king, Urraca and Teresa, married the Counts Raymond and Henry of Burgundy. Leon and Castile escaped from the provincialism (with an Islamic accent) of the Mozarabic tradition only to fall into an inadequate Europeanism—the net of Cluniac and Burgundian interests. While the Spaniards, under the protection of Santiago, were fighting against the Almorávides, the dioceses were being populated with French bishops, most of them of Cluniac origin, and the crown of Alfonso VI was about to pass to the head of a foreigner, Raymond of Burgundy. For Cluny, Spain was a second Holy Land in which she could create a kingdom like that of Jerusalem, only very near to the Pyrenees. In their form the French imperial designs in 1100 were analogous of those of 1800; the Napoleon of that time was that abbot of abbots, Hugh of Cluny.

The Independence of Portugal as the Indirect Result of Santiago

Such was the course of the Spanish life with which we are now concerned, and whose total quality we should not lose sight of. Santiago, once he was born into the life of belief, unfolded his religiopolitical virtues; the great dimensions of his personality caused him to be accepted in parts far from Spain with the same faith as in his own land. So inimitable was his originality that all attempts to replace him failed, as happened in the case of Saint-Jean-d'Angély.

---

[22] One cannot accept the explanation that Cluny was called upon because the campaigns of Almanzor and his immediate successors left the Spanish monasteries in ruins. In the first place, the great monasteries were still occupied by their own communities when they were turned over to the Burgundian monks, and it was for this reason even difficult at times to install the foreigners in the monastic properties. Moreover, the destruction wrought by Almanzor has been exaggerated: for instance, life was only briefly interrupted in the monastery of Abellar, near Leon; Abbot Tehodus received donations in 994, 997, and 1001, the year in which he was replaced by Abbot Fredenandus. It was not Almanzor but the Navarrese who destroyed Abellar in 1034 and 1035. (Cf. J. E. Díaz-Jiménez, in *Boletín de la Historia*, XX [1892], 149–150.)

The pilgrimage was the result of his international validity, and within its broad stream flowed the elements of piety, prestige, corruption, and material wealth. Aquitaine and Burgundy used the pilgrimage for their own benefit, with a view to the domination of Christian Spain.[23] The weakness of Alfonso VI, and the urgent need he felt to gain prestige for himself and his kingdom, made him a docile instrument of the policy of Cluny, which was also the agent of the imperial policy of the papacy. He first married Inez of Aquitaine (a reminder of the activities of Cluny as carried on by the duchy of Aquitaine and the kingdom of Navarre); then he married Constance, the daughter of the Duke of Burgundy. His sons-in-law, Henry and Raymond, belonged to the ducal house of Burgundy, just as did their relative, Abbot Hugh of Cluny. The death of Count Raymond, heir to Alfonso's throne, disturbed Cluny's plans with respect to Leon and Castile, plans that at that time were being concentrated on Portugal, a fief granted by Alfonso VI to his son-in-law, Count Henry. Thus, the independence of Portugal, arrived at by indirect but very clear routes, is inseparable from the cult that arose around Santiago.

With great acumen, Carolina Michaëlis de Vasconcellos and Teófilo Braga wrote that "only *events* made an independent state out of Portugal, and created little by little in her inhabitants the sense of being a separate people."[24] But now these events must be regarded in the indirect light shed upon them by the Apostle Santiago and Burgundian imperialism. The same motives that brought the Cluniac monks to establish their monasteries at strategic places along the route of the pilgrimage also brought Count Henry to Spain; for these same reasons he married Teresa, an illegitimate daughter of Alfonso VI, and thus he also received in fief the lands to the south of Galicia. Henry was annoyed to see the better luck of his cousin Raymond, married to the firstborn and legitimate daughter, Urraca; and there was serious friction between them, very harmful to the Cluniac policy. Abbot Hugh sent an emissary who obtained an agreement between both counts: upon the death of the king, the rich treasure of Toledo would be divided, two parts to go to Raymond and the

---

[23] The international interventions of the eleventh century must not be confused in kind with those of our own times, aimed merely at bringing about military and economic advantages. The people of the eleventh century lived in God and felt His power, just as today we feel the action of physical forces and are conscious of them. In the eleventh century there was no separation of the spiritual and the temporal; and the proportion in which values were assigned to each of those aspects of life, and the greater or lesser accent on each of them, introduced decisive differences among the peoples of Europe. It would be a mistake, then, to interpret the policy of the French religious orders as insincere maneuvering with the sole end of improving their financial situation. In the tenth, eleventh, and twelfth centuries, nothing in the human sphere was consciously opposed to the divine.

[24] *Geschichte der portugiesischen Literatur*, in Gröber's *Grundriss*, II, 2, p. 129.

rest to Henry, who would also receive the land of Toledo in fief, and if not Toledo, then Galicia.

The death of Raymond of Burgundy disarranged everything; the King died in 1109, and his widow, Urraca, occupied the throne for so long as it would take the child Alfonso VII to reach his majority. Many of the nobles feared lest a woman would not be able to face the dangers which beset Leon and Castile, and perhaps because they wanted to counter the French influences, they advised Urraca to marry King Alfonso I of Aragon—an excellent idea in theory, in which was already to be discerned the intention of uniting all the Christians of the Peninsula into a single kingdom. But the time for Ferdinand and Isabella had not yet arrived, and the marriage begot great disasters, for Alfonso I did not take possession of the kingdom; he devastated it like a cruel invader. The church of Santiago, the Cluniac monks, and the county of Portugal opposed the Aragonese.

We still know nothing of what lay beneath these events; but it is permissible to think that the chaos created by that intestine war was due to the impossibility of harmonizing the interests of the French clergy, the personality of Leon and Castile, and the violence of Alfonso I, who went so far as to kill with his own hands a Galician nobleman who was holding onto the skirts of Queen Urraca, a refuge considered inviolable. Such chaos was used to good advantage by Count Henry (d. 1112) and his widow Teresa, who had already assumed the title of queen in 1115 and thus soothed her feeling of inferiority in birth and rank to Queen Urraca, her half sister.[25] The French interests gained more supporters in the Portuguese county with the arrival of the Knights Templar and the Cistercian monks, just as closely allied with Burgundy as Cluny was. What decided the matter was that Henry and Teresa had as an heir Afonso Henriques, who from his youth showed excellent gifts as both a soldier and a ruler, gifts that were enhanced by the atmosphere of rebellion built up by his father and so well described in the chronicle of the archbishop Rodrigo Jiménez de Rada at the beginning of the thirteenth century:

Already in the lifetime of Alfonso VI, Count Henry of Burgundy began to rebel a little, although so long as the king lived, Henry did not withdraw his homage; he continued to do his best in throwing the Moors back from the border, but in the lands he retook, he kept the sovereignty for himself. In spite of this, he came with all his people when he was called to the aid of the royal army, or to attend at court. Alfonso VI, out of kindness, or rather out of weakness, tolerated Henry's moves toward independence because Henry was his son-in-law; and in this Alfonso showed great lack of foresight.[26]

---

[25] P. B. Gams, *Kirchengeschichte von Spanien* (1876), III, 64 ff.

[26] *De rebus Hispaniae*, VII, 5, in *Hispaniae Illustratae ... Scriptores Varii* (Francoforti, 1603), II, 114.

Such were the "events" that were at the roots of the independence of Portugal, and little by little they produced motives for her separation from Castile and Leon. Portugal was born as the result of the ambition of Count Henry, supported by Burgundy and Cluny, and by the weakness of Alfonso VI, this kind of thing being the very food of civil wars. Portugal was born and grew out of her will not to be Castile; to this fact she indubitably owes great accomplishments as well as certain wretched experiences.

Burgundy tried to bring about in Castile what the Normans had done in England some years before; that is, she tried to install a foreign dynasty. The struggles with Islam and Castilian vitality caused the project to miscarry, but they did not prevent the birth of a kingdom on the west side of the Peninsula. That kingdom did not arise out of its own existence—as happened in the Castile of Fernán González—but out of exterior ambitions. The proof of this is that the Hispano-Galician tradition of Portugal remained intact; the eloquent sign of this is the total lack of epic poetry. If the initial rebellion of the Portuguese had proceeded from the inner will of the people, as in Castile, Count Henry, or his son Afonso Henriques, would have been converted into epic themes. But the foreigners who came to populate the land were unable to create any kind of national epic, and the Galicians who came from the north went on being lyrical dreamers. Their will to fight came to them from the outside. The only poetic aureole surrounding Afonso Henriques is fitted to a model drawn from Galicia and Santiago: the victory of Ourique (1139), after which Alfonso was proclaimed king, took place on June 25, the feast of the Apostle; Christ himself appeared in the course of the battle, and left the imprint of his five wounds in the form of the five *quinas*[27] of the Portuguese coat of arms. Portugal came into being by struggling against Islam on her southern border (led and helped by northern European people) and against Castile with her rear guard. That little detached piece of Galicia developed the spirit of a besieged city which the Spain of Philip II with its grandeur among the clouds could not assimilate. The suspicion and resentment with which she regarded Castile were the emotional fires in which Portugal was forged, but she was born originally of the

---

[27] *Quinas* or "fives" is the popular designation of the Portuguese shield, so called because it consists of five shields arranged in the shape of a cross, with a cross made of five coins on each of the five shields. Father Juan de Mariana says in his history (X, 17) that some people believe "stulte scilicet et inaniter" ("no doubt foolishly and vainly") that the five small shields are the five wounds of Christ and not an allusion to the five banners of the five Moorish chieftains conquered at Ourique. In the Spanish version of his history, Mariana writes with more caution, and instead of "stulte scilicet et inaniter" he says "no sé si con fundamento bastante" ("I doubt whether with sufficient foundation"). Thus, in 1600, Father Mariana's critical reason expressed itself candidly in Latin, which few read, but not in the common language.

energetic impulse of Burgundy, Cluny, and the Knights Templar in
the eleventh and twelfth centuries. Lisbon was captured in 1147 by
an army made up largely of foreigners.

If my view regarding the origin of the Portuguese nation is to
be accepted as valid, it is necessary to put in abeyance, at least
temporarily, the way the Portuguese themselves feel about their
history. Vitally speaking, to be sure, the belief that Portugal was
already in existence before the twelfth century is not an error but
a fable like the one about Spain's origin which is favored by many
Spaniards. The belief that Portugal brought herself into being and
was not the result of forces external to her is part of the very existence of that nation. If the people who occupied the territory below
the Minho River had felt themselves to be an extension of Galicia,
Leon, and Andalusia, they would not, I daresay, have achieved their
wonderful discoveries, nor would we have the works of Gil Vicente,
Luis de Camoens, Eça de Queiroz, and many others.

The cold facts of Portugal's past are to the Portuguese nation as
the historically documented personage of the Cid is to the Cid of
literature. The legend of Portugal, which is of course as much a
part of Portuguese reality as the facts are, asks us to believe that the
region situated between the Minho and Douro rivers had, before
the twelfth century, certain peculiar characteristics betokening a
national self-awareness; the inhabitants were already looking toward
Lisbon and Santarém, still in Muslim hands, as a prolongation of
Portugal. But the cold fact is that what was to become Portugal
did not, before it came under the rule of Henry of Burgundy, possess a collective awareness that set it apart from Galicia and Leon.
The special geographical or prehistoric characteristics of a given
region do not necessarily imply the capacity for constituting a separate political state. Yet it is no less true that in failing to be objective,
the historical awareness of the early Portuguese produced an interpretation of the past which became a fruitful part of the authentic
history of the Portuguese people: to exist as a Portuguese consists,
among other things, in not feeling oneself to be an appendage of
Spain—from Spain, as a Portuguese proverb says, there comes neither
a good wind nor a good marriage. This dissociation impelled the Portuguese to increase their historical dimension backward in the past
and to seek imperial expansion. The heroic impulse that carried as
far as Hormuz and Malacca was but a part of the effort to find non-
Spanish national roots. The Spaniards, for their part, sank their roots
in Iberia to free themselves from the Judao-Islamic shadow.

According to certain historians, the people who dwelt between
the Minho and the Tagus in the eighth and ninth centuries already
displayed an attitude of expectation, waiting to become themselves,

that is, Portuguese. The *Annales Portugalenses veteres* (from the beginning of the twelfth century) mention the taking of Coria by Alfonso VI of Leon and Castile in 1077. Some would take this remark as evidence that the Portuguese of that time already believed that the town of Coria was "the key to the Tagus Valley, and certainly within their sphere of interest" (Pierre David, *Etudes historiques sur la Galice et le Portugal du VIe au XIIe siècle* [1947], p. 332).

Portugal, *finis terrae*, had always dreamed of escaping her narrow confines:

> The Lusitanian realm,
> Where the land ends and the sea begins.
>
> (*The Lusiads*, III, 20)

+ It is impossible to understand the formation of the immense Portuguese empire solely in terms of economic or statistical analysis. During the sixteenth, seventeenth, and eighteenth centuries, Portuguese was the linguistic vehicle that brought Western civilization to the East Indies (David Lopes, *A expansão da língua portuguesa no Oriente* [1936]). The Dutch, the English, and the Danes communicated with the indigenous population in that language, and Protestant missionaries were still spreading their gospel in Portuguese in 1800.

+ The expansionist energy of that people, counting few more than a
+ million inhabitants in the sixteenth century, surpasses measurement. The Portuguese preceded Castile in African and Atlantic enterprises;[28] by the years between 1427 and 1432, the Portuguese were
+ already established in the Azores. The Messianic and imperialist drive
+ of the Jews was as intense in Portugal as in Castile.

Spain and Portugal are not inwardly happy nations, and they never have been. To this inner disquietude shared with Spain, Portugal adds the resentful and therefore repressed awareness that her past has not been entirely her own. Portugal wanted and believed a history of her own, and she did this with such intensity that she was successful little by little in incorporating both an imagined history and the practice of imagining it into the process of her authentic existence. The imperial enterprises; the enduring imprint of Portugal in Brazil, in the East Indies, and in Africa; the imposing figures of Vasco da

---

[28] The enterprises were begun in the fourteenth century and finally carried through to a successful conclusion by Prince Henry the Navigator (1394–1460). For bibliography concerning this matter, see Fortunato de Almeida, *História de Portugal* (1924), II, 26 ff. The importance of the Portuguese efforts in Africa is properly appreciated in such works as the monumental *Anais de Arzila* by Bernardo Rodrigues, which covers the years 1508 to 1550 (ed. David Lopes [2 vols.; Lisbon, 1915–1919]); or in the *Chrónica do descobrimento e conquista de Guiné*, which was completed by Gomes Eannes de Azurara in 1448 (Viscount of Carreira ed. [Paris, 1841]). That the Portuguese still maintain their African colonies (Angola, Mozambique) is a natural projection of the national and international greatness of their past.

Gama, Afonso de Albuquerque, Ferdinand Magellan—all this and more have motivated the recreation of the origins of Portugal. Historical consciousness has transformed that which had no intrinsic value as objective reality into human poetic reality. A great novelist does not work differently.

But let us now examine the objective background of this great history. A Brazilian scholar describes it correctly:

The rebellion and independence [in the twelfth century] had meant the dismembering of the Hispano-Christian empire that was on the way to being established; and the existence of Portugal depended on her not accepting the Spanish imperialist ideas. Portuguese nationalism was a historical and moral position opposed to Spanish political ideology: the policy of Spain was to direct its forces centripetally; Portuguese policy, to find centrifugal moral and material forces that would provide it with a historical destiny outside the Spanish orbit. . . . Portugal found herself an illustrious past on the plane of universal history, but not within the perspective of Spanish history.[29]

In the twelfth century, the Portuguese structure of life was no different from the Galaico-Leonese; so the differentiation of Portugal from Leon could not consist in wishing to be, or in going on being, herself, but rather, in finding some way of not being like her relatives and neighbors. It is obvious, then, that the militant impetus and support for that Peninsular vivisection could not arise spontaneously from the Galician-speaking people who dwelt to the south of the Miño and were spreading out in the wake of victories achieved in the reconquest by Ferdinand I and Alfonso VI of Leon and Castile. The initial motivation of that rebellion does not lie in the proto-Portuguese character of the county that Alfonso VI granted Henry of Burgundy in fief, but in the fact that the count was a Burgundian. There is, of course, no trace of such reasons in the historical consciousness of the Portuguese, for if the kingdom of Lusitania was to exist at all, it had to forget its real origin. And this consciousness in turn created retroactively a belief in the primordial reality of Portugal. In the process of human history, children can give life to their fathers, as well as the other way around. That is why two apparently contradictory ways of understanding the origin of Portugal —my own and that of the Portuguese historians who opposed it—can both be true. I would say metaphorically that our conceptions of history became true and harmonious in an ideal space of multiple dimensions.

It is easy to understand why the origins of the kingdom of Portugal are veiled in legend and obscurity. It has not been possible to locate the Battle of Ourique (1139), the most important event in the Portuguese reconquest. The name of the defeated Moorish king is

---

[29] A. Soares Amora, *O Nobiliário do Conde D. Pedro* (São Paulo, 1948), p. 62.

equally unknown. The story of the taking of Santarém (1143) is found in an account that is by any critical standards apocryphal. Foreign participation in the reconquest of the land that eventually corner of Europe, although these foreigners bore the brunt of the came to be Portugal was both considerable and decisive. Of the reign of Afonso Henriques, the first Portuguese king (1128–1185), little is known. The Portuguese chronicles did not incorporate into their national history the activities of foreigners who came to that far war against the Moors, as did not happen in Spain, regardless of the number of foreigners present there.[30] The contemporary accounts of the conquest of Lisbon (1147) were composed by an Englishman and two Germans, and these left no doubt concerning the secondary role that fell to the Christians of the Peninsula in that enterprise.[31] When the city surrendered, "the name of the Franks was glorified in all Spain. . . . One of our own, Gilbert of Hastings, was chosen bishop of Lisbon with the consent of the king" (Alfredo Pimenta, *Fontes medievais da História de Portugal,* I, 122). In 1149 Afonso Henriques gave this bishop thirty-two houses: "xxxii domos cum omnibus suis hereditatibus ubicumque illas invenire potuerit."[32] The fleet engaged in the conquest of Lisbon had weighed anchor in England with 169 ships manned by Englishmen, Germans, Flemings, Frenchmen, and Gascons. The towers raised for the conquest of the city were the work of Flemings, Englishmen, and an engineer from Pisa. All the booty was for the foreigners, who, through a pact with the Moors, took for themselves the gold, the silver, the clothing, the horses, and the mules, and gave the city to the king: "Regi civitatem redderent" (*ibid.,* p. 129, 139). The chronicler of these international forces proudly writes that "the soldiers of the king of Spain [regis Hispaniae—he does not say Portugal] gave battle from a wooden tower," even though they were frightened by the Moor's missiles, until the Teutons came to their aid (donec Theutonici eis auxilio venerant). "When the Saracens saw the Lorrainese going up into the tower, such panic came over them that they gave up their arms" (*ibid.,* p. 132).

Information concerning the taking of Silves (1189) comes from a German writing in 1191. According to him, it was the foreign crusaders or adventurers who took the lead in the action (*ibid.,* 162–

---

[30] See Carolina Michaëlis de Vasconcellos, *Cancioneiro da Ajuda,* II, 692–698. The erroneous etymology of Portugal which was current in the fifteenth century is significant: "Portus Galliae." County Henry and his son Afonso Henriques gave many towns and lands to the Burgundians and the French.

[31] Alfredo Pimenta, *Fontes medievais da História de Portugal* (1948), I, 107–140.

[32] A. E. Reuter, *Documentos da chancelaria de Afonso Henriques* (Coimbra, 1938), p. 219.

163). And foreigners also participated in the taking of other cities—
Alcor and Alcácer.

The history of Portugal in the twelfth century is a tissue of shadows
and gaps. David Lopes, through his fortunate aquaintance with
Arabic sources, has added to our meager knowledge of Gerald the
Fearless (Geraldo Sem Pavor), a chieftain contemporary with
Afonso Henriques.[33] It was Gerald, not the king, who conquered
Trujillo, Evora, Cáceres, Montánchez, Juromenha, and Badajoz. Falling out with the king, Gerald went to Morocco, where the Moors,
fearing he would betray them, cut off his head. It is somewhat surprising that the Portuguese should compare this figure with the Castilian Cid merely because both personages became subjects of Moorish kings. But a great deal is known of the Cid, and of Gerald, very
little. The one served as subject for poetry in Latin and Romance,
whereas the other is remembered only in fragmentary Christian and
Arabic anecdotes. Besides, Gerald seems to be a foreigner judging
not only from his name but also from his epithet (Sem Pavor), which
seems French rather than Portuguese. In the middle of the tenth century, the third duke of Normandy was called "Richard Sans Peur."
From the little of his life that has come down to us, Gerald appears
to have helped the king on some occasions, and on others, not. His
loyalty to the monarch is not like that of Rodrigo Díaz, the Cid.
In any case, one wonders why neither the chronicles nor any other
documents have anything to say about such a prominent person, no
matter what his relations with the king may have been. Gerald was
very likely quite as foreign as the dynasty that founded the Portuguese kingdom and as the conquerors of Lisbon.

Transcending the bare reality of these facts, the Portuguese created
the work of art that is their history-life. They owed their independence from Leon and Castile to the fact that the lands to the south
of Galicia had been given to a Burgundian house at a time when the
Burgundians were the most dynamic and energetic people of Europe.
Against this foreign background there later developed a distinctive
national feeling though common traditions and geographical proximity ensured the preservation of numerous links with the rest of the
Peninsula.

It is futile for some foreigners to try to construct a history of
Portugal founded on geopolitics, on natural boundaries, on climate
and prehistory. In certain instances such attempts may flatter the
national *amour propre*, but such a result is obtained at the price of
muting all that which affects the "historifiable" level of a people, all
that which justifies devoting thought to it, valuing it, and distinguish-

---

[33] "O Cid português: Geraldo Sempavor," *Revista Portuguesa de História*, I
(1941), 93–104.

ing it from savage people who have no true history but who also
possess natural boundaries, economics, commerce, and the like. It is
our habit to term "scientific" those studies of history which are insensitive to all values that are not, almost literally, earthbound—as
if a student of footwear might deem worthy of interest only clogs
or rope-soled sandals. Any other approach is considered old-fashioned
bourgeois "mysticism."[34] But Portuguese life is a good deal more
than crops, river channels, and the boundaries of certain prehistoric
settlements.

Galicia, the older sister of Portugal—closely unified with Leon and
Castile by the bonds of the pilgrimage—remained the while in a state
of passive receptivity, enjoying the wealth attracted by the Apostle,
benefiting from the reflected homage paid by the masses of pilgrims
to the relic enshrined in Santiago. With such fury did the pilgrims
dispute the privilege of praying beside the sacred tomb that they
would sometimes kill each other, so that it would be necessary to
reconsecrate the church, a complicated ceremony which the pope
authorized to be simplified on account of the frequency of such disturbances. Galicia immobilized herself: doing nothing, she obtained
everything—visits from kings and magnates, luxury, the poetry of
troubadours, active trade, endless donations. The star clouds of the
Milky Way, through which galloped Santiago's charger, came down
and penetrated into the depths of the Galician soul. Missing the fer-
ment provided by the Templars and the Burgundians and not forced
to go outside himself to extend his land at the price of his blood, the
Galician did not become a conqueror like his Portuguese brother.
This is not to say that the Galician, beginning with his archbishops,
did not fight bravely in the army of the kings of Leon and Castile,
as he had once done against the Norman invaders. Clerics and knights
were present, and to their honor, in the major battles: Almeria, Cordova, Seville, Tarifa. But they always participated as *auxiliary* troops
of the king. Nor did the Galician language conquer new dominions
as Portuguese was doing, because Galician imperialism was receptive
and not aggressive, or, one might say, it consisted in irradiating the
prestige of the Apostle throughout all Christendom;[35] that prestige
kept alive the special characteristics peculiar to Galicia.

---

[34] In a recent important study of the city of Pisa "in the early Renaissance,"
everything is treated except "la grandeur intellectuelle et artistique de la cité
qui, avec Leonardo Fibonacci et Burgundio, donnait à l'Occident la science
arabe et le droit romain, et qui, dans les années même qu'il étudie, appelle sur
les chantiers du plus bel ensemble d'édifices religieux que jamais ville ait con-
struit, le rénovateur de la grande sculpture classique, Nicolas d'Apulie, dit
Nicolas Pisano, dont le nom n'est même pas prononcé" (Yves Renouard, in
Annales [Paris, 1962], no. 1, pp. 141–142).
[35] The apostolic prestige of Galicia did, however, lead to a wider use of
Galician, which was the language used in notarial documents in Zamora and

When the springs of foreign piety were exhausted, the Galician limited himself to spreading out over other lands, with gentle melancholy, the excess of his amorous and fecund population. For centuries Compostela, the lovely recluse, received flattery and homage worthy of Rome; yet such glory did not permit her to exercise an imperial Catholicity beyond her own walls, in spite of the fact that she possessed great dominions in the south of France, in Italy, and in other parts of Europe. The *antistes totius orbis* had no orb. He could not even gain for himself the primacy of *las Españas*.

The beliefs and customs prevailing from the ninth century to the seventeenth made the forms and the horizons of Galician life what they are. The constant proximity to the mysteries of the shrine gave rise to skepticism and irony; under the vault of the cathedral were heard songs that accentuated the "human, clever, licentious element."[36] Machiavelli noticed the contrast between the irreligiosity of Rome and the continued presence of the pontiff in the capital of the Christian world, and something like this happened in Galicia. To take the best advantage of the pilgrim demanded quick, sharp wits; in the end an antiheroic skepticism and a rare talent for political intrigue came to be dominant. The finest gifts of the Galician soul were concentrated in its prodigious lyric poetry, always atremble with disappointed melancholy; on the other hand, Galicia felt quite disinclined to cultivate the heroic epic or, later, the drama, genres in which Italy too showed no particular eminence. It is no accident, then, that Father Feijoo (1676–1764) was a Galician; his ironic spirit and his critical mind enabled him to go into battle against false miracles and popular superstitions with an energy proportional to the paralysis into which Galicia had fallen. The long Galician connection with Santiago was, then, much more essential for that region than the often claimed Celtic or Suevian character, both quite dubious. This looking back to remote Celtic or Suevian origins is just another aspect of the Spanish *vivir desviviéndose*. To the militant and imperious dimension of Castilian life, there corresponded in Galicia the lordly and spectacular dimension of the faith, as clearly evidenced by the grandeur and enormous vitality of Galician abbeys up to the nineteenth century.

Literature and Disorder

The primary stimulus for the monastic invasion of Spain was the holy war against Islam, of which, as I shall demonstrate later, other European peoples knew nothing through personal experience. Ru-

---

Salamanca as late as the beginning of the thirteenth century, and in the lyric poetry written by Alfonso the Learned and others.

[36] A. López Ferreiro, *Historia de la Iglesia de Santiago*, V, 369.

dolph Glaber (d. 1050) says that in the time of King Sancho of Navarre "the army was so scant that the monks of that region found themselves forced to take up arms."[37] The chronicler did not know that the motive for the monastic readiness to fight was not so much the reduced size of the army as the example of the Muslims, for among them the struggle with the infidel was very often associated with monasticism. In any event, the former statement is our first testimony concerning activities that two centuries later were to be organized in the form of military orders. It was already known in France that death incurred while fighting the Saracens opened the gates of paradise, as may be inferred from the vision of a holy monk described by Rudolph Glaber: "His church was invaded by a multitude that filled it completely; all were wearing white albs and red stoles. The bishop who led them said the mass and then explained that all had perished while fighting the sons of Hagar in Spain, and how, in the march to glory, they had stopped in that monastery (in *Patrologia*, vol. 142, col. 641). Without such visions, Archbishop Turpin would not have fought against the Saracens in the *Chanson de Roland*:

> Li arcevesque i fiert de sun espiet.   (1, 682)

Nor would he have sent the souls of all who died around him to heaven:

> Tutes vos anmes ait Deus li Glorius!
> En pareïs les metet en sentes flurs.   (2, 196–197)

Thus an air of wonder was built up around the land of the Apostle, to which, when all was said and done, came many more pilgrims than crusaders. Christian Europe lent feeble assistance to Spain, because Christ's sepulcher was not in Seville, and the road to Santiago's was cleared of the enemy. Only in poetry did Charlemagne fight to free it.

The liberality of the kings and of the lesser folk towards the Burgundian monasteries reached its maximum in the eleventh century with 375 gifts of land and populated villages; in the twelfth century the number of gifts went down to 138,[38] even though the influence of France continued to be intense; but Cluny was falling into decay, and the Cistercians, newly established, no longer made so much of an impression on the owners of land. The Abbey of Cîteaux, near Dijon, sprang up in 1098 under the protection of the Duke of Burgundy, and great was the success of the ascetic mysticism there, magnified by the glorious figure of Bernard de Clairvaux. Alfonso VII, forgetful of Cluny, concentrated his affections on the new

---

[37] "Historiarum libri quinque," in *Patrologia*, vol. 142, col. 640.
[38] Pérez de Urbel, *op. cit.*, II, 450.

white friars, whose monasteries spread profusely in the course of the twelfth century. The architectural marvels of Poblet in Catalonia, Las Huelgas in Burgos, and Alcobaça in Portugal stand out among them. Spain continued to be incapable of finding national forms in which to express her religious feeling, and she came out from under one Burgundian pressure only to go under another, very broad in scope but only slightly connected with the route of the pilgrims. Cluny was decaying along the road to Santiago, and thus I find an explanation for the clamorous propaganda initiated by those monks and centered in the falsification of the so-called *Codex Calixtinus*, attributed to Pope Calixtus II, Guido of Burgundy, brother of the Count Raymond known to us as Alfonso VI's son-in-law. One part of the famous manuscript refers directly to the Apostle and to the pilgrimage—sermons about Santiago, offices, liturgy, and a description of the road to Compostela, valuable as the first tourist's guide written in Europe.[39] This first part is really a *Book of Santiago*, less important in a literary way than its continuation, the *Chronicle of the Pseudo-Turpin*, containing a supposed history of Charlemagne and Roland. The fabulous account glorifies the Emperor for his conquest of Spain, and Roland as the hero of Roncevaux; it scarcely mentions Santiago, although the entire subject is related to places along the route of the pilgrims. I think that Bédier is right in connecting this chronicle with the road to Santiago, while C. Meredith-Jones has the idea that its object was to incite a crusade. But calling people to a crusade by glorifying events that took place along the *via francigena*—was this not the most effective propaganda? If those to whom the crusade was being preached were not attracted to the final goal of the crusade—that is, the fight against the infidel—they would at least go and visit the holy places that preserved the imprint of such glorious events. The *Chronicle of the Pseudo-Turpin* made use of the epic accounts of the Battle of Roncevaux, a place situated on the road to Santiago, for the purpose of propaganda.

But we would not exhaust the meaning of the eleventh and twelfth centuries in Spain if we presented them only as centuries under the yoke of Burgundian monasticism. This intervention was solicited by very Christian kings who were seeking a better relationship with God for their peoples through the free institution of monasticism rather than through the centralized hierarchy of the Church. There was no feeling of loss in this, for in the Kingdom of God there were no frontiers. On the other hand, Alfonso VI yielded unwillingly to the pressures of Pope Gregory VII, who forced him to institute the use of the Roman in place of the Mozarabic rite, finally supressed only

---

[39] Cf. C. Meredith-Jones, *Historia Karoli Magni et Rotholandi, ou Chronique du pseudo-Turpin* (Paris, 1936). See p. 43 of this work for the contents of the codex, and the abundant bibliography on pp. 353–357.

through the combined action of the Pope and the Cluniac monks.[40] Toward the monks themselves there was no resistance. Their mission, though taking a different direction, was analogous to that of the emigrant Mozarabs from the south: the filling of cultural voids in the Christian kingdoms through help from the outside, a tendency always visible to a greater or lesser degree in later centuries, including the twentieth.

This situation was due mainly to circumstances created by the Arabic occupation. Before the Arabs came, Visigothic Hispania had been linked to what was left of culture in the Mediterranean world; trade with Byzantine ships even went up the Spanish rivers as far as Merida, Cordova, and Saragossa. Hispano-Visigoths who had fled from the Saracen invasion evangelized important regions of Europe, and it was St. Pirminius who founded the monasteries of Reichenau and Murbach, whither he carried many codices rescued from Spain.[41] The land of St. Isidore and St. Eugene of Toledo played no mean role alongside the other fragments of the Roman Empire, as we have seen in chapter vi. But the "Spanishness" of Spanish history was to begin in the northwestern zone of the Peninsula, a region of little strength until it received support from the faith in Santiago, the Anti-Mohammed. The kingdoms of Leon and Castile put their faith in Santiago; and, thanks to them, Navarre, Aragon, and Catalonia were not an extension of France, as Catalonia had been at the beginning of the reconquest. Muslim writers called the Catalans "Franks" (as they were also called in the *Poema del Cid* in 1140), whereas the Christians of the north were "Galicians" to the same writers, a fact that is explainable by the great significance of the Christian "Mecca." Behind the Catalans stood the prestige of the Carolingian Empire, behind the rest of the Christians, that of the Galician Santiago. The

---

[40] The Cluniac monks were the first to call the attention of King Sancho the Great of Navarre to the peculiarity of the Mozarabic or Toledan rite; but the Roman rite was first introduced in Aragon, in the monastery of San Juan de la Peña, in 1071. In 1076 it was adopted in Navarre and in 1078, in Leon and Castile (P. Kehr, "Wie und wann wurde das Reich Aragon ein Lehen der römischen Kirche?" in *Sitzungsberichte der preussischen Akademie der Wissenschaften* [1926], pp. 204–208; Menéndez Pidal, *La España del Cid*, p. 239). Aragon became a feudatory state of the popes in order to protect herself from Castilian pressure; had it not been for the invasion of the Almorávides, Alfonso VI would have extended his domain as far as the Ebro River, and the small kingdom of Aragon would have been reduced to insignificance. The acceptance of papal protection, however, brought with it the adoption of the Roman rite and the religious policy of Cluny, which was the representative of the papacy and of European life. For their part, Castile and Leon could not remain isolated from European Christianity, or, in this instance, Cluny; the Mozarabic horizon—which is to say, the horizon of al-Andalus—began to turn toward Europe in the declining years of the eleventh century. We are still concerned here, consequently, with the complex of new religious, political, and economic problems created by the pilgrimage to Santiago.

[41] Pérez de Úrbel, *op. cit.*, I, 352, 527.

number of Galicians in Arabic Spain was not enough to blanket the memory of the Asturians and Leonese; but the Asturians and Leonese had no distinguishing feature that made them stand out, as had the Galicians. Spanish Navarre, for its part, was dangerously exposed to annexation by France, and did not belong entirely to Spain until Ferdinand the Catholic incorporated it into the kingdom.[42]

The Christians to the south of the Pyrenees gravitated toward France and were slow in opposing the Muslims, precisely because, as a result of its submission to the Carolingian Empire at the end of the eighth century, the sub-Pyrenean area of the Peninsula possessed a more "Occidental" way of life than did Galicia and Asturias. Nevertheless, it was among the Galicians and Asturians that the cohesive force arose with the necessary aptitude to give some sort of organization to the rude and divided Christians of the ninth century. With that force, the kingdom of Leon began to acquire political structure and an inciting ideal, militant and religious in character, strong enough to oppose a similar ideal possessed by the enemy. Through the monks from outside, the Christian caste was joined to the rest of Europe in a union made painful for the Castilian because it required him at one and the same time to affirm proudly his own way of life and to lament not becoming what he might have wished to be. This coming out of itself and then folding back upon its own self was the shuttlelike process of Spanish history. This process allowed Spain to submit to what was foreign without totally renouncing what was her own, whether good or bad. Such surrender was opposed by the energy of the Christian caste, an ultimate *quid* that must remain beyond the grasp of the historian, for it is as inexplicable as all other creative acts in a national life that merits consideration as history.

This process is already evident in the eleventh and twelfth centuries. Cluny and the Cistercians did not modify religiosity; they did not encourage the militant caste to give itself over to passive meditation, partly because they themselves rarely practiced that religious art in Spain. Almost from their beginnings, the monasteries of Cluny abounded in sterile controversies among the monks, the vassals, and the royal house, sterile in that no party came out of them with an advantage. Of all the foundations of the foreign orders, the abbey at Sahagún, chosen by Alfonso VI for his burial place, was perhaps the richest. Around the abbeys, towns grew up composed of people from everywhere, attracted by the wealth of the road to Santiago: "Gascons, Bretons, Germans, Englishmen, Burgundians, Normans, Tolosans, Provençals, Lombards, and many other tradesmen of divers

---

[42] Exaggerating a good deal, J. A. Brutails says: "The Navarre of the Middle Ages belongs perhaps more to France than to Spain" (*Documents des archives de la chambre des comptes de Navarre* [1890], p. ii).

nations and foreign tongues."[43] Such a list helps us to imagine something of the social conditions that prevailed and the type of life that went on along the road to Santiago. The abbot of Sahagún was lord over that amorphous multitude, which showed frequent disrespect toward the authority of the monastery. On the death of Alfonso VI (1109), the townspeople revolted tumultuously, and for a long time anarchy dominated the seigniory. Alfonso I of Aragon invaded Leon and Castile, and the religious community suffered a great many indignities. The rebellion broke out again later on, and this continued like an endemic disease until the thirteenth century. We are not interested here in the details but simply in observing how the original purpose of the coming of the monks—the organization of life around a spiritual principle—turned into a struggle between greedy parties in which each band aspired to take advantage of the wealth that had fallen into the lap of the other. "The townsmen of Sahagún made peaceful use of their trades, and carried on their business in great tranquillity; thus, they came and *brought with them from everywhere* goods of gold as well as silver and even many cloths of divers weaves, so that the townsmen and the dwellers there were very rich, and were provided with many pleasant things. But since offensive and harmful agitation and great arrogance and pride are likely to rule in the abundance and multiplication of temporal things, the hearts of the said townsmen began to swell up with pride, as usually happens when people of low birth and humble condition are given an excess of temporal things" (*Las crónicas anónimas de Sahagún*, ed. J. Puyol, p. 33). The throng of enriched merchants attacked the monastery, which by the mere fact that it was the target of such an attack showed that it had lost prestige and authority and that it was very much mixed up in "temporal things." The townsmen were joined by the peasants, who called their conspiracy a "brotherhood," a brotherhood that is the distant ancestor of what would one day be the Christian caste that arose against the Jewish caste—even at times against the royal power—and which was disciplined into an army by Ferdinand and Isabella. The brotherhood of Sahagún refused to pay its taxes and killed the Jews who were to be found in the neighborhood of the monastery—another antecedent of the massacres at the end of the fourteenth century—because the Spanish-Christian people has always found it extremely difficult to invent new forms of bourgeois authority, shared common life, and economy. In the frequent disturbances in Sahagún, the dominant spirit was demagoguery, a corollary of the excess of foreigners and of the shaky equilibrium among the castes. In those slaughters there was no discernible outline of the organization of a class of craftsmen, because the whole thing revolved

---

[43] *Las crónicas anónimas de Sahagún*, ed. J. Puyol, p. 32.

around wealth "brought in," not produced, and it fell prey to the greed of monks, merchants, the bourgeoisie, and the peasants. Neither did Sahagún forge for itself any form of intellectual culture. There remained the artistic beauty of the magnificent abbey, which later fell into ruin.

The internal situation of other Cluniac monasteries between 1259 and 1480 is well known, thanks to the documents published by Ulysse Robert.[44] In some of them, the abbots and friars lived with their mistresses and reared their children in the monastery; kings, great lords, and bishops, for their part, confiscated the monastic properties to increase their own wealth. All coveted the already existing wealth, but none was able to turn it into lasting benefits—and this, in turn, anticipates the futile confiscation of ecclesiastical properties in the nineteenth century, easy to justify, no doubt, but disastrous; for the state did not succeed in taking advantage of that wealth in either Spain or Spanish America, and many of the architectural and artistic treasures of the military orders and the Church fell into ruin or were dispersed. There had vanished from around Spanish Cluny that aura of faith which had caused Alfonso VI, calling himself Emperor of Spain, to donate to Cluny in 1079 the monastery of Santa María de Nájera, "juxta ipsam viam que ducit apud Sanctum Jacobum."[45]

Apogee and Decline of the Belief in Santiago

That disposition of life which I have called "theobiosis" (see above, p. 414), habit, and intertwined selfish interests kept the belief in the Apostle alive and beyond dispute until the beginning of the seventeenth century. It is outside my purpose here to relate the details of its vicissitudes, a task which, in any event, has already been performed admirably by A. López Ferreiro in the eleven volumes of his history and by the authors of the *Peregrinaciones a Santiago de Compostela* (see p. 381, n. 1). My desire now is only to indicate how exalted a rank the belief in Santiago held in the hierarchy of Spanish values. It is for this reason that I emphasize so strongly what the monarchs felt and said about it. Alfonso VII said that he had conquered Coria in 1147 with the help of Santiago: before he took Baeza, the Apostle's hand, grasping a fiery sword, appeared to him. The Apostle's efficacious zeal was repaid with offerings and solemn acts of homage; when Louis VII of France came to Castile because evil rumors were spreading that his wife (the daughter of Alfonso VII) was not a legitimate child, the best way to dissipate those doubts and put a seal upon the good accord existing between the two kings was to organize a pil-

---

[44] "Etat des monastères espagnols de l'ordre de Cluny aux XIIIe et XVe siècles," *Boletín de la Academia de la Historia*, XX (1892), 321–431.
[45] *Recueil des chartes de l'abbaye de Cluny*, IV, 666.

grimage to Compostela. Alfonso VII "and the kings Don Sancho and Don Fernando, his sons, and the king of [Spanish] Navarre" accompanied the French king; "the king and his sons showed such courtesies and such marvelous honors to the pilgrim king at each of the stations and vigils that he had to keep" that Louis VII returned to his own country filled with joy.[46]

In 1228 Alfonso IX of Leon said that on account of the "singular watch of the Apostle our kingdom and all of Spain still lives." In 1482 Isabella the Catholic called Santiago the "light and patron and guide of the kingdom of Spain,"[47] just as Alfonso VI had said earlier (see p. 417) that the "government of all Spain" was founded on Santiago. For such reasons the Catholic Sovereigns had a hospital built for pilgrims in Santiago which was of a beauty and grandeur unknown in Europe at that time.

The masses of the people continued to trust in their patron saint even in the sixteenth and seventeenth centuries,[48] although they were not always followed in their faith by a new social class unknown in the preceding centuries: certain learned writers—whose existence and activities are an expression of those circumstances I have called "conflictive"—maintained opinions in opposition to the traditions popular among the masses. The effect of their opinions on the belief in Santiago is examined later in this book; but for the moment we must dwell a little longer on what was happening in Compostela in the Middle Ages.

Belief in the *ex machina* power of the Apostle stimulated the mili-

---

[46] *Crónica General*, p. 657a.

[47] López Ferreiro, *op. cit.*, V, Appendix, p. 44; VII, 407. Santiago sometimes intervened in French victories, although in a different form. Philip Augustus told the prisoners captured at the Battle of Bouvines (1214) that not he but St. James, the patron of Liège, had conquered them (v, 80). The French king, like a good believer, thought that his victory was a punishment visited by God on the enemy because they had offended the patron of Liège. There may be an influence of the Spanish Santiago here, albeit reduced to purely spiritual limits. There is no visible miracle during the battle; the white charger does not gallop through the air above the armies; and, most important of all, Philip Augustus had not entrusted the direct administration of his nation to any saint.

[48] In 1535 Santiago appeared "visibly to the Spaniards, for they and the Indians saw him, riding on a beautiful white horse," according to Garcilaso the Inca in his *Comentarios reales*, II, ii, 24. In 1626 the general Don Diego Flores de León made a public deposition telling how, thanks to the Apostle, he conquered 7,000 Chilean Indians with only 260 Spaniards. In 1639 the Marquis of Flores-Dávila vanquished the whole army of Abdelcader in Oran with 500 Spaniards, thanks to the help of "a horseman dressed in a white waistcoat, armed with lance and shield, and riding on a horse" (López Ferreiro, *op. cit.*, IX, 319–321). Friar Vicente Palatino, to prove that the war against the American Indians was just, says that during one of Hernán Cortés' battles in Mexico, "a man on a white horse appeared, and slaughtered the Indians mightily, and his horse likewise destroyed them by biting and kicking them." If the war had been unjust, God would not have sent Santiago to fight on the side of the Spaniards ("Tratado de derecho y justicia de la guerra . . ." [1559], in L. Hanke and A. Millares, *Cuerpo de documentos del siglo XVI* [Mexico, 1943], p. 24).

tancy of Leon and Castile at a critical time and contributed effectively to reinforcing the awareness of political value, from the point of view of the Christian caste, of religious faith. Kings, clergy, and people could not realize that they had to do something to modify things around them while they were trusting in both the invincible sword of the Patron of Spain and in the value of an economy built on conquest and the spoils of battle. When the need for Santiago's help was not urgent, attention was directed toward the treasures that were collected through international piety, and which the kings exploited by having recourse now to cleverness and now to violence. Alfonso X was given what he demanded, although he was forced to declare that he demanded it "as a favor and not by right."[49] To be sure, the Learned King never went on a pilgrimage to Compostela; he was more interested in the cult of the Virgin—whom he exalts in his *Cantigas*—in accord with the new European sensibility of the thirteenth century. Alfonso X's indifference to Santiago (which no doubt explains López Ferreiro's lack of sympathy for the monarch) is due to a complicated variety of causes—above all, to a personal temperament that was more lyrical and intellectual than epic and bellicose, but perhaps also to the Jewish atmosphere of his court.

In the apostolic city there was a continual buzz of foreign tongues, and the multicolored spectacle of the milling crowd. Inside the church, kept open constantly, it was necessary to impose order on the mob of pilgrims who struggled violently to install themselves near the sacred tomb. The different national groups at times fought among themselves, as we have already seen, to enjoy the passionately coveted privilege, and it was not unusual for them to leave behind the germs of plagues that decimated the population. Princes, great lords, merchants, beggars, and sharpers,[50] in a milling jumble, adored

---

[49] López Ferreiro, *op. cit.*, V, 220. Alfonso VII subjected Archbishop Gelmírez to continued harassment (*ibid.*, IV, 208, 214).

[50] I think a large number of words having to do with the life of the rabble were introduced into Spanish through the pilgrimage: *arlote* ("idler"), *belitre* ("low, mean"), *bufón* ("buffoon"), *gallofero* ("vagabond"), *jaque* ("braggart"), *jerigonza* ("argot"), *ribaldo* ("ribald"), *pícaro*, *titerero* ("one who operates a puppet show"), *truhán* ("scoundrel"), and many others, from French or its dialects. Don Cristóbal Pérez de Herrera writes in 1598: "Eight or ten thousand Frenchmen and Gascons, who come [into Spain] to make pilgrimages through these realms, pass by the Hospice in Burgos every year and are given lodging and food there without pay, for two or three days. . . . It is said that in France eligible daughters are promised in dowery as much as can be amassed on a journey to Santiago and back, as if the men were going to the Indies instead of coming to Spain *with their gadgets and trinkets*" ("Discurso del amparo de los legítimos pobres," in Diego Clemencín, *Notas al Quijote*, II, 54). An echo of the beggars from southern France can still be heard in the Galician and Portuguese expression *andar à moina* ("beg alms"), from Gascon *moina*, Latin *eleemosyna* (H. Kahane and R. Kahane, in *Language*, XX [1944], 83–84). Moreover, ne'er-do-well outlaws were not the only foreigners for whom Galicia was a popular place of visitation. In 1541 Antonio de Guevara, the bishop of Mondo-

the Apostle and offered gifts, the protection and use of which became a great problem for the cardinal-canons. Each pilgrim received written testimony of his visit, and each brought the shell (*venera*), a symbol of the Apostle, whose sale constituted an important business for some fivescore merchants. Lodging for that unsettled mass of people, and the control of the riches that came in, kept clerics and laymen busy, and produced frequent conflicts between the Church and the townspeople. Then, too, there was the military activity of the clergy, who were forced to ride with the army when the king needed them, since the priest was at the same time a man of arms. Religious sentiment was thus intermingled with bureaucracy, military service, liturgy, law suits, and financial activities.

The archbishops tried to impose good customs by force of sanctions and external rules, but one can easily imagine how ineffective these were. For centuries the diocesan councils ordered the priests to use the tonsure, to dress as priests, and not to bear arms. In 1289 these orders were still without effect. The Council of 1289[51] forbade the clergy to wear beards, even—curiously enough—if they were young, or to wear clothing that was striped, green, or red; or to gamble with dice in public; or to participate with their arms in fights between soldiers and citizens; or to keep concubines publicly, either in their own houses or in those of other people. In addition, the priests were forbidden to practice sorcery, spells, prophecies, and divinations. The lack of a well-documented history of religious life in Spain makes it impossible to provide further details.

Although none of these practices was limited exclusively to the clergy of Compostela, one cannot help contrasting the divinity of the Apostle with the conduct of his nearest servants, conduct not attributable, as López Ferreiro so innocently puts it, to the "turbulence of the times"; for virtue has always been surrounded by turbulence. Resistance to the law was connected with the excessive predominance of a very special form of religion that was not interested in creating social bonds in the kingdom of this world. When conduct is not supported by internal-external criteria, those who are not saints are anarchists. The quality that is so inexactly called Spanish individualism (see chapter ix) is the residue of a history that was almost solely supported by the belief in the incalculable power of God and of the visionary and courageous human will. The principles from which authority emanated were too sublime and could not reach down to

---

ñedo, could still say "that many French clerics and others from other lands, and many monks from diverse orders pass through our bishopric, saying masses, and even being rectors of many churches. . . . Oftentimes the French clergy cannot be understood . . . and many of the native clerics of the dioceses do not have enough to eat because there are so many foreign ones" ("Constituciones sinodales," in R. Costes, *Antonio de Guevara, Sa vie* [1925], p. 62).

[51] López Ferreiro, *op. cit.*, V, Appendix, pp. 116, 235.

the point of shaping the prosaic task of hour-to-hour existence. But, returning to my central idea, if the Christian caste had not been inspired by the unifying stimuli of a yearning faith and a will toward empire, the reconquest of the Peninsula would have been carried out by foreigners, not by Spaniards, and there would have been no *Quixote*, no new countries whose language is Spanish, or many other things.

The pendulum oscillated in Santiago between submission to the procurers of heavenly favor, and chaotic and even criminal rebelliousness. During the civil quarrels between Peter the Cruel (d. 1369) and his brother Henry, Count of Trastámara, the archbishop, Don Suero de Toledo, rather inclined toward the latter; Henry was already lord of almost the entire kingdom, and his fief of Trastámara was located in Galicia. Fleeing from his brother, King Peter passed through Santiago in 1365, and gave the county of Trastámara, as a fief, to his friend and faithful vassal, Don Fernando de Castro; Don Fernando and the king being uncertain of the loyalty of the archbishop, decided to eliminate him. The king summoned the prelate, who had taken refuge in the castle of Rocha, and had him assassinated[52] as he approached the cathedral. The dean suffered the same fate, except that his ebbing strength allowed him to commend his soul to God at the altar of the Apostle.

After King Peter was assassinated by his brother Henry, Don Fernando de Castro continued to be powerful. The townsmen, taking his part against the church of Santiago, drove out the new archbishop, Don Rodrigo de Moscoso, who in turn placed the rebellious city under interdict. The spiritual sanction did not frighten the enraged citizens; they burst into the cathedral (Tuesday in Holy Week, April 1, 1371) and barred the doors of the cathedral treasury hall with iron, imprisoning the canons—called cardinals in Compostela—who had taken refuge there and forbidding them to have anything to eat or drink. The canons stayed there for nine days, and they came out alive only because their relatives got food to them behind the backs of their jailers.[53]

---

[52] Apart from any other consideration, the See of Compostela had to lean toward France in international politics: Henry was supported by the king of France; Peter, by the king of England. When King Peter assassinated the archbishop, he committed one more cruel deed, but he did eliminate a serious enemy, albeit too late for any advantage.

[53] One of the victims has left a poignant account in Galician of what happened: "E de mais foron buscar todos los outros coengos e personas que eran enna villa, a sus casas. E por forza trouxeron a o cardeal dom Afonso Pérez e a o cardeal dom Afonso Gonzáles ... e ensarraronnos con os outros enno dito Tesouro, e mandaron dar pregón por toda a villa que nihum non fose ousado de les dar pan nen vino, nen outra cousa ninhua. ... E alguus seus parentes e criados ascundudamente les davan vino e vianda por que se manteveron. E os vellos e fracos que non podian sair, ouveron de fazer enno dito Tesouro aquelo

When Henry II had made himself secure on the throne, he bestowed his love and gifts on the ill-treated church of Compostela with prodigality. López Ferreiro says that "it seems that Don Enrique [i.e., Henry II] sincerely believed that he owed a large part of his good fortune to the Apostle" (*Historia de la Iglesia de Santiago*, 198). The apostolic Church fared well or badly according as it was blown upon by the winds of belief or the gales of capital sins. Everyone lived in accidental groupings gathered around Santiago's fortuitous benefits, which frequently occasioned quarrels and disturbances. Santiago enjoyed pontifical splendor: The castle of Rocha, built in 1223, was an imitation of the castle of Santangelo in Rome, and the so-called cardinals were parish priests of the churches of the city, just like the cardinals of Rome. But even such glory afforded no protection against trouble.

The receipts of Santiago provided for everything, however, and the pilgrimages did not diminish until well into the seventeenth century. The kings, to be sure, no longer went to Santiago as they had done in the twelfth century, because the monarchy no longer needed the Apostle to conquer the Saracens, and the Spaniards of the Christian caste (see chapter iii) had come to view all aspects of human existence, all human endeavors, according to the criteria of faith. The primacy of faith and hope remained unchallenged, but their perspective was different. There was still the *plus ultra* but now it was the Spanish Empire, where one could be magnified as a churchman or as a conqueror; the feverish desire to become a hidalgo, to be pure of blood, bound the temporal and the eternal together, because, in the long run, to wait for graces rained down from heaven or to wait for the favors of fortune from all the Utopias amounted to the same thing.

Until the fifteenth century, roughly, belief was chiefly attached to Santiago (the only apostolic city in Spain was the one consecrated to him), though other guiding stars had already appeared next to him: the Virgin of Guadalupe in the province of Cáceres, for example (whose later appearance in Mexico gave rise to a cult which still possesses great vigor in that country).[54] In the long run, the belief origi-

---

que e necessario e se non pode escussar" (López Ferreiro, *op. cit.*, VI, Appendix, p. 142).

[54] In the sixteenth century, St. Joseph intervened in the public and official life of Mexico, just as Santiago had done before and the Virgin of Guadalupe was to do later, as may be seen in this ruling from a Mexican council: "Because the entire Commonwealth, in both its ecclesiastical and its secular constituency, has with great persistence begged us to order the keeping and celebrating of the feast of the glorious St. Joseph . . . and the receiving of him as the advocate and patron of this new Church, and especially for him to be the advocate and intercessor against tempests, thunder, lightning, and hail, with which this land is much afflicted," the Council of 1555 decided that St. Joseph should be the patron of the Mexican ecclesiastical province (*Concilios provinciales celebrados en la ciudad de México en 1555 y 1565* [Mexico, 1769], p. 67). The singular

nally attached to Santiago found new channels, even including faith
in the monarchy. This aspect of faith acquired Messianic overtones
and prestige in the time of the Catholic Sovereigns, while Philip II
was venerated almost as if he were a caliph. From the sixteenth century on, moreover, there is discernible a faith in the projection of
the individual, of his own personal valor (the valor that, in Quevedo
and Gracián, reached the status of almost divine myth). A man like
Alvar Núñez Cabeza de Vaca must have felt himself to be some sort
of superhuman force after having crossed the North American continent from Florida to the Pacific Coast and having subdued savage
Indians in all that region by no other means than his wits and valor.
It was the epoch of the cult of heroic leaders, *caudillos*, from Gonzalo
de Córdoba to Don Juan of Austria or the Duke of Osuna. The halo
of prestige that once shone from the heavenly captain, Santiago, now
rested over the human hero, who had been rare in the Middle Ages
(Fernán González, the Cid). Spain, in her own way in the sixteenth
century, began to exalt certain purely human values found in figures
of the triumphant caste. We are accustomed, in part for this reason,
to speak of this period as the Spanish Renaissance, but the accepted
meanings of the word Renaissance scarcely apply to what was happening in Spain.

The nationalization of the religious orders, already oblivious of
their French connections with Cluny and the Cistercians, contributed
to the displacement of the horizon formerly outlined by the rays
from Santiago. Once the wars within Spain were at an end, with
neither Moors nor Jews to convert or expel, the conquering religion
permeated the whole of social life, and overflowed its former banks
in the form of hundreds of thousands of monks and nuns, swarming
in cities, countryside, and villages. The Middle Ages had had recourse
to religion according as each individual had needed it; now religion
enveloped people like the air around them (see chapter ix) and had
been converted from an end in life to a means of livelihood. It was
the epoch in which religious hypocrisy, as a source of wealth, became
a subject for narrative and dramatic literature in the works of Quevedo and others (for example, Tirso de Molina's *Marta la piadosa*).

The innumerable monasteries and nunneries created a second Spain
inside Spain, and each order fought to spread its prestige and popu-
larity at the expense of others. Their founders (St. Augustine, St.
Dominic, St. Ignatius, etc.) came to be like spiritual monarchs who
bestowed the honors of nobility on each professing novice, and these
were indeed hidalgos in a divine fashion, an aspect doubtless of importance, because public opinion was shaped much more by religious

---

thing about this example is not the matter of belief, which can exist in any
place and at any time, but rather the high importance attached to it, and the
fact that it is treated in a public document as if it were a physical principle.

orders than by laymen, who were lacking a definite social structure
and especially lacking an organ of expression comparable to the pulpits, very similar in function to today's press and political forum. In
truth, there was none but sacred oratory. The pride of the orders in
their "nobility" was translated into a parochialism of the spirit which
split even further the already precarious unity of the inhabitants of
the Peninsula, who had no civil bond save the common reverence for
the person of the king, a reverence that, however, was not strong
enough to prevent the definitive separation of Portugal from Spain,
or to keep Catalonia from trying the same thing, or even to forestall
the signs of rebellion in Aragon in the seventeenth century.

In such a brittle, fragile society it was to be expected that the faith
in the invincible Apostle would not remain incorruptible. To understand this fact, it has been necessary to survey in the preceding pages
various aspects of Spanish society which at first glance might seem
unrelated to the belief in Santiago. By this time Madrid was the center
of Spain. Santiago was now far away and without any kind of economic tie with the kingdom. Writers of the first order, like the historian Father Juan de Mariana, denied his authenticity; Cervantes,
who spoke with trembling emotion of Paul the Apostle as "a knight
errant in life [but] a steadfast foot-soldier saint in death" (*Don
Quixote*, II, 58), could speak ironically of Santiago's unrelenting
"knight errantry." So weak did Santiago's dominion become that one
religious order rose up against him and tried to dethrone him; failing
to accomplish so much, it confronted him with a rival power, to share
his already diminished sovereignty. This is the significance of the fact
that the discalced, or reformed, Carmelites succeeded in persuading
King Philip III and the pope to establish St. Theresa, in a new and
unheard-of arrangement, as a copatron of Spain.

The country rose up as if it were a question that affected the existence of the whole kingdom. Pulpits trembled and tracts issued forth
in torrents.[55] The only one of these that has been reprinted is Quevedo's *Su espada por Santiago* ("His Sword for Santiago"), addressed
to Philip IV in 1628.[56] The disposition of Spanish life went on functioning in the seventeenth century as in the tenth. Life was grounded
in faith, and faith was the origin, directly or indirectly, of every activity. This did not preclude the possibilities of changes in the position of the believer with respect to his belief. There was no more land
in Spain to be reconquered to the cry "Santiago!" The gigantic bulk
of Spanish political institutions during the seventeenth century caused
the country to assume more of a bureaucratic than a military appear-

---

[55] Some of these are to be found in the library of the Hispanic Society of
America. Cf. Clara L. Penny, *A List of Books Printed 1601–1700*, pp. 624–626.

[56] In *Biblioteca de Autores Españoles*, XLVIII. The page numbers in parenthesis following subsequent quotations from this work refer to this edition.

ance. Even more numerous than the offices in charge of public affairs
were the churches, monasteries, convents, and other religious estab-
lishments occupied with spiritual matters.

The dispute between the partisans of Santiago and those of St. Theresa looked at times like the arguing of two legal adversaries. Although the opponents of the exclusive patronage of Santiago may not
have been rationalist skeptics (or even men who reasoned scientifically as Feijoo did in the eighteenth century), their criticism of the
efficacy in heaven of the Patron of Spain showed a tendency towards
rationalism: if the belief that Santiago fought on his horse above the
clouds had to be rejected, and if private judgment should be preferred
to traditional faith, then the way was open for other pious traditions
to be exploded by reason. The Spaniards of the seventeenth century
were neither willing nor able to run such a frightful risk. This is why
the vacuum that resulted when a belief was brought into question was
not filled (as was beginning to happen outside Spain) by rational
judgments concerning men and nature detached from ecclesiastical
guidance. In Spain, when a belief grew weak there were many others
ready to replace it. It is a corollary of this that the Spain of the seventeenth century should seem more "medieval" than does the Spain of
the fifteenth, although it would be meaningless to think of a seventeenth century more "reactionary" than the Middle Ages, for the
essential thing is not the age, but the people who are living each moment as they can and as it is given them to live. In Spain it was impossible to argue with no weapons save those of reason, a situation I
have attempted to explain in my book *De la edad conflictiva: El
drama de la honra* (Madrid: Taurus, 1963).

In 1550 the Spaniard had attained a zenith of glory by being what
he was. For centuries he had been the master of Moors and Jews who
had discovered and learned whatever could then be known. He had
benefited from European technical skills and their products, for
which he exchanged the magical powers of his Santiago. Then he had
discovered and taken possession of an immense empire, which yielded
incalculable riches. Once it had been accepted that intellectual activity was a Hispano-Judaic peculiarity, it was impossible for the
Spanish Christian to do other than to withdraw into the fortress of
the nobility (*hidalguía*) of the pure caste. It is understandable, therefore, why beliefs got out of control in the seventeenth century, in a
countercharge against the gesture to combat them, feeble as this may
have been; they were no longer expressed with that innocent simplicity of the eleventh and twelfth centuries, when even the possibility
of disputing them was not suspected. But in the seventeenth century
people did not breathe a "normal" air of belief but rather something
like an oxygen of faith; and this excessively tense situation has upset
many observers. Moreover, as I have already demonstrated, by the

time Christians, Moors, and Jews had ceased to live together in Spain, Spanish Catholicism had already absorbed the totalitarian religiosity characteristic of the Moors and the Jews.

The same thing that happened to religious beliefs happened to everything else—the monarchy, love, virtue, honor—all were galvanized in the seventeenth century with a view to self-defense. In a vital situation of this kind, belief and thought, desire and duty, illusion and disappointment, appear in a conflict that in Spain presents singular characteristics and values. In the seventeenth century life expresses itself in binary formulas, each of whose terms increases or decreases as an inverse function of the other. Thus it happens that the Carmelite friar, Gaspar de Santa María, a native of Granada, can say that if the body of Santiago were interred in Galicia, he could not have ridden into battle on horseback.[57] More than this, he laughs at those who believe that Santiago's horse causes the thunder with his hoofbeats; and since those who believe this are mostly common folk, he casts his ridicule in the mold of the popular speech of Granada:

> The thunder of the cloud,
> Says Johnny,
> Is made by our Santiago's horsey.
> (*El ruido que al tronar la nube suena,*
> *como dice* Juanico,
> *lo hace de Santiago el* caballico.)
> (*Biblioteca de Autores Españoles*, XLVIII, 456)

The grotesque poem in which these lines occur was written by Fray Gaspar in reply to Quevedo's *Su espada por Santiago*, which assails St. Theresa's copatronage of Spain. The Carmelite friar's poem is divided into a first part falsely attributed to Quevedo and then a reply to him. With perverse intention (full-fledged literary wars scarcely existed in Spain before the seventeenth century), Quevedo is made to say:

> Teresa, we know well
> Owes to Santiago the light she drinks
> For it is Santiago that brought light to Spain.

The rebuttal reads:

> But we should not say that she drinks light.
> Light that is drunk—I'll pay you with a gongorism,
> Is owed to Saint-Gin, and not to Saint-Jim.

---

57   El cuerpo de Santiago está en Galicia,
      que el orbe nos codicia;
      de donde *cierto infiero,*
      que no anduvo en las lides caballero.
      (The body of Santiago is in Galicia,
      which is the envy of the world;
      wherefore *I infer with certainty*
      that he did not go riding his horse into battles.)
      (*Biblioteca de Autores Españoles*, XLVIII, 453)

Or, as the passage goes in Spanish:

> Así Teresa, es cosa conocida
> Que a Santiago le debe,
> Pues que a España dió luz, la luz que bebe. . . .
> Mas decir no se debe
> Jamás que bebe luz: luz que se bebe
> (Con Góngora te pago),
> A *San-Trago* se debe, y no a *San-Tiago.*[58]

(pp. 451, 453)

The moment rational criticism is brought to bear on a matter of faith, faith is shattered. This is what happens to Santiago, whose name, symbolically, splits in two. The first part retains as it were a fragment of sanctity while the second merges grotesquely with the atmosphere of the tavern. Everything goes to pieces in life and in the mediocre poetry of the monk from Granada: He has faith in St. Theresa and he destroys Santiago with his reason; his true name is Gaspar de Santa María, and he uses the pseudonym Valerio Villavicencio; he divides his poem into two parts, of which he falsely attributes the first to Quevedo; and to cap it all, he cracks open the very name of Santiago so that he may split it into a *San* and a *Trago* (rather than *Iago*). This radical duality in both art and life in the seventeenth century—a characteristic I have been discussing for many years now—has as its base the breaking up of the compact unity of certain beliefs—ranging from Santiago to personal honor—which had hitherto never been questioned in Spain. In this century the awareness of the process I call *vivir desviviéndose*—in a sense a kind of construction by destruction—reaches a maximum intensity, and all literature is impregnated with it. In the sixteenth century, many things were censured, and especially practices and customs, but nothing was attacked by its roots. But seventeenth-century Spain, which owed so much to Santiago, renounced him, not through its ignorant masses, but through its clerics and theologians. Reacting against this, Quevedo writes things hard to believe, things I have before called ultramedieval:

> In the ancient annals and histories you will find that 4,700 open and decisive battles were fought in Spain against the Moors, counting the battles in Castile, Aragon, Portugal, and Navarre; you will find that 11,015,000 and some odd Moors died in these battles; you will find that the holy Apostle, *fighting personally and visibly, gave us victories and death to such numberless enemies.* (p. 439)

---

[58] The original Spanish poem turns upon a malicious pun, untranslatable, the purport of which may be grasped in the following literal version, only slightly worse in English than in Spanish.

Quevedo is made to say: "Since Santiago brought the light (of the Gospel) to Spain, it is manifest that Theresa owes to him the light she drinks."

The Carmelite replies: "But we should never say that Theresa drinks light: should she have drunk light, the light would come from a holy draught of wine (San-Trago) and not from Santiago (I take my cue from Góngora)."

Santiago's adversaries used their skepticism to try to destroy him, but not to build any kind of truth founded on rational thought; they limited themselves to killing one belief and replacing it with another, in an equally ultramedieval fashion. But once the advocates of the patronage of St. Theresa had found out how to destroy the rival belief by rational criticism, they could not forget what they had learned, and the new belief had to live in uncomfortably close quarters with rational weapons used to combat its enemy. The patronage of St. Theresa rose out of the dying embers of the belief in Santiago, in what appeared to be a patronal duality, and as such, highly characteristic of the seventeenth-century style of life, for it integrated the *no* and the *yes* of the rejection of Santiago and the affirmation of Theresa. In the same way, the hordes of political medicine men that devised one fantastic scheme after another to solve the problems of the kingdom believed in the schemes because they had lost faith in the efficacy of the king and his government. And once started, this process continued. A symbol and expression of the life that was simultaneously possible and impossible was the play on words, the pun, the rejection of words that expressed the elementary experience of everyone ("table," *mesa*), in favor of metaphors ("squared pine," *cuadrado pino*) that would endow the ordinary references with a new and striking content—as Góngora does. Or else, the writer destroys belief in the reality of things, suffocating them under the shroud of nothingness—as the nihilists Quevedo and Gracián prefer to do. And, as we shall see later, the themes of Arabic literature continued to exist in the seventeenth-century Spanish literature alongside the now familiar despairing attitude of the Jews.

The conflict that at its inception was a tension between the worldliness of the cathedral chapter at Compostela and the shining star of the warrior-Apostle—an earth unmanageable and a heaven unattainable—now unfolds in the broader terms of the life that is impossible and possible at one and the same time. It seems to me a misguided abstraction to relate the schism between illusions and daily life experienced in seventeenth-century Spain only to contemporary circumstances in the rest of Europe, such as the special situation created by the Council of Trent. Those things we call the Renaissance, the Counter-Reformation, or the baroque were lived by the Spaniards from within their own existence, and this existence was established on a base of extremely peculiar habits, tasks, and interests. If we forget this, we shall reduce the history of the Spanish seventeenth century to an abstract international pattern. One day we shall have to view the problem of what is called Mannerism and the baroque from the standpoint that these and other like cultural phenomena express concrete vital situations—at the same time that they are imitations, frequently artistically dead, of expressive forms that have already been socially accredited on a national or international basis. Considered in themselves alone, as abstract and generic entities, such terms as Renaissance, Mannerism, and baroque create nothing, nor do they explain anything worthy of the historian's attention and respect.

Quevedo, a Knight of Santiago, felt that he was being reduced to the status of a commoner when he saw how Spain's great patron was being snatched away from him only to be sacrificed to the ideal of the Carmelites, who, in Quevedo's opinion, were weak and effeminate. "How can the fathers of the Reformed Order [the Discalced Carmelites] expect Santiago to give you arms [he is addressing the king], and then beg you to turn them against him; how can they beseech you to find your own sword at his altar, and then ask you to take the sword he holds in his hand and give it to St. Theresa, whose very children have had her depicted with a spinning-wheel?" (p. 443). Quevedo had toppled all values; the world around him seemed like a tapestry turned wrong side out; but he clung to his cult of bravery and boldness, the only railings his unsteady soul[59] could lean upon as it looked into the abyss of nothingness. He disposed of institutions, persons, and things with one gigantic, sarcastic epitaph, but he sprang up like a tiger when anyone probed at the foundations of his *castizo* nobility, the foundations of the ultimate reason for his existence. Thus it was that he defended the prestige of the Apostle with absurd statistics about battles and deaths in a way that would have been inconceivable in he twelfth and thirteenth centuries, when for the Leonese and the Castilians their faith was as natural as the air they breathed.

With this contrast in mind, one can sense very distinctly the situation of the Spaniard of the seventeenth century: he could not overcome his belief by means of rational analysis and confidence in the useful efficacy of that process, and yet he could not go on living within the belief with the same security as before, because critical thought had begun to triumph in other European countries. Wherefore the frenetic efforts to "rationalize" the belief and make it tangible through the search for relics and miracles, efforts that were more abundant than ever in the seventeenth century; wherefore also the extreme styles—Quevedo, Góngora, Gracián—the beautiful projection of existences without inner repose that floated over a human vacuum and lacked ideas or "things" on which they might rest. Noth-

---

[59] "Not missing on the road [to hell] were *many* ecclesiastics, *many* theologians. I saw *some* soldiers, but *few*; for along the other path [the one leading to paradise], *infinite numbers* were going in *ordered file, glorious in their triumphant honor*" (*El sueño del infierno*). For Quevedo all is chaos, save the order created by valor, which stimulates him to literary expression of exalted nobility in which he ceases to present a skeptical grimace. The words "ordered file" reveal the only earthly value in which he truly believed and in which his anguished existence could affirm itself.

ing could now change the Hispanic condition and the immense interests created by it. By the time Cervantes appeared, it was useless for him to prefer St. Paul and to treat Santiago ironically, just as it was for Father Mariana to label as old wives' tales the accounts of the hoofbeats of Santiago's white charger or the stories of Christ's wounds on the Portuguese shield. All this was a trifling gesture without consequences; people tenaciously went on believing that the issues of life were decided in heaven, where, indeed, there was to be found a special secretariat for Hispanic affairs: "She is a good sister [St. Theresa] and therefore loves Spain; *as its business representative in heaven, in payment of her wages, she asks for the honor of being the patron saint*" (p. 437). The Saint required that her services be paid for with the honor of being the patroness of Spain, as Quevedo puts it in a sentence that is notable for the mixture of commercial jargon (*librar gajes*, "to pay wages") with the language of a faith that defied quantitative measurement.

The whole affair was debated as in a case at law. The partisans of St. Theresa said: "If we look at this claim according to the style of lawsuits, which, for our sins, it is . . . ," and "so long as she cease not her intercessions, the kingdom cannot fail to reserve for her the name of patroness" (p. 435). To this Quevedo replies: "Christ wished that only his *cousin* should be the patron" (p. 435), wherein there is still a residue of the faith in the Apostle on account of his relationship with Jesus. Now he is a cousin; formerly he was a brother. In the face of such a claim, the Carmelites brought up strong arguments: No one could say how long King Philip II would have remained in purgatory if Theresa of Avila had not gotten him out of there on the eighth day, "because it would not have taken a fantastic imagination to think that he was supposed to have a long sojourn in purgatory" (p. 438). This was written thirty years after Philip II's death, by a Carmelite from an aristocratic family—so that we can add here one more voice to the chorus of those dissatisfied with the person and policy of the Prudent King (see p. 335, n. 22). But this is to digress. What is interesting is that the intimate details of purgatory should be dealt with here so plainly, as if there were postal service between this visible world and the next. (It is not surprising that Baltasar Gracián read from the pulpit a letter that came from hell itself.) Certain clergy, moreover, were of the opinion that St. Theresa ought to be preferred because she was a woman and God would have to grant her petitions, "or Christ himself would blush with shame to see her denied" (p. 445).

At the time when Santiago was the true star by which Spain guided her fortunes, the visible and operative society was in all respects masculine. In the seventeenth century, society was an all-encompassing entity, and within its scope women had made their presence felt as an active theme in life and art. Gallantry as a literary motif in the novel and the theater is a sign of the social character love had acquired. Nunneries were the "divine" counterpart of European salons, and nuns on earth or saints in glory (María de Agreda, Juana Inés de la Cruz, St. Theresa) were to Spain or to Mexico what Madame de Rambouillet and Madame de Sévigné were to France. It made no difference whether the ladies dwelt in glory or on earth: "If there is any saint—man or woman—known today who has won hearts through bewitching charm, it is St. Theresa" (p. 436). It is therefore not surprising that St. Theresa was on the point of officially sharing the supervision of Hispanic affairs in the other world with Santiago. Pope Paul V, at the insistence of the Carmelites and King Philip III, had declared St. Theresa copatron of Spain in 1618, but the majority persisted in their devotion to Santiago: there was a greater sympathy for the attitude of the soldier than for the attitude of mystic contemplation. In spite of popular feeling, Philip IV, more a man of letters than of arms, joined the partisans of Theresa, and brought about the Pope's confirmation of the copatronage. One might say, without the slightest intention of impropriety, that the salons favored Theresa and the people favored the Apostle. The force of popular tradition prevailed against the King. In 1627, Pope Urban VIII revised the earlier brief and left the clergy and the people free to accept or reject the copatronage of Theresa,[60] with the result that her equality of status with Santiago became a reality in the Carmelite monasteries and virtually nowhere else. As late as 1812, the Cortes (Parliament) of Cadiz incorporated the copatronage of the two saints into their legislation, and their decree was still legally in force during the reign of Isabella II, dethroned in 1868. Whatever the reason, there still subsisted in nineteenth-century Spain traces of the religious structure of the state, of that mixed Occidental and Oriental religiosity that we have seen to be characteristic of the Spaniards.

Although Santiago ceased to attract attention, St. Theresa did not replace him as a national figure; and the conflict between the ideal of the soldier incarnate in the Apostle and the longing for feminine tenderness were eventually harmonized in the cult of the Virgin of the Column (Virgen del Pilar), in which are to be found reminiscences of the militant divinity of the "son of thunder."[61] In 1808 this

---

[60] This brief (dated July 21, 1627) says that the Saint may continue to be patroness, "sine tamen praeiuditio, aut innouatione, vel diminutione aliqua Patronatus sancti Jacobi Apostoli in universa Hispaniarum regna." I cite from the first page of the brief, of which I possess a copy most kindly sent to me by Don Fermín Bouza Brey.

[61] The Virgin of Guadalupe (in Estremadura) was also a center from which Hispanic energy radiated. Cortés and Pizarro, also from Estremadura, were

Saragossan Virgin acted as "captain of the Aragonese troops" against the French invaders, and in the twentieth century her image was granted the "honors of a captain-general"—a feeble and belated spark from the warrior cults, of which the antecedents are by now familiar to the reader. In these cults are revealed the structural functioning of Spanish life.

It is pertinent at this point to make one further observation concerning Quevedo's little treatise *Su espada por Santiago*. Quevedo was the first Spanish chronicler of current events, and the currency of the events derived in this instance from the fact that feelings previously locked in the subconscious had emerged into public discussion, because Spanish life had acquired a social dimension due, in part, to the volume acquired by the public "opinion" that created and destroyed an individual's caste purity. Material circumstances, such as the absence of war against the Moors, did not provide the only basis for the Santiago crisis. It was also a consequence of the change of direction that took place in religion in the second half of the sixteenth century, thanks to the mysticism of St. Theresa and St. John of the Cross, who pointed out for the first time, or at least for the first time in the supreme form that was theirs, the way of religious inwardness. Remote and hidden currents of Islamic spirituality came to the surface of life and mingled with currents flowing from other kinds of foreign mysticism.

But extraordinary as it was, the mysticism of the sixteenth century was ephemeral and, in volume, meager, and not only because it had to submit to the repressions of the Church and the Inquisition. In this as in other instances, it is undoubtedly more fruitful to look for the explanations of history in the authentic preferences of a people rather than in the obstacles that may have hindered the expression of these preferences (after all, if the Spaniards had truly preferred not to have the Inquisition, they would have suppressed it). Not only Quevedo but also the religious orders disliked the reforms of the Carmelites, who cultivated solitude with God and practiced manual labor, as the Hieronymites had done in the fourteenth century.[62] Living by manual labor was plebeian and, in the final analysis, an activity proper to Moors and Jews but as repugnant to a Knight of Santiago as to a mendicant friar. These Carmelites, opposed to mendicancy, were the people who advanced the cause of St. Theresa as copatron. Their mystic religiosity provoked the disdain of Quevedo,

---

much indebted to her. In Mexico, shortly after the Spanish conquest, there appeared an image of the Virgin which was also given the name of Guadalupe. The priest Hidalgo began his rebellion against the Spanish regime in 1810 carrying as his standard an image of the Virgin of Guadalupe.

[62] It was Portuguese Hieronymites who hand-printed the translation of the mystic Henry Herpius, *Espelho de perfeiçao* (Coimbra, 1535).

who says that before Theresa "this kind of prayer had been treated of in Spain" by Gómez García in his book *Carro de dos vidas* (Seville, 1500). "There is nothing at all in this book except discussions of mystical theology: rapture, ecstasy, visions, internal unions, in a compilation of everything written by such saints and learned authors as Richard [of St. Victor] and St. Bonaventure" (p. 448). His polemical intent and the frequent aridity of his soul concealed the values in Theresa's work from Quevedo; but the lack of comprehension displayed by the Franciscan order is surprising, for it should have looked with more favor on any form of divine love. However, the order's tradition of mendicancy and its popular roots turned it against the Carmelites. The Franciscans scornfully referred to the Carmelites' claim that they worked diligently and were reviving the rigorous life "without any burden to the community, but rather with much benefit to it, because *they must work and earn their bread with their hands.* . . . Since this appeared to have the blessing of heaven, they were allowed to establish foundations; and looms and other tools for doing honest work that would earn bread were installed in the convents." The project failed, as the superior general of the Franciscans happily affirms: "If some part of it was carried out, that lasted but a few days; look now at the multitude of convents that have been founded by this reformed order, and see whether they are only in deserted places, and whether they live from the labor of their hands, and whether they beg for alms and have income from rents" (p. 447).

Around the year 1600 the Carmelites were trying to do what the Brethren of the Common Life, in Flanders, and then the Spanish Hieronymites had been doing since the fourteenth century, that is, to give themselves over to divine contemplation and the cultivation of honest craftsmanship, for social ends. The superior general of the Franciscans indicated the failure of the Carmelites, and in my *Aspectos del vivir hispánico* (Santiago, Chile, 1949) I have pointed out that the Hieronymites also failed to produce lasting results. The Hispano-Christian disposition of life rejected serene contemplation as well as manual labor, both of which, I repeat, were practiced openly by the Sufistic Muslims in their own way. The Carmelites had been reformed by St. John of the Cross, whose mystic vocabulary translates in certain essential respects the vocabulary of Ibn 'Abbād of Ronda (see above, p. 217). In the seventeenth century St. John's order was seeking to integrate physical with spiritual enterprises, and it is precisely his order that reacts against Santiago's militant spirit and makes a plea for the loving, "charming" protection of the Saint of Avila. But the effect of this plea on Spanish sensibilities was slight. Like the other efforts that have run counter to deeply rooted inclinations, this one amounted to nothing more than a gesture. In repressing the progress of spirituality of the inward kind, the Inquisition was in harmony with the firmly established preferences of the triumphant caste.

The violent polemic (a far cry from the *pax Domini*) over the question of a single or dual patronage for Spain confirms the idea that Santiago is an essential ingredient of Hispanic history. Quevedo felt this with a lively intensity: "God made him patron of Spain, *which no longer existed*, against the time when, through his intercession, his teaching, and his sword, *Spain should once again exist*" (p. 445). "Everything is owed" to Santiago (p. 438). To this militant and political conception, the Carmelites opposed the claim that "before Theresa very little had been known" about God (p. 449). Thus, a pragmatic and activist conception of the divine clashed with the experience of God in pure contemplation. Between the absolute alternatives of militant activism and the passive mendicant life, no room was left for diligent labor, for the intellectual concern with "things," as much the works of God as were the words of Holy Writ.

I have not sought to write a history of Santiago of Galicia in the usual sense but to understand the phenomenon as a response to Mohammedan aggressiveness, just as the fact that those who were once "Roman-Goths" came to call themselves "Christians" was due to the domination by Muslims of what had formerly been Hispano-Roman-Gothic territory. Belief strengthened the fighting impulse and made it efficacious, whereas both intellectual and practical work were made difficult. When the belief fell into decay in the seventeenth century, no kind of earthly impulse could replace it, once the other two castes had been exterminated. Since that time the Spaniard has lived questioning himself ever more sharply about the validity of a past that isolated Spain ever more radically in each succeeding period from the life of other peoples, whose life was constantly being renewed. With a clear awareness of his collective dimensions, the Spaniard has lived in the tension created by simultaneous impulses toward progress and regression. A number of people have thought it desirable to revive the sociopolitical program of Ferdinand and Isabella—a chimera that did not lend itself to rational analysis and was finally converted into another "belief." In the eighteenth century the enormous task of rectifying the course of collective life was begun, and as a result there appeared works and men of extraordinary importance in various fields, from Feijoo and Jovellanos to Goya and the group of scientists and scholars whose names honor the reign of Charles III. The process of *vivir desviviéndose*, of a life constantly torn between affirmation and denial, continued to stimulate the efforts of superior people.

This long and tortuous process now becomes comprehensible once the authentic history of the Spaniards has been firmly grounded on the reality, unique in Europe, of its three castes. The phenomenon of

Santiago has allowed us to see the two faces of the first centuries of the reconquest: one turned both toward and away from the Islam of al-Andalus; the other, directed toward European Christianity. The coming of the Cluniac monks in the eleventh century and the Cistercians in the twelfth was instigated by the kings and nobles of the Christian caste, a group that was clearly delimited by its religious faith. While the historian's vision has been directed by the abstract fantasy that "the Spaniards"—as an apparently homogeneous body— did such and such a thing, it has not been possible to perceive the peculiar form taken by the cultural action of European Christianity on the Hispano-Christians of the eleventh and twelfth centuries. Even though it was well known that the kings and their nobles practiced private customs and carried on public activities which reveal a complex of Christian, Islamic, and Judaic origins (clothing, baths, city life, building methods and architectural forms, the ways of collecting taxes, etc.), opinions about eleventh- and twelfth-century life have been formulated as if so odd a situation had not existed. But here we have before our eyes the epitaphs on the tomb of Ferdinand the Holy (see above, p. 60) as an enduring testimonial to how those circumstances affected the feelings and thoughts of "the Spaniards" of three faiths; therein is revealed the inner functioning of the opinions and scale of values held by Spaniards with respect to the possible harmony or antagonism among the three castes.

The fact that the Christian caste was not much interested in cultivating the learning of other European Christians may be noted immediately in the scant attention paid to literature in Latin, whereas from Italy to Scandinavia much emphasis was placed upon it, as, indeed, had happened in Visigothic Hispania. The cultural renascence fostered by Cluny and the Cistercians (or by the secular clergy) affected vernacular literature (for example, the *mester de clerecía*) and, in a very special way, Romanesque art—a subject that has recently been treated in masterful fashion by Juan Antonio Gaya Nuño.[63] He finds that the southern half of Spain is linked by its architecture to the Oriental culture that had entered Spain by way of Africa: "The mosques and their minarets, the patios filled with orange trees, the Moorish palaces, the *casbah* with its narrow little streets lined by whitewashed buildings . . . I accept with pride all this African element in our southern Spain," as well as "the glorious hybrid Mudejar style. . . . But at the same time I boast that the other half of Spain, the northern part, should be Romanesque and European" ("Teoría del románico español," *Boletín de la Universidad Com-*

---

[63] "Teoría del románico español," *Boletín de la Universidad Compostelana* (Santiago de Compostela) (1960), pp. 77–93.

postelana [1960], (p. 83). In "the great Spain of that twelfth century, which was so European, so attentive to the most modern conquests of an international and highly original plastic art," it was possible for a small Galician, Catalan, or Castilian village "to adopt . . . aesthetic forms that were triumphing at that very moment in other small villages in Wales, Champagne, or the Palatinate" (*ibid.*, 85–86). "The most homogeneous possible Spain was forged then, and in the shelter of this great art" (*ibid.*, 86). This was indeed so, though I would add that this homogeneity did not Europeanize the *mind* of the Christian caste, despite the fact that the forms of artistic expression to be found throughout all northern Spain were in harmony with the contemporary art of the rest of Europe (as even those who are little versed in art history could recognize at the international exposition of Romanesque art in Barcelona in 1961). It should be taken into account, on the other hand, that in the north of Spain in the twelfth century, foreign monks and clerics, especially French, were abundant.

Nevertheless, it is still true that the religious feelings expressed in those monuments did not function in Spain as they did in other "Romanic" countries likewise affected by the Cluniac spirit of "catholicity" and ecclesiastical imperialism. In the rest of Europe, between the eleventh and the twelfth centuries, there began to spring up amid the thick growth of monkish theology a type of thought which was secularly oriented. Around 1100 an anonymous ecclesiastic composed some bold treatises in York (England) which tended to invalidate the idea of papal supremacy represented by Cluny and Gregory VII. John Wyclif read and absorbed these writings several centuries later; but even if they had been ignored, at the time of their composition, they represented an energetic protest against the doctrine that the state should be subordinate to the Church. Furthermore, they are, I believe, related to the naturalist and scientific tendencies of such Englishmen as Roger Bacon and of other Europeans who were interested in utilizing the occult powers of nature and in discovering the divine order in them. From that natural order, which is the work of God, the "Anonymus Eboracensis" deduces that priests should marry because *fecunditas* and *virginitas* are all the same to God. In addition, he places the king above the priest, since the consecration given to the king is for him alone, whereas the priest is consecrated only as the member of a group.[64]

The struggles between the papacy and the Empire were contemporaneous with the great diffusion of Romanesque art in Europe, with the beginnings of what would become secular instruction in

---

[64] The treatises cited may be found in the *Libelli de Lite Regum et Pontificum, Monumenta Germaniae Historica*. See Brackmann, *op. cit.*, pp. 36 ff.

the universities, and especially, with the thought that inspired the teaching: "Credo ut intelligam" (Anselm of Canterbury). Manifestations of this secular spirit appear even before the end of the eleventh century; in my opinion, secular tendencies lie behind the autonomous decision by the king of France that he and his successors would possess the grace of curing scrofula (see above, p. 430).

The Romanesque churches from Galicia to Catalonia, both the magnificent and the humble ones, were like spiritual fortresses—advance bastions designed to protect the dominant faith against two opposed religious creeds. The Christian Gonzalo de Berceo (thirteenth century) expresses a similar attitude of wariness, this time on the part of the Jews, in a famous watch song in which the Jews gathered around Christ's sepulcher sing to each other that they must be vigilant against the theft of Christ's body from them:

> Keep watch, O Jewish community,
>   oh, keep watch!
> that they may not steal from you the Son of God.
> (*Velat, aljama de los judíos,*
>   *¡eya velar!*
> *que non vos furten ei Fijo de Dios.*)
>
>   (*Duelo de la Virgen*)

The Cluniac monks and the Cistercians were called by the kings, not only to perform a purely sacerdotal function, but also to take over the ministry of spiritual crusades. The trail of Romanesque churches left by their religious action (direct or indirect) is the visible sign of the Christians' steadfast will that the Moors and Jews should not snatch from them the basis of their collective identity, both political and social. As Gaya Nuño acutely suggests, the Romanesque monuments carried on what might be called a dialogue with the people: "In the towns many church porticos provided" a center in which "the Church of the time wisely offered a meeting place, shelter, sun, shade, conversation, and an agreeable atmosphere to the citizens." "If at times [their sculptures and bas-reliefs] showed forth the iconography of the Old and New Testaments, at other times they were limited to scenes . . . of normal daily life. . . . This partial secularization of an art that in its origins was religious was of considerable importance in the success it achieved" (*op. cit.*, pp. 86–87).

So, indeed, the figurative element in Romanesque art was partially secularized; but from the roots of that Romanesque religiosity there did not spring intellectual and critical activities like those found in the rest of Europe. It has, thus, once more been demonstrated that each cultural phenomenon, when viewed as a living reality, depends much less on geography and economy than on the functioning of the dwelling place of life within which it exists; it may undergo modifications before it becomes an enterprise suitable to the new structural functioning. In the northern half of the Peninsula, the whole complex of European Romanesque culture was not treated or managed with the same vitality as in Italy or Scandinavia, where, in the eleventh and twelfth centuries, people were forging their own dwelling places of life (which today appear as eminently worthy subjects of history) in their own peculiar and unique fashion. There is only one form of Italian or Scandinavian—or Spanish—life.

XII · THE ISLAMIC PERSPECTIVE OF
THREE CHRISTIAN INSTITUTIONS

Military Orders

Between the twelfth and fifteenth centuries, the powerful orders of Calatrava, Santiago, and Alcántara occupy the foreground of history as a military and political force. In them may be glimpsed the first outlines of the future permanent army of Ferdinand and Isabella. They had their origin in the religiosity, at once spiritual and warlike, of the Christian caste. In the fourteenth century their character was already more political than religious, and their extensive properties gave them a power that at times dwarfed that of the king and gave rise to frequent internecine wars that retarded the progress of the reconquest. In some instances, the knights commanders of the orders tyrannized the towns of their commanderies, and thus fostered not only hatred between the people and the nobility but also a kind of unproductive particularism. In the fifteenth century—perhaps the only period in which the nobility fully sensed its mission of guidance—a few of the grand masters of the orders were distinguished by their interest in culture and left noteworthy imprints on the spiritual aspects of religion, on scholarship, and on literature. (Thanks to the protection of the nobility, the cultural activities of a considerable number of members of the Hebrew caste were made possible.) Their economic hegemony lasted till the dawn of the nineteenth century, and even in our own day their colorful uniforms have ornamented the ceremonies of the court, as the decorative feature of an aristocracy that has long since lost any authentic role in society. Spain's noble class was both unwilling and unable to preserve from ruin the marvelous shrines of Calatrava and Uclés, seats of the ancient grand masters. Like many other reflections of the past, the orders, to use the words of Quevedo, had for a long time been nothing more than "a word and an empty form."[1]

---

[1] Calatrava—church, monastery, and castle—was demolished in 1804. M. Danvila writes in 1888: "The outcries of good citizens have not kept neglect and

We have no adequate history of the military orders, in spite of the fact that there are many documents extant pertaining to them. Not having access to these materials, I am interested at present only in what may have a bearing on the relations between Islam and the Christian kingdoms. The dominant notion today is that the Spanish orders grew up as a replica of the Hospitalers and Templars of France, established in Spain in the twelfth century.[2] In the face of this assertion, a few Spanish Arabists of the twentieth century have thought that the beginnings of the Spanish orders are to be sought in Islam.[3] But long before them José Antonio Conde, in his *Historia de la dominación de los árabes en España* ([Madrid, 1820], I, p. 619), had said: "The military orders both in Spain as well as among the Eastern Christians came out of these *morabitos.*" No one, however, paid any attention to Conde's theory. For my part, I think that the problem would be badly posed if we thought that we had to choose between the European and the Muslim origin, since the orders of the Hospitalers and the Templars would be incomprehensible without the Oriental model, a matter to which modern books on the Templars make no reference.[4] One must keep clearly in view the fact that only in the Muslim world is the life of rigorous asceticism fused with the life of combat against the infidel. On this point the thesis of Miguel Asín Palacios is irrefutable. It is no matter of chance, then, that the orders in question were born in the twelfth century in lands that were Christian outposts against Islam—Palestine and Spain—and not someplace else. The Templars, "pauperi commilitones Christi," started out by protecting the pilgrims from the attacks of the infidels along the routes to Jerusalem, and before them the Hospitalers had busied themselves with the care of the poor and sick who got to the Holy City. But amongst the Muslims "charitable and beneficent work (caring for the poor, the sick, and the leprous, acting as ser-

---

bad weather from bringing about the disappearance of the last remains of Calatrava" (*Boletín de la Academia de la Historia*, XII [1888], 125). The monastery and the best parts of the town of Uclés were deserted and fell into decay in the middle of the nineteenth century. The archives and the library almost disappeared. In 1860 a commission of archivists was sent "literally to disinter the books and papers from the midst of saltpeter and filth of every kind" (J. M. Escudero de la Peña, in *Boletín de la Academia de la Historia*, XV [1889], 308–309).

[2] See, for example, H. Prutz, *Entwicklung und Untergang des Tempelsherrenordens* (1888), p. 8: "Ein Seitenstück bietet der Ritterorden von S. Jago." The same thing comes up in J. Piquet, *Les Templiers: Etude de leurs opérations financières* (1939): "Les Ordres du Temple et de l'Hôpital excitaient une grande jalousie en Espagne, car la plupart der Frères étaient des étrangers; aussi la tendence fut-elle à la création d'Ordres militaires nationaux" (p. 234).

[3] J. Oliver Asín, *Origen árabe de "rebato, arrobda" y sus homónimos* (1927). According to Miguel Asín Palacios, "the *ribāṭ* is the exact model of the military orders" (*Islam cristianizado*, pp. 137, 141).

[4] See, for example, G. A. Campbell, *The Knights Templars* (1937).

vants to the spiritual leaders, etc.) had occupied the lives of not a few ascetics [for centuries], although these people were not given a distinguishing name based on their profession; on the other hand, those who practiced jointly the devout and the military life, defending the frontiers in monasteries that were at the same time barracks (*ribāṭs, rápitas*), were called 'almorávides' " (*Islam cristianizado*, p. 141).[5]

One cannot, by taking an exclusively Christian point of view, understand how the practice of ascetic discipline and military action can be reconciled in the same person—just as the Bible alone provides no key to the understanding of Santiago *Matamoros*. The Church, it is well known, has always frowned on the idea that priests should kill human beings (for that reason, the Inquisition somewhat disingenuously handed over its victims to the secular authorities for execution). The Muslims, on the other hand, and centuries before the military orders appeared, had the institution of the *ribāṭ* (singular, *rābiṭa*), or hermitages "in which the 'almorávides,' that is, the holy men who alternated between asceticism and the defense of the borders, lived in retirement." Thus it is that *ribāṭ* also means "holy war, especially defensive holy war," and that in Spain and Portugal there are so many places named *Rábida, Rápita*, and the like. From *ribāṭ*, as J. Oliver Asín has shown, come the words *rebato* ("sudden, unexpected attack; alarm; fit of passion"), and *arrebatar* ("to snatch away," etc.), and the old *arrobda* ("advanced guard"). The adoption of such words presupposes the prior existence of the things they signify.[6] If, then, we look at the matter from the other side of the borders of Christendom, the birth of the military orders seems extremely natural, just as it should seem in the highly Islamized Spain of the twelfth century (where an Apostle of Christ devoted himself to decapitating infidels). Nor, by the same token, should it be surprising to find that in the *Poema del Cid* (1140) Bishop Jerome—not

---

[5] Miguel Asín Palacios, *Vidas de santones andaluces*, p. 157, translates the biography of Abūl-l-'Abbās Aḥmad b. Hammām as it is related by Ibn 'Arabī in his "Epistle of Holiness": He was very fervent. He continually moaned for the health of his soul, like a mother who has lost her only son. One day he said to Ibn 'Arabī: "What I shall do is betake me to the frontiers of Islam, to the front lines of the enemy, and in some one of the *rábidas* there I shall consecrate myself to the holy war till I die." He did in fact go away to one of the frontiers, to a place called Juromenha (in Portugal), where he took up his residence until, sometime later, he returned to Seville, gathered up the things he needed for his new way of life as a warrior-monk. This happened at the end of the twelfth century, although such examples had been common in Islam for a long time.

[6] "The multiplication of *rābitas* in Spain, and their possible confusion with *ribāṭ*, are connected with the great movement of mystic piety which, starting in Persia, had brought about the substitution of monasteries—*khānaka* in the east, *zāwia* in Barbary—for the foundations more military than religious, of the heroic age of Islam" (G. Marçais, in *Encyclopedia of Islam, s.v.* "ribāṭ").

a legendary figure like Turpin in the *Chanson de Roland*, but a historical personage—fights fiercely in the vanguard of the Christians. Furthermore, as has been noted in the discussion of Santiago, the type of the warrior-bishop which appears in the medieval French epic probably has to be included in the same oriental current, which it would be absurd to try to limit to Spain in those centuries. In *Le Jeu de Saint Nicolas*, by Jean Bodel (end of twelfth century), an angel appears to the Christians in the battle and says: "You will be destroyed fighting in the service of God, but you will receive the crown of glory." In France the feelings that inspired the holy war most certainly disappeared with the crusades, whereas in Spain they were still alive in the sixteenth century. When it was discovered in 1568 that the Moors in Granada had revolted, "even the friars in the Monastery of St. Francis left their cells and came out into the square armed." Later, at a critical moment for the village of Dúrcal (in the Alpujarras), "there appeared eight religious, four Franciscan friars and four Jesuits, saying that they wished to die for Jesus Christ, since the soldiers did not dare to do so; but the captain, Gonzalo de Alcántara, did not consent to this" (Luis del Mármol, *Rebelión y castigo de los moriscos de Granada*, Book V, chap. 2).

Now let us see how those at the pinnacle of twelfth-century spiritual Christianity, that is to say, in the Abbey of Clairvaux, reacted to this Islamic innovation. The first master of the Order of the Knights Templar, Hugh of Paynes, came from Jerusalem to France to obtain the approval of the new order, and with this objective he went to his friend, the future St. Bernard, then the abbot of Clairvaux, the most influential person in Christendom—who, it was said, named popes and yet renounced the office for himself. Hugh sought to persuade the Abbot to lend support of his pen to the creation of that strange institution, whose rule was finally approved by the Council of Troyes (1128). This was the motive behind St. Bernard's celebrated sermon "De laude novae militiae," in response to repeated requests from the new master: "Three times, if I do not mistake, have you beseeched me, my beloved Hugh, to write for you and your companions in arms a sermon that would raise your spirits."[7] Hugh had to beg the Abbot three times, then, to write in favor of the Templars, and St. Bernard remained undecided, waiting for someone to do it better than he, for fear that his support of the new institution would be adjudged an ill-considered act of temerity ("sed ne levis praecepsque culparetur assensio"). Ultimately he decided to write the sermon because, apparently, the new order needed to be defended and explained. All this reveals that crusaders returning to

---

[7] J. P. Migne, *Patrologia*, S.L., vol. 182, col. 921 ff.: "Semel, et secundo, et tertio, ni fallor, petiisti a me, Hugo charissime, ut tibi tuisque commilitonibus scriberem exhortationis sermonem."

Europe from Palestine were bringing back a novelty that was discordant with the Christian tradition: "A new kind of militia, of which nothing was known until now" ("Novum inquam militiae genus, et saeculis inexpertum").[8] St. Bernard lets himself be carried away by enthusiasm for the holy war, which Christendom had received from Islam by injection, as it were: "How gloriously they return from the battle! How blessedly do they perish in it like martyrs!" ("Quam gloriosi revertuntur victores de proelio! quam beati moriuntur martyres in proelio!"). His enthusiasm was strange indeed, for according to St. Bernard, it was not even lawful to kill another man in self-defense: "It is a lesser evil to lose the body than the spirit" ("De duobus malis, in corpore quam in anima levius sit"). But for the new knights, the defense of God was authority for everything "because their war is God's war, and they need have no fear either of the sin of killing the enemy or of the risk of their own death" ("proeliantur proelia Domini sui, nequaquam metuentes aut de hostium casde peccatum, aut de sua nece periculum").

This is the way European Christendom was penetrated by a doctrine and certain habits that had been familiar to Islam for centuries, although they were novel and unheard of for the French monks of Cîteaux and Cluny. To give oneself over to contemplative ascesis and to spill the blood of the enemy were compatible activities for the Muslim, bcause in him the distance between the corporeal and the spiritual, between the mundane and the divine, was obliterated. The most contradictory attitudes are thus integrated in the vital unity of the person. And just as there could be a harmony between the strictest piety and bloody warfare, so there were mystic sects that abandoned themselves to the love of God by means of contemplating a "présence charnelle," feeling an ecstatic pleasure in the presence of "la beauté d'un jeune visage admiré."[9] This harmony between opposing values, something contradictory according to Christian principles, became accessible in Jerusalem to all who were affected by a strange and splendid culture, whose modes of curious spirituality were adopted, just as its ways of living were imitated. King Baldwin I dressed like an Oriental, and in his customs, ceremonies, and pomp, he resembled a Muslim monarch. This fact is well known, because it is a visible and tangible phenomenon; but there has been an unwillingness to see that the mixture of religious piety and bloody violence was like an Oriental garment for the Christian spirit. Although he ended by being enthusiastic, Bernard de Clairvaux's astonishment

---

[8] Apropos of this, the editors of the *Patrologia* quote a passage from a letter of Peter the Venerable, abbot of Cluny (1156): "Quis non laetetur, quis non exsultet, processisse vos, non ad simplicem, sed ad *duplicem* conflictum. Estis monachi virtutibus, milites actibus."

[9] L. Massignon, *La passion d'Al-Hallaj*, p. 798. Asín, Palacios, *Islam cristianizado*, p. 327.

nevertheless gives a measure of the great distance that separated the new military orders from the Christian conception of life. If the Templars were accepted and if they subsequently accumulated incalculable riches, this was because only those knights were devoted to a continuous and regular struggle for the possession of the Holy Places, where the dominion of the Christians was more than insecure. So insecure was it that with the fall of St. John of Acre toward the end of the thirteenth century, the entire undertaking of the crusades collapsed, and with it, the *raison d'être* of the Templars. They had begun as a pseudomorphosis of the Almorávides, the holy warriors of Islam. In spite of such an origin, they soon came under the influence of that aspect of French life that was more sensuous than ascetic, and the order was transformed into a banking society which for nearly two centuries made commercial traffic possible between Europe and the Orient.[10] History expresses the interaction between a special form of collective life and certain changing but very concrete circumstances. The Templars were converted into the bankers of the kings and were almost completely "desanctified." When Christian rule disappeared from Palestine, King Philip the Fair of France got the pope to dissolve the order, appropriated its immense riches, and, to secure his title to the property, ordered the grand master and many of his knights, first to be subjected to exquisite tortures and then to be burned at the stake (1310–1314).

This means that at the beginning of the fourteenth century the French monarchy was already able to rid itself of an annoying competitor, in this case an organization whose main power resided in its religious character rather than its military strength, estimated at some 15,000 men. Alongside these material and immediate causes, there must be kept in mind a strange quality in the Templars' religiosity. This religiosity in no way resembled that of the other orders, against which the power and envy of the civil authority still remained ineffectual. There was something in the Templars that was incompatible with French life, and a sign of this is the legend about their incontinence and their heresies. Their bellicose piety was tolerated so long as they lived in Palestine; but when they were forced to live once more in the country of their origin, the conflict became patent between church and war, between spirituality and profane business transactions—opposites that could no longer be integrated in the rationalized life of France, where a banker was a banker and a religious was a religious. They had lost their mythic halo and showed only their naked reality, open to the cupidity of the great and the resentment and disrespect of the lowly. They could not keep from

---

[10] Cf. Piquet, *op. cit.*

disappearing, even though, as the victims of a sadistic and covetous Inquisition, they may inspire our pity.

The incompatibility of the Order of the Templars with the neat separation of heaven and earth, faith and reason, characteristic of French life, serves as a reference point for understanding by contrast the prolonged splendor of the military orders in Spain. There, as in Palestine, the *Almorávides* of the *rábidas* made converts. The orders of Calatrava, Santiago, and Alcántara were constituted in the second half of the twelfth century, during the reigns of Sancho III and Alfonso VIII of Castile; and, indeed, it is more than likely that before that time there had been Christian ascetics who included the slaying of Moors among their pious duties. Thus we can see why it is that the origin of these Spanish orders is concealed in a certain chronological vagueness, a fact that in no way contradicts the idea that the Templars furnished an example for the organization of the Spanish warrior-ascetics into regular communities.[11] Let us recall briefly the known facts. The orders of the Hospitalers and the Templars spread over the Christian kingdoms in the first third of the twelfth century, especially in Aragon and Catalonia. They were given castles, towns, vassals, and lands in recognition of the services they had rendered in the war against the infidels. Their prestige reached its highest point when, in 1134, Alfonso I of Aragon named as heirs to his kingdom the Knights of the Holy Sepulcher, the Hospitalers, and the Templars. If this act expresses on the one hand the ardent spirit of religious reconquest which animated the monarch, on the other it reveals how weak the political personality of Aragon still was in 1134. Aragon, Navarre, and Catalonia, connected in so many way, were less united politically at that time than were Castile, Leon, and Galicia. The ceding of Aragon to the military orders was both a sign of exalted religious faith and an expression of little confidence in the solidarity of the Aragonese monarchy. As might have been expected, the will of Alfonso the Warrior could not be carried out, for he was actually succeeded on the throne by Ramiro II, called the Monk. Alfonso I had beclouded the boundaries between heaven and earth in his testament; perhaps by that illusory solution to his kingdom's problems he was compensating for very real discouragements and disappointments.

The Templars also benefited from the munificence of the kings of Castile, although to a lesser degree. When Alfonso VII captured the town of Calatrava (Ciudad Real), he charged the Order of the

---

[11] This suggests a comparison with what happened in the fourteenth century to the religious of the Spanish Order of the Hieronymites, who for a period of time impossible to determine, lived dispersed, as hermits, until their rule was approved by the Pope in 1373.

Knights Templar with its defense—proof that there still did not exist in Castile any organized militia of that character.[12] Ten years later the Templars declared themselves unable to hold that key position on the frontier against the Moors, and they informed King Sancho III that "they could not attack against the great power of the Arabs, . . . for they were not adequately equipped to stand against them. Moreover, the King himself had not found any among the great men of Castile that would dare to face the danger of that place" (*Crónica General*, p. 666). Two monks, Raimundo de Fitero and Diego Veláz-quez, offered themselves to the King for the defense of Calatrava, and raised a large army for that purpose. Out of this crusade came the Order of Calatrava. But let us note rather the example that its two founders presented: one a monk to begin with, Raimundo de Fitero, who threw himself into the fight against the infidel; the other Diego Velázquez, a former knight who became a monk and as such entered the same struggle. This was probably not the first instance in which this happened, even though documents may be lacking to prove that it happened before.[13]

The orders of Santiago and Alcántara appear to have been or-ganized about this same time, a fact that lends support to the idea that their institutional model was the Franco-Islamic Order of the Templars. In the face of such a complicated set of circumstances, I would venture to suggest that if the Spanish orders did indeed owe the manner in which they were organized to the example of the Templars, the substance that made their existence possible was Hispano-Islamic.[14] What would have otherwise been the disorganized action of guerrilla fighters for the faith, crystallized into a regular force, recognized by the civil authority. I do not believe that the Knights Templars could have inspired the asceticism and heroism displayed by the first knights of Calatrava at precisely the moment when the Templars were abandoning their difficult position on the frontier in 1158, whatever the reasons may have been for their with-drawal. I insist again that the fight against the Moor in Spain did not need to be especially organized in order to present the combination of heroic warfare and an extreme devotion to the faith, a phenomenon

---

[12] At the same time, the King entrusted the government of the conquered fortress to Rabbi Juda, son of the illustrious Rabbi Josef ben Ezra. Fidel Fita conjectured that the Templars accepted this authority because of their Masonry and certain Jewish rites performed in the course of their initiation (*Boletín de la Academia de la Historia*, XIV [1889], 267). But the reason behind such co-operation lies in the bonds established among the castes and in the tolerance so habitual in the Christian kingdoms.

[13] The date of the first mention of the order is 1158, when Sancho III gives Calatrava to Raimundo de Fitero, "ut defendatis eam a paganis inimicis crucis Christi," and to whom in the future might be, "vestri ordinis et ibi Deo servire voluerint" (*España sagrada*, L, 413).

[14] For another example of Spanish *matter* and foreign *form*, see above, p. 346.

that must have occurred in a disorganized way at every turn. It might be presumed, then, that the primitive organization of the Knights of Calatrava, far from arising as a jealous emulation of the Templars' might, may have been rather the reaction of militant asceticism against an instant of faintheartedness on the part of the foreign institution. This in no way denies that the economic and political structure of the Spanish orders had as its model the precedent of the Templars—beginning with the name of the head, *maestre* ("master"), which is a gallicism. A Christian-Islamic substance was remolded in the French form.

Muslim tradition and the immediate example of the Templars took on a peculiarly Castilian meaning in the military orders. Belief, the warrior spirit, and the prestige of the monarchy are expressed conjointly in a single passage of *De rebus Hispaniae*, a chronicle penned by the archbishop Rodrigo Jiménez de Rada (1180?–1247), and in the version of this Latin text incorporated in the *Crónica General*. The beauty and meaning of these passages have hitherto passed unnoticed. In Jiménez de Rada we can see clearly the most authentic dimensions of Castilian existence and of its cultural possibilities. He wrote decent Latin, he knew Arabic and took advantage of this knowledge in his historical works, he was educated in Bologna and Paris, he ruled the Spanish Church from the primatial see in Toledo, and in his best days he fought for his faith and his king on the greatest occasion to mark the centuries-old struggle between the Christians and the Moors, that is, in the decisive Battle of Las Navas de Tolosa (1212), won by Alfonso VIII. The Archbishop was an aristocratic Castilian who had refined his culture, thanks to contacts with Islam and Christian Europe.[15]

Through almost the entirety of *De rebus Hispaniae* the style is simply narrative and devoid of poetic intention. But in the treatment of the great deeds of Alfonso VIII, the king most admired by Jiménez de Rada, the prose becomes consciously artistic; parallelism and a kind of rhyme become features of the sentences:

> In manu robusta vastavit eos [the Moors],
> et in cordis magnificentia coegit eos;
> succendit ignibus civitates,
> et succidit viridia deliciarum;
> replevit terram timore suo,
> conclusit Arabes adventu suo.

---

[15] To help Alfonso VIII in his war against the Almohades, people came to Toledo "from many lands and different in their customs, their ways of dressing, and their tongues; and *because it pleased the king*, the Archbishop of Toledo [i.e., Don Rodrigo Jiménez de Rada], resided there in those days, so that through his wisdom the discord among the differing peoples might be eased" (*Crónica General*, p. 689a).

Once Cuenca, the city situated among jagged rocks, was taken,

> rupes eius factae sunt perviae,
> et aspera eius in planicies.[16]

The same kind of prose continues to the end of the chapter. The version in the *Crónica General* reads thus:

> And he destroyed them with strong hand,
> and he reduced them with the magnitude of his heart;
> he burned their cities and their other dwellings,
> he cut down their orchards and the places where they
> found their delights and took their pleasures.[17]

The Latin text recalls the parallelism of certain passages in the Bible:

> Halitus eius prunas ardere facit,
> et flamma de ore eius aggreditus.
>
> (Job 41:12)

And English readers will recognize the verbal echoes of the passage made familiar by Handel's *Messiah*: "Prepare ye the way of the Lord, make straight in the desert a highway for our God. Every valley shall be exalted, and every mountain and hill shall be made low: and the crooked shall be made straight, and the rough places plain" (Isaiah 40:3–4). In the Vulgate, however, the rhythmic correspondence between the beginnings of the phrases as well as between their endings is lacking.

But what is of special interest is the heightening of the poetic tension in the chapter that follows in *De rebus Hispaniae* (VII, 27), the title of which is "Item de magnalibus et piis operibus nobilis Aldephonsi" ("About the great and pious deeds of the noble King Alfonsus"). It has as its theme, albeit in prose, a real piece of poetry, a canticle to the military orders and to the foundation of the commandery of the Order of Santiago by King Alfonso. Here are the finest sentences in this rather inaccessible text:

> Cepit Alarconem in rupibus sempiternis,
> et firmavit seras defensionis;
> aldeis multis dotavit illud,
> ut abundaret in eo incola fidei;
> constituit fortis in munimine,
> ut esset Arabibus via necis; . . .
> alcarias rupium domuit populis,

---

[16] Rodrigo Jiménez de Rada, *De rebus Hispaniae*, VII, 26, in *Hispaniae Illustratae ... Scriptores Varii* (Francoforti, 1603), I, 124. I have broken the prose down into verselike lines so as to render its rhythmic structure more perceptible.
[17] In Spanish:
> Et destrúxolos con rezia mano,
> et encogiólos con la grandeza de su coraçón;
> quemoles las çipdades et las otras pueblas,
> cortoles las huertas et los logares de sus annazaes,
> o fazían sus deleytes et tomavan sus solazes.

et duritiam ilicis convertit in vias.
In Uclesio statuit caput ordinis,
et opus eorum ensis defensionis;
persecutor Arabum moratur ibi,
et incola eius defensor fidei;
vox laudantium auditur ibi,
et iubilus desiderii hilarescit ibi;
rubet ensis sanguine Arabum,
et ardet fides charitate;
mentium execratio est cultori daemonum,
et vita honoris credentium in Deum . . .
Rex Aldephonsus educavit eos [the knights of the orders],
et possessionibus pluribus ditavit eos, . . .
et sustulit sarcinam paupertatis,
et superaddidit divitias competentes,
multiplicatio eorum corona principis;
qui laudabant in Psalmis, accinti sunt ense,
et qui gemebant orantes, ad defensionem patriae;
victus tenui[s] pastus eorum;
et asperitas lanae tegumentum eorum;
disciplina assidua probat eos,
et cultus silentii comitatur eos;
frequens genuflexio humiliat eos,
et nocturna vigilia macerat eos;
devota oratio erudit illos,
et continuus labor excercet eos.
Alter alterius observat semitas,
et frater fratrem ad disciplinam.[18]

Against the general poverty of Latin literature in Castile, the text transcribed above stands out in sharp relief as an authentic fragment of Castilian autobiography, a genuine vibration of the disposition of Castilian life, of its *vividura*. According to Jiménez de Rada, it was Alfonso VIII (1158–1214) who organized the knights of Santiago and of Calatrava, both spiritually and economically: "educavit eos." He praises no other king so extensively and so warmly: the conquest of Cordova by Ferdinand III (1236) was an accomplishment of capital importance for the progress of the reconquest, yet it is recounted by Jiménez de Rada in a simple and prosaic style. But the memory of the Battle of Las Navas de Tolosa and of the leader who made such a splendid victory possible lived in the heart of the spirited Archbishop just as Lepanto and Don Juan of Austria were to live in the heart of Cervantes centuries later. Alfonso VIII's achievement in warfare on the frontier had as its counterpart in the interior of the kingdom the great feat of organizing those holy armies. It is perfectly consistent with the Castilian life structure that this battling archbishop should employ an exceptionally poetic style to exalt the monarch he personally preferred, *his* king, and to magnify the half-

---

[18] Jiménez de Rada, *op. cit.*, p. 125.

religious, half-military orders in a style biblical in its rhythm and, in its metaphors, close to Arabic literature, with which Jiménez de Rada was well acquainted. The chronicler does not find his inspiration in the literature of classical Antiquity; his art is limited indeed, if we measure him against writers more versed in classical Latin. His grave and austere morality is Castilian, and his purpose is not to cultivate exuberant and ornate expression, but to pay reverent homage to the King, to the military orders, and to his own conscience—an exemplary instance of Castilian personalism and integralism.

This is the way of *Crónica General* (pp. 679–680) turns the foregoing Latin passage into Castilian: "Este rey don Alfonso preso a Alarcón ... que está en peñas que nunca fallesçrán. ... Las alcarias de las peñas domólas con pueblos, et tornó en uvas sabrosas la dureza de la enzina," and so on. That is:

This king Don Alfonso seized Alarcón . . . which is built on everlasting rocks. . . . The lonely settlements in the stony wilds were tamed by the King through the building of towns. The hardness of the oak turned into sweet-tasting grapes.[19] The King won the town of Uclés, and established therein the Grand Master of the Order of Santiago, whose duty it is to fight with the sword in defense of the land. The fighters against the Arabs and defenders of our faith dwell there. Voices are heard there of those praising God; their songs, full of the hope for victory, rise in joy. Their sword reddens with Arabian blood. The faith that springs from their hearts is kindled in love and charity, and their wrath falls upon those who honor and worship the spirit of evil; life and honor are for those who believe in God. . . . This king, Alfonso, raised up and nurtured these knights, and he enriched them with many possessions. . . . And he took from them the burden of poverty, and added to them besides fitting riches; the increase in the number of them is the glory of the King; the virtuous teaching of the order's friars is a crown for the Prince. Those who [in the monasteries] sang psalms in praise of God, today gird on the knight's sword. Those who once groaned in prayer have risen up in defense of the land. Their food is meager, their clothing of rough wool. Daily discipline proves them and makes them good. They keep the rule of silence; humility they learn from frequent genuflexion. The night watch makes them thin in body. The prayer of humility teaches them wisdom. Daily toil makes them used to daily toil; and one brother keeps watch over the discipline of another.[20]

---

[19] The misunderstanding of the Latin original (let me here thank Ramón Menéndez Pidal for calling my attention to the Latin source of this passage) has produced a curious yet pretty expression. The Latin says: "Et duritiam ilicis convertit in vias" ("the hardness of the oak was made into roads") just as Jiménez de Rada says earlier, referring to Cuenca, "Rupes eius factae sunt perviae, et aspera eius in planicies" ("her stony places were made passable and her rough places were made into plains"). For *vias* the Castilian translator read *uvas*, and then came out with the phrase "the hardness of the oak he turned into sweet-tasting grapes."

[20] The *Crónica general* translates the three last sentences: "El trabajo cutiano los da usados a ello; ell una de éstas guarda las carreras de la otra, et el frayre al

Thanks to Rodrigo Jiménez de Rada, then, thirteenth-century Castilian possesses a small piece of ascetic literature marked by high feeling and the authentic projection of a historical moment and of the spirit of the people who experienced it. Such, in effect, was the meaning of the military orders during the reign of Alfonso VIII, when the rugged ground of Cuenca was incorporated into Christendom. The lyric tension of the chronicler makes him allude to the "everlasting rocks" and the "hard oaks" growing among them. The result is a bit of incipient landscape poetry. This rude solidity was a fitting background for those monk-warriors, the hope and support of the Crown of Castile, when, following the defeat of Alarcos, the victory at Las Navas de Tolosa (1212) established forever the superiority of the Christians. The Archbishop's joyous optimism is mirrored in his well-sung Latin and through it in the text of the *Crónica General*. It would be hard to find in the Castilian prose and poetry of the thirteenth century another passage like this one, so dense with strong metaphor and inspired by both the Bible and the ascetic Islamic tradition.

Consistent with the method that governs the structure of the present book, I should now remind the reader that it is less important to demonstrate the analogy between the military orders and the Muslim *ribāṭ* than it is to include this fact within the totality of this Christian life whose perspective was limited by a Muslim horizon. It is this life that is manifested in the institution of the hermit-warrior and in the literary expression of a life so oriented. The fact that the institution of the hermit-warrior was subsequently converted into something different must be related to the fact that the dangerous vigil on the frontiers had become less pressing, while the confidence that the Muslims would no longer win a decisive battle had greatly increased. The military orders began to forget their asceticism, and to orient themselves anew, now in terms of the wealth of their lands and political and social prestige, a prestige that grew ever less authentic. The exercise of a power now lacking in purpose gave rise to the disparagement of that power and, once again, to disobedience

---

frayre, a las disciplinas" (p. 680). But the Latin original says: "Each brother of the orders observes the path [i.e., the conduct] of the other; each gives the other an example of discipline." The Castilian translator was not always accurate. Hence the obscurity of the sentence that begins "Ell una de éstas guarda." A thorough understanding of the *Crónica General* would require a detailed comparison with its sources, a gigantic task that would reveal a great deal of the inner quality of Castilian culture. It is curious, for instance, that "erudit" (in the sentence "devota oratio erudit illos") is translated by "los enseña et los faze enseñados": knowledge that is not authentically incorporated into the life of the learner is no knowledge at all.

(see chapter ix). This accounts for the monstrous knights commanders immortalized by Lope de Vega in *Fuente Ovejuna* and in *El comendador de Ocaña*, who are related in name only to those of the twelfth and thirteenth centuries. Lope could never have said of his *comendadores* what was said of the medieval ones: "And of rough wool was their vesture."

This negative aspect of the orders is what was perceived by popular feeling starting in the fifteenth century, when the foreground of history was beginning to be occupied by the rural masses, who were destined to annihilate the Jews and conquer America. For the common folk, the powerful knights personified what is called in the Spanish language of today *señoritismo*—idleness, sensuality, and the misuse of the privileges that come with the possession of riches. The beautiful dirge "Los Comendadores de Córdoba"[21]—two Andalusian *señoritos* who found their death in a hapless amorous adventure—already shows (fifteenth century) the light in which the knights commanders of the orders appeared to the common people. Lope de Vega was eventually to become the interpreter of that sentiment, precisely because it was the other side of the tapestry of glorious deeds; the theme was no longer epic but replete with dramatic conflicts.

It is much rarer that the bright points in the history of the orders should be emphasized, because, with a few exceptions, since the fifteenth century, literature has customarily expressed (see chapter ix) sentiments opposed to any form of authority or institutionalized justice (*La Celestina*, the *Quixote*, the picaresque novel, *El alcalde de Zalamea*, etc.). In the realm of chronicles and local histories, we have nothing to give us insight into the activities of the orders in those zones where they exercised their authority; and we especially feel the lack of such works during the fifteenth century, a period in which, as I have said before, the doctrine of *noblesse oblige* came nearer to being a reality than at any other time in Spanish history.

---

21   Oh knights commanders,   *¡Los comendadores*
To my sorrow I saw you!   *por mi mal os vi!*
I saw you;   *¡Yo vi a vosotros,*
You, me!   *vosotros a mí!*

. . . .

The knights commanders   *Los comendadores*
Of Calatrava   *de Calatrava*
Left from Seville   *partieron de Sevilla*
At an ill-starred hour,   *en hora menguada,*
For the city   *para la ciudad*
Of Cordova in the plain,   *de Córdoba la llana,*
With rich steeds   *con ricos trotones*
And golden spurs.   *y espuelas doradas.*
Handsome pages they bring   *Lindos pajes llevan*
Preceding them.   *delante de sí.*

(Cf. *Biblioteca de Autores Españoles*, XVI, 697.)

One would like to have some intimate acquaintance with Luis de Guzmán, a grand master of Calatrava, who, under the influence of little-known currents of religious thought, was seized with the desire to read an accurate version of the Old Testament, and, to be able to do this, paid large sums of money to Rabbi Arragel of Guadalajara. For ten years that Hebrew scholar worked in the town of Maqueda, a fief of the Order of Calatrava near Toledo, and at the end of this period the Grand Master received from him a handsome manuscript, illustrated with miniatures of the finest workmanship and containing besides the text a scholarly gloss, prepared, it would seem, in collaboration with the Grand Master himself.[22]

There is another episode of great importance, yet known to us only in its most general, external lines. Don Juan de Zúñiga, the last grand master of the Order of Alcántara, at the close of the fifteenth century, attended in Salamanca the classes of Antonio de Nebrija, who brought the new Latinity of the humanists from Italy to Spain. The pupil became the Maecenas of the teacher, whom he took to his Zalamea palace (Cáceres), where he established a scholarly academy in which figured the two Hebrew astronomers, Abraham Zacuto and Abasurto.[23] An illustration shows Nebrija dressed in the

---

[22] Cf. A. Paz y Melia, "La Biblia de Arragel," in *Homenaje a Menéndez y Pelayo*. The manificent text was published in 1922, at the expense of the Duke of Alba. The transcription was made by A. Paz y Melia and J. Paz. This was not the first time, moreover, that a grand master of the orders had taken advantage of the talents of a Jew to further the ends of culture. Don Lorenzo Suárez de Figueroa, grand master of Santiago, ordered Don Jacob Çadique of Uclés to translate the *Libro de sabios e philosophos e de otros ejemplos e doctrinas muy buenas* from Catalan to Castilian, a task that was finished in 1402 (J. Rodríguez de Castro, *Biblioteca española de los escritores rabínicos* [Madrid, 1781], I, 263). Jacob Çadique had been baptized, a consequence, no doubt, of the massacres of 1391. The book he translated must be something like the *Libro de la saviesa* of the Catalonian Jew, Jahuda. It is evident, then, that the great lords of the orders were interested in didactico-moral literature, that birthright of the Arabs and Jews for which the Christians had such a highly cultivated taste.

[23] Cf. F. Cantera, *El judío salmantino Abraham Zacut* (1935). Zacuto was not a Portuguese but a Salamancan, and very much the protégé of the learned bishop Gonzalo de Vivero (d. 1480), who heaped honors on him in life and left him an inheritance in his will. After the Bishop's death, Zacuto found patronage in the palace of the Grand Master of Alcántara, whom he describes as "a lover of all the sciences and learned in them, so that, attracted by his fame, all wise and lettered men leave their lands and their birthplace to seek [near him] true peace and full perfection"; at his side, "men of letters have refreshment and reward." The most detailed account of the academy created around Don Juan de Zúñiga is to be found in Alonso de Torres Tapia, *Crónica de la Orden de Alcántara* (1763), II, 569: "The Grand Master was a friend of good learning; and besides the religious that he kept there [in Zalamea] with him, he brought from without men distinguished in letters: the bachelor [of law] Friar Gutierre de Trijo; the master Friar Domingo, a theologian of the Order of Preachers; the Doctor de la Parra [a convert from Judaism who became a physician at the court of the Catholic Sovereigns]; *Abasurto*, a Jew by birth and an astrologer; the master *Antonio de Lebrija* [who was almost surely of the Jewish caste]; and the choir-

habit of a knight of Alcántara and giving instruction in humane letters to the grand master and his household.[24]

I have no idea how extensive or how profound the learning was that he imparted, or what repercussions the grand master's cultural initiative may have had within the order. It is noteworthy, in any case, that Estremadura, where the order had its landholdings, could claim a certain literary and humanistic culture in the first half of the sixteenth century—a culture that now seems to me to be in large measure the work of Jewish converts living under the protection of the grand masters of Alcántara, the Duke of Alba, and other great lords. The Spanish drama was born toward the end of the fifteenth century with Juan del Encina, a cleric who had studied at the University of Salamanca, located in the territory just to the north of Estremadura, and served to satisfy the artistic appetite of the courts of the prince Don Juan and the Duke of Alba, in Alba de Tormes (Salamanca). After this, the new art turned southward for further propagation, and the result is found in the works of the Estremadurans Torres Naharro, Miguel de Carvajal, Sánchez de Badajoz, Díaz Tanco, and others; of their lives, we know very little, and of their works only a very few examples have been preserved. The University of Salamanca, the clergy, and the Order of Alcántara were in close contact with one another in Estremadura, although research in Spanish archives would be necessary before one would have an adequate foundation for a discussion of this matter. It may be possible one day to prove that the University of Salamanca, the Hieronymite Monastery of Guadalupe (in Estremadura, and filled with converts from Judaism), and the Order of Alcántara were centers in which the Hispano-Judaic culture found refuge for the last time in the shadow of certain illustrious aristocrats.

---

master Solórzano, the best musician known to those centuries. Master Antonio taught him Latin, and he [the Grand Master] had given the habit [of the order of Alcántara] with the commandery of the town to Master Antonio's son, Friar Marcelo de Lebrija. The Jewish astrologer explained the *Esfera* [probably the books on astronomy translated by the Order of Alfonso the Learned] to him, and everything that it was permissible to know about his art. And he was such an enthusiast that in one of the upper rooms of his house he caused to be painted the heavens with all their planets, stars, and signs of the zodiac. Today the painting is faded from age." Zacuto wrote a *Brief Treatise on Celestial Influences* (*Tratado breve de las influencias del cielo* [1486]) "for the help of the Grand Master's physicians" (Cantera, *op. cit.*, p. 87). Concerning Abasurto, cf. Professor J. Gillet, *Torres Naharro's Propalladia*, III, 630. This is what might be called a Renaissance court, in which, very much in the Spanish fashion, Dominican theologians mingled with Jewish astronomers and humanists of Jewish origins educated in Italy. Yet for the meaning of this "Renaissance" we must not turn to Italy but to the ancient tradition of the Spanish Peninsula, a tradition maintained by the great lords of the orders like an echo of that most splendid of courts presided over by Alfonso the Learned in the thirteenth century.

[24] In an article by A. Paz y Melia in *Revista de Archivos* (1898), p. 8.

Holy War

To imagine European life after the rise of Islam without bearing in mind the now hostile, now harmonious relationships between Christians and Muslims during that period causes certain historians to close their eyes to what is *expressed* by the documents they cite. Texts from the ninth, tenth, and eleventh centuries issuing from the papal chancellery show constant awareness of the nearby powerful presence of the Muslim states, just as today Western governments make no pronouncements on international affairs (or even their own internal affairs) which do not reflect, directly or indirectly, the consciousness that a large part of humanity is ruled at this time by the quasi-religious ideology of Marxism. If the documents of the eleventh century display anxiety and fear with respect to Islam, today these feelings seem to have been transmuted in some historians into a retrospective antipathy toward the Muslim world. While the Belgian historian Henri Pirenne believes that, without Mohammed, Charlemagne would be inconceivable[25]—which is, indeed, an exaggerated notion—others think that European Christianity was completely self-contained and that the "holy war" and the initial impulse that animated the Crusades can be perfectly well explained without Islam. As might be expected, the historical opinions in this instance reflect the value judgments of the historian, a fact that is of even more importance in dealing with the history of Spain than in the consideration of the histories of the rest of Europe. Spanish historians fight to Europeanize themselves retrospectively and even go to the extreme of converting into "Spaniards" the Muslims of al-Andalus.[26]

My personal preferences lead me to accept the existence of what I believe to have been the reality of European and Hispanic life in the ninth, tenth, and eleventh centuries—and that is, a constant oscillation between antagonism and the sharing of a common life between the Christian and Islamic peoples. This too is a form of "partisanship," which I believe to be true and maintain[27] in the attempt to explain

---

[25] Henri Pirenne, *Mahomet et Charlemagne* (Paris and Brussels, 1937).

[26] The revulsion against all things Islamic is ancient in its origins and tends to cloud the mind. Long ago Petrarch heaped all kinds of insults on Arabic literature in a letter addressed to a physician. In the histories of Italian literature, no reference is made to the Arabic structure of the *Decameron*. In 1840 the Englishman Thomas Fuller said that the diffusion of Islam, "that cursed doctrine," was like "the spreading of leprosy." See *The History of the Holy War*, pp. 8–9.

[27] A similar point of view is expressed by Carlo M. Cipolla; speaking of the monetary reforms of a certain caliph in the seventh century, he says that the relationship between gold and silver in the Islamic world was reflected in the West, "because the two zones [East and West] were never completely isolated from one another" (*Annales* [Paris, 1962], no. 1, p. 136).

to myself who the Spaniards were and how they came to be themselves, a problem of which I was unaware thirty years ago—and which many would prefer to continue to ignore.

The war against the Muslims in Spain and in Palestine, however different its purposes and its results may have been, was inspired by the *ŷihād*, or the Muslim doctrine of holy war. The magnitude and the form of that inspiration matter less than the fact that such a special type of war did exist. A good deal has been written about the Crusades and the holy war.[28] One study, distinguished by the excellence of its documentation,[29] considers the possible connection between the holy war and the Muslim *ŷihād*: the author wonders especially whether "the Christians were aware of the role played by the *ŷihād* in the ninth and tenth centuries among the Muslims of the western basin of the Mediterranean" (Carl Erdmann, *Die Entstehung des Kreuzzugsgedankens*, p. 27). In my opinion it is inconceivable that Popes Leo IV, in 848, and Urban II, in 1095, should have been ignorant of the fact that the Muslim chieftains reminded their armies, when they were urging them on to fight against the unbelievers, that Mohammed had promised a paradise of exquisite delights to those who might lose their lives in that combat. Dazzled by the prospect of eternal pleasure, as certain for him as the rising of the sun and the moon, the Muslim fought ferociously. The efficacy of that stimulus is reflected in what the people of the "house of Islam" conquered in less than a century—from Persia to Hispania. To judge the effect of such a major occurrence on the spirit of those who were directing Christendom, it is not necessary to be an expert Orientalist nor even to read Arabic, as Carl Erdmann thinks (*op. cit.*, p. 27). Nor is it advisable, at least with respect to al-Andalus, to consider the holy war as an economic enterprise, as Richard Konetzke maintains:[30] "Material gain seems to have been the most obvious stimulus of the 'holy war,' for both the state and for the individual." The fact that the Moors should have fought with the hope of obtaining rich booty does not invalidate the significance of the fact that those who lost their lives during a military skirmish expected to win paradise. Earthly gains might be added to celestial ones, but the latter were assured to all those who fought against the infidel. E. Lévi-Provençal (quoted by Konetzke) understands the matter clearly: "With the mystic impulse of offering one's own life 'pour le bon combat' there was often mingled the manifest purpose, or at least the tacit hope, of

---

[28] See my book *De la edad conflictiva: El drama de la honra* (Madrid: Taurus, 1963), pp. 95–98.

[29] Carl Erdmann, *Die Entstehung des Kreuzzugsgedankens* (Stuttgart, 1935).

[30] "Islam und christliches Spanien im Mittelalter," in *Historische Zeitschrift* (1957), p. 586. The author is not sympathetically attracted to the object of his study and, like so many others, misunderstands it.

winning, through the sacrifice of one's own life, some material benefit."[31] But this fact does not deprive the holy war of its meaning; the
basic meaning would be lost only if it should be demonstrated (and
no one has attempted to do so) that the Muslim did not believe in the
reward promised by Allah, through his prophet Mohammed, to those
who lost their lives fighting against Christians. Lévi-Provençal mentions the "volunteers for the holy war," desirous of "keeping, at
least once in their lives, the canonical precept of *ŷihād*" (*Histoire de
l'Espagne musulmane*, III, 79).

A number of Westerners have taken a point of view which I
would call "Christian" and have falsified the meaning of the *ŷihād*
by trying to probe into the religious sincerity of the Muslim fighter
(as if we should say that the hermit's life was a farce because there
have been hypocritical hermits). I point this out for no critical
motive but only to underline once more the necessity of situating
ourselves within the vital functioning of human events, which are always "inhabited" by an interacting "someone" and "something." The
leaders of the Christian forces in the Peninsular kingdoms, in Rome,
and in Cluny had a full awareness of the fearful efficacy of the promise made by the Koran. If the struggle between Christians and Moors
had been no more than a matter of earthbound economics, as Konetzke thinks, the popes and lesser Church dignitaries would not have
imitated the koranic formula of the *ŷihād*; but Pope Leo IV followed
it in 848 when he promised eternal bliss to those who died fighting
against the Muslims who occupied Sicily: "regna ille caelestia minime
negabuntur."[32] When he preached his holy war, this pope made
use of the same spiritual weapon brandished by Islam. And the author
of the *Poema del Cid*, who knew very well that the Cid and his followers were greatly interested in booty, nevertheless infused the
spirit of the holy war, of the *ŷihād*, into those who fought furiously:

> You would have seen . . . so many white banners turn red
> with blood, so many horses without their riders.
> The Moors cry, "Mohammed!" and the Christian,
> "Santiago!"
>
> (ll. 728–731)

In both camps there were people greedy for earthly goods and highly
soiled in spirit; but both groups of believers fought with the assurance
that when they died they would attain a choice place in their respective paradises.

In Islam no distinction is made between religious and secular wars,
for "any war between Muslims and non-Muslims may be a *ŷihād*,
with its appropriate incentives and rewards" (*Encyclopedia of Islam*,

---

[31] *Histoire de l'Espagne musulmane* (1953), III, 104.
[32] See my *De la edad conflictiva*, p. 95.

s.v. "ŷihād"). The Mohammedan clung to what was written in the Koran: "Fight for the cause of God against whosoever may fight against you. . . . Kill them wheresoever you may find them, and cast them forth from whatever place they may have thrown you out" (II: 186–187). "Believers who are seated in their houses free from care shall not be treated like those who valorously aid the cause of God with their fortune and with their persons. God has assigned a place above those who are seated in their houses to those who truly fight with their persons and with their fortune. He has made divine promises to all. But God has assigned to the brave a beautiful reward, higher than that of those who are seated tranquilly in their houses, a post selected for them, and pardon, and mercy; because he is clement and merciful" (IV: 97–99).

Just as Leo IV could not have been unaware in 848 of the nature of the religious belief held by the forces that had conquered Sicily in 827 as they listened to the recital of suras from the Koran, so also Urban II could not have been ignorant of it when he solemnly proclaimed his Crusade in 1095 at the Council of Clermont. As I demonstrate, there is nothing in the Bible, or in St. Augustine, or in any other father of the Church like what Urban II wrote between 1089 and 1091 to the Counts of Besalú, Roussillon, and Cerdeña when he was exhorting them to fight against the Saracens in Tarragona: "Whosoever dies on this expedition for the love of God and his brothers should by no means doubt that he will find pardon for his sins and will partake of eternal life, thanks to the most benevolent mercy of *our* God."[33]

The Pope says "of our God" because he knows that in the enemy camp it is the custom to invoke the clemency and mercy of Allah, the Muslim God. The popes had already referred to the problem of the likeness or disparity between the two religions, which was bound to happen after four hundred years of war, hostility, and accords between Christians and Muslims. But since readers may be confused by the capricious negation of this basic historical situation by some historians, it is necessary to spend a little time refuting such naïve misunderstandings. Gregory VII, in his eagerness to rule over all the Christian kingdoms, tried to maintain friendly relations with al-Nāṣir, a Mauretanian prince, and gave as his reason the essential oneness of the God of the Christians and the God of the Mohammedans: "Vnum Deum, licet diverso modo, credimus et confitemur" ("We believe, we

---

[33] "In qua uidelicet expeditione si quis pro Dei et fratrum suorum dilectione occubuerit, peccatorum profecto suorum indulgentiam et eterne uite consortium inuenturum se ex clementissima Dei nostri miseratione non dubitet" (P. Kehr, "Papsturkunden in Katalonien," in *Abhandlungen der Gesellschaft der Wissenschaften zu Göttingen*, Philological-Historical Section, n.s., XVIII, 2 [Berlin, 1926], pp. 287–288).

acknowledge one God, though in a different way").[34] For this pope the difference between Christian and Muslim belief was one of external forms, not of essence. Thus it was possible to accept the idea that the clemency and mercy of God would free from all sin any Christian who lost his life fighting against the Muslims: Popes Leo IV and Urban II expressly said that this was so. This belief was the central point in the holy war, and *not* that the purpose of the war should be the defense of God's Church, or an attack upon its enemies, or that the war should be waged under God's protection. These latter things had happened before Islam existed; but since the eighth century, when the Muslims had already snatched extensive and prized territories away from the Western Christian Empire, the principles and the feelings that animated the fighters against Islam had been affected by those of their formidable enemy. Only confusion results from arguments—such as those made by Erdmann (*op. cit.*, p. 89)— as to whether the reconquest in Spain was truly a fight for the faith (*Glaubenskämpfe*). Nor is it pertinent to classify as "romantic" the opinion that the war had a "missionary" purpose; we are, in fact, dealing with something more complex, namely, *the intermingling of warlike activities with the peaceful ones resulting from tolerance and a shared common life.* We have seen this very well in the cited documents issued by the papal chancellery: Gregory VII seeks the friendship of a Muslim prince under the shelter of that one God in whom two rival, hostile beliefs coincide; Urban II avails himself of a belief of Islamic origin in order to move certain great Catalonian lords to take up the holy war. None of this is incompatible with the survival of the Augustinian idea of the opposition between the state of God and the state of Satan or with the accustomed blessing of the army as it marches into combat, and so on (Erdmann, *op. cit.*, p. 73). To fight for a cause pleasing to God, or to pray for divine favor, or to receive signs of supernatural aid has nothing to do, however, with the reflection of the doctrine of the *ŷihād* in the words of Popes Leo IV and Urban II.

If such things happened at the topmost levels of Christendom, it was most natural that the doctrine of the *ŷihād* should be all too familiar to the Christians of the Iberian Peninsula, beginning with the Mozarabs. Karl Heisig has dealt with the last-named group in an excellent article about the *Chanson de Roland*,[35] which I mentioned only briefly in the first edition of this book because it seemed unnecessary to insist on a matter that appeared to be already settled. In view, however, of the lack of comprehension displayed by certain

---

[34] *Gregorii VII Registrum*, ed. E. Caspar, lib. III, 21. See F. Cognasso, *La genesi delle crociate* (Turin, 1934), p. 38.
[35] "Geschichtsmetaphysik des Rolandsliedes," in the *Zeitschrift für romanische Philologie* (1935), LV, 1–87.

medievalists, it is necessary to demonstrate in more detail the special "sacramental" character—in the sense of absolution of sins—which the war against the Muslims frequently had for the Christian.

Toward the middle of the ninth century the formerly peaceful relations between Muslims and Mozarabs in Cordova were converted into mutual and fierce animosity. A state of collective delirium arose among the Christians, and many of them suffered martyrdom for their faith. 'Abd al-Raḥmān II tried to pacify this spiritual revolt, but a few fanatics put up strong resistance. In this connection the matter of prime interest for us now is the work of the Mozarabic writer Eulogius, *Memoriale Sanctorum*; in the first book, written in 851, he urges Christian believers to fight against the Muslims ("bellum parare incredulis")[36] in a manner which could well be called "sacramental" from a Catholic point of view. According to him, those who fight to kill Muslims "should not be concerned if sins that have not been atoned for remain in them, or if they come to suffer martyrdom stained by any uncleanliness of vice, for they will appear before Christ in order to be crowned and freed from all guilt, thanks to the triumphant banner of their martyrdom."[37] Karl Heisig (*op. cit.*, p. 19) perceived, as might have been expected, the connection between this and the koranic doctrine: "To all those who fall fighting 'on God's road' the joys of paradise will be granted without further question." According to Heisig the coincidence between these two doctrines pronounced in the same territory and at the same time excludes the possibility that the origin of the ideas of Eulogius could be other than Islamic. In this instance as in so many others we are faced with a close contact between peoples which produced both violent opposition and inevitable similarities. At any rate, Heisig believes that Eulogius, spurred on by the exaltation of his polemic against the Koran, sought in the Old Testament for texts that might support his anti-Mohammedan campaign, "although the decisive motivation behind his turning a posteriori to ancient biblical evidence was, without doubt, the Islamic precept." I accept the reasonableness of this contention, but it should be clearly stated that none of the texts from the Old Testament or from the Gospels which were gathered together and adduced by Eulogius coincide in meaning with the previously cited koranic suras. To be sure, in the Bible the death of the guilty appears pleasing to Yahweh: "And Samuel said, As thy sword hath made women childless, so shall thy mother be childless among

---

[36] See F. J. Simonet, *Historia de los mozárabes* (Madrid, 1903). The works of Eulogius were edited by Cardinal Lorenzana: *Sanctorum patrum Toletanorum opera*, II, 391–642. They appear also in Migne's *Patrologia*, S.L., vol. 115, cols. 731–870.

[37] "Si culpis obnoxii maneant, et ex qualibet sorde vitiorum infecti ad martyrium veniant, nihil impedit; cum omnibus martyriali tropaeo deletis ad Christum coronandi accedant" (*Patrologia*, vol. 115, p. 855).

women. And Samuel hewed Agag in pieces before the Lord in Gilgal" (I Samuel 15:33). Psalm 116 (115 of the Vulgate) is, however, a hymn of thanksgiving for restored health: "I love the Lord, because he hath heard my voice and my supplications. ... I will pay my vows unto the Lord now in the presence of all his people. Precious in the sight of the Lord is the death of his saints" (vv. 1, 14, 15), or, as in the Latin text adduced by Eulogius: "Pretiosa est in conspecto Domini mors sanctorum ejus" ("The death of God's hallowed ones is beautiful in his sight"). A text from Matthew (10:39) also seems relevant to Eulogius in the justification of his Christian version of the *ŷihād*. He cites it thus: "Si quis voluerit animam suam salvam facere, perdet eam, et qui perdiderit animam suam propter me, in vitam aeternam custodiet eam" ("He that findeth his life shall lose it: and he that loseth his life for my sake shall find it"); and indeed it does seem to agree with the sense of the previously cited sura: "Believers who are seated in their houses free from care shall not be treated like those who valorously aid the cause of God with their fortune and with their persons" (Koran IV:97). But the text from the Vulgate really says: "Qui invenit animam suam, perdet illam; et qui perdiderit animam suam propter me, inveniet eam" ("He that findeth his life shall lose it: and he that loseth his life for my sake shall find it"). St. Matthew does not say that "in vitam aeternam custodiet eam" ("he will preserve it in the life eternal").

In other words, however much we may search in the Old and New Testaments, we will find nothing that agrees with the koranic doctrine. What St. Matthew said (which is in accordance with other texts from the Gospels) about "finding and losing one's life" resembles not at all the doctrine of "Lose your life fighting against the infidel, and by that alone you shall enjoy the delights of paradise."

The Islamic precept certainly belongs in the same general class with ideas about the sacrifice of one's person or one's goods in an offering to God in order that the creature may be bound more tightly to his Creator; but reduced to so abstract a form the precept would not serve to explain what happened at that point when two differing religions both came to practice the doctrine of holy war. What appears in the Koran as the *outward* passage of the person from the field of battle to paradisiacal joy, without reference to the person's inner *state*, was perforce translated on the Christian side into an absolution of the sins of those who fight against the infidel. Eulogius' reference to "the uncleanliness of vice" in the combatant makes clearly visible the form in which the koranic doctrine was to be Christianized. For the state of the soul, the consciousness of the individual soul, had been the enormous and decisive innovation of Christianity.

In sum, when we deal with the human phenomenon of the "holy

war," we must proceed in one way when it is the expression of Christian life and in another when it is an expression of Islamic life. The Christian, as we have already seen, put an inward meaning into koranic suras which had lacked that aspect; we historians, in our turn, should not inject a Christian meaning into the koranic holy war and deny the reality of the existence of the ŷihād when those who obeyed the religious precept of taking part in it were animated by the greed for material gain or when they were pirates or highwaymen. Neither the secondary motivations of the ŷihād nor the inward uncleanness of the combatant kept the Muslim holy war from being the ŷihād.

Aside from all this, if the manner in which Eulogius formulated the doctrine of holy war had been normal and easily relatable to the Christian tradition, the French monks (or, rather, the Frankish monks) Usuard and Odilard who went to Cordova in 858 would have been able to comprehend what the Mozarabic doctrine of holy war meant. The purpose of their journey was to carry back the bodies of St. George and St. Aurelius to the monastery of Saint-Germain-des-Prés (see Heisig, *op. cit.*, p. 25). Another monk from that monastery, Aimoin, wrote the account of their perilous trip (*Patrologia*, S.L., vol. 115, cols. 941–948) and explained how they felt with respect to the Mozarabs who had died as martyrs for the purpose of upholding a spiritual opposition to the infidel. But neither Aimoin nor the two other monks, Usuard and Odilard, understood the way in which Eulogius interpreted the texts from the Old Testament. That the Christian should suffer martyrdom passively seemed thoroughly logical to those monks, but active physical combat against the infidel seemed meaningless to them. "Ninth-century France ['the kingdom of the Franks,' as I would say] was not yet prepared to accept such ideas, while in Spain, from the moment of their conception there, they were kept alive all during the long struggle between the Christian and the Mohammedan faiths" (Heisig, *op. cit.*, p. 26).

As late as the twelfth century, as has already been noted (p. 474), the future St. Bernard of Clairvaux hesitated a long time before deciding to give his approval to those who would confer a sacred character on the act of putting to death the enemies of the Christian faith. Nor does his hesitancy cast doubt on the fact that certain popes had already sponsored the Islamic idea of holy war at an earlier time, for ideas and feelings do not always progress down through the centuries in synchronic alignment.

As early as the *Poema del Cid* we may find expression of the belief that death received in combat against the Moors led to eternal glory. Bishop Jerome absolves the followers of the Cid before they attack the Almorávides in the following words:

The one who should die here fighting face to face,
I absolve him from his sins, and God shall have his soul.

(ll. 1704–1705)

Making the salvation of the soul depend on not turning one's back on the enemy emphasizes less the Christian than the militant spirit; the promise of absolution given in advance by the bishop shows the effect of the Islamic doctrine of holy war much more than it does the spirituality of the Church. References to the holy war are also made in a translation of the *Historia Gothica* of Jiménez de Rada, archbishop of Toledo; the latter says to King Alfonso VII, beside whom he fought at the Battle of Las Navas de Tolosa: "Sire, if you go to your death, all [who die with you] will go up with you into paradise."[38] But in other references to the holy war in the twelfth and thirteenth centuries Islamic and Christian doctrine are harmonized in a way not found among the Mozarabs of the ninth century. Following the Latin text of Jiménez de Rada, the *Crónica General* narrates the Battle of Las Navas de Tolosa and reports that on the eve of the battle the Archbishop of Toledo walked among the men "encouraging them . . . and pardoning all their sins most humbly and most devoutly" (p. 699). And later: "they all confessed and, having partaken of the sacred body of Our Lord Jesus Christ, they all prepared themselves and provided themselves with full armor" (p. 700). Still later, in the same *Crónica*, when the chronicler recounts the defense of the fortified town of Martos (Jaen), he reflects popular belief rather than the ecclesiastical point of view and forgets to mention the necessity of previous confession. At a critical moment a knight named Diego Pérez de Vargas harangues his fellow soldiers in the following words: "Those of us who do not succeed in getting through and who die today, shall save our souls and shall go to our glory in paradise" (p. 738).

In the fourteenth century Prince Juan Manuel also brings together Islamic and Christian precepts with regard to the holy war, just as the Archbishop of Toledo and the editors of the *Crónica General* had done before. In his *Libro de los Estados* he writes that God permitted the Moors to conquer the lands "that formerly belonged to the Chris-

---

[38] See p. 123 of the translation, entitled *La Estoria Gótica*, ed. E. Lidforss (Lund, 1876). The *Historia Gothica* is the short title of the *Rerum in Hispania gestarum Chronicon*, translated in various forms since the thirteenth century and used by the editors of the *Crónica General* (see B. Sánchez Alonso, "Versiones en romance de las crónicas del Toledano," in *Homenaje a Menéndez Pidal* (1925), I, 341–354). The passage quoted in the text appears as follows in the *Crónica General*, p. 701: "Sennor, si a Dios plaze esso, corona nos viene de victoria, esto es de vençer nos," etc. ("Sire, if it should please God, a crown shall come to us from this victory, that is, if we should conquer"). In the version cited in our text, however, the translator was interested in emphasizing the immediate connection between death and ascension into paradise.

tians [he does not say 'to the Spaniards']" in order that the Christians might have just cause to fight with the Moors to recover their lands and so that "those who should die [in the war], having fulfilled the commandments of Holy Church, might be *martyrs*, or, in other words, that their souls might be cleared of the sin that they committed." In a later passage of the same book it is said that those who "go out against the Moors" should "go well confessed and with amends made for their sins in so far as they might be able"; and that they should think that just as Jesus Christ "wished to suffer death on the cross to redeem sinners, so also do they go prepared to receive *martyrdom* and death to defend and exalt the holy Catholic faith."[39] Now the idea that those who died fighting against the Moors were martyrs is of Islamic origin, nor was it originally motivated by the goal of saving Europeans from the African menace.[40] The fact that Europeans in general found it convenient for the frontier with Islam to be as far removed as Castile and Aragon does not mean that Castilians and Aragonese suffered martyrdom for the sake of the Provençals and the French but that they were adapting to their Christian faith the Mohammedan concept of the *ŷihād*, as it is expressed here once again by a Muslim writer: "In al-Andalus there are not to be seen any eyes save those that keep watch to satisfy God, any warriors save those who fight on the road of God. Whosoever dies in that state, *dies a martyr*: whosoever lives [that is, even those who do not die in the war] is blessed, for the holy war and those who make it are pillars on the road [to God]."[41] The Almohades who fell before Santarém (Portugal) in 1184 "died as martyrs."[42] This way of referring to those who died in religious struggles may even be found in a Christian gloss to the Bible translated by Arragel around 1420: "Whoever in the service of God receives death for the true and Catholic faith from the hand of a heretic ... not only does not suffer [in the other life] but rather will have a reward for his deed: for without doubt *martyrs* do not die."[43] As I. Goldzieher has said, "The holy war imposed by the Koran is one of the surest ways to achieve *martyrdom*."[44]

This is the type of martyrdom to which Prince Juan Manuel was referring; he was thoroughly familiar with Islamic beliefs and ways of life, which he relates very closely to Christianity in the case of the

[39] *Biblioteca de Autores Españoles*, LI, 294, 324–325.

[40] As is maintained by R. Menéndez Pidal in *La España del Cid* (1947), p. 637.

[41] *Descripción de España* (or, in other words, of al-Andalus), by the writer called the "Anonymous of Almería," translated by René Basset in *Homenaje a don Francisco Codera*, p. 641.

[42] See Dozy, *Recherches*, II, 457.

[43] Duke of Alba ed., I, 116a. This gloss is doubtless the work of one of Rabbi Arragel's Christian collaborators.

[44] I. Goldzieher, *Le dogme et la loi de l'Islam* (1920), p. 97.

holy war. For that reason he finds it necessary to make it clear that not "all who die in the war against the Moors are martyrs or saints; for those who go there robbing and raping women and committing many and very evil sins, and even those who go solely to seize wealth from the Moors, or for the money they receive [to do combat], or to gain fame in this world, rather than for right intention and the defense of the faith and the land of the Christians—of all these, even though they may die, God alone, who knows hidden things, knows what it is to become of them" (*op. cit.*, p. 324). Prince Juan Manuel tries to resolve the conflict between the *ŷihād* and Christianity, since for the latter, as noted already, war against the infidel could not rightly have a "sacramental" character. Aware of this difficulty and at the same time not wishing to negate the redeeming power of the *ŷihād*, he then proposes several ways out of the impasse. We may, for example, trust that sinners fallen in battle have repented their evil deeds and that God, who knows everything, "is merciful unto them and saves them." For our subtle Prince Juan Manuel, the point of final contrition may set the soul right with God without need of the sacraments, for he knows that souls are not condemned on account of their good or evil life but on account of their final repentance and through the faith they have put in divine mercy. Thus it happens that people who "have lived a good life lose their souls: and *all this lies in the mercy and pity of God*"—which sentiment leans somewhat toward the koranic doctrine. But the learned prince thought it necessary to rectify his position in some measure and goes on to say: "[to be sure], hope is brighter for the man who lives a good life and dies a good death, *according to the law and faith of the Christians.*" Still the clever mind continues to play with the problem, and he proceeds: "Yet those sinners who die and are killed by the Moors *should have much better hope of salvation than those other sinners who do not die in the war against the Moors*" (*ibid.*). For all these reasons, those who go to fight against the infidel with good intentions and with their minds fixed on the redemptive death of Jesus Christ, are, if they die, "without any doubt holy and upright *martyrs.*"

If such a comparison may be permitted, Prince Juan Manuel's ideas about the holy war show all the characteristics of Mudejar art, in other words, an intricate blend of Islamic imitation in the words of the Mozarab Eulogius in the ninth century, as well as in the statements of Popes Leo IV and Urban II, has now been intermingled with Christian meaning in the Castile of the twelfth, thirteenth, and fourteenth centuries.

In the prose of Don Juan Manuel the holy war appears as a problem that the author analyzes in spiritual, moral, and theological terms. No less could have been expected when, as a result of the convergence between Christian, Islamic, and Judaic cultures, the Castilian of sensitive but morally strict soul began to treat as never before states of consciousness which until then had been only latent or barely uttered in stammers. In addition to the prose of Don Juan Manuel, like manifestations of this mutation may be found in the poetry of the Archpriest of Hita, the anguished philosophical and moral experience of Rabbi Santob of Carrión, the new sensitivity toward epic themes displayed in the early ballads or *romances*, and the ascetic, contemplative inwardness of the Hieronymite order. In the midst of the environment that produced all these things Don Juan Manuel, author of the *Libro de Patronio*, treats the institution of holy war with delicate half-Christian, half-Islamic nuances; by this time the holy war was an institution firmly rooted in the ethical and religious sensibilities of a Castilian of the highest rank. Don Juan Manuel could not be unaware of its origins, for he knew and valued highly his enemies who were at the same time his friends, the Muslims. If it were not, he says, "for the false sect in which they live, and because they are not armed or mounted so as to suffer blows like knights . . . , I would say that in all the world there are not such fine soldiers, nor any so expert in war, or so fit to make so many conquests" (*op. cit.*, p. 323). Don Juan Manuel distinguishes—as one had done previously in Castile—between the inner and outer accidental qualities of a man, and the man himself, what he calls "the man in himself" ("el hombre en sí"). A Moorish knight, with his erring faith rectified and with suitable armor, would be worth as much as the best of Castilian warriors. Let us leave aside the question as to whether such an opinion is right or not; my only interest at this moment has been to reveal in some measure the mentality and the spirit of the man who submitted to such penetrating analysis the institution of holy war, always so ambiguous in meaning for the Christians.

Tolerance

Just as the fact that those who undertook the reconquest of al-Andalus came to call themselves "Christians" reflects the opposition between these people and the "Moors," so was the constitution by both the northern and the southern peoples of a society made up of three castes of believers affected and conditioned by the Islamic doctrine of religious tolerance. The Koran says: "Fight therefore against them [the unbelievers] until they cease persecuting you, and the only worship be that of Allah; but if they desist, then let there be no hostility, save against the wicked" (II, 189). "Let there be no violence in religion. Now is the right way made distinct from error" (II, 257). "But if thy Lord had pleased, verily all who are in the earth would have believed together. Wilt thou compel men to become believers? No soul can believe but by the permission of God" (X, 99-100).

The Koran, itself a product of religious syncretism, was a monument of tolerance to begin with, since there appear combined in it Islamic beliefs and those of Judaism and Christianity. An anticipatory suggestion of the Sufistic idea that all paths lead to God is to be found in the Koran, and the Koran itself is founded (I venture to think) on the belief that nothing outside the divine essence is substantial or certain. The lack of stability in all human things even made it possible to think that "the roads that lead to God are as numerous as the souls of men."[45]

With occasional exceptions, tolerance was practiced throughout the Muslim world,[46] and the persecution of the Mozarabs in Cordova during the ninth century was directed more "against those who were politically rebellious than against unbelievers on account of their religion."[47] At a later period, in the eleventh and twelfth centuries, when the Almorávides and the Almohades instituted fanatical persecutions of both Christian and Jewish communities, the Christian kingdoms had already modeled their social customs according to the example offered by an earlier al-Andalus. We have already seen (chapter iii) how the kings were received when they made solemn entries into cities, and how the three faiths were harmoniously grouped around the sepulcher of Ferdinand III. We should also bear in mind the religious syncretism displayed by the forged Gospels found in Granada at the end of the sixteenth century (see chapter vii).

Muslim tolerance, implicit in the very constitution of the new faith, was fostered by political necessity as the boundaries of the Mohammedan empire, which had sprung up almost overnight, were pushed outward at a dizzying rate of speed. Many people were drawn toward so victorious a faith, the bearer of delightful promises and paradisiacal hopes, because the Byzantine Empire was weak and chaos and uncertainty reigned in wide areas of what had been the Roman Empire. The new religious message combined spiritual attractions with sensual ones, the fury of conquest and a stable political structure with the possibility of giving oneself over to ascesis and mystic meditation. Monotheistic religions were not felt to be mortal enemies, for, according to Mohammed, "his message coincided at some points with the faith of the Jews and that of the Christians."[48] As we have seen, certain Moors in Granada said that the Lord's Prayer appeared in one *hadiz*[49] as an Islamic prayer.

---

[45] *Ibid.*, p. 143.
[46] *Ibid.*, p. 29.
[47] Lévi-Provençal, *Histoire de l'Espagne musulmane* (1950), I, 227.
[48] Tor Andrae, *Mahomet: Sa vie et sa doctrine* (1945), p. 92.
[49] The *hadiz* is the documented form which preserves the sacred tradition

There is no doubt that one of the factors in Muslim tolerance was economic self-interest, that is, the collection of taxes paid by conquered Christians and Jews; but the mixture of economic and spiritual motives is no more characteristic of Mohammedanism than of Christianity. It would be folly, however, to deny the spiritual meaning of the two religions throughout the centuries only because of the zeal with which taxes in the form of tithes and first fruits were imposed and collected—or because the Mozarab paid a head tax or *ŷizyah*.[50]

But aside from these considerations, and from the fact that no religion is entirely faithful to its own creed, we must bear in mind that, in addition to the precept which demanded tolerance for Christians and Jews, there were forms of mysticism in which an antidogmatism and psychological relativism with respect to belief formed the very heart of religious experience. The mystic Ibn 'Arabī (1164–1240), a Muslim born in Murcia, expresses himself in the following words:

> My heart can take on any form: it is a pasture for
> gazelles and a monastery for Christian monks.
> A temple for idols, and for the Kaaba of the pilgrims,
> and for the tables of the Torah, and for the book
> of the Koran.
> I follow the religion of love: whatever the direction
> of the camels of my love, my religion and my
> faith are there.[51]

Such ambiguous expressions are unthinkable on the Christian side. We have noted several times the idea or feeling that the ways which lead to God are various (see chapter iii); but to say that Christians, Muslims, and Jews worship the same God is not equivalent to thinking that *all* roads lead to God, for in the latter instance belief is reduced to indifference. But what doubtless penetrated into Castilian thought was the doctrine of tolerance as it is formulated in the Koran. Alfonso the Learned says, for example:

> By good words and appropriate preaching should the Christians seek
> to convert the Moors and make them believe our faith . . . , not by force

---

(*Sunna*) of what the Prophet expressed orally (I. Goldzieher, *op. cit.*, pp. 34, 35).

[50] For a discussion of the spread of Mohammedanism, see T. W. Arnold, *The Preaching of Islam* (London, 1913).

[51] *The Tarjumān Al-Ashwāq*, translated by R. A. Nicholson (London, 1911), p. 67. In the commentary the author makes on his own poem we read: " 'My heart has become capable of every form,' as another has said, 'The heart is so called from its changing,' for it varies according to the various influences by which it is affected in consequence of the variety of its states of feeling; and the variety of its feelings is due to the variety of the Divine manifestations that appear to its inmost ground" (*ibid.*, p. 69). For the true Mohammedan, the heart—and everything else—must have been like a weathervane, having no other meaning save that which is given by the breath of God. In the light of all this, how much easier is it to understand a volatile spirit like that of Lope de Vega!

or compulsion [Koran: "Let there be no violence in religion"], for if it were the will of our Lord to lead them to it and to make them believe it by force, He would constrain them if He wished to [Koran: "But if thy Lord had pleased, verily all who are in the earth would have believed together"]; but He is not pleased by the service which men do for Him out of fear, but by that which is done willingly, and without any compulsion. (*Partidas*, VII, XXV, 2).[52]

Don Juan Manuel, in his *Libro de los Estados*, expresses himself in the same fashion in the fourteenth century: "There is war between the Christians and the Moors, and there will be, until the Christians have regained the lands that the Moors took from them by force; for *neither because of the law nor because of the sect that they hold to*, would there be war between them; for Jesus Christ never commanded us to kill or to constrain people in order that they should embrace His law; for He has no desire for forced service but only for that which is done readily and freely" (p. 294).

The great historian Menéndez Pidal, citing this passage from Juan Manuel in *La España del Cid* (1947), p. 632, rightly observes that religiosity loses, "precisely in the Middle Ages . . . , a certain racial intolerance that it displays earlier in the Christian-barbarian epoch." It seems to me, however, that the matter will continue to be confused and unintelligible if we continue to speak (as I used to do also) of the "Middle Ages," or an abstract "religiosity," or "race," for the truth is that Juan Manuel's ideas about tolerance derive from those of Alfonso the Learned in his *Partidas*, and, as we have seen, they are a simple imitation of the koranic doctrine. If we are to understand the passage from the tolerance prevailing in the Christian kingdoms (with the exception of certain isolated instances of anti-Jewish persecution) to the aggression of the "little people" against the Jews in 1391—and of the inquisitors after 1481—we cannot view the process as an abstract phenomenon typical of an "epoch"; both the tolerance and the persecution arose from the varying situations of each caste with respect to the others. In each "epoch" of the past of the authentic (and not the legendary) Spaniards we must ask ourselves what were the desires and the possibilities of each of the three castes we have seen gathered around the sepulcher of Ferdinand the Holy in 1252— and around that of the Catholic Sovereigns in 1516, though by this time two of the castes had been reduced to the role of mute and suffering shadows.

The slow or rapid passage from tolerance to intolerance in the Christian caste depended on the power the upper classes wielded over the lower classes. In 1212 at the Battle of Las Navas de Tolosa

---

[52] The Moorish jurists were inspired by the same doctrine: "The profession of the Muslim faith, when it is forced, has no validity in religious law" (I. Goldzieher, *op. cit.*, p. 257, where there is cited a similar decision at the end of the seventeenth century).

the lower classes still were not playing a dominant role and were not feared by their lords. In his account of the battle the Archbishop of Toledo says that some people "terga vertentes fugere videbantur. Quod attendens Aldephonsus nobilis vidensque *quosdam plebeia vilitate quid deceat non curare*, [he exclaimed] 'Archiepiscope, ego et vos his moriamur.' "[53] The *Crónica General* translates this passage as follows: "Some of our people began to show fear, and turning their backs, it seemed that they were fleeing. And when the most noble king Don Alfonso saw what some of the *base common people* were doing, that they had not thought to observe *what was ill done*, he said to the Archbishop in the hearing of everyone: 'Archbishop, you and I shall die here' " (p. 701*b*). And after the great victory, the Archbishop said to the King: "Be mindful of the grace of God, which made up for all that you were lacking . . . : and remember likewise *your knights*, by whose aid you came to such great glory and so much honor among the kings of Spain" (p. 702*b*). In the first half of the thirteenth century the action of a strong and respected minority made itself felt in Castile.

Some two centuries later these same common people attacked the Jews of Seville (in 1391) and massacred thousands of them. The *Crónica de Enrique III* relates the episode in words which should be compared with those of the text just cited: "The people of the towns, partly because of such sermons [preached by the archdeacon, Ferrant Martínez], partly out of a desire to steal, and furthermore having no fear of the King [Henry III] on account of his youth and because of the discord among the lords of the kingdom . . . set no value on the letters of the King, nor did the cities, the towns, or the knights respect his commandments; therefore this evil came to pass."[54]

It should be borne in mind at this point that the fundamental motivation of the violent intolerance that began at the end of the fourteenth century was, on the one hand, the weakening of the authority held by the seignorial class and, on the other, the increase in the size of the Christian population. The gap between the Christian caste and the two others with respect to material wealth could no longer be bridged by the authority of the upper classes or by any spiritual principle. Finally a day would come when the Catholic Sovereigns had an urgent need for the "common people" to further their militant imperial enterprises, and with it would come at last the annihilation of the two castes which no longer possessed any possible defense. Nevertheless, there were some exceptions, as in the case of Tarazona (Saragossa), where in 1391 Christians and Jews

---

[53] Jiménez de Rada, *De rebus Hispaniae*, Book VIII, Chap. X, in *Hispania illustrata ... Scriptores Varii*, II, 135.
[54] See *Biblioteca de Autores Españoles*, LVIII, 177*b*.

skillfully came to an agreement designed not to break the traditional peace between Christians, Moors, and Jews.[55]

It is understandable that Raymond Lully (d. 1315) should have written his *Libro del gentil y los tres sabios* in Arabic rather than in his own Catalan. In this book a Christian, a Moor, and a Jew talk amiably, expounding the contents of their respective faiths without a trace of acrimony. Without doubting the orthodoxy of Lully's Christianity, one may still be quite sure that here he let himself be carried away by his enthusiasm for a kind of religion in which the faiths of the three Hispanic castes might all be contained. Just as the three religions live together side by side juridically in the legislation of Alfonso X's *Partidas*,[56] so they also dwell together harmoniously in the intellectual dreaming of Raymond Lully, after the model of Yehuda ha-Leví in the *Cuzari*.[57] What appears in the Mallorcan mystic as lyrical enthusiasm centered in the heart is converted, in Alfonso X, into a very Castilian juridical objectivity. Lully's sympathetic feelings for the infidel break out in sentences such as these: "Let our soul in prayer not forget the infidels, who are of our flesh and blood, being like us in species and form. The ignorance of faith and of science that there is in them comes from the lack of masters to teach them."[58] It must be remembered, however, that the vital

---

[55] *Sefarad* (1947), pp. 66–75. See the discussion in Chap. II about the *entrée* of the Bishop of Palencia in 1486. In this period the Jews were still offering up public prayers for rain (*Sefarad* [1958], p. 282).

[56] Among other humane laws pertaining to the Jews, we find this one: "And because the synagogue is a house where the name of God is praised, we forbid that any Christian should dare to break into it or to take from it anything by force" (VII, XXV, 4).

[57] As we have seen before, Sufism made a positive effort to becloud the frontiers that separated the different religious confessions. Some Sufists went so far as to argue that "with the knowledge of divine unity an element of union was given to humanity, whereas the different religious laws were the cause of the separation." These ideas are plainly present in the works of Raymond Lully, where they are in perfect harmony with the exalted illuminism of his lyric soul. Rationalist Deism was preceded in Europe by emotional situations in which Islam and Christianity were brought into harmony. Guillaume Postel, with his *Alcorani, seu legis Mahometi, et Evangelistarum Concordiae libre* (Paris, 1543), was trying to bring the Koran and the Gospel into agreement not in order to enrich "the ancient dream of unity *of the Middle Ages*" (as Lucien Febvre says in *Le problème de l'incrovance religieuse au XVIe siècle* [1947], p. 116) but because he was an Arabist who had been in the Orient, who had written an Arabic grammar, etc. As always happens, we are dealing here with a problem of life and not only of ideas, which will remain impenetrable for those who view it from the standpoint of inoperative suppositions. The dehumanized phantom of the "Middle Ages" bears some resemblance to the phlogiston of ancient chemistry.

[58] *Evast y Blanquerna*, Chap. XL, in Ramon Llull, *Obras literarias*, ed. M. Batllori and M. Caldentéy (Madrid, 1948), p. 255.

and legal harmony among Christians, Moors, and Jews was not an aspect of the theological and metaphysical order of the so-called Middle Ages, whose spirit was most perfectly incarnate in Dante and Thomas Aquinas. The period in Spain that was contemporary with the Middle Ages was something quite singular, as we can see when we examine Spanish history in its totality. Spanish tolerance was the result of a *modus vivendi*, not of a theology.[59]

To Alfonso the Learned and his follower Don Juan Manuel, the Moor was a political rival to be conquered and not a religious enemy to be exterminated. (Yet the Spanish Christian was at the same time implacable toward the heretic who divided his own faith.) The infidel—Moor or Jew—had a "book" just as the Christian did (as the Koran says) and was worthy of respect for this reason. But the conception of tolerance lost its power, as we have seen, when the Muslim ceased to inspire fear and admiration, and when the masses of the people began subjecting the Jews to a relentless persecution, at the end of the fourteenth century.

The power of kings and nobles stood out against so strange and complex a situation, and that power in turn enabled that heterogeneous collection of peoples to participate in a common life without excessive friction. The Church (especially certain religious orders) did all in its power to break up this common life from the end of the thirteenth century, while from the end of the fourteenth century the energies of the people were turned against the Jews. They did not attack the Mudejar population because they feared reprisals against Christian captives in Granada. After the end of the fifteenth century, Spain was ruled by only one caste. No longer was it thought that the Moors ought to live "among the Christians, keeping their own law, and not condemning ours" (*Partidas*, VII, XXV, 1). If we are to understand the difference between the mild laws of Alfonso the Learned with respect to the Jews and the savage Visigothic ones in the *Fuero Juzgo*[60] of the seventh century, we must remember the five

---

[59] Tolerance had reached down to the lowest layers of the Spanish people, to judge by certain local laws, based on the law of custom: "And the Jews shall have rights as Christians do; for whoever shall wound or kill a Jew, shall pay the same fine as if the victim were a Christian, or as if he had killed a citizen of Salamanca" (*Fuero de Salamanca*, ed. by Américo Castro and Federico de Onís, p. 202).

[60] "Let them not keep their Passover, let them not be married under their own law, let them not be circumcised." Let the Jew that does not have his children baptized "receive a hundred lashes, and let his head be shorn, and let him be cast out of the land, and let his goods come into the hands of the king," etc. (*Fuero Juzgo*, Book XII, titles ii and iii). The situation of the Jews during the Visigothic period has been studied by Solomon Katz, *The Jews in the Visigothic and Frankish Kingdoms of Spain and Gaul* (1937). The Visigothic monarchs had serious difficulty in carrying out their rigorous laws against the Jews, because the Jews bribed the clergy (Katz, *op. cit.*, p. 13) and were protected by the nobles (p. 19).

hundred years of Islam which lie between the two codes of law—
and the society of the three castes thanks to which the social structure and horizon of the Spaniard were formed.

During those five hundred years, one belief was opposed to the
other and at the same time considerable interconnection developed
between them, as in the case of Lully. Ibn Ḥazm made a detailed study
of the skepticism that suspended all judgment concerning the truth or
falsity of any philosophic system or religion: "Every demonstration
in support of a thesis or dogma is offset by another demonstration
against it." This, as Miguel Asín Palacios observes, had already been
said by the thinkers of Alexandria.[61] In his *Critical History of
Religions* Ibn Ḥazm refers to those who think that "there must be
amongst all the religions one that is authentic, but it has not manifested itself clearly and evidently to anyone, and therefore God has
imposed on no one the obligation to profess it" (Asín, *Cultura Española*, p. 302).

How it got there I do not know, but there is a spark of the idea of a
universal religion in Franciscanism. When asked why he collected the
writings of pagans with the same solicitude as those of Christians, St.
Francis replied that it was "because in them he found the letters of
which the name of God is composed. What there is of good in those
writings belongs neither to paganism nor to humanity, but only to
God, who is the author of all goodness."[62] Long before St. Francis, a
Jew from al-Andalus named Ibn Paquda had written in the eleventh
century: "The rabbis say that whoever utters a wise word, even if he
belongs to the Gentiles, is called a sage."[63]

Poetic reflections of the religious breadth of medieval Spain are to
be found in the *Cantigas* of Alfonso the Learned (see above, p. 431):
the Virgin saves a Moorish woman with her infant daughter (no.
205); a king of Morocco defeats his enemy with the help of a banner
of the Virgin (no. 181); the Moors bring back from the sea into
which they had cast it an image of the Virgin, so that they may catch
fish once more (no. 183); etc. We may recall also the Jewish supplications for relief from drought (see above, p. 503); in one instance,
the prayers were authorized by the cathedral chapter of Seville.

During the years of Christian-Islamic-Judaic intermingling, the
spiritual communication among the three beliefs made it possible for
Alfonso the Learned to base his doctrine of tolerance on the Koran
without feeling that he was offending the Church of which he was a

---

[61] *Cultura Española* (1907), V, 299.

[62] A. F. Ozanam, "Les poètes franciscains en Italie," quoted by Father Michel-
Ange, in *Etudes Franciscaines*, XXII (1909), 610. Duns Scotus finds the imprint
of God in everything, for "In commendando enim Christum, malo excedere
quam deficere a laude" (3, Dist. XIII, qua est. 4, no. 9) (*ibid.*).

[63] *Duties of the Heart*, ed. by M. Hyamson (1925), p. 16.

faithful son. But this passed, and Spanish life took other directions. True, as late as the reign of Juan II, the famous Muslim architect, Abderrahman from Segovia, designed the ground plan of the charter-house of El Paular (see above, p. 206); and at the beginning of the six-teenth century Bishop Antonio de Guevara could say: "To call a person a Moorish dog, or to call him an unbelieving Jew . . . is to use words of great temerity and even of little Christianity. . . . To call a convert a 'dog of a Moor' or 'pig of a Jew' is to call him a perjurer, a false witness, a heretic."[64] And we have already seen other humane remarks with reference to the Moriscos (p. 248). But as time went on, the Spaniard became more and more intolerant, because the motives had disappeared that had created common interests and reciprocal respect after the people forced the expulsion of all those who resisted entrance into the Christian community. The Aragonese Count of Sástago, Don Artal de Alagón, wrote in 1593:

Do not mix with any other family. The Christian family follows this rule by neither admitting nor hearing the errors of the infamous nations that are removed from God. . . . Although [Jesus Christ] came to redeem everyone, we see that he told the gentile Canaanite woman that it was not reasonable to give the children's bread to the dogs, meaning to say by this that so long as the gentiles did not change their opinions and recognize and receive His law, they were to be treated as dogs.[65]

With the adversaries of the Catholic faith eliminated (by expulsion or by forced conversion), the Spanish Catholics followed the same procedure in the sixteenth century that the Moors and Jews had followed within their own religions. That is, it was not tolerated within Judaism or Mohammedanism that a man should depart from his belief: "The Inquisition is a popular institution which functions constantly in Islam, and *for searching out and denunciation*" it is in-dependent of the ordinary tribunals. At the end of the tenth century, Almanzor won sympathy of the Mohammedan masses as well as the doctors of law *(faqihs)* "by organizing a true and official Inquisition, or purge, of all the libraries of the realm, not excepting even the royal library of Al-Hakam II" (Miguel Asín Palacios, *Abenmasarra* [1914],

---

[64] "Epístola XIV" in the second part, in *Biblioteca de Autores Españoles*, XIII, 213b.
[65] *Concordia de las leyes divinas y humanas* (Madrid, 1593), fol. 104r. The crisis in the sentiment of tolerance, and the basing of war against the infidel on purely religious motives are inseparable phenomena revealing a change in the historical horizon. But in the last analysis, the quest for "just causes" on which to base the wars against the American Indians derives from those same remote circumstances. Before the discovery of America, the King of Portugal, Don Duarte, wrote concerning the justification of the war against the Moors: "The Holy Father admonishes us to wage such a war, and none of the faithful, unless he disobeys the Pope, *must have any doubt about its justice*" (*Leal Conselheiro*, ed. J. M. Piel [1942], Chap. XVIII).

pp. 24, 91). Indeed, the Spanish Jews had a genuine Inquisition for the purpose of prosecuting those of their coreligionists who departed from their orthodoxy.

It must be clear to the reader of the foregoing pages, however, that the religious exclusionism of the Catholic caste in the sixteenth century (with its concept of an ecclesiastical state) drew more inspiration from the Judaic spirit infused into Spanish life than it did from Islam. Up until the present moment, the Muslims have allowed Jews to share their life in Morocco, Turkey, and other countries; the Holy See likewise extended such privileges to the Jews in the sixteenth century.

All these facts, the reasons for which I shall discuss in the following chapter, are linked to the different ways in which the king of France and the kings of Spain were called. In the treaty of Corbeil (1258) between St. Louis and James the Conqueror, the former is simply mentioned as "Ludovicus, Dei gratia, Francorum rex . . . ," while Don Jaime bears the titles of King of Aragon, Majorca, Valencia, Count of Barcelona and Urgel, Lord of Montpellier.[66] The reason for this difference is that the name of the king of France is linked to a Romano-Germanic tradition, while the name of several of the Christian kings (Leon, Castile, Navarre, Aragon) bears the implications of an Arabic meaning. The name of the king of France (*roi*) is derived from the Latin *rex*, a word related to *regere*, and thus having the meaning "he who rules and commands with supreme authority within a territory." The Christian kings of the Peninsula, however, are the kings of several kingdoms and territories that were not kingdoms but cities and lands conquered by them. The military nature of the sovereign underlies those titles that were given to the kings of Castile and Aragon. James I of Aragon, as we saw previously, also bore the title of King of Valencia and Majorca; as for James II, it is sufficient to cite here the beginning of a letter addressed to him by Nasar I, the king of Granada in 1314: "To the very noble Don Jaime, by the grace of God, King of Aragon, Valencia, Sardinia, Corsica, and Count of Barcelona: from me, Don Nasar, by the same grace, King of Granada, Malaga, Algeciras, Ronda, Guadix, and *amir al-moslemin* (prince of the faithful), I salute thee . . ."[67]

---

[66] *Colección de documentos del archivo de la Corona de Aragón* (Barcelona: Pedro de Bofarull, 1850), vol. VI, 130.

[67] A. Giménez Soler, *Don Juan Manuel* (Zaragoza, 1932), p. 437. That royal dignity was conditioned by transcendental circumstances that were obligatory to mention, is clearly shown in these Aragonese documents dated 1124: "Regnante Domino nostro Ihesu Cristo et sub eius imperio ego Adefonsus *dominans* in Aragone, in Superarvi [Sobrarbe] et in Ripacurcia [Ribagorza]." The king commands in the name of God and is lord of different territories. Their number in-

The parallelism between the titles given to the king of Aragon by the king of Granada and his own titles prompted me to deduce that *malik*, or king in Arabic, means "he who possesses what he has conquered by arms." Islamic law distinguishes between the *khalifa* (sovereign who rules by spiritual authority) and the *malik*, who receives his effective sovereignty (*mulk*) only by virtue of what he has conquered.[68] The Christian kings, consequently, would be similar to the *muluk* (the rulers of the princely *taifa* states), who arose in al-Andalus upon the disintegration of the caliphate of Cordova. When the Almorávides invaded Muslim territory of the Peninsula in the eleventh century, the *alfaquíes* exiled those *muluk*, a fact which at that time would have been impossible to do to a caliph.[69]

I now observe that in the war against Granada, Don Rodrigo Ponce de León, Marqués de Cádiz, had a clear idea of that royal dignity among the Moors. When Boabdil was taken prisoner by the Catholic Sovereigns in 1483, Don Alonso de Cárdenas, grand master of the military Order of Santiago, advised the king Don Fernando not to free such an illustrious captive. The Marqués de Cádiz, better acquainted with Muslim customs and laws, was adverse to this tactical move because "the Moors have such little faith in their kings, and they have such little respect for them, that they can make or break a king if he is free; if their ruler is held captive, as we have seen on several occasions, and as we see with this king who is in prison, this is even more true. We are already advised that those who were subject to his rule changed their allegiance for that of his father [Muley Hacén], and deprived the son of the title of king which they had given him. . . . Thus we cannot rightly say that we have captured a king, but merely a private personage."[70] Acting wisely on the advice of his counselor, Don Fernando freed Boabdil, who thus became more useful to him as a rival of his father than as a prisoner.

---

creased in this other document of the same year: "Ego Adefonsus, rex in Pampilona et in Aragon, in Superarvi et Ripacurcia, in Tutela et Çaragoça," J. M. Lacarra, "Documentos para el estudio de la reconquista y repoblación del Valle del Ebro," in *Estudios de Edad Media de la corona de Aragón* (Zaragoza, 1946), II, 433–434.

[68] Professor James Monroe has informed me, to confirm my suspicions, of the Arabic origin of the fact that the Christian kings bore the titles of sovereigns of several kingdoms, including cities and territories which had never been kingdoms.

[69] Muslim influence over the Christian monarchs is further evident in the fact that Alfonso VIII of Castile, the victor over the Almohades in the decisive battle of Las Navas de Tolosa (1212), coined money with Arabic inscriptions, on which, instead of the title *amīr al-Muslimīn*, he wrote *amīr al-Qatulaqīn*, that is, "he who commands over the Catholics," Philip K. Hitti, *History of the Arabs* (1967), p. 542.

[70] Hernando del Pulgar, *Crónica de los Reyes Católicos*, ed. J. de Mata Carriazo (Madrid, 1943), II, 87.

The Population of the Christian Kingdoms
from the Eighth to the Fifteenth Centuries

J UST AS THE NOUN *español* gradually became a center
toward which several other nouns such as Castilian, Leonese, Aragonese, and Navarrese gravitated and converged in the Peninsula, as was
shown in the first chapter, so a similar phenomenon also occurred
among the diverse peoples who made up the population of the
Christian kingdoms. These kingdoms were first designated as a group
by a religious term—Christians—without analogy anywhere else in
Europe, because they were combating a heterogeneous mixture of
adversaries whose common denominator was their belief in Mohammedanism. Berbers from Africa, converts to Islam who were the
descendants of Goths and Hispano-Romans, Arabs from the Near
East, and, later, groups of former captives of Slavic origin all fought
against the Christians of the north. Both Muslim and Christian territories contained a sizable number of Jews which increased simultaneously in the Christian kingdoms as the reconquest progressed. When
Alfonso VI conquered Toledo in 1085, many Moors and Jews chose
to remain in the city and live side by side with the Mozarabs, those
direct descendants of the Christians who had been living there since
the eighth and ninth centuries as a result of the system of tolerance
characteristically practiced, as we saw in chapter xii.

The warrior caste imposed its name "Christians" on all those who
lived under the authority of the Christian kings; yet the present-day
Jews of Spanish descent continue to call themselves "Sephardim"
(Spaniards) and the Moriscos (baptized Moors) expelled from Spain
in 1609 formed groups of *andalusís* in North Africa, until the eighteenth century, an eloquent indication that they still considered al-

Andalus or Muslim Spain as their homeland. In the tenth century the Mozarabs who had migrated northward from al-Andalus built a chapel for the Christian cult around 940 in a pure Arabic style at Celanova, Galicia. Moriscos expelled from Spain in the seventeenth century erected a mosque in Tunis whose façade resembles a baroque church. The casual observer attaches no importance to the phenomenon that two extraordinary works of art, the two synagogues in Toledo, were preserved as Christian churches. Furthermore, when Ferdinand III conquered Cordova in 1236 he did not destroy its magnificent mosque, although a section of it was rebuilt as a Christian cathedral in the sixteenth century within the mosque itself. These vital phenomena, as well as others discussed in previous chapters and yet to be explained, will enable me to summarize the dramatic complexity of Spanish history. In addition, they clearly indicate the necessity of reorienting our spirit and intellect toward an adequate understanding of a truly unique people. In this chapter I shall attempt to explain how the peculiar circumstances and interaction of those three castes—Christian, Muslim, and Hebrew—ultimately resulted in the lack of a European Middle Ages in Spain, and at the same time had far-reaching consequences throughout the course of Spanish history.

*Castile During the Centuries
of the Reconquest*

The point of departure for the history of those who began to call themselves *españoles* in the thirteenth century, but only truly became Spaniards in the sixteenth century when they succeeded in creating an empire, arose out of the bellicose impetus of the county of Castile in the tenth century, which proclaimed itself an independent kingdom in the following century. Only among the Castilians did an epic poetry arise that took its inspiration from contemporary themes that narrated the exploits of Count Fernán González, the seven Infantes de Lara, and the Cid. Although the anonymous *Cantar de Mio Cid*, dating from the twelfth century, is the only known surviving work of its genre,[1] Menéndez Pidal has shown that the origins of this poetry dealing with a collective theme—this point should be emphasized—probably date back to the last years of the tenth century. With this poetry the spoken dialect of Castile, different from the one used in Visigothic Hispania, achieved the status of a literary language, a phenomenon of primary historical importance that has nothing to do

---

[1] Nothing remains of the narrations or *cantares* of the eleventh century because the original manuscripts were lost. A major factor in this loss was the change in the form of writing from the Visigothic script used prior to the thirteenth century to the later use of the French script. The *Cantar de Mio Cid*, originally composed around 1140, has been preserved in a fourteenth-century copy.

with demography. The dialects spoken in the kingdoms of Leon and
Aragon, similar to those of the Visigothic period, never attained a
literary level. The Catalans first expressed themselves lyrically in
Provençal, and when their own language began to be used for literary
purposes it was not to recount the prowess of some national hero.
The Castilian epic lost its creative force in the thirteenth century,
although in the second half of the fourteenth its themes reappeared,
along with others of international inspiration, in the epicolyrical
romances (ballads) in brief form. The poetic repertory of the
Romancero, the entire corpus of traditional balladry, consists of all
that was sung in the Castilian epic and narrated in the chronicles. It
became an expressive vehicle for what had been sung previously in
the gests and narrated in the chronicles, for some local event or anecdote, for an event of national scope, or for what had been brought
to Castile on the winds of local and foreign folklore, all of which was
emptied artistically into the mold of the Castilian *Romancero* and
transferred to the popular Galaico-Portuguese or Catalan song in the
same metrical form. Audible traces of this Castilian poetic "imperialism" at an anonymous and popular level can still be heard today from
Chile and New Mexico to the Balkans, where it is preserved by
groups of Spanish-speaking Jews.

This is just a brief and incidental mention of a subject so broad
that it cannot be discussed more fully now. I only wish to emphasize
that nothing similar occurred to the east or west of Castile in Leon,
Galicia, Aragon, or Catalonia. We should keep in mind the peculiar
origin of the name *Castilla* as opposed to the other regions and kingdoms that eventually made up the future Spain. The name *Galicia* is a
continuation of the Roman *Gallaecia*. *León* is another survival of the
Roman past, whose origin is derived from the name of the Roman
legion (Legio VII Gemina) billeted in the camp site occupied by the
present-day capital. Navarre and Aragon owe their names to geographical circumstances (*nava*, "an uncultivated terrain between two
mountains"; and the river *Aragón*). The name Cataluña does not appear until the end of the eleventh century and its origin is unknown.[2]

The name *Castilla*, however, is derived from the Latin plural
castella (castles).[3] It is significant that the name of the capital of
Old Castile, Burgos, is also a plural, because, as the *Crónica General*

---

[2] See F. Udina Martorell in *Estudios de Edad Media de la Corona de Aragón*
(Saragossa), VII, 549–577. The etymology of the adjective *catalán* is also vague
or unknown.

[3] "In the ninth century the name *Castella* (the castles), applied to the contested
frontier of the kingdom of Asturias, begins to be heard in history" (R. Menéndez
Pidal, *Orígenes del español* [Madrid, 1950], p. 472). The Muslims translated *Castella* as *al-quilá*, whose singular form is Alcalá, a common toponym in Spain. For
al-Quilá see E. Lévi-Provençal, "España musulmana," in *Historia de España*, ed.
R. Menéndez Pidal, IV, 1360.

says (*op. cit.*, p. 473), its founder built up the city "among some small castles" (entre unos burguetes). The origins of Castile, then, are directly related to warlike activities (offensive and defensive fortresses) and not to traditional or geographical circumstances. This is a clear indication that the combative rhythm of the Castilian was quicker, more active, and livelier than that of his other comrades-in-arms in the reconquest. The "melody" of history is represented by its volitional, willful, and intentional line imposed on the main theme; the rest is an indispensable "accompaniment."

At the end of the tenth or the beginning of the eleventh century the inhabitants of that fortified Castile began to sing in epic poetry of the prowess and deeds of Count Fernán González. According to legend, he is credited with achieving the independence of the county of Castile from the kingdom of Leon. At this point the Castilian dialect imposed itself as a written means of communication. The minstrel who composed the *Cantar del Cid* speaks of the hero's homeland in terms of "Castilla la Gentil" (Castile "the noble"). No other kingdom was extolled in such glowing and complimentary terms.

The castles and fortified villages of early, primitive Castile are not mentioned here merely to accentuate the warlike nature of that human aggregate in relation to the Spain of the future. I am particularly interested in calling attention to the projective nature and character of the Castilians, to their will to organize themselves as an independent entity with a single language, a unique body of laws, and a literature unparalleled in other centers that arose as a consequence of resistance to Muslim domination. The unity formerly grouped around the Visigothic monarchy with its seat in Toledo, the geographical center of the Peninsula, had been shattered forever. The initial heroic reaction begun in Asturias in the eighth century and later pursued by the Leonese kings lacked the necessary dynamic impulse to lead the others. The kingdom of Leon "was an antiquated monarchy, stubbornly intent on preserving the Visigothic legal code and the strong clerical tendency of the kingdom that had already been destroyed."[4] Whether it is based on actual tradition or mere legend, it is a significant fact that those Visigothic laws were burned in Burgos by the Castilians as a sign of protest against the kingdom of Leon to which they were subject.

Today it is difficult to imagine how those eleventh-century Castilians saw themselves in relation to or in opposition to those peoples in the other regions of the Peninsula who had been fighting the Muslims for three hundred years. In the year 1000 Castile was still a county, whereas Asturias, Leon, Navarre, and Aragon had been or were in the process of becoming kingdoms. Tenth-century Castile was

---

[4] R. Menéndez Pidal, *La epopeya castellana* (Madrid, 1959), p. 43.

a dependency of the antiquated kingdom of Leon.[5] The Catalan counties comprised a special group apart with a particular set of circumstances because they were linked to the Frankish monarchy until the eleventh century. The Castilians of that "tiny corner of land" (pequeño rincón), mentioned in the eleventh-century *Cantar del conde Fernán González*, preserved the memory of their modest but heroic beginnings. Echoes of that *cantar* are found in the *Poema de Fernán González*, the learned work of a thirteenth-century monk composed around 1250:

> Estonce era Castiella un pequeño rincón
> era de castellanos Montes d'Oca mojón ...[6]
> Castiella la Vieja, al mi entendimiento,
> mejor es que lo al, porque fue el cimiento,
> ca conquirieron mucho, maguer poco conviento.

> Castile was then only a tiny corner of land,
> and Montes de Oca the Castilians' border....
> Old Castile, in my opinion,
> is the best, for it laid the foundation,
> although it numbered few inhabitants,
> it conquered a large share.

In contrast to the other Christians in the Peninsula, the Castilians firmly believed that they were self-sufficient and self-reliant, and in full possession of their own traditions. Single-handedly they extended their borders, increasing their territory with the lands taken from the Moors, and at the same time they took special advantage of the benefits of the Mudejars and Jews who became subjects of the king and lords of Castile. It was the only Peninsular kingdom that slowly forged and kept alive the collective memory of its past in a particular form of poetry that embellished the narrative sections with the imagination and sentiments of the anonymous minstrel. One of the oldest preserved *cantares de gesta* is *Los Infantes de Lara*, dating from the end of the tenth or beginning of the eleventh century.[7] The theme

---

[5] It is well known but sometimes overlooked that the Visigoths could never have bequeathed any sense of centralized unity to the groups who began to oppose the Muslims in the eighth century. According to R. Menéndez Pidal, the Visigothic monarchy was already beset by internal division and ill-fated on the arrival of the Muslims (*Historia de España*, III, lv). "The Visigothic State died of natural causes; it was not the victim of tradition or an act of treason. For years it had been afflicted by a serious illness—internal rivalries struggling for possession of the throne and the absence of any political spirit or idea of obligation toward the state" (M. Torres López, *op. cit.*, III, 139). The saying "ser de los godos" ("to be of Gothic lineage") as an expression of Spanishness is mere rhetorical vanity and serves as a good example of the erroneous idea they had about themselves.

[6] The Montes de Oca lie east of Burgos separating Castile from Navarre. Ed. A. Zamora Vicente, *Clásicos castellanos*, p. 128, *coplas* 170 and 157.

[7] R. Menéndez Pidal was able to reconstruct *La leyenda de los Infantes de Lara*

and subject matter deal with the death of the sons of an illustrious Castilian lord who were betrayed by their uncle in order to avenge an offensive act against his wife. The *cantar* reflects the intimate relationship existing in the tenth century between the Castilians and the Muslims of the caliphate of Cordova when moments of peace alternated with strife and fierce hatred, as will be explained later in this chapter. Ruy Velázquez, the Infantes' uncle, sends his brother-in-law Gonzalo Gustioz to Cordova with a letter written in Arabic to the powerful Moorish chieftain Almanzor asking him to kill the emissary and to send a band of Moors to waylay the Infantes and to kill them in an ambush set up by their own uncle. The seven young noblemen are slain together with the tutor who had raised them. According to custom, he was obliged to accompany into battle those whom he had educated and instructed in the arts of war. The seven Infantes and their tutor, Nuño Salido, perished and, as it was customary among Muslims, their eight heads were taken to Cordova where they were shown to the Infantes' father who was about to be put to death by Almanzor. The climax of that famous tragedy of hatred and avenged honor was immortalized in the ballad that begins:

> Pártese el moro Alicante
> víspera de San Cebrián
> ocho cabezas llevaba,
> todas de *hombres de alta sangre.*

> The Moor Alicante departed
> on the eve of St. Ciprian;
> eight heads he carried,
> all of men of high-born blood.

The Infantes' father enumerates the characteristic virtues of each of his sons and together "they comprise a catalog of those virtues of a typical thirteenth-century knight" (Menéndez Pidal, p. 26). The content and obvious historical basis for the nucleus of this legend (Menéndez Pidal, p. 453) are of less interest to me at this point than the very fact of the legend's survival, which is not due to the tragic intensity of the event narrated by the minstrels, but to the position of the Castilians in respect to it. The victims of this family tragedy were great lords of Castile; the entire episode took place within Castilian territory and in places whose names are still preserved today in the geography of the region.

If it were a matter of dealing with strangers, foreigners, and an unknown or fictitious geography, what had happened at the end of

---

(1934) with the help of the chronicles containing prose versions of the *cantar* and also with the ballads that had preserved the most significant scenes of the ancient *cantar de gesta* in poetic form.

the tenth century would not have given rise to a legend and a poetry that the Castilians have kept alive for over seven hundred years. It is evident that the historical and traditional aspects of this form of literature, transmitted orally, depended on a set of very specific human circumstances and conditions rather than on any abstract traditionalism. Although it is true that the possibility of an epic literature is related to Germano-Gothic traditions, as Menéndez Pidal has correctly deduced, the fact that those poetic roots flourished only in Castile obliges us, in this case, to concede more importance to the "Castilianness" of the epic than to its probable Visigothic ancestry.[8] Isidore of Hispalis once alluded to the *cantica majorum*, to the lays of his ancestors. The Goths ruled politically the entire Peninsula, but these *cantares de gesta* appeared to take root only in Castile.

In discussing the historicity of the epic, it is necessary to distinguish between the fact that the *cantares* referred to an event that had actually taken place and the idea that those *cantares* also brought the poeticized figures and their circumstances closer in time and place to the level of the minstrel and his audience. Given these circumstances, it is understandable that the minstrels who recited the Castilian epic were able to correlate the time of the literary happening or event with that of their listeners. It is a well-known fact that in the successive versions of the *cantar* of the Infantes de Lara, the frontiers of Muslim territory began to recede as the reconquest continued to advance. In addition, if those *cantares* had dealt with non-Castilian themes, they would not have become rooted in the collective conscience of the people or passed through successive phases of Castilian tradition such as the *cantares de gesta*, chronicles, ballads, and the popular theater of the seventeenth century. In this case it is more important to observe the course of life than to contemplate the sources from which it sprang forth. In the picaresque novel, *Guzmán de Alfarache*, by Mateo Luján de Sayavedra, the pseudonym of Juan Martí, the famous picaro briefly sketches for his master the entire history of Spain together with its glories and its heroes.[9] His Italian master is astonished at Guzmán's extensive knowledge. Guzmán professes to have seen "some books in Spain, and even though he had not personally seen them, everything that he had narrated was common knowledge and well-known facts which had been handed down by oral tradition, by word of mouth, and it is more difficult to ignore those facts than to know them." In 1602 Juan Martí has Guzmán mention "Count Fernán González, the first lord of Castile, from whose line the kings of Spain are descended."

The historicity of the Castilian epic expressed the Castilians' interest

---

[8] See R. Menéndez Pidal, *La epopeya castellana* (1959), pp. 23 ff.
[9] Bibl. Aut. Esp., III, Part II, Bk. I, chap. 3, 369–370.

in being present and in participating actively in the making of history itself. Moreover, their continuous warlike activity and attachment to an insistence upon the awareness of their own existence and identity obliged the Castilians to be chiefly concerned about *who* they were and where they came from, and to pay little attention to the study and knowledge of visible and material things. The offensive or defensive enterprise, either in conjunction with the neighboring Christian kingdoms or with the Moors, consumed the total energy of the Castilians, because what was at stake was the very existence of the Castilian people and not any cultural problem, either philosophical or religious. Customs and usages occupied the topsoil of their existence and not the subsoil from which unexpected fruits come forth and flourish when they are encouraged by new methods of cultivation. It is significant that the Castilian language has moved more slowly than French or English, whose thirteenth-century texts are almost unintelligible to those who are familiar with these languages only in their present-day form. The Castilian language of that century, on the contrary, requires little effort to be understood in comparison with the other tongues.

The Castilian of the first centuries of the reconquest was the only one who posed the problem of his very existence as a Castilian per se. The others—Navarrese, Leonese, Aragonese, and Catalans—also fought to survive and subsist and extend their territories, but the Castilian did all this and, in addition, he adorned his initial intellectually barren existence with the awareness of his own personality. Those lines quoted from the *Poema de Fernán González* exemplify the confession of a handful of self-made men who "conquered much, though they were few in number." When these verses were written around 1250, Castile had already taken from the Moors Toledo (1085); Cordova (1236), the ideological center of Muslim power; and Seville (1248). Castile was gradually becoming an entity with a clearly defined structure and purpose as is evident in these lines from the same poem:

> com ella es mejor de las sus vezindades,
> assí sodes mejores cuantos aquí morades;
> omnes sodes sesudos, *mesura heredades*; . . .
> Pero de toda España, Castiella es mejor,
> porque fue de los otros el comienço mayor,
> guardando e temiendo siempre a su señor;
> quiso acrecentarla assí el Criador.   (*coplas* 156–157)

> as she is better than her neighbors,
> thus you who live here are also superior;
> you are sensible, wise, and prudent, qualities you inherited . . .
> But Castile is the best in all Spain,
> because in former times it had the most glorious beginnings,
> and has always respected and feared its lord;
> thus did the Creator ordain it to grow and multiply.

In *copla* 477 he again repeats the words, "You are prudent, men of common sense, and think before you act" (sois sesudos, sois reflexivos, mesurados). The author lived during the time of Ferdinand III, a period of great military triumphs. Perhaps he would not have expressed himself in the same manner if he had written during the succeeding reigns of Alfonso X and Sancho IV. In any event, though the Castilians were capable of giving themselves over fully to undisciplined violence in practice, their literature still dealt primarily with solemn, grave moral themes or heroic subjects in the thirteenth century. During this same period Catalan and Galician literatures were entirely different in subject matter and treatment. Castile's bellicose enterprise, which formed the very core of its political and economic life, did not offer a propitious climate for a literature of the imagination or individualized loves, without any relationship to the modes of thought and sensibility of the Castilians. This was possible in "Western Europe," in the centers of learning at Paris and other places during the same period for reasons I shall discuss in the following section, but heroic deeds, moralizing reflection, and religious beliefs inspired the literature of Castile between the eleventh and fourteenth centuries.

The continuity of Castilian life revolved around the *ser*, the very core of the Castilian's existence, his own self-esteem and his character and conduct rather than around specific cultural manifestations such as schools of philosophy or art which arose beyond Castile's frontiers. Castile centered its interest in its *hombría castellana*, in the Castilian as a human being in all his manly aspects, and in turn transformed this theme into a prolonged present by virtue of which that *pequeño rincón*, the "tiny corner of land," ultimately succeeded in fusing its boundaries with those of Spain as a whole. Eventually its frontiers coincided with those of a pyramidal Spain in an apex of beliefs and respect at the top, even though it was not altogether unified at its base on a plane of mutual political, cultural, and economic interests. For these very reasons, exemplified by the Castilian's awareness of his own uniqueness, together with singular circumstances unparalleled in the rest of Europe, it was impossible for Castile to follow the course of Western European culture or to participate in the so-called Middle Ages, the causes of which I shall attempt to analyse in the following section.

Why the Concept of the European
"Middle Ages" Was Not Possible in Spain

The Christian caste began to increase its population and territories as it fought against the Muslims, augmenting its number with Mozarabs, who were Christians but whose culture and language were Arabic. In the thirteenth century the Christian armies made great advances after their victory at the decisive battle of Las Navas de Tolosa in 1212. The annexation of Valencia, Cordova, Seville, and other cities contributed to increasing the Mudejar population (those who professed the Islamic faith) as well as the number of Jewish subjects whose native language by this time was Castilian or Catalan. These conditions gave rise to a phenomenon without analogy or parallel anywhere in Europe at this time. The significance of all this is that the life and culture of the Christian population were conditioned by those who were not of the same religion. In European cities during this same period there were internal differences between classes and economic and cultural levels, but there were no religious differences manifested in the triple form in which they were found in Spain. For this reason it is impossible to pour out blind, abstract figures concerning population data or rational class distinctions to explain the problems confronting this heterogeneous population in the Christian kingdoms. Those analytic methods entirely overlook the main factor that the intrinsic condition, religion, and customs of these peoples were the primary determinants in everything that happened in those kingdoms under Christian sovereignty, determinants that eventually led to the formation of an empire and to the apparent consolidation of Spain under one single religion—the Catholic one—in the sixteenth century.

Paradoxically, as a result of the aforementioned conditions, the Christian kingdoms continued to increase their dominions at the cost of being affected by Judeo-Islamic ways of living, primarily because religion served to characterize and differentiate people socially. At the same time, Arabic culture left its profound mark on certain material areas of Christian domination, as is evidenced by the numerous examples of words, expressions, and customs of Arabic origin dealt with extensively in chapters vii and viii. It is also very significant that royal personages were sometimes buried in Arabic shrouds and clothing bearing Arabic inscriptions.[10] According to Manuel Gómez Moreno, the Castile of the twelfth and thirteenth centuries "gravitated between two poles. . . . Burgos represented the attraction toward Europe. The other pole was Toledo," which had received its Oriental culture by way of the Jews and the Moors; it had its own unique art and industry. The tombs of the members of the royal families buried at the convent of Las Huelgas in Burgos were embellished with "magnificent vestments of an Eastern type that had penetrated the Christian mode of living in the same manner as Muslim science, philosophy, and literature became accessible to them through Latin versions" (*El panteón real de las Huelgas de Burgos*, pp. 99–100).

This statement is only partially accurate. It is a well-known fact

---

[10] See illustrations in Manuel Gómez Moreno, *El panteón real de las Huelgas de Burgos* (Madrid, 1946).

that during this period the knowledge of important aspects of Greek culture penetrated Europe by way of the Arabs of al-Andalus, whose works were, in turn, translated into Latin in Toledo with the help of Mozarabs and Jews.[11] It is also often heard or read that Spain served as a bridge between Greek culture and the European culture of the Middle Ages. In spite of such rhetoric, the truth is that even before the twelfth century foreigners had journeyed to Muslim Seville and to other parts of al-Andalus, that vast territory below the Christian kingdoms, to translate scientific or technical works in order to take advantage of them in their own countries.[12] As early as the tenth century, French scholars from the School of Chartres, avid for knowledge of Arabic philosophy and science, had made use of Arabic learning. As J. M. Millás Vallicrosa says, the culture of al-Andalus "quickly spread beyond its own borders and shone brilliantly on the horizon among European Christians."[13]

In brief, Greek culture and Arabic thought, aside from their influence on one lone Toledan scholar, Gundisalvus, and outside Castile, on the great figure of Raymond Lully, did not have any visible effect on the Christian kingdoms. Although it has been well known for many years, no attempt has been made to explain why the Christian kingdoms in the Peninsula were scarcely affected by that culture. Neither the Castilians nor the Aragonese were interested in cultivating the philosophy of Averroës, Avempace, or Ibn Gabirol, or in creating a philosophy of their own. They did not want to or were not able to draw upon the thought or scientific techniques of the Moors who were their enemies in one sense and models in so many others. The truth is that these philosophers bore fruit in Europe and not in the Christian kingdoms.

What is even worse is the fact that Spanish historians close the door on any possible explanation of this phenomenon when they consider those philosophers, scientists, or scholars of al-Andalus as *españoles*, or when they compare the translations of astrological works at the court of Alfonso X of Castile in the thirteenth century with the reactions provoked by the thought of certain Muslims in Christian

---

11 "In Spain the natural development of monastic life had been broken by the Moorish invasion and the religious wars that followed . . . . The knowledge that Spain spread over Europe in this period had not found a place in her own monastic libraries; indeed, the whole of twelfth-century manuscripts in Spain today is disappointingly small." Ch. J. Haskins, *The Renaissance of the Twelfth Century* (Harvard, 1933), pp. 41-43.

12 Ibn Abdūn said this without hiding his annoyance at this fact in his *Sevilla a comienzos del siglo XII*, trans. E. Lévi-Provençal and E. García Gómez, p. 173.

13 See E. Gilson, *La philosophie au moyen âge* (1947), pp. 377 ff; J. M. Millás Vallicrosa, *Las traducciones orientales de la Biblioteca de la Catedral de Toledo* (1942); J. Ferrater Mora, *Diccionario de filosofía* (1965), for details concerning the famous School of Translators in Toledo and Greco-Arabic influence in Europe.

Europe. One of the most notable examples is the presence of the thought of Averroës (Ibn Rushd) in the *Summa Theologica* of St. Thomas Aquinas.[14] But if Averroës is called *español*,[15] what explanation is there for the fact that there were never any followers of Averroës among the Spaniards? Ramón Menéndez Pidal also confuses the issue by stating that "the school [of translators] at Toledo was signaled out as unique among the episcopal schools of Europe which performed important scholarly services at that time because it transmitted Arabic science and learning to the Latin world which was so greatly in need of such knowledge."[16]

Actually it was not a Castilian Christian at all who took the initiative in calling attention to the philosophy and science of the Muslims. The study of Greco-Arabic thought actually began in the twelfth century when Raymond de Sauvetat, a French archbishop of Toledo (1125–1151), ordered Aristotle as well as Arabic and Jewish philosophers to be translated into Latin. One of these translators was the archdeacon of Segovia, Domingo Gundisalvo (Dominicus Gundisaluus, sometimes called Gundisalino because a copyist misread his Latin name Gundisaluus).[17] He is the only Castilian of that period mentioned in the histories of philosophy and the sole outstanding Castilian figure in that group of inquisitive and curious Europeans who was able to perceive the possibilities of Greek thought brought to Europe by way of the Arabs. In spite of his originality, however, his thought was closely related to that of the Muslim philosophers of his time. In the middle of the twelfth century Gundisalvus translated works by Avicenna and Ibn Gabirol from the Arabic with the help of the Jewish convert, Johannes Hispanus (known as Ibn-Dāwūd). He is also the author of *De divisione philosophiae*, a classification of the sciences in which he added to the Quadrivium physics, psychology, metaphysics, and economy, whose existence had been revealed by the translations of Aristotle. His most important works, *De processioni mundi*, *De anima*, and *De immortalitate animae*, were strongly influenced by the authors Gundisalvus was translating. He believed that God does not create the soul directly, but rather it is created through angels, who do not create it from nothingness, but from "spiritual matter." The corporeal and spiritual substances, insofar as they come from God, are incorruptible and infinite. I do not propose to discuss Gundisalvus's ideas at this point, but simply wish to emphasize that he is an isolated case of a Castilian philosopher whose presence began to be

---

[14] M. Asín Palacios, *Huellas del Islam* (1941), pp. 18–69.

[15] See M. Cruz Hernández, "Averroës, filósofo español," in *Historia de la filosofía española: Filosofía hispano-musulmana* (Madrid, 1957), II, 27.

[16] "Sicilia y España antes de las Vísperas sicilianas," in *Bolletino*, III (Palermo, 1955), 9.

[17] See Gilson, *La philosophie . . .*

felt in Europe in Guillaume d'Auvergne, St. Bonaventure, and Albertus Magnus.[18]

All these facts were brought to light in 1843 when A. Jourdain published his *Recherches sur les anciennes traductions latines d'Aristote* in Paris. Menéndez y Pelayo contributed additional information,[19] although he was partially responsible for creating some of the "myths" when he refers to Muslim culture in the Peninsula as "Spanish": "There were hardly any Arabs among these philosophers. Most of them were Syrians, Persians, or Spaniards." A more modern historian, E. Gilson, does not fall into the same trap. Referring to Ibn-Ṭufayl who was born in Cadiz around 1100 and died in Morocco in 1185, Gilson writes: "He was a man of encyclopedic knowledge, like all those Arabs whose learning and scholarship surpassed that of the Christians of his time" (*La philosophie au moyen âge*, p. 359). It would be more accurate to apply the term "Muslims" to those writers whose language and beliefs were Arabic and whose works constituted the most enduring and valuable aspects of that civilization from the ninth to the twelfth century. In the Muslim West philosophy and science flourished together with those same disciplines whose roots were not Arabic in origin. Ibn-Sīna (980–1037), or Avicenna as he is better known in Latin, was a native of Bukhara, a region far to the east of the Caspian Sea, originally a part of the Persian Empire and incorporated into the caliphate in the eighth century. The great mathematician, al-Battāni (877–918), born in Haran, Mesopotamia, was not an Arab either. It is important to bear in mind these and other analogous examples and facts in order to understand the conflict that arose later between two sectors of the Muslim world. A disastrous rivalry was built up between two groups of people, one of whom felt the vanity and pride of their Arabic ancestry, of originally belonging to a tribe of Bedouins or nomads capable of building an empire, but who at the same time sensed their cultural inferiority with respect to those people in the Persian Empire or in broad areas of the Byzantine Empire who considered themselves the heirs of those who had Hellenized the lands now inhabited by Mohammedan and Arabic-speaking peoples.

Ibn Khaldūn (1332–1406), the last important representative of Muslim thought after its eclipse in the thirteenth century, explains, clearly and accurately, the reasons for the rise and fall of philosophical and scientific knowledge in the Eastern and Western domains of Islam.[20]

---

18 See J. A. Endres, "Die Nachwirkung von Gundisalinus' *De immortalitate animae*," *Philosophisches Jahrbuch*, XII (1900), 382–392; in addition, the important study by M. Asín Palacios, *Abenmasarra y su escuela* (Madrid, 1914), pp. 114–120, for the meaning of "spiritual matter" in Gundisalvus and other philosophers before and after him; also see bibliography, note 13.

19 *Historia de los heterodoxos españoles* (1882), (ed. Madrid, 1965), I, 410–444.

20 *The Muqaddimah* (*An Introduction to History*), trans. Franz Rosenthal, ed. and abridged by N. J. Dawood (Princeton, 1967).

When the Muslims conquered vast areas of the Byzantine Empire in Asia in the eighth century, they began to hear the bishops and priests of their Christian subjects speak of philosophy and science. Because man's thinking capacity directs its desire for knowledge toward the intellectual sciences, the caliph al-Manṣūr (r. 754–775) requested translations of mathematical works from the emperor of Byzantium who sent him Euclid's treatise and several works on physics (Gilson, pp. 374–375).

The mere fact that the first contacts with Greek culture reached these Muslims by way of Christian ecclesiastics does not explain why later followers of Islam were completely uninterested in knowing anything about Hellenistic literature. According to evidence of the discovery of manuscripts by Homer and playwrights, as well as by orators and poets, Greek was still being read and studied when the Arabs conquered Egypt in the middle of the seventh century, even though its literary tradition was not continued in written form.[21] The Muslims were interested in translating and using the botanist, Dioscorides, for practical purposes, but not Sophocles, Aristophanes, or Sappho. Only a small minority assiduously cultivated the philosophic and scientific learning of ancient Greece, because these disciplines remained outside the sphere and structure of Islamic sensibility insofar as its world vision and way of life were concerned or affected. Achilles, Oedipus, and Lysystrata did not find their way into the Arabic language, an excellent vehicle for expressing the sensitive, imaginative flow of a narrative form or a particular type of poetry. In Greek literature, however, the artistically idealized figure is occasionally the victim of his fate, but he is able to reason with himself and argue with the superhuman powers beyond his control. In Islamic literature it was not possible to pose any conflict between man and the gods that might have given rise to characters such as Agamemnon, Electra, and Orestes. It was inconceivable and forbidden to satirize or treat the gods skeptically. On this point East and West inevitably diverged. Gerbertus d'Aurillac (who became Pope Silvester in 999) could write a treatise on geometry and at the same time cultivate his interest in the Latin classics. He read the *Achileid* of Statius and Cicero, whose style he tried to imitate ("Cum studio bene vivendi semper conjunxi studium bene dicendi"); he searched avidly for commentaries of Terence (Gilson, p. 229). None of the various dialects into which Arabic was divided within its vast dominions could ever develop into a literary language different from the fixed and consecrated style perpetuated by the Koran. By contrast, Latin continued to be written

---

[21] See H. Iris Bell, *Egypt from Alexander the Great to the Arab Conquest* (Oxford, 1948), p. 61.

among European Christians until the eighteenth century, and the Romance and Germanic languages began to be cultivated for literary purposes in the eleventh century. The use and value of a language depends on circumstances alien to its mere grammatical structure.

The linguistic phenomenon that occurred in Western Europe was not able to take place in Muslim-dominated lands for the same reasons that "the ability to cultivate scientific and philosophic thought" was only continued for a short time and under particular conditions, according to Ibn-Khaldūn. The Muslim historian relates that the caliph al–Ma'mūn (r. 813–833), considered to be an educated man for his time and anxious to encourage intellectual activity, sent ambassadors to Byzantium in search of scientific works that would later be translated into Arabic. "Muslim scholars and scientists studied Greek sciences assiduously, and . . . they made so much progress that they were able to refute the arguments of the First Master (Aristotle) on many points." Al-Fārābī and Ibn-Sīna in the East and Averroës (Ibn-Rushd) and Avempace (Ibn-Baŷŷa) in Muslim Spain were held to be some of the greatest figures of Islam; "and there were others who also attained similar intellectual stature in the sciences" (Ibn-Khaldūn, *The Muqaddimah*, p. 374). Much later, however, cultural activity in Muslim Spain came to a standstill; a few sporadic traces remained, but now the studious scholars "are controlled by orthodox religious scholars" (p. 375). Further on Ibn-Khaldūn mentions vaguely that science and philosophy were cultivated "in the land of Rome [at the University of Bologna?] and along the adjacent shore of the country of the European Christians [England?]. . . . God knows better what exists there" (p. 375).

In spite of its ups and downs, the study of philosophy and science continued uninterrupted from the ninth century until modern times in Christian Western Europe, while these disciplines were strangled by Muslim orthodoxy in the twelfth century. Only in the fourteenth century did the solitary, exceptional figure of Ibn-Khaldūn appear to pose for himself the problem of the rise and fall of civilizations. In the Muslim world from this time on, the pursuit of secular knowledge and thought was condemned as sinful activity by the undisputed authority of the *alfaquíes* (the expounders of the Koran) and in general, by the common people as well.

We can approach this phenomenon from several angles without losing sight of our ultimate aim, which is to explain why the Christian kingdoms between the twelfth century and the modern era (1500) reacted so feebly both to that Muslim culture that was so close to them and to Western Europe, whose faint echoes had remotely reached Ibn-Khaldūn. Our problem has now become bifurcated: on the one hand, it is a question of understanding the reasons for the gradual disappearance of Muslim science and philosophy and, on the other, why the Peninsular kingdoms remained so impervious to that culture.

A recent study by James T. Monroe, *The Shu' Ūbiyya in al-Andalus* (the Muslims of non-Arabic descent in Muslim Spain),[22] has shed new light on the first aspect of the question. Professor Monroe has translated and commentated the *risala* or literary epistle of Abū 'Amīr ibn Garcia and five arguments against it. Ibn Garcia was a Basque who had been captured by the Moors as a young child. His sire, the Muslim king of Denia in the eleventh century, who was of Christian descent, raised Ibn Garcia in the faith and culture of Mohammed. From its very beginnings the population of al-Andalus, as I have emphasized on other occasions, was composed of a heterogeneous mixture of peoples of different ancestry; the smallest number came from Arabia, the largest group was of Berber and particularly of Roman-Gothic origin. A large majority of these last peoples chose to become Muslims, and in this manner a "caste" of converts was formed, analogous in many ways to the "caste" of Jewish converts who accepted baptism willingly or reluctantly during the fifteenth century.

The conflicting situations created by the Shu'ūbiyya were not comparable, however, to those which existed between New and Old Christians in the Spain of the sixteenth and seventeenth centuries, primarily because of the prominent position of many Muslims of non-Arabic descent. The king of Denia, Ali ibn Mujāhid (r. 1044–1076), in whose reign Monroe believes that the *risala* of Ibn Garcia was composed, as we have seen, was of Christian ancestry. In addition, these neo-Muslims boasted of their scientific and cultural knowledge, since the men of the highest intellectual level were not descended from Arab Bedouins. Ibn Garcia says: "The non-Arabs are wise, mighty in knowledge, endowed with insight into natural philosophy and the sciences of exact logic, such as the bearers of astronomy, music, and the experts in arithmetic and geometry . . ." (Monroe, pp. 13–14). Two centuries prior to Ibn Garcia, the aforementioned caliph, al-Mamūn, who was chiefly responsible for the introduction of Greek thought in the Muslim world, had been accused of being a "prince of disbelievers" by one of his courtiers.[23] It was probably not by sheer accident that the man responsible for introducing and encouraging Greek thought in the Islamic world was the son of a Persian mother and in turn was married to a Persian wife. Al-Mamūn was not of pure Arabic descent and, besides, he believed as the Mutakellemim or "dis-

---

[22] Berkeley, Los Angeles, and London: University of California Publications: Near Eastern Studies (1970), vol. 13.

[23] De Lacy O'Leary, *How Greek Science Passed to the Arabs* (London, 1948), p. 162.

senters" did, that man is responsible for his actions, that he can exercise his free will, that God does not determine the course of human action, and that it is possible to attain salvation by rational means. Obviously Greek dialectics supplied all the necessary ammunition for this trend of thought.[24] Logically the orthodox Muslims and the masses adhered to the traditional norms imposed on them by the *alfaquíes*: "The Koran, the Word of the Prophet, and the I-don't-know."[25] Eventually this last formula became the prevailing one in determining the course of Muslim civilization. In spite of the fact that a cultural movement of a very high level was achieved in the eleventh and twelfth centuries, superior in many respects to that of Christian Europe, there was an underlying tension created by the contrast between the high military-political level of Islam in the Near East as well as in al-Andalus and the awareness of the primitive and illiterate origins of those who had helped to create it. This conflict may possibly explain the rivalry and struggles for power between the neo-Muslims and those of pure Arabic descent, and at the same time provide a clue to the minority nature of the movements in science as well as the religious sects who supported them. Consequently, the attempts of the neo-Muslim Ibn Garcia to erase the social distinction between the people of his caste and those of remote Muslim descent were in vain, because in the eyes of the latter group he was looked upon as an outcast. One of his adversaries replies to him: "Get you hence, O very ignorant apostate and depraved religious hypocrite" (Monroe, p. 13). This is merely an example of what happened to the caliph al-Mamūn, who was accused of being the "prince of disbelievers" instead of being called by his title, the "prince of believers" (amir al-muʾminīn) because in 830 he had founded the House of Wisdom (al-Bayt al-Hikmah) in Bagdad.

The philosopher Ibn Masarrah (883–931), who was also of non-Arabic descent, flourished in al-Andalus in the following century. Because of his "pantheistic and almost atheistic" ideology, according to the Muslims of Cordova, he was forced to take refuge in the East.[26]

---

[24] A bibliography of this complex theological, philosophical problem may be found in M. Cruz Hernández, *Filosofía hispano-musulmana* (Madrid, 1957), I, 37 ff.

[25] Asín Palacios, *Abenmasarra* . . . , p. 19, calls this formula of the *alfaquíes* "stubborn agnosticism."

[26] See Asín Palacios, *op. cit.* The father of this philosopher revealed his non-Arabic descent in his physical characteristics: "The blond color of his hair and fair skin made him pass, in the eyes of the inhabitants of Basora, for a Sicilian, a Norman, or one of some northern stock"; for this reason he was vulnerable "to being sold as a slave" (p. 30). Asín's study, like those of other distinguished Spanish scholars, occasionally loses sight of or deforms the subject dealt with because of that traditional error discussed and combated in this book. The author believes that the assimilation of Eastern culture did not invalidate "the eternal law of the continuity of Iberian thought" (p. 29). Asín acknowledges the absence of philosophy in Visigothic Hispania because "The indigenous tradition had been broken (!) without any link to Islam" (p. 17). He cites Seneca, who we have said

He returned at the beginning of the reign of Abd-al-Rahmān III (912–961), having become "a more tolerant and avid scholar" (Asín, p. 36). Ibn Masarrah's works were not destroyed until after his death, probably because of the caliph's protection, but the philosopher left such a broad and deep imprint that Asín was able to reconstruct the essence of his doctrine. It is beyond the scope of this topic to discuss his philosophy at this point, but it is significant that both in Eastern and Western centers of Islam thinkers arose who were interested in a rational interpretation of their faith, which, incidentally, none of them attempted to destroy, and who wished to spread Ibn Masarrah's doctrines. These theories inevitably disappeared, as Ibn Khaldūn said sorrowfully in the same tone as he vaguely referred to the study of sciences in Christian Europe.

From a historical standpoint Ibn Khaldūn's lament and Ibn Masarrah's predicament are understandable if we bear in mind that Greek rational thought was able to penetrate certain areas of the Mohammedan world because the Arabs had occupied parts of the Byzantine Empire that were too weak to resist the advancing onslaught of the Bedouins who were fascinated by the promises of the Koran and at the same time seduced by the echoes and traces of Hellenistic and Judeo-Hellenistic culture. The circumstances that had brought about a Judeo-Neoplatonic-Christian harmony six centuries earlier, together with the orientation of the new religion toward the Greco-Roman lands in the West, began to make themselves felt when Islam's power consolidated itself in the vast territories of the Abbassid caliphs in Persia, Assyria, and Egypt in the second half of the eighth century. The Koran ended up by confronting the Gnosis (the only wisdom is that attained by mystical means); along with this came astrology, magic spells, love potions, and other popular beliefs. The commentators of the Koran found themselves in an atmosphere full of forms of spirituality as varied and contradictory as those used by the Prophet to construct that motley syncretic collection of beliefs. Resonances of the Old and New Testaments lived side by side with magical daydreams and the experience of the Bedouin, proud of being a nomad and of his genealogy at the same time. The conflicts between reason and faith were minimal, and to settle those quarrels scholars had recourse to the philosophy that had enlightened the minds of the Hellenes and Hellenized peoples a thousand years earlier. Under the protection of the Abbassid caliphs, as in the earlier case of al-Mamūn, there was a gradual renaissance of Aristotelian thought, that is, of scholastic philosophy which opened the way for theological controversy.

---

before was not a Spaniard but a Roman, and St. Isidore, who was not a philosopher at all.

The ultimate consequence of this heterogeneous mixture of beliefs was the defeat of certain schools of thought, nourished by the habits of intelligent discourse, that had originated in the upper cultural circles but had not flourished spontaneously on every social level. Islam could not withstand the powerful opposition of the *alfaquíes*, the orthodoxy that was supported by the masses, and the peoples of Islam again returned to their former state, because trees, both vegetable and social, grow from their roots, not from their tops. The last of the great Muslim thinkers, Ibn-Rushd or Averroës (1126–1198), proposed a dual method of expounding theology, one for the learned and a separate one for laymen and the masses: "Muslim leaders should prohibit books of religious science for those who are not versed in it. . . . He who reveals the content of these books contradicts the precepts of divine law, for it is harmful to the highest class of superior beings, since these books rigidly state that they be known thoroughly only by those who have the proper instruction to know them profoundly."[27]

The lawgivers, theologians, and common people were the staunch enemies of any type of secular science. In spite of this, the Almohade caliph Yaqūb Yusūf (r. 1163-1184) employed both Ibn-Rushd and Ibn-Ṭufayl as his physicians in Marrakesh and bestowed honor and favor on them. Acting on the ruler's orders, the vizier suggested that Ibn-Rushd undertake his great task of commentating Aristotle. Upon the death of that benevolent caliph, his successor Yaqūb al-Manṣūr retained Ibn-Rushd as his physician, but exiled him to Lucena near Cordova in order to pacify public opinion. The caliph found it necessary to ingratiate himself with his subjects while he was preparing the great army that was to win the important Battle of Alarcos in 1195, so disastrous for Alfonso VIII of Castile (Léon Gauthier, p. ii). According to Gauthier, it is mere hearsay that the masses hostile to Ibn-Rushd succeeded in convincing the caliph that the philosopher was a heretic. After the victory at Alarcos the philosopher returned from exile and continued to serve as the caliph's court.

I might point out here that the same thing happened at an African court at the end of the twelfth century as had occurred in Bagdad during the ninth century when the jurists and theologians looked upon the caliph al-Mamūn as a "bad" Muslim. At the highest, most splendid moment of the caliphate of Cordova al-Ḥakam II, "the Learned" (r. 961–976), amassed an extensive library, said to contain 400,000 volumes, and encouraged all types of intellectual activity; but before he died he repented of this sin of such great magnitude that he advised his successor to study only religious books.[28] In order to ingratiate himself with the anticultural demagogues, the invincible leader Al-

---

27 Fasl al-Maqāl, *Traité décisif*, trans. Léon Gauthier (Algiers, 1948), pp. 21-22.
28 Julián Ribera, *La enseñanza entre los musulmanes españoles*, pp. 14-15.

manzor, "the Victorious," established "a veritable official inquisition" and purged all the libraries, including the magnificent one of al-Ḥakam II, at the end of the tenth century.[29] Almanzor won his victories with the help of the zealous impetus of the masses, fired by their enthusiasm for the Mohammedan faith. Consequently in view of this opposition, there was no hope for the survival of any type of rational thought cultivated by philosophers, scientists, and mathematicians, in spite of the good intentions of a few caliphs and certain groups desirous of encouraging intellectual efforts. The origins of Islamic might, its swift and fiery victories over the fallen Persians, Byzantines, Berbers, and Roman-Goths in the Iberian Peninsula, made it very difficult to convince broad sectors of public opinion of the need to reconcile their belief in Allah and the promises of paradise with the actual reality He had created for them on earth. Over a period of five centuries a handful of intelligent Muslims made an effort to develop their capacity for rational discourse, initiated by a minority of thinkers; in addition, they even tried to make the genealogy of the non-Arabs compatible with that of the descendants of the Arabic companions of Mohammed. It is significant that the only important religious controversy in Islam was more of a genealogical than a doctrinary nature. The Shiites differed from the orthodox Sunnites because the former believed that the true imams (the prayer leaders in the mosque) were descended from Ali and Fatima, Mohammed's daughter.[30] All these facts support the theory that the neo-Muslims (studied by J. T. Monroe) aspired to form an independent group or "caste" based on the fact that they were not descended from "Arabs, possessors of mangy camels," but on the contrary were made up of people of "Roman origin and blond, Byzantine lineage, fostered by the possessors of inner virtue, lineal glory, and greatness among the blond ones; they did not pasture sheep or different varieties of beasts of burden" (*History of the Arabs*, p. 24). The five violent retorts to Ibn Garcia's *risala* reflect the viewpoint of the dominating masses who stifled any possible intellectual or individualized activity among Muslims.

The evidence discussed in this section also confirms the present-day ideas of a few Muslims concerned with their position of inferiority with respect to Western peoples. A version of Amir Shakib Arsalan's work, *Our Decline and its Causes*,[31] published in Pakistan, states: "Where and what is the state of the Muslims today and that of their predecessors who marched, shouting, into the jaws of death, in order

---

[29] Asín Palacios, *Abenmasarra* . . . , pp. 24 and 91. According to this Arabic scholar, the denunciation of an impious act is mandatory in Islam; the Inquisition was an institution of a popular nature, independent of the tribunals of justice insofar as the seeking out and denunciation of heresy were concerned.

[30] For a bibliography of this subject, see Philip K. Hitti, *History of the Arabs* (1967), pp. 247 ff.

[31] Lahore: Ashraf Press (1962).

to defend their holy faith, and who were often disappointed at not finding death while seeking it along their path of duty. 'It smells of Paradise'—these are their words with which those gallant soldiers of Islam urged their steeds forward" (p. 10). The author adds that "the worst enemies of the Muslims are Muslims themselves" (p. 39), because they try to adopt the policies of their enemies in Morocco and other places. It is equally noteworthy that this Muslim should censure his coreligionists for imitating foreign science (p. 104), forgetting "with what zeal and enthusiasm" all the sciences were formerly taught at the Muslim universities in Cordova and other cities; "how glorious was the galaxy of geniuses and scholars produced by Islam." Apparently it is unusual for some educated Muslims to realize that the Mohammedans themselves, with their own beliefs and "genealogies," made it impossible for the Islamic peoples to place themselves on the same level with the West because they were incapable of studying and utilizing the laws of nature for their own benefit.

A similar situation occurred in Spanish historiography, although in a very different form. Except for the aforementioned Gundisalvus, there is still no logical explanation for the absence of a philosophy or science as such among the Christians of the reconquest. Perhaps this is why the Muslim and Jewish authors of al-Andalus are called "españoles," in order to compensate for such an obvious vacuum. Outside Castile, however, there was one great figure, Raymond Lully (1235–1315), whose thought gravitated toward the religion of the Sufis and Muslim doctrine rather than toward Christian European philosophy. He knew only Catalan and Arabic.[32] But neither Gundisalvus nor Lully could fill the vacuum of original thought between Galicia and Aragon during the centuries of the reconquest, inaccurately called the "Middle Ages"; the merit and originality of this period in Spain lies in a different direction.

Our own carelessly written histories (and I am as responsible as any for not having revolted against my teachers fifty years ago) have neglected to clarify once and for all that Roman-Visigothic Hispania did not will a single original thinker to posterity. Historians have let themselves be carried away by the currents of the medieval chroniclers. We already saw in the first chapter that the *Crónica General*, written at the end of the thirteenth century, referred to the pre-Roman and Hispano-Roman inhabitants of the Iberian Peninsula as *españoles*. Today some people still continue to believe and write that Trajan and Seneca were fellow countrymen of the present-day Span-

---

[32] Asín Palacios proves this in his *Abenmasarra* . . . , pp. 123–126. According to his own declaration, his works were translated from Catalan into Latin on two occasions.

iards. But even the *Crónica General* does not call either the Goths or the Christians who fought against the Moors *españoles*, as we have already seen.

Thanks to these detours and circumlocutions I can understand why Spanish historians and foreigners who follow their example are not surprised at the fact that there are "Spaniards" in Spain when "Frenchmen" do not yet exist in France, nor "Italians" in Italy. Ferdinand Lot writes: "St. Hilary of Poitiers, a Gaul," and shortly afterward he mentions "the Spaniard," Aurelius Prudentius, and "the Spaniard," Paulus Orosius.[33] In French, the term *gallo-romain* is used, but not *hispano-romain*, because the erroneous terminology of Spanish historians has confused foreigners. By virtue of inventing a fictitious past in order to avoid unpleasant realities, the authentic past loses its problematic aspect and fuses into a block with the present, leaving both periods of time subject to a false interpretation.

As for Seneca, Karl A. Blüher's work, *Seneca in Spanien*,[34] has placed things in their proper perspective. Seneca began to be known in Spain in the thirteenth century only after his work had been studied and acknowledged in the rest of Europe. "Spain never actually cultivated Senecanism on her own account" ("Eine isolierte Entwicklung hat es in Spanien nie gegeben," p. 7). Seneca left a deep mark on the Spanish mind as a "scholar" or wise man; for this reason, that Roman, a native of Cordova ("der aus Córdoba gebürtige Römer"), symbolized the height of "wisdom and learning" for the masses (p. 488). Perhaps Blüher does not put sufficient emphasis on the relationship between the false "Spanishness" of Seneca and the Spanish tendency to adapt as its own everything that originated within its geographical boundaries, oblivious of the human-temporal factors. Foreigners unconsciously accept this cultural imperialism; thus Blüher also calls Prudentius a *Spanier* (p. 22), just as the French do.

In the same line of thought, St. Isidore of Hispalis (Seville was the name the Muslims gave to the city) was a great compiler of cultural information used widely in medieval Europe, but he did not make any original contribution to philosophy of his own.[35] The Arianism

---

[33] *La fin du monde antique et le début du moyen âge* (1928), (ed. 1968), pp. 168–171. On page 422 he speaks of the "société gallo-franque," not of French society.

[34] Munich: Francke Verlag (1969).

[35] A. Schmekel, *Isidorus von Sevilla, sein System und seine Quellen* (Berlin, 1914). In discussing St. Isidore's thought, Dom Justo Pérez de Urbel writes: "His principal source was a work that had been a common one for all those who had written about these same subjects. . . . He did not attempt to formulate new theories, but to merely summarize the old ones and compile them into an organic whole, as he himself loyally confesses" in *Historia de España*, ed. R. Menéndez Pidal (Madrid, 1963), III, 451, 459. In E. A. Thompson's recent book, *The Goths in Spain* (Oxford, 1969), he speaks only of Goths and Romans: "The old Roman population were left to live their old form of life. . . . The Gothic nobility gov-

of the Visigothic kingdom (Reccared was converted in 589) contributed to the isolation of the Visigothic monarchy, for it was unlikely that the Arians would have changed their religion so abruptly. Clovis, the first king of the Franks, had been baptized in 496, thus becoming the first Catholic sovereign to establish close ties with the Church of Rome. The wave of missionary activity that brought Christianity to the British Isles first passed through France, where it prepared the way for the propagation of classical studies, and then made it possible for the Anglo-Saxons of York and the Irish monks to adorn the Frankish kingdom with such figures as Alcuin (735–804) and the Irishman, John Scotus Erigena (810–877). No one has ever clarified why no figure arose in Roman-Gothic Hispania comparable to the Roman Boethius (470–525?). Having been educated in Rome and Athens, he was naturally well acquainted with Greco-Roman culture, and later he became attached to the court of Theodoric, the king of the Ostrogoths. Boethius was falsely accused of treason and witchcraft and executed in Pavia. While in prison he wrote his famous work, *De consolatione philosophiae*, and translated Aristotle and the third-century Alexandrian philosopher, Porphyry, in addition to contributing to formulating the philosophical terminology of the Middle Ages. J. Ferrater Mora rightly calls him "the last Roman and the first scholastic."[36]

Either directly or indirectly, Greek thought found its way to the British Isles and France. John Scotus Erigena introduced Neoplatonism in the Middle Ages; Alcuin, a propagator of culture, but not a philosopher, had already written in one of his letters to Charlemagne the famous phrase: "Perhaps a new Athens shall arise in the land of the Franks" ("forsan Athenae nova perficeretur in Francia"). In this manner a combination of illusory desires and realities was gradually built up, first by way of the Anglo-Saxons and later by the Muslims. In the thirteenth century the University of Paris, as Gilson says, gradually became "a clearing house for the intellectual transactions of Christianity" (*La philosophie au moyen âge*, p. 416). The most unusual characteristic of this unique situation was the fact that, although it was actually produced in France, the "clergie" Chrétien de Troyes (1135–1183?) was so proud of in the twelfth century was not French in the following century. As Gilson observes (*op. cit.*, p. 416), scholars lectured in Latin, the international language of the Middle Ages at the University of Paris; these scholars were the Englishmen Alexander of Hales, Roger Bacon, and William of Ockham; Duns Scotus was a Scot, Albertus Magnus and Eckhardt were Germans; St. Bonaventure

---

erned the Gothic population and the Roman nobility the Roman population, while the Gothic king and his highest officials decided policy for them all" (p. 312). Finally the fable that the Goths were "Spaniards" has begun to vanish.

[36] *Diccionario de filosofía* (Buenos Aires, 1965), I, 218.

and St. Thomas Aquinas were Italians; Siger came from Brabant, and Boethius from Dacia. United under the spiritual guidance of pontifical Rome, the countries of Western Europe lacked linguistic and intellectual boundaries or frontiers from the time of Charlemagne to that of Luther.[37] This unity was broken in the wake of the so-called period of the Renaissance, through a process that took on a particular shape and direction in each individual country, without any strict synchronization.

Aside from the intellectual aspects of the Middle Ages that occurred in conditions quite different from those below the Pyrenees, there is another distinction which must be made at this point. In twelfth-century France an awareness of the reality and value of a secular or "objectivized" culture, as we might say pedantically, was already in existence, while nothing comparable to this was possible in Castile during the same period. The fact that this idea was lived as an authentic reality can be seen by its adaptation in literature. Chrétien de Troyes knew and was aware, from what he had learned from certain chronicles, that what we call "Western civilization" today had its origin in Greece, then passed on to Rome, and through her to France in an unbroken line:

> Puis la chevalerie vint à Rome
> et de clergie la somme,
> qui maintenant en France est venue.[38]

The modes of life and literature of medieval France, reflected in the *romans* of Chrétien de Troyes composed at the end of the twelfth century for the pleasure and amusement of Countess Marie de Champagne and the ladies of her court, are quite alien to the conditions prevailing in the kingdoms of Spain and particularly Castile at that time. It was possible for the Frenchman to put his *ser*, the essence of his being as a person, in parenthesis and to become interested in activities of an aesthetic or philosophical nature. Pierre Abélard (1079–1142) had schools for the study of philosophy which were

---

[37] A slight indication of what might have been the Hispanic participation in that cooperative system of culture was the presence in Carolingian France of two Visigoths who had fled the Peninsula during the Muslim occupation. Agobard, born in 769, became archbishop of Lyon in 816 and, according to Gilson (*op cit.*, p. 190), he was "one of the bright lights of the Carolingian Church." Theodolf (d. 831) was the bishop of Orleans and wrote poetry in Latin (*De libris quos legere solebam*), a work which proves his familiarity with the great classical writers (Virgil, Ovid, Horace, Lucan, Cicero). For other illustrious Hispano-Gothic refugees, see R. del Arco (*Historia de España*, ed. R. Menéndez Pidal) VI, 420. Max Manitius discusses Agobard and Theodolf extensively in his *Geschichte der lateinischen Literatur des Mittelalters* (1911), pp. 380–390 and 537–543.

[38] See "Presencia del Sultán Saladino en las literaturas románicas" in my book *Hacia Cervantes* (Madrid: Taurus, 1967), p. 66, for the sources and meaning of this text.

not limited to Paris alone. After quarrelling with his teacher Guillaume de Champeaux in Paris, he went off to teach at Melun and was so successful that he had to transfer his school to Corbeil.

All this is very elementary common knowledge. I merely wish to emphasize here that during the first half of the twelfth century in France men could already become aroused and excited by the questions that Pierre Abélard posed, since his ideas challenged the modes of philosophical and theological thought in vogue at this time. To a great extent this was no longer possible in Muslim-dominated lands. In another direction, the *romans* of Chrétien de Troyes opened new horizons of love and wonder for a few aristocratic ladies fascinated by the problems that the knights of their courtly world created for themselves out of the conflicts between the realities of love and the obligation to behave in a dignified manner. The *matière de Bretagne* invented by Geoffrey of Monmouth (*ca.* 1100–1154) enlivened the sensibilities of Europe for centuries with its tales of King Arthur and the knightly deeds of his courtiers. The *romans* of Chrétien (*Yvain, Erec, Lancelot, Perceval*), composed in "beau français à pleines mains," combined the fantasy of the cycle of Bretagne with the delicate nuances of courtly love sung by the Provençal troubadours. By the end of the twelfth century a "secularized" climate of thought and sensibility was already possible in the circles of a cultured, refined minority of Northern France, including Champagne which had not yet been annexed to the French crown. For reasons we have already analyzed and are about to discuss, the term "Spanish Middle Ages" in a Western European sense is not valid.

Toward a New Chronological
Arrangement of Spanish History

In view of the above references to the cultural situations to the north and south of the Christian kingdoms in the Peninsula, it is apparent that the chronological arrangement of the history of the Spaniards must be based on two factors: what they have been effectively in a given time and space and what they did in reality as "pre-Spaniards." It was the Christians of the kingdoms of Castile, Leon, and Aragon who gave themselves the name *español*, not the Goths, Hispano-Romans, or Iberians. The centuries of the reconquest must be arranged chronologically in a particular way, taking as a point of departure what the inhabitants of the Peninsula themselves did and understood as a temporal reality, rather than superimpose on them an abstract, nonexperiential time that was not lived by these people. The Castilians or Catalans, to take two outstanding examples, did not use their idle time or their mental efforts to rationalize their beliefs or to question the reality and nature of the genres and classifications of species they perceived. The great European controversies concerning realism and nominalism, the truths of faith and those demonstrable by reason, were not combated on an international scope in the monasteries of Castile or Aragon-Catalonia.[39]

Because of the peculiar circumstances prevailing in Castile when Alfonso VIII founded his school of studies at Palencia around 1208, he sent for masters from France and Italy, but not from anywhere in the Christian Peninsula. In the part of the *Crónica General (ed. cit.,* pp. 685–686) dealing with the founding of the monastery of Las Huelgas and a hostel for the pilgrims who stopped at Burgos on their way to Santiago, there is a section on the university. The king, who was always guided by divine inspiration in everything he did, "sent to France and Lombardy for scholars, in order that in these lands [of Castile] the teaching of knowledge should not decrease during his reign, for it is through these schools of learning that God rectifies and resolves many things, and in turn the educated men of high birth *(fecho de la cavallería)* in the kingdom also benefit; and he gathered together teachers of all the sciences in Palencia," a convenient place for the clerics from all the Spains to meet. Knowledge would be given to them like manna in the mouths of the hungry in the desert, "according to the archbishop Don Rodrigo de Toledo." At this point the *Crónica* actually follows the *De rebus Hispaniae* of Rodrigo Jiménez de Rada *(Liber* VII, *cap.* 34), although the archbishop of Toledo only specifies, "He sent for learned men from France and Italy in order that the teaching of science should never cease in his realm" ("sapientes a Gallia et Italia convocavit, ut sapientiae disciplina a regno suo nunquam abesset").[40] The translator of the *Crónica* felt it necessary to justify the social usefulness of those teachings; hence the reason for additions he made. "Educated men of high birth" *(caballería)* refers, in this case, to the dignity and prestige of the kingdom where such learning exists, for, "as the ancients said, the wisdom of the law is another form of *caballería* or chivalry, a weapon to combat the dauntless or to right wrongs" *(Partida II, tit. x, ley 3).* The person who mentioned the foundation of the college of studies at Palencia in the *Crónica General* had the same idea about culture as those who drew up the code of the *Siete Partidas,* the compendium of religious, ethical, political, and juridical principles necessary for the

---

[39] Petrus Hispanus, who was elected pope in 1276 as John XXI, and cited in the histories of medieval philosophy, was actually a Portuguese from Lisbon who spent most of his life and engaged in cultural activities in France and Italy. See J. Ferrater Mora, *Diccionario . . .* T. and J. Carreras Artau include him in their *Historia de la filosofía española* (1939), I, 101–144. I believe, however, that the case of Pedro Hispano in the thirteenth century is comparable to that of Jorge Santayana (1863–1952) who was born in Madrid, but whose work and philosophy were North American, for they bear no relationship to anything Spanish.

[40] Madrid (1793), p. 174.

functioning of an ideal society, formulated at the time of Alfonso X. Both the archbishop and the *Crónica* mention that the University of Palencia ceased to function for a time, "although by the grace of God, it has continued to exist." That center of studies was the origin of the University of Salamanca founded in the middle of the thirteenth century, even though its prestige as a center of learning did not begin to spread to other parts of Europe or to make its influence felt until the end of the fifteenth century.

The concept of *fecho de la cavallería*, encompassing the dignity, self-esteem, prestige, and influence of the person himself, obsessed the ruling classes of Castilian society to such an extent that there was no possibility of cultivating any type of knowledge other than that related to personal conduct and the good government of society. Speculative thought or the study of the human body and its functioning did not concern scholars in Castile or in the other Christian kingdoms.[41] The Castilian was primarily interested in his dealings with persons of another caste, not another race, with whom he had to live side by side or to combat. He could not bring himself to accept them as equals nor could he reject them completely. Consequently those other castes of Jews and Muslims prevented the Castilian Christian from seeing or studying the world of things.

The Role of the Mudejars in Relation to the Other Two Castes

The legend of Bernardo del Carpio, in which Christians and Moors fight side by side against Charlemagne, is a poetic reflection of what actually happened in the daily life of the Mudejars: "Marzil, the king of Saragossa, led his large armies of *Moors and Navarrese* . . .; they joined forces and he and Bernardo fought together against the Emperor Charles" (*Crónica General, ed. cit.*, p. 353). We have already seen how members of the royal families were buried in Moorish vestments in the convent of Las Huelgas at Burgos. As late as the fifteenth century Christians, Moors, and Jews continued to work together and cooperate on mutual projects. In 1437 the bishop of

---

[41] In thirteenth-century Castile there is nothing comparable either in Latin or the vernacular to the treatise on ophthalmology by Mohammad al-Ghâfiqi, born near Pedroche, Cordova, possibly in the twelfth century. The work is of little scientific importance, but it is pertinent here only because of the fact that it was possible to write it at that time. The author relates, for example, how he treated a case of closed eyelids (*iltizâq* in Arabic): "In Cordova I treated a case of congenital iltizâq in a month-old child, and at first I thought of operating to separate the lids. But after meditating on nature's own action I did not do anything. A year later the lids separated on their own accord." Unpublished work by the Hispano-Arabic occulist, Mohammad ibn Qassum ibn Aslam al-Ghâfiqi, "Le guide d'oculistique," trans. Max Meyerhoff (Barcelona: Laboratoires du Nord de l'Espagne, Masnou, 1933), p. 31.

Avila, Don Alonso de Madrigal, ordained that "all men and women, be they Christians, Moors, or Jews, must contribute with wood, lime, or brick to the work" of building the church of San Nicolás.[42] The same was true in the kingdom of Aragon in 1504, even though the Jews had been officially expelled from Spain in 1492. "On 22 August 1504, after consulting the Muslim masters of works, Christians, and Jewish bankers of the city [of Saragossa], the City Council" gave the order for "the construction of the Torre Nueva and appointed two Christians, two Muslims, and one Jew," whom we assume had already been baptized, to take charge of the work.[43]

Another piece of evidence is also eloquent of the true nature of the Spanish past. At the Cortes (parliament) of 1367 held at Burgos, after the partisans of Henry II had proclaimed him king in opposition to his brother Peter I, the representatives complained that there were fortresses still under the command of Jews and Moors and asked that they be turned over to the Christians. King Henry opposed this request, "because there is no reason to do so, for the Jews would be harmed considerably" ("porque non es razón de lo fazer, ca se destruirían los judíos").[44] Even though this situation was the result of a civil and fratricidal war between the two rival brothers Peter I and Henry II, it is symptomatic of the social context created by five hundred years of coexistence.

The scholarly architect, Fernando Chueca, has written that the Mudejar style is the only true Spanish style, a theory that supports what I have said in this and in other books about such an important social phenomenon. The Romanesque was the "creation of monastic Europe" and the Gothic, "a French style par excellence"; but according to Chueca, the Mudejar is "an attitude or state of mind rather than an artistic style, seen in the context of a very particular set of circumstances in the history and the Spanish society of the Middle Ages."[45] Menéndez y Pelayo had already perceived that the "Mudejar is the only peculiarly Spanish type of construction that we can be proud of"; to which Chueca adds: "That type of construction is the only one that took root most strongly in our Peninsula, quantitatively speaking." All this "necessitates a revision that may reveal many things to us and tear down that apparent Christian-European unanimity that many scholars believe in or refuse to stop believing" (Chueca, p. 116).

---

[42] News of the discovery of these documents was published by the daily *ABC* (Madrid), 5 Sept. 1967.

[43] F. Abbad Ríos, *Guías artísticas de España: Zaragoza* (1952), p. 80, contains a photograph of that very beautiful Mudejar tower, shamefully torn down a few years ago.

[44] *Cortes de León y Castilla*, Academia de la Historia (Madrid, 1863), II, 146.

[45] "Aragón y la cultura mudéjar," *Zaragoza*, revista de la Diputación provincial, XXIX (1969), 113–125.

A keen observer of Mudejar construction in Spain would probably arrive at the same conclusions as I have: in order to comprehend the history of the Spaniards, it is necessary to situate them in a historiological space that is peculiarly theirs, as I believe, somewhere between Western and Eastern civilizations. The authentic Spaniards (not Viriatus, Trajan, or Isidore of Hispalis) molded their own unique shape—the reason or logos of their historical being—by opposing simultaneously both Europe and the East, and at the same time letting themselves be affected and seduced by both civilizations. I find that the concept of "the conflictive" is an increasingly effective way of getting at the core of the maximum creations of the Spaniards. Related to this ambivalent form of life is the idea of *vivir desviviéndose*, life as the process of simultaneous adoption and rejection, a dialectic between two opposing extremes which I have used since my first historical essays.

In the twelfth and thirteenth centuries Toledo became the setting for two opposing intellectual operations: the use and manipulation of Greco-Arabic philosophy so that English, French, and German scholars could reap the benefits of the study and translation of those works; at the same time, the Castilian Christians did not take part in these purely intellectual activities. A handful of Muslims succeeded in going beyond the horizon of the divine word as it was interpreted by the *alfaquíes*. As we have already seen, these heroic efforts ultimately failed, and, as a result, the Muslim remained enclosed and immobile behind the wall of his belief without any possibility of regaining the lost territories and cities of his former al-Andalus. The Christian, on the contrary, was sustained by the hope of expanding his frontiers without disturbing the inner calm of his mind. The newly conquered cities of Cordova (1236) and Seville (1248) were a source of wonder for those relatively crude Christians. Cordova, "the patron and example of other peoples of Andalusia, was swept clean of the dirt of Mohammed on that day. . . . So great is the bounty of the city of Cordova and such are its delights and luxury that the people, upon hearing the praises of this city, came from all parts of Spain to dwell here and populate it, and hasten to come here . . . as if to the wedding of a king" (*Crónica General*, ed. cit., pp. 733, 734).

By the middle of the thirteenth century the Moors of al-Andalus were already in a state of cultural and military decline, but their cities and lands fell into the hands of Christians from the north like wealth and magnificence gained by warlike means without the aid or need for any type of science or philosophy. They were not concerned with the future possibilities of speculative thought, but merely interested in the practical effort to gain access to something beyond—in other words, to a future of grandeur and power. The rearguard, however, still combined the Mudejars and Jews, now subject to the will of the nobles and church hierarchies, but in possession of a technical knowledge and industrial skill unparalleled in Europe. If we take into account the composition and functions of each human group that comprised the population of the Christian kingdoms, we can readily understand the difference between the tasks of the foreign translators who came to Toledo or Seville in the twelfth century to translate the philosophy and science of the Arabs into the Latin of medieval Europe, and the role of Jewish scholars from Castile or Mudejars in Toledo who were ordered to do translations of astronomical, astrological, moral, or juridical works, encouraged and patronized by King Alfonso the Learned and his collaborators. But Averroës did not beget any Averroists in the Christian kingdoms, and if he was read occasionally, it was only to expound his errors.[46] The cultural activity fostered at the court of Alfonso the Learned was oriented toward practical rather than scientific or theoretical ends. The astronomical works translated from the Arabic were not of interest or important for what they revealed about the nature of the stars, but for how their movements influenced men's lives. For this reason they were translated into Castilian rather than Latin, which was the language of a minority. One of these works was *El libro conplido en los iudizios de las estrellas*[47] (*A Complete Treatise on the Predictions, Prejudged Influences, and Forecasting of the Stars*) by Ibn Abī'r-Riŷāl, translated into Castilian by Yehuda ben Moshe who, at the very beginning of his translation, emphasizes his personal worth as well as the learning of the Jews who had attained a high social level at the court of Ferdinand III and his son Alfonso X. In sum, this is the great difference between the translations from the Arabic done for certain foreigners so that they might better understand Aristotle and the thought of his Muslim commentaries, and the other types of translation intended for use and enjoyment only in Castile at the court of a learned king, and at the same time with a view toward enhancing the prestige of Judaic culture in Castile. Without establishing this basic difference between the translations made for export and those intended for use of the king, his court, and the Jews, it is impossible to comprehend the full meaning of Arabic-Judaic-Christian cultural activities that took place in Toledo in the twelfth and thirteenth centuries.

The process of cultural preeminence by which the Jews in the Christian kingdoms reached their height at the court of Alfonso X, "the Learned" (r. 1252–1284), had been prepared long before that time. In order to perceive the true meaning of this strange fact from a European viewpoint, it will suffice to read the translator's preface

---

[46] For example, by Alvaro de Oviedo. See Marie-Thérèse d'Alverny and Georges Vajda, "Marc de Tolède," *Al-Andalus*, XVI (1951), 99.
[47] Ed. Gerold Hilty (Madrid: Real Academia Española, 1954).

to that work on "los iudizios de las estrellas." The translator writes: "Let us praise and thank God, our true, omnipotent father, who in this our time has seen fit to grant us in this world a lord who is a lover of righteousness and bestower of benefits and praises" (p. 3). He mentions "God, the true father"; the Jew expressed and practiced his religion freely, and began by affirming, not without a certain arrogance, that his is the "true" God. This is followed by praises to the king which clearly indicate the reasons for the influential status of the Jews at court. King Alfonso sought out those scholars because he was "a lover of truth, avid for learning and science, and a compiler of doctrines and teachings." In present-day language we might say that the king was neither a scholar nor a philosopher, but a mere dilettante avid for culture and for people at whose service to put it. For this reason "he gathers around him wise men and those who delve into learning," scholars who could make knowledge readily available to him. In turn, he rewards them with "wealth and benefits"; he remunerates them and heaps favors on them. The king had created for himself a court of "intellectuals." Each one of those scholars was a specialist in a particular subject that he brought down to the level of those who were not acquainted with his field. "Each one of them worked to explain and divulge his specialized knowledge and to translate that wisdom into the Castilian language for the praise and glory of the name of God and for the honor and prestige of said lord, His Majesty Don Alfonso." As a young man, he "loved and attracted to his person wisdom and scholarship, and made up for the lack of ladinos [learned persons] because of the scarcity of books written by good philosophers." When Yehuda ben Moshe discovered the book of Ibn Abï'r-Riŷāl, "so worthy, complete, and adequate in all things pertaining to astronomy, he translated it from the Arabic language into Castilian" for the glory of God and his sovereign (p. 3).

In this manner there converged the curiosity and munificence of a Christian monarch, the astronomical or astrological knowledge of a Muslim, and the technical scholarship of a Jew who translated that knowledge and wisdom concerning the essence and conduct of human beings into Castilian: "He who is born when the Sun, the lord of life, enters the first phase of Aries, which is the phase of Mars, shall be powerful, valiant, and lordly and shall be fond of slaughter, arms, and horses and other similar activities" (p. 9). Arabic science and technical knowledge were imported by the Castilian Christian because of their practical and artistic efficacy, as in the case of Mudejar art. The Jew served as an intermediary between the Moor and the Christian in many ways, and through him the Castilian of the dominant caste was able to become master of his lands, conqueror of the Moor, and eventually executor of the Hispano-Hebrew prophecies of imperial domination of the world.

The purely intellectual activities cultivated by Muslims in the Near East and al-Andalus until the twelfth century had vanished, because it became impossible for the Mohammedan to reconcile inquisitive reasoning with his fixed mode of living, totally immersed as he was in his religious beliefs. Western man was able to go by the principle "Dios a su hora—mi pensar a la suya" ("God at his proper time—and my thoughts at theirs"). For him, the difficult paths of what was formerly called heterodoxy were made practicable and compatible. For the Muslim, there was no way out except the extermination of heterodoxy. Europe and the English-speaking countries eventually accepted the reality that there are many ways of being a Christian, just as there are numerous ways in which each individual poses the problem of the relationship between his evident finite being and the no less apparent transcendency which is inaccessible to him. This process has not taken place in Spain because of the simple fact that its population had to exist at one and the same time united and divided since Christians, Jews, and Moors had Hispanized themselves in distinct and contrary forms, not because of the working of any sinister *fatum*. I realize that this way of thinking is unpalatable to those who prefer to cling to the fiction of Spaniards having existed in Roman times or who imagine the centuries of the reconquest to have been like those of the rest of Europe that was structuring itself simultaneously, between the tenth and sixteenth centuries, by reason and belief, without their contradicting each other. This was true in the so-called Middle Ages, but since that process of harmony–disharmony did not take place in Spain, it is meaningless to try to fit the past life of the Spaniards into molds that are absolutely foreign to it.

My convictions become even clearer on this arduous road of historiological thought when I am confronted with the tactless outbursts of ardent adversaries to my methods. Spain's most important present-day Arabist wrote in 1966 that the Arabs were mere "invaders" and "pillagers" of Spain.[48] In order to put forth such a rash judgment, it was necessary to put in parentheses the enormous amount of Arabic toponyms, the mosque at Cordova, the Alhambra, the entire corpus of Mudejar architecture, the great number of Arabic words that existed and are still used in Spanish, or institutions such as the *hijodalgo* (hidalgo) modeled on Arabisms such as *ibn al-duniā* (the son of wealth); *algo* in Old Castilian meant "the sum of one's fortune, riches." I might add to what I have been saying in this and other works of mine for more than twenty years, that in no European country other than Spain does a radio or television announcer sign off with this Muslim phrase to his listeners, "hasta mañana, *si Dios quiere*"

---

[48] See my *"Español", palabra extranjera: razones y motivos* (Madrid: Taurus, 1970), pp. 9 ff.

("until tomorrow, *God willing*") which is the exact translation of *in shā al-lāh*. Its slight variant in pure Arabic is *wa shā al-lāh*, the common Spanish expression *ojalá*, "y quiera Dios" ("and may God will it").

The Moors lived and fought with the Christians as a people fully conscious of their own individuality and personality which they staunchly defended even after the loss of the kingdom of Granada in 1492. In 1499 they rebelled in Granada and were crushed in 1501 and obliged to accept the religion of their secular enemies, contrary to the terms of their surrender agreement in 1492: "On the condition that we were to remain like the Mudejars before us, namely, the inhabitants of the old territory, and that we were to be allowed to remain in enjoyment [of the right] to call to prayer and [to celebrate] our ritual oration. . . ."[49] The vanquished Moors of Granada could not continue to live in harmony with the Christians as the Mudejars did before that time and after Cordova, Valencia, and Seville were conquered in the thirteenth century. In spite of this, they still retained the hope of recovering their former grandeur and power. For this reason they again rebelled in 1568 during Philip II's reign, and were finally expelled in 1609. Instead of yielding submissively to the immense power of imperial Spain, they judged it already to be without sufficient spirit and force. This error in judgment led to the bloody uprising of the Moriscos in the Alpujarras region of Granada and to their eventual expulsion. Their totally religious concept of life exalted the sense of their own grandeur and importance and their innate right to exert it. The Muslims of Spain never lost sight of the sense of their political dimension; in this sense they coincided with those who, imbued with a spirit as Oriental as their own, ended up by annihilating them.

The Role of the Jews
in the Caste System

The entire picture of the Spanish phenomenon begins to take shape as a group of persons comprising three castes who were uncomfortable as a direct outcome of their inevitable coexistence. Spain's imperial grandeur in the sixteenth century was forged by a combination of factors: the Castilian's tenacious awareness of his superiority and self-reliance, evident even prior to this time in his epic poetry and ballads; the Moor and later the Mudejar's technical skill used to advantage by the Castilian Christians as well as others in the Peninsula; and, finally, the technical knowledge, financial administration, cul-

---

[49] James T. Monroe, "A Curious Morisco Appeal to the Ottoman Empire," *Al-Andalus*, XXI (1966), 296.

ture, and imperialistic utopian idea of the Castilian Hebrews. Without these Castilian Jews, and the converts in the fifteenth century, it is impossible to explain either the long and complicated undertaking of the reconquest or the aspiration to extend the Spanish Empire to unknown and remote lands.

If we attempt to superimpose the chronological divisions of Western Europe on Spain's past, as we saw in the previous section, we overlook the basic fact that the population of the Christian kingdoms during the centuries of the reconquest was made up of heterogeneous castes. There were no "racial" differences, as the books repeat, because physically they all looked more or less alike. As an example I shall cite a thirteenth-century text: "The Jews live together with the Christians in the towns and they both dress alike"; for this reason, the Jews were obliged "to wear some distinguishing mark on their heads . . . so that the people can differentiate between a Jew and a non-Jew" (*Partida* VI, *tit.* xxiv, *ley* 11). In previous chapters I mentioned several examples to prove that the word *casta* (caste) originated in Spain and was used to designate the people of three different religions who comprised its population. As late as 1633 Fray Agustín Salucio wrote: "Laws were never made excluding [from the priesthood] those who are of the caste of Jews (*casta de judíos*) . . . merely because of the unjust indignation that the faithful have against those who killed our Lord Jesus Christ."[50]

Historically speaking, it would be incorrect to refer to the Jews in generic terms. For this reason I shall begin in the present in order to look back on the past from our modern vantage point. Shortly before 1930 the philologist M. A. Luria visited the poor, isolated, and antiquated community of Jews in Monastir (present-day Bitolj, Yugoslavia), a village south of Macedonia. In the course of a conversation with two old women about Spain and its language, one of them was overtly surprised to observe that the language spoken in Spain was very similar to that of Monastir; her companion quickly and proudly replied: "¡Ma somuz ispañolis!" ("But we are Spaniards").[51] The two old ladies in that remote community saw themselves as Jews, to the very core of their being, yet at the same time they also felt that they had been deprived of a collective dimension and a situation as real and actual for them as that of a monarch in exile whose crown was forcibly taken from him. If one prods slightly into the Sephardic Jew's sensibility, one discovers his Jewishness, and at the same time the feeling of missing his old Spanish roots. Much has been written

---

[50] "Discurso acerca de la justicia . . . en los estatutos de limpieza de sangre," *Semanario Erudito*, XV (Madrid, 1788). Concerning Salucio, see Albert A. Sicroff, *Les controverses des Statuts de "pureté de sang" en Espagne* (Paris: Didier, 1960), pp. 186 ff.

[51] *A Study of the Monastir Dialect of Judeo-Spanish* (New York, 1930), p. 9.

about this well-known phenomenon, but the entire historical complex on which it is based or which it forms a part of is not often presented in its true perspective, because it is a rather unpleasant theme for both Jewish and Spanish historians or for those who delight in reducing history to ciphers or abstractions. As I mentioned before, a famous French historian attributed the expulsion of the Jews by the Catholic sovereigns to a population surplus, ignoring the fact that only those who refused to be baptized were expelled.[52] In addition, those who insist on treating the Hispanic Jews generically, in the same way as they deal with Jews in other regions of the diaspora, disfigure the historical features of this unique people. The German Jews spread throughout Eastern Europe spoke Yiddish (*jüdisch* or "Jewish" in German); their collective name, Ashkenazim, is derived from a Hebrew proper noun or person, not from a particular geographical place. The name Sephardim, however, is derived from the Hebrew word for Spain, "Sefarad." Although the Jews never succeeded in organizing themselves as a particular entity, they did reach the point where they considered the land of Spain, Sefarad, as their homeland; and for this reason they continue to call themselves Sephardim, or "Spaniards," the descendants of those who were expelled from Spain in 1492.

The impressive corpus of moving Judeo-Spanish dirges collected in Larache and Tetuan, Morocco, by Manuel Alvar is an eloquent example of this deep-rooted attachment of the Sephardim to their spiritual and cultural heritage.[53] Several examples of these dirges, a sorrowful echo of voices submerged for five hundred years, refer specifically, in my opinion, to the tragic exile and the cultural prestige of the Castilian Jews:

Aljamí honrados,	Illustrious sages
grandes de Castilla,	*grandes* of Castile
los sacaban žorreados	dragged through the streets
por toda la villa ...	of the town ...
. . . .	. . . .
Decía la gente:	Our people cried out:
"¡qué negra mancilla!"	"Our honor is tarnished!"
. . . .	. . . .
Mataban a los chiquitos,	Little children were slaughtered,
los enfilaban en lanzas,	their heads stuck on lances,
salían las madres	their mothers cried like goats;
deshonraban a las arasbas,	young maidens were dishonored,
mataban a los mancebos.	youths were killed.

In spite of the remote and generic allusions to persecutions or po-

---

[52] Braudel, *La Méditerranée*, I, 380. See also my *"España," palabra extranjera* ..., pp. 62–68.

[53] *Endechas judeo-españolas*, rev. ed. (Madrid: C.S.I.C., 1969), p. 147. For the phonetic transcription see page 85.

groms indicative of the tragedy of those hapless Jews, the outcry of those who had been renowned throughout Castile and had shared in the prestige, hopes, and expectations of the highest ruling classes centuries earlier still comes through. Today all this lies buried under the gravestones of the Jewish cemetery in Tetuan known as the *Cementerio de Castilla* (*Endechas judeo-españolas*, p. 24).

It is highly significant that those Jews dragged through the streets of the town were called "grandes de Castilla," which made them the equals of the "grandes omnes de Castiella" (*Crónica General*, ed. Menéndez Pidal, p. 666) and of those who were called "grandes de España," the highest title granted to the Spanish nobility in the sixteenth century. This title is also an example of Spanish parallelism, having its counterpart in the Arabic word, *al-kābir*, meaning noble, eminent, important; used in the plural it refers to persons of the highest social rank, because *grande* in this case is a noun, not an adjective. In Hebrew, *Kābir*, meaning great, is also used as a noun signifying "the powerful one." The Castilians endowed a Latin word with a Judeo-Islamic meaning, while the Jewish subjects of a lesser social status exalted their own personal worth to a par with the greatness and stature of their legal lords. This sense of grandeur specifically refers here to an absolute concept affecting the intrinsic worth of the person himself, rather than depending directly on his rank or noble title, in contrast to other countries where the title "grand duke" is used, as in Russia, Italy, or Germany.[54] This same word came into use in English at the end of the sixteenth century as "grandee," not as a translation (in this case impossible) of a peculiarly Spanish concept, but as a result of the English pronunciation of the word.

The Sephardic Jew has still kept alive this awareness of his Spanishness and the past grandeur and prestige of his sages, comparable in status to the noble lords of Castile for five centuries. Those dirges, still sung by Moroccan Sephardim, are significant historical documents which clearly show the positive aspect of the relationship between the Castilians of different castes. The prominent and influential position occupied by many Castilian Jews is a well-known fact, although few people have bothered to deduce the consequences of that intrinsic feeling of "Castilianness." If the title *grandes de Castilla* appears in the aforementioned dirge, this means that the ancestors of the present-day Sephardic Jews actually bore that title and, furthermore, in a characteristically Spanish manner. If Spain was different from Western Europe, the art and literature of those other countries is different from the art and literature of Spain which filled the lands of its empire with beautiful monuments that are still admired today after three centuries of domination.

---

[54] See Paul-Betz, *Deutches Wörterbuch* (1966), p. 376.

One of those *grandes de Castilla* was Rabbi Mosé Arragel of Guadalajara. Legally he was a "serf" (*siervo*) of the king of Castile and the humble vassal of the grand master of the military order of Calatrava, Don Luis de Guzmán, although the rabbi, well aware of his own merit and self-esteem, considered himself to be as great a lord as his master. In 1420 Don Luis de Guzmán ordered the rabbi to translate the Old Testament into Castilian and to commentate it for him. The very fact that a great Christian lord should ask a Hebrew scholar to read and unravel the meaning of the sacred text is surprising in itself, but such cultural contacts of this kind were traditional in Spain. It is no less astonishing that a Jew like Rabbi Arragel should reply to his lord in the following manner: "The kings and lords of Castile were so renowned that their Jewish subjects, endeavoring to reflect the magnificence of their sires, were the most learned, the most illustrious Jews in all the realms of the Diaspora, and as such excelled in four preeminent virtues: lineage, wealth, goodness, and learning. The kings and lords of Castile, in turn, have always acknowledged that the learned Jews of Castile are responsible for discovering and compiling all or almost all the rights, laws, and other sciences [of the kings and lords] in their realm. We Jews and the Jews of other kingdoms in all the realms of the diaspora also recognize that we are governed by the doctrine of the Sacred Law [the Torah], also revealed and interpreted by the Castilian Jews."[55] In other words, the magnificence and prestige of the Castilian Jews was on the same level with and at the same time dependent upon the kings and lords of Castile of whom they were loyal subjects. The last echoes of that awareness of cultural superiority among the Jews of Castile have come down to our time in the form of those dirges still sung in the Jewish quarters of Morocco.

The learned Jews of Castile mentioned in the Spanish text of Rabbi Arragel should now be related to the Hebrew word *ḥaḥamim* (sages or learned men) preceded by the Arabic article *al* and the phrase, *grandes de Castilla*, which taken together, encompass all the reasons that justify their preeminence, according to Rabbi Arragel. At the beginning of the fifteenth century the Jew was conscious of his superiority in learning over the Christian and boasted of it, a fact that ultimately had disastrous consequences for the Jew and for the study of science among Christians, as I shall explain in the following chapter. In a prior passage of the same letter the rabbi contrasts, in a roundabout manner, although the meaning is clear, the high cultural level of the Jews in comparison with the scant learning of the Christians, as we have already seen in the translator's introduction to *El*

---

[55] *Biblia de la Casa de Alba*, published by the Duke of Alba (Madrid, 1920), p. 3.

libro conplido en los iudizios de las estrellas, composed for the use of King Alfonso X of Castile. Rabbi Arragel says that the kings of Castile preferred to be the sires of a few wise Christians in exchange for keeping all the Jews in bondage, but at the same time the sovereign encouraged their zeal for knowledge, treated them benevolently, and bestowed favors on them: "The emperors of Spain and particularly the magnanimous kings and lords of Castile were especially interested in having only a few learned Christians as their vassals and in extending their domain and captivity over those born of Jewish descent, even though these Jews were always treated with the utmost kindness and benevolence, and much honor was bestowed upon them."

The *Partidas* of Alfonso X explain that the reasons the Christians tolerate the Jews living among them were "to keep them in bondage forever, so that they might never forget that they are the descendants of those who had crucified our Lord Jesus Christ" (VII, xxiv, 1). This was the legal and Christian point of view. Rabbi Arragel, representing the Hispano-Hebrew viewpoint, says that, although the Castilian Jews lived in captivity, the kings still found them useful as a veritable seedbed of learned men and scholars from which there came forth human plants conscious of their preeminence and whose knowledge was useful and radiated prestige both at court and in noblemen's mansions. This singular factor cannot be explained by quoting population figures or data on the occupations and habits of Jews, or even the persecutions and the ultimate exile of the Jews. The Hispanic Jew was unique among the other Jews of the diaspora, precisely because his presence in the Christian kingdoms of Spain was structured and functioned within a complex set of factors that would never have been possible without him. The religious policies and attitudes of the Castilian kings had no counterpart in the so-called Europe of the Middle Ages, and because of these peculiar circumstances it is once again inaccurate to continue speaking of the Spanish Middle Ages.

The Fuero Real (Royal Privilege) of 1255 containing a compilation and systematic collection of the laws governing Castile states: "We shall see to it that no Jew dare to read any books that speak of his law and are contrary to it, or have such books hidden in his house. If anyone should have them in his possession or if they are found, they shall be burned publicly at the door of the synagogue" (*Libro* IV, *tit.* ii, *ley* 1). This law decreed for Castile, Leon, and Andalusia in the reconquered territories by Alfonso X was also promulgated for the town of Madrid in 1263.[56] In the thirteenth century the laws of the kingdom carefully watched over and preserved the Jewish as well as Christian orthodoxy. The sovereigns of Castile protected the official Judaism of the rabbis against the heresies among them, the most

---

[56] A. García-Gallo, *Manual de historia del derecho español,* II, 209.

notable being Karaism, whose partisans accepted biblical revelation instead of rabbinical tradition.[57] It is not feasible to interpret this fact, inconceivable in Western Europe, as a trap set for the Jews simply as a means of collecting fines. In 1391 King John I of Aragon ordered Mossé Faquim to be punished because he had violated the precepts of both the Christian religion and the mosaic law; he had drunk Christian wine, eaten pork, and done business on Saturday.[58] The Christian kings protected Jewish orthodoxy for reasons that are linked to the very structure of the Christian courts where Jewish officials held high positions of authority throughout the entire reconquest, first as Jews religiously so before the fifteenth century, and later as Jews and Christians of Jewish origin in the fifteenth and sixteenth centuries. The *Crónica de Alfonso XI* says: "The king [Alfonso XI, r. 1312–1350] appointed a Jew by the name of Don Yuzaf de Ecija as his *almojarife* on the advice of his uncle Don Felipe, because it had been the custom in Castile for many years to appoint Jews as royal tax collectors."[59] Even after the expulsion of the Spanish Jews important men of Jewish extraction who were nationally and internationally renowned, such as Miguel Pérez de Almazán, Ferdinand the Catholic's Secretary of State, and Antonio Pérez, who held the same position under Philip II,[60] continued to play prominent roles in court affairs. Not only were the Jews in charge of financial matters in the Christian kingdoms, but they also served as ambassadors even during the reign of the Catholic Sovereigns.[61] In the field of practical science, "the role of the Jewish physicians and intellectuals was important in the development of medieval medicine."[62] In addition, there were other areas of Peninsular culture in which Hispanic Jews were involved; they are discussed in works by Baer, Neuman, J. Amador de los Ríos, Léon Poliakov (*Histoire de l'antisémitisme de Mahomet aux*

---

[57] J. Amador de los Ríos, *Historia social y política de los judíos de España* (Madrid, 1960), pp. 880–883; and Yitzhak Baer, *A History of the Jews in Christian Spain* (Philadelphia, 1961), I, 390.

[58] Baer, *Die Juden im christlicen Spanien* (Berlin, 1929), I, 646. A. A. Neuman, *The Jews in Spain*, I, 128, believes that the kings watched over the religious conduct of the Jews with the object of making them pay fines, as I say in the text.

[59] Bibl. Aut. Esp. LXIV, 199.

[60] Antonio Pérez's father had already played an important role at court during the king's youth. G. Marañón, *Antonio Pérez*, I, 19, believes that this Pérez family was of Jewish origin.

[61] For information on these diplomatic functions from the ninth to the fourteenth century, see Y. Baer, *A History of the Jews*, I, 49, 177. Alfonso VI (1065–1109) sent his ambassador, Ibn Sālib, to collect the tribute money exacted from the king of Seville, al-Mu'tamid (R. Dozy, *Histoire des musulmans d'Espagne* [1932], III, 119). Fernando IV of Castile sent his *almojarife*, Don Samuel, as ambassador to the king of Granada (A. Giménez Soler, *Don Juan Manuel*, p. 286).

[62] Luis S. Granjel, *Historia de la medicina española* (1962), p. 24. The author holds the chair of Professor of the History of Medicine at the University of Salamanca.

Marranes [Paris: Calmann-Lévy, 1961]), as well as in my *Realidad histórica de España* (Mexico: Porrúa, 1954), which I hope to republish in the near future.

Rabbi Arragel's letter to his lord the grand master, the pitiful lamentations still kept alive today among the Spanish Jews of Morocco, the coincidence between the meaning of *grande* in Castilian, Arabic, and Hebrew and the role of the Jews in Castilian society, all bear witness to the fact that the Christians, Moors, and Jews were quite aware of one another. Each of the three castes competed zealously to outdo the other and gain supremacy and power, the Castilians with arms on the battlefield, and the Hebrews and Mudejars with their many indispensable activities. There is nothing comparable to this unique situation in Europe at that time; therefore, it is understandable that the culture of the Christian kingdoms was not like that of the European ones. The human activities pursued here were oriented toward practical and immediately visible ends. There was no time nor room for theoretical meditation; the pure effectiveness of calm contemplation was impossible. The condition and the reputation of the man who did the thinking was imposed between the thinker and his thoughts. When scholars write about the necessity for warlike activity and the depopulation of the center of the Peninsula, their theories do not explain why the cultural activity of the kingdoms of Leon and Castile, in the areas markedly dominated by the Christians, was at a minimum. Those who had fought against the Moor had identified the warrior's profession with the awareness of belonging to the politically dominant caste. Furthermore, those who had accomplished this to the greatest extent were the Castilians, who realized their superiority more keenly because of the imperious esteem placed on their own persons. The power of the dominating caste was constantly being tested as the kingdoms of Castile and Aragon began to conquer Muslim territories and cities and to live with the conquered Moors and Jews who had come from the south and become increasingly numerous in their dominions.

This unique structuring of Spanish society contained within it the very seeds of its disintegration. In the case of the Jews, in particular, along with the strong sentiment of magnificence and pride they had built up, there was the increasing anguish of menacing pogroms, together with their rejection by a society influenced by the Inquisition since 1481, full of baptized Jews and Old Christian Castilians whose prestige grew considerably after the surrender of Granada. These converts, consequently, could not tolerate the fact that they had to share their preeminence with other Jews who also bore the title "Don," were influential members of the court, and boasted too of their superiority. From all this we can reach the conclusion that an accurate subtitle for a true history of Spain might be, "a conflict between three incompatible sovereignties."

If we cannot reconstruct and relive the past, we can hardly begin to comprehend the history of the Spaniards and the reasons for those harsh, strident dissonances between man's personal mode of living and his collective existence, between what is evident today and what lies hidden in the problematic past.

Spain in Relation to its Mythical "Western" Tradition

In spite of all the evidence in the previous sections to prove that the course of Spanish history does not fit into traditional molds, histories of Spain by both Spanish and foreign writers continue to build their hypotheses on fables and omissions. An excellent example of this is the four-volume work by the American scholar, Otis H. Green, to attempt to prove that Spain and the Western tradition are one and the same. According to his interpretation, Spain and the Spaniards come out immaculately clean and free of Judeo-Islamic antecedents.[63] The very title of the book (*Spain and the Western Tradition* [Wisconsin, 1966] implies a "contradictio in adjecto," because if the Spaniards had been wholly included in the Western tradition just as England, France, Italy and Germany were, structured by a sense of "courtly love," the father of the "dolce stil nuovo," it is evident that the Spaniards would never have been what they are today. In addition, they would never have done any of the important things they have been doing since the tenth century when they began to sing their epic poetry or in the twentieth which has seen the flourishing of the poetry of Antonio Machado, Juan Ramón Jiménez, and García Lorca among others, as well as the painting of Pablo Picasso. In brief, a more urgent task at the moment than writing a history of Spain itself is the initial need to clarify why it has not been written and why historians with their misconceptions, myths, or attempts to conceal evidence take issue with any attempt to demolish their great magical sideshow, that *retablo de maravillas* which, even today, comprises the bulk of those visions written about Spain's past.

New terms must be coined to explain these present undertakings; I should like to propose the neologism "historical hatement" (*odicio*) instead of judgment to give some sort of a name to this seeming prejudice. There are no Jews or Muslims in the cumulative index of Professor Green's extensive work. In his bibliography he does men-

---

[63] Francisco Márquez, in his article "Sobre la occidentalidad cultural de España," *Revista de Occidente* (Madrid), January 1970, has clearly refuted the fundamental error and fallacy inherent in Green's work.

tion Albert A. Sicroff's work on the *Statuts de "pureté de sang"* . . . but the author's name does not appear in the index of names nor does he make use of Sicroff's main hypothesis. In like manner, Green mentions but does not use my *De la edad conflictiva*,[64] because his whole historical pile of cards would come tumbling down. He does not take into account documents such as the one I published on the investigation of counselors of Charles V by the noted jurist, Lorenzo Galíndez de Carvajal (d. 1534), a text which has been known since 1842 and proves that there is no lack of documents about the Spaniards' past,[65] but simply the absence of a desire to perceive their true meaning. An essential requisite to be a counselor to the emperor was that he be the son or grandson of *labradores*, that is, of peasants, farmers, or people who tilled the soil. Galíndez proposed to fill two vacant posts with "Dr. Vázquez and Licenciado Medina, *oidores* (judges) from Valladolid, who are very learned men (*letrados*) . . . and virtuous and clean (*limpios*) men, descendants by birth of *labradores*." This simple fact proves sufficiently that sixteenth-century Spain thought and felt about the being and merits of the persons involved in a peculiar way, without any relationship to the value judgments and criteria in effect during the same period in Western Europe. Note that a candidate to be a royal counselor was not required to have Catholic ancestors, nor to have a clean criminal record, nor even to be a nobleman. What was required was that his parents, or at least his grandparents, should belong to the lowest class of society, those who earned their livelihood by working the land, farmhands living at the level of the soil, without any possibility or opportunity of acquiring any type of craftsmanship, technical skill, or culture. In sum, the ideal was that the ancestor of a counselor of His Imperial Majesty, the lord of half the world, should be illiterate, that he should lack even the elementary knowledge or technical experience to be a bricklayer, muleteer, tailor, or itinerant salesman. By no means should he be a physician, pharmacist, or—an hidalgo! Neither the status of hidalgo nor one's patent of nobility guaranteed beyond the shadow of a doubt that the royal counselor was free from Jewish or Moorish ancestry. This piece of evidence which I brought to light and published after a century or more of oblivion is like the proverbial peak of an iceberg, very indicative, in this case, of the collective frenzy already prevailing in Spanish society in the first third of the sixteenth century. Ironically, not even the emperor him-

---

[64] Madrid: Taurus, 1963; also translated as *Le drame de l'honneur* (Paris: Klincksieck, 1965) and *L'Età dei Conflitti* (Milan: Ricciardi, 1970).

[65] First published in the *Colección de documentos inéditos para la historia de España* (Madrid, 1842), I, 122, and brought to light again in my *De la edad conflictiva*, p. 197.

self was free from stain, since Juana Enríquez, the mother of his grandfather, Ferdinand the Catholic, was of Jewish ancestry.[66]

Upon reexamination of this invaluable report addressed to the emperor by Dr. Galíndez de Carvajal, I now note that the two counselors he proposed are, in his judgment, "muy buenos *letrados*," very learned men, a fact that at first sight would not strike the reader as unusual. In 1490 Alonso de Palencia says in his *Universal Vocabulario*,[67] that "*letras* are the sciences and teaching or doctrines, and a *letrado* is one who is knowledgeable in this type of learning." Today Spaniards use the term *letrado* to refer specifically to a lawyer, by virtue of a truly surprising semantic specialization. Behind the transformation of this word lies the drama of Spanish culture between the fifteenth and seventeenth centuries. The ultimate consequence of all this was that the "sciences and doctrines" mentioned by Alonso de Palencia in 1490 ended up by being reduced to the knowledge and practice of law. The chasm of culture between 1490 and 1611 had widened. Around 1600 there was no study of Greek or mathematics in Spain, and those who did engage in intellectual activity were oriented toward jurisprudence or theology, not because of the "Counter-Reformation," as several respectable scholars insist upon rather elusively, but in order to evade all suspicion of Judaism. In his famous dictionary, *Tesoro de la lengua castellana* (1611), Sebastián de Covarrubias says with a slight tone of irate and repressed protest: "*Letrado*, he who studies letters, and [in our time] the lawyer jurists have usurped this name" ("Letrado, el que profesa letras, y hanse alzado con este nombre los juristas abogados"). He implies that the lawyers deforced a name that did not rightfully belong to them, and a few of his contemporaries also reacted indignantly, as far as they were able, against such a social confusion that had gone too far.

A contemporary of Sebastián de Covarrubias, Miguel de Cervantes, gave a novelistic form to that calamitous situation in the *Quixote* (XX, 16) where he has two generations, Don Diego de Miranda and his son Don Lorenzo, confront each other. The father is very annoyed that Don Lorenzo is not studying "the science" of law or that "Queen of all the sciences, Theology." The son had spent six years studying Latin and Greek at Salamanca and now, at the very moment of Don Quixote's visit, he spends all his time "trying to find out if Homer wrote such and such a verse of the Iliad correctly . . . or if one should interpret Virgil's lines in one way or another." Don Quixote and Cer-

---

[66] See my "*Español*," *palabra extranjera* . . . , pp. 38 ff. As I say there, the Jewish ancestry of Doña Juana Enríquez is not mentioned in the two biographies of that woman who was the wife of King John of Aragon.

[67] The part written in Spanish has been made workable in a version by John M. Hill (Madrid: Real Academia Española, 1957), p. 105.

vantes side with Don Lorenzo, not with his father, in a passage that many people continue to take literally because they insist on denying the ironic intent insinuated by the author. But neither Spain nor the *Quixote* are comprehensible if the historian cannot tie up the loose ends left undone by the flow of life. The key fact that the emperor's counselors had to be children of people who lacked the most rudimentary requisites of a craft or culture gives us a historical clue to use as proof against the misconstrued, twisted, and malicious attempts to deform the real facts.

Professor Green also overlooks or conceals a passage from a sermon by Philip II's preacher, Father Alonso de Cabrera: "We have gone from one extreme to the other—men have chosen to be dissolute, or at least to appear so, in order to avoid being hypocrites, just as there were those who chose to become stupid and did not want to learn to read rather than be taken for heretics" (*De la edad conflictiva*, p. 179). Since the Jews had a reputation for being the most intelligent and learned men, they purposely chose to appear ignorant and illiterate on the surface in order to avoid the risk of being earmarked as Jews.

The works of Juan de Mal Lara, Cervantes, Quevedo, and Fray Luis de León confirm these same ideas. Professor Green quotes the humanist Juan de Mal Lara (IV, 323) fifteen times, but he neglects to mention a phrase in his *Filosofía vulgar* (1568, *cap*. vi, 61) that says, "Things have gone to such an extreme that it is a sign of noble lineage not to know how to write one's own name," a phrase cited in my *De la edad conflictiva* (p. 178). Green says with incredible aplomb: "Literature is ever unreliable as a social document" (IV, 166). How, then, can we interpret his assertion that he finds no "trace of despair" in the works of Fray Luis de León (II, 375)? If that "despair" does not refer to the society in which the writer lived, what other meaning can it possibly have? As in other cases, Green carefully hides that desperate cry of Fray Luis in Book II of *Los nombres de Cristo*, mentioned before in chapter x; there are kings "who think they are lords just because they keep law and order, not only to affront their own subjects, but also to perpetuate this shame for endless generations." Is this not a direct allusion to the *sanbenitos* with the names of those families who had been tried and sentenced by the Inquisition that hung in the churches for an indefinite length of time? How can we say, then, that the literature of the Spaniards "is ever unreliable as a social document?" Green repeats several times that the persecutions of culture in Spain were similar to those in Europe, but he neglects to say that Hobbes was able to publish his *Leviathan*, a very controversial book for its time, in England in 1651. Furthermore, Spanish culture was in such a state in 1756 that there was no type of physics other than that of Aristotle, because he was considered to be an "Old Christian" in the opinion of fools; and Galileo, Descartes, and Newton were Jews and dangerous heretics according to these same people.[68] Green is careful not to mention a passage in Quevedo, whom he has read thoroughly: "In order to be a knight or hidalgo, even though you are a Moor or Jew, pretend your handwriting is bad . . . and go where you are not recognized" (Bibl. Aut. Esp., XXIII, 481). It was a well-known fact then, and confirmed today, that people who changed their residence often in sixteenth- and seventeenth-century Spain were looking for places where their family ancestry was unknown.

Just because atrocities were committed during the sixteenth and seventeenth centuries in Europe does not put the Spaniards on the same level with Western civilization, but rather with Spanish civilization itself. An honest and accurate historian must explain, first of all, the circumstances that made the Spanish Empire possible. Spanish civilization is not favored by distorting the facts or "stacking the cards" to take advantage of some "hatement."

The past, present, and future of Spain was shaped in a particular way because of and within a set of truly unique circumstances. Men were already aware that the Christian kingdoms were different from Europe, as we saw in the thirteenth-century *Crónica General* that says anachronistically that the cavalry gathered by the Ebro River sided with the Romans against the Carthaginians because the latter were Africans and the Romans were Europeans. In the fifteenth century Fernán Pérez de Guzmán condemns the Muslim domination and puts the blame for it on the defeat of Roderic, the last Visigothic king: "Because of King Roderic, Count Don Julian opened the doors of Spain to the Africans. The sad consequence of what I have said is still very much with us." (The Moorish kingdom of Granada had not yet been conquered when he wrote this.) The account of Spain's invasion and occupation is judged to be "a sad, lamentable history, unworthy of verse and prose." The author says this in his *Loores de los claros varones de España*,[69] a very meaningful text, to grasp the significance of the marginal position of the Christian kingdoms in a cultural sense in relation to medieval Europe. Pérez de Guzmán mentions the archbishop-chronicler, Rodrigo Jiménez de Rada: "He was born in Navarre,/ raised in Castile;/ and educated in the sciences at Paris." The author does not speak of a single university, but of "learned scholars from Cordova," which, according to him, was "worthy of being called,/ another Athens,/ if we recall with pride Seneca/ and Lucan/ and Avén Ruiz (Averroës) the pagan/ whose Commentary gives us pleasure./ If the Egyptian scholar,/ Rabí Moisén (Maimonides),/ wrote/ that Moré (*Guide for the Perplexed*) . . ./ the Hispanic kingdom will do well to recall/ and not in vain/ that I called Cordova

---

[68] See Paulino Garagorri, "Xavier de Munibe," *Revista de Occidente* (Madrid, 1964).

[69] Nueva Bibl. Aut. Esp., XIX, 626, 718, 738.

another Athens,/ and my observation is based on a firm foundation." The memory of Athens is evoked in the fifteenth century just as Chrétien de Troyes had done in twelfth-century France, but for reasons different from those put forth by Pérez de Guzmán. As usual, the Spaniard had fallen into that ever present trap of calling Seneca and Lucan Spaniards, and he completed his cultural survey with a Muslim who had been so mythified by this time that the name Averroës appears as Avén Ruiz, because, I believe, he had read in Dante: "Averroís, che il gran comento feo" (*Inferno*, IV, 144). Rabí Moisén is a reference to Maimonides who left Cordova and went to Egypt where he wrote his Moreh, the Hebrew name for the *Guide for the Perplexed*. This reference in itself is unusual because Pérez de Guzmán used the Hebrew word, while he did not know Averroës's name, which had been strangely Hispanized by way of Dante's reference; what better proof that Muslim wisdom was admired and appreciated while those who had made it possible were despised? Pérez de Guzmán did not know what he was talking about when he mentioned "Avén Ruiz" by way of Dante; Averroës, as I have said, left no traces among the Christians of Castile or Aragon, although he was translated into Hebrew by Jews living in the Peninsula or originally from there.[70] His philosophy affected much of the philosophical and theological thought of medieval Europe, but not that of the Christians in the peninsular kingdoms isolated from Europe of the Middle Ages.

It is noteworthy, however, that Maimonides was present, because the lords of Castile were surrounded by learned Hebrews as Castilian as themselves. Pérez de Guzmán mentions the *Moreh Nebuchim* in Hebrew at a time when Rabbi Arragel of Guadalajara was translating the Old Testament for his lord, Don Luis de Guzmán, the master of Calatrava; in those same years the master of the order of Santiago, Don Gómez Suárez de Figueroa, asked the Jewish convert Pedro de Toledo to translate the *Moreh Nebuchim*,[71] which later found its way into the library of the Marqués de Santillana. The cultural activity of the Castilian Hebrews was extremely effective in the highest aristocratic circles. This situation was part of a long-standing tradition: the kings and noblemen needed the financial, medical, and technical aid and even knowledge of the child-raising ways of those who were legally "servants," condemned to perpetual bondage by virtue of their descent from those who had crucified Christ. This absurd tradition— valid until the Second Vatican Council annulled it a short time ago as

---

[70] For the influence of Averroës outside Christian Spain, see M. Cruz Hernández, *Filosofía hispano-musulmana*, II, 207–245.

[71] See Mario Schiff, *La bibliothèque du Marquis de Santillane* (1905), p. 428. According to Hebrew scholars, the translation is not very good; I gave a microfilm of the work to an American scholar, who, to my knowledge, has not published it.

meaningless—largely contributed to shaping society in the Christian kingdoms and to making it incompatible with medieval Europe and impervious to European ways of thinking. The Christian kingdoms were incapable of creating spontaneously from within themselves forms of life and intellectual activities like those of Western Europe. This imbalance is still true today when Spanish newspapers speak of the "*presence* of Spain in Europe," which indicates, even to someone who is not a psychiatrist, that the fear of Spain being absent from Europe still persists, and that it is necessary to continue importing "Europeanism." People in the Peninsula will never free themselves from this predicament until they decide to get rid of the image of their past, hidden by layers of falsehoods that contribute to encouraging works whose purpose is to perpetuate the deception that Spain constructed and articulated its history upon a "Western tradition." If the Spaniards themselves do not publish works to show the Europeans something they do not know about Spanish past and present history, Spain will not be able to free itself from the cultural stagnation that makes it possible for foreigners to publish such books on Spanish civilization.

As a consequence, the historian of the Spaniards is constantly confronted with difficulties that are nonexistent for those who write about the past of peoples who are completely Western or completely Eastern. The Spaniards' particular problem is that they began to constitute themselves as a single entity by simultaneously rejecting and assimilating the civilization of al-Andalus (including that of the Jews), and at the same time receiving from Western Europe what was imported by the pilgrims to Santiago and also by those who were interested in reaping the profits of political and economic conditions existing in the Christian kingdoms. An example of that receptive attitude toward the Muslim south and European north is reflected in the aforementioned convent of Las Huelgas at Burgos, founded at the end of the twelfth century by Leonore Plantagenet, the wife of Alfonso VIII, where members of the royal family are buried in the pantheon both in Moorish style and Christian European dress (M. Gómez Moreno, *op. cit.*, pp. 7, 68, 73, 76). We have seen how the religious orders of Cluny and Cîteaux affected the life and politics of Castile; and later, in the fourteenth century, how England and France took opposite sides in the fratricidal war between the brothers Peter I of Castile and Henry of Trastámara. Innumerable examples of this type could be cited to describe how the population of the Christian kingdoms came to be made up.

The military advances of the reconquest did not unify the conquerors either culturally or as a single caste; the mere possession of Valencia, Cordova, and Seville did not free the Christians from their obligations, but rather forced them to live together with the Moors and Jews and increased those very obligations. Because the kingdoms of Castile and Aragon had to take the Muslims into account, they could not put themselves on the same level with the kingdoms of Europe in which those unique conditions did not prevail. As late as the fourteenth century the best prose writer of the time, Don Juan Manuel (1282–1349?), wrote in his *Libro de los Estados*: "In truth, I say to you, my sire (Infante) that they [the Moors] are such good men of arms and know so much about war and wage it so well that" if it were not for their false religion and the fact that they do not fight so well on horseback, "I would say that no one in the world has so many good men at arms or is so adept at war or so well equipped for so many conquests." The previous text was cited in chapter xii in reference to the "holy war," but it is used here in another context to reinforce and complete what Don Juan Manuel says later on: "The first thing men need to conquer the Moors, so that they will not be tricked by all their arts and skills, is that they must fight against the Moors bearing this thought in mind constantly . . . that just as Our Lord Jesus Christ died to redeem the sinners, fortune will come to him who dies defending and exalting the Holy Catholic faith; for undoubtedly there are saints and true martyrs among those who die defending our faith in this manner" (Bibl. Aut. Esp., LI, 323–324).

Behind all this lies something more than the scholarly proof of the Castilians' having incorporated the koranical institution of the holy war into their ideal of collective life, because when Don Juan Manuel was writing, the reconquest had already accomplished its main objectives and decisive victories. At the same time, the Christians' bellicose superiority was unquestionable. The mention of "arts and skills" of the Moors in matters of war and insistence on exalting "the Holy Catholic faith" of their Castilian adversaries makes it clear that the horizon of life of both groups was religious, not secular. Similarly, when they were no longer fighting each other and the Muslims lived in submission under Christian domination or as Mudejars in the Christian kingdoms, Don Juan Manuel was advised that, in accordance with the Gospel, "no man of any other law [in our case, Moors and Jews] should be tricked or coerced forcibly to believe in the law of the Gospel" (*Libro de los Estados*, ed. cit., p. 289). The adoption of the Muslim point of view in the case of religious tolerance and living together differed "from the common belief held in Europe at that time," according to a scholar who was well acquainted with the work of Don Manuel and in addition writes that "in all probability it can be stated that he was familiar with the Arabic language."[72] Paradoxically, that "living-togetherness" of believers of different faiths made it pos-

---

[72] A. Giménez Soler, *Don Juan Manuel* (Saragossa, 1932), pp. 133–136.

sible for Don Juan Manuel to call "the Moors to his aid . . . to provoke conflicts with the king of Castile" (Giménez Soler, p. 134).

From the eighth to the end of the fifteenth century the Moors were endowed with a political dimension because the Christians were fighting against them during that time; once they were conquered and lived under Christian domination as Mudejars they became endowed with a social dimension and, as such, they stood out as a group against which to project the idea expressed by Don Juan Manuel, which is equally valid for the kingdoms of Castile and Aragon. In 1283 King Peter III of Aragon addressed his loyal Saracen subjects of the kingdoms of Valencia to the effect that he was at war with the French, "in which we have need of your services . . . and to inform you further of this situation, I am sending our loyal emissary (*alphaquim*) Don Samuel." Note that the king's emissary was a high-ranking Jew, for the king called him "Don Samuel." The king continues: "We beg of you and command you" ("perque us pregam e us manam") to choose from each assembly or quarter of Moors a group of crossbowmen and lancers provided with all the necessary equipment and weapons. The king promises them a good salary with added benefits.[73] In this case, the king "begs and orders," undoubtedly working in accordance with the custom of recruiting Moors specialized in the arts of fighting on foot and horseback; this was by no means a "European" custom, but apparently a very common occurrence in a peninsular Christian kingdom.

Taking a chronological leap forward to 1559, we observe that an extremely anti-semitic author admits the possibility that a Moor might be a nobleman. Juan Arce de Otálora, a magistrate in the chancery of Valladolid, recalls having granted a patent of nobility to a Moor; and, returning again to the past, he observes that "among those Saracens or Moors, mention is made of the lineage of *hidalgos*, such as in the time of the Almorávides of Africa, who were sent for by King Don Alonso VI on the advice of Abenabet, the king of Seville, his father-in-law, the father of Doña Zaida, the sixth wife of this King Don Alonso."[74] The author also mentions the noble Abencerraje family of Granada "et aliae plures familiae." No matter how adverse the Moors had been to the Christian cause, they had fought bravely for eight centuries and had become exalted with a halo of valor. Their science and philosophy meant little to the Christians of Castile, but their daring, bravery, and chivalry were idealized in the *Romancero* and in tales dealing with Morisco themes in the sixteenth century.

---

[73] *Colección de documentos inéditos del Archivo de la Corona de Aragón*, ed. Próspero de Bofarull (Barcelona, 1850), VI, 196.

[74] *Summa nobilitatis Hispanicae* (Salamanca, 1559), p. 193.

In contrast to the Moors, the Jews distinguished themselves less as a group than as individuals. Between the eleventh century and 1492 it is possible to cite numerous Jews who held influential positions at the courts of Castile and Aragon or lived side by side with the *grandes* of these kingdoms as administrators of public and private finance, as physicians, and as ambassadors and scholars.[75] Since it is not my purpose to accumulate facts, but to emphasize the *functional* nature of those diverse components of the population of the future Spaniards and the outcome of those circumstances, I shall mention only a few examples. We have already seen how Rabbi Arragel reminded his lord, the master of Calatrava, of the cultural superiority of the Hispano-Hebrews, to which we must also add their influence as the preceptors of noble families. In 1321 King James II of Aragon wrote to his daughter Constanza, the wife of Don Juan Manuel: "Daughter, we received your letter . . . regarding your newborn son. . . . With God's help he will survive. . . . But, daughter, do not, as is your custom, nurse him and raise him in the way the Jews advise."[76]

In his life, in his works (particularly *El Conde Lucanor*), and in his opinions, Don Juan Manuel reflects the dual action of the Moors and Jews on his radically Christian person. We saw how he spoke of the Moors in generic terms, and now we shall see how he felt in particular about his physician when he drew up his will: "Because Don Solomon, my physician, is a Jew, and cannot and should not be my executor (*cabeçalero* in Old Spanish, *albacea* in modern Spanish),[77] but because I have always deemed him so loyal, which is almost impossible to believe or express in words, I beg Doña Blanca, my wife, and my children to follow his advice in business and in all matters, because I am

---

[75] Abundant data can be found in Yitzhak Baer, *A History of the Jews in Christian Spain* (Philadelphia, I, 1961; II, 1966). *Die Juden im christlichen Spanien* (Berlin, I, 1929; II, 1936) by the same author contains a magnificent collection of documents which have never been reedited and are inaccessible today.

[76] A. Giménez Soler, p. 501, published a fragment of this letter. I have the complete text (Archivo de la Corona de Aragón, *Reg.* 247, folio 320), thanks to Don Federico Udina. The king says nothing specific in it other than his order not to have his grandson raised, according to custom, by Jews.

[77] It is worthy of note that the Arabic word *albacea* is used today instead of the term of Latin origin, *cabezalero*, in this case. The *cabezalero* was so called because he was near the pillow (*cabezal* or almohada), that is, the head (*cabeza*) of the dying person who made his will. This is another case of the substitution of a word of Latin origin by one of Arabic origin, and an indication that the pillows (*almohadas*) were made by Moorish artisans rather than Christians. The legal code of the *Partidas* (VI, i, 1) uses both *cabeçalero* and *testamentario* without differentiating between them; but it does use the word *albacea* (III, xviii, 62) to refer to those in charge of "selling the deceased man's possessions," a task usually reserved for Moors or Jews whose language was full of Arabisms. These sales often took place at *almonedas* (auctions), again an Arabic word. The form of the language and the manner of expression bear witness to the constant interaction of the population of the Christian kingdoms.

certain that they will profit from his counsel, for if he were a Christian, I know full well that I would leave everything in his hands."[78] Both these texts reflect clearly the intimate way of life of the highest families of the Spanish nobility who raised their children in the manner advised by the Jews whose services, in turn, were transmitted as an inheritance to successive generations.

Juan Ruiz, the Archpriest of Hita and author of *El libro de buen amor* (*The Book of Good Love*), was the best poet of the reconquest period and a contemporary of Don Juan Manuel. His book deals with themes of European literature in a style full of Oriental reflections, without any comparison in Europe. The author says that he has composed "many songs and poems (*cantigas*) . . . for Jewish and Moorish women" (line 6175, ed. G. Chiarini), and before this, the go-between, Trotaconventos, converses with a Moorish girl who replies in Arabic to the four questions Trotaconventos asks and begs her to answer '*alá wudd*' (with love).[79] If Giménez Soler reasonably assumed that Don Juan Manuel knew Arabic, there is no less reason to suppose the same to be true of the Arcipreste de Hita. People of three beliefs and two languages intermingled for centuries. When the Cid conquered Valencia in 1093, he designated the surveillance of its towers to certain men because they had been raised "with Moors and spoke like them and were familiar with their ways and customs" (*Crónica General*, p. 588). In 1236 Ferdinand III took Cordova with the aid of his best *algaraviados*, the bilingual Christians in his armies who, disguised as Moors, could not be taken as enemies because they spoke the same language (*Crónica General*, p. 730). The names of those bilingual Christians who were the first to scale the walls of Cordova were by no means Arabic. The *Crónica* mentions Alvar Colodro and Benito de Baños, whose names sounded as Castilian as that of Juan Ruiz in the following century. Those who ignore or refuse to accept the makeup of Castile's population as it really was also reject any Oriental traces in the themes or stylistic arrangement and structure of the *Libro de buen amor*. This is not the place to discuss the highly original form in which this unique poetry artistically combines Near Eastern and Western traits. The same is true of the prose of *El Conde Lucanor* by Don Juan Manuel.

About a century later the composition of Castile was still the same, when two Czech noblemen, Baron Leon von Rosmithal and Gabriel Tetzal, visited the kingdom between 1465 and 1467. The latter describes the estates of the Count of Haro, in the region of La Rioja,

---

[78] See Mercedes Gailbrois, *Boletín de la Academia de la Historia* (1931), XCIX, 25.

[79] See J. Oliver Asín, "La expresión 'alá ud' en *El libro de Buen Amor*," *Al-Andalus* (1956), pp. 212–214.

province of Logroño, thus: "On his lands and even at his court there are Christians, Moors, and Jews. They say that the count is a Christian [!] but one cannot tell what religion he professes. He lets everyone live in peace with their own belief."[80] This kind of observation or evidence has never been used to any advantage so that people might realize, from a European point of view, that fifteenth-century Castile did not give the foreigner an impression of resembling any European country. Where else outside of Spain could a great lord have Moors and Jews as his vassals and in addition accept them as a part of his court? From a European viewpoint, that piece of noble politics did not seem to be compatible with the fact that the lord was a Christian. It was an actual situation, though, within the non-Western tradition of Castile and Aragon. These same factors readily explain that certain Europeans (Ariosto among them) in the sixteenth century erroneously thought that the Spaniards were descendants of the Jews or Marranos.

While the inaccurate practice of calling "the Middle Ages" those centuries of living together of three castes and sporadic importation of European customs, there can be no solution to the ills that afflict Spanish historiography, nor will it be possible to establish any dividing line between the malicious slander (every country suffers from the same malady) and the lack of understanding caused by the ignorance of what is simply a uniqueness or peculiarity. As far back as 1904 Antoine Thomas commented that Roger Bacon was horrified to observe that a Latin text translated from the Arabic in Spain had introduced vernacular words, which the thirteenth-century philosopher termed a "vile thing."[81] It was by no means a question of an insidious error. In Castile Latin was not used as a means of scholarly or scientific expression, primarily for the reasons I have discussed before; there was no science of philosophy as such to express in that international language common to Western Europe. The Aragonese-Catalan court had more contacts with Europe than Castile through the region later known as Catalonia, which was an extension of the French monarchy, the so-called Marca Hispanica.[82] But in spite of the great figure of Raymond Lully, who did not know Latin and at times wrote in Arabic, neither Aragon nor Catalonia made any contribution to the development of modern science and thought.

The Castilians, as we have said repeatedly, had lived for centuries

---

[80] *Viajes de extranjeros por España y Portugal*, ed. J. García Mercadal (Madrid, 1952), I, 295.

[81] "Roger Bacon et les étudiants espagnols," *Bulletin Hispanique*, VI, 18–28.

[82] See H. Finke, *Acta Aragonensia. Quellen zur deutschen italienischen französischen, spanischen zur Kirchen un Kulturgeschichte aus den diplomatischen Korrespondenz Jaymes II (1291–1327)*, pp. 1908–1922.

with the Moors or fought against them. Menéndez Pidal was probably correct when he surmised that Alfonso X took his inspiration from the Taifa states, those small principalities of al-Andalus that rivaled each other "in encouraging brilliant academies where the most illustrious men collaborated side by side."[83] The example or emulation of those Muslim courts may also have contributed to the fact that they were limited insofar as they used as a written language the same one that was spoken by the kings. In spite of the dialectical differences in spoken Arabic, the written language used was that of the Koran, or classical Arabic (just as the Byzantines made an effort to perpetuate the Greek of Plato and Aristotle as a written language insofar as it was possible). In this way another non-European phenomenon arose: the language spoken by the Castilians was the same one that the Jews of Castile used as their written language in the books of astronomy or doctrinary treatises or that the Christians used in the juridical works (*Siete Partidas*) promulgated by the royal council. The Jews, who were very influential in scholarship and public administration at that time, rarely studied Latin because "they mistrusted and feared it; ultimately it was the language of those who had destroyed their temple and had brought the Chosen People down to that condition of slavery and baseness and had accused them of deicide. The Vulgate was written in Latin in accordance with Christian dogma and contrary to the biblical concept of the Jews; the most terrible decrees had been propagated against them in that language."[84] Neuman also concurs with that idea: "Latin never replaced Arabic as a medium of Jewish culture. Not only was it linguistically alien but it was also spiritually hostile and historically inimical."[85] When Abraham ibn Ezra went to France in the middle of the twelfth century he dictated his work (called in Spanish *Fundamentos de las Tablas astronómicas*) to a scribe in Latin.[86]

As I pointed out several years ago, the Castilian Jews were able to give free rein to their aversion for Latin and encourage the use of the vernacular or spoken tongue for astronomy or other sciences. But the mere facts do not reveal the meaning behind them—this is the fundamental illness of Spanish historiography. I have not emphasized until now that one of the reasons why there were no cultural movements in the Christian kingdoms analogous to those in Europe from the

---

83 "España y la introducción de la ciencia árabe en Occidente," *Estudios segovianos*, II (1952), 22–23. In this study, as in others, the author anachronistically confuses what we call "Spain" today with the Muslims connected with Near Eastern culture, who had nothing to do with "Spaniards," as I have said before.

84 M. Steinschneider, *Die hebraeischen Übersetzungen des Mittelalters*, p. 461.

85 A. A. Neuman, *The Jews in Spain*, II, 90.

86 See J. M. Millás Vallicrosa, *El libro de los fundamentos de las Tablas astronómicas* (Madrid, 1947), pp. 17, 66.

eleventh to the fourteenth centuries was the resistance of the Castilian Hebrews to the use of the only language that the so-called medieval culture used to express these movements. Another factor was that the Castilian Christians had not only been occupied since the tenth century in the arduous task of combating the Moors, according to the usual excuse for their intellectual inactivity, but also they wished to magnify their own importance as Castilians in relation to the other Christian inhabitants of the Peninsula. The problem for the Castilians during this time was to achieve such a high degree of vital tension that they could single themselves out as a people, and, as such, assert their feelings of superiority over the Navarrese, Aragonese, Leonese, and Galicians. At the beginning of the twentieth century, Pedro Corominas had already made observations of a human-economic nature[87] which were not taken into account in historiography because history had not integrated economy with the basic factor in Castile's heterogeneous population—the fact that Christians lived side by side with Jews and Mudejars who were their subjects and at the same time conditioned their way of life. Castile, on the other hand, moved under the double pressure of its Moorish enemy and France to the north which had been introducing into Castile since the eleventh century everything that was convenient for its ecclesiastic and economic interests. For the Frenchman of the Île de France (Corominas does not say this), his land was a fertile one where he could be both seigneur and farmer, but for the Castilian, his land was a place where he could live and which at the same time he had to defend. As late as the year 1000, after three centuries of fighting the Moor, Almanzor, the Muslim chieftain, was still able to overrun the land at will, and in his campaigns he went as far north as Galicia and Soria. In 1282, after Cordova and Seville had been conquered, the Banu Marín of Morocco, called in by Alfonso X, went up "almost as far as Madrid," and "finally retreated to Algeciras because winter had set in," not because the Castilians had forced a retreat.[88] For a long time the area between the frontier of Castile, south of the Duero and north of the Tagus, was either deserted or practically uninhabitable. In addition, Aragón, at the time of the reconquest, was considered a foreign country, just as Leon had been until the beginning of the thirteenth century. The king of Leon, Alfonso IX, invaded and ransacked Castilian land regularly.[89]

---

[87] El sentimiento de la riqueza en Castilla (Madrid: Residencia de Estudiantes, 1917), p. 122.

[88] Luis García de Valdeavellano, "Los días penosos del Rey Sabio," Residencia: Revista de la Residencia de Estudiantes (Mexico, 1963), p. 34.

[89] An echo of the ancient rivalries and hostilities between Castile and Leon is found in the ballad, "Castellanos y leoneses tienen grandes divisiones ..." ("Castilians and Leonese have great divisions or differences of opinion"), which, ac-

The nature of Castilian soil must be related to the historical circumstances and conditions that had made the man who inhabited it a defensive human being for centuries. Corominas rightly observed that the riches a man could manipulate with his hands were more important to him than the inanimate land; the spoils of war took precedence over the territorial acquisition itself. Trees did not interest him; "the tree—the big and the small—for my grandfather" ("el árbol y el arboyuelo, para mi abuelo"). This lack of interest in the land itself is linked to what I have called the "imperative dimension of the individual," and related to what Corominas had written in 1917, although I have not had his text available until now; he speaks of "the will to dominate men and things" (*El sentimiento*, p. 122). The Castilian did not consider his home a stable or pleasant place, but rather a frontier outpost constantly on the verge of being attacked by Moorish or Christian enemies. Sancho the Elder of Navarre (d. 1035), the father of Ferdinand, the first king of Castile, slept by his horse, because the kings at that time had these animals "in their chambers [where] they slept with their wives, so that when they heard the call to arms, they could have their horses and arms ready without delay, in order to leave in a hurry" (*Crónica General*, p. 474).

If we now take into account what I explained in chapter xi, it is clear that Castile was obliged to "import" Europeanism, but it could not situate itself, by its own initiative, within the political-cultural community called the European Middle Ages. Bellicose conditions and the "meddling" of Europeans in the affairs of the pilgrimages to Santiago forced the Castilians to develop their own original personality. They did not bother to foment culture; they cultivated the art of being "lords" rather than exercize the faculties of the intellect or imagination. They did not develop a philosophy or science of their own, but they did create personal ways of being that would, in the future, make possible imperial enterprises and literary forms of expression still admired and studied throughout the world. The Spaniards lived alongside Europe, but ultimately they were so alien to it that as late as the first half of the nineteenth century they found themselves without any means to establish effective contacts with their own past. Extraordinary personalities arose as individuals, but as a people they discovered themselves from what foreigners had written and made manifest of their great achievements. Calderón's plays were edited, published, and studied in Germany; Lord Holland was an avid

cording to R. Menéndez Pidal, was inspired by a "poetic narration," the common source of the ballad and of the *Crónica* of 1344 which describes the hostile encounter between Count Fernán González of Castile and King Ordoño of León in the tenth century. See *Homenaje a Menéndez Pelayo* (Madrid, 1899), pp. 441 and 451.

scholar and collector of Lope de Vega's manuscripts; George Ticknor, an American educated at Heidelberg, wrote a history of Spanish literature at a time when no one in Spain was capable of doing a similar task.

The extreme radicalisms of our time offer a more propitious opportunity than ever to bring the authentic history of the Spaniards to the foreground. If the truth is stripped bare, or if shameful acts are legalized that were illegal in many countries only a short time ago, there is no reason why countries should be reluctant to show youth the genetic processes of their grandeur and misery. If children are taught that the notion that the stork brought them is a stupid legend, or something of the sort, then why should people be afraid to make books available to youth which would uncover the reasons for the political disunity of the Italians, the phenomenon of German Hitlerism, the absence of democracy in Russia, the cultural insufficiency of the Spaniards, or racial crises in the United States? The contrast between a civilization that has put men on the moon and the state of degradation and total absence of direction of today's youth in many of the most progressive nations is all too clear. The United States, with all its laws and democratic traditions, has not closed the legal and moral gap separating the whites from the blacks. Furthermore, it is becoming increasingly difficult in civilized countries for teachers and students to properly fulfill their indispensable obligation of keeping culture alive and making it grow. In short, the concepts of progress and cultural underdevelopment are not as clear and challenging as they were half a century ago. The notions of evolution and social revolution have been affected by doubt and skepticism; the so-called advanced countries no longer have implicit faith in the principles that motivated and stimulated their progressive advancement; and countries in the process of revolution have freed themselves from the yoke of the czar's cossacks or from the subtle cruelties of the Chinese Empire only to be treated as flocks of sheep pent up within the folds of their borders, confined to thinking, writing, working, or moving in accordance with the norms imposed by an iron-handed bureaucracy.

From all this we can ultimately conclude that it is not morally or intellectually legitimate to reduce history to ciphers or dogmatic principles such as population figures, class struggles, or economic progress, in other words, to establish the premises a priori in the historiographic work based on the type of social organization pleasing to the writer or to season the past in such a way that it ends up coinciding with the personal tastes of the man who is forging his history. Whatever the future may uncover, the past cannot be the object of any manipulation, as historians have done until now, by excluding

Moors and Jews from Spanish history and arbitrarily forcing upon it a "Western Middle Ages." I realize the serious problem confronting foreign Hispanists who try to write or teach an <u>authentic</u> history of the Spaniards, because they are obliged to move among those who teach forms of Western civilization (Anglo-Saxon, French, German). This difficulty is further complicated by the Spaniards' own resistance to accepting the fact that their true history is inconceivable without Moors or Jews; on the other hand, they have no choice but to exclude from it the Romans and Visigoths, as was clearly shown at the beginning of this work.

This is the reason for the apparent disorder of my historical work which seems to irritate many people. Actually I have tried to interweave together with references of what happened in Spain the indubitable fact that Spanish scholars themselves have felt obligated, either knowingly or inadvertently, to write fabulous, fallacious histories or to avoid the motivating factors of the so-called Spanish decadence. The problem, strictly speaking, is not how the Spaniards passed from hegemony to decline, but how the deficiencies and defects created by the dizzying force of human motivation reduced this course to an almost total state of immobility. The attempts to make Spanish history comprehensible by means of the accumulation of documents or economic research fail completely in this respect and only serve to foment political or religious causes, to fire personal grudges or flatter nationalistic vanity, or, in the long run, to hide or evade what the historian does not know how to present to his readers or students in an acceptable, coherent, and positive form.

XIV · PROBLEMS AND PERIODS
IN SPANISH HISTORY

From the Caste Struggle
to Imperial Grandeur

A HISTORY OF THE SPANIARDS based on the new form of Peninsular population initiated in the eighth century would prove an excellent opportunity to overcome traditional hatred and cultural obstacles and also to cure the Spaniards' blindness about themselves. Even if the Christians ultimately did away with the Moors' military power and the Jews' haughty social pretentions, it is useless to deny or ignore the existence of those unique forms of living that arose from eight centuries of coexistence. When the Spaniards were confronted with their own history, their refractory reaction to their own peculiar mode of being became very evident in the fifteenth century when rivalries began to arise between the Jewish converts and those of their own caste. Here is a clear example of this situation. In the middle of the fifteenth century Fray Alonso de Oropesa, the general of the Hieronymite order, wrote a still unpublished work, "Lumen ad revelationen gentium," in which he attempted to explain the sincerity or insincerity of the Jewish converts to Christianity. Fray Alonso says that he is an Old Christian, but that he would not mind if he had not been born an Old Christian because he would be "no less happy to be the son of Abraham, from whose flesh Christ was born, and even be proud of it."[1] Sigüenza says that in chapter 24 of his work Oropesa reprimands the secular and ecclesiastical princes for permitting these "devilish" people to "communicate with and live together with the faithful and to confide their estates to them, make these people their overseers, give them tithes and other incomes

---

[1] Fray José de Sigüenza, *Historia de la orden de San Jerónimo* (*1600*), Nueva Bibl. Aut. Esp., I, 371. The future St. Ignatius of Loyola said the same thing later when his order was founded; at the beginning he had no reservations about accepting New Christians. Diego Laínez, the second general of the Society of Jesus, was of Jewish descent.

to make them grow rich" (p. 871). In the middle of the fifteenth century the princes of the church took advantage of the Jews to collect tithes and lived in close contact with the descendants of those who had crucified Christ. We saw that a century earlier Don Juan Manuel, the grandson of Ferdinand the Holy, spoke highly of his Jewish physician and entrusted the Jews with the upbringing of his children. A similar collaboration took place even earlier in the thirteenth century when the aforementioned Fuero Real of 1263 forbade Jews to have unorthodox books in their homes and ordered those books to be burned at the door of the synagogue. In the eleventh and twelfth centuries the Castilian kings, Alfonso VI, VII, and VIII, helped exterminate the Karaite heresy, a dangerous one for the rabbis and the Talmud. The preeminence of all the Hispanic Jews in the highest strata of the nobility and the church (this had also taken place in the kingdom of Aragon, although in a slightly different form) was the result and reflection of the position the Jews had occupied at the Muslim courts of al-Andalus, where they were not persecuted as they had been prior to this time under the Visigoths. For this reason the economy and culture of the Christian kingdoms were inseparable from the form and structure of the Peninsular population itself, and very different from Europe at this time.

If we have found faults and flaws in the Spanish past, upon comparing it with the culture that made possible the thought and technology of Western Europe and the United States, it is no less certain that, thanks to the conflicts created by those faults and "non-Europeanisms," Spain has achieved highly unique virtues and creations that are equally valid and admired beyond its borders. One of the aims of my work is to attempt to show how the entire history of the Spaniards, from the reconquest to the present, has been sustained or impelled by the struggle between the person and his circumstances. By this concept I do not mean the well-known idea of Ortega y Gasset, "Yo soy yo y mi circunstancia"; I refer specifically to the conflict created by men living together with other men, following the example of the Moors, consciously or not, and at the same time needing to conquer them or do without them; making use of the Jews, living together with them, and accepting their prayers alongside those of the Christians at a moment of devastating drought as the cathedral chapter of Seville did even in the fifteenth century, and at the same time attempting to suppress them; feeling the desire and need to cultivate science and secular, or speculative, knowledge, and refraining from doing so in order not to give the impression of being Jewish; exterminating the American Indians in the Antilles and later preserving them on the continent,[2] with the result that today Hispanoamerica

---

[2] Professor R. R. Palmer has placed this phenomenon in its proper perspective,

finds itself in a situation both of coexistence and feeling a repulsion of a racial nature, not of a caste system, comparable, in its schematic outline, to that which existed in the Christian kingdoms among Christians, Moors, and Jews and later among Christians of different ancestries. Again I must return to my idea that one of the most important and decisive aspects of the Hispanic world is that men, as absolute human beings, have interposed themselves and still do today to some extent between man and his nonhuman circumstances.

All this has had far-reaching consequences. The Spaniards created for themselves a very unique civilization, one of whose most outstanding aspects was to affirm man's absolute or combative worth and self-reliance against his environment. The feats performed by the Spaniards in the lands they discovered and eventually conquered had no parallel in Europe. The naive attempt to "Europeanize" Spanish history appears ridiculous, because there was nothing in the Western tradition of Europe to make these feats comprehensible. The Spaniards were the only ones in the sixteenth century capable of discovering and exploring the Amazon river as Orellana did, or of crossing the future United States from Florida to California as Alvar Núñez Cabeza de Vaca did, or of dominating a powerful empire as Hernán Cortés did. The very fact that the Mexicans have benefited from the Spanish conquest today and hate Cortés to the extent that no street or monument in Mexico bears his name, is one more case in point of that peculiar Spanish battle of man against his circumstances. In relation to this singular phenomenon I shall relate a small anecdote: the word *hombre* (man, pronounced with an aspirated "h") found its way into the English of the American Southwest, and during the last World War a division from Texas wore this word on the sleeve patch of its uniform. A touch of humor? The echo of Castilian *hombría*, or a long-lost or long-ignored voice?

All this proves how ineffective it is to attempt to explain the imperial expansion of the Castilians merely by their greed for wealth. Historians neglect to mention that many Europeans had this same desire to become rich, but only the Spaniards—and this is the central point—were able to create a situation that made it possible to exploit the Indians and at the same time to achieve great economic benefits in inhospitable, remote lands never trodden by white men and inhabited by experts in the effective use of poisoned arrows or darts.

What I have termed man's struggle against his circumstances was

---

without resorting to historical "hatement": "It may be observed not only that the Spanish Empire let the Indians survive, but in all the long record of European expansion the Spanish are the only people (with some exception for the Portuguese in Brazil, and possibly for the Russians) who have ever really Europeanized a large non-European mass in its own native environment" (*A History of the Modern World* [New York: Knopf, 1950], p. 95).

not only expressed in fearless undertakings; it is also found in literary forms related to peculiar modes of existence in Spanish society. *La Celestina*,[3] many plays written during the first half of the sixteenth century, and picaresque novels such as *Lazarillo de Tormes*, *Guzmán de Alfarache*, and *Quixote* were conceived by writers on the fringe of a society obsessed by pride, vanity, and the terror of belonging or not belonging to the Old Christian caste, to the "Chosen People," as the Israelites were in biblical times.

The Disintegration of the Caste System and Its Consequences for Spain

The Castilian Christian's lack of interest in intellectual activity and technical concern made it very difficult for him to do without the collaboration of Jews and Mudejars before 1500 and of Moriscos after that time.[4] The contradictory opinions about the Jews and Moriscos are very indicative symptoms of a conflict that had been expressed in many ways and facets throughout the course of several centuries. But conflict is one thing and the awareness of living in a constant state of conflict is another. Moreover, if the Jews and Moors created insoluble problems for the Christians, eventually the Jews, and to a lesser extent the Moors and Moriscos, suffered the consequences deeply in the anguish and anxiety of their very existence.

Salomón Ben Verga's very significant work, *Chébet Jehudá (The Rod of Judah)*,[5] written after the expulsion of the Jews in 1492, is favorable to the Sephardim, but at the same time the author is very aware of the conditions that had brought about the great catastrophe suffered by that essential component of the Spanish population. In discussing the reasons for their exile, Ben Verga points out that the principal one was "the religious hatred and the desire of those who

---

[3] A forthcoming study by Professor Francisco Márquez on Fray Antonio de Guevara, the famous bishop of Mondoñedo, will enable us to include him in this group of people who are situated face to face with their circumstances.

[4] "Anything that had to do with the arts of construction [in the kingdom of Aragón] was in the hands of Morisco craftsmen in the sixteenth century; around 1550 the beautiful merchant's exchange was built by Moriscos in Saragossa," as well as other important buildings (María Soledad Carrasco, *El problema morisco en Aragon en el reinado de Felipe II* [Madrid, 1969], p. 40). In addition to the section on the Moriscos in chapter vii of this book, there is the opinion voiced by the Jesuit Pedro de León in 1610: "Brothers, give us your customs and partake of our faith" (cited in A. Domínguez Ortiz, *Crisis y decadencia de la España de los Austrias* [Barcelona: Ariel, 1969], p. 33). Bartolomé Leonardo de Argensola, the well-known Aragonese author (1562–1631), said that the Moriscos *"were useful and good in their moral and ethical aspects, in spite of the fact that they were not Christians"* (cited in M. S. Carrasco, p. 26). I have italicized this phrase, which is very expressive of the conflict that has been making Spanish life difficult for many centuries.

[5] Trans. Francisco Cantera (Granada, 1927).

command to subject the other inhabitants of the world to their religion and faith" (p. 219). In this work the memories of harmony and controversy between Jews and Christians and among the Jews themselves become meshed and interwoven. There was a permanent psychological imbalance of attraction and aversion in the Christian kingdoms, in addition to the inevitable contrasts and differences present in any society where the strong and weak live together. Ben Verga explains this situation perhaps more clearly than anyone else in the fifteenth and sixteenth centuries: "I have never known an intelligent man who truly hated the Jews. They are hated only by the masses or lower classes. This is justified by the fact that the Jew himself is proud and haughty and always wants to be the leader; he does not realize that his people are poor exiles and slaves who wander rejected from one country to another, no matter how hard they try to appear as lords and governors, and this is why the common people hate them" (p. 65).

These outbursts of sincerity explain what inevitably happened, particularly in Castile where the lower strata of Christian society began to rise in the ranks and the way became clear for them to govern those who had formerly dominated them as *grandes de Castilla* without being Christians. This situation cannot be explained away by a simplified rationale of a mere "class struggle," because in the case of the Spaniards during the centuries of the reconquest the driving force was the ultimate domination of the population, not the liberation of the oppressed. Chance alone cannot explain why an original idea of a democratic-socialistic nature has never taken root or been utilized to a large extent in Spain. Ben Verga says: "There are three principal kinds of envy: that of religion, of women, and of riches, and Israel has all three types just like any other people; but by constant dealing with the people, the Jewish men of Spain began to set their eyes on the daughters of the people," without thinking that if "the young lady was seduced, he had begot a son for the idolatrous cult." Because of their greed for wealth, "the Jews entered the professions and businesses of the Christians." Another cause of their downfall was "pride, for some of our people became proud and ambitious and thought they could rule over the Christians who were the true lords of the country. Because of this vane pride a disastrous event occurred in the very year of the expulsion [1492]. On the night of the Feast of Atonement [Yom Kippur] men began to argue over the seating arrangements in the synagogue, and each one seized a candle in the Hecal [place between the atrium and the sanctuary] and beat his neighbor over the head" (pp. 219–220).[6]

---

[6] When the funeral services were to be held in Seville for Philip II, December 1598, they had to be postponed because of an argument between the members of the city council and the Inquisition involving protocol over the seating arrangements. Philip III had to settle the matter. Cervantes composed one of his most

The image of that authentic Spain, made up and torn apart by three conflicting wills to command and dominate the others, is gradually taking shape. We may recall the words of Abén Humeya, the leader of the Moorish rebellion in La Alpujarra against the omnipotent Philip II (chapter vii, note 49): "Do you not realize that we have been in Spain and this land has been ours for nine hundred years?" In spite of that crushing defeat of Granada in 1581, a few Aragonese Moriscos still believed that they could restore the "Moorish kingdom of Saragossa"[7] with the help of the Sultan of Turkey.

Both the real and the illusory themes of the reconquest have become interwoven in the threads of that splendid tapestry of a grandiose and melancholy Spain. After eight centuries of warring against the Moor—a long series of magnificent, valiant points rather than a continuous unbroken line—the Christian lord was accustomed to living off the booty he had captured, off the land cultivated by the Mudejar in the vast southern and eastern regions of the Peninsula, and off the administrative and technical abilities of the Jew who was always available to serve the hierarchies of the aristocracy and the church. When the secular battle ended (the War of Granada lasted ten years), the immense areas of the Spanish Empire began to increase, as if they had dropped into the Spaniards' lap by some miraculous fortune. In 1525 much of Italy was in the hands of the emperor Charles V; in the far-off Indies the Castilians began to take possession of the lands they had conquered in easily fought battles, easily fought when the extent of the conquered lands is considered. The phrase in the *Quixote* (I, 8), "Risk everything at a single blow" ("Aventurarlo todo a la [ventura] de un solo golpe"), would be a fitting motto for the Spain that was finally governed militarily and inquisitorially by the dominating caste.

Since 1480 the Inquisition and royal treasury had begun to swell with the enormous wealth and material possessions, impossible to figure in round numbers, of those accused of practicing Judaism. All these factors add up to the inevitable and definitive rupture of the coexistence of the three castes (1492, 1609). Castile and Aragon completed what I have called the "interior reconquest,"[8] the domestic reconquest, without substituting "Europeanism" for their ancient customs of war and command.

Now the Spaniards began to create for themselves the problematic situation in which one was or was not an Old Christian or an *hidalgo*

---

bitter and satirical poems on that pompous tumulus built for the solemn occasion ("Voto a Dios que me espanta tal grandeza . . ."), which apparently was of no use to anyone.

[7] See M. S. Carrasco, *El problema morisco* . . . , p. 40.

[8] "La reconquista interior," *La realidad histórica de España* (Mexico, 1954), p. 488.

who was automatically exempt from paying taxes. What they had actually "reconquered" was their ancient and exclusive right to aspire to their personal "grandeur" as Old Christians, a rank that had been coveted for centuries by the Muslims (see chapter vii, note 86, on al-kābir) and by the Jews. It was not easy, however, to trace the dividing line between the Christians of pure descent and those whose blood had been contaminated by Judaism. Thus the great historical trial began and reached such proportions that it has still not been resolved, because it is a subject that irritates present-day Spaniards and foreigners. I shall try to explain it briefly. The Christian Castilians succeeded in rising above the Jews and Mudejars through their military prowess (the War of Granada, the conquest of the kingdom of Naples, the domination of vast areas of the Americas), not through their intellectual superiority or technical know-how. The Old Christians were confronted by equally zealous "caste" rivals in the many Christians of remote or near Jewish descent (neither judicial authority nor public opinion took this difference into account). One outcome of this rivalry was the tendency of the so-called New Christians to distinguish themselves culturally. When I called attention to this phenomenon several years ago, it provoked a reaction, sometimes absurdly aggressive, among those who accused me of depriving Spain of some of its most important figures in the fields of science and thought. Although people had suspected for many years that the philosopher Luis Vives was of Jewish parentage, the mere mention of this fact in a book provoked violent reactions among the Spaniards because of their retrospective anti-Semitism.[9] In spite of all this, in the fields of secular culture and religious spirituality the New Christians occupy prominent places in the foreground: Antonio de Nebrija, Francisco Sánchez de las Brozas ("el Brocense"), Gonzalo Fernández de Oviedo, José de Acosta, Andrés Laguna, St. Theresa de Jesús, St. John of Avila, Fernando de Rojas (the author of La Celestina),[10] and Miguel de Cervantes, etc. I assume that people will be equally shocked to learn that the great Jesuit thinker, Francisco Suárez, was also of more or less remote Jewish extraction. In my book Español, palabra extranjera . . . I showed that the mother of King Ferdinand the Catholic was of Jewish descent. I shall not go into detail about this particular matter here, because I only wish to explain at this point why Spain could not raise herself to the same level as Europe in cultural aspects, primarily because of having identified any intellectual occupation with Jewish

---

[9] The Procesos inquisitoriales contra la familia judía de Luis Vives have finally been published by M. de la Pinta Llorente and J. M. de Palacio (Madrid, 1964).

[10] The publication of La Celestina as an anonymous work by a Barcelona publisher in 1966 is an extreme case of anti-Semitism. The saying "better dead than red" could be paraphrased in certain Spanish circles by "better anonymous than Jewish."

descent. This situation is comparable to what had occurred in the twelfth and thirteenth centuries when Muslim science and philosophy passed through Toledo on its way to Europe without affecting the Castilian mind. The latter was logically more concerned with subduing the Moors in the Peninsula and asserting its political superiority over the Leonese and Aragonese than in meditating on the fundamental truths of reason and faith or in discovering the nature of the visible or invisible world.

In the sixteenth century this concern for the personal worth and valor and self-esteem of the individual as such absorbed the Spaniard's entire scale of values, outlook, and capacity for judgment. He dominated Italy, Flanders, and the rest of his empire by sheer tension between his willpower and bravery and self-reliance, on the one hand, and the lack of scientific knowledge and techniques to cope with those fabulous feats he had accomplished, on the other. Mathematicians and engineers, however, could be imported from other countries. Italian technicians worked in Spain on projects such as the one to bring water up to the city of Toledo from the Tagus river, and later experts lent their services in Flanders and other parts of the empire.[11] Since personal daring and determination could not be acquired at any price, it was understandable that the Castilians developed to a maximum that warlike dimension of their "virtues," closer in meaning to the *virtus* of the ancient Romans. We might recall here that the *cantares de gesta*, the epic poems, and later the collections of ballads dealing with the reconquest were particularly Castilian forms of literature from the tenth to the beginning of the fourteenth century; during this period neither Arabic nor European lyrical poetry affected the Castilians' sensibility to any extent. The oral poetry of the ballads in the form of brief poems comprised an expressive literary baggage that anyone could easily carry around with him in his memory. These ballads arose in the middle of the fourteenth century, precisely when the Castilian lower classes began to become consciously aware of their power against the *grandes*. Juan de Mena and the Marquis de Santillana, erudite writers of the first half of the fifteenth century, classify this type of poetry as "rustic" and sung by "the people of base and servile condition."[12] But at the end of that same century these ballads were

---

[11] The lack of artillerymen in seventeenth-century Spain is a good example of this point. In 1617 Philip III asked the Count de Gondomar, his ambassador in London, to send him some "artillery experts." Gondomar sent "Guillermo Crader" who "has served in the armada of the crown for many years" (*Documentos inéditos para la Historia de España* [Madrid, 1936], I, 116). In 1614 the same ambassador says that Spain owes the English merchant, Guillelmo (William) Caley, money for having outfitted "the army of Flanders with cloth for uniforms," which was "a very important service"; this Englishman "owes money here," says Gondomar, "and has to pay a high interest" because he lent his services to the king of Spain (*op. cit.*, p. 112).

[12] See my "*Español*," *palabra extranjera . . .*, p. 52.

sung at the court of Queen Isabella. In 1519, before Hernán Cortés had made his final decision to conquer Mexico, "a knight called Alonso Hernández Puerto Carrero went to Cortés and said to him: 'It seems to me, Sir, that those knights have been telling you . . .

Cata Francia, Montesinos,	Look at France, Montesinos,
cata París, la ciudad:	look at Paris, the city:
cata las aguas del Duero	look at the waters of the Duero
do van a dar en el mar.	that flow out to the sea.

I say to you, look over those rich lands and know how to govern them well.' And Cortés, who fully understood the meaning of those words, replied:

Denos Dios ventura en armas	May God grant us fortune at arms,
como al paladín Roldán.[13]	like the paladin Rolland."

The tactical advice of a subordinate—"Be daring, my lord"—go ahead and risk everything, was given in verses from the *Romancero*, the collection of ballads that everyone carried in his head; and his leader replied in an equally poetic manner.

Returning to the central theme, I have emphasized that the Castilian Christians did not win out over the Moors and Jews through their superior knowledge or technical skill; the Moor was conquered on the battlefield, and the Jew who aspired through his culture to be a *grande de Castilla* was pushed aside and finally eliminated on the premise that the Christian was brave and courageous, while the Jew was cowardly. The Muslim was crushed with tangible and visible weapons, the Jew with psychological warfare. In the oldest documents that mention Jews in Castile and Aragon,[14] their legal status was that of serfs of the Christian kings; in reality, however, this was not true, because they exerted their superiority and will to command from an inferior social position, as I explain in my *Realidad histórica* . . . (p. 444). The weapon used to knock them off their pedestal was to accuse them of being "cowards," incapable of accomplishing those feats of command and bravery the Castilian displayed first in the War of Granada and later on a universal scale in the sixteenth century.

During this same period the Jewish converts and their descendants began to cultivate intellectual activities which the Old Christians had scorned and judged incompatible with their warlike enterprises. This peculiar situation gave rise to a notable phenomenon in the sixteenth century. Those people of Jewish descent who aspired to stand out in some way begin to write philosophical, scientific, and spiritual works superior to those written by their ancestors, who had been more out-

---

[13] Bernal Díaz del Castillo, *Verdadera historia de la conquista de la Nueva España* (Mexico: Porrúa, 1960), vol. I, chap. xxxvi, 122. R. Menéndez Pidal, *Romancero hispánico* (1953), II, 226.

[14] See J. Amador de los Ríos, Y. Baer, A. A. Neuman, and Léon Poliakov.

standing as transmitters of culture rather than creators of original thought or works of significant literary value. Before the expulsion few Jews had reached the intellectual or literary heights of their descendants such as Luis Vives, Gómez Pereira, Francisco Suárez, Luis de León, Francisco de Vitoria, Huarte de San Juan, Cervantes, or Góngora. Nationalistic anti-Semites raise an uproar and try to invalidate the evidence that this intellectual creation or artistic expression was a reflection of that oppressive social situation by which public opinion tried to tarnish the reputation of Jews by calling them Jews, just because some of their remote ancestors had professed that religion. Fortunately, in recent years, the social and intellectual climate has relaxed somewhat, and the publication of inquisitorial documents relating to the family of St. Theresa by N. Alonso Cortés, the ones mentioned before in Luis Vives, and works such as those by Albert Sicroff and Francisco Márquez, in addition to my *De la edad conflictiva*, have forced people to adopt a more cautious approach in dealing with this problem.

This matter was further complicated by the fact that the Sephardic Jews themselves produced few great thinkers of international renown after the expulsion. Except for the *Dialoghi d'amore* (Rome, 1535) by León Hebreo (Judas Abravanel), whose traces can be found throughout sixteenth-century literature, no single work of great literary merit was produced among the Sephardim in exile, even though it was possible for their Christian descendants in Spain to do so. While these New Christians wrote outstanding works in spite of great obstacles, they did not live under the dogmatic censorship of the rabbis. Baruch Spinoza (Benito Espinosa, 1632–1677), an outstanding thinker, lived in solitude as an outcast, tormented by the fanaticism of his coreligionists in Holland. Uriel da Costa committed suicide. The Sephardic communities inevitably had to give in to their scant literary possibilities, because they lived in isolated environments where their language was not spoken and it was impossible to print their works in Spain. A similar situation occurred in which it was impossible for a scholar to cultivate the study of mathematics or Greek culture without being accused of being a Jew. For different reasons, a council of "six eminent rabbis" was created in 1529 in Salonika and shortly afterward in Constantinople to pass judgment on anything written in Spanish or Hebrew.[15]

It is certainly true that life was not pleasant for some notable New Christians who felt themselves to be links in a long chain of insults "that never end," as Fray Luis de León wrote. The *Lazarillo de Tormes* was published as an anonymous work; Mateo Alemán, the

---

15 Mihael Molho, "La producción literaria castellana en Oriente en el siglo XVI," in *Studies in Honor of M. J. Benardete* (New York: Las Américas Publishing Co., 1965), p. 335.

author of *Guzmán de Alfarache*, had to bribe the emigration officials to be able to go to the Indies, which was forbidden for New Christians; Cervantes apparently could not bribe anyone in his two attempts to go to the Indies, but, thanks to such unpleasant circumstances, he was able to write his *Quixote*. An outstanding philosophical work by Antonio Gómez Pereira, *Antoniana Margarita* (Madrid, 1554), was published in Latin, and has never been reedited or translated in spite of the fact that it contains many ideas later expressed by others. Judges in the chancelleries of Granada and Valladolid accepted gratifications in exchange for granting false patents of nobility to New Christians, so that they could pass themselves off as Old ones.

Several years ago I attempted to explain why the Spaniards deviated from the general course of Western culture as a direct result of the conflict between Spaniards of Christian descent and those of Jewish ancestry, not as the consequence of any inherent incapacity to cultivate certain disciplines.[16] As a résumé of what actually happened, I shall cite the following examples. At the end of the sixteenth century the Augustinian friar Diego de Zúñiga taught astronomy at the University of Salamanca according to Copernicus, but because his theory was judged to be contrary to biblical doctrine, the erroneous theory of Ptolemy was again reinstated. During those same years several illustrious professors of Salamanca, such as the poet Fray Luis de León, were incarcerated by the Inquisition on charges of interpreting the Old Testament in the light of the original Hebrew text. Luis de León was freed after five years of unjust imprisonment, but that scandalous trial was symptomatic of more profound states of opinion. Fray Diego de Zúñiga, the partisan of Copernicus, wrote a Latin commentary of the Book of Job: "In our time certain ignorant and cowardly men immediately raise a commotion on the slightest pretext, saying that those who expound the Sacred Writings are Judaizers if they do not relate all their meanings to a purely mystical sense of context or if they accept the plain, simple, and obvious interpretation of some Hebrew."[17]

Culture and Judaism eventually became synonymous terms and, as a result, scientific research, study, and teaching became impossible or fell into disuse in the seventeenth century. Later, in 1727, Fray Benito Jerónimo Feijoo, an outstanding and unusual figure for his time, wrote in a personal letter that he was aware that new roads were being opened in physics, but that they were opposed by "an Inquisitor general who is so enamored of outmoded and antiquated thought that

---

[16] *De la edad conflictiva* where I explain how culture and honor eventually became incompatible.

[17] Quoted in P. Pedro M. Vélez, *Observations al libro de Aubrey F. G. Bell sobre Fray Luis de León* (1931), p. 207.

he threatens to hurl a lightning bolt at any book that mentions some-thing about the infinite that is unknown in Spain."[18] Feijoo echoes what Pedro Simón Abril had written at the end of the sixteenth cen-tury in an unpublished work, "Filosofía natural": "Our nation has little warmth or enthusiasm for anything concerning the desire for knowledge" (Garagorri, p. 63).

In 1786, after Feijoo's personal observations, Count Peñaflorida, Xavier de Munibe, published his *Los aldeanos críticos* (*The Village Critics*), a book erroneously included in the works of Padre José Francisco Isla and published as such in the Biblioteca de Autores Españoles, XV, a century ago. No one had been aware of the meaning of Munibe's sarcastic references to Spanish science in the eighteenth century until Paulino Garagorri developed this theme in his article on Xavier de Munibe in the *Revista de Occidente* in 1964. This cul-tural situation prevailed in the eighteenth century as an obvious re-sult of the problems and theories I have analyzed in *De la edad con-flictiva*. Munibe writes in his fierce invective against the intellectual narrowmindedness of his contemporaries: "Why does anyone have to pay attention to any heretical dogs, atheists, and Jews like Newton, who was a terrible arch-heretic . . . , [like] Galileo de Galileis, whose very name implies that he must have been an arch-Jew or proto-Hebrew, and others whose names cause people to shudder?" (BAE, XV, 375). On the previous page he says: "Thanks to the very rev-erend father and teacher, Fray Benito Feijoo, it is known" that people like Newton and Descartes actually existed.

Of Cowards and Chosen Ones; The History of Spain as Attraction and Repulsion

The above accumulation of facts was necessary to eventually arrive at our final goal, that is, to determine the peculiarity of sixteenth-and seventeenth-century Spain with respect to other countries. This aim, in turn, is an indispensable step prior to clarifying subsequent historical events and conditions.[19]

The legend of Jewish cowardice that lent further support to the legal condition of those who were absurdly accused of deicide had been vanquished. The Castilian Jews themselves had also spoken of their lack of fighting spirit. Ben Verga (*op. cit.*, p. 62) says: "And what shall we say of the cowardice in their hearts? If a hundred Jews are in the plaza and a single Christian boy comes and says: 'Let's

---

[18] Quoted in Paulino Garagorri, *Españoles razonantes* (1969), p. 58, who refers to the facsimile edition of G. Marañón, in *Las ideas biológicas del P. Feijoo*, p. 1934.

[19] See appendix, "Observations on bullfights and autos da fé."

have it out with the Jews!' everyone runs away. . . . Their natural cowardice cannot stand either their own death or that of their enemies by virtue of the divine curse, as the Bible says: 'I shall instill fear in their hearts, and they shall flee at the rustling of a leaf in the wind' " (Lev. 26:14), (p. 36). But Ben Verga quoted that curse in a slightly different context from the biblical one in which Yahweh hurls his wrath against those who do not heed or practice his commandments (Lev. 26:14). The Jews may have believed that their own guilt had caused them to be abandoned by the hand of God and, in turn, to be exposed to the worst punishments. A similar idea is expressed by Don Alonso de Cartagena, the bishop of Burgos and son of Don Pablo de Santa María, also a bishop of Burgos who had previously been a rabbi in that city and become a convert to Christianity after the atrocious massacre and sack of 1391. According to Don Alonso, the cowardice of the Israelites was like a fungus produced by their lack of faith in Christ; that disease disappeared once they were baptized ("quod ex rubigine infidelitatis habebant, per lavacrum sublato").[20] Don Alonso adds that many of them fight with ardent fervor ("in actibus bellicis competenti audacia militare"); a singular phenomenon, since before baptism they were held to be cowards and actually were ("ante sublationem impedimenti timidiores putabantur et erant").

The magical power attributed to baptism by Don Alonso de Cartagena in the first half of the fifteenth century indicates how tense the controversy had already become between the baptized Jews and their excoreligionists. It made no difference how many generations of baptisms separated them from their Hispano-Hebrew ancestors. Many learned men expressed the same opinions as the magistrate Juan Arce de Otálora, whom I have mentioned on several occasions because of the profound significance of his words for Spanish history and culture: "The hidalgos of Spain have always served the kings and kingdom in wars both with their persons and their possessions." He continues in Latin: "These people never go to war except as physicians and surgeons" ("Isti nunquam ad bella pergunt, nisi vel medici, vel chirurgi") . . . "They are also pharmacists, dyers, merchants, and fraudulent contractors" ("Sunt etiam pharmacopolae, pigmentarii, mercatores, et satrapae").[21] With these words he condemned the professions of medicine and surgery, together with business and small trades and crafts.[22] This work is a prime example of the crux of the

---

[20] *Defensorum unitatis Christianae*, ed. P. M. Alonso ((Madrid, 1963), p. 215.

[21] *Summa nobilitatis Hispanicae* (1559), p. 188. This work was written in a mixture ot Hispanized Latin and Castilian.

[22] Rodrigo de Dueñas, "perhaps the most opulent businessman in Castile" (Ramón Carande, *Carlos V y sus banqueros*, II, 128–129), was a member of the Consejo de Hacienda (Ministry of Public Finance) in 1555. Prince Philip, the future

Spanish historical problem: history does not depend solely on economy or the "law of numbers." Spanish history, at any rate, depends on how the Spaniards situated themselves in relation to their economic problems because of the unusual way in which their population was made up. The history of Spain cannot be compared with that of Western Europe in this respect.

What is extraordinary in the Spaniards' case and what has harmed Spanish historiography is the fact that the anti-Semitism I am discussing was an obvious outcome of having incarnated the Jewish concept of lineage in the Old Christian caste. This concept is non-existent among European Christians, but it is common among Muslims and Jews, as we saw in Ibn Garcia's defense of the New Mohammedans and his derision of the Old ones (see chapter xiii, p. 524). Once again we return to the concept of the *hidalgo* (*hijo de algo*), "son of wealth and fortune," which is an Arabic parallelism, and the same concept of *benē tovim* (*hijos de buenos*), "sons of good," discussed in chapter vii.

At this point I should like to propose the idea of "adoptions and repulsions" as a more accurate characteristic of the history of the Spaniards than the previous ones. *Vivir desviviéndose*, or "the history of an insecurity," is also valid as a conjecture about that peculiar and problematic human reality. When I wrote *De la edad conflictiva* in 1961, I concentrated on the sixteenth and seventeenth centuries, believing rather than thinking that this particular period gave rise to "conflicts" that were less acute prior to this time. While it is true that the conflicts created by several centuries of coexistence of people of three beliefs culminated in that period, it is equally valid to argue that those conflicts—the necessity to accept and reject, to exist under a regime of "adoptions and repulsions"—arose from a historical source whose turbulence took on triple and constantly changing reflections. The Muslim occupation enabled the Jew to move much more freely than he had under Visigothic tyranny.[23] This is the usual historical explanation for Jewish support of those new occupants of most of the Peninsula, particularly of Toledo, the ancient capital of the Visigothic monarchy. At this point in the eighth century the struggle and rivalry among three peoples began. No one of them was powerful enough to completely subjugate the other two, yet not weak enough to resign

---

King Philip II, wanted to keep him there, because "he needed a person who had practical experience in matters of exchange." In spite of the prince's wishes, Rodrigo de Dueñas was deprived of his post by the finance minister because he was "the grandson of a renegade Jew and the son of a dyer."

[23] "Egica . . . aimed to deprive the Jews of the capacity to earn a living." In 694 "it was reported that in some parts of the world the Jews had rebelled against their Christian rulers and that many of them had been killed by the kings" (E. A. Thompson, *The Goths in Spain*, pp. 246-247). They could not build new synagogues and many of the old ones were destroyed (pp. 53 and 247).

itself to total submission.[24] The final decisive blow was struck by the Christian caste, led by the military and political supremacy of Castile. Moreover, as we saw before, the Castilian language was more uniform and intelligible to all the Castilians, while in the thirteenth-century kingdom of Leon, an Asturian-Leonese could not understand a Galician and, in the kingdom of Aragon, an Aragonese could not understand a Catalan. Castile austerely shut itself up in its epic-bellicose activity at the expense of renouncing cultural aspects—a shortcoming that would later have serious consequences and even prevent it from joining other regions (Catalonia, Basque Provinces, Galicia), like convergent rivers flowing serenely and without longing for their former courses.[25] Unfortunately, the otherwise intelligent and forceful Queen Isabella made the grave mistake of excluding the Aragonese and Catalans from the imperial enterprise begun at the end of her reign, as she stated in her will: Granada, the Canary Islands and "all those lands discovered and yet to be discovered, conquered or yet to be conquered, shall remain in *my* kingdoms of Castile and Leon."[26] The Jewish converts, who had become very influential since the reign of John II (1406–1454), contributed largely to encouraging the imperial designs of the Castilians and to convincing them that anything was possible and could be obtained with the help of their loyal, obliging Jewish subjects. Without the collaboration of Don Abraham Senior and particularly Don Isaac Abravanel, the War of Granada might have dragged on for who knows how long. The Christians were brave and daring, but they had a difficult time solving the more practical and immediate problems of provisioning their army and navy.

This leads us back to that fantastic image the Christian had gradually built up in his mind of the Jew as a mixture of efficiency and cowardice. This idea is reflected in an expressive anecdote, worth many sterile documents, told around the middle of the sixteenth century: "Cavallos [Ceballos?] used to say in Seville that the best way to show that the Jews were stupid was to prove that the work they did was so perfect that no other man could do it. Thus, if a

---

[24] In the eleventh century the Jews even attempted to take over Granada and, as I said before, their power in Castile was considerable; there is no other logical explanation for the Christian kings legally and forcibly protecting Jewish orthodoxy. For the importance of the Jews in the Moorish kingdom of Granada, see David Gonzalo Maeso, *Garnata al-Yahūd* (Granada in the history of Spanish Judaism), University of Granada, 1963. See also Frederick P. Bargebuhr, *El palacio de la Alhambra en el siglo XI* (Mexico: Cultura, 1966).

[25] Picardy, Burgundy, and Provence, regions independent from France (until the 17th, 15th, and 13th centuries), are now just a part of France.

[26] Alonso de Santa Cruz, *Crónica de los Reyes Católicos*, ed. J. de Mata Carriazo (Seville, 1951), I, 95 and 355. Carriazo (I, lxvii) has good reason to suppose that Santa Cruz was a convert. Reasons for "psychological separatism" went much farther back than Queen Isabella's time.

Christian needed shoes, he told the Jew: 'Go and fetch me some shoes.' And the Jew, who had no cloth, thread, soles, or needles, went up to a mountain and picked a certain kind of grass to use as thread, another for cloth, another for soles, and another for an awl, and in four hours he delivered the finished shoes. Everything those stupid people do is perfect: they can smell like a dog, hear like a wild boar, see like a lynx; hence, the Jews' senses are perfect, but they lack intelligence and wits, because if the *ocri* [?] or tiger comes along and says something to them, they put their hands over their eyes and wait; they do not run away or defend themselves."[27] The comparison between the technique of a craftsman and the biological characteristics of animals is monstrous.

The above anecdote takes us to the very core of the Spaniards' sociohistorical problem. Everything was easy for the Jew; he acted under the influence of some magical power, and at the same time he was incapable of fleeing or defending himself when attacked by his enemy. Those contemptible human beings, who contaminated the very professions in which they were skilled, had instilled in the minds of the Spaniards the Semitic idea of lineage, that the body was worth more than the works accomplished by the person, because biological descent took precedence over those very works. In the course of the sixteenth century the scale of values became ever more unbalanced, resulting in the concept that it was more important to establish *who* the person was rather that evaluate his capacity for work or thought; it was imperative to take into account his own personal worth or nobility or such factors as illustrious forbears. Positive values were replaced by negative ones revolving around *not* belonging to the Jewish caste; all this was the result of having Judaized the criteria for value judgments in the Spain of Charles V. This situation reached such absurd and fantastic proportions that even in the case of a person whose ancestry had been unquestionably Christian for centuries, if that person succumbed to the temptation of taking up tasks or professions that the majority deemed even slightly tinged with Judaism, all the saints and *grandes de Castilla* among his ancestors were of no avail. As I have said before, intellectual activity was particularly vulnerable to this collective frenzy, as illustrated by the fact that the title *letrado* was not granted to the scholar in the humanities or in any other type of scientific knowledge, but was the exclusive property of lawyers, as the lexicographer, Sebastián de Covarrubias, said without hiding his indignation (see chapter xiii, p. 551).

Spanish historians were slow to realize the real truth about the history of their country because they refused to admit the obvious

---

27 F. J. Sánchez Cantón, "Floreto de anécdotas y noticias diversas," in *Memorial Histórico Español* (Madrid: Real Academia de la Historia, 1948), LVIII, 41.

connection between the imperial and literary and artistic grandeur of the Spaniards and the collective conscience of those who had triumphed over Moors and Jews and now felt themselves to be a people chosen by God, just as Israel had been. The works of several writers of that period confirm this idea. Fray Juan de Salazar says: "Similar happenings occur in every period, and the singular way in which God has chosen and governed the Spanish people prove that they were chosen by His Grace, just as the Chosen Ones [the Hebrews] in biblical times."[28] "The Hebrews waited a long time to set their eyes on the land of promise, and in this respect they are like the Spanish people who also wandered for many years through the deserts of Spain, commonly called mountains, before finding their beloved homeland and land of promise. . . . The Hebrews had great difficulty in taking possession of the land of promise by virtue of work and sweat; they fought bravely and arduously with lance in hand, at the cost of much bloodshed by their own people, and finally won out over its inhabitants" (pp. 77–78). This man's blindness, ignorance, and hallucinations were indispensable to sustaining his absurd imagination. This quotation is not selected as an example of historical criticism; it is rather meant to reveal the Spaniards' own beliefs about themselves and because that very historiography, so in need of revision and annulment, has been built on this type of belief and hypothesis, and not on rational knowledge. Father Salazar writes: *"Our ancient Spaniards,* sustained by their courage and prudence, held out for two hundred years against the Romans, who had overcome the French [!] in only nine years. With the same prudence and valor they subdued the Moors [in eight centuries!] and recovered Spain from their hands. . . . Their bravery and daring went beyond the world known by the ancients to discover and conquer the new world called America" (p. 49).

Such parallelisms between the Spaniards and Hebrews appear constantly: Samson "was the executioner and destroyer of the Philistines" and the Cid was "the whip and terror of the Moors" (p. 81). Bernardo del Carpio was likened to Gideon. In imitation of Solomon, Philip II built "the famous and wondrous edifice of San Lorenzo . . . in the Escorial, in imitation of the famous temple" of Jerusalem (p. 82). The anonymous author of the *Vida de Estebanillo González* (1646) repeats this idea that the Escorial is "a sumptuous temple, the work of the second Solomon in emulation of the first."[29] In spite of all this rhetoric, Padre Salazar ignores or refuses to acknowledge the presence of the Jews who surrounded the kings in the days before their expulsion: "How can I describe those fortunate and joyful days

---

[28] *Política española* (Logroño, 1619), ed. Miguel Herrero (Madrid: Instituto de Estudios Políticos, 1945), p. 73.
[29] Bibl. Aut. Esp., XXXIII, 303.

when Spain was ruled by those zealous Christian kings, the Sanchos and Alfonsos, whose counselors of state were bishops and abbots!" (p. 63). The Catholic sovereigns were more interested in "preserving the purity of our sacrosanct religion in their lands" than increasing their royal income because "it decreased" with the expulsion of "the Moors and Jews who did not wish to receive our holy faith" (p. 66). True to form, the author demands "antiquity of lineage" and "illustrious and pure blood" as requisites for any public office and admission to the university colleges: "Before being admitted to these colleges they must undergo a thorough investigation. . . . It is not sufficient for them to be of noble birth [*bien nacidos*], but it must also be required that *it has never been heard to the contrary* that they are not of noble birth" (p. 111).

For this good friar, Philip III's Spain was the double of the land of Israel; the religious content was different, but the structure and totalitarianism of the religious belief was identical for him. He even cites the case of a latter-day Joshua, a master of the order of Santiago, who commanded the sun to stand still in the course of a victorious battle against the Moors (p. 80). It is necessary here to mention only briefly an important book recently published in Spain,[30] by Alfonso Martínez Albiach, which should be evaluated in the light of the historical arguments I have been discussing throughout this book. In spite of its good intentions, it confirms my idea of the furious anti-Semitism of the Spaniards that was a direct result of the opposition to Jewry held so tenaciously by Spain's using the concept of lineage unrelated to any Western European standards for measuring the worth and merits of human beings. This work states: "We shall see [in Spain] two ideological stages: *a*) The establishment of theocracy in Spain, according to the Israelite model, by way of messianic prophecy and the biblical support of the Old Testament, and *b*) The surpassing of the Israelite model by investing Spanish history with a concept of theology by which Spain considered itself more qualified than Israel to be God's chosen people" (p. 15).

All that has been said so far is an attempt to make an important contribution to the clarification of that perplexing problem of who the Spaniards are, how they are made up, and their ultimate worth as a nation. All this must be done by taking into account the process of simultaneous adaptation (adoption) and rejection that has conditioned the history of this illustrious people with its grandeur, misfortunes, and misery from its very beginnings. I must now end this book, which

---

[30] Alfredo Martínez Albiach, *Religiosidad hispana y sociedad borbónica* (Burgos: Facultad teológica, 1969).

is actually only an introduction to the history of the Spaniards. Until now I have used the idea of a dwelling place of life (*morada vital*) as an immanent concept. Now I see that the dwelling place is really an ideal one to which that human entity called the "Spaniard" must be adjusted. In this book I have presented only the framework for what I consider a transcendental idea, because it was not entirely possible to discuss what the Spaniards have done in a series of chapters for two reasons: first, it was indispensable to put an end to those legends conceived about the present-day people called the "Spaniards"; and second, it was necessary to provide a basis for and give meaning to what the inhabitants of the Iberian Peninsula have done, a fact which is still incomprehensible today because people insist on projecting over the Spaniard human forms that are incompatible with the true reality of his historical profile. Until now the reality of the Spaniards had been floating in "castles in the air," or resting on a formless, imaginary base. As a result of such an abnormal situation it has been necessary to begin by constructing a theoretical house or dwelling as a kind of framework to house that entity called "Spain" in a proper form. Someday I hope to furnish that dwelling, but here in conclusion, I shall offer the following outline for that possible history.

Chronological Divisions for a
Future History of the Spaniards

A) Disappearance of the Roman-Visigothic duality and beginning of the reconquest in the eighth and ninth centuries.

B) A living-togetherness (*convivencia*) in the Christian kingdoms from the tenth to the end of the fifteenth century of people of three castes: Christian, Jewish, and Mudejar.

C) Religious exclusivism: imperial, artistic, and literary grandeur from 1500 to 1700 (a conflict between the individual person and collective opinion—Cervantes, Gracián, cultural paralysis).

D) Crisis in the eighteenth century with the rise of a foreign dynasty, intellectual hermeticism, and attempts at Europeanization; tension between the imported culture and traditional modes of living: Feijoo, Jovellanos, Godoy, Goya.

E) From 1800 to the fall of the monarchy in 1931: the Spaniards have to choose openly between continuing tradition (Carlist Wars) and modern political solutions. What had been lived as a fixed, stable present in the seventeenth century now arises as a situation that is longed for nostalgically, or as something that one desires might happen in another manner (some prominent Spaniards would have three or four centuries of their past completely erased). The whole period is characterized by a feeling of uncomfortable instability combined with utopian longings of a contrary nature (anarchism, separatism, imperialism). Brilliant manifestations of literature and art arise in the course of the nineteenth and twentieth centuries, but only sporadic, isolated examples of science and thought arise that hardly affect the traditional course or tone of Spanish life.

Holy War

IN THE EARLY NINETEENTH CENTURY it was still felt that war in defense of the sovereignty of the king of Spain was holy and of divine origin. The Spaniards' War of Independence against the French (1808–1814) was inspired by both political and religious motives; and in 1821 the last Spanish government official in Mexico with viceregal powers addressed a proclamation to the rebels against Spanish authority whose tone recalls the words of Alonso de Cartagena in the fifteenth century (quoted above, p. 151): "The king of England makes war, but his are not holy [*divinal*] wars [like those of the kings of Castile]." When Juan Ruiz de Apodaca, Count of Venadito and last viceroy of Mexico, abandoned the city of Mexico in July of 1821, the field marshal, Francisco Novella, was left in command of the loyal forces. From Novella's proclamation directed to the inhabitants of Puebla, I have excerpted the following significant phrases:

Citizens of Puebla: Your Viceroy speaks to you for the last time. You will already have learned how the perfidious Iturbide plans to open the floodgates of the Town of Tenepantla to inundate you: Have no fear, I have cannons and bayonets. . . . The perfidious Iturbide wants you to proceed without Spain to set up a separate government. . . . I have no one to whom I can entrust you, because [I fear] that afterward you would complain of your commanders;[1] but I will say to you that our Holy Religion is in danger. . . . The Roman Pontiff does not wish you to do this, and the priests will rather leave here. *This is heaven's war*, and the *Apostle Santiago* [is] always on the side of the Spaniards.[2]

---

[1] Earlier Novella had threatened to bring in the commander, Manuel de la Concha, whose cruel repression was notorious. Novella, on the other hand, was well known for his humane feelings.

[2] The text of the proclamation may be found in *Adiciones a la "Imprenta en la Puebla de los Angeles" de J. T. Medina* (*Colección Florencio Gavito*), Prefacio y compilación bibliográfica de Felipe Teixidor (Mexico, 1961), p. 565. For the situation in Mexico at that time, see William S. Robertson, *Iturbide of Mexico* (Duke University Press, 1952).

Luis de Granada and the Converts

Luis de Carvajal (El Mozo), burned by the Mexican Inquisition in 1596, declared before the tribunal of the Holy Office on October 21 of that year, that Manuel de Lucena told him "that he had a friend in the mines of Pachuca, whose name was Juan del Cassal, . . . with whom, because he was a man of very good disposition . . . he had dared to discuss very important things in the law of Moses; and that from these conversations there had arisen doubts about religion in the said Juan del Cassal, and that [the latter] had answered him: 'I wish to see in what law we live, and if we are in error.' " And *on the advice* of the said Manuel de Lucena, Juan del Cassal had asked Lucena to buy for him the *Símbolo de la Fe*, by Friar Luis de Granada, and Lucena had bought it for him.[3]

It is obvious that if Manuel de Lucena recommended the reading of a work by Luis de Granada to a man whom he wished to convert to Judaism, it must have been because he considered that reading to be suitable for his purpose. In other words, long before Lorenzo Escudero declared in 1658 that "having read in the books of Friar Luis de Granada had made him a Jew" (see above, p. 331), the works of the great Christian religious writer were used for Jewish purposes. Escudero did not say what work by Luis de Granada he had read; Lucena does say specifically that he used the *Introducción al Símbolo de la Fe*. I imagine that converts who tended to revert back to Judaism must have been attracted by the idea that God manifested himself in the marvels of the world, described in such beautiful and captivating terms by Luis de Granada, for it is a concept that harmonizes very well with the doctrine of the Psalmist that "the Heavens declare the glory of God." Some converts must have deemed it more pleasing to disregard the belief that God is revealed through his Church and to direct their faith instead toward Nature as a direct expression of its infinite Creator. The whole matter should be examined and discussed in greater detail.

---

[3] *Procesos de Luis Carvajal (El Mozo)* (Mexico: Publicaciones del Archivo General de la Nación, 1935), p. 432.

APPENDIX · OBSERVATIONS ON
BULLFIGHTS AND AUTOS DA FÉ

THE CASE OF THE SPANIARDS is anomalous. This is not because they have been the only ones to suffer fraticidal wars and sanguinary revolutions for religious as well as political reasons. The anomaly consists in the fact that outside of Spain religious and political wars or revolutions created stable structures or at least firm arrangements in which violence appears as a means oriented toward a specific goal and not simply as the expression of one's anger at a chronic malaise. The Lutheran and Calvinist revolutions ultimately led to religious freedom and the secularization of the state; the French Revolution ended in a true constitutional regime still effective in France and in other European countries.

When the connecting link between unbridled violence and the achievement of a stable end, beneficial for the majority and later maintained without coercion, does not seem possible or is not apparent, the people feel oppressed and politically helpless and abandoned. The other side of the social coin of aimless violence is an apparent calm paralysis on the surface and the longing for renewed arbitrary violence pent up in the dark recesses of the mind. It is equally true that oppressive regimes sometimes ended up by giving the impression that they had not been dictatorial because no one had even thought of an alternate possibility or the means of a social organization different from the one rooted in tradition. I am more concerned, here, with this aspect of the experiential living situation of those who have endured in the past and must still endure paralytic and inflexible forms of government in the present, rather than discuss the demographic, economic, or other diverse facets of those regimes.

As an example of this situation, I shall discuss the institution of the Holy Office or Inquisition which played such a powerful role in Spanish history. While it was notorious for effectively exterminating heretics, it was even more prominent because of the great spectacle that its autos da fé presented to the people for over three centuries. These were enacted in such an exalted atmosphere of solemn ceremony that the spectacular setting concealed the total absence of a Christian spirit.

Elsewhere heretics and witches were burned, but in spite of blindness of such magnitude, there arose reactions of intelligence or humanity that ultimately resulted in opening the eyes of even the most stubborn reactionaries. Calvin had Michael Servetus burned on a slow flame, but his fellow countryman, Montaigne, taking St. Augustine (*City of God*, XIX, xviii) as his point of departure, thought: "qu'il vaut mieux pancher vers le doute que vers l'asseurance és choses de difficile preuve et dangereuse creance" (*Essais*, ed. Pléiade, III, xi). Montaigne voices his opposition, his "resveries," to "opinion ou coutume," that lets itself be carried away by its "pensée tumultuaire et vacillante." He deems the expulsion of the Jews from Portugal, and before then in Castile, as inhumane; children under fourteen were forcibly seized "d'entre les mains des peres et des meres," and taken to places where they were raised as Christians. Many Jews committed suicide and killed their own children (I, xiv). Commenting on the burning of witches, so common in the Europe of his time, Montaigne believes that those poor unfortunate creatures were mentally deranged and should have been cured rather than burned. Like his contemporary, Cervantes, that extraordinary, profound thinker skillfully glides over certain points without taking a direct stand on anything. In the 1588 edition of the *Essais*, however, he inserted this magnificent phrase which I recalled years ago: "Apres tout, c'est mettre ses conjectures à bien haut pris que d'en fair cuire un homme tout vif" (*ed. cit.*, Bk. III, chap. xi). Whatever the reasons those people may have had for burning a human being at the stake either for witchcraft or anything else (Montaigne refrains from being more explicit), they were conjectural, or "problematic," as we say today; but those who condemned a person to be burned (or in our time to be gassed or to work in mines at glacial temperatures that exterminate their victims, or to undergo similar horrors because they do not belong to a race judged to be humanly sublime, or because they do not choose to submit to certain political dogmas), those who did this or continue to do similarly "set an excessively high price to be paid for those conjectures," as the admirable Montaigne wrote.

Violence based on suspicion or hearsay provoked reactions from foreigners like Montaigne, but it was never so complete and dogmatic as in seventeenth-century Spain. The Flemish bookdealer, Baltasar Moretus, happened to be in Madrid in June 1680 and had the opportunity to witness a very solemn auto da fé,[1] attended by King Charles II and the *grandes* of the realm with an ostentatious display of soldiers

---

[1] See Maurits Sabbe, *Baltasar Moretus en Madrid*, trans., prologue, and notes by A. Rodríguez Moñino (Madrid: V. Suárez, 1934). In his commentary the translator utilizes the *Relación* of that auto da fé by José del Olmo, Madrid, 1680.

and the attendance of an immense multitude of commoners. The captain of a company of soldiers of the faith carried a "bundle of kindling to His Majesty's chamber." The Duke of Pastrana received it and, in turn, showed it to "the Queen, Our Lady, Doña María Luisa de Borbón." The bundle of kindling was returned to the captain with the message that "his Majesty commanded that it be carried in his name, and that it should be the first to be thrown onto the flames." The king authorized the auto da fé in the same manner as he also "gave his authorization to fight" to those noblemen who fought the bulls on horseback (p. 59). In the auto that took place on 30 June 1680, everyone was amazed at the king's display of endurance and vigor: "His Majesty watched on the balcony starting at eight in the morning without being affected by the intense heat. . . . He did not leave the balcony for a quarter of an hour even to eat. . . . God had made him so superior and independent of human influence" (p. 54).

My purpose at this point is not to censure or to praise; I only try to understand history as a living and lived entity, with the ultimate goal of situating and ordering it within its own singular, not generic, human structure. Today those autos da fé and the religious totalitarianism of the seventeenth-century Spaniards seem to us to be a macabre stupidity, a shadowy hollow; Baltasar Gracián spoke of "the cave of Nothingness," not realizing that those vacuums complemented his own deficient being with hallucinations that, on being transcended, endow his being with its full meaning and reality. What would remain, what would become of history or personal lives if we eliminate from them what is considered today to be (from several contradictory points of view) false, absurd, nonsensical hallucination or inhuman cruelty? Nothing, beginning with religion itself, would be immune from such criticism.

The author of that account of the auto da fé of 30 June 1680, José del Olmo, was the mere mouthpiece for what the rest of his fellow countrymen believed and felt. For these people, Charles II, that last shrunken residue of the Spanish Hapsburgs, was going to be eternal: God "must have granted us the favor of making the great planet of Spain eternal" (p. 54). The "planet" was also taken seriously by his Flemish subjects, the forbears of those who, years later, would accommodate the Belgian nation within the framework provided and preserved for them by the Spanish monarchs of the House of Austria. Baltasar Moretus marveled at the religious fervor of the Spaniards. After attending a "beautiful mass" sung in the church of Los Mínimos, he wrote in his diary (9 June 1680): "The altar was sumptuously adorned, and I might add that I find Spain expends greater sums on divine offices than Flanders, and the sodalities and images of Our Lady are held in higher esteem than in France and elsewhere." In other words, Spanish religiosity was not the same as the French or

Flemish variety, because it existed and was structured within a network of beliefs and values peculiar to its own mode of living and feeling. The Spanish language contains an effective medium of two verbs, *ser* and *estar*, to express the concept "to be"; the absolute dimension of what one is (*es*), his essence, becomes relative when the subject is situated (*está*) in relation to time, space, or a particular living experience (*vivencia*), the vital disposition of one's way of life. Catholicism will be in essence (*será*) what the church dictates from Rome, but it is being lived (*está*) in one form or another, in a different manner in Charles II's Spain, in Louis XIV's France, or among the Indians of Chichicastenango, Guatemala, who venerate the smoke produced by the incense of copal on the steps of the church of Santo Tomás.

We should not be led to believe, however, that José del Olmo was indulging in servile flattery when he called Charles II (for us today, a miserable degenerate), "the great planet of Spain." The monarchical institution still preserved its magic halo and its rays continued to illuminate the desires for imperial grandeur which had arisen in the fifteenth century in the midst of hallucinatory prophecies converted into reality a century later. Charles II attended the bullfights amid clouds of pomp and circumstance, outdone only by the ceremonies of the autos da fé. Baltasar Moretus describes one such event. The royal carriage appeared escorted by three companies of guards. Moretus emphasizes in his notes that all the soldiers were well dressed and that Monsieur Nicolas du Pont, Moretus's agent in Madrid and an "archier" of the first company, was one of the finest looking men in the king's entourage (p. 58). On the balcony occupied by the court, the Admiral of Castile "would occasionally address the king and take off his hat; when he did not converse with His Majesty, he kept his hat on, which was the privilege of the highest ranking *grandes*." Such formulas of protocol did not go overlooked by the young patrician from Antwerp, who ardently desired both "to be accepted among the Spanish nobility" (p. 58) and to preserve his monopoly on the sale of religious books in Spain and the Indies. The Spanish Church had to import them because it was incapable of printing them. The young Moretus was one of many foreigners, subjects of His Catholic Majesty, who prospered at the expense of the inertia of that Spain which was exhausted, pompous, and still under delusions of grandeur. One day he attended mass at the church of the Santísima Trinidad, where the papal nuncio gave his benediction to three hundred priests who were ordained, each of whom was provided with a newly bought Roman missal. In this way Moretus was able to estimate how many missals he could send to Spain (p. 43); he combined business interests with the desire for nobility, which he finally attained in 1695 (p. 65). For him, Spain represented the source of material wealth and socially recognized honor, dispensed by the king of Spain whose Flemish subjects were descendants of the vassals of the dukes of Burgundy. This dome of ennobling prestige was a refuge for those who would eventually call themselves Belgians, as I have said before, in spite of their linguistic divisions, because human collective groups do not live by economy or demography alone.

The affluent Antwerp merchant was not shocked by the brutalities of the autos da fé or the bullfights. If we take the point of view of the Spaniards of that time, the sacrifices of heretics or ferocious beasts were equally symbolic and solemn ritual acts. In order to understand such strange facts in the West, it is necessary to observe them at a mental distance far from present-day eyes. The Spanish Empire arose and attracted the attention and fears of Europeans as a religious-political institution. According to Góngora, the Escorial was a temple erected by "the greatest king of the faithful,"[2] whose prime national and international mission was to exterminate heresy (the Protestant kings of England did not adopt a political program of extending their religion throughout the world). If the voice of the people was expressed in the romances,[3] the way the exquisite poet Góngora called Philip II was an exact transcription of miramolín (in Arabic amir al-ámuminín), or "prince of believers."[4]

During the reign of the Catholic Sovereigns, religion and imperial policies already formed an indissoluble unity as in Islamic countries. Furthermore, in the course of the sixteenth century—as we have seen —an indelible line was being drawn between the Christians of pure Christian descent and others of Jewish ancestry. That question did not exist in the fifteenth century for Henry IV of Castile, Queen Isabella's brother, who was anxious to eradicate intercaste hatred, so disastrous in many ways for Spanish civilization. That unfortunate monarch, a misfit in many ways, had at least one humane characteristic and performed a praiseworthy act as well as an astute political move: "In the month of April (1465), when the lord king Don Enrique was in Toledo, he made peace between the members of two rival brotherhoods, one of converts and the other of Old Christians who had quarreled with each other. This king went to each and every member,

---

[2] In the sonnet beginning "Sacros, altos, dorados capiteles."

[3] In De la edad conflictiva (1963), I quote a ballad composed around 1539 in which the anonymous poet imagines Charles V bringing the religion of the Spaniards to Armenia, Egypt, and India: "To those in a sheepfold [he must enclose them; the sacraments are food] on which they may feed." In another ballad appears "The great Philip II [sublime king of Spain] God has granted him the power to govern . . . most of the world" ("Dios en gobierno le ha dado").

[4] "Fuesse (Alfonso VI) pora tierra de moros, e derechamientre pora Almiramomelín que era en Córdova" ("The King Alfonso VI went straight to the land of the Moors, and directly to Almiramomelín [the prince of believers] who was in Cordova") (Primera Crónica General, ed. Menéndez Pidal, p. 556).

brother by brother, to make peace between them. And he made them swear as a single body and donated ten thousand maravedís, in concept of heredity forever, for their common cause, so that these two brotherhoods might be united in a single entity."[5]

Collectivized Belief and
Individualized Valor

Henry IV, an inept, defiled, and incompetent human being, acted wisely in the case of the two rival brotherhoods. He intended that Castilians of different lineages should live in peaceful harmony, although subsequent history has made it apparent that his royal initiative could never be converted into a norm as I have explained in chapter xiv. Seen from this vantage point, both the auto da fé and the bulls killed by noble *grandes* seem to me to take on a meaning which has already vanished in our time. The significance of these rituals was very obvious in 1680, as we have already seen, both for the subjects of His Catholic Majesty and those who were not born in Spain. The auto da fé not only eliminated a heretic, an intruder in the bosom of the sole possible belief, but it also served as a solemn offering of a human being to the Divinity (in pagan Rome, the "suovetaurilia," a sacrifice of a pig, a sheep, and a bull was offered to the gods: in more remote times a human being was sacrificed to God, an act abolished by Yahweh in the case of Isaac). In the seventeenth century criminals were hanged or quartered in public, although without pomp and circumstance; the auto da fé, on the contrary, became increasingly more spectacular and ostentatious, because the ritualistic aspect and the liturgy of the "act" were as important as the extermination of the heretic. That drawn-out and extremely complex spectacle was the symbol of the collective form and dimension of the Spanish people who were totally immersed in their belief. At the end of the seventeenth century, as we have seen in this book, the space occupied by secular culture was minimal. This is clearly evident in the names given to people, rivers, or mountains at that time by men who had their minds set on advocations of the Virgin or on the human personality of Christ. I shall cite only a few examples: Pilar (after the Virgin of the Column in Saragossa), Peligros (Danger), Camino (Way), Circuncisión, the river Brazos de Dios (the Arms of God in Texas), or Sierra de la Sangre de Cristo (Blood of Christ mountain range in New Mexico).

If religion filled and encompassed the totality of the Spaniard's collective spirit, valor and bravery ended as the expression of his own personal worth and dignity as an individual. Each person believed in

---

[5] "Los anales de García Sánchez, jurado de Sevilla," ed. Juan de Mata Carriazo, *Anales de la Universidad hispalense* (1953), XIV, 50.

the Divine, just like everyone else, and in communion with everyone: the individual as such, however, acquired recognition of himself as a true and absolute being when he performed an outstanding and unique act of valor (*denodar* in Spanish means to be noteworthy or outstanding, but originally had the meaning of *denotarse*, to be noticed or to stand out as an individual from the crowd). He who was absorbed in and unrecognized among the anonymous mass of believers might be singled out individually for his bravery. In order to prevent any attempt at likening the Spanish situation to other superficially similar ones, however, I shall say that the individual trait of bravery and valor referred to here acquires its full dimension only within the context of specifically Spanish circumstances. To prove in public that one was capable of performing a fearless individual feat carried with it an aura of a collectively prestigious dimension in Spain, for it clearly and visibly proved that the brave, fearless person possessed such a virtue because he belonged to the caste of Old Christians, and, as such, was of authentic, clean birth. It was a well-known fact and echoed in the literature of the time that in spite of all the elaborate attempts to prove the purity of one's blood, it was still possible for a knight of a military order to be of Jewish descent (Lope de Vega has a villager remind the grand master of a military order of this in his play, *Fuenteovejuna*). As we have seen in chapter xiv, according to an absurd and accepted tradition, a member of the Jewish caste was automatically considered a coward.[6] This belief makes it possible to comprehend the spectacular significance that the participation of the noble lords or *grandes* acquired in the fighting of brave bulls.

At the beginning of the fifteenth century, bullkilling was an occupation of commoners and outsiders. "On 18 March 1401, Johan of Santander, 'bullkiller,' acknowledges having received from the treasurer of the kingdom (of Navarre), Johan Caritat, the sum of 10 florins for his work in killing a bull at Pamplona in the presence of Charles the Noble."[7] Customs were very different in seventeenth-century Castile. In Baltasar Moretus's notes on his journey to Madrid (1680), he describes a bullfight presided over by the king. The bulls killed some of the horses of the knights who fought on horseback, and in order to avenge that insult, the knights continued to fight on

---

[6] To show how Cervantes reacted against this deep-rooted, popularly held belief, see my *Cervantes y los casticismos* (1967), p. 129. There is also an indirect attack on the idea that valor was the exclusive attribute of Old Christians, when Sancho Panza, an arch-Old Christian, becomes frightened out of his wits in the adventure of the fulling mills, in contrast to the unshakable courage of his master: "Such great fright had entered his heart, that he did not dare to separate himself from his master, even for a nail's breadth" (*Quixote*, I, 20). Thus history, life, and literary expression are once again united in a coherent structure.

[7] Juan Reglá, *History of Spain*, ed. R. Menéndez Pidal, XVI, 398.

foot "face to face" (Moretus, p. 59). Prior to that time literature offers many examples of valuable evidence referring to the "lances of skill and valor," taken as a symbol of Spanish courage displayed in so many tests of bravery.[8] The central theme of the "lances" is an encounter between a courageous man and a ferocious beast. "Don Antonio Guino, sponsored by the Duque de Cea, offered one of the best displays of lancework ever seen in the plaza against a very brave bull . . . and his horse also displayed as much serenity and bravery as his master" (Cossío, op. cit., p. 841). Cossío discreetly attempts to explain the flourishing of aristocratic bullfighters in the sixteenth century by saying that it was "an homage to chivalry," motivated by the books of chivalry, "without any other purpose than that of the exemplary display of courage and noble effort" (p. 842). In my opinion, however, the implied problem is much more complex and is related to the status of the individual in Spanish society, whose human structure had not yet been brought to light when Cossío was writing his monumental work on the history of Spanish bullfighting.

Don Quixote says to Don Diego de Miranda: "He truly seems to be a gallant knight who makes a successful lance thrust against a brave bull in the midst of a great plaza and witnessed by His Majesty" (II, 17). Don Quixote himself, however, does not challenge bulls, nor does any character in Cervantes's novel, for that matter; the spectacle is merely discussed and reflected through that problematic knight-errant. Valor and daring constituted its essential ingredients; the author created a figure who ran upstream against the current of popular values—a New Christian in contrast to an Old one—opposed and harmonized in a form that was not apparent until now. In this new novelistic context there was no room for a knight who could make any positive affirmation about his bravery, for it was primarily a question of hurling a recently born literary figure against a society and a literature founded on the supposition that valor was the exclusive patrimony of a particular caste, and thus impossible to dignify the one deprived of it by birth. Don Quixote ultimately had no use for the knight who confronted a bull in the eyes of the unanimous, reverent masses. For this reason, after Don Quixote renders verbal homage to all those knightly feats so greatly admired in his time, he continues adversely: "but above all these qualities, it seems better to be an errant knight who wanders through *deserts* and *solitudes* . . . in search of dangerous adventures" (II, 17).

It was already a great risk and feat to confront and compare a notable New Christian (Don Quixote) with a very cowardly Old

---

8 "Relación de la fiesta real de toros, 4 May 1623," in José María de Cossío, *Los Toros*, IV, 838.

Christian (Sancho Panza) without arousing the fury of a society completely absorbed by religion. This was true to such an extent that the two aspects of that society I have been discussing, the bullfights and autos da fé, were two sides of the same question that sometimes ended by coinciding on the same point. The Jesuit Pedro de Guzmán wrote in 1614 that it was customary to hold bullfights in honor of the patron saints of towns because people believed that "the meat of the dead bull on these saints' days was kept as a relic and served as a talisman against fevers and other illnesses and as a remedy against hailstorms. May the patron saint have mercy on and remedy those who hold such beliefs."[9] Father Guzmán was not fond of the bullfights; he did not voice his opinion on the autos da fé.

The absolute, individual figure of the knight affirming his raison d'être against a ferocious beast aroused admiration and incited other individuals to realize themselves in the supreme isolation of their bravery and daring. The prowess of the knight, victorious over the bull, united both its purpose and its end in one single act. It only remained for this feat to be duplicated in the imagined reality of poetry; perhaps Góngora was the only poet capable of accomplishing this task of such great magnitude: "Al Marqués de Velada, Herido (1623) de un Toro que mató luego achuchillado" ("To the Marquis de Velada, wounded [in 1623] by a bull he later killed with his sword"):

should have
been translated

> Con razón, gloria excelsa de Velada,
> te admira Europa, y tanto, que celoso
> su robador mentido pisa el coso,
> piel este día, forma no alterada.

> Buscó tu fresno, y extinguió tu espada
> en su sangre su espíritu fogoso:
> si de tu arena ya lo generoso
> poca arena dejó calificada.

> Lloró su muerte el Sol, y del segundo
> lunado signo su esplendor vistiendo,

> a la satisfacción se disponía;
> cuando el monarca deste y de aquel Mundo
> dejar te mandó el circo, previniendo
> no acabes dos planetas en un día.[10]

---

[9] This text was already cited by Diego Clemencín in his notes to the *Quixote* (1833), II, 17. The extraordinary work by P. de Guzmán, *Bienes del honesto trabajo y daños de la ociosidad* (Madrid, 1614), has been mentioned by me on other occasions. It states that "In many kingdoms, not only of the faithful, but also of infidels and heretics (such as those of La Rochelle), their governors take especial care and attention to see that there are no idlers in their republics, which largely accounts for their happiness" (pp. 119–120).

[10] Mythology becomes meaningful and serves as a supernatural background for the prowess of the Marqués de Velada. In one form or another, life contained an aura of wonder. That geographical Europe which admired the Marquis,

The ultimate problem was to discover the way that led to the affirmation of one's own personal being as an individual, to find one's own outstanding worth and self-esteem, with one's unquestionable right to be oneself. A Spaniard did not achieve this awareness of his personal identity by creating something "depersonalized," abstract, and neutral (for instance, a scientific theory); he was looking for and attracted by something identified with, attached to and dependent upon its creator. Seen from this viewpoint, even the knights of military orders were suspect of tainted ancestry if they did not back up their person by the demonstration of superhuman, absolute valor. This sublime courage had the value of gold in contrast to the depreciated value of copper coins, or, in our time, of paper money that becomes worthless through inflation and devaluation. According to Góngora, in 1588 the court was filled with "habits and patched up capes"; in other words, lords of Jewish descent had gained entry into the military orders through bribes, deceit, and tricks; they had passed themselves off as hidalgos so they would not have to pay *pechos* (taxes).

> Casas y pechos, todo a la malicia.[11]
> (Houses and taxes, everything on the sly.)

In conclusion, everything revolved around the question of whether or not one was an hidalgo, a New or Old Christian. In this manner, the charge of a ferocious bull served as a "reactive" or reagent to clearly prove that a person (in most cases a member of the upper classes) was who he pretended to be. As a final illustration, I shall cite part of a sonnet composed in honor of the Duke of Maqueda, who remained firmly in his saddle when his horse bucked wildly after the Duke had performed a good *suerte* with the bull:

> Por derribaros, de soberbia armado,
> diligencias en que estrellas han perdido
> la silla, el animal enfurecido
> más alabanza os dio que os dio cuidado.

---

is also the beautiful woman (Europa) carried off by Jupiter who disguised himself as a bull (*mentido*, deception), at the beginning of the *Soledades* of Góngora. He also becomes a real bull, jealous of the fame of the Marqués de Velada. If the wounded Marquis shed blood which ennobled the arena (sand) it touched, the Marquis's lance and later his sword killed the sanguinary spirit of the bull. "The Sun becried its death"—it rained during that fiesta celebrated on 4 May (Góngora, *Obras*, ed. Millé y Giménez, p. 1155). "The God of light shed tears," —the sun shone again, and a second bull whose horns in the shape of a half-moon symbolized its splendor, prepared to take revenge for the death of the first bull. But the King, who presided over the fiesta, ordered Velada to leave the plaza so that he would not kill two planets in one day.

[11] According to Covarrubias's *Tesoro* (1611), a *casa a la malicia* is "built in such a way that it cannot be divided or shared because it has two inhabitants," so that it will be free of the royal order of having to lodge outsiders in houses having three storys. The houses appeared from the outside to have only two storys.

Poca le pareció su valentía
al toro, presunción de la rivera,
para desalentar vuestra osadía.

Vuestro caballo os duplicó la fiera;
mas en vos vencen arte y valentía,
juntas a la que os lleva y os espera.[12]

In short, the autos da fé and the fighting of brave bulls in seventeeth-century Spain came to be spectacles endowed with sacred significance, although in different forms. We have already seen that the bullfight was a vehicle for the display of arrogant bravery and courage; now we shall quote writers who occasionally viewed the auto da fé with admiration for those who, at times, faced the torture of the bonfire with equally unflinching heroism. In 1544 the Portuguese Inquisitor, João de Mello, wrote to King John II of Portugal: "I certify to Your Highness that nothing astonishes me more than to see how Our Lord gave human weakness so much patience, to see sons lead their parents to the stake, wives lead their husbands, and brothers lead each other; and not one of them spoke a single word, nor cried, nor made any gesture other than taking leave of each other with their blessings as if they were leaving to return the following day. In like manner the Christian martyrs chose to be devoured by the beasts rather than accept paganism."[13] This parallel between both types of behavior had already been noted by such a shrewd observer as Don Francisco de Quevedo. In a letter to the Conde-Duque de Olivares in 1624, Quevedo proposes to the Inquisition that "any man who, alive and impertinent [in other words, without renouncing his heresy], lets himself be burned, may he be burned alive with the same secret he had when taken into custody. . . . The common people esteem life and health so highly that when they see someone who rejects life and seeks death joyfully and resolutely, they do not know whether to call him crazy or rash; and if they do not praise him, they look upon him in awe and extol him. . . . *'It's hardly credible that he did not utter one word or complain!'* [people say]. Nero and all those who beheaded or burned Christians without knowing what they were doing propagated our faith."[14]

Neither the Count-Duke, Philip IV's minister, nor the Inquisition

---

[12] *Obras completas*, ed. Blecua, I, 262. The proud bull attacked his adversary with such fury that even the greatest star of bullfighting would have been un-horsed; but the animal was unsuccessful and in his fury he gave you more glory than worries. The bull, the pride of the Jarama river bank where he was raised, proved valorous and when the horse bucked, the bull became even more enraged and brave. The horse matched his bravery and, together, horse and rider will go on to future honor, glory, and valor.

[13] J. Lúcio d'Azevedo, *História dos Christãos Novos Portugueses* (1922), p. 452.

[14] Bibl. Aut. Esp., XLVIII, 525–527.

paid attention to Quevedo's proposal, because the spectacular function of the auto da fé was more important than the minimal risk that rebellion and heresy might be propagated. In the auto da fé, the bullfight, and the plays of Lope de Vega, the popular masses had the opportunity to participate collectively and to reinforce their own pride as Old Christians. On these occasions Spanish unanimity wore its finest clothes. No matter what the denouement of Lope de Vega or his followers' plays might be, these works echoed the beliefs, expectations, sentiments, and value judgments of their audience.

During the time of the reconquest in the Christian kingdoms and after the reign of the Catholic sovereigns, not one single heresy of national origin arose with the possibility of gaining some social foothold. Even though heresy among the Jews (Karaites) and Muslims (Mutazilites) was stamped out by their orthodox factions, nevertheless, it was still possible among these people to voice some opposition to official doctrine.

The reality offered by nature or created by the minds of other non-Hispanic men remained quiet, given to magic (such as that worked by the sanctified meat of the bull), or intentionally ignored or unknown as it revolved around the incommensurable absolute of valor as conceived by Spain. The problem posed by the confrontation between man and beast is ultimately resolved by the destruction of one or the other; this gives rise to a noble gesture, as magnanimous as it is sterile. It is necessary to insist on this idea as a present that will not engender futures, and thus reduce the admirer and the object of his admiration to a static quietism. In an effort to escape this ultimately devastating inertia, outside Spain the cult of wonder and the miraculous began to align itself with the struggle against the tenacious obstacle offered by reality disguised as appearance in a stubborn effort to conceal its true nature. For centuries people had died of appendicitis because they were ignorant of the nature and function of the human body.

Even though the leap we are about to take may seem exaggerated, the Spaniards have been killing each other with astonishing frequency as a result of that collective structure fabricated in the sixteenth century whose authentic nature many people insist on ignoring or revealing. Spanish historiography, until recent years, has been in keeping with the mentality of those who believed that the meat of a bull killed as an offering to a saint was an effective remedy against hailstorms. Even in the twentieth century this historiography has oscillated between the poles of fable and hallucination. In another sense, an anarchist who disapproved of the explanation I offer in this book for the origins of political anarchism among many Spaniards, attributes its failure in the last civil war to the fact that it preferred "the man to the skilled technician." Don Luis de Góngora, Don

Francisco de Quevedo, and all those who decided that any sort of technical activity left a spot on or tainted the lineage of the technician or manual craftsman, felt and evaluated human reality and nature in exactly the same manner.

In conclusion, what may seem to many to be an excessively high price to pay today (a moat between Western culture and Spain) was not so for the majority of Spaniards at that time. The writings of Luis de León, Padre Juan de Mariana, Cervantes, and others were either not understood or probably sounded like pure nonsense. The Spanish monarch was the lord of immense areas of the known world. What right, then, do we have to feel the acute lack of this intellectual struggle with reality? Besides, His Catholic Majesty compensated for this lack of what his Castilians were incapable of doing in the field of military engineering or in the art of printing by importing technical assistants from Italy or Flanders. The architectural grandeur of Spain's temples, palaces, mansions, and fountains continued at full strength until the end of the eighteenth century. In one sense it incarnated and monumentalized the beliefs and veneration of the faithful masses. The awareness and consciousness of the Spaniards' greatness was so deeply rooted in their subconscious that even in our time it has given rise to hallucinatory phenomena and, in the long run, it is responsible for the ingenuous fables created by Spanish historiography. Ultimately, to perceive and grasp the dramatic sense of history is as necessary and at least as important as the study of the rising and falling graphs of economy or public and private property.

INDEX

Alfonso VIII (king of Castile), 112,
555; and the Battle of Alarcos, 18,
231–232, 527; and the Battle of Las
Navas de Tolosa, 232, 236; deeds of,
described by Jiménez de Rada, 479–
482; foreign scholars used by, 165;
and the Karaite heresy, 567; love affair of, 72; school founded by, 534

Alfonso IX (king of Leon): importance of Santiago to, 450; not "Spanish," 232; raids of, into Castile, 231–
232, 562

Alfonso X (king of Castile; the Learned), 11, 45, 61, 193–194, 407; and the
Banu Marín, 562; cultural activity at
the court of, 259, 538, 546; disbelief
in the miraculous powers of French
kings, 430; Jews at court of, 538; poetry written by, 443 n; and Santiago,
417, 451; scholars patronized by, 538–
539; and the taifa states, 561; tolerance of, 500–501, 504–506. See also
Primera Crónica General; Siete Partidas

Alfonso XI (king of Castile), 547
Alhambra (palace), 56
Aljamía, 249
Al-kābir (noble, eminent), 544
Almanzor, 223–224, 399, 433n, 562; Inquisition of, 506, 527–528; in the Poema de Fernán González, 411; tem-
ple of St. James the Apostle de-
stroyed by, 418; in tragedy of Infan-
tes, 514
"Al Marqués de Velada ... " ("To the
Marquis de Velada ...'"), 596
Almeria, 9, 227
Almohades, 77, 231; defeat of, 224; per-
secution of Christians and Jews by,
204, 499
Almorávides, 77, 433; and the forma-
tion of European military orders,
476–477; muluk exiled by, 508; per-
secutions of Christians and Jews by,
204, 499; the term, 473
Alonso, Amado, 19 n
Alonso de Herrera, Gabriel, 242
Alphonsine Astronomical Tables, 194
Alpujarra, 78, 246, 294; land of, 237;
martial clergy in, 474; uprisings in,
8, 236, 541
Altamira, cave paintings of, 20, 25, 31
Alvar, Manuel, Judeo-Spanish dirges
collected by, 543
Alvarez de Villasandino, Alonso, 282
Alvarez Gato, Juan, 329–330, 332
Alvitus (bishop), 184
Amadís, 85, 260
Amador de los Ríos, J., 547

Amazon River, 568
America: Spanish actions in, 96; Spanish monks and Indians of, 354
Amezúa, A. G. de, 349–350
Analects of Al-Maqqarī, 399
Anarchism, 292–293, 296, 345–347, 371–
373, 375; background for, 329; of
converts, 399; of the municipal councillors, 341; "native," 324–325; "practical," 324
Anarcho-syndicalism, 357–358, 363, 371
Andalucía, Arabic name, 265
Andalus, al-, 16 n, 50; basis of strength
of, 214; caste in, 53–54, 62–63; confusion regarding, 228; conservatism
of, 230; culture of, 56–57, 519; effects
of existence of, 212; and the French,
204; heterogeneous peoples of, 55,
230; importance of, in Spanish history, 555; Moors of, in decline, 537;
muluk of, 508; Muslim nature of, 27–
28; mysticism in, 217; politico-religious structure of, 137; and the po-
sition of Jews, 567; and Spanish Ara-
bists, 229; taifa states of, 561; waning
power of, 16
Andalusia, agitation against Jews in, 91
Andalusians: appeal of anarchism to,
362–363; groups of, in North Africa
(Andalusís), 509–510
Angelino, Banu, 230
Anglia, the term, 151 n
Anglo-Saxons, secular identity of, 15
Annales Portugalenses veteres, 438
"Anonymus Eboracensis," 468
Anselm, St., 191, 469
Anti-intellectualism: of Christian
Spain, 551–553, 576; of Fernández de
Navarrete, 314–316, 322
Antilles, Indians of, exterminated, 567
Antioch, Battle of, 394
Antoniana Margarita, 576
Anzuelo de Fenisa, El ("Fenisa's Fish-
hook"), 161
Apellido ("summons to battle";
"family name"), 102
Apostle, the. See James the Apostle;
Santiago Apóstol
Apostles, the, 398
Aquitaine, 434
'Ār, 263
Arabic gospels, fraudulent, 238–241
Arabic language, 28, 125
Arabic words: in Catalan, 255; pertain-
ing to public functions, 80, 307–308;
in Spanish, 9, 217, 249 n, 253–259; in
Spanish and Portuguese, 57, 255–259
Arabisms, in Spanish, 260–266, 540–541,
558 n